ALSO BY WALTER ISAACSON

Benjamin Franklin: An American Life

Kissinger: A Biography

The Wise Men: Six Friends and the World They Made
(with Evan Thomas)

Pro and Con

Benjamin Franklin, by Charles Amédée Philippe Vanloo

A
BENJAMIN
FRANKLIN
READER

Including: THE AUTOBIOGRAPHY,
Poor Richard's Almanac, Silence Dogood's letters, Polly Baker's trial,
bagatelles to his French girlfriends, the closing speech at the
Constitutional Convention, letters to Jefferson and Adams
and Washington, and many other wonderful writings from
America's favorite Founder

EDITED AND ANNOTATED BY

WALTER
ISAACSON

SIMON & SCHUSTER
NEW YORK   LONDON   TORONTO   SYDNEY   SINGAPORE

SIMON & SCHUSTER
Rockefeller Center
1230 Avenue of the Americas
New York, NY 10020

For information about special discounts for bulk purchases,
please contact Simon & Schuster Special Sales:
1-800-456-6798 or business@simonandschuster.com

Designed by Jaime Putorti

Manufactured in the United States of America

10   9   8   7   6   5   4   3   2   1

Library of Congress Cataloging-in-Publication Data
Franklin, Benjamin, 1706–1790.
   [Selections. 2003]
   A Benjamin Franklin reader / edited and annotated by Walter Isaacson.
      p.   cm.
   "Including: THE AUTOBIOGRAPHY, Poor Richard's Almanac, Silence
Dogood's letters, Polly Baker's trial, bagatelles to his French girlfriends, the closing
speech at the Constitutional Convention, letters to Jefferson and Adams and
Washington, and many other wonderful writings from America's favorite Founder."
   1. Franklin, Benjamin, 1706–1790—Archives.   2. United States—Politics and
government—To 1775—Sources.   3. United States—Politics and government—
1775–1783—Sources.   4. Franklin, Benjamin, 1706–1790.   5. Statesmen—United
States—Biography.   6. Scientists—United States—Biography.   7. Printers—
United States—Biography.   I. Isaacson, Walter.   II. Title.
E302.F82   2003
973.3'092—dc22   2003055788

ISBN 0-7432-5782-0

Photo Credits:

American Philosophical Society: iv, 356
Corbis: 258
Beinecke: 8, 268
The Historical Society of Pennsylvania: 44, 132
Rosenbach Museum & Library: 92, 186
Huntington Library: 396–397

CONTENTS

Part 6: American Rebel

Part 7: Ambassador in Paris

PART 8: CONSTITUTIONAL SAGE

PART 9: THE AUTOBIOGRAPHY

CHRONOLOGY

1763   Postal inspection trip from Virginia to New England. French and Indian War ends.
1764   Paxton Boys crisis. Defeated in bitter Assembly election. Returns to London as agent.
1765   Stamp Act passes.
1766   Testifies in Parliament against Stamp Act, which is repealed.
1767   Townshend duties imposed. Travels to France.
1768   Wages press crusade in London on behalf of the colonies.
1769   Second visit to France.
1770   Townshend duties repealed except on tea. Made agent for Massachusetts.
1771   Begins *Autobiography*. Visits Ireland and Scotland.
1773   Writes parodies "Rules by Which a Great Empire May Be Reduced to a Smaller One" and "Edict of the King of Prussia." Boston Tea Party.
1775   Returns to Philadelphia. Battles of Lexington and Concord. Elected to Second Continental Congress. Proposes first Articles of Confederation.
1776   William removed as royal governor, imprisoned in Connecticut. Declaration of Independence. Goes to France with Temple and Benny.
1777   Settles in Passy, feted throughout Paris.
1778   Treaties of alliance and commerce with France.
1779   Salons of Madames Brillon and Helvétius. John Paul Jones's *Bonhomme Richard* defeats the *Serapis*.
1781   Appointed (with Adams and others) to negotiate, in Paris, peace with Britain.
1785   Last meeting with William. Returns to Philadelphia.
1787   Constitutional Convention. Elected president of Pa. Society for Promoting the Abolition of Slavery.
1790   Dies on April 17 at age 84.

KEY CHARACTERS

JOHN ADAMS (1735–1826). Massachusetts patriot, second U.S. president. Worked with Franklin editing Jefferson's draft of the Declaration of Independence in 1776. Arrived in Paris April 1778 to work with Franklin as commissioner.

BENJAMIN "BENNY" FRANKLIN BACHE (1769–1798). Son of Sally and Richard Bache, traveled to Paris with grandfather Franklin and cousin Temple in 1776.

RICHARD BACHE (1737–1811). Struggling merchant who married Franklin's daughter Sally in 1767. They had seven children who survived infancy: Benjamin, William, Louis, Elizabeth, Deborah, Sarah, and Richard.

ANDREW BRADFORD (1686–1742). Philadelphia printer and publisher of the *American Weekly Mercury,* he became a competitor of Franklin's and supported the Proprietary elite.

ANNE-LOUISE BOIVIN D'HARDANCOURT BRILLON DE JOUY (1744–1824). Franklin's neighbor in Passy, Madame Brillon was an accomplished harpsichordist who became one of Franklin's favorite female friends. Wrote *Marche des Insurgents* to commemorate American victory at Saratoga.

PETER COLLINSON (1694–1768). London merchant and scientist who helped Franklin set up the library and furnished him with electricity tracts and equipment.

FRANCIS DASHWOOD, BARON LE DESPENCER (1708–1781). British politician postmaster who protected and then had to fire his friend Franklin as the deputy postmaster for America. At his country house, Franklin had the pleasure of hearing his hoax "An Edict from the King of Prussia" fool people.

ABIAH FOLGER FRANKLIN (1667–1752), Born on Nantucket, she married Josiah Franklin in 1689 and had ten children, including Benjamin.

DEBORAH READ FRANKLIN (1705?–1774). Franklin's loyal, common-law wife, she was raised on Market Street in Philadelphia and never left that neighborhood for the rest of her life. She first saw Franklin in October 1723 when he straggled off the boat into Philadelphia. She married John Rogers, who abandoned her. Entered common-law union with Franklin in 1730. Two children: Francis "Franky" who died at age 4 and Sarah "Sally."

JAMES FRANKLIN (1697–1735). Franklin's brother and early master, he started the *New-England Courant* in 1721 and was a pioneer in provocative American journalism.

JANE FRANKLIN [MECOM] (1712–1794). Franklin's youngest sister and favorite sibling.

JOSIAH FRANKLIN (1657–1745). A silk dyer born in Ecton, England, he was the youngest son of a large family and migrated to America in 1683, where he became a candlemaker. Had seven children by his first wife Anne Child and ten (including Benjamin) by his second wife Abiah Folger Franklin.

SARAH "SALLY" FRANKLIN [BACHE] (1743–1808). Loyal only daughter, married Richard Bache in 1767. Served as hostess and homemaker when Franklin returned to Philadelphia in 1776 and then 1785.

[WILLIAM] TEMPLE FRANKLIN (c. 1760–1823). Illegitimate son of William Franklin. Grandfather helped to raise and educate him, brought him back to America in 1775, took him to Paris in 1776, retained his loyalty in struggle with the boy's father. Had his own illegitimate children. Published a haphazard collection of his grandfather's writings.

WILLIAM FRANKLIN (c. 1730–1813). Illegitimate son raised by Franklin. Accompanied him to England, became a Tory sympathizer, appointed royal governor of New Jersey, remained loyal to the crown and split with his father.

ANNE-CATHERINE DE LIGNIVILLE HELVÉTIUS (1719–1800). Franklin's close friend in France. Widowed in 1771 from wealthy philosopher Claude-Adrien Helvétius. Franklin proposed marriage, more than half-seriously, in 1780.

LORD HILLSBOROUGH (1718–1793). Wills Hill, the first Marquis of Downshire and the Viscount of Hillsborough, Britain's colonial secretary from 1768–72 and Franklin's antagonist.

DAVID HUME (1711–1776). Scottish historian and philosopher, he was (with Locke and Berkeley) one of the greatest British empirical analysts. Franklin befriended him in London and visited him in Edinburgh in 1759 and 1771.

SAMUEL KEIMER (c. 1688–1742). A London printer, he moved to Philadelphia in 1722 and gave Franklin his first job there the following year. Franklin had a stormy relationship with him, became his competitor, and Keimer left for Barbados in 1730.

COTTON MATHER (1663–1728). Prominent Puritan clergyman and famed witch-hunter who succeeded his father Increase Mather as pastor of Boston's Old North Church. His writings inspired Franklin's civic projects.

THOMAS PENN (1702–1775). Son of William Penn, he became, in 1746, the primary Proprietor of Pennsylvania, based in London with his brother Richard. He was one of Franklin's foremost political enemies.

JOSEPH PRIESTLEY (1733–1804). Theologian who turned to science. Met Franklin in 1765. Wrote a history of electricity (1767) that stressed Franklin's work. Isolated oxygen and other gases.

SIR JOHN PRINGLE (1707–1782). Physician who became Franklin's close English friend and traveling companion.

CATHERINE RAY [GREENE] (1731–1794). Met Franklin on his 1754 trip to New England and became his first major young female flirtation. Married in

1758 William Greene, who became governor of Rhode Island, but remained a friend of Franklin. (She signed her name "Caty," but Franklin tended to address her as "Katy" or "Katie.")

JONATHAN SHIPLEY, BISHOP OF ST. ASAPH (1714–1788). Anglican bishop at whose house Twyford, near Winchester, Franklin began his autobiography.

MARGARET STEVENSON (1706–1783). Franklin's landlady on Craven Street, off the Strand, and occasional companion in London.

MARY "POLLY" STEVENSON [HEWSON] (1739–1795). Mrs. Stevenson's daughter, longtime flirtatious young friend and intellectual companion to Franklin. Married in 1770 to medical researcher William Hewson. Widowed in 1774, visited Franklin in Paris in 1785, moved to Philadelphia in 1786 to be at his deathbed.

WILLIAM STRAHAN (1715–1785). London printer who became Franklin's close friend via letters before even meeting him in person. Franklin wrote but did not send a famous "you are my enemy" letter to him during the Revolution, but they actually remained friends.

BENJAMIN VAUGHAN (1751–1835). Franklin's close friend in London, he compiled many of Franklin's papers and helped to negotiate with him the final peace treaties with Britain.

CHARLES GRAVIER, COMTE DE VERGENNES (1717–1787). French foreign minister, 1774–1787, with whom Franklin negotiated an alliance.

A

BENJAMIN FRANKLIN

READER

INTRODUCTION

When he was a young teenager working as an apprentice at his brother's printing shop in Boston, Benjamin Franklin, America's original apostle of self improvement, devised a wonderful little method to teach himself how to be a powerful and persuasive writer. He would read the essays of Joseph Addison and Richard Steele in *The Spectator*, the irreverent London daily that flourished in 1711–12, take notes, jumble them up, set them aside, and then return to them a few days later to see how well he could replicate the original. Sometimes he would even turn the notes into poetry, which helped him expand his vocabulary by forcing him to search for words with the right rhythm or rhyme, before trying to recreate what Addison and Steele had written.

When he found his own version wanting, he would correct it. "But I sometimes had the pleasure," he recalled, "of fancying that in certain particulars of small import I had been lucky enough to improve the method or the language, and this encouraged me to think that I might possibly in time come to be a tolerable English writer, of which I was extremely ambitious."

More than making himself merely "tolerable," he became the most popular writer in colonial America. He may also have been, as the great literary historian Carl Van Doren has flatly declared, "the best writer in America" during his lifetime. (The closest rival for that title would probably be the preacher Jonathan Edwards, author of such vivid sermons as "Sinners in the Hands of an Angry God," who was certainly more intense and literary, though far less felicitous and amusing.) Franklin's self-taught style, as befitting a protégé of Addison and

Steele, featured a direct and conversational prose, which was lacking in poetic flourish but was powerful in its directness and humor.

Franklin's father had originally intended to send the last of his sons to Harvard to study for the ministry, but observing his cheeky impertinence, especially about matters of religion, he decided that it would be a waste of money. Instead, he decided to apprentice the young boy at age 12 to his older brother James, who had learned the print trade in London and returned to Boston to open up shop and start the first feisty and independent newspaper in the colonies.

The print trade was a natural calling for young Franklin. "From a child I was fond of reading," he recalled, "and all the little money that came into my hands was ever laid out in books." Indeed, books were the most important formative influence in his life, and he was lucky to grow up in Boston where libraries had been carefully nurtured since the Arabella brought fifty volumes along with the town's first settlers in 1630.

Franklin was able to sneak books from the other apprentices who worked for booksellers, as long as he returned the volumes clean. "Often I sat up in my room reading the greatest part of the night, when the book was borrowed in the evening and to be returned early in the morning, lest it should be missed or wanted."

His favorite was John Bunyan's *Pilgrim's Progress,* the saga of the tenacious quest by a man named Christian to reach the Celestial City, which was published in 1678 and quickly became popular among the Puritans and other dissenters who settled Boston. As important as its religious message, at least for Franklin, was the refreshingly clean and sparse prose style it offered in an age when writing had become clotted by the richness of the Restoration. "Honest John was the first that I know of," Franklin correctly noted, "who mixed narration and dialogue, a method of writing very engaging to the reader."

A central theme of Bunyan's book—and of the passage from Puritanism to Enlightenment, and of Franklin's life—was contained in its title: progress, the concept that individuals, and mankind in general, move forward and improve based on a steady increase of knowledge and the wisdom that comes from conquering adversity. Christian's famous opening phrase sets the tone: "As I walked through the wilderness of this world . . ." Even for the faithful, this progress was not solely the handiwork of the Lord but also the result of a human struggle, by individuals and by communities, to triumph over obstacles.

Likewise, another Franklin favorite—and one must pause to marvel at a twelve-year-old with such tastes in leisure pursuits—was Plutarch's *Lives,* which is also based on the premise that individual endeavor can change the course of history for the better. Plutarch's heroes, like Bunyan's Christian, are honorable men who believe that their personal strivings are intertwined with the progress of mankind. History is a tale, Franklin came to believe, not of immutable forces but of human endeavors.

His writing style, as well as his belief in the power of the written word to encourage useful civic endeavors, was also influenced by two books he borrowed from his father's little library shelf: Daniel Defoe's *Essay on Projects* and Cotton Mather's *Bonifacius: Essays to Do Good.* Throughout his life as an author and publisher, he believed that writing should primarily be judged by its practical effects and usefulness. He had little use for the ethereal artistic and sublime poetic aspirations of the Romantic period that was beginning to flower near the end of his life. Instead, he was an avatar of the Enlightenment, with its belief in reason, practicality, direct prose and earthly enquiry. To that he added the wit he found in Addison, Steele, Defoe and later Jonathan Swift.

His first significant published writings came when he was only sixteen and he invented the pseudonym Silence Dogood to get himself published in his brother's paper. (His jealous brother would not have printed them if he had known the true author.) Like many other witty writers of the Enlightenment, he was partial to pseudonyms and hoaxes, and he wrote his last such piece, a purported speech by a member of the divan of Algiers defending the enslavement of Christians, on his deathbed at eighty-four.

After running away from his apprenticeship in Boston at 17, Franklin settled in Philadelphia, where he soon launched his own print shop and newspaper. He perfected various tricks of the trade to build circulation: gossip, sex, crime and humor. But he also used his pen to encourage worthy civic endeavors and, later, to push his political views.

His Poor Richard's almanacs combined humor and his penchant for self-improvement to become far and away the best-selling books of the era. And he used his talent to create a great media empire that included franchised print shops and newspapers throughout the colonies and then a distribution system, the colonial postal service, that tied them all together and helped give an advantage to his own content.

His output was wondrously diverse and prolific. He wrote pointed tales and humorous hoaxes, amusing essays, letters both chatty and sophisticated, scientific treatises, detailed charters for civic associations, political tracts, plans for uniting the colonies, propaganda pieces supporting the American cause in Britain and then France, and bagatelles to his French female friends. All together his writings fill what will be forty-two volumes, each averaging about seven hundred pages, of which thirty-seven have already been published by the masterly editors of his papers at Yale University.

In this book, I have assembled some of his most revealing, amusing and significant works. I tried to pick those that gave the best insight into Franklin's personality and into his influence on the American character. I also chose a few of them, I must admit, simply because I found them delightful, and I want to convey what a fun (although complex) person Franklin was.

I have presented the pieces chronologically, for the most part, because they thus provide an insight into the evolution of his own life and thinking. To put them in context, they are accompanied by short introductions or explanations that draw from the biography I wrote, *Benjamin Franklin: An American Life*. One exception to the chronological order is the *Autobiography*. He wrote it in four installments, beginning in 1771 and ending in 1789 a year before his death, and I have included it all as one coherent narrative, as he intended, at the end of this volume.

Franklin's writings likewise flow together to give a narrative of both his own pilgrim's progress and that of the new nation he helped to shape. He was the greatest inventor of his time, but the most interesting thing that he invented, and continually reinvented, was himself. America's first great publicist, he was, in his life and in his writings, consciously trying to create a new American archetype. In the process, he carefully crafted his own persona, portrayed it in public, and polished it for posterity.

Partly it was a matter of image. As a young printer in Philadelphia, he carted rolls of paper through the streets to give the appearance of being industrious. As an old diplomat in France, he wore a fur cap to portray the role of backwoods sage. In between, he created an image for himself as a simple yet striving tradesman, assiduously honing the virtues—diligence, frugality, honesty—of a good shopkeeper and beneficent member of his community.

But the image he created was rooted in truth. Born and bred a member of the leather-aproned class, Franklin was, at least for most of his life, more comfortable with artisans and thinkers than with the established elite, and he was allergic to the pomp and perks of a hereditary aristocracy. Throughout his life he would refer to himself, first and foremost, as a printer and writer. And it was through these crafts that he was able to influence, more than any of the other Founders, the character and personality of the American nation.

PART I

THE YOUNG APPRENTICE

THE
New-England Courant.

From M O N D A Y March 26. to M O N D A Y April 2. 1 7 2 2.

Honour's a Sacred Tye, the Law of Kings,
The Noble Mind's Distinguishing Perfection,
That aids and strengthens Vertue where it meets her,
And Imitates her Actions where she is not,
It ought not to be sported with ——————— Cato.

To the Author of the New-England Courant.
Sagulahock, March 20.

SIR,
HONOUR is a Word that Sounds big and makes a most ravishing Entrance into Men's Ears, while a Just and proper Notion of it, is mistaken by most, and the Rules and Measures of it, are comply'd with but by few.

Hence it comes to pass, that some who make a conspicuous Figure in the World, (thro' their Ignorance of this Noble Principle,) falsly imagine themselves to be treading in the Paths of Honour, while they are but greedily pursuing their Ambitious Designs, and Impatiently Gratifying their Lusts of Pride and Covetousness.

Honour indeed, according to the vulgar Notion of it, is nothing more than an empty Name. The Actions of many Men, speak their Sentiments of it; and render it Obvious, that they suppose it to consist only in Flattering Titles, and high Posts and Preferments, be they Acquir'd in the most Shameful and Dishonourable Ways. But how often do such Precipitate themselves into Open Shame? and when they fondly imagine they have grasp'd the Airy Phantom, and arriv'd to the utmost Pitch of Honour, Behold, it Vanishes into nothing, perishes even in the using, and leaves a lasting Brand of Infamy on their Memory.

Now seeing nothing is more pernicious, than a Principle of Action not rigidly apprehended, it may not be improper; First, To hint at some Things, which have the Shadow and Appearance of Honour, but in reality are Infamous and Dishonourable; and Then, to give some brief Description of this Superior Principle.

With respect to Posts of Honour and Honourary Titles, (and some Men have no other Idea of Honour than what results from such Empty Names as these,) it may be said in the Words of an Ingenious Writer, " But whatever Wealth " and Dignities Men may arrive at, they ought to consider, " that every one stands as a Blot in the Annals of his Coun- " try, who arrives at the Temple of Honour, by any other " Way than through that of Vertue". He that advanceth himself to Posts of Honour, by cursed Bribery, or sordid Flattery, or by other base and unworthy Arts, lays his Honour in the Dust, and Exposes himself to lasting Infamy and Reproach. It is also highly Dishonourable for a Man, when any particular Accomplishment is requisite to Qualify him for Preferment, to climb thereto by Sham Pretences, and meer Imposture. He that will thus Impose on the World, it is no Wonder, if he Act by Secret Commissions, and carry on Designs in the Dark that are ruinous to his Country, and Infamous to himself. But the true Reason why Men are guilty of such Actions is, Their Breasts were never once warm'd with one single Spark of true Honour.

It is also Dishonourable for men to rise to Places of Honour, by Calumny and Detraction, or other sordid Arts, which them Envy, Ambition, or Avarice prompt them to Improve, the more easily to undermine and supplant others, who are perhaps more Righteous and worthy of Honour than themselves.

But above all, how vile and inglorious is it, for Men hotly to pursue Preferment with this Design and View, that they may Squeese and Oppress their Brethren; that they may Crush and Trample them in the Dust? How amazing is it, that Men who pretend to Reason and Religion, should thus Desire to Act the Tyrant and the Brute! May we not reasonably conclude of Such, that they never yet Entertain'd a Just Idea of true Honour. The Driving of such Men, is commonly like the Driving of the Son of Nimshi; and to such a high Degree of Impetuosity, do their Passions sometimes swell, that the Man is Dismounted, loses the Reins, and is Dragg'd whither the fury of the Beast directs.

Men of Arbitrary Spirits, what wont they comply with? Through what Rules of Vertue and Humanity will they not break, that they may attain their Ends? Too many such there are, (says Mr. Dummer, in his Defence of the N.E. Charters, pag. 41.) who are contented to be Saddled themselves, provided they may Ride others under the chief Rider.

Men of Tyrannical Principles, with what abhorrence are they to be Look'd on, by all who have any Sense of Honour? Such, it may be presum'd, had they Power equal to their Will, would soon, not only Sacrifice Honour, and Conscience, but even all Mankind, to their Voracious Appetites. They are to be Esteem'd, (as Dr Cotton Mather calls them) the Basest of Men. Such Sons of Nimrod, Nero, & old Lewis, are viler than the Earth they tread on; it groans under them as an Intolerable Plague, and insupportable Burthen. Tyranny and Honour, cannot Reign together in the same Breast.

And (to mention nothing more) it is very Dishonourable, for Men to make rash and hasty Promises, relating to any Thing Wherein the Interest of the Publick is nearly concern'd, and then to say, they will retain their Integrity forever, or till Doomsday, pretending it is for fear of violating their Word and Honour. The Talents, Interest, or Experience of such Men (says one) make them very often useful in all Parties, and at all Times. They Ridicule every Thing, as Romantick, that comes in Competition with their present Interests; and treat those Persons as Visionaries, who dare stand up in a corrupt Age, for what has not its Immediate Reward annexed to it.

But let us now change the Scene, and see what true Honour is. And no doubt, the reverse of what has been said is truly Honourable. True HONOUR, (says a Learned Writer) defines it) is the Report of Good and Vertuous Actions, issuing from the Conscience into the Discovery of the PEOPLE with whom we live, and which (by a Reflection on our selves) gives us the Testimony of what others believe concerning us, and to the Soul becomes a great Satisfaction. True Honour, (says another) tho' it be a different Principle from Religion, is that which Produces the same Effects. The Lines of Action, tho' drawn from different Parts, terminate in the same Point. Religion Embraces Vertue, as it is enjoin'd by the Laws of GOD; Honour as it is Graceful and Ornamental to Humane Nature. The Religious Man fears, a Man of Honour scorns to do an ill Action. A Noble Soul, would rather die, than commit an Action that should make his Children Blush, when he is in his Grave, and be look'd upon as a Reproach to those who shall live a Hundred Years after him.

In a Word, He is the Honourable Man, who is Influenc'd and Acted by a Publick Spirit, and fir'd with a Generous Love to Mankind in the worst of Times; Who lays aside his private Views, and foregoes his own Interest, when it comes in competition with the Publick: Who dare adhere to the Cause of Truth, and Manfully Defend the Liberties of his Country when boldly Invaded, and Labour to retrieve them when they are Lost. Yea, the Man of Honour, (when contracted sordid Spirits desert the Cause of Vertue and the Publick) will stand himself alone, and (like Atlas) bear up the Massy Weight on his Shoulders: And this he will do, in Spite of Livid Envy, Snaky Malice, and vile Detraction.

This is true Honour indeed; and the Man who thus Gloriously acquits himself, shall shine in the Records of Fame, with a peculiar Lustre: His Name shall be mention'd with Reverence in Future Ages, and all Posterity shall call him Blessed.

PHILANTHROPOS

To the Author of the New-England Courant.

SIR,
IT may not be improper in the first Place to inform your Readers, that I intend once a Fortnight to present them, by the Help of this Paper, with a short Epistle, which I presume will add somewhat to their Entertainment.

And since it is observed, that the Generality of People, now a days, are unwilling either to commend or disparate what they read, until they are in some measure informed who or what the Author of it is, whether he be poor or rich, old or young, a Schollar or a Leather Apron Man, &c. and give their Opinion of the Performance, according to the Knowledge which they have of the Author's Circumstances, it may not be amiss to begin with a short Account of my past Life and present Condition, that the Reader may not be at a Loss to judge whether or not my Lucubrations are worth his reading.

At the time of my Birth, my Parents were on Ship-board in their Way from London to N England: My Entrance into this troublesome World was attended with the Death of my Father, a Misfortune

SILENCE DOGOOD INTRODUCES HERSELF

Benjamin Franklin did not like being apprenticed to his older brother. "I fancy his harsh and tyrannical treatment of me," Franklin later speculated, had the affect of "impressing me with that aversion to arbitrary power that has stuck to me through my whole life." That was a bit unfair to poor James, whose newspaper in Boston, *The New-England Courant,* was the first feisty and independent publication in the colonies and taught young Benjamin how to be cheeky about establishment authority.

Franklin knew that his brother would never knowingly print his pieces. So one night he invented a pseudonym, disguised his handwriting, and slipped an essay under the printing house door. His brother's friends who gathered the next day lauded the anonymous submission, and Franklin had the "exquisite pleasure" of listening as they decided to feature it on the front page of the next issue.

Silence Dogood was a slightly prudish widowed woman from a rural area, created by a spunky unmarried Boston teenager who had never spent a night outside of the city. Despite the uneven quality of the essays, Franklin's ability to speak convincingly as a woman was remarkable, and it showed his appreciation for the female mind.

By creating Mrs. Dogood, Franklin invented what became the quintessential genre of American folk humor: the wry and self-deprecating homespun character whose feigned innocence and naïveté is disarming but whose wicked little insights poke through the pretensions of the elite and the follies of everyday life.

The echoes of Joseph Addison are apparent from the outset of the Silence Dogood essays. In Addison's first *Spectator* essay, he wrote: "I have observed, that a reader seldom peruses a book with pleasure 'till he knows whether the writer of it be a black or a fair man, of a mild or choleric disposition, married or a bachelor . . ." Franklin likewise began his first Dogood essay by justifying an autobiographical introduction from his fictional narrator.

Sir,

It may not be improper in the first place to inform your readers, that I intend once a fortnight to present them, by the help of this paper, with a short epistle, which I presume will add somewhat to their entertainment.

And since it is observed, that the generality of people, now a days, are unwilling either to commend or dispraise what they read, until they are in some measure informed who or what the author of it is, whether he be *poor* or *rich, old* or *young,* a *scholar* or a *leather apron man,* &c. And give their opinion of the performance, according to the knowledge which they have of the author's circumstances, it may not be amiss to begin with a short account of my past life and present condition, that the reader may not be at a loss to judge whether or no my lucubrations are worth his reading.

At the time of my birth, my parents were on ship-board in their way from London to n. England. My entrance into this troublesome world was attended with the death of my father, a misfortune, which though I was not then capable of knowing, I shall never be able to forget; for as he, poor man, stood upon the deck rejoicing at my birth, a merciless wave entered the ship, and in one moment carried him beyond reprieve. Thus, was the *first day* which I saw, the *last* that was seen by my father; and thus was my disconsolate mother at once made both a *parent* and a *widow.*

When we arrived at Boston (which was not long after) I was put to nurse in a country place, at a small distance from the town, where I went to school, and past my infancy and childhood in vanity and idleness, until I was bound out as an apprentice, that I might no longer be a charge to my indigent mother, who was put to hard shifts for a living.

My master was a country minister, a pious good-natured young man, and a bachelor: he labored with all his might to instill virtuous and godly principles into my tender soul, well knowing that it was the most suitable time to make deep and lasting impressions on the mind, while it was yet untainted with vice, free and unbiased. He endeavored that I might be instructed in all that knowledge and learning which is necessary for our sex, and denied me no accomplishment that could possibly be attained in a country place; such as all sorts of needle-work, writing, arithmetic, &c. And observing that I took a more than ordinary delight in reading ingenious books, he gave me the free use of his library, which though it was but small, yet it was well chose, to inform the understanding rightly, and enable the mind to frame great and noble ideas.

Before I had lived quite two years with this reverend gentleman, my indulgent mother departed this life, leaving me as it were by my self, having no relation on earth within my knowledge.

I will not abuse your patience with a tedious recital of all the frivolous accidents of my life, that happened from this time until I arrived to years of discretion, only inform you that I lived a cheerful country life, spending my leisure time either in some innocent diversion with the neighboring females, or in some shady retirement, with the best of company, *books.* Thus I past away the time with a mixture of profit and pleasure, having no affliction but what was imaginary, and created in my own fancy; as nothing is more common with us women, than to be grieving for nothing, when we have nothing else to grieve for.

As I would not engross too much of your paper at once, I will defer the remainder of my story until my next letter; in the meantime desiring your readers to exercise their patience, and bear with my humors now and then, because I shall trouble them but seldom. I am not insensible of the impossibility of pleasing all, but I would not willingly displease any; and for those who will take offence where none is intended, they are beneath the notice of Your Humble Servant,

Silence Dogood

SILENCE DOGOOD ON COURTSHIP

The Dogood essays exhibit a literary dexterity that was quite subtle for a 16-year-old boy. "I am courteous and affable, good humored (unless I am first provoked) and handsome, and sometimes witty," Mrs.

Dogood writes in the second one. The flick of the word "sometimes" is particularly deft, as is his jab at redundancy when he has her promise to write "briefly, and in as few words as possible." In addition, Franklin imbued Mrs. Dogood with that aversion to "arbitrary government and unlimited power" that he helped to make part of the American character. Having lost her husband, a minister, she is now spending time with another minister, who is teaching her a few sentences of Latin and Greek so that she can toss them into her writings in a manner that "will not only be fashionable, and pleasing to those who do not understand it, but will likewise be very ornamental."

SILENCE DOGOOD # 2, THE NEW-ENGLAND COURANT, APRIL 16, 1722

Sir,

Histories of lives are seldom entertaining, unless they contain something either admirable or exemplar: and since there is little or nothing of this nature in my own adventures, I will not tire your readers with tedious particulars of no consequence, but will briefly, and in as few words as possible, relate the most material occurrences of my life, and according to my promise, confine all to this letter.

My reverend master who had hitherto remained a bachelor (after much meditation on the eighteenth verse of the second chapter of Genesis), took up a resolution to marry; and having made several unsuccessful fruitless attempts on the more topping sort of our sex, and being tired with making troublesome journeys and visits to no purpose, he began unexpectedly to cast a loving eye upon me, whom he had brought up cleverly to his hand.

There is certainly scarce any part of a man's life in which he appears more silly and ridiculous, than when he makes his first onset in courtship. The awkward manner in which my master first discovered his intentions, made me, in spite of my reverence to his person, burst out into an unmannerly laughter: however, having asked his pardon, and with much ado composed my countenance, I promised him I would take his proposal into serious consideration, and speedily give him an answer.

As he had been a great benefactor (and in a manner a father to me) I could not well deny his request, when I once perceived he was in earnest. Whether it was love, or gratitude, or pride, or all three that made me consent, I know not; but it is certain, he found it no hard matter, by the help of his rhetoric, to conquer my heart, and persuade me to marry him.

This unexpected match was very astonishing to all the country round about, and served to furnish them with discourse for a long time after; some approving it, others disliking it, as they were led by their various fancies and inclinations.

We lived happily together in the height of conjugal love and mutual endearments, for near seven years, in which time we added two likely girls and a boy to the family of the Dogoods: but alas! When my sun was in its meridian altitude, inexorable unrelenting death, as if he had envied my happiness and tranquility, and resolved to make me entirely miserable by the loss of so good an husband, hastened his flight to the heavenly world, by a sudden unexpected departure from this.

I have now remained in a state of widowhood for several years, but it is a state I never much admired, and I am apt to fancy that I could be easily persuaded to marry again, provided I was sure of a good-humored, sober, agreeable companion: but one, even with these few good qualities, being hard to find, I have lately relinquished all thoughts of that nature.

At present I pass away my leisure hours in conversation, either with my honest neighbor Rusticus and his family, or with the ingenious minister of our town, who now lodges at my house, and by whose assistance I intend now and then to beautify my writings with a sentence or two in the learned languages, which will not only be fashionable, and pleasing to those who do not understand it, but will likewise be very ornamental.

I shall conclude this with my own character, which (one would think) I should be best able to give. *Know then,* that I am an enemy to vice, and a friend to virtue. I am one of an extensive charity, and a great forgiver of *private* injuries: a hearty lover of the clergy and all good men, and a mortal enemy to arbitrary government and unlimited power. I am naturally very jealous for the rights and liberties of my country; and the least appearance of an encroachment on those invaluable privileges, is apt to make my blood boil exceedingly. I have likewise a natural inclination to observe and reprove the faults of others, at which I have an excellent faculty. I speak this by way of warning to all such whose offences shall come under my cognizance, for I never intend to wrap my talent in a napkin. To be brief; I am courteous and affable, good humored (unless I am first provoked,) and handsome, and sometimes witty, but always, sir, your friend and humble servant,

Silence Dogood

SILENCE DOGOOD ATTACKS HARVARD

Of the fourteen Dogood essays that Franklin wrote between April and October of 1722, the one that stands out both as journalism and self-revelation is his attack on the college he never got to attend. Many of the classmates he had bested in grammar school had just entered Harvard, and Franklin could not refrain from poking fun at them. The form he used was an allegorical narrative cast as a dream, similar to that in Bunyan's *Pilgrim's Progress*. Addison had also used the form somewhat clumsily in an issue of *The Spectator* that Franklin had read, which recounted the dream of a banker about an allegorical virgin named Public Credit.

SILENCE DOGOOD # 4, *THE NEW-ENGLAND COURANT*, MAY 14, 1722

> *An sum etiam nunc vel Graec loqui vel Latin docendus?*
> —Cicero

Sir,

Discoursing the other day at dinner with my reverend boarder, formerly mentioned, (whom for distinction sake we will call by the name of Clerics,) concerning the education of children, I asked his advice about my young son William, whether or no I had best bestow upon him academical learning, or (as our phrase is) *bring him up at our college:*

he persuaded me to do it by all means, using many weighty arguments with me, and answering all the objections that I could form against it; telling me withal, that he did not doubt but that the lad would take his learning very well, and not idle away his time as too many there nowadays do. These words of Clericus gave me a curiosity to inquire a little more strictly into the present circumstances of that famous seminary of learning; but the information which he gave me, was neither pleasant, nor such as I expected.

As soon as dinner was over, I took a solitary walk into my orchard, still ruminating on Celsius's discourse with much consideration, until I came to my usual place of retirement under the *great apple-tree;* where having seated my self, and carelessly laid my head on a verdant bank, I fell by degrees into a soft and undisturbed slumber. My waking thoughts remained with me in my sleep, and before I awaked again, I dreamt the following dream.

I fancied I was traveling over pleasant and delightful fields and meadows, and through many small country towns and villages; and as I passed along, all places resounded with the fame of the temple of learning: every peasant, who had wherewithal, was preparing to send one of his children at least to this famous place; and in this case most of them consulted their own purses instead of their children's capacities: so that I observed, a great many, yea, the most part of those who were traveling thither, were little better than dunces and blockheads. Alas! Alas!

At length I entered upon a spacious plain, in the midst of which was erected a large and stately edifice: it was to this that a great company of youths from all parts of the country were going; so stepping in among the crowd, I passed on with them, and presently arrived at the gate.

The passage was kept by two sturdy porters named *riches* and *poverty,* and the latter obstinately refused to give entrance to any who had not first gained the favor of the former; so that I observed, many who came even to the very gate, were obliged to travel back again as ignorant as they came, for want of this necessary qualification. However, as a spectator I gained admittance, and with the rest entered directly into the temple.

In the middle of the great hall stood a stately and magnificent throne, which was ascended to by two high and difficult steps. On the top of it sat learning in awful state; she was appareled wholly in black, and surrounded almost on every side with innuerable volumes in all languages. She seemed very busily employed in writing something on half a sheet of paper, and upon enquiry, I understood she was preparing a paper, called, *The New-England Courant.* On her right hand sat *English,* with a pleasant smiling countenance, and handsomely attired; and on her left were seated several *antique figures* with their faces veiled. I was considerably puzzled to guess who they were, until one informed me, (who stood beside me,) that those figures on her left hand were *Latin, Greek, Hebrew,* &c. And that they were very much reserved, and seldom or never unveiled their faces here, and then to few or none, though most of those who have in this place acquired so much learning as to distinguish them from *English,* pretended to an intimate acquaintance with them. I then enquired of him, what could be the reason why they continued veiled, in this place especially: he pointed to the foot of the throne, where I saw *idleness,* attended with *ignorance,* and these (he informed me) were they, who first veiled them, and still kept them so.

Now I observed, that the whole tribe who entered into the temple with me, began to climb the throne; but the work proving troublesome and difficult to most of them, they withdrew their hands from the plow, and contented themselves to sit at the foot, with madam *idleness* and her maid *ignorance,* until those who were assisted by diligence and a docile temper, had well nigh got up the first step: but the time drawing nigh in which they could no way avoid ascending, they were fain to crave the assistance of those who had got up before them, and who, for the reward perhaps of a *pint of milk,* or a *piece of plumb-cake,* lent the lubbers a helping hand, and sat them in the eye of the world, upon a level with themselves.

The other step being in the same manner ascended, and the usual ceremonies at an end, every beetle-scull seemed well satisfied with his own portion of learning, though perhaps he was *even just* as ignorant as ever. And now the time of their departure being come, they marched out of doors to make room for another company, who waited for entrance: and I, having seen all that was to be seen, quitted the hall likewise, and went to make my observations on those who were just gone out before me.

Some I perceived took to merchandizing, others to traveling, some to one thing, some to another, and some to nothing; and many of them from henceforth, for want of patrimony, lived as poor as church mice, being unable to dig, and ashamed to beg, and to live by their wits it was impossible. But the most part of the crowd went along a large beaten path, which led to a temple at the further end of the plain, called, *the temple of theology*. The business of those who were employed in this temple being laborious and painful, I wondered exceedingly to see so many go towards it; but while I was pondering this matter in my mind, I spied *pecunia* behind a curtain, beckoning to them with her hand, which sight immediately satisfied me for whose sake it was, that a great part of them (I will not say all) traveled that road. In this temple I saw nothing worth mentioning, except the ambitious and fraudulent contrivances of Plagius, who (notwithstanding he had been severely reprehended for such practices before) was diligently transcribing some eloquent paragraphs out of Tillotson's *works,* &c., to embellish his own.

Now I bethought my self in my sleep, that it was time to be at home, and as I fancied I was traveling back thither, I reflected in my mind on the extreme folly of those parents, who, blind to their children's dullness, and insensible of the solidity of their skulls, because they think their purses can afford it, will needs send them to the temple of learning, where, for want of a suitable genius, they learn little more than how to carry themselves handsomely, and enter a room genteelly, (which might as well be acquired at a dancing-school,) and from whence they return, after abundance of trouble and charge, as great blockheads as ever, only more proud and self-conceited.

While I was in the midst of these unpleasant reflections, Clericus (who with a book in his hand was walking under the trees) accidentally awaked me; to him I related my dream with all its particulars, and he, without much study, presently interpreted it, assuring me, *that it was a lively representation of* Harvard college, *etcetera.* I remain, sir, your humble servant,

Silence Dogood

SILENCE DOGOOD'S RECIPE FOR POETRY

When he was in London, Franklin's brother James saw how Grub Street balladeers would churn out odes and hawk them in the coffee-houses. So he had put Benjamin to work not only pushing type but also producing poetry. Young Benjamin wrote two works based on news stories, both dealing with the sea: one about a family killed in a boating accident, and the other about the killing of the pirate known as Blackbeard. They were, as Franklin recalled, "wretched stuff," but they sold well, which "flattered my vanity."

Herman Melville would one day write that Franklin was "everything but a poet." His father Josiah, no romantic, in fact preferred it that way, and he put an end to Benjamin's versifying. "My father discouraged me by ridiculing my performances and telling me verse-makers were generally beggars; so I escaped being a poet, most probably a very bad one." A year or so later, Silence Dogood lampooned the formula for poetry and eulogies in Boston.

SILENCE DOGOOD # 7, *THE NEW-ENGLAND COURANT,* JUNE 25, 1722

Give me the Muse, whose generous Force, Impatient of the Reins,
Pursues an unattempted Course, Breaks all the Critic's Iron Chains
—Watts

Sir,

It has been the complaint of many ingenious foreigners, who have traveled amongst us, *that good poetry is not to be expected in New England.* I am apt to fancy, the reason is, not because our countrymen are altogether void of a poetical genius, nor yet because we have not those advantages of education which other countries have, but purely because we do not afford that praise and encouragement which is merited, when any thing extraordinary of this kind is produced among us: upon which consideration I have determined, when I meet with a good piece of New England poetry, to give it a suitable encomium, and thereby endeavor to discover to the world some of its beauties, in order to encourage the author to go on, and bless the world with more, and more excellent productions.

There has lately appeared among us a most excellent piece of poetry, entitled, *an elegy upon the much lamented death of Mrs. Mehitebell Kitel, wife of Mr. John Kitel of Salem, &c.* It may justly be said in its praise, without flattery to the author, that it is the most *extraordinary* piece that ever was wrote in New England. The language is so soft and easy, the expression so moving and pathetic, but above all, the verse and numbers so charming and natural, that it is almost beyond comparison,

> *The muse disdains those links and chains,*
> *Measures and rules of vulgar strains,*
> *And over the laws of harmony a sovereign queen she reigns.*

I find no English author, ancient or modern, whose elegies may be compared with this, in respect to the elegance of stile, or smoothness of rhyme; and for the affecting part, I will leave your readers to judge, if ever they read any lines, that would sooner make them *draw their breath* and sigh, if not shed tears, than these following.

> *Come let us mourn, for we have lost a wife, a daughter, and a sister,*
> *who has lately taken flight, and greatly we have mist her.*

In another place,
Some little time *before she yielded up her breath, she said, I never shall hear one sermon more on earth. She kissed her husband* some little time *before she expired, then leaned her head the pillow on, just out of breath and tired.*
But the threefold appellation in the first line

> *A wife, a daughter, and a sister,*

must not pass unobserved. That line in the celebrated Watts,

> *Gunston the just, the generous, and the young,*

is nothing comparable to it. The latter only mentions three qualifications of *one* person who was deceased, which therefore could raise grief and compassion but for *one*. Whereas the former, (*our most excellent poet*) gives his reader a sort of an idea of the death of *three persons*, viz.

A wife, a daughter, and a sister,

which is *three times* as great a loss as the death of *one*, and consequently must raise *three times* as much grief and compassion in the reader.

I should be very much straitened for room, if I should attempt to discover even half the excellencies of this elegy which are obvious to me. Yet I cannot omit one observation, which is, that the author has (to his honor) invented a new species of poetry, which wants a name, and was never before known. His muse scorns to be confined to the old measures and limits, or to observe the dull rules of critics;

Nor Rapin gives her rules to fly, nor Purcell notes to sing.
—Watts

Now 'tis pity that such an excellent piece should not be dignified with a particular name; and seeing it cannot justly be called, either *epic, Sapphic, lyric,* or *Pindaric,* nor any other name yet invented, I presume it may, (in honor and remembrance of the dead) be called the kitelic. Thus much in the praise of *kitelic poetry.*

It is certain, that those elegies which are of our own growth, (and our soil seldom produces any other sort of poetry) are by far the greatest part, wretchedly dull and ridiculous. Now since it is imagined by many, that our poets are honest, well-meaning fellows, who do their best, and that if they had but some instructions how to govern fancy with judgment, they would make indifferent good elegies; I shall here subjoin a receipt for that purpose, which was left me as a legacy, (among other valuable rarities) by my reverend husband. It is as follows,

A recipe to make a New England funeral elegy.

For the title of your elegy. Of these you may have enough ready made to your hands; but if you should choose to make it your self, you must be sure not to omit the words *aetatis suae,* which will beautify it exceedingly.

For the subject of your elegy. Take one of your neighbors who has lately departed this life; it is no great matter at what age the party died, but it will be best if he went away suddenly, being *killed, drowned,* or *froze to death.*

Having chose the person, take all his virtues, excellencies, &c. And if he have not enough, you may borrow some to make up a sufficient quantity: to these add his last words, dying expressions, &c. If they are to be had; mix all these together, and be sure you *strain* them well. Then season all with a handful or two of melancholy expressions, such as, *dreadful, deadly, cruel cold death, unhappy fate, weeping eyes,* &c. Have mixed all these ingredients well, put them into the empty scull of some *young Harvard*; (but in case you have neer a one at hand, you may use your own,) there let them ferment for the space of a fortnight, and by that time they will be incorporated into a body, which take out, and having prepared a sufficient quantity of double rhymes, such as, *power, flower; quiver, shiver; grieve us, leave us; tell you, excel you; expeditions, physicians; fatigue him, intrigue him;* &c. You must spread all upon paper, and if you can procure a scrap of Latin to put at the end, it will garnish it mightily; then having affixed your name at the bottom, with a *moestus composuit,* you will have an excellent elegy.

N.B. This recipe will serve when a female is the subject of your elegy, provided you borrow a greater quantity of virtues, excellencies, &c. sir,

Your servant, Silence Dogood

SILENCE DOGOOD ATTACKS THE PURITAN THEOCRACY

After his brother was jailed for three weeks for criticizing the authorities, Franklin used Mrs. Dogood to attack the link between church and state that was then the very foundation of Massachusetts government. At one point she asks, "Whether a Commonwealth suffers more by hypocritical pretenders to religion or by the openly profane?" Unsurprisingly, she concludes the former is worse, and she aims a barb at the governor, Thomas Dudley, a minister who had become a politician.

SILENCE DOGOOD # 9, *THE NEW-ENGLAND COURANT,* JULY 23, 1722

Corruptio optimi est pessima.

Sir,

It has been for some time a question with me, whether a commonwealth suffers more by hypocritical pretenders to religion, or by the openly profane? But some late thoughts of this nature, have inclined me to think, that the hypocrite is the most dangerous person of the two, especially if he sustains a post in the government, and we consider his conduct as it regards the public. The first artifice of a *state hypocrite* is, by a few savory expressions which cost him nothing, to betray the best men in his country into an opinion of his goodness; and if the country wherein he lives is noted for the purity of religion, he the more easily gains his end, and consequently may more justly be exposed and detested. A notoriously profane person in a private capacity, ruins himself, and perhaps forwards the destruction of a few of his equals; but a public hypocrite every day deceives his betters, and makes them the ignorant trumpeters of his supposed godliness: they take him for a saint, and pass him for one, without considering that they are (as it were) the instruments of public mischief out of conscience, and ruin their country for God's sake.

This political description of a hypocrite, may (for ought I know) be taken for a new doctrine by some of your readers; but let them consider, that *a little religion, and a little honesty, goes a great way in courts.* 'Tis not inconsistent with charity to distrust a religious man in power, though he may be a good man; he has many temptations to propagate *public destruction* for *personal advantages* and security: and if his natural temper be covetous, and his actions often contradict his pious discourse, we may with great reason conclude, that he has some other design in his religion besides barely getting to heaven. But the most dangerous hypocrite in a commonwealth, is one who *leaves the gospel for the sake of the law:* a man compounded of law and gospel, is able to cheat a whole country with his religion, and then destroy them under *color of law:* and here the clergy are in great danger of being deceived, and the people of being deceived by the clergy, until the monster arrives to such power and wealth, that he is out of the reach of both, and can oppress the people without their own blind assistance. And it is a sad observation, that when the people too late see their error, yet the clergy still persist in their encomiums on the hypocrite; and when he happens to die *for the good of his country,* without leaving behind him the memory of *one good action,* he shall be sure to have his funeral sermon stuffed with *pious expressions* which he dropt at such a time, and at such a place, and on such an occasion; than which nothing can be more prejudicial to the interest of religion, nor indeed to the memory of the person deceased. The reason of this blindness in the clergy is, because they are honorably supported (as they ought to be) by their people, and see nor feel nothing of the oppression which is obvious and burdensome to every one else.

But this subject raises in me an indignation not to be born; and if we have had, or are like to have any instances of this nature in New England, we cannot better manifest our love to religion and the country, than by setting the deceivers in a true light, and undeceiving the deceived, however such discoveries may be represented by the ignorant or designing enemies of our peace and safety.

I shall conclude with a paragraph or two from an ingenious political writer in the *London Journal,* the better to convince your readers, that public destruction may be easily carried on by *hypocritical pretenders to religion.*

A raging passion for immoderate gain had made men universally and intensely hard-hearted: they were every where devouring one another. And yet the directors and their accomplices, who were the acting instruments of all this outrageous madness and mischief, set up for wonderful pious persons, while they were defying almighty god, and plundering men; and they set apart a fund of subscriptions for charitable uses; that is, they mercilessly made a whole people beggars, and charitably supported a few *necessitous* and *worthless* favorites. I doubt not, but if the villainy had gone on with success, they would have had their names handed down to posterity with encomiums; as the names of other *public robbers* have been! We have *historians* and ode makers now living, very proper for such a task. It is certain, that most people did, at one time, believe the *directors* to be *great and worthy persons*. And an honest country clergyman told me last summer, upon the road, that sir john was an excellent public-spirited person, for that he had beautified his chancel.

Upon the whole we must not judge of one another by their best actions; since the worst men do some good, and all men make fine professions: but we must judge of men by the whole of their conduct, and the effects of it. Thorough honesty requires great and long proof, since many a man, long thought honest, has at length proved a knave. And it is from judging without proof, or false proof, that mankind continue unhappy. I am, sir, Your humble Servant,

Silence Dogood

SILENCE DOGOOD PROPOSES CIVIC IMPROVEMENTS

Picking up on the ideas of Mather and Defoe for voluntary civic associations, Franklin devoted two of his Silence Dogood essays to the topic of relief for single women. For widows like herself, Mrs. Dogood proposes an insurance scheme funded by subscriptions from married couples. The next essay extends the idea to spinsters and cheekily notes that those who claim the money and then marry will have to repay it if they unduly brag about their husbands. In these essays, Franklin was being gently satirical rather than fully serious. But his interest in civic associations would later become more earnest when he became established as a young tradesman in Philadelphia.

SILENCE DOGOOD # 10, *THE NEW-ENGLAND COURANT*,
August 13, 1722

> *Optim societas hominum servabitur.*
> —Cicero

Sir,

Discoursing lately with an intimate friend of mine of the lamentable condition of widows, he put into my hands a book, wherein the ingenious author proposes (I think) a certain method for their relief. I have often thought of some such project for their benefit my self, and intended to communicate my thoughts to the public; but to prefer my own proposals to what follows, would be rather an argument of vanity in me than good will to the many hundreds of my fellow-sufferers now in New England . . .

Suppose an office to be erected, to be called *An Office Of Insurance For Widows*, upon the following conditions:

Two thousand women, or their husbands for them, enter their names into a register to be kept for that purpose, with the names, age, and trade of their husbands, with the place of their abode, paying at the time of their entering 5s. down with 1s. 4d. per quarter, which is to the setting up and support of an office with clerks, and all proper officers for the same; for there is no maintaining such without charge; they receive every one of them a certificate, sealed by the secretary of the office, and signed by the governors, for the articles hereafter mentioned.

If any one of the women becomes a widow, at any time after six months from the date of her subscription, upon due notice given, and claim made at the office in form, as shall be directed, she shall receive within six months after such claim made, the sum of 500 in money, without any deductions, saving some small fees to the officers, which the trustees must settle, that they may be known.

In consideration of this, every woman so subscribing, obliges her self to pay as often as any member of the society becomes a widow, the due proportion or share allotted to her to pay, towards the 500 for the said widow, provided her share does not exceed the sum of 5s.

No seamen's or soldiers' wives to be accepted into such a proposal as this, on the account before mentioned, because the contingences of their lives are not equal to others, unless they will admit this general exception, supposing they do not die out of the kingdom.

It might also be an exception, that if the widow that claimed had really, bona fide, left her by her husband to her own use, clear of all debts and legacies, 2000 she should have no claim; the intent being to aid the poor, not add to the rich. But there lies a great many objections against such an article: as

1. It may tempt some to forswear themselves.
2. People will order their wills so as to defraud the exception.

One exception must be made; and that is, either very unequal matches, as when a woman of nineteen marries an old man of seventy; or women who have infirm husbands, I mean known and publicly so. To remedy which, two things are to be done.

1. The office must have moving officers without doors, who shall inform themselves of such matters, and if any such circumstances appear, the office should have 14 days time to return their money, and declare their subscriptions void.
2. No woman whose husband had any visible distemper, should claim under a year after her subscription.

One grand objection against this proposal, is, how you will oblige people to pay either their subscription, or their quarteridge.

To this I answer, *by no compulsion* (though that might be performed too) but altogether voluntary; only with this argument to move it, that if they do not continue their payments, they lose the benefit of their past contributions.

I know it lies as a fair objection against such a project as this, that the number of claims are so uncertain, that no body knows what they engage in, when they subscribe, for so many may die annually out of two thousand, as may perhaps make my payment 20 or 25 per ann., and if a woman happen to pay that for twenty years, though she receives the 500 at last she is a great loser; but if she dies before her husband, she has lessened his estate considerably, and brought a great loss upon him.

First, I say to this, that I would have such a proposal as this be so fair and easy, that if any person who had subscribed found the payments too high, and the claims fall too often, it should be at their liberty at any time, upon notice given, to be released and stand obliged no longer; and if so, *volenti non fit injuria;* every one knows best what their own circumstances will bear.

In the next place, because death is a contingency, no man can directly calculate, and all that subscribe must take the hazard; yet that a prejudice against this notion may not be built on wrong grounds, let's examine a little the probable hazard, and see how many shall die annually out of 2000 subscribers, accounting by the common proportion of burials, to the number of the living.

Sir William Petty in his *Political Arithmetick,* by a very ingenious calculation, brings the account of burials in London, to be 1 in 40 annually, and proves it by all the proper rules of proportioned computation; and I'll take my scheme from thence. If then one in forty of all the people in England should die, that supposes fifty to die every year out of our two thousand subscribers; and for a woman to contribute 5s. To every one, would certainly be to agree to pay 12 10s. per ann. upon her husband's life, to receive 500 when he did, and lose it if she did first; and yet this would not be a hazard beyond reason too great for the gain.

But I shall offer some reasons to prove this to be impossible in our case; first, Sir William Petty allows the city of London to contain about a million of people, and our yearly bill of mortality never yet amounted to 25,000 in the most sickly years we have had, plague years excepted, sometimes but to 20,000, which is but one in fifty: now it is to be considered here, that children and ancient people make up, one time with another, at least one third of our bills of mortality; and our assurances lies upon none but the middling age of the people, which is the only age wherein life is any thing steady; and if that be allowed, there cannot die by his computation, above one in eighty of such people, every year; but because I would be sure to leave room for casualty, I'll allow one in fifty shall die out of our number subscribed.

Secondly, it must be allowed, that our payments falling due only on the death of husbands, this one in fifty must not be reckoned upon the two thousand; for 'tis to be supposed at least as many women shall die as men, and then there is nothing to pay; so that one in fifty upon one thousand, is the most that I can suppose shall claim the contribution in a year, which is twenty claims a year at 5s. each, and is 5 per ann. And if a woman pays this for twenty years, and claims at last, she is gainer enough, and no extraordinary loser if she never claims at all: and I verily believe any office might undertake to demand at all adventures not above 6 per ann. and secure the subscriber 500 in case she come to claim as a widow.

I would leave this to the consideration of all who are concerned for their own or their neighbor's temporal happiness; and I am humbly of opinion, that the country is ripe for many such *Friendly Societies,* whereby every man might help another, without any disservice to himself. We have many charitable gentlemen who yearly give liberally to the poor, and where can they better bestow their charity than on those who become so by providence, and for ought they know on themselves. But above all, the clergy have the most need of coming into some such project as this. They as well as poor men (according to the proverb) generally abound in children; and how many clergymen in the country are forced to labor in their fields, to keep themselves in a condition above want? How then shall they be able to leave any thing to their forsaken, dejected, and almost forgotten wives and children. For my own part, I have nothing left to live on, but contentment and a few cows; and though I cannot expect to be relieved by this project, yet it would be no small satisfaction to me to see it put in practice for the benefit of others. I am, sir, &c.

Silence Dogood

SILENCE DOGOOD # 11, *THE NEW-ENGLAND COURANT,*
August 20, 1722

Neque licitum interea est meam amicam visere.

Sir,

From a natural compassion to my fellow creatures, I have sometimes been betrayed into tears at the sight of an object of charity, who by a bare relation of his circumstances, seemed to demand the assistance of those about him. The following petition represents in so lively a manner the forlorn state of a virgin well stricken in years and repentance, that I cannot forbear publishing it at this time, with some advice to the petitioner.

> *To Mrs. Silence Dogood.*
> *The humble petition of Margaret Aftercast,*
> *Sheweth,*

1. That your petitioner being puffed up in her younger years with a numerous train of humble servants, had the vanity to think, that her extraordinary wit and beauty would continually recommend her to the esteem of the gallants; and therefore as soon as it came to be publicly known that any gentleman addressed her, he was immediately discarded.

2. That several of your petitioners humble servants, who upon their being rejected by her, were, to all appearance in a dying condition, have since recovered their health, and been several years married, to the great surprise and grief of your petitioner, who parted with them upon no other conditions, but that they should die or run distracted for her, as several of them faithfully promised to do.

3. That your petitioner finding her self disappointed in and neglected by her former adorers, and no new offers appearing for some years past, she has been industriously contracting acquaintance with several families in town and country, where any young gentlemen or widowers have resided, and endeavored to appear as conversable as possible before them: she has likewise been a strict observer of the fashion, and always appeared well dressed. And the better to restore her decayed beauty, she has consumed above fifty pounds worth of the most approved *cosmetics*. But all wont do.

Your petitioner therefore most humbly prays, that you would be pleased to form a project for the relief of all those penitent mortals of the fair sex, that are like to be punished with their virginity until old age, for the pride and insolence of their youth.

And your petitioner (as in duty bound) shall ever pray, &c.

Margaret Aftercast

Were I endowed with the faculty of match-making, it should be improved for the benefit of Mrs. Margaret, and others in her condition: but since my extreme modesty and taciturnity, forbids an attempt of this nature, I would advise them to relieve themselves in a method of *friendly society;* and that already published for widows, I conceive would be a very proper proposal for them, whereby every single woman, upon full proof given of her continuing a virgin for the space of eighteen years, (dating her virginity from the age of twelve,) should be entitled to 500 in ready cash.

But then it will be necessary to make the following exceptions.

1. That no woman shall be admitted into the society after she is twenty five years old, who has made a practice of entertaining and discarding humble servants, without sufficient reason for so doing, until she has manifested her repentance in writing under her hand.

2. No member of the society who has declared before two credible witnesses, *that it is well known she has refused several good offers since the time of her subscribing,* shall be entitled to the 500 when she comes of age; that is to say, *thirty years.*

3. No woman, who after claiming and receiving, has had the good fortune to marry, shall entertain any company with encomiums on her husband, above the space of one hour at a time, upon pain of returning one half the money into the office, for the first offence; and upon the second offence to return the remainder. I am, sir, your humble servant,

Silence Dogood

A DISSERTATION ON LIBERTY
AND NECESSITY

A year after he had run away to Philadelphia, Franklin traveled to London, where he worked for 18 months in two of the city's best print shops. Among the books he helped to publish was an edition of William Wollaston's *The Religion of Nature Delineated,* an Enlightenment tract which argued that religious truths were to be gleaned through the study of science and nature rather than through divine revelation. With the intellectual spunk that comes from being youthful and untutored, Franklin decided that Wollaston was right in general but wrong in parts, and he set out his own thinking in a piece in which he mixed theological premises with logical syllogisms to get himself quite tangled up. He inscribed it to his erstwhile friend James Ralph, who had absconded on some debts he owed him. The result was, as Franklin later conceded, so shallow and unconvincing as to be embarrassing. He printed a hundred copies, called it an "erratum," and burned as many as he could retrieve.

In his defense, philosophers greater and more mature than Franklin have, over the centuries, gotten lost when trying to sort out the question of free will and reconcile it with that of an all-knowing God. The primary value of his "Dissertation" lies in what it reveals about Franklin's willingness to abandon Puritan theology.

LONDON, 1725

A Dissertation on Liberty and Necessity, &c. To Mr. J. R.
Sir,

I have here, according to your request, given you my *present* thoughts of the *general state of things* in the universe. Such as they are, you have them, and are welcome to them; and if they yield you any pleasure or satisfaction, I shall think my trouble sufficiently compensated. I know my scheme will be liable to many objections from a less discerning reader than your self; but it is not designed for those who can't understand it. I need not give you any caution to distinguish the hypothetical parts of the argument from the conclusive: you will easily perceive what I design for demonstration, and what for probability only. The whole I leave entirely to you, and shall value my self more or less on this account, in proportion to your esteem and approbation.

Sect. I. Of liberty and necessity.

I. *There is said to be a* first mover, *who is called* god, *maker of the universe.*

II. *He is said to be all-wise, all-good, all powerful.*

These two propositions being allowed and asserted by people of almost every sect and opinion; I have here supposed them granted, and laid them down as the foundation of my argument; what follows then, being a chain of consequences truly drawn from them, will stand or fall as they are true or false.

III. *If he is all-good, whatsoever he doth must be good.*

IV. *If he is all-wise, whatsoever he doth must be wise.*

The truth of these propositions, with relation to the two first, I think may be justly called evident; since, either that infinite goodness will act what is ill, or infinite wisdom what is not wise, is too glaring a contradiction not to be perceived by any man of common sense, and denied as soon as understood.

V. *If he is all-powerful, there can be nothing either existing or acting in the universe against or without his consent; and what he consents to must be good, because he is good; therefore* evil *doth not exist.*

Unde malum? Has been long a question, and many of the learned have perplexed themselves and readers to little purpose in answer to it. That there are both things and actions to which we give the name of *evil,* is not here denied, as *pain, sickness, want, theft, murder,* &c. But that these and the like are not in reality *evils, ills,* or *defects* in the order of the universe, is demonstrated in the next section, as well as by this and the following proposition. Indeed, to suppose any thing to exist or be done, *contrary* to the will of the almighty, is to suppose him not almighty; or that something (the cause of *evil*) is more mighty than the almighty; an inconsistence that I think no one will defend: and to deny any thing or action, which he consents to the existence of, to be good, is entirely to destroy his two attributes of *wisdom* and *goodness.*

There is nothing done in the universe, say the philosophers, *but what God either does, or* permits *to be done.* This, as he is almighty, is certainly true: but what need of this distinction between *doing* and *permitting?* Why, first they take it for granted that many things in the universe exist in such a manner as is not for the best, and that many actions are done which ought not to be done, or would be better undone; these things or actions they cannot ascribe to God as his, because they have already attributed to him infinite wisdom and goodness; here then is the use of the word *permit;* he *permits* them to be done, *say they*. But we will reason thus: if God permits an action to be done, it is because he wants either *power* or *inclination* to hinder it; in saying he wants *power*, we deny him to be *almighty;* and if we say he wants *inclination* or *will*, it must be, either because he is not good, or the action is not *evil*, (for all evil is contrary to the essence of *infinite goodness*). The former is inconsistent with his before-given attribute of goodness, therefore the latter must be true.

It will be said, perhaps, that God *permits evil actions to be done, for wise ends and purposes*. But this objection destroys itself; for whatever an infinitely good God hath wise ends in suffering to *be*, must be good, is thereby made good, and cannot be otherwise.

VI. *If a creature is made by god, it must depend upon god, and receive all its power from him; with which power the creature can do nothing contrary to the will of god, because God is almighty; what is not contrary to his will, must be agreeable to it; what is agreeable to it, must be good, because he is good; therefore a creature can do nothing but what is good.*

This proposition is much to the same purpose with the former, but more particular; and its conclusion is as just and evident. Though a creature may do many actions which by his fellow creatures will be named *evil*, and which will naturally and necessarily cause or bring upon the doer, certain *pains* (which will likewise be called *punishments;*) yet this proposition proves, that he cannot act what will be in itself really ill, or displeasing to god. And that the painful consequences of his evil actions *(so called)* are not, as indeed they ought not to be, *punishments* or unhappinesses, will be shown hereafter.

Nevertheless, the late learned author of *the religion of nature*, (which I send you herewith) has given us a rule or scheme, whereby to discover which of our actions ought to be esteemed and denominated *good*, and which *evil*: it is in short this, every action which is done according to *truth*, is good; and every action contrary to truth, is evil: to act according to truth is to use and esteem every thing as what it is, &c. Thus if *a* steals a horse from *b*, and rides away upon him, he uses him not as what he is in truth, viz. The property of another, but as his own, which is contrary to truth, and therefore *evil*. But, as this gentleman himself says, (sect. I. Prop. Vi.) In order to judge rightly what any thing is, it must be considered, not only what it is in one respect, but also what it may be in any other respect; and the whole description of the thing ought to be taken in: so in this case it ought to be considered, that *a* is naturally a *covetous* being, feeling an uneasiness in the want of B's horse, which produces an inclination for stealing him, stronger than his fear of punishment for so doing. This is *truth* likewise, and *a* acts according to it when he steals the horse. Besides, if it is proved to be a *truth,* that *a* has not power over his own actions, it will be indisputable that he acts according to truth, and impossible he should do otherwise.

I would not be understood by this to encourage or defend theft; 'tis only for the sake of the argument, and will certainly have no *ill effect.* The order and course of things will not be affected by reasoning of this kind; and 'tis as just and necessary, and as much according to truth, for *b* to dislike and punish the theft of his horse, as it is for *a* to steal him.

VII. *If the creature is thus limited in his actions, being able to do only such things as God would have him to do, and not being able to refuse doing what God would have done; then he can have no such thing as liberty, free-will or power to do or refrain an action.*

By *liberty* is sometimes understood the absence of opposition; and in this sense, indeed, all our actions may be said to be the effects of our liberty: but it is a liberty of the same nature with the fall of a heavy body to the ground; it has liberty to fall, that is, it meets with nothing to hinder its fall, but at the same time it is necessitated to fall, and has no power or liberty to remain suspended.

But let us take the argument in another view, and suppose ourselves to be, in the common sense of the word, *free agents.* As man is a part of this great machine, the universe, his regular acting is requisite to the regular moving of the whole. Among the many things which lie before him to be done, he may, as he is at liberty and his choice influenced by nothing, (for so it must be, or he is not at liberty) choose any one, and refuse the rest. Now there is every moment something *best* to be done, which is alone then *good,* and with respect to which, every thing else is at that time *evil.* In order to know which is best to be done, and which not, it is requisite that we should have at one view all the intricate consequences of every action with respect to the general order and scheme of the universe, both present and future; but they are innumerable and incomprehensible by any thing but omniscience. As we cannot know these, we have but as one chance to ten thousand, to hit on the right action; we should then be perpetually blundering about in the dark, and putting the scheme in disorder; for every wrong action of a part, is a defect or blemish in the order of the whole. Is it not necessary then, that our actions should be overruled and governed by an all-wise providence? How exact and regular is every thing in the *natural* world! How wisely in every part contrived! We cannot here find the least defect! Those who have studied the mere animal and vegetable creation, demonstrate that nothing can be more harmonious and beautiful! All the heavenly bodies, the stars and planets, are regulated with the utmost wisdom! And can we suppose less care to be taken in the order of the *moral* than in the *natural* system? It is as if an ingenious artificer, having framed a curious machine or clock, and put its many intricate wheels and powers in such a dependence on one another, that the whole might move in the most exact order and regularity, had nevertheless placed in it several other wheels endowed with an independent *self-motion*, but ignorant of the general interest of the clock; and these would every now and then be moving wrong, disordering the true movement, and making continual work for the mender; which might better be prevented, by depriving them of that power of self-motion, and placing them in a dependence on the regular part of the clock.

VIII. *If there is no such thing as free-will in creatures, there can be neither merit nor demerit in creatures.*

IX. *And therefore every creature must be equally esteemed by the creator.* These propositions appear to be the necessary consequences of the former. And certainly no reason can be given, why the creator should prefer in his esteem one part of his works to another, if with equal wisdom and goodness he designed and created them all, since all ill or defect, as contrary to his nature, is excluded by his power. We will sum up the argument thus, when the creator first designed the universe, either it was his will and intention that all things should exist and be in the manner they are at this time; or it was his will they should *be* otherwise i.e. In a different manner: to say it was his will things should be otherwise than they are, is to say somewhat hath contradicted his will, and broken his measures, which is impossible because inconsistent with his power;

therefore we must allow that all things exist now in a manner agreeable to his will, and in consequence of that are all equally good, and therefore equally esteemed by him.

I proceed now to show, that as all the works of the creator are equally esteemed by him, so they are, as in justice they ought to be, equally used . . .

[Editor's note: Franklin includes a second, longer section arguing that pleasure and pain are always equal in the life of each individual.]

I am sensible that the doctrine here advanced, if it were to be published, would meet with but an indifferent reception. Mankind naturally and generally love to be flattered: whatever sooths our pride, and tends to exalt our species above the rest of the creation, we are pleased with and easily believe, when ungrateful truths shall be with the utmost indignation rejected. What! Bring ourselves down to an equality with the beasts of the field! With the *meanest* part of the creation! 'Tis insufferable! But, (to use a piece of *common* sense) our *geese* are but *geese* though we may think them *swans;* and truth will be truth though it sometimes prove mortifying and distasteful.

PLAN OF CONDUCT

While in London, Franklin lamented that his life had so far been rather confused because he had never outlined a design for how to conduct himself. A very methodical man, he produced the first such plan during his eleven-week voyage back to Philadelphia in 1726. Rule one he had already mastered. Rule three he likewise had little trouble following. As for two and four, he would henceforth preach them diligently and generally make a show of practicing them, though he would sometimes be better at the show than the practicing.

1726

Those who write of the art of poetry teach us that if we would write what may be worth the reading, we ought always, before we begin, to form a regular plan and design of our piece: otherwise, we shall be in danger of incongruity. I am apt to think it is the same as to life. I have never fixed a regular design in life; by which means it has been a confused variety of different scenes. I am now entering upon a new one: let me, therefore, make some resolutions, and form some scheme of action, that, henceforth, I may live in all respects like a rational creature.

1. It is necessary for me to be extremely frugal for some time, till I have paid what I owe.

2. To endeavor to speak truth in every instance; to give nobody expectations that are not likely to be answered, but aim at sincerity in every word and action, the most amiable excellence in a rational being.

3. To apply myself industriously to whatever business I take in hand, and not divert my mind from my business by any foolish project of growing suddenly rich; for industry and patience are the surest means of plenty.

4. I resolve to speak ill of no man whatever, not even in a matter of truth; but rather by some means excuse the faults I hear charged upon others, and upon proper occasions speak all the good I know of every body.

ADVICE TO HIS SISTER ON HER MARRIAGE

Franklin's lifelong advocacy of industry and frugality first appears in a letter to his younger sister Jane when she was getting married. He had thought of sending her a tea table, he said, but his practical nature got the better of him. Spinning wheels and tea sets would become, for him, symbols of industry versus indulgence that he would return to in Poor Richard's Almanac and other writings.

Dear Sister,

I am highly pleased with the account captain Freeman gives me of you. I always judged by your behavior when a child that you would make a good, agreeable woman, and you know you were ever my peculiar favorite. I have been thinking what would be a suitable present for me to make, and for you to receive, as I hear you are grown a celebrated beauty. I had almost determined on a tea table, but when I considered that the character of a good housewife was far preferable to that of being only a pretty gentlewoman, I concluded to send you a *spinning wheel*, which I hope you will accept as a small token of my sincere love and affection.

Sister, farewell, and remember that modesty, as it makes the most homely virgin amiable and charming, so the want of it infallibly renders the most perfect beauty disagreeable and odious. But when that brightest of female virtues shines among other perfections of body and mind in the same person, it makes the woman more lovely than an angel. Excuse this freedom, and use the same with me. I am, dear Jenny, your loving brother,

B. Franklin

A NEW CREED AND LITURGY

Upon his return to Philadelphia, Franklin showed little interest in organized religion and even less in attending Sunday services. Still, he continued to hold some basic religious beliefs, among them "the existence of the Deity" and that "the most acceptable service of God was doing good to man." He was tolerant toward all sects, particularly those that worked to make the world a better place. Because he believed that churches were useful to the community, he paid his annual subscription to support the town's Presbyterian minister, the Rev. Jedediah Andrews.

One day Andrews prevailed upon him to sample his Sunday sermons, which Franklin did for five weeks. Unfortunately, he found them "uninteresting and unedifying since not a single moral principle was inculcated or enforced, their aim seeming to be rather to make us good Presbyterians than good citizens." Franklin reverted to spending his Sundays reading and writing on his own.

Franklin began to clarify his religious beliefs through a series of essays and letters. In them he adopted a creed that would last his lifetime: a virtuous, morally-fortified and pragmatic version of deism. Unlike most pure deists, he concluded that it was useful (and thus probably correct) to believe that a faith in God should inform our daily actions; but his faith was devoid of sectarian dogma, burning spirituality, deep soul-searching, or a personal relationship to Christ.

The first of these religious essays was a paper "for my own private use," written in November 1728. His opening affirmation, "I believe there is one Supreme most perfect being," was an important statement, since some mushier deists shied from even going that far. Some commentators read this essay as an embrace by Franklin of some sort of polytheism, with a bevy of gods overseeing various realms and planets. But Franklin seems to be speaking more figuratively than literally. (Given the difficulties Franklin sometimes seems to have in believing in one God, it seems unlikely he could find himself believing in many.)

NOVEMBER 20, 1728

Articles of Belief and Acts of Religion
Here will I hold, If there is a Power above us (And that there is,
all Nature cries aloud, Thro all her Works), He must delight in Virtue
And that which he delights in must be Happy.
—Cato

First Principles

I Believe there is one Supreme most perfect Being, Author and Father of the Gods themselves.

For I believe that Man is not the most perfect Being but One, rather that as there are many Degrees of Beings his Inferiors, so there are many Degrees of Beings superior to him.

Also, when I stretch my Imagination thro and beyond our System of Planets, beyond the visible fixed Stars themselves, into that Space that is every Way infinite, and conceive it filled with Suns like ours, each with a Chorus of Worlds for ever moving round him, then this little Ball on which we move, seems, even in my narrow Imagination, to be almost Nothing, and my self less than nothing, and of no sort of Consequence.

When I think thus, I imagine it great Vanity in me to suppose, that the *Supremely Perfect,* does in the least regard such an inconsiderable Nothing as Man. More especially, since it is impossible for me to have any positive clear Idea of that which is infinite and incomprehensible, I cannot conceive otherwise, than that He, *the Infinite Father,* expects or requires no Worship or Praise from us, but that he is even infinitely above it.

But since there is in all Men something like a natural Principle which inclines them to Devotion or the Worship of some unseen Power;

And since Men are endowed with Reason superior to all other Animals that we are in our World acquainted with;

Therefore I think it seems required of me, and my Duty, as a Man, to pay Divine Regards to Something.

I conceive then, that the Infinite has created many Beings or Gods, vastly superior to Man, who can better conceive his Perfections than we, and return him a more rational and glorious Praise. As among Men, the Praise of the Ignorant or of Children, is not regarded by the ingenious Painter or Architect, who is rather honored and pleased with the Approbation of Wise men and Artists.

It may be that these created Gods, are immortal, or it may be that after many Ages, they are changed, and Others supply their Places.

Howbeit, I conceive that each of these is exceeding wise, and good, and very powerful; and that Each has made for himself, one glorious Sun, attended with a beautiful and admirable System of Planets.

It is that particular wise and good God, who is the Author and Owner of our System, that I propose for the Object of my Praise and Adoration.

For I conceive that he has in himself some of those Passions he has planted in us, and that, since he has given us Reason whereby we are capable of observing his Wisdom in the Creation, he is not above caring for us, being pleased with our Praise, and offended when we slight Him, or neglect his Glory.

I conceive for many Reasons that he is a *good Being,* and as I should be happy to have so wise, good and powerful a Being my Friend, let me consider in what Manner I shall make myself most acceptable to him.

Next to the Praise due, to his Wisdom, I believe he is pleased and delights in the Happiness of those he has created; and since without Virtue Man can have no Happiness in this World, I firmly believe he delights to see me Virtuous, because he is pleased when he sees me Happy.

And since he has created many Things which seem purely designed for the Delight of Man, I believe he is not offended when he sees his Children solace themselves in any manner of pleasant Exercises and innocent Delights, and I think no Pleasure innocent that is to Man hurtful.

I *love* him therefore for his Goodness and I *adore* him for his Wisdom.

Let me then not fail to praise my God continually, for it is his Due, and it is all I can return for his Many Favors and great Goodness to me; and let me resolve to be virtuous, that I may be happy, that I may please Him, who is delighted to see me happy. Amen.

PART 2

THE PHILADELPHIA PRINTER

Numb. 422.

THE

Pennſylvania GAZETTE.

Containing the freſheſt Advices Foreign and Domeſtick.

From January 6. to January 13. 1736,7.

Nothing more like a Fool than a drunken Man.
                                        Poor Richard.

IS an old Remark, that Vice always endeavours to aſſume the Appearance of Virtue: Thus Covetouſneſs calls itſelf *Prudence*; *Prodigality* would be thought *Generoſity*; and ſo of others. This perhaps ariſes hence, that, Mankind naturally and univerſally approve Virtue in their Hearts, and deteſt Vice; and therefore, whenever thro' Temptation they fall into a Practice of the latter, they would it poſſible conceal it from themſelves as well as others, under ſome other Name than that which properly belongs to it.

But DRUNKENNESS is a very unfortunate Vice in this reſpect. It bears no kind of Similitude with any ſort of Virtue, from which it might poſſibly borrow a Name; and is therefore reduc'd to the wretched Neceſſity of being expreſs'd by diſtant round-about Phraſes, and of perpetually varying thoſe Phraſes, as often as they come to be well underſtood to ſignify plainly that A MAN IS DRUNK.

Tho' every one may poſſibly recollect a Dozen at leaſt of the Expreſſions us'd on this Occaſion, yet I think no one who has not much frequented Taverns would imagine the number of them ſo great as it really is. It may therefore ſurprize as well as divert the ſober Reader, to have the Sight of a new Piece, lately communicated to me, entitled

The DRINKERS DICTIONARY.

A
HE is Addled,
He's caſting up his Accounts,
He's Afflicted,
He's in his Airs.

B
He's Biggy,
Bewitch'd,
Block and Block,
Boozy,
Bow'd,
Been at Barbadoes.
Piſs'd in the Brook,
Drunk as a Wheel-Barrow,
Burdock'd,
Buskey,
Buzzey,
Has Stole a Mancher out of the Brewer's Basket,
His Head is full of Bees,
Has been in the Bibbing Plot,
Has drank more than he has bled,
He's Bungey,
As Drunk as a Beggar,
He ſees the Bears,
He's kiſs'd black Betty,

He's had a Thump over the Head with Sampſon's Jaw-bone,
He's Bridgey,

C
He's Cat,
Cagrin'd,
Capable,
Cramp'd,
Cherubimical,
Cherry Merry,
Wamble Crop'd,
Crack'd,
Concern'd,
Half Way to Concord,
Has taken a Chirriping-Glaſs,
Got Corns in his Head,
A Cup to much,
Coguy,
Copey,
He's heat his Copper,
He's Crocus,
Catch'd,
He cuts his Capers,
He's oeen in the Cellar,
He's in his Cups,
Non Compos,
Cock'd,
Curv'd,
Cut,
Chipper,
Chickery,
Loaded his Cart,
He's been too free with the Creature,
Sir Richard has taken off his Conſidering Cap,
He's Chap-fallen,

D
He's Diſguiz'd,
He's got a Diſh,
Kill'd his Dog,
Took his Drops,
It is a Dark Day with him,
He's a Dead Man,
Has Dipp'd his Bill,
He's Dagg'd,
He's ſeen the Devil,

E
He's Prince Eugene,
Enter'd,
Wet both Eyes,
Cock Ey'd,
Got the Pole Evil,
Got a braſs Eye,
Made an Example,

He's Eat a Toad & half for Breakfaſt.
In his Element,

F
He's Fiſhey,
Fox'd,
Fuddled,
Sore Footed,
Frozen,
Well in for't,
Owes no Man a Farthing,
Fears no Man,
Crump Footed,
Been to France,
Fluſh'd,
Froze his Mouth,
Fetter'd,
Been to a Funeral,
His Flag is out,
Fuzl'd,
Spoke with his Friend,
Been at an Indian Feaſt.

G
He's Glad,
Groatable,
Gold-headed,
Glaiz'd,
Generous,
Booz'd the Gage,
As Dizzy as a Gooſe,
Been before George,
Got the Gout,
Had a Kick in the Guts,
Been with Sir John Goa,
Been at Geneva,
Globular,
Got the Glanders.

H
Half and Half,
Hardy,
Top Heavy,
Got by the Head,
Hiddey,
Got on his little Hat,
Hammeriſh,
Looſe in the Hilts,
Knows not the way Home,
Got the Hornſon,
Haunted with Evil Spirits,
Has Taken Hippocrates grand Elixir,

I
He's Intoxicated,
Jolly,
Jagg'd,
Jambled,

Going

THE FIRST ABORTION CONTROVERSY

When Franklin decided he wanted to start a newspaper, his former employer, a quirky printer named Samuel Keimer, beat him to it. So Franklin began writing for an older paper in Philadelphia, published by an established gentleman named Andrew Bradford, in hopes of putting Keimer out of business. Keimer decided to serialize an encyclopedia as a way to build circulation, and in the first installment included the entry on "abortion." So Franklin, using the pseudonym of two outraged women, "Celia Shortface" and "Martha Careful," manufactured the first known abortion debate in America.

THE AMERICAN WEEKLY MERCURY, JANUARY 28, 1729

Mr. Andrew Bradford,

In behalf of my self and many good modest women in this city (who are almost out of countenance) I beg you will publish this in your next *Mercury*, as a warning to Samuel Keimer: that if he proceed farther to expose the secrets of our sex, in that audacious manner, as he hath done in his *gazette*, no. 5. Under the letters, a.b.o. to be read in all *taverns* and *coffee-houses*, and by the vulgar: I say if he publish any more of that kind, which ought only to be in the repository of the learned; my sister Molly and my self, with some others, are resolved to run the hazard of taking him by the beard, at the next place we meet him, and make an example of him for his immodesty. I subscribe on the behalf of the rest of my aggrieved sex. Yours,

Martha Careful

Friend Andrew Bradford,

I desire thee to insert in thy next *Mercury*, the following letter to Samuel Keimer, for by doing it, Thou may perhaps save Keimer his ears, and very much oblige our sex in general, but in a more particular manner. Thy modest Friend, Celia Shortface.

Friend Samuel Keimer,

I did not expect when thou puts forth thy advertisement concerning Thy *Universal Instructor,* (as Thou art pleased to call it,) That, thou would have Printed such things in it, as would make all the modest and virtuous women in Pennsylvania ashamed.

I was last night in company with several of my acquaintance, and thee, and *thy indecencies,* was the subject of our discourse, but at last we resolved, that if thou continue to take such scraps concerning us, out of thy great dictionary, and publish it, as thou hath done in thy *Gazette,* No. 5, to make thy ears suffer for it: And I was desired by the rest, to inform thee of our resolution, which is that if thou proceed any further in that *scandalous manner,* we intend very soon to have thy right ear for it; therefore I advise thee to take this timely caution in good part; and if thou canst make no better use of thy dictionary, sell it at thy next *luck in the bag;* and if thou hath nothing else to put in thy *Gazette,* lay it down, I am, thy troubled friend,

Celia Shortface

THE BUSY-BODY

The next week, as part of his crusade to put Keimer out of business, Franklin launched a series of classic essays for Bradford's paper, signed Busy-Body. "By this means the attention of the public was fixed on that paper," Franklin later recalled, "and Keimer's proposals, which we burlesqued and ridiculed, were disregarded." The Busy-Body was a scold and a tattler in the tradition of the character "Isaac Bickerstaff" that the English essayist Richard Steele had created, thus adding gossip columnist to the list of Franklin's American firsts. He readily admitted that much of this was "nobody's business," but "upon mature deliberation" and "out of zeal for the public good," he volunteered "to take nobody's business wholly into my own hands."

BUSY-BODY #1, *THE AMERICAN WEEKLY MERCURY*, FEBRUARY 4, 1729

Mr. Andrew Bradford,

I design this to acquaint you, that I, who have long been one of your *courteous readers,* have lately entertained some thoughts of setting up for an author my self; not out of the least vanity, I assure you, or desire of showing my parts, but purely for the good of my country.

I have often observed with concern, that your *Mercury* is not always equally entertaining. The delay of ships expected in, and want of fresh advices from Europe, make it frequently very dull; and I find the freezing of our river has the same effect on news as on trade. With more concern have I continually observed the growing vices and follies of my country-folk. And though reformation is properly the concern of every man; that is, *Every one ought to mend One;* yet 'tis too true in this case, that *what is every Body's Business is no Body's Business,* and the business is done accordingly. I, therefore, upon mature deliberation, think fit to take *no Body's Business* wholly into my own hands; and, out of zeal for the public good, design to erect my self into a kind of *censor morum;* proposing with your allowance, to make use of the *Weekly Mercury* as a vehicle in which my remonstrances shall be conveyed to the world.

I am sensible I have, in this particular, undertaken a very unthankful office, and expect little besides my labor for my pains. Nay, 'tis probable I may displease a great number of your readers, who will not very well like to pay 10*s.* a year for being told of their faults. But as most people delight in censure when they themselves are not the objects of it, if any are offended at my publicly exposing their private vices, I promise they shall have the satisfaction, in a very little time, of seeing their good friends and neighbors in the same circumstances.

However, let the fair sex be assured, that I shall always treat them and their affairs with the utmost *decency* and respect. I intend now and then to dedicate a chapter wholly to their service; and if my lectures any way contribute to the embellishment of their minds, and brightening of their understandings, without offending their *modesty,* I doubt not of having their favor and encouragement.

'Tis certain, that no country in the world produces naturally finer spirits than ours, men of genius for every kind of science, and capable of acquiring to perfection every qualification that is in esteem among mankind. But as few here have the advantage of good books, for want of which, good conversation is still more scarce, it would doubtless have been very acceptable to your readers, if, instead of an old out-of-date article from Muscovy or Hungary, you had entertained them with some well-chosen extract from a good author. This I shall sometimes do, *when I happen to have nothing of my own to say that I think of more consequence.* Sometimes, I propose to deliver lectures of morality or philosophy, and (because I am naturally inclined to be meddling with things that don't concern me) perhaps I may sometimes talk politicks. And if I can by any means furnish out a weekly entertainment for the public, that will give a rational diversion, and at the same time be instructive to the readers, I shall think my leisure hours well employed: and if you publish this I hereby invite all ingenious gentlemen and others, (that approve of such an undertaking) to my assistance and correspondence.

'Tis like by this time you have a curiosity to be acquainted with my name and character. As I do not aim at public praise I design to remain concealed; and there are such numbers of our family and relations at this time in the country, that though I've signed my name at full length, I am not under the least apprehension of being distinguished and discovered by it. My character indeed I would favor you with, but that I am cautious of praising my self, lest I should be told *my trumpeters dead:* and I cannot find in my heart, at present, to say any thing to my own disadvantage.

It is very common with authors in their first performances to talk to their readers thus, *if this meets with a* suitable *reception;* or, *if this should meet with* due *encouragement, I shall hereafter publish, &c.* This only manifests the value they put on their own writings, since they think to frighten the public into their applause, by threatening, that unless you approve what they have already wrote, they intend never to write again; when perhaps, it may not be a pin matter whether they ever do or no. As I have not observed the critics to be more favorable on this account, I shall always avoid saying any thing of the kind; and conclude with telling you, that if you send me a bottle of ink and a quire of paper by the bearer, you may depend on hearing further from Sir, Your most humble Servant,

The Busy-Body

FRANKLIN THE EDITOR

The excitable Keimer responded with limp doggerel: "With scornful eye, I see your hate, / And pity your unhappy fate." But Keimer was soon driven out of business, and fled to Barbados. On the way to the boat he sold his paper, *The Pennsylvania Gazette,* to Franklin in October 1729.

There are many types of newspaper editors. Some are crusading ideologues who are blessed with strong opinions, partisan passions, or a desire to bring low authority. Benjamin's brother James was in this category. Some are the opposite: they like power and their proximity to it, are comfortable with the established order and feel vested in it. The Philadelphia printer Andrew Bradford was such.

And then there are those who are charmed and amused by the world, and delight in charming and amusing others. They tend to be skeptical of both orthodoxies and heresies, and they are earnest in their desire to seek truth and promote public betterment (as well as sell papers). There fits Franklin. He was graced—and afflicted—with the trait so common to journalists, especially ones who have read Swift and Addison once too often, of wanting to participate in the world while also remaining a detached observer. As a journalist he could step out of a scene, even one that passionately engaged him, and comment on it, or on himself, with a droll irony. The depths of his beliefs were often concealed by his knack of engaging in a knowing wink, as was evident in the first editorial he wrote.

THE PENNSYLVANIA GAZETTE, OCTOBER 2, 1729

The Printer to the Reader.

The Pennsylvania Gazette being now to be carried on by other hands, the reader may expect some account of the method we design to proceed in.

There are many who have long desired to see a good newspaper in Pennsylvania; and we hope those gentlemen who are able, will contribute towards the making this such. We ask assistance, because we are fully sensible, that to publish a good news-paper is not so easy an undertaking as many people imagine it to be. The author of a gazette (in the opinion of the learned) ought to be qualified with an extensive acquaintance with languages, a great easiness and command of writing and relating things cleanly and intelligibly, and in few words; he should be able to speak of war both by land and sea; be well acquainted with geography, with the history of the time, with the several interests of princes and states, the secrets of courts, and the manners and customs of all nations. Men thus accomplished are very rare in this remote part of the world; and it would be well if the writer of these papers could make up among his friends what is wanting in himself.

Upon the whole, we may assure the public, that as far as the encouragement we meet with will enable us, no care and pains shall be omitted, that may make *The Pennsylvania Gazette* as agreeable and useful an entertainment as the nature of the thing will allow.

THE LESSONS OF MISPRINTS

In a classic canny maneuver, Franklin corrected an early typo—he had reported that someone "died" at a restaurant when he meant to say "dined" at it—by composing a letter from a fictitious "J.T." that discoursed on other amusing misprints. For example, one edition of the Bible quoted David as saying he was "wonderfully mad" rather than "made," which caused an "ignorant preacher to harangue his audience for half an hour on the subject of spiritual madness." Franklin then went on (under the guise of J.T.) to praise Franklin's own paper, point out a similar typo made by his rival Bradford, criticize Bradford for being generally sloppier, and (with delicious irony) praise Franklin for not criticizing Bradford.

THE PENNSYLVANIA GAZETTE, MARCH 13, 1730

Printerum est errare.

Sir,

As your last paper was reading in some company where I was present, these words were taken notice of in the article concerning governor belcher, [*after which his excellency, with the gentlemen trading to New England,* died *elegantly at Pontacks*]. The word *died* should doubtless have been *dined,* Pontacks being a noted tavern and eating-house in London for gentlemen of condition; but this omission of the letter (*n*) in that word, gave us as much entertainment as any part of your paper. One took the opportunity of telling us, that in a certain edition of the bible, the printer had, where David says I *am fearfully and wonderfully made,* omitted the letter (*e*) in the last word, so that it was, I *am fearfully and wonderfully mad;* which occasioned an ignorant preacher, who took that text, to harangue his audience for half an hour on the subject of *spiritual madness.* Another related to us, that when the company of stationers in England had the printing of the bible in their hands, the word (*not*) was left out in the seventh commandment, and the whole edition was printed off with *thou shalt commit adultery,* instead of *thou shalt not,* &c. This material *erratum induced the crown to take the patent from them which is now* held by the king's printer. The *Spectator's* remark upon this story is, that he doubts many of our modern gentlemen have this faulty edition by E.M., and are not made sensible of the mistake. A third person in the company acquainted us with an unlucky fault that went through a whole impression of common-prayerbooks; in the funeral service, where these words are, *we shall all be changed in a moment, in the twinkling of an eye,* &c. The printer had omitted the (*c*) in *changed,* and it read thus, *we shall all be hanged,* &c. And lastly, a mistake of your brother news-printer was mentioned, in *the speech of James*

Prouse written the night before he was to have been executed, instead of I *die a Protestant,* he has put it, I *died a Protestant.* Upon the whole you came off with the more favorable censure, because your paper is most commonly very correct, and yet you were never known to triumph upon it, by publicly ridiculing and exposing the continual blunders of your contemporary. Which observation was concluded by a good old gentleman in company, with this general just remark, that whoever accustoms himself to pass over in silence the faults of his neighbors, shall meet with much better quarter from the world when he happens to fall into a mistake himself; for the satirical and censorious, whose hand is against every man, shall upon such occasions have every man's hand against him. I am, Sir, your Friend, &c.

J.T.

RULES FOR MARRIAGE

In September of 1730, Franklin entered into a common-law marriage with Deborah Read, the girl who had laughed at him years earlier when he straggled as a runaway into Pennsylvania. Because she had been married once before to a man who then ran away, they could not enter into an official marriage out of fear of being charged with bigamy. It was a very practical marriage, more a fond partnership than a passionate romance. A month after they began living together as man and wife, he published a set of rules for marital happiness that reflected both the nature of his marriage and his penchant for making funny lists. He apologized for aiming his advice at women, since men were in fact more faulty, "but the reason is because I esteem them better disposed to receive and practice it."

Fortunately for him, Deborah tended to share his practical views. In general she had plain tastes, a willingness to work, and a desire to please her spouse. Of course, as he might have pointed out, the same could be said of him. And so they settled into a partnership that was

both more and less than a conventional marriage. A tireless collabora-
tor both in the house and at work, Deborah handled most of the accounts and expanded their shop's inventory to include ointments made
by her mother, crown soap made by Franklin's Boston relatives, coffee,
tea, chocolate, saffron, cheese, fish and various other sundries.

THE PENNSYLVANIA GAZETTE, OCTOBER 8, 1730

Rules and Maxims for Promoting Matrimonial Happiness

Ver novum, ver jam canorum, vere natus Orbis est:
Vere concordant amores, vere nubent alites
—Catul

Faelices ter, & amplius,
Quos irrupta tenet Copula: nec malis
Divulsis Querimoniis
Suprema citius solvet amor die.
—Horat

The happy state of matrimony is, undoubtedly, the surest and most
lasting foundation of comfort and love; the source of all that endearing
tenderness and affection which arises from relation and affinity; the grand
point of property; the cause of all good order in the world, and what alone
preserves it from the utmost confusion; and, to sum up all, the appointment of infinite wisdom for these great and good purposes. Notwithstanding, such is the perverseness of human nature, and so easy is it to
misuse the best of things, that by the folly and ill-behavior of those who
enter into it, this is very often made a state of the most exquisite
wretchedness and misery; which gives the wild and vicious part of
mankind but too much reason to rail against it, and treat it with contempt.
Wherefore, it highly becomes the virtuous of both sexes, by the prudence
of their conduct, to redeem this noble institution from those unjust reproaches which it at present labors under, and restore it to the honor and
esteem it merits, by endeavoring to make each other as happy as they can.

I am now about to lay down such rules and maxims as I think most
practicable and conducive towards the end and happiness of matrimony. And these I address to all females that would be married, or are

already so; not that I suppose their sex more faulty than the other, and most to want advice, for I assure them, upon my honor, I believe the quite contrary; but the reason is, because I esteem them better disposed to receive and practice it, and therefore am willing to begin, where I may promise myself the best success. Besides, if there is any truth in Proverbs, *Good Wives* usually make *Good Husbands.*

RULES and MAXIMS for promoting Matrimonial Happiness.
Addressed to all Widows, Wives, *and* Spinsters.

The likeliest way, either to obtain a *good husband,* or to keep one *so,* is to be *good* yourself.

Never use a *lover* ill whom you design to make your *husband,* lest he either upbraid you with it, or return it afterwards: and if you find, at any time, an inclination to play the tyrant, remember these two lines of truth and justice.

Gently shall those be *ruled,* who *gently* swayed;
abject shall those *obey,* who *haughty* were *obeyed.*

Avoid, both before and after marriage, all thoughts of managing your husband. Never endeavor to deceive or impose on his understanding: nor give him *uneasiness* (as some do very foolishly) to *try* his temper; but treat him always beforehand with sincerity, and afterwards with *affection* and *respect.*

Be not over sanguine before marriage, nor promise your self felicity without alloy, for that's impossible to be attained in this present state of things. Consider beforehand, that the person you are going to spend your days with, is a man, and not an angel; and if, when you come together, you discover any thing in his humor or behavior that is not altogether so agreeable as you expected, *pass it over as a humane frailty:* smooth your brow; compose your temper; and try to amend it by *cheerfulness* and good-nature.

Remember always, that whatever misfortunes may happen to either, they are not to be charged to the account of *matrimony,* but to the accidents and infirmities of humane life, a burthen which each has engaged to assist the other in supporting, and to which both parties are equally exposed. Therefore, instead of *murmurs,* reflections, and *dis-agreement,* whereby the *weight* is rendered abundantly more *grievous,* readily put your shoulders to the yoke, and make it easier to both.

Resolve every morning to be *good-natured* and CHEERFUL that day: and if any accident should happen to break that resolution, suffer it not to put you out of temper with every thing besides, and especially with your husband.

Dispute not with him, be the occasion what it will; but much rather deny yourself the trivial satisfaction of having your own will, or gaining the better of an argument, than risk a quarrel or create an heart-burning, which it's impossible to know the end of.

Be assured, a woman's power, as well as happiness, has no other foundation but her husband's esteem and love, which consequently it is her undoubted interest by all means possible to preserve and increase. Do you, therefore, study his temper, and command your own; enjoy his satisfaction with him, share and sooth his cares, and with the utmost diligence conceal his infirmities.

Read frequently with due attention the matrimonial service; and take care in doing so, not to overlook the word *obey.*

In your prayers be sure to add a clause for grace to make you a good wife; and at the same time, resolve to do your utmost endeavor towards it.

Always wear your wedding ring, for therein lies more virtue than usually is imagined. If you are ruffled unawares, assaulted with im-proper thoughts, or tempted in any kind against your duty, cast your eyes upon it, and call to mind, who gave it you, where it was received, and what passed at that solemn time.

Let the tenderness of your conjugal love be expressed with such de-cency, delicacy and prudence, as that it may appear plainly and thor-oughly distinct from the designing fondness of an harlot.

Have you any concern for your own ease, or for your husband's es-teem? Then, have a due regard to his income and circumstances in all your expenses and desires: for if necessity should follow, you run the greatest hazard of being deprived of both.

Let not many days pass together without a serious examination how you have behaved as a wife, and if upon reflection you find your self guilty of any foibles or omissions, the best atonement is, to be ex-actly careful of your future conduct.

I am fully persuaded, that a strict adherence to the foregoing rules would equally advance the honor of matrimony, and the *glory* of the *fair sex:* and since the greatest part of them, with a very little alteration, are as proper for husbands as for wives to practice, I recommend them accordingly to their consideration, and hope, in a short time, to receive acknowledgments from *married persons* of *both sexes* for the benefit they receive thereby.

And now, in behalf of my *unlearned readers,* I beg leave of my learned ones, to conclude this discourse with Mr. *Creech*'s translation of that part of *Horace* which I have taken for the motto of this paper.

> Thrice happy *they,* that free from *strife,*
> maintain a *love* as long as life:
> whose fixt and binding vows,
> no intervening *jealousy,*
> no *fears* and no *debates* untie;
> and *death* alone can loose.

A SCOLDING WIFE

Franklin's affection for Deborah grew from his pride at her industry; many years later, when he was in London arguing before the House of Commons that unfair taxes would lead to boycotts of British manufac-turers, he asserted that he had never been prouder than when he was a young tradesman and wore only clothes that had been made by the spinning wheel of his wife.

But Deborah was not merely a submissive or meek partner to the man she often addressed (as he did her) "my dear child" and whom she sometimes publicly called "Pappy." She had a fierce temper, which Franklin invariably defended. "Don't you know that all wives are in the right?" he asked a nephew who was having a dispute with Deborah. Soon after their marriage, he wrote a piece called "A Scolding Wife," in which he defended assertive women by saying they tended to be "active in the business of the family, special good housewives, and very careful of their husband's interests."

THE PENNSYLVANIA GAZETTE, JULY 5, 1733

Sir,

'Tis an old saying and a true one, that *there is no Conveniency without an Inconveniency:* For aught I know, there might be a saying not less true, though more new, *That there is no Inconveniency without a Conveniency.*

However, there is the Inconveniency (as 'tis commonly thought) of a Scolding Wife, which has conveniencies enough in it, to make it (when rightly considered) esteemed a happiness. For I speak from experience, (as well as a long course of observation) women of that character have generally sound and healthy constitutions, produce a vigorous offspring, are active in the business of the family, special good housewives, and very careful of their husband's interest. As to the noise attending all this, 'tis but a trifle when a man is used to it, and observes that 'tis only a mere habit, an exercise, in which all is well meant, and ought to be well taken. For my own part, I sincerely declare, that the meek whining complaints of my first wife, and the silent affected discontent in the countenance of my second, gave me (either of them) ten times the uneasiness that the clamor of my present dear spouse is capable of giving. 'Tis my opinion, in short, that their freedom of speech springs from a sense they have, that they do their duty in every part towards their husbands, and that no man can say, *black is* (the white of) *their eye.* . . .

A WITCH TRIAL AT MOUNT HOLLY

Among Franklin's famous spoofs in a report on a purported witch trial, which was a delightful parody of Puritan mystical beliefs clashing with scientific experimentation. Cotton Mather, who had been lampooned in James Franklin's paper but who later befriended Benjamin, had been involved in the Witch Trials of Salem.

THE PENNSYLVANIA GAZETTE, OCTOBER 22, 1730

Burlington, Oct. 12. Saturday last at *Mount-Holly,* about 8 miles from this place, near 300 people were gathered together to see an experiment or two tried on some persons accused of witchcraft. It seems the accused had been charged with making their neighbors' sheep dance in an uncommon manner, and with causing hogs to speak, and sing psalms, &c. To the great terror and amazement of the king's good and peaceable subjects in this province; and the accusers being very positive that if the accused were weighed in scales against a bible, the bible would prove too heavy for them; or that, if they were bound and put into the river, they would swim; the said accused desirous to make their innocence appear, voluntarily offered to undergo the said trials, if 2 of the most violent of their accusers would be tried with them. Accordingly the time and place was agreed on, and advertised about the country; the accusers were 1 man and 1 woman; and the accused the same. The parties being met, and the people got together, a grand consultation was held, before they proceeded to trial; in which it was agreed to use the scales first; and a committee of men were appointed to search the men, and a committee of women to search the women, to see if they had any thing of weight about them, particularly pins. After the scrutiny was over, a huge great bible belonging to the justice of the place was provided, and a lane through the populace was made from the justice's house to the scales, which were fixed on a gallows erected for that purpose opposite to the house, that the justice's wife and the rest of the ladies might see the trial, without coming amongst the mob;

and after the manner of *Moorfields,* a large ring was also made. Then came out of the house a grave tall man carrying the holy writ before the supposed wizard, &c. (as solemnly as the sword-bearer of *London* before the Lord Mayor) the wizard was first put in the scale, and over him was read a chapter out of the books of *Moses,* and then the bible was put in the other scale, (which being kept down before) was immediately let go; but to the great surprise of the spectators, flesh and bones came down plump, and outweighed that great good book by abundance. After the same manner, the others were served, and their lumps of mortality severally were too heavy for *Moses* and all the prophets and apostles. This being over, the accusers and the rest of the mob, not satisfied with this experiment, would have the trial by water; accordingly a most solemn procession was made to the millpond; where both accused and accusers being stripped (saving only to the women their shifts) were bound hand and foot, and severally placed in the water, lengthways, from the side of a barge or flat, having for security only a rope about the middle of each, which was held by some in the flat. The accuser man being thin and spare, with some difficulty began to sink at last; but the rest every one of them swam very light upon the water. A sailor in the flat jumped out upon the back of the man accused, thinking to drive him down to the bottom; but the person bound, without any help, came up some time before the other. The woman accuser, being told that she did not sink, would be ducked a second time; when she swam again as light as before. Upon which she declared, that she believed the accused had bewitched her to make her so light, and that she would be ducked again a hundred times, but she would duck the devil out of her. The accused man, being surprised at his own swimming, was not so confident of his innocence as before, but said, *if I am a witch, it is more than I know.* The more thinking part of the spectators were of opinion, that any person so bound and placed in the water (unless they were mere skin and bones) would swim till their breath was gone, and their lungs filled with water. But it being the general belief of the populace, that the women's shifts, and the garters with which they were bound helped to support them; it is said they are to be tried again the next warm weather, naked.

A PRINTER'S CREED

Franklin had a lot of fun with his paper, but there was one belief he held deeply and sincerely: that of the value of a free press. When he was criticized for something he printed that was considered profane, he responded with what is the classic defense of journalistic freedom and opposition to censorship. Yet it is noteworthy that he also includes a section on how such freedom also carries with it a duty to act responsibly.

THE PENNSYLVANIA GAZETTE, JUNE 10, 1731

Being frequently censured and condemned by different persons for printing things which they say ought not to be printed, I have sometimes thought it might be necessary to make a standing apology for my self, and publish it once a year, to be read upon all occasions of that nature. Much business has hitherto hindered the execution of this design; but having very lately given extraordinary offence by printing an advertisement with a certain *N.B.* At the end of it, I find an apology more particularly requisite at this juncture, though it happens when I have not yet leisure to write such a thing in the proper form, and can only in a loose manner throw those considerations together which should have been the substance of it.

I request all who are angry with me on the account of printing things they don't like, calmly to consider these following particulars.

1. That the opinions of men are almost as various as their faces; an observation general enough to become a common proverb, *so many men so many minds.*

2. That the business of printing has chiefly to do with men's opinions; most things that are printed tending to promote some, or oppose others.

3. That hence arises the peculiar unhappiness of that business, which other callings are no way liable to; they who follow printing being scarce able to do any thing in their way of getting a living, which

shall not probably give offence to some, and perhaps to many; whereas the smith, the shoemaker, the carpenter, or the man of any other trade, may work indifferently for people of all persuasions, without offending any of them: and the merchant may buy and sell with Jews, Turks, heretics, and infidels of all sorts, and get money by every one of them, without giving offence to the most orthodox, of any sort; or suffering the least censure or ill-will on the account from any man whatever.

4. That it is as unreasonable in any one man or set of men to expect to be pleased with every thing that is printed, as to think that nobody ought to be pleased but themselves.

5. Printers are educated in the belief, that when men differ in opinion, both sides ought equally to have the advantage of being heard by the public; and that when truth and error have fair play, the former is always an overmatch for the latter: hence they cheerfully serve all contending writers that pay them well, without regarding on which side they are of the question in dispute.

6. Being thus continually employed in serving all parties, printers naturally acquire a vast unconcernedness as to the right or wrong opinions contained in what they print; regarding it only as the matter of their daily labor: they print things full of spleen and animosity, with the utmost calmness and indifference, and without the least ill-will to the persons reflected on; who nevertheless unjustly think the printer as much their enemy as the author, and join both together in their resentment.

7. That it is unreasonable to imagine printers approve of every thing they print, and to censure them on any particular thing accordingly; since in the way of their business they print such great variety of things opposite and contradictory. It is likewise as unreasonable what some assert, *that printers ought not to print any thing but what they approve;* since if all of that business should make such a resolution, and abide by it, an end would thereby be put to free writing, and the world would afterwards have nothing to read but what happened to be the opinions of printers.

8. That if all printers were determined not to print any thing until they were sure it would offend no body, there would be very little printed.

9. That if they sometimes print vicious or silly things not worth reading, it may not be because they approve such things themselves, but because the people are so viciously and corruptly educated that good things are not encouraged. I have known a very numerous impression of *Robin Hood's Songs* go off in this province at *2s.* per book, in less than a twelvemonth; when a small quantity of *David's psalms* (an excellent version) have lain upon my hands above twice the time.

10. That notwithstanding what might be urged in behalf of a man's being allowed to do in the way of his business whatever he is paid for, yet printers do continually discourage the printing of great numbers of bad things, and stifle them in the birth. I my self have constantly refused to print any thing that might countenance vice, or promote immorality; though by complying in such cases with the corrupt taste of the majority, I might have got much money. I have also always refused to print such things as might do real injury to any person, how much soever I have been solicited, and tempted with offers of great pay; and how much soever I have by refusing got the ill-will of those who would have employed me. I have heretofore fallen under the resentment of large bodies of men, for refusing absolutely to print any of their party or personal reflections.

In this manner I have made my self many enemies, and the constant fatigue of denying is almost insupportable. But the public being unacquainted with all this, whenever the poor printer happens either through ignorance or much persuasion, to do any thing that is generally thought worthy of blame, he meets with no more friendship or favor on the above account, than if there were no merit in it at all. Thus, as Waller says,

> *Poets loose half the praise they would have got*
> *Were it but known what they discreetly blot;*

Yet are censured for every bad line found in their works with the utmost severity. . . .

I take leave to conclude with an old fable, which some of my readers have heard before, and some have not.

A certain well-meaning man and his son, were traveling towards a market town, with an ass which they had to sell. The road was bad; and the old man therefore rid, but the son went a-foot. The first passenger they met, asked the father if he was not ashamed to ride by himself, and suffer the poor lad to wade along thro the mire; this induced him to take up his son behind him: he had not traveled far, when he met others, who said, they were two unmerciful lubbers to get both on the back of that poor ass, in such a deep road. Upon this the old man gets off, and let his son ride alone. The next they met called the lad a graceless, rascally young jackanapes, to ride in that manner thro the dirt, while his aged father trudged along on foot; and they said the old man was a fool, for suffering it. He then bid his son come down, and walk with him, and they traveled on leading the ass by the halter, till they met another company, who called them a couple of senseless blockheads, for going both on foot in such a dirty way, when they had an empty ass with them, which they might ride upon. The old man could bear no longer; my son, said he, it grieves me much that we cannot please all these people: let us throw the ass over the next bridge, and be no farther trebled with him.

Had the old man been seen acting this last resolution, he would probably have been called a fool for troubling himself about the different opinions of all that were pleased to find fault with him: therefore, though I have a temper almost as complying as his, I intend not to imitate him in this last particular. I consider the variety of humors among men, and despair of pleasing every body; yet I shall not therefore leave off printing. I shall continue my business. I shall not burn my press and melt my letters.

SEX SELLS

Along with such high-minded principles, Franklin employed some more common strategies to push papers. One ever reliable method, which had particular appeal to the rather raunchy young publisher, was the time-honored truth that sex sells. Franklin's *Gazette* was spiced with little leering and titillating items. In the issue a week after his "Apology for Printers," for example, Franklin wrote about a husband who caught his wife in bed with a man named Stonecutter. The next issue had a similar short item about a horny constable, who had "made an agreement with a neighboring female to *watch* with her that night" and then mistakenly climbs into the window of a different woman, whose husband was in another room. And then there was the story of the sex-starved woman who wanted to divorce her husband because he could not satisfy her. After her husband was medically examined, however, she moved back in with him.

THE PENNSYLVANIA GAZETTE, JUNE 17, 1731

Friday night last, a certain St-n-c-tt-r was, it seems, in a fair way of dying the Death of a Nobleman; for being caught napping with another man's wife, the injured husband took the advantage of his being so fast asleep, and with a knife began very diligently to cut off his head. But the instrument not being equal to the intended operation, much struggling prevented success; and he was obliged to content himself for the present with bestowing on the aggressor a sound drubbing. The gap made in the side of the st-n-c-tt-r's neck, though deep, is not thought dangerous; but some people admire, that when the person offended had so fair and suitable an opportunity, it did not enter into his head to turn st-n-c-tt-r himself.

THE PENNSYLVANIA GAZETTE, JUNE 24, 1731

Sure some unauspicious cross-grained planet, in opposition to *Venus*, presides over the affairs of love about this time. For we hear, that on Tuesday last, a certain c-n-table having made an agreement with a neighboring female, to *watch* with her that night; she promised to leave a window open for him to come in at; but he going his rounds in the dark, unluckily mistook the window, and got into a room where another woman was in bed, and her husband it seems lying on a couch not far distant. The good woman perceiving presently by the extraordinary fondness of her bedfellow that it could not possibly be her husband, made so much disturbance as to wake the good man; who finding somebody had got into his place without his leave, began to lay about him unmercifully; and 'twas thought, that had not our poor mistaken gallant, called out manfully for help (as if he were commanding assistance in the king's name) and thereby raised the family, he would have stood no more chance for his life between the wife and husband, than a captive L——between two thumb nails.

THE PENNSYLVANIA GAZETTE, JULY 29, 1731

We are credibly informed, that the young woman who not long since petitioned the governor, and the assembly to be divorced from her husband, and at times industriously solicited most of the magistrates on that account, has at last concluded to cohabit with him again. It is said the report of the physicians (who in form examined his *abilities,* and allowed him to be in every respect sufficient,) gave her but small satisfaction; whether any experiments *more satisfactory* have been tried, we cannot say; but it seems she now declares it as her opinion, that *George is as good as de best.*

ANTHONY AFTERWIT ON MARRIAGE

Before he had entered into a union with Deborah, Franklin had courted a woman from a wealthier family. Dowries being common for such matches, Franklin sought to negotiate one of approximately £100. When the girl's family replied that they could not spare that much, Franklin suggested rather unromantically that they could mortgage their home. The girl's family broke off the relationship, either out of outrage or (as Franklin suspected) in the hope that the courtship had gone so far that they would elope without a dowry. Resentful, Franklin refused to have anything more to do with the girl.

Franklin satirized the process in the *Gazette* a few years later, after he had married Deborah without a dowry, using the pseudonym An-

thony Afterwit. The piece also returned to his theme of the virtue of frugality. Afterwit, after complaining about having to elope with no dowry,
goes on to ridicule his wife for adopting the airs and spending habits of
a gentlewoman, including her desire for a tea set.

The Anthony Afterwit essay had an interesting side effect. His fictional wife, Abigail Afterwit, was the name of a character that had been
created by Franklin's brother James almost a decade earlier in the *New-
England Courant*. James, who had since moved to Rhode Island,
reprinted the Anthony Afterwit piece in his own paper along with a reply
from a Patience Teacraft. Benjamin in turn reprinted the reply in his
Philadelphia paper, and the following year he visited his brother for an
emotional reconciliation.

THE PENNSYLVANIA GAZETTE, JULY 10, 1732

Mr. *Gazetteer*,

I am an honest tradesman, who never meant harm to any body.
My affairs went on smoothly while a bachelor; but of late I have met
with some difficulties, of which I take the freedom to give you an
account.

About the time I first addressed my present spouse, her father gave
out in speeches, that if she married a man he liked, he would give with
her £200 on the day of marriage. 'Tis true he never said so to me, but he
always received me very kindly at his house, and openly countenanced
my courtship. I formed several fine schemes, what to do with this same
£200 and in some measure neglected my business on that account: but
unluckily it came to pass, that when the old gentleman saw I was pretty
well engaged, and that the match was too far gone to be easily broke
off; he, without any reason given, grew very angry, forbid me the house,
and told his daughter that if she married me he would not give her a
farthing. However (as he foresaw) we were not to be disappointed in
that manner; but having stole a wedding, I took her home to my house;
where we were not in quite so poor a condition as the couple described
in the scotch song, who had

Neither pot nor pan,
but four bare legs together;

For I had a house tolerably furnished, for an ordinary man, before. No thanks to dad, who I understand was very much pleased with his politick management. And I have since learned that there are old curmudgeons (so called) besides him, who have this trick, to marry their daughters, and yet keep what they might well spare, till they can keep it no longer: but this by way of digression; *a word to the wise is enough.*

I soon saw that with care and industry we might live tolerably easy, and in credit with our neighbors: but my wife had a strong inclination to be a *gentlewoman.* In consequence of this, my old-fashioned looking-glass was one day broke, as she said, *no mortal could tell which way.* However, since we could not be without a glass in the room, *my dear,* says she, *we may as well buy a large fashionable one that Mr. Such-a-one has to sell; it will cost but little more than a common glass, and will be much handsomer and more creditable.* Accordingly the glass was bought, and hung against the wall: but in a week's time, I was made sensible by little and little, that the table was by no means suitable to such a glass. And a more proper table being procured, my spouse, who was an excellent contriver, informed me where we might have very handsome chairs *in the way;* and thus, by degrees, I found all my old furniture stowed up into the garret, and every thing below altered for the better.

Had we stopped here, we might have done well enough; but my wife being entertained with *tea* by the good women she visited, we could do no less than the like when they visited us; and so we got a tea-table with all its appurtenances of *china* and *silver.* Then my spouse unfortunately overworked herself in washing the house, so that we could do no longer without a *maid.* Besides this, it happened frequently, that when I came home at *one,* the dinner was but just put in the pot; for, *my dear thought really it had been but eleven:* at other times when I came at the same hour, *she wondered I would stay so long, for dinner was ready and had waited for me these two hours.* These irregularities, occasioned by mistaking the time, convinced me, that it was absolutely necessary *to buy a clock;* which my spouse observed, *was a great ornament to the room!* And lastly, to my grief, she was frequently troubled with some ailment or other, and nothing did her so much good as *riding;* and *these hackney horses were such wretched ugly creatures, that*—I bought a very fine pacing mare, which cost £20 and hereabouts affairs have stood for some months past.

I could see all along, that this way of living was utterly inconsistent with my circumstances, but had not resolution enough to help it. Till lately, receiving a very severe dun, which mentioned the next court, I began in earnest to project relief. Last Monday my dear went over the river, to see a relation, and stay a fortnight, because *she could not bear the heat of the town.* In the interim, I have taken my turn to make alterations, *viz.* I have turned away the maid, bag and baggage (for what should we do with a maid, who have (except my boy) none but our selves). I have sold the fine pacing mare, and bought a good milk cow, with £3 of the money. I have disposed of the tea-table, and put a spinning wheel in its place, which methinks *looks very pretty:* nine empty canisters I have stuffed with flax; and with some of the money of the tea-furniture, I have bought a set of knitting-needles; for to tell you a truth, which I would have go no farther, I *begin to want stockings.* The stately clock I have transformed into an hour-glass, by which I gained a good round sum; and one of the pieces of the old looking-glass, squared and framed, supplies the place of the great one, which I have conveyed into a closet, where it may possibly remain some years. In short, the face of things is quite changed; and I am mightily pleased when I look at my hour-glass, *what an ornament it is to the room.* I have paid my debts, and find money in my pocket. I expect my dame home next Friday, and as your paper is taken in at the house where she is, I hope the reading of this will prepare her mind for the above surprising revolutions. If she can conform to this new scheme of living, we shall be the happiest couple perhaps in the province, and, by the blessing of god, may soon be in thriving circumstances. I have reserved the great glass, because I know her heart is set upon it. I will allow her when she comes in, to be taken suddenly ill with the *headache,* the *stomach-ache,* fainting-fits, or whatever other disorder she may think more proper; and she may retire to bed as soon as she pleases: but if I do not find her in perfect health both of body and mind the next morning, away goes the aforesaid great glass, with several other trinkets I have no occasion for, to the vendue that very day. Which is the irrevocable resolution of, Sir, Her loving husband, *and* Your very humble servant,

Anthony Afterwit

Postscript, You know we can return to our former way of living, when we please, if *Dad* will be at the expense of it.

CELIA SINGLE RESPONDS

Less sexist than most men of his day, Franklin also aimed his barbs at men. Afterwit's letter was answered two weeks later by one from Celia Single. With the delightful gossipy voice of Franklin's other female characters, such as Silence Dogood, Single recounts a visit to a friend whose husband is trying to replicate Afterwit's approach. A raucous argument ensues.

THE PENNSYLVANIA GAZETTE, JULY 24, 1732

My Correspondent Mrs. Celia, *must excuse my omitting those circumstances of her letter, which point at people* too plainly; *and content herself that I insert the rest as follows.*

Mr. *Gazetteer,*

I must needs tell you, that some of the things you print do more harm than good; particularly I think so of my neighbor the tradesman's letter in one of your late papers, which has broken the peace of several families, by causing difference between men and their wives: I shall give you here one instance, of which I was an eye and ear witness.

Happening last *Wednesday* morning to be in at Mrs. C————ss's, when her husband returned from market, among other things which he had bought, he showed her some balls of thread. *My dear,* says he, I *like mightily those stockings which I yesterday saw neighbor* Afterwit *knitting for her husband, of thread of her own spinning: I should be glad to have some such stockings my self: I understand that your maid* Mary *is a very good knitter, and seeing this thread in market, I have bought it, that the girl may make a pair or two for me.* Mrs. *Careless* was just then at the glass, dressing her head; and turning about with the pins in her mouth, lord, child, says she, *are you crazy? What time has* Mary *to knit? Who must do the work, I wonder, if you set her to knitting?* Perhaps, my dear, *says he,* you have a mind to knit 'em yourself; I remember, when I courted you, I once heard you say you had learned to knit of your mother. I *knit stockings for you,* says she, *not I truly; there are poor women enough in town, that can knit; if you please you may employ them.* Well, but my dear, *says he,* you know a penny saved is a penny got, a pin a day is a groat a year, every little makes a nickel, and there is neither sin nor shame in knitting a pair of stockings; why should you express such a mighty aversion to it? As to *poor* women, you know we are not people of quality, we have no income to maintain us, but what arises from my labor and industry; methinks you should not be at all displeased, if you have an opportunity to get something as well as my self. I *wonder,* says she, *how you can propose such a thing to me; did not you always tell me you would maintain me like a gentlewoman? If I had married* Capt.————, *he would have scorned even to mention knitting of stockings.* Prithee, *says he, (a little nettled)* what do you tell me of your captains? If you could have had him, I suppose you would; or perhaps you did not very well like him: if I did promise to maintain you like a gentlewoman, I suppose 'tis time enough for that when you know how to behave like one; mean while 'tis your duty to help make me able. How long do you think I can maintain you at your present rate of living? *Pray,* says she, (somewhat fiercely, and dashing the puff into the powder-box) *don't use me after this manner, for I assure you I won't bear it. This is the fruit of your poison* newspapers; *there shall come no more here, I promise you.* Bless us, *says he,* what an unaccountable thing is this! Must a tradesman's daughter, and the wife of a tradesman, necessarily and instantly be a gentlewoman? You had no portion; I am forced to work for a living; if you are too great to do the like, there's the door, go and live upon your estate, if you can find it; in short, I don't desire to be troubled—what answer she made, I cannot tell; for knowing that a man and his wife are apt to quarrel more violently when before strangers, than when by themselves, I got up and went out hastily: but I understood from *Mary,* who came to me of an errand in the evening, that they dined together pretty peaceably, (the balls of thread that had caused the difference, being thrown into the kitchen fire) of which I was very glad to hear.

I have several times in your paper seen severe reflections upon us women, for idleness and extravagance, but I do not remember to have once seen any such animadversions upon the men. If I were disposed to be censorious, I could furnish you with instances enough: I might mention Mr. *Billiard,* who spends more than he earns, at the green table; and would have been in jail long since, were it not for his industrious wife: Mr. *Husselcap,* who often all day long leaves his business for the rattling of halfpence in a certain alley: Mr. *Finikin,* who has seven different suits of fine clothes, and wears a change every day, while his wife and children sit at home half naked: Mr. *Crownhim,* who is always dreaming over the checker-board, and cares not how the world goes, so he gets the game: Mr. *T'otherpot* the tavern-haunter; Mr. *Bookish,* the everlasting reader; Mr. *Tweedledum,* Mr. *Toot-a-toot,* and several others, who are mighty diligent at any thing beside their business. I say, if I were disposed to be censorious, I might mention all these, and more; but I hate to be thought a scandalizer of my neighbors, and therefore forbear. And for your part, I would advise you, for the future, to entertain your readers with something else besides people's reflections upon one another; for remember, that there are holes enough to be picked in your coat as well as others; and those that are affronted by the satyrs you may publish, will not consider so much who *wrote,* as who *printed:* take not this freedom amiss, from,

> Your Friend and Reader,
> Celia Single

IN PRAISE OF GOSSIP

In his first Busy-Body essay, Franklin had defended the value of nosiness and tattling. Now that he had his own paper, he made it clear that the Gazette was pleased, indeed proud, to continue this service. Using the same tone as the Busy-Body, Franklin wrote an anonymous essay defending gossip and followed it the next week by a fake letter from the aptly named Alice Addertongue urging his paper to print more gossip. Franklin, who was then 26, had Alice identify herself, with an edge of irony, as a "young girl of about thirty-five."

The Pennsylvania Gazette, September 7, 1732

> *Impia sub dulci melle venena latent.*
> —Ovid
> *Naturam expellas furca licet, usq; recurret.*
> —Horace

There is scarce any one thing so generally spoke against, and at the same time so universally practiced, as *censure* or backbiting. All divines have condemned it, all religions have forbid it, all writers of morality have endeavor's to discountenance it, and all men hate it at all times, except only when they have occasion to make use of it. For my part, after having frankly declared it as my opinion, that the general condemnation it meets with, proceeds only from a consciousness in most people that they have highly incurred and deserved it, I shall in a very fearless impudent manner take upon me to oppose the universal vogue of mankind in all ages, and say as much in behalf and vindication of this decried virtue, as the usual vacancy in your paper will admit.

I have called it a virtue, and shall take the same method to prove it such, as we commonly use to demonstrate any other action or habit to be a virtue, that is, by showing its usefulness, and the great good it does to society. What can be said to the contrary, has already been said by every body; and indeed it is so little to the purpose, that any body may easily say it: but the path I mean to tread, has hitherto been trod by no body; if therefore I should meet with the difficulties usual in tracing new roads, and be in some places a little at loss, the candor of the reader will the more readily excuse me.

The first advantage I shall mention, arising from the free practice of *censure* or *backbiting*, is, that it is frequently the means of preventing powerful, political, ill-designing men, from growing too popular for the safety of a state. Such men are always setting their best actions to view, in order to obtain confidence and trust, and establish a party: they endeavor to shine with false or borrowed merit, and carefully conceal their real demerit: (that they fear to be evil spoken of is evident from their striving to cover every ill with a specious pretence;) but all-examining censure, with her hundred eyes and her thousand tongues, soon discovers and as speedily divulges in all quarters, every the least crime or foible that is a part of their true character. This clips the wings of their ambition, weakens their cause and party, and reduces them to the necessity of dropping their pernicious designs, springing from a violent thirst of honor and power; or, if that thirst is unquenchable, they are obliged to enter into a course of true virtue, without which real grandeur is not to be attained.

Again, the common practice of *censure* is a mighty restraint upon the actions of every private man; it greatly assists our otherwise weak resolutions of living virtuously. *What will the world say of me, if I act thus?* Is often a reflection strong enough to enable us to resist the most powerful temptation to vice or folly. This preserves the integrity of the wavering, the honesty of the covetous, the sanctity of some of the religious, and the chastity of all virgins. And, indeed, when people once become regardless of censure, they are arrived to a pitch of impudence little inferior to the contempt of all laws humane and divine.

The common practice of *censure* is also exceedingly serviceable, in helping a man to *the knowledge of himself*, a piece of knowledge highly necessary for all, but acquired by very few, because very few sufficiently regard and value the censure past by others on their actions. There is hardly such a thing as a friend, sincere or rash enough to acquaint us freely with our faults; nor will any but an enemy tell us of what we have done amiss, *to our faces;* and enemies meet with little credit in such cases, for we believe they speak from malice and ill-will: thus we might always live in the blindest ignorance of our own folly, and, while every body reproached us in their hearts, might think our conduct irre-proachable: but thanks be to providence, (that has given every man a natural inclination to backbite his neighbor) we now hear of many things said *of* us, that we shall never hear said *to* us; (for out of goodwill to us, or ill will to those that have spoken ill of us, every one is willing enough to tell us how we are censured by others,) and we have the ad-vantage of mending our manners accordingly.

Another vast benefit arising from the common practice of backbit-ing, is, that it helps exceedingly to a thorough *knowledge of mankind,* a science the most useful of all sciences. Could we come to know no man of whom we had not a particular experience, our sphere of knowledge of this sort would certainly be narrow and confined, and yet at the same time must probably have cost us very dear. For the crafty tricking vil-lain would have a vast advantage over the honest undesigning part of men, when he might cheat and abuse almost every one he dealt with, if none would take the liberty to characterize him among their acquain-tance behind his back.

Without saying any more in its behalf, I am able to challenge all the orators or writers in the world, to show (with solid reason) that the few trifling inconveniencies attending it, bear any proportion to these vast benefits! And I will venture to assert to their noses, that nothing would be more absurd or pernicious than a law against backbiting, if such a law could possibly take effect; since it would undoubtedly be the great-est encouragement to vice that ever vice met with, and do more to-wards the increasing it, than would the abolishing of all other laws whatsoever.

I might likewise have mentioned the usefulness of *censure* in society, as it is a certain and an equal punishment for such follies and vices as the common laws either do not sufficiently punish, or have provided no punishment for. I might have observed, that were it not for this, we should find the number of some sorts of criminals increased to a degree sufficient not only to infest, but even to overthrow all good and civil conversation: but it is endless to enumerate every particular advantage arising from this glorious virtue! A virtue, which whoever exerts, must have the largest share of public spirit and self-denial, the highest benevolence and regard to the good of others; since in this he entirely sacrifices his own interest, making not only the persons he accuses, but all that hear him, his enemies; for all that deserve censure (which are by far the greatest number) hate the censorious;

> *That dangerous weapon, wit,*
> *frightens a million when a few you hit:*
> *whip but a cur as you ride thro' a town,*
> *and strait his fellow curs the quarrel own:*
> *each knave or fool that's conscious of a crime,*
> *though he escapes now, looks for it another time.*

A virtue! Decried by all that fear it, but a strong presumption of the innocence of them that practice it; for they cannot be encouraged to offend, from the least prospect of favor or impunity; their faults or failings will certainly meet with no quarter from others. And whoever practices the contrary, always endeavoring to excuse and palliate the crimes of others, may rationally be suspected to have some secret darling vice, which he hopes will be excused him in return. A virtue! Which however ill people may load it with the opprobrious names of *calumny, scandal,* and *detraction,* and I know not what; will still remain a virtue, a bright, shining, solid virtue, of more real use to mankind than all the other virtues put together; and indeed, is the mother or the protectress of them all, as well as the enemy, the destructress of all kinds of vice. A virtue, innately, necessarily, and essentially so; for——but, dear reader, large folio volumes closely written, would scarce be sufficient to contain all the praises due to it. I shall offer you at present only one more convincing argument in its behalf, *viz.* That you would not have had the satisfaction of seeing this discourse so agreeably short as I shall make it, were it not for the just fear I have of incurring your *censure,* should I continue to be troublesome by extending it to a greater length.

THE PENNSYLVANIA GAZETTE, SEPTEMBER 12, 1732

Mr. *Gazetteer,*

I was highly pleased with your last week's paper upon scandal, as the uncommon doctrine therein preached is agreeable both to my principles and practice, and as it was published very seasonably to reprove the impertinence of a writer in the foregoing Thursday's *Mercury,* who at the conclusion of one of his silly paragraphs, laments, forsooth, that the *fair sex* are so peculiarly guilty of this enormous crime: every blockhead ancient and modern, that could handle a pen, has I think taken upon him to cant in the same senseless strain. If to *scandalize* be really a *crime,* what do these puppies mean? They describe it, they dress it up in the most odious frightful and detestable colors, they represent it as the worst of crimes, and then roundly and charitably charge the whole race of womankind with it. Are they not then guilty of what they condemn, at the same time that they condemn it? If they accuse us of any other crime, they must necessarily *scandalize* while they do it: but to *scandalize* us with being guilty of *scandal,* is in itself an egregious absurdity, and can proceed from nothing but the most consummate impudence in conjunction with the most profound stupidity.

This, supposing, as they do, that to scandalize is a crime; which you have convinced all reasonable people, is an opinion absolutely erroneous. Let us leave then these idiot mock-moralists, while I entertain you with some account of my life and manners.

I am a young girl of about thirty-five, and live at present with my mother. I have no care upon my head of getting a living, and therefore find it my duty as well as inclination, to exercise my talent at censure, for the good of my country folks. There was, I am told, a certain generous emperor, who if a day had passed over his head, in which he had conferred no benefit on any man, used to say to his friends, in Latin, *diem perdidi,* that is, it seems, I *have lost a day.* I believe I should make use of the same expression, if it were possible for a day to pass in which I had not, or missed, an opportunity to scandalize somebody: but, thanks be praised, no such misfortune has befell me these dozen years.

Yet, whatever good I may do, I cannot pretend that I first entered into the practice of this virtue from a principle of public spirit; for I remember that when a child, I had a violent inclination to be ever talking in my own praise, and being continually told that it was ill manners, and once severely whipped for it, the confined stream formed itself a new channel, and I began to speak for the future in the dispraise of others. This I found more agreeable to company, and almost as much so to my self: for what great difference can there be, between putting your self up, or putting your neighbor down? *Scandal,* like other virtues, is in part its own reward, as it gives us the satisfaction of making our selves appear better than others, or others no better than ourselves.

My mother, good woman, and I, have heretofore differed upon this account. She argued that scandal spoilt all good conversation, and I insisted that without it there could be no such thing. Our disputes once rose so high, that we parted tea-table, and I concluded to entertain my acquaintance in the kitchen. The first day of this separation we both drank tea at the same time, but she with her visitors in the parlor. She would not hear of the least objection to any ones character, but began a new sort of discourse in some such queer philosophical manner as this; I *am mightily pleased sometimes,* says she, *when I observe and consider that the world is not so bad as people out of humor imagine it to be. There is something amiable, some good quality or other in every body. If we were only to speak of people that are least respected, there is* such a one *is very dutiful to her father, and methinks has a fine set of teeth;* such a one *is very respectful to her husband;* such a one *is very kind to her poor neighbors, and besides has a very handsome shape;* such a one *is always ready to serve a friend, and in my opinion there is not a woman in town that has a more agreeable air and gait.* This fine kind of talk, which lasted near half an hour, she concluded by saying, I *do not doubt but every one of you have made the like observations, and I should be glad to have the conversation continued upon this subject.* Just at that juncture I peeped in at the door, and never in my life before saw such a set of simple vacant countenances; they looked somehow neither glad, nor sorry, nor angry, nor pleased, nor indifferent, nor attentive; but, (excuse the simile) like so many blue wooden images of rye dough. I in the kitchen had already begun a ridiculous story of Mr.—'s intrigue with his maid, and his wife's behavior upon the discovery; at some passages we laughed heartily, and one of the gravest of mamas company, without making any answer to her discourse, got up *to go and see what the girls were so merry about:* she was followed by a second, and shortly after by a third, till at last the old gentlewoman found herself quite alone, and being convinced that her project was impracticable, came her self and finished her tea with us; ever since which *Saul also has been among the prophets,* and our disputes lie dormant.

By industry and application, I have made my self the center of all the *scandal* in the province, there is little stirring but I hear of it. I began the world with this maxim, *that no trade can subsist without returns;* and accordingly, whenever I received a good story, I endeavored to give two or a better in the room of it. My punctuality in this way of dealing gave such encouragement, that it has procured me an incredible deal of business, which without diligence and good method it would be impossible for me to go through. For besides the stock of defamation thus naturally flowing in upon me, I practice an art by which I can pump scandal out of people that are the least inclined that way. Shall I discover my secret? Yes; to let it die with me would be inhuman. If I have never heard ill of some person, I always impute it to defective intelligence; *for there are none without their faults, no not one.* If she is a woman, I take the first opportunity to let all her acquaintance know I have heard that one of the handsomest or best men in town has said something in praise either of her beauty, her wit, her virtue, or her good management. If you know anything of humane nature, you perceive that this naturally introduces a conversation turning upon all her failings, past, present, and to come. To the same purpose, and with the same success, I cause every man of reputation to be praised before his competitors in love, business, or esteem on account of any particular qualification. Near the times of *election,* if I find it necessary, I commend every candidate before some of the opposite party, listening attentively to what is said of him in answer: (but commendations in this latter case are not always necessary, and should be used judiciously;) of late years I needed only observe what they said of one another freely; and having for the help of memory taken account of all informations and accusations received, whoever peruses my writings after my death, may happen to think, that during a certain term, the people of Pennsylvania chose into all their offices of honor and trust, the veriest knaves, fools and rascals in the whole province. The time of election used to be a busy time with me, but this year, with concern I speak it, people are grown so good natured, so intent upon mutual feasting and friendly entertainment, that I see no prospect of much employment from that quarter.

I mentioned above, that without good method I could not go thro my business: in my father's life-time I had some instruction in accounts, which I now apply with advantage to my own affairs. I keep a regular set of books, and can tell at an hour's warning how it stands between me and the world. In my *daybook* I enter every article of defamation as it is transacted; for scandals *received in,* I give credit; and when I pay them out again, I make the persons to whom they respectively relate *debtor.* In my *journal,* I add to each story by way of improvement, such probable circumstances as I think it will bear, and in my *ledger* the whole is regularly posted.

I suppose the reader already condemns me in his heart, for this particular of *adding circumstances;* but I justify that part of my practice thus. 'Tis a principle with me, that none ought to have a greater share of reputation than they really deserve; if they have, 'tis an imposition upon the public: I know it is every ones interest, and therefore believe they endeavor, to conceal *all* their vices and follies; and I hold, that those people are *extraordinary* foolish or careless who suffer a *fourth* of their failings to come to public knowledge: taking then the common prudence and imprudence of mankind in a lump, I suppose none suffer above *one fifth* to be discovered: therefore when I hear of any persons misdoing, I think I keep within bounds if in relating it I only make it *three times* worse than it is; and I reserve to my self the privilege of charging them with one fault in four, which, for aught I know, they may be entirely innocent of. You see there are but few so careful of doing justice as my self; what reason then have mankind to complain of *scandal?* In a general way, the worst that is said of us is only half what *might* be said, if all our faults were seen.

But alas, two great evils have lately befallen me at the same time; an extreme cold that I can scarce speak, and a most terrible toothache that I dare hardly open my mouth: for some days past I have received ten stories for one I have paid; and I am not able to balance my accounts without your assistance. I have long thought that if you would make your paper a vehicle of scandal, you would double the number of your subscribers. I send you herewith account of *4 knavish tricks, 2 cracked almonds, 5 culdms, 3 drubbed wives,* and *4 henpecked husbands,* all within this fortnight; which you may, as articles of news, deliver to the public; and if my toothache continues, shall send you more; being, in the mean time, your constant reader,

Alice Addertongue

I thank my correspondent Mrs. Addertongue for her good-will; but desire to be excused inserting the articles of news she has sent me; such things being in reality no news at all.

THE DISCUSSION CLUB

Franklin was a consummate networker. He liked to mix his civic life with his social one, and he merrily leveraged both to further his business life. This approach was displayed when he formed a club of young workingmen, in the fall of 1727 shortly after his return to Philadelphia, that was commonly called "The Leather Apron Club" and officially dubbed "The Junto."

Franklin's little club was composed of enterprising tradesmen and artisans, rather than the social elite who had their own fancier gentlemen's clubs. At first the members went to a local tavern for their Friday evening meetings, but soon they were able to rent a house of their own. There they discussed issues of the day, debated philosophical topics, devised schemes for self-improvement, and formed a network for the furtherance of their own careers.

The enterprise was typical of Franklin, who seemed ever eager to organize clubs and associations for mutual benefit, and it was also typically American. As the nation developed a shopkeeping middle class, its people balanced their individualist streaks with a propensity to form clubs, lodges, associations and fraternal orders. Franklin epitomized this Rotarian urge and has remained, after more than two centuries, a symbol of it.

Besides being amiable clubmates, the Junto members often proved helpful to one another personally and professionally. Franklin also used the Junto to push his belief that the best method of discussion was gentle Socratic questioning rather than disputatious assertions and argument. It was a style he would urge upon the Constitutional Convention 60 years later.

PHILADELPHIA, 1732

Previous question, to be answered at every meeting.

Have you read over these queries this morning, in order to consider what you might have to offer the Junto [touching] any one of them? viz.

1. Have you met with any thing in the author you last read, remarkable, or suitable to be communicated to the Junto? particularly in history, morality, poetry, physic, travels, mechanic arts, or other parts of knowledge.

2. What new story have you lately heard agreeable for telling in conversation?

3. Hath any citizen in your knowledge failed in his business lately, and what have you heard of the cause?

4. Have you lately heard of any citizens thriving well, and by what means?

5. Have you lately heard how any present rich man, here or elsewhere, got his estate?

6. Do you know of any fellow citizen, who has lately done a worthy action, deserving praise and imitation? or who has committed an error proper for us to be warned against and avoid?

7. What unhappy effects of intemperance have you lately ob-served or heard? of imprudence? of passion? or of any other vice or folly?

8. What happy effects of temperance? of prudence? of moderation? or of any other virtue?

9. Have you or any of your acquaintance been lately sick or wounded? If so, what remedies were used, and what were their effects?

10. Who do you know that are shortly going voyages or journeys, if one should have occasion to send by them?

11. Do you think of any thing at present, in which the Junto may be serviceable to *mankind?* to their country, to their friends, or to themselves?

12. Hath any deserving stranger arrived in town since last meeting, that you heard of? and what have you heard or observed of his character or merits? and whether think you, it lies in the power of the Junto to oblige him, or encourage him as he deserves?

13. Do you know of any deserving young beginner lately set up, whom it lies in the power of the Junto any way to encourage?

14. Have you lately observed any defect in the laws of your *country,* [of] which it would be proper to move the legislature for an amendment? Or do you know of any beneficial law that is wanting?

15. Have you lately observed any encroachment on the just liberties of the people?

16. Hath any body attacked your reputation lately? and what can the Junto do towards securing it?

17. Is there any man whose friendship you want, and which the Junto or any of them, can procure for you?

18. Have you lately heard any member's character attacked, and how have you defended it?

19. Hath any man injured you, from whom it is in the power of the Junto to procure redress?

20. In what manner can the Junto, or any of them, assist you in any of your honorable designs?

21. Have you any weighty affair in hand, in which you think the advice of the Junto may be of service?

22. What benefits have you lately received from any man not present?

23. Is there any difficulty in matters of opinion, of justice, and injustice, which you would gladly have discussed at this time?

24. Do you see any thing amiss in the present customs or proceedings of the Junto, which might be amended?

Any person to be qualified, to stand up, and lay his hand on his breast, and be asked these questions; viz.

1. Have you any particular disrespect to any present members? *Answer.* I have not.

2. Do you sincerely declare that you love mankind in general; of what profession or religion soever? *Answ.* I do.

3. Do you think any person ought to be harmed in his body, name or goods, for mere speculative opinions, or his external way of worship? *Ans.* No.

4. Do you love truth's sake, and will you endeavor impartially to find and receive it yourself and communicate it to others? *Answ.* Yes . . .

Queries to be asked the Junto

Whence comes the dew that stands on the outside of a tankard that has cold water in it in the summer time?

Does the importation of servants increase or advance the wealth of our country?

Would not an office of insurance for servants be of service, and what methods are proper for the erecting such an office?

Qu. Whence does it proceed, that the proselytes to any sect or persuasion generally appear more zealous than those who are bred up in it?

Answ. I suppose that people *bred* in different persuasions are nearly zealous alike. He that changes his party is either sincere, or not sincere; that is he either does it for the sake of the opinions merely, or with a view of interest. If he is sincere and has no view of interest; and considers before he declares himself, how much ill will he shall have from those he leaves, and that those he is about to go among will be apt to suspect his sincerity: if he is not really zealous he will not declare; and therefore must be zealous if he does declare. If he is not sincere, he is obliged at least to put on an appearance of great zeal, to convince the better, his new friends that he is heartily in earnest, for his old ones he knows dislike him. And as few acts of zeal will be more taken notice of than such as are done against the party he has left, he is inclined to injure or malign them, because he knows they contemn and despise him. Hence one renegade is (as the proverb says) worse than 10 Turks.

Qu. Can a man arrive at perfection in this life as some believe; or is it impossible as others believe?

A. Perhaps they differ in the meaning of the word perfection.

I suppose the perfection of any thing to be only the greatest the nature of that thing is capable of;

Different things have different degrees of perfection; and the same thing at different times.

Thus an horse is more perfect than an oyster yet the oyster may be a perfect oyster as well as the horse a perfect horse.

And an egg is not so perfect as a chicken, nor a chicken as a hen; for the hen has more strength than the chicken, and the chicken more life than the egg: yet it may be a perfect egg, chicken and hen.

If they mean, a man cannot in this life be so perfect as an angel, it may be true; for an angel by being incorporeal is allowed some perfections we are at present incapable of, and less liable to some imperfections that we are liable to.

If they mean a man is not capable of being so perfect here as he is capable of being in heaven, that may be true likewise. But that a man is not capable of being so perfect here, as he is capable of being here; is not sense; it is as if I should say, a chicken in the state of a chicken is not capable of being so perfect as a chicken is capable of being in that state. In the above sense if there may be a perfect oyster, a perfect horse, a perfect ship, why not a perfect man? That is as perfect as his present nature and circumstances admit?

Quest. Wherein consists the happiness of a rational creature?

Ans. In having a sound mind and a healthy body, a sufficiency of the necessaries and conveniencies of life, together with the favor of god, and the love of mankind.

Qu. What do you mean by a sound mind?

A. A faculty of reasoning justly and truly in searching after and discovering such truths as relate to my happiness. Which faculty is the gift of god, capable of being improved by experience and instruction, into wisdom.

Q. What is wisdom?

A. The knowledge of what will be best for us on all occasions and of the best ways of attaining it.

Q. Is any man wise at all times, and in all things?

A. No; but some are much more frequently wise than others.

Q. What do you mean by the necessaries of life?

A. Having wholesome food and drink wherewith to satisfy hunger and thirst, clothing and a place of habitation fit to secure against the inclemencies of the weather.

Q. What do you mean by the conveniencies of life?

A. Such a plenty.

And if in the conduct of your affairs you have been deceived by others, or have committed any error your self, it will be a discretion in you to observe and note the same, and the defailance, with the means or expedient to repair it.

No man truly wise but who hath been deceived.

Let all your observations be committed to writing every night before you go to sleep.

Query, whether it is worth a rational man's while to forego the pleasure arising from the present luxury of the age in eating and drinking and artful cookery, studying to gratify the appetite for the sake of enjoying healthy old age, a sound mind and a sound body, which are the advantages reasonably to be expected from a more simple and temperate diet.

Whether those meals and drinks are not the best, that contain nothing in their natural tastes, nor have any thing added by art so pleasing as to induce us to eat or drink when we are not athirst or hungry or after thirst and hunger are satisfied; water for instance for drink and bread or the like for meat?

Is there any difference between knowledge and prudence?

If there is any, which of the two is most eligible?

Is it justifiable to put private men to death for the sake of public safety or tranquility, who have committed no crime?

As in the case of the plague to stop infection, or as in the case of the Welshmen here executed.

Whether men ought to be denominated good or ill men from their actions or their inclinations?

If the sovereign power attempts to deprive a subject of his right, (or which is the same thing, of what he thinks his right) is it justifiable in him to resist if he is able?

What general conduct of life is most suitable for men in such circumstances as most of the members of the Junto are; or, of the many schemes of living which are in our power to pursue, which will be most probably conducive to our happiness?

Which is best to make a friend of, a wise and good man that is poor; or a rich man that is neither wise nor good? Which of the two is the greatest loss to a country, if they both die?

Which of the two is happiest in life?

Does it not in a general way require great study and intense application for a poor man to become rich and powerful, if he would do it, without the forfeiture of his honesty?

Does it not require as much pains, study and application to become truly wise and strictly good and virtuous as to become rich?

Can a man of common capacity pursue both views with success at the same time?

If not, which of the two is it best for him to make his whole application to?

HOW TO PLEASE IN CONVERSATION

In a newspaper piece that he wrote shortly after forming the Junto, Franklin stressed the importance of deferring—or at least giving the appearance of deferring—to others. "Would you win the hearts of others, you must not seem to vie with them, but to admire them," he sagely counseled.

The older he got, the more Franklin learned (with a few notable lapses) to follow his own advice. He used silence wisely, employed an indirect style of persuasion, and feigned modesty and naiveté in disputes. "When another asserted something that I thought an error, I denied myself the pleasure of contradicting him," he recalled when writing his autobiography. Instead, he would agree in parts and suggest his differences only indirectly.

The method would become, often with a nod to Franklin, a staple in modern management guides and self-improvement books. Dale Carnegie, in his book *How to Win Friends and Influence People,* draws on Franklin's rules for conversation. Carnegie's rules include: "The only way to get the best of an argument is to avoid it." "Show respect for the other person's opinions. Never say, 'You're wrong.,' " "Call attention to people's mistakes indirectly," and "Ask questions instead of giving direct orders."

THE PENNSYLVANIA GAZETTE, OCTOBER 15, 1730

To *please* in *conversation* is an art which all people believe they understand and practice, though most are ignorant or deficient in it. The bounds and manner of this paper will not allow a regular and methodical discourse on the subject, and therefore I must beg leave to throw my thoughts together as they rise.

The two grand requisites in the art of pleasing, are *complaisance* and *good nature. Complaisance* is a seeming preference of others to our selves; and *good nature* a readiness to overlook or excuse their foibles, and do them all the services we can. These two principles must gain us their good opinion, and make them fond of us for their own sake, and then all we do or say will appear to the best advantage, and be well accepted. *Learning, wit,* and *fine parts,* with *these,* shine in full luster, become wonderfully agreeable, and command affection; but without *them,* only seem an assuming over others, and occasion envy and disgust. The common mistake is, that people think to please by setting themselves to view, and showing their own perfections, whereas the easier and more effectual way lies quite contrary. Would you win the hearts of others, you must not seem to vie with, but admire them: give them every opportunity of displaying their own qualifications, and when you have indulged their vanity, they will praise you too in turn, and prefer you above others, in order to secure to themselves the pleasure your commendation gives.

But above all, we should mark out those things which cause dislike, and avoid them with great care. The most common amongst these is, *talking overmuch,* and robbing others of their share of the discourse. This is not only incivility but injustice, for every one has a natural right to speak in turn, and to hinder it is an usurpation of common liberty, which never fails to excite resentment. Besides, great talkers usually leap from one thing to another with so much rapidity, and so ill a connection, that what they say is a mere chaos of noise and nonsense; though did they speak like angels they still would be disagreeable. It is very pleasant when two of these people meet: the vexation they both feel is visible in their looks and gestures; you shall see them gape and stare, and interrupt one another at every turn, and watch with the utmost impatience for a cough or a pause, when they may crowd a word in edgeways: neither hears nor cares what the other says; but both talk on at any rate, and never fail to part highly disgusted with each other. I knew two ladies, gifted this way, who by accident traveled in a boat twenty miles together, in which short journey they were both so extremely tired of one another, that they could never after mention each other's name with any temper, or be brought in company together, but retained a mutual aversion which could never be worn out.

The contrary fault to this, and almost as disobliging, is that of seeming wholly unconcerned in conversation, and bearing no other part in the discourse than a *no* or *yes* sometimes, or an *hem*, or perhaps a *nod* only. This inattention and indifference appears so like disrespect, that it affronts the desire we all possess of being taken notice of and regarded, and makes the company of those who practice it tiresome and insipid. Such is the vanity of mankind, that minding what others say is a much surer way of pleasing them than talking well our selves.

Another error very common and highly disagreeable, is to be ever speaking of our selves and our own affairs. What is it to the company we fall into whether we quarrel with our servants, whether our children are forward and dirty, or what we intend to have for dinner to morrow? The sauciness of a Negro, the prattle of a child, the spoiling a suit of clothes, the expenses of housekeeping, or the preparation for a journey, may be to ourselves matters of great importance, as they occasion us pain or pleasure; but wherein are strangers concerned, or what amusement can they possibly receive from such accounts? Opposite to this, but not less troublesome, is the impertinent inquisitiveness of some people which is ever prying into and asking ten thousand questions about the business of others. To search after and endeavor to discover secrets, is an unpardonable rudeness; but what makes this disposition worse, it is usually attended with an ill-natured, ungenerous, and mischievous desire of exposing and aggravating the mistakes and infirmities of others. People of this turn are the pest of society, and become both feared and hated. On these two heads it may be useful always to remember, that we never ought to trouble people with more of our own affairs than is needful for them to know, nor enquire farther into theirs than themselves think fit to tell us.

Story-telling is another mistake in conversation, which should be avoided by all who intend to please. It is impossible to hear a long insipid trifling tale, void of wit or humor, drawn in by neck and shoulders, and told merely for the sake of talking, without being uneasy at it. Besides, people this way given are apt to tell the same string of stories, with all their rambling particulars, again and again over; without considering, that whatsoever pleasure themselves may find in talking, their hearers wish their tongues out. Old folks are most subject to this error, which is one chief reason their company is so often shunned.

Another very disagreeable error, is, a spirit of *wrangling* and *disputing,* which some perpetually bring with them into company: insomuch, that say whatever you will, they'll be sure to contradict you: and if you go about to give reasons for your opinion, however just they be, or however modestly proposed, you throw them into rage and passion. Though, perhaps, they are wholly unacquainted with the affair, and you have made yourself master of it, it is no matter, the more ignorant they are you still find them the more positive, and what they want in knowledge they endeavor to supply by obstinacy, noise and fury: and when you press hard upon them, instead of argument they fly to personal reproaches and invectives. Thus every trifle becomes a serious business, and such people are continually involved in quarrels.

Raillery is a part of conversation, which to treat of fully would require a whole paper; but now, I have only room to observe that it is highly entertaining or exceedingly disobliging, according as it is managed, and therefore we ought to use it with all the caution possible. Natural infirmities, unavoidable misfortunes, defects, or deformities of any kind, should never be the subject of it, for then it is not only impertinent, but affronting and inhuman. It's like salt, a little of which in some cases gives a relish, but if thrown on by handfuls, or sprinkled on things at random, it spoils all. Raillery supposes wit; but agreeable as wit is, when it takes a wrong turn it becomes dangerous and mischievous. When wit applies it self to search into, expose, and ridicule the faults of others, it often inflicts a wound that rankles in the heart, and is never to be forgiven. To rally safely, and so as to please, it is requisite that we perfectly know our company: its not enough that we intend no ill, we must be likewise certain what we say shall be taken as we intend it; otherwise, for the sake of a jest we may lose a friend, and make an inveterate enemy. I shall say no more on this head, but that we ought to use it sparingly; and whatever opportunities may offer of showing our parts this way, so soon as any body appears uneasy at it, and receives it with a grave face, both good manners and discretion advise to change the subject for something else more harmless.

Akin to raillery, and what oftentimes goes along with it, is *scandal.* But if people hereby think to gain esteem, they unhappily are mistaken; for everybody (even those who hear them with a seeming pleasure) considers them with a kind of horror. No ones reputation is safe against such tongues: all in turn may expect to suffer by them. Insensible of the ties of friendship, or the sentiments of humanity, such creatures are mischievous as bears or tigers, and are as much abhorred and feared.

There are many more mistakes which render people disagreeable in conversation, but these are the most obvious; and whosoever avoids them carefully can never much displease. I shall only add, in a few words, what are the most likely means to make a man be well accepted.

Let his air, his manner, and behavior, be easy, courteous and affable, void of every thing haughty or assuming; his words few, expressed with modesty, and a respect for those he talks to. Be he ever ready to hear what others say; let him interrupt no body, nor intrude with his advice unasked. Let him never trouble other people about his own affairs, nor concern himself with theirs. Let him avoid disputes; and when he dissents from others propose his reasons with calmness and complaisance. Be his wit ever guided by discretion and good nature, nor let him sacrifice a friend to raise a laugh. Let him not censure others, nor expose their failings, but kindly excuse or hide them. Let him neither raise nor propagate a story to the prejudice of anybody. In short, be his study to command his own temper, to learn the humors of mankind, and to conform himself accordingly.

PART 3

POOR RICHARD AND FRIENDS

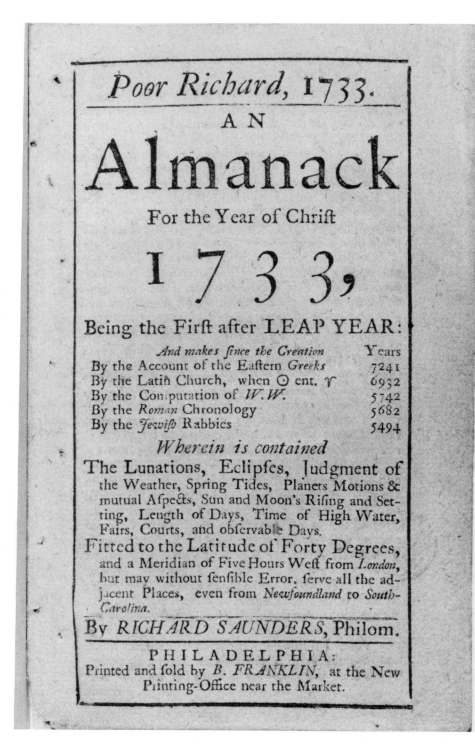

Poor Richard, 1733.

A N

Almanack

For the Year of Christ

1 7 3 3,

Being the First after LEAP YEAR:

And makes since the Creation	Years
By the Account of the Eastern *Greeks*	7241
By the Latin Church, when ☉ ent. ♈	6932
By the Computation of *W.W.*	5742
By the *Roman* Chronology	5682
By the *Jewish* Rabbies	5494

Wherein is contained

The Lunations, Eclipses, Judgment of the Weather, Spring Tides, Planets Motions & mutual Aspects, Sun and Moon's Rising and Setting, Length of Days, Time of High Water, Fairs, Courts, and observable Days.

Fitted to the Latitude of Forty Degrees, and a Meridian of Five Hours West from *London*, but may without sensible Error, serve all the adjacent Places, even from *Newfoundland* to *South-Carolina*.

By RICHARD SAUNDERS, Philom.

PHILADELPHIA:
Printed and sold by *B. FRANKLIN*, at the New Printing-Office near the Market.

The first Poor Richard's Almanac

INTRODUCING POOR RICHARD

Poor Richard's Almanac, which Franklin began publishing at the end of 1732, combined the two goals of his doing-well-by-doing-good philosophy: the making of money and the promotion of virtue. It became, in the course of its twenty-five-year run, America's first great humor classic. The beleaguered Richard Saunders and his nagging wife Bridget (like their predecessors Silence Dogood, Anthony Afterwit and Alice Addertongue) helped to continue his development of the genre of American folk humor featuring the naïvely wicked wit and homespun wisdom of characters who seem to be charmingly innocent but are sharply pointed about the pretensions of the elite.

In format and style, it was like other almanacs, most notably that of Titan Leeds, who was publishing, as his father had before him, Philadelphia's most popular version. The name Poor Richard, a slight oxymoron pun, echoed that of Poor Robin's Almanac, which was published by Franklin's brother James. Franklin, however, added his own distinctive flair. He used his pseudonym to permit himself some ironic distance, which allowed him to poke fun at his pecuniary motives for publishing it. He also ginned up a running feud with his rival Titan Leeds by predicting and later fabricating his death, a prank borrowed from Jonathan Swift.

POOR RICHARD'S ALMANAC FOR 1733

Courteous Reader,

I might in this place attempt to gain thy favor, by declaring that I write almanacs with no other view than that of the public good; but in this I should not be sincere; and men are nowadays too wise to be deceived by pretences how specious soever. The plain truth of the matter is, I am excessive poor, and my wife, good woman, is, I tell her, excessive proud; she cannot bear, she says, to sit spinning in her shift of tow, while I do nothing but gaze at the stars; and has threatened more than once to burn all my books and rattling-traps (as she calls my instruments) if I do not make some profitable use of them for the good of my family. The printer has offered me some considerable share of the profits, and I have thus begun to comply with my dame's desire.

Indeed this motive would have had force enough to have made me publish an almanac many years since, had it not been overpowered by my regard for my good friend and fellow-student, Mr. Titan Leeds, whose interest I was extremely unwilling to hurt: but this obstacle (I am far from speaking it with pleasure) is soon to be removed, since inexorable death, who was never known to respect merit, has already prepared the mortal dart, the fatal sister has already extended her destroying shears, and that ingenious man must soon be taken from us. He dies, by my calculation made at his request, on Oct. 17. 1733, 3 ho. 29 m. *P.M.* At the very instant of the # of # and #: by his own calculation he will survive till the 26th of the same month. This small difference between us we have disputed whenever we have met these 9 years past; but at length he is inclinable to agree with my judgment; which of us is most exact, a little time will now determine. As therefore these provinces may not longer expect to see any of his performances after this year, I think my self free to take up the task, and request a share of the public encouragement; which I am the more apt to hope for on this account, that the buyer of my almanac may consider himself, not only as purchasing an useful utensil, but as performing an act of charity, to his poor friend and servant,

R. Saunders

POOR RICHARD VS. MR. LEEDS

Leeds fell into the trap, albeit with good humor, and in his own almanac for 1734 (written after the date of his predicted death) called Franklin a "conceited scribbler" who had "manifested himself a fool and a liar." Franklin, with his own printing press, had the luxury of reading Leeds before he published his own 1734 edition. In it Poor Richard responded that all of these defamatory protestations indicate that the real Leeds must indeed be dead and his new almanac a hoax by someone else.

Poor Richard's Almanac for 1734

Courteous Readers,

Your kind and charitable assistance last year, in purchasing so large an impression of my almanacs, has made my circumstances much more easy in the world, and requires my grateful acknowledgment. My wife has been enabled to get a pot of her own, and is no longer obliged to borrow one from a neighbor; nor have we ever since been without something of our own to put in it. She has also got a pair of shoes, two new shifts, and a new warm petticoat; and for my part, I have bought a second-hand coat, so good, that I am now not ashamed to go to town or be seen there. These things have rendered her temper so much more pacific than it used to be, that I may say, I have slept more, and more quietly within this last year, than in the three foregoing years put together. Accept my hearty thanks therefore, and my sincere wishes for your health and prosperity.

In the preface to my last almanac, I foretold the death of my dear old friend and fellow-student, the learned and ingenious Mr. Titan Leeds, which was to be on the 17th of October, 1733, 3 h. 29 m. PM at the very instant of the # of # and #. By his own calculation he was to survive till the 26th of the same month, and expire in the time of the eclipse, near 11 a clock, a.m. At which of these times he died, or whether he be really yet dead, I cannot at this present writing positively assure my readers; for as much as a disorder in my own family demanded my presence, and would not permit me as I had intended, to be with him in his last moments, to receive his last embrace, to close his eyes, and do the duty of a friend in performing the last offices to the departed. Therefore it is that I cannot positively affirm whether he be dead or not; for the stars only show to the skilful, what will happen in the natural and universal chain of causes and effects; but 'tis well known, that the events which would otherwise certainly happen at certain times in the course of nature, are sometimes set aside or postponed for wise and good reasons, by the immediate particular dispositions of providence; which particular dispositions the stars can by no means discover or foreshow. There is however, (and I cannot speak it without sorrow) there is the strongest probability that my dear friend is *no more;* for there appears in his name, as I am assured, an almanac for the year 1734, in which I am treated in a very gross and unhandsome manner; in which I am called *a false predictor, an ignorant, a conceited scribbler, a fool, and a liar.* Mr. Leeds was too well bred to use any man so indecently and so scurrilously, and moreover his esteem and affection for me was extraordinary: so that it is to be feared that pamphlet may be only a contrivance of somebody or other, who hopes perhaps to sell two or three years almanacs still, by the sole force and virtue of Mr. Leeds's name; but certainly, to put words into the mouth of a gentleman and a man of letters, against his friend, which the meanest and most scandalous of the people might be ashamed to utter even in a drunken quarrel, is an unpardonable injury to his memory, and an imposition upon the public.

Mr. Leeds was not only profoundly skilful in the useful science he professed, but he was a man of *exemplary sobriety,* a most *sincere friend,* and an *exact performer of his word.* These valuable qualifications, with many others so much endeared him to me, that although it should be so, that, contrary to all probability, contrary to my prediction and his own, he might possibly be yet alive, yet my loss of honor as a prognosticator, cannot afford me so much mortification, as his life, health and safety would give me joy and satisfaction. I am, courteous and kind reader, your poor friend and servant,

R. Saunders

ON THE DEATH OF INFANTS

Two years into their marriage, in October of 1732, Franklin and Deborah had a son, Francis Folger Franklin, known as Franky. For the rest of his life, Franklin would marvel at the memory of how precocious, curious and special Franky was.

These were, alas, destined to be only sad memories. In one of the few searing tragedies of Franklin's life, Franky died of smallpox just after his fourth birthday. On his grave Franklin wrote a simple epitaph: "The delight of all who knew him."

The memory of Franky was one of the few things ever to cause Franklin painful reflections. When his sister Jane wrote to him in London years later with happy news about his grandsons, Franklin responded that it "brings often afresh to my mind the idea of my son Franky, though now dead thirty-six years, whom I have seldom since seemed equaled in everything, and whom to this day I cannot think of without a sigh." Adding to the poignancy, Franklin had written for his paper, while Franky was still alive, an unusually deep rumination on "The Death of Infants," which was occasioned by the death of a neighbor's child. Drawing on his observations of the tiny Franky, he described the magical beauty of babies.

THE PENNSYLVANIA GAZETTE, JUNE 20, 1734

> *Ostendunt Terris hunc tantum Fata, neque ultra*
> *Esse sinunt.*
> —Virgil

It has been observed by Sir *William Petty* in his *Political Arithmetick*, that one half of mankind, which are born into this world, die, before they arrive to the age of *sixteen*, and that an half of the remaining part never measure out the short term of thirty years. That this observation is pretty just, every inquisitive person may be satisfied by comparing the several bills of mortality, published in *Europe*, for some years past; even a cursory view of any common burial place may, in a great measure evidence the truth of it.

Many arguments, to prove a *future state*, have been drawn from the unequal lot of good and bad men upon earth, but no one seems to carry a greater degree of probability in it, than the foregoing observation.—, to see virtue languish and repine, to see vice prosperous and triumphant, to see a *dives* faring deliciously every day, and rioting in all the excess of luxury and wantonness; to see a Lazarus poor, hungry, naked, and full of sores, lying at his door, and denied even the crumbs that fall from his table, the portion of his dogs, which dogs are more charitable, more human than their master: such a view, I confess, raises in us a violent presumption that there is another state of retribution, where the just and the unjust will be equally punished or rewarded by an impartial judge. On the other hand, when we reflect on the vast numbers of infants, that just struggle into life, then weep and die, and at the same time consider, that it can be in no wise consistent with the justice and wisdom of an infinite being, to create to no end, we may very reasonably conclude, that those animated machines, those *men* in miniature, who know no difference between good and evil, who are incapable of any good offices towards their fellow-creatures, or of serving their maker, were made for good and wise designs and purposes, which purposes, and designs transcend all the limits of our ideas and all our present capacities to conceive. Should an able and expert artificer employ all his time and his skill in contriving and framing an exquisite piece of *clockwork,* which, when he had brought it to the utmost perfection wit and art were capable of, and just set it a-going, he should suddenly dash it to pieces; would not every wise man naturally infer, that his intense application had disturbed his brain and impaired his reason?

Let us now contemplate the body of an infant, that curious engine of divine workmanship. What a rich and artful structure of flesh upon the solid and well compacted foundation of bones! What curious joints and hinges, on which the limbs are moved to and fro! What an inconceivable variety of nerves, veins, arteries, fibers and little invisible parts are found in every member! What various fluids, blood and juices run thro' and agitate the innumerable slender tubes, the hollow strings and strainers of the body! What millions of folding doors are fixed within, to stop those red or transparent rivulets in their course, either to prevent their return backwards, or else as a means to swell the muscles and move the limbs! What endless contrivances to secure life, to nourish nature, and to propagate the same to future animals! Can we now imagine after such a survey, that so wise, so good and merciful a creator should produce *myriads* of such exquisite machines to no other end or purpose, but to be deposited in the dark chambers of the grave, where each of the dead lie in their cold mansions, in beds of darkness and dust. The shadows of a long evening are stretched over them, the curtains of a deep midnight are drawn around them, *the worm lies under them, and the worm covers them.* No! The notion of annihilation has in it something so shocking and absurd, reason should despise it; rather let us believe, that when they drop this earthly vehicle they assume an ethereal one, and become the inhabitants of some more glorious region. May they not help to people that infinite number of *starry* and *planetary* worlds that roll above us: may they not become our better *genii*, our guardian angels, watch round our bed and our couch, direct our wandering paths thro' the maze and labyrinth of life, and at length conduct us safe, even us, who were the instruments of their passing thro' this valley of sorrow and death, to a land of peace and the mountains of paradise?—but these are things that belong to the provinces of light and immortality, and lie far beyond our mortal ken.—

I was led into this train of thinking by the death of a desirable child, whose beauty is now turning a pace into corruption, and all the loveliness of its countenance fled for ever. Death sits heavy upon it, and the sprightliness and vigor of life is perished in every feature and in every limb. If the foregoing reflections should urge any one forward in the paths of virtue, or yield any consolation to those in the like circumstances, and help to divert the stream of their sorrow into a better channel, I shall hope my thoughts have been employed to good purpose. When nature gave us tears, she gave us leave to weep. A long separation from those who are so near a-kin to us in flesh and blood, will touch the heart in a painful place, and awaken the tenderest springs of sorrow. The sluices must be allowed to be held open a little; *nature* seems to demand it as a debt to *love*. When *Lazarus* died, *Jesus* groaned and wept.

I shall only add by way of conclusion an *epitaph* upon an infant: it is taken from a tombstone in a little obscure village in England, that seems to have very little title to any thing so elegantly poetical, which renders it the more remarkable.

Read this and weep—but not for me;
Lament thy longer Misery:
My Life was short, my Grief the less;
Blame not my Hast to Happiness!

POOR RICHARD DENIES HE IS FRANKLIN

Although Franklin loved the freedom afforded by writing under the thin disguise of Poor Richard, he occasionally poked through the veil in a humorous way. Some of his pseudononymous pieces he made sure remained anonymous, but usually it was well known that he was the writer. At the end of 1735, he made fun of this process by having Poor Richard, in his preface for 1736, pretend to protest about those who thought he was merely a fictional invention of his printer Franklin.

Poor Richard's Almanac for 1736

Loving Readers,

Your kind acceptance of my former labors, has encouraged me to continue writing, though the general approbation you have been so good as to favor me with, has excited the envy of some, and drawn upon me the malice of others. These ill-willers of mine, despited at the great reputation I gained by exactly predicting another man's death, have endeavored to deprive me of it all at once in the most effectual manner, by reporting that I my self was never alive. They say in short, *that there is no such a man as I am;* and have spread this notion so thoroughly in the country, that I have been frequently told it to my face by those that don't know me. This is not civil treatment, to endeavor to deprive me of my very being, and reduce me to a non-entity in the opinion of the public. But so long as I know my self to walk about, eat, drink and sleep, I am satisfied that *there is really such a man as I am,* whatever they may say to the contrary: and the world may be satisfied likewise; for if there were no such man as I am, how is it possible I should appear publicly to hundreds of people, as I have done for several years past, in print? I need not, indeed, have taken any notice of so idle a report, if it had not been for the sake of my printer, to whom my enemies are pleased to ascribe my productions; and who it seems is as unwilling to father my offspring, as I am to lose the credit of it. Therefore to clear him entirely, as well as to vindicate my own honor, I make this public and serious declaration, which I desire may be believed, to wit, *that what I have written heretofore, and do now write, neither was nor is written by any other man or men, person or persons whatsoever.* Those who are not satisfied with this, must needs be very unreasonable.

My performance for this year follows; it submits itself, kind reader, to thy censure, but hopes for thy candor, to forgive its faults. It devotes itself entirely to thy service, and will serve thee faithfully: and if it has the good fortune to please its master, 'tis gratification enough for the labor of poor

R. Saunders

FAITH VERSUS GOOD WORKS

Franklin's objection to the Calvinist theology of the Puritans of Boston and the Presbyterians of Philadelphia was based on its insistence that salvation could come only through God's grace rather than through good works. In 1734, a preacher from Ireland named Samuel Hemphill came to Philadelphia and began preaching the doctrine of good works, much to Franklin's pleasure. But the local synod put him on trial for heresy. In a fictional dialogue Franklin printed in his paper, he defended Hemphill and his doctrine.

THE PENNSYLVANIA GAZETTE, APRIL 10, 1735

Mr. Franklin,

You are desired by several of your Readers to print the following Dialogue. *It is between Two of the Presbyterians Meeting in this City. We cannot tell whether it may not be contrary to your Sentiments, but hope, if it should, you will not refuse publishing it on that Account: nor shall we be offended if you print any thing in Answer to it. We are yours, &c.*

A.B.C.D.

S. Good Morrow! I am glad to find you well and abroad; for not having seen you at Meeting lately, I concluded you were indisposd.

T. *'Tis true I have not been much at Meeting lately, but that was not occasioned by any Indisposition. In short, I stay at home, or else go to Church, because I do not like Mr. H. your new-fangled Preacher.*

S. I am sorry we should differ in opinion upon any account; but let us reason the point calmly; what offence does Mr. H. Give you?

T. *'Tis his preaching disturbs me: he talks of nothing but the duties of morality: I do not love to hear so much of morality: I am sure it will carry no man to heaven, and I do not think it fit to be preached in a Christian congregation.*

S. I suppose you think no doctrine fit to be preached in a Christian congregation, but such as Christ and his apostles used to preach.

T. *To be sure I think so.*

S. I do not conceive then how you can dislike the preaching of morality, when you consider, that morality made the principal part of their preaching as well as of Mr. H's. What is Christ's sermon on the mount but an excellent moral discourse, towards the end of which, (as foreseeing that people might in time come to depend more upon their *faith* in him, than upon *good works,* for their salvation) he tells the hearers plainly, that their saying to him, *Lord, lord,* (that is, professing themselves his disciples or *Christians*) should give them no title to salvation, but their *doing* the will of his father; and that though they have prophesied in his name, yet he will declare to them, as neglecters of morality, that he never knew them.

T. *But what do you understand by that expression of Christ's,* doing the will of my father?

S. I understand it to be the will of God, that we should live virtuous, upright, and good-doing lives; as the prophet understood it, when he said, *what doth the lord require of thee, o man, but to do justly, love mercy, and walk humbly with the lord thy God.*

T. *But is not faith recommended in the new testament as well as morality?*

S. 'Tis true, it is. Faith is recommended as a means of producing morality: our savior was a teacher of morality or virtue, and they that were deficient and desired to be taught, ought first to *believe* in him as an able and faithful teacher. Thus faith would be a means of producing morality, and morality of salvation. But that from such faith alone salvation may be expected, appears to me to be neither a Christian doctrine nor a reasonable one. And I should as soon expect, that my bare believing Mr. Grew to be an excellent teacher of the mathematics, would make me a mathematician, as that believing in Christ would of it self make a man a Christian.

T. *Perhaps you may think, that though faith alone cannot save a man, morality or virtue alone, may.*

S. Morality or virtue is the end, faith only a means to obtain that end: and if the end be obtained, it is no matter by what means. What think you of these sayings of Christ, when he was reproached for conversing chiefly with gross sinners, *the whole,* says he, *need not a physician, but they that are sick;* and, I *come not to call the righteous, but sinners, to repentance:* does not this imply, that there were good men, who, without faith in him, were in a state of salvation? And moreover, did he not say of Nathaniel, while he was yet an unbeliever in him, and thought no good could possibly come out of Nazareth, *behold an Israelite indeed, in whom there is no guile!* That is, *behold a virtuous upright man.* Faith in Christ, however, may be and is of great use to produce a good life, but that it can conduce nothing towards salvation where it does not conduce to virtue, is, I suppose, plain from the instance of the devils, who are far from being infidels, *they believe,* says the scripture, *and tremble.* There were some indeed, even in the apostles days, that set a great value upon faith, distinct from good works, they merely idolized it, and thought that a man ever so righteous could not be saved without it: but one of the apostles, to show his dislike of such notions, tells them, that not only those heinous sins of theft, murder, and blasphemy, but even *idleness,* or the neglect of a man's business, was more pernicious than mere harmless infidelity, *he that neglects to provide for them of his own house,* says he, *is* worse *than an infidel.* St. James, in his second chapter, is very zealous against these criers-up of faith, and maintains that faith without virtue is useless, *wilt thou know, o vain man,* says he, *that faith without works is dead;* and, *show me your faith without your works, and I will show you mine by my works.* Our savior, when describing the last judgment, and declaring what shall give admission into bliss, or exclude from it, says nothing of *faith* but what he says against it, that is, that those who cry *lord, lord,* and profess to have *believed* in his name,

have no favor to expect on that account; but declares that 'tis the practice, or the omitting the practice of the duties of morality, *feeding the
hungry, clothing the naked, visiting the sick,* &c. In short, 'tis the doing or
not doing all the good that lies in our power, that will render us the
heirs of happiness or misery.

T. *But if faith is of great use to produce a good life, why does not Mr. H.
Preach up faith as well as morality?*

S. Perhaps it may be this, that as the good physician suits his physic
to the disease he finds in the patient, so Mr. H. May possibly think,
that though faith in Christ be properly first preached to heathens and
such as are ignorant of the gospel, yet since he knows that we have been
baptized in the name of Christ, and educated in his religion, and called
after his name, it may not be so immediately necessary to preach *faith*
to us who abound in it, as *morality* in which we are evidently deficient:
for our late want of charity to each other, our heart-burnings and bick-
erings are notorious. St. James says, *where envying and strife is, there is
confusion and every evil work:* and where confusion and every evil work
is, *morality* and good-will to men, can, I think, be no unsuitable doctrine. But surely *morality* can do us no harm. Upon a supposition that
we all have faith in Christ already, as I think we have, where can be the
damage of being exhorted to good works? Is virtue heresy; and universal benevolence false doctrine, that any of us should keep away from
meeting because it is preached there?

T. *Well, I do not like it, and I hope we shall not long be troubled with
it. A commission of the synod will sit in a short time, and try this sort of
preaching.*

S. I am glad to hear that the synod are to take it into consideration.
There are men of unquestionable good sense as well as piety among
them, and I doubt not but they will, by their decision, deliver our profession from the satirical reflection, which a few uneasy people of our
congregation have of late given occasion for, to wit, that the Presbyterians are going to persecute, silence and condemn a good preacher, for
exhorting them to be honest and charitable to one another and the rest
of mankind.

T. *If Mr. H. Is a Presbyterian teacher, he ought to preach as Presbyterians use to preach; or else he may justly be condemned and silenced by our*

church authority. We ought to abide by the Westminster confession of faith; and he that does not, ought not to preach in our meetings.

S. The apostasy of the church from the primitive simplicity of the gospel, came on by degrees; and do you think that the reformation was of a sudden perfect, and that the first reformers knew at once all that was right or wrong in religion? Did not Luther at first preach only against selling of pardons, allowing all the other practices of the Romish church for good? He afterwards went further, and Calvin, some think, yet further. The Church of England made a stop, and fixed her faith and doctrine by 39 articles; with which the Presbyterians not satisfied, went yet farther; but being too self-confident to think, that as their fathers were mistaken in some things, they also might be in some others; and fancying themselves infalliable in *their* interpretations, they also tied themselves down by the Westminster confession. But has not a synod that meets in King George the seconds reign, as much right to interpret scripture, as one that met in Oliver's time? And if any doctrine then maintained is, or shall hereafter be found not altogether orthodox, why must we be for ever confined to that, or to any, confession?

T. But if the majority of the synod be against any innovation, they may justly hinder the innovator from preaching.

S. That is as much as to say, if the majority of the preachers be in the wrong, they may justly hinder any man from setting the people right; for a *majority* may be in the wrong as well as the *minority*, and frequently are. In the beginning of the reformation, the *majority* was vastly against the reformers, and continues so to this day; and, if, according to your opinion, they had a right to silence the *minority*, I am sure the *minority* ought to have been silent. But tell me, if the Presbyterians in this country, being charitably inclined, should send a missionary into Turkey, to propagate the gospel, would it not be unreasonable in the Turks to prohibit his preaching?

T. It would, to be sure, because he comes to them for their good.

S. And if the Turks, believing us in the wrong, as we think them, should out of the same charitable disposition, send a missionary to preach Mahometanism to us, ought we not in the same manner to give him free liberty of preaching his doctrine?

T. It may be so; but what would you infer from that?

S. I would only infer, that if it would be thought reasonable to suffer a Turk to preach among us a doctrine diametrically opposite to Christianity, it cannot be reasonable to silence one of our own preachers, for preaching a doctrine exactly agreeable to Christianity, only because he does not perhaps zealously propagate all the doctrines of an old confession. And upon the whole, though the *majority* of the synod should not in all respects approve of Mr. H's doctrine, I do not however think they will find it proper to condemn him. We have justly denied the infallibility of the pope and his councils and synods in their interpretations of scripture, and can we modestly claim *infallibility* for our selves or our synods in our way of interpreting? Peace, unity and virtue in any church are more to be regarded than orthodoxy. In the present weak state of humane nature, surrounded as we are on all sides with ignorance and error, it little becomes poor fallible man to be positive and dogmatical in his opinions. No point of faith is so plain, as that *morality* is our duty, for all sides agree in that. A virtuous heretic shall be saved before a wicked Christian: for there is no such thing as voluntary error. Therefore, since 'tis an uncertainty till we get to heaven what true orthodoxy in all points is, and since our congregation is rather too small to be divided, I hope this misunderstanding will soon be got over, and that we shall as heretofore unite again in mutual *Christian Charity.*

T. I wish we may. Ill consider of what you've said, and wish you well.

S. Farewell.

POOR RICHARD BLAMES HIS PRINTER

In the preface for his 1737 edition, Poor Richard turns his attack on another almanac writer, John Jerman, for making weather predictions that were so vague as to be useless. He does concede, however, that his own weather predictions are sometimes off by a few days. This he blames on his "printer" (i.e., Franklin) for moving his predictions around a bit in order to fit in the holidays. Since he had noted the previous year that Franklin was getting the credit for what Poor Richard wrote, it was only fair that he also take the blame.

POOR RICHARD'S ALMANAC FOR 1737

Courteous and kind Reader,

This is the fifth time I have appeared in public, chalking out the future year for my honest countrymen, and foretelling what shall, and what may, and what may not come to pass; in which I have the pleasure to find that I have given general satisfaction. Indeed, among the multitude of our astrological predictions, 'tis no wonder if some few fail; for, without any defect in the art itself, 'tis well known that a small error, a single wrong figure overseen in a calculation, may occasion great mistakes: but however we almanac-makers may *miss it* in other things, I believe it will be generally allowed *that we always hit the day of the month,* and that I suppose is esteemed one of the most useful things in an almanac.

As to the weather, if I were to fall into the method my brother J——n sometimes uses, and tell you, *snow here or in New England, rain here or in South Carolina, cold to the northward, warm to the southward,* and the like, whatever errors I might commit, I should be something more secure of not being detected in them: but I consider, it will be of no service to any body to know what weather it is 1000 miles off, and therefore I always set down positively what weather my reader will have, be he where he will at the time. We modestly desire only the favorable allowance of *a day or two before* and *a day or two after* the precise day against which the weather is set; and if it does not come to pass accordingly, let the fault be laid upon the printer, who, 'tis very like, may have transposed or misplaced it, perhaps for the conveniency of putting in his holidays: and since, in spite of all I can say, people will give him great part of the *credit* of making my almanacs, 'tis but reasonable he should take some share of the *blame.*

I must not omit here to thank the public for the gracious and kind encouragement they have hitherto given me: but if the generous purchaser of my labors could see how often his *five pence* helps to light up the comfortable fire, line the pot, fill the cup and make glad the heart of a poor man and an honest good old woman, he would not think his money ill laid out, though the almanac of his

Friend and Servant, R. Saunders

were one half blank Paper.

THE DRINKER'S DICTIONARY

Franklin was ambiguous when writing about drinking. He was a temperate man who nevertheless enjoyed the joviality of taverns. In one famous *Gazette* piece, destined to become a poster in countless pubs, he produced a "Drinker's Dictionary" listing 228 or so synonyms for being drunk.

THE PENNSYLVANIA GAZETTE, JANUARY 13, 1737

> *Nothing more like a Fool than a drunken Man.*
> —Poor Richard

'Tis an old remark, that vice always endeavors to assume the appearance of virtue: thus covetousness calls itself *prudence;* prodigality would be thought *generosity;* and so of others. This perhaps arises hence, that mankind naturally and universally approve virtue in their hearts, and detest vice; and therefore, whenever through temptation they fall into a practice of the latter, they would if possible conceal it from themselves as well as others, under some other name than that which properly belongs to it.

But DRUNKENNESS is a very unfortunate vice in this respect. It bears no kind of similitude with any sort of virtue, from which it might possibly borrow a name; and is therefore reduced to the wretched necessity of being express's by distant round-about phrases, and of perpetually varying those phrases, as often as they come to be well understood to signify plainly that A MAN IS DRUNK.

Though every one may possibly recollect a dozen at least of the expressions used on this occasion, yet I think no one who has not much frequented taverns would imagine the number of them so great as it really is, it may therefore surprise as well as divert the sober reader, to have the sight of a new piece, lately communicated to me, entitled

The Drinker's Dictionary

A

He is Addled, He's casting up his Accounts, He's Afflicted, He's in his Airs.

B

He's Biggy, Bewitch'd, Block and Block, Boozy, Bowz'd, Been at Barbadoes, Piss'd in the Brook, Drunk as a Wheel-Barrow, Burdock'd, Buskey, Buzzey, Has Stole a Manchet out of the Brewer's Basket, His Head is full of Bees, Has been in the Bibbing Plot, Has drank more than he has bled, He's Bungey, As Drunk as a Beggar, He sees the Bears, He's kiss'd black Betty, He's had a Thump over the Head with Sampson's Jawbone, He's Bridgey.

C

He's Cat, Cagrin'd, Capable, Cramp'd, Cherubimical, Cherry Merry, Wamble Crop'd, Crack'd, Concern'd, Half Way to Concord, Has taken a Chirriping-Glass, Got Corns in his Head, A Cup to much, Coguy, Copey, He's heat his Copper, He's Crocus, Catch'd, He cuts his Capers, He's been in the Cellar, He's in his Cups, Non Compos, Cock'd, Curv'd, Cut, Chipper, Chickery, Loaded his Cart, He's been too free with the Creature, Sir Richard has taken off his Considering Cap, He's Chap-fallen.

D

He's Disguiz'd, He's got a Dish, Kill'd his Dog, Took his Drops, It is a Dark Day with him, He's a Dead Man, Has Dipp'd his Bill, He's Dagg'd, He's seen the Devil.

E

He's Prince Eugene, Enter'd, Wet both Eyes, Cock Ey'd, Got the Pole Evil, Got a brass Eye, Made an Example, He's Eat a Toad & half for Breakfast. In his Element.

F

He's Fishey, Fox'd, Fuddled, Sore Footed, Frozen, Well in for't, Owes no Man a Farthing, Fears no Man, Crump Footed, Been to France, Flush'd, Froze his Mouth, Fetter'd, Been to a Funeral, His Flag is out, Fuzl'd, Spoke with his Friend, Been at an Indian Feast.

G

He's Glad, Groatable, Gold-headed, Glaiz'd, Generous, Booz'd the Gage, As Dizzy as a Goose, Been before George, Got the Gout, Had a Kick in the Guts, Been with Sir John Goa, Been at Geneva, Globular, Got the Glanders.

H

Half and Half, Hardy, Top Heavy, Got by the Head, Hiddey, Got on his little Hat, Hammerish, Loose in the Hilts, Knows not the way Home, Got the Hornson, Haunted with Evil Spirits, Has Taken Hippocrates grand Elixir.

I

He's Intoxicated.

J

Jolly, Jagg'd, Jambled, Going to Jerusalem, Jocular, Been to Jerico, Juicy.

K

He's a King, Clips the King's English, Seen the French King, The King is his Cousin, Got Kib'd Heels, Knapt, Het his Kettle.

L

He's in Liquor, Lordly, He makes Indentures with his Leggs, Well to Live, Light, Lappy, Limber.

M

He sees two Moons, Merry, Middling, Moon-Ey'd, Muddled, Seen a Flock of Moons, Maudlin, Mountous, Muddy, Rais'd his Monuments, Mellow.

N

He's eat the Cocoa Nut, Nimptopsical, Got the Night Mare.

O

He's Oil'd, Eat Opium, Smelt of an Onion, Oxycrocium, Overset.

P

He drank till he gave up his Half-Penny, Pidgeon Ey'd, Pungey, Priddy, As good conditioned as a Puppy, Has scalt his Head Pan, Been among the Philistines, In his Prosperity, He's been among the Philippians, He's contending with Pharaoh, Wasted his Paunch, He's Polite, Eat a Pudding Bagg.

Q

He's Quarrelsome.

R

He's Rocky, Raddled, Rich, Religious, Lost his Rudder, Ragged, Rais'd, Been too free with Sir Richard, Like a Rat in Trouble.

S

He's Stitch'd, Seafaring, In the Sudds, Strong, Been in the Sun, As Drunk as David's Sow, Swampt, His Skin is full, He's Steady, He's Stiff, He's burnt his Shoulder, He's got his Top Gallant Sails out, Seen the yellow Star, As Stiff as a Ring-bolt, Half Seas over, His Shoe pinches him, Staggerish, It is Star-light with him, He carries too much Sail, Stew'd Stubb'd, Soak'd, Soft, Been too free with Sir John Strawberry, He's right before the Wind with all his Studding Sails out, Has Sold his Senses.

T

He's Top'd, Tongue-ty'd, Tann'd, Tipium Grove, Double Tongu'd, Topsy Turvey, Tipsey, Has Swallow'd a Tavern Token, He's Thaw'd, He's in a Trance, He's Trammel'd.

V

He makes Virginia Fence, Valiant, Got the Indian Vapours.

W

The Malt is above the Water, He's Wise, He's Wet, He's been to the Salt Water, He's Water-soaken, He's very Weary, Out of the Way.

The phrases in this dictionary are not (like most of our terms of art) borrowed from foreign languages, neither are they collected from the writings of the learned in our own, but gather's wholly from the modern tavern-conversation of tipplers. I do not doubt but that there are many more in use; and I was even tempted to add a new one my self under the letter B, to wit, *brutify'd:* but upon consideration, I fear's being guilty of injustice to the brute creation, if I represented drunkenness as a beastly vice, since, 'tis well-known, that the brutes are in general a very sober sort of people.

HOW TO WRITE AN ALMANAC

By the time he was ready to publish his fifth edition of Poor Richard's in 1738, Franklin was publishing the most popular almanac in the colonies. Humor had been the key to his success. In a little parody he published as a letter to his paper from "Philomath," the name for almanac writers, he took the opportunity to poke fun at his rivals for being far too weighty and serious.

THE PENNSYLVANIA GAZETTE, OCTOBER 20, 1737

Sir,

As I am a great lover of all works of ingenuity, and the authors of them, so more especially am I a great reader and admirer of those *labors of the learned,* called *almanacs.*

As I am a considerable proficient in this sort of learning; and as at this time of the year, copies of almanacs for the next year usually come to the press, long before they are wanted: and as I have laid out many a six-pence among your customers, the profit whereof has in a great measure redounded to you: so I may reasonably hope to be looked on as a good customer, and claim a favorable place in your paper.

I have a large volume in manuscript by me, on the important subject of *almanac-making,* which I may in time communicate to the public; but at present I am willing to oblige them, with only a taste of my skill, which (if I have any title to the art of prognostication) will certainly make them long for the whole.

My present design, is to give to you and the public, *a short essay,* upon the talents requisite in *an almanac-writer,* by which it will plainly appear, how much the community is indebted to men of such *great and uncommon parts and sagacity.*

An *almanac-writer,* sir, should be born one like a poet; for as I read among the works of the learned, *poeta nascitur non fit;* so it is a maxim with me, that *almanackorum scriptor nascitur not fit.* Gifts of nature, sir, completed by rules of art, are indispensably necessary to make a great man this way, as well as any other.

The first thing requisite in an *almanac-writer,* is, *that he should be descended of a great family, and bear a coat of arms,* this gives luster and authority to what a man writes, and makes the common people to believe, that *certainly this is a great man.* I have known almanac-writers so curious and exact in this particular, that they have been at the expense and charge of a wooden cut in the frontispiece, with their arms emblazoned, and surrounded with a label, expressing the name of the family. This, sir, made a great impression, I confess, upon myself and others, and made those works to go off well.

If the author who was *born to be an almanac-maker,* has the misfortune to be meanly descended, but yet, has a true genius; if he has by him, or can borrow a book, entitled the peerage of *England,* he may safely borrow a coat, (if there happens to be a peer of his own name) by reason, we are so great a way distant from the earl marshal of that part of *Great Britain* called *England.*

The next talent requisite in the forming of *a complete almanac-writer,* is a sort of gravity, which keeps a due medium between dullness and nonsense, and yet has a mixture of both. Now you know, sir, that grave men are taken by the common people always for wise men. Gravity is just as good a picture of wisdom, as pertness is of wit, and therefore very taking. And to complete an almanac-maker, in this particular, he should write sentences, and throw out hints, that neither himself, nor any body else can understand or know the meaning of. And this is also a necessary talent. I will give you some instances of this way of writing, which are almost inimitable, such as these, *Leeds, Jan. 23. 1736*. Beware, the design is suspected. *Feb. 23. The world is bad with somebody. Mar. 27. Crimes not remitted. April 10. Cully mully puff appears. May 21 the sword of Satan is drawn. June 7. The cat eat the candle.* Now, sir, why should the sword of Satan be drawn to kill the cat on the 21st day of *May*, when it plainly appears in print, that the cat did not eat the candle till the 7th of June following? This question no man but an astrologer can possibly answer.

In the next place, I lay it down as a certain maxim or position, that *an almanac-writer should not be a finished poet, but a piece of one,* and qualified to write, what we vulgarly call doggerel; and that his poetry should bear a near resemblance to his prose. I must beg *Horace's* and my lord *Roscommon's* pardon, if I dissent from them in this one particular. I will give you their rule in my lord's English translation, and save myself the trouble of transcribing the Latin of *Horace*.

> *But no authority of gods nor men*
> *allow of any mean in poesy.*

This might for all I know be a rule for poetry among the ancients, but the moderns have found it troublesome, and the most of them, have wholly neglected it for that reason. Witness the author's verses, whose praise I am now celebrating, *December* 1736.

> *Now is my 12 months task come to conclusion,*
> *lord free us from hatred, envy and confusion.*
> *All are not pleased, nor never will i'th' main.*
> *Feuds and discords among us will remain.*
> *Be that as 'twill, however I'm glad to see,*
> *envy disappointed both at land and sea.*

I do not pretend to say, that this is like the poetry of Horace, or lord *Roscommon,* but it is the poesy of an astrologer, it is his own and not borrowed; it is occult and mysterious. It has a due degree of that sort of gravity, which I have mentioned: in short, it is formed upon the rules which I have laid down in this short essay.

I could further prove to you, if I was to go about it, that *an almanac-writer* ought not only to be a piece of a wit, but a very wag; and that he should have the art also to make people believe, that he is almost a conjurer, &c. But these things I reserved for my greater work, and in the mean time, until that appears, I desire to remain, *Sir, Your very humble Servant,*

Philomath

POOR RICHARD'S WIFE TAKES HER TURN

Richard and Bridget Saunders did, in many ways, reflect Benjamin and Deborah Franklin. In the almanac for 1738, Franklin had the fictional Bridget take a turn at writing the preface for Poor Richard. It came at the time when Franklin's newspaper pieces were poking fun at the pretensions of wives who acquire a taste for fancy tea services. Bridget Saunders announced to the reader that she read the preface her husband had composed, discovered he had "been slinging some of his old skits at me," and tossed it away. "Forsooth! all the world must know that Poor Dick's wife has lately taken a fancy to drink a little tea now and then." Lest the connection be missed, she noted that the tea was a present from "the printer."

POOR RICHARD'S ALMANAC FOR 1738

Preface by Mistress Saunders
Dear Readers,

My good man set out last week for Potowmack, to visit an old stargazer of his acquaintance, and see about a little place for us to settle and end our days on. He left the copy of his almanac sealed up, and bid me send it to the press. I suspected something, and therefore as soon as he was gone, I opened it, to see if he had not been flinging some of his old skits at me. Just as I thought, so it was. And truly, (for want of somewhat else to say, I suppose) he had put into his preface, that his wife Bridget was this, and that, and the other. What a peasecods! Cannot I have a little fault or two, but all the country must see it in print! They have already been told, at one time that I am proud, another time that I am loud, and that I have got a new petticoat, and abundance of such kind of stuff; and now, forsooth! All the world must know, that poor dick's wife has lately taken a fancy to drink a little tea now and then. A mighty matter, truly, to make a song of! 'Tis true, I had a little tea of a present from the printer last year; and what, must a body throw it away? In short, I thought the preface was not worth a printing, and so I fairly scratched it all out, and I believe you'll like our almanac never the worse for it.

Upon looking over the months, I see he has put in abundance of foul weather this year; and therefore I have scattered here and there, where I could find room, some *fair, pleasant, sunshiny, &c.* for the good-women to dry their clothes in. If it does not come to pass according to my desire, I have shown my good-will, however; and I hope they'll take it in good part.

I had a design to make some other corrections; and particularly to change some of the verses that I don't very well like; but I have just now unluckily broke my spectacles; which obliges me to give it you as it is, and conclude Your loving Friend,

Bridget Saunders

POOR RICHARD DEFENDS
ASTROLOGY AND WIT

Franklin loved poking fun at superstition, and writing as Poor Richard, a purported astrologer, he explained how the stars can be used to predict that it will rain sometime in April. He also defended his recipe for almanacs, which in the parlance of today's magazines might be called high/low: some worthy wisdom about morality embedded in some idle chatter and humor. It's a good formula for making money, he says, even if his printer Franklin, for whom he professes high regard, pockets most of it.

POOR RICHARD'S ALMANAC FOR 1739

Kind Reader,

Encouraged by thy former generosity, I once more present thee with an almanac, which is the 7th of my publication. While thou art putting pence in my pocket, and furnishing my cottage with necessaries, Poor Dick is not unmindful to do something for thy benefit. The stars are watched as narrowly as old Bess watched her daughter, that thou mayst be acquainted with their motions, and told a tale of their influences and effects, which may do thee more good than a dream of last years snow.

Ignorant men wonder how we astrologers foretell the weather so exactly, unless we deal with the old black devil. Alas! 'Tis as easy as pissing abed. For instance; the stargazer peeps at the heavens thro a long glass: he sees perhaps Taurus or the great bull, in a mighty chase, stamping on the floor of his house, swinging his tail about, stretching out his neck, and opening wide his mouth. 'Tis natural from these appearances to judge that this furious bull is puffing, blowing, and roaring. Distance being considered, and time allowed for all this to come down, there you have wind and thunder. He spies perhaps Virgo (or the virgin); she turns her head round as it were to see if any body observed her; then crouching down gently, with her hands on her knees, she looks wistfully for a while right forward. He judges rightly what she's about: and having calculated the distance and allowed time for its falling, finds that next spring we shall have a fine April shower. What can be more natural and easy than this? I might instance the like in many other particulars; but this may be sufficient to prevent our being taken for conjurors. O the wonderful knowledge to be found in the stars! Even the smallest things are written there, if you had but skill to read. When my brother J—m-n erected a scheme to know which was best for his sick horse, to sup a new-laid egg, or a little broth, he found that the stars plainly gave their verdict for broth, and the horse having supped his broth; now, what do you think became of that horse? You shall know in my next.

Besides the usual things expected in an almanac, I hope the professed teachers of mankind will excuse my scattering here and there some instructive hints in matters of morality and religion. And be not thou disturbed, o grave and sober reader, if among the many serious sentences in my book, thou findest me trifling now and then, and talking idly. In all the dishes I have hitherto cooked for thee, there is solid meat enough for thy money. There are scraps from the table of wisdom, that will if well digested, yield strong nourishment to thy mind. But squeamish stomachs cannot eat without pickles; which, 'tis true are good for nothing else, but they provoke an appetite. The vain youth that reads my almanac for the sake of an idle joke, will perhaps meet with a serious reflection, that he may ever after be the better for.

Some people observing the great yearly demand for my almanac, imagine I must by this time have become rich, and consequently ought to call myself *Poor Dick* no longer. But, the case is this, when I first begun to publish, the printer made a fair agreement with me for my copies, by virtue of which he runs away with the greatest part of the profit. However, much good may it do him; I do not grudge it him; he is a man I have a great regard for, and I wish his profit ten times greater than it is. For I am, dear reader, his, as well as thy Affectionate Friend,

R. Saunders

A DEFENSE OF RELIGIOUS TOLERANCE

Franklin's freethinking and unorthodox religious views, especially his belief that salvation was more likely to come by doing good works rather than merely through God's grace alone, unnerved his family. In a letter to his parents in 1738, he provided an eloquent defense of the virtue of religious tolerance and a bit of humility about doctrine (including mixing up Matthew 26 with Matthew 25). These were among the great contributions he made to the American character. His views were echoed a few years later in letters he wrote to his sister Jane and then his brother John.

To Josiah and Abiah Franklin, April 13, 1738

Honored Father and Mother,

I have your favor of the 21st of March in which you both seem concerned lest I have imbibed some erroneous opinions. Doubtless I have my share, and when the natural weakness and imperfection of human understanding is considered, with the unavoidable influences of education, custom, books and company, upon our ways of thinking, I imagine a man must have a good deal of vanity who believes, and a good deal of boldness who affirms, that all the doctrines he holds, are true; and all he rejects, are false. And perhaps the same may be justly said of every sect, church and society of men when they assume to themselves that infallibility which they deny to the popes and councils. I think opinions should be judged of by their influences and effects; and if a man holds none that tend to make him less virtuous or more vicious, it may be concluded he holds none that are dangerous; which I hope is the case with me. I am sorry you should have any uneasiness on my account, and if it were a thing possible for one to alter his opinions in order to please others, I know none whom I ought more willingly to oblige in that respect than your selves: but since it is no more in a man's power *to think* than *to look* like another, methinks all that should be expected from me is to keep my mind open to conviction, to hear patiently and examine attentively whatever is offered me for that end; and if after all I continue in the same errors, I believe your usual charity will induce you rather to pity and excuse than blame me. In the mean time your care and concern for me is what I am very thankful for.

As to the freemasons, unless she will believe me when I assure her that they are in general a very harmless sort of people; and have no principles or practices that are inconsistent with religion or good manners, I know no way of giving my mother a better opinion of them than she seems to have at present, (since it is not allowed that women should be admitted into that secret society). She has, I must confess, on that account, some reason to be displeased with it; but for any thing else, I must entreat her to suspend her judgment till she is better informed, and in the mean time exercise her charity.

My mother grieves that one of her sons is an Arian, another an Armenian. What an Armenian or an Arian is, I cannot say that I very well know; the truth is, I make such distinctions very little my study; I think vital religion has always suffered, when orthodoxy is more regarded than virtue. And the scripture assures me, that at the last day, we shall not be examined what we *thought*, but what we did; and our recommendation will not be that we said *lord, lord,* but that we did good to our fellow creatures. See Matth. 26.

To Jane Mecom, Philadelphia, July 28, 1743

Dearest Sister Jenny,

I took your Admonition very kindly, and was far from being offended at you for it. If I say any thing about it to you, 'tis only to rectify some wrong opinions you seem to have entertained of me, and that I do only because they give you some uneasiness, which I am unwilling to be the occasion of. You express yourself as if you thought I was against worshipping of God, and believed Good Works would merit Heaven; which are both Fancies of your own, I think, without Foundation. I am so far from thinking that God is not to be worshipped, that I have composed and wrote a whole Book of Devotions for my own use: And I imagine there are few, if any, in the world, so weak as to imagine, that the little good we can do here, can *merit* so vast a reward hereafter. There are some Things in your New England doctrines and worship, which I do not agree with, but I do not therefore condemn them, or desire to shake your belief or practice of them. We may dislike things that are nevertheless right in themselves. I would only have you make me the same allowances, and have a better opinion both of morality and your brother. Read the Pages of Mr. Edwards's late Book entitled *Some Thoughts Concerning The Present Revival Of Religion In New England* from 367 to 375; and when you judge of others, if you can perceive the fruit to be good, don't terrify your self that the tree may be evil, but be assured it is not so; for you know who has said, *Men do not gather Grapes of Thorns or Figs of Thistles*. I have not time to add but that I shall always be,

Your affectionate Brother

P.S. It was not kind in you to imagine when your sister commended Good Works, she intended it a reproach to you. Twas very far from her thoughts.

TO JOHN FRANKLIN, PHILADELPHIA, MAY, 1745

. . . Our people are extremely impatient to hear of your success at Cape Breton. My shop is filled with thirty inquiries at the coming in of every post. Some wonder the place is not yet taken. I tell them I shall be glad to hear that news three months hence. Fortified towns are hard nuts to crack; and your teeth have not been accustomed to it. Taking strong places is a particular trade, which you have taken up without serving an apprenticeship to it. Armies and veterans need skilful engineers to direct them in their attack. Have you any? But some seem to think forts are as easy taken as snuff. Father Moody's prayers look tolerably modest. You have a fast and prayer day for that purpose; in which I compute five hundred thousand petitions were offered up to the same effect in New England, which added to the petitions of every family morning and evening, multiplied by the number of days since January 25th, make forty-five millions of prayers; which, set against the prayers of a few priests in the garrison, to the Virgin Mary, give a vast balance in your favor.

If you do not succeed, I fear I shall have but an indifferent opinion of Presbyterian prayers in such cases, as long as I live. Indeed, in attacking strong towns I should have more dependence on *works,* than on *faith;* for, like the kingdom of heaven, they are to be taken by force and violence; and in a French garrison I suppose there are devils of that kind, that they are not to be cast out by prayers and fasting, unless it be by their own fasting for want of provisions. I believe there is Scripture in what I have wrote, but I cannot adorn the margin with quotations, having a bad memory, and no Concordance at hand; besides no more time than to subscribe myself, &c.

A BALLAD FOR DEBORAH

Although they shared values, Franklin was far more worldly and intellectual than his wife was, or ever wanted ever to be. During her adult life, Deborah never seems to have spent a night away from her home on Market Street within two blocks of the house where she was raised. Franklin, on the other hand, loved to travel, and although he would occasionally express some hope that she would accompany him, he knew that she was not so inclined. They respected each other's independence, perhaps to a fault. For fifteen of the last seventeen years of Deborah's life, Franklin would be away, including when she died. He would also, as we shall see, form close friendships and diverting flirtations with other women—though no committed romantic or sexual relationships—and his letters to Deborah, while frequent and chatty, were rarely emotionally or intellectually engaging.

Nevertheless, their mutual affection, respect, loyalty and devotion—and their sense of partnership—would endure. The only extant painting of Deborah makes her seem like a sensible and determined woman, plump and plain but not unattractive. It was a relationship that did not inspire great romantic verse, but it did produce an endearing ballad that he put into the mouth of Poor Richard. In it Franklin paid tribute to "My Plain Country Joan," his nickname for Deborah, and blessed the day he made her his own.

I SING MY PLAIN COUNTRY JOAN, C. 1742

Of their Chloes and Phillisses Poets may prate
I sing my plain Country Joan
Now twelve Years my Wife, still the Joy of my Life
Blest Day that I made her my own,
My dear Friends
Blest Day that I made her my own.

Not a word of her shape, or her face, or her eyes,
Of flames or of darts shall you hear:
Though I beauty admire, 'tis virtue I prize,
Which fades not in seventy years,
My dear Friends

In Health a Companion delightful and dear,
Still easy, engaging, and Free,
In Sickness no less than the faithfullest Nurse
As tender as tender can be,
My dear Friends

In peace and good order my household she guides,
Right careful to save what I gain;
Yet cheerfully spends, and smiles on the friends
I've the pleasure to entertain,
My dear Friends

She defends my good Name ever where I'm to blame,
Friend firmer was ne'er to Man giv'n,
Her Compassionate Breast, feels for all the Distrest,
Which draws down the Blessing from Heavn,
My dear Friends

Am I laden with Care, she takes off a large Share,
That the Burthen ne'er makes to reel,

Does good Fortune arrive, the Joy of my Wife,
Quite Doubles the Pleasures I feel
My dear Friends

In Raptures the giddy Rake talks of his Fair,
Enjoyment shall make him Despise,
I speak my cool sense, that long Experience,
And Enjoyment have changd in no wise,
My dear Friends

The best have some faults, and so has my Joan,
But then they're exceedingly small,
And now, I'm used to 'em, they're so like my own,
I can scarcely feel them at all,
My dear Friends
I can scarcely see them at all.

Were the fairest young Princess, with Million in Purse
To be had in Exchange for my Joan,
She could not be a better Wife, mought be a Worse,
So I'd stick to my Joggy alone
My dear Friends
I'd cling to my lovely old Joan.

REASONS TO CHOOSE AN OLDER MISTRESS

Throughout his life, Franklin was an unabashed admirer of women, and never prudish. His list of bawdy reasons for preferring older women as mistresses is now, at least in some circles, one of Franklin's most famous pieces, but it was suppressed by his grandson and other compilers of his papers throughout the nineteenth century as being too indecent to print.

OLD MISTRESSES APOLOGUE, JUNE 25, 1745

My dear friend,

I know of no medicine fit to diminish the violent natural inclinations you mention; and if I did, I think I should not communicate it to you. Marriage is the proper remedy. It is the most natural state of man, and therefore the state in which you are most likely to find solid happiness. Your reasons against entering into it at present, appear to me not well-founded. The circumstantial advantages you have in view by postponing it, are not only uncertain, but they are small in comparison with that of the thing itself, the being *married and settled.* It is the man and woman united that make the complete human being. Separate, she wants his force of body and strength of reason; he, her softness, sensibility and acute discernment. Together they are more likely to succeed in the world. A single man has not nearly the value he would have in that state of union. He is an incomplete animal. He resembles the odd half of a pair of scissors. If you get a prudent healthy wife, your industry in your profession, with her good economy, will be a fortune sufficient.

But if you will not take this counsel, and persist in thinking a commerce with the sex inevitable, then I repeat my former advice, that in all your amours you should *prefer old women to young ones.* You call this a paradox, and demand my reasons. They are these:

1. Because as they have more knowledge of the world and their minds are better stored with observations, their conversation is more improving and more lastingly agreeable.

2. Because when women cease to be handsome, they study to be good. To maintain their influence over men, they supply the diminution of beauty by an augmentation of utility. They learn to do a 1000 services small and great, and are the most tender and useful of all friends when you are sick. Thus they continue amiable. And hence there is hardly such a thing to be found as an old woman who is not a good woman.

3. Because there is no hazard of children, which irregularly produced may be attended with much inconvenience.

4. Because through more experience, they are more prudent and discreet in conducting an intrigue to prevent suspicion. The commerce with them is therefore safer with regard to your reputation. And with regard to theirs, if the affair should happen to be known, considerate people might be rather inclined to excuse an old woman who would kindly take care of a young man, form his manners by her good counsels, and prevent his ruining his health and fortune among mercenary prostitutes.

5. Because in every animal that walks upright, the deficiency of the fluids that fill the muscles appears first in the highest part: the face first grows lank and wrinkled; then the neck; then the breast and arms; the lower parts continuing to the last as plump as ever: so that covering all above with a basket, and regarding only what is below the girdle, it is impossible of two women to know an old from a young one. And as in the dark all cats are gray, the pleasure of corporal enjoyment with an old woman is at least equal, and frequently superior, every knack being by practice capable of improvement.

6. Because the sin is less. The debauching a virgin may be her ruin, and make her for life unhappy.

7. Because the compunction is less. The having made a young girl *miserable* may give you frequent bitter reflections; none of which can attend the making an old woman *happy*.

8thly and lastly they are *so grateful!!*

Thus much for my paradox. But still I advise you to marry directly; being sincerely your affectionate friend.

POLLY BAKER'S TRIAL

"The Speech of Miss Polly Baker" is a tale of sex and woe told from a woman's point of view, a literary device often used by Franklin that displayed his ability to appreciate the other sex. It purports to recount the speech of a young woman on trial for having a fifth illegitimate child. The light humor of the piece hides the fact that it is actually a sharp attack on hypocritical customs and unfair attitudes toward women and sex. Franklin, who had fathered an illegitimate child before his marriage but taken responsibility for it, is particularly scathing about the double standard that subjects her, but not the men who had sex with her, to humiliation. First published in London, it was then frequently reprinted in England and America without people realizing that it was fiction. Only thirty years later did Franklin reveal that he had written it as a hoax.

THE GENERAL ADVERTISER, APRIL 15, 1747

The Speech of Miss Polly Baker, before a Court of Judicature,
At Connecticut near Boston in New England; where she
was prosecuted the fifth time, for having a bastard child: which
influenced the court to dispense with her punishment,
and induced one of her judges to marry her the next day.

May it please the honorable bench to indulge me in a few words: I am a poor unhappy woman, who have no money to fee lawyers to plead for me, being hard put to it to get a tolerable living. I shall not trouble your honors with long speeches; for I have not the presumption to expect, that you may, by any means, be prevailed on to deviate in your sentence from the law, in my favor. All I humbly hope is, that your honors would charitably move the governors' goodness on my behalf, that my fine may be remitted.

This is the fifth time, gentlemen, that I have been dragged before your court on the same account; twice I have paid heavy fines, and twice have been brought to public punishment, for want of money to pay those fines. This may have been agreeable to the laws, and I don't dispute it; but since laws are sometimes unreasonable in themselves, and therefore repealed, and others bear too hard on the subject in particular circumstances; and therefore there is left a power somewhat to dispense with the execution of them; I take the liberty to say, that I think this law, by which I am punished, is both unreasonable in itself, and particularly severe with regard to me, who have always lived an in-

offensive life in the neighborhood where I was born, and defy my enemies (if I have any) to say I ever wronged man, woman, or child. Ab-
stracted from the law, I cannot conceive (may it please your honors)
what the nature of my offence is. I have brought five fine children into
the world, at the risk of my life; I have maintained them well by my
own industry, without burdening the township, and would have done it
better, if it had not been for the heavy charges and fines I have paid.

Can it be a crime (in the nature of things I mean) to add to the
number of the king's subjects, in a new country that really wants people? I own it, I should think it a praise-worthy, rather than a punishable
action. I have debauched no other woman's husband, nor enticed any
youth; these things I never was charged with, nor has any one the least
cause of complaint against me, unless, perhaps, the minister, or justice,
because I have had children without being married, by which they have
missed a wedding fee. But, can ever this be a fault of mine? I appeal to
your honors.

You are pleased to allow I don't want sense; but I must be stupefied
to the last degree, not to prefer the honorable state of wedlock, to the
condition I have lived in. I always was, and still am willing to enter into
it; and doubt not my behaving well in it, having all the industry, frugality, fertility, and skill in economy, appertaining to a good wife's character. I defy any person to say, I ever refused an offer of that sort: on the
contrary, I readily consented to the only proposal of marriage that ever
was made me, which was when I was a virgin; but too easily confiding
in the person's sincerity that made it, I unhappily lost my own honor, by
trusting to his; for he got me with child, and then forsook me: that very
person you all know; he is now become a magistrate of this country;
and I had hopes he would have appeared this day on the bench, and
have endeavored to moderate the court in my favor; then I should have
scorned to have mentioned it; but I must now complain of it, as unjust
and unequal, that my betrayer and undoer, the first cause of all my
faults and miscarriages (if they must be deemed such) should be advanced to honor and power in the government, that punishes my misfortunes with stripes and infamy.

I should be told, 'tis like, that were there no act of assembly in the
case, the precepts of religion are violated by my transgressions. If mine,

then, is a religious offence, leave it to religious punishments. You have already excluded me from the comforts of your church-communion. Is not that sufficient? You believe I have offended heaven, and must suffer eternal fire: will not that be sufficient? What need is there, then, of your additional fines and whipping? I own, I do not think as you do; for, if I thought what you call a sin, was really such, I could not presumptuously commit it. But, how can it be believed, that heaven is angry at my having children, when to the little done by me towards it, God has been pleased to add his divine skill and admirable workmanship in the formation of their bodies, and crowned it, by furnishing them with rational and immortal souls.

Forgive me, gentlemen, if I talk a little extravagantly on these matters; I am no divine, but if you, gentlemen, must be making laws, do not turn natural and useful actions into crimes, by your prohibitions. But take into your wise consideration, the great and growing number of bachelors in the country, many of whom from the mean fear of the expenses of a family, have never sincerely and honorably courted a woman in their lives; and by their manner of living, leave unproduced (which is little better than murder) hundreds of their posterity to the thousandth generation. Is not this a greater offence against the public good, than mine? Compel them, then, by law, either to marriage, or to pay double the fine of fornication every year.

What must poor young women do, whom custom have forbid to solicit the men, and who cannot force themselves upon husbands, when the laws take no care to provide them any; and yet severely punish them if they do their duty without them; the duty of the first and great command of nature, and of nature's god, *increase and multiply.* A duty, from the steady performance of which, nothing has been able to deter me; but for its sake, I have hazarded the loss of the public esteem, and have frequently endured public disgrace and punishment; and therefore ought, in my humble opinion, instead of a whipping, to have a statue erected to my memory.

PART 4

THE PUBLIC CITIZEN

PLAIN TRUTH:

O R,

SERIOUS CONSIDERATIONS

On the PRESENT STATE of the

CITY of *PHILADELPHIA*,

A N D

PROVINCE of *PENNSYLVANIA*.

By a TRADESMAN of *Philadelphia.*

*Capta urbe, nihil fit reliqui victis. Sed, per Deos immortales, vos
ego appello, qui semper domos, villas, signa, tabulas vestras, tan-
tæ æstimationis fecistis ; si ista, cujuscumque modi sint, quæ am-
plexamini, retinere, si voluptatibus vestris otium præbere vultis ;
expergiscimini aliquando, & capessite rempublicam. Non agitur
nunc de sociorum injuriis ; LIBERTAS & ANIMA nostra in du-
bio est. Dux hostium cum exercitu supra caput est. Vos cunctamini
etiam nunc, & dubitatis quid faciatis ? Scilicet, res ipsa asperæ
est, sed vos non timetis eam. Imo vero maxume ; sed inertiâ &
mollitiâ animi, alius alium exspectantes, cunctamini ; videlicet,
Diis immortalibus confisi, qui hanc rempublicam in maxumis peri-
culis servavere. NON VOTIS, NEQUE SUPPLICIIS MULIE-
RIBUS, AUXILIA DEORUM PARANTUR : vigilando, agen-
do, bene consulendo, prospere omnia cedunt. Ubi socordiæ tete at-
que ignaviæ tradideris, nequicquam Deos implores ; irati, infesti-
que sunt.* M. POR. CAT. *in* SALUST.

Printed in the YEAR MDCCXLVII.

"Plain Truth," 1747

A CALL TO ARMS FOR THE
MIDDLING PEOPLE

Most of the voluntary associations that Franklin formed—a Junto, library, philosophical society, even fire squad—did not usurp the core functions of government. But in 1747, he proposed something that was, though he may not have quite realized it, far more radical: a military force that would be independent of Pennsylvania's colonial government.

Franklin's plan for a volunteer Pennsylvania militia arose because of the feckless response by the colony's government to the ongoing threats from France and her Indian allies. The Assembly, dominated by pacifist Quakers, dithered and failed to authorize any defenses, and the Proprietors refused to submit their lands to any taxes for defense. So in November 1747, Franklin stepped into the breach by writing a vibrant pamphlet entitled "Plain Truth," signed by "a Tradesman of Philadelphia." It includes a warning that sounds like a Puritan terror sermon, and it climaxes with his memorable rallying cry to his fellow middle class, "the middling people, he farmers, shopkeepers and tradesmen of this city and country."

The result was the formation of a private militia. Thomas Penn, the colony's proprietor, was appalled. "This association is founded on a contempt to government," he wrote, "a part little less than treason." In a subsequent letter, he called Franklin "a sort of tribune of the people" and "a dangerous man."

By the summer of 1748, the threat of war passed and the Militia Association disbanded, without any attempt by Franklin to capitalize on his new power and popularity. But the lessons he learned stayed with him. He realized that the colonists might have to fend for themselves instead of relying on their British governors, that the powerful elites deserved no deference, and that "we the middling people" should be the proud sinews of the new land. It also reinforced his belief that people, and perhaps someday colonies, could accomplish more when they joined together rather than remained "separate filaments of flax," when they formed unions rather than stood alone.

*Plain Truth: or, Serious Considerations On the Present State of the
City of Philadelphia, and Province of Pennsylvania*

It is said the wise Italians make this proverbial remark on our nation, viz. *The English* feel, *but they do not* see. That is, they are sensible of inconveniencies when they are present, but do not take sufficient care to prevent them: their natural courage makes them too little apprehensive of danger, so that they are often surprised by it, unprovided of the proper means of security. When 'tis too late they are sensible of their imprudence: after great fires, they provide buckets and engines: after a pestilence they think of keeping clean their streets and common shores: and when a town has been sacked by their enemies, they provide for its defense, &c. This kind of after-wisdom is indeed so common with us, as to occasion the vulgar, though very significant saying, *when the steed is stolen, you shut the stable door.*

But the more insensible we generally are of public danger, and indifferent when warned of it, so much the more freely, openly, and earnestly, ought such as apprehend it, to speak their sentiments; that if possible, those who seem to sleep, may be awakened, to think of some means of avoiding or preventing the mischief before it be too late.

Believing therefore that 'tis my duty, I shall honestly speak my mind in the following paper . . .

You have, my dear countrymen, and fellow citizens, riches to tempt a considerable force to unite and attack you, but are under no ties or engagements to unite for your defense. Hence, on the first alarm, *terror* will spread over all; and as no man can with certainty depend that another will stand by him, beyond doubt very many will seek safety by a speedy flight. Those that are reputed rich, will flee, thro fear of torture, to make them produce more than they are able. The man that has a wife and children, will find them hanging on his neck, beseeching him with tears to quit the city, and save his life, to guide and protect them in that time of general desolation and ruin. All will run into confusion, amidst cries and lamentations, and the hurry and disorder of departers, carrying away their effects. The few that remain will be unable to resist. *Sacking* the city will be the first, and *burning* it, in all probability, the last act of the enemy. This, I believe, will be the case, if you have timely notice. But what must be your condition, if suddenly surprised, without previous alarm, perhaps in the night! Confined to your houses, you will have nothing to trust to but the enemy's mercy. Your best fortune will be, to fall under the power of commanders of kings' ships, able to control the mariners; and not into the hands of *licentious privateers.* Who can, without the utmost horror, conceive the miseries of the latter! When your persons, fortunes, wives and daughters, shall be subject to the wanton and unbridled rage, rapine and lust, of *Negroes, mulattoes,* and others, the vilest and most abandoned of mankind. A dreadful scene! Which some may represent as exaggerated. I think it my duty to warn you: judge for yourselves.

'Tis true, with very little notice, the rich may shift for themselves. The means of speedy flight are ready in their hands; and with some previous care to lodge money and effects in distant and secure places, though they should lose much, yet enough may be left them, and to spare. But most unhappily circumstanced indeed are we, the middling people, the tradesmen, shopkeepers, and farmers of this province and city! We cannot all fly with our families; and if we could, how shall we subsist? No; we and they, and what little we have gained by hard labor and industry, must bear the brunt: the weight of contributions, extorted by the enemy (as it is of taxes among ourselves) must be surely borne by us. Nor can it be avoided as we stand at present; for though we are numerous, we are quite defenseless, having neither forts, arms, union, nor discipline. And though it were true, that our trade might be protected at no great expense, and our country and our city easily defended, if proper measures were but taken; yet who shall take these measures? Who shall pay that expense? On whom may we fix our eyes with the least expectation that they will do any one thing for our security?

Should we address that wealthy and powerful body of people, who have ever since the war governed our elections, and filled almost every seat in our assembly; should we entreat them to consider, if not as friends, at least as legislators, that *protection* is as truly due from the government to the people, as *obedience* from the people to the government; and that if on account of their religious scruples, they themselves could do no act for our defense, yet they might retire, relinquish their power for a season, quit the helm to freer hands during the present tempest, to hands chosen by their own interest too, whose prudence and moderation, with regard to them, they might safely confide in; secure, from their own native strength, of resuming again their present stations, whenever it shall please them: should we remind them, that the public money, raised *from all,* belongs *to all;* that since they have, for their own ease, and to secure themselves in the quiet enjoyment of their religious principles (and may they long enjoy them) expended such large sums to oppose petitions, and engage favorable representations of their conduct, if they themselves could by no means be free to appropriate any part of the public money for our defense . . . Our late governor did for years solicit, request, and even threaten them in vain. The council have since twice remonstrated to them in vain. Their religious prepossessions are unchangeable, their obstinacy invincible. Is there then the least hope remaining, that from that quarter any thing should arise for our security?

And is our prospect better, if we turn our eyes to the strength of the *opposite party,* those great and rich men, merchants and others, who are ever railing at Quakers for doing what their principles seem to require, and what in charity we ought to believe they think their duty, but take no one step themselves for the public safety? They have so much wealth and influence, if they would use it, that they might easily, by their endeavors and example, raise a military spirit among us, make us fond, studious of, and expert in martial discipline, and effect every thing that is necessary, under god, for our protection. But envy seems to have taken possession of their hearts, and to have eaten out and destroyed every generous, noble, public spirited sentiment. *Rage* at the disappointment of their little schemes for power, gnaws their souls, and fills them with such cordial hatred to their opponents, that every proposal, by the execution of which *those* may receive benefit as well as themselves, is rejected with indignation. *What,* say they, *shall we lay out our money to protect the trade of Quakers? Shall we fight to defend Quakers? No; let the trade perish, and the city burn; let what will happen, we shall never lift a finger to prevent it.* Yet the Quakers have *conscience* to plead for their resolution not to fight, which these gentlemen have not: *con-*

science with you, gentlemen, is on the other side of the question: *conscience* enjoins it as a duty on you (and indeed I think it such on every man) to defend your country, your friends, your aged parents, your wives, and helpless children: and yet you resolve not to perform this duty, but act *contrary* to *your own* consciences, because the Quakers act *according* to *theirs*. Till of late I could scarce believe the story of him who refused to pump in a sinking ship, because one on board, whom he hated, would be saved by it as well as himself. But such, it seems, is the unhappiness of human nature, that our passions, when violent, often are too hard for the united force of *reason, duty* and *religion*.

Thus unfortunately are we circumstanced at this time, my dear countrymen and fellow-citizens; we, I mean, the middling people, the farmers, shopkeepers and tradesmen of this city and country. Thro the dissensions of our leaders, thro *mistaken principles* of *religion,* joined with a love of worldly power, on the one hand; thro *pride, envy* and *implacable resentment* on the other; our lives, our families and little fortunes, dear to us as any great man's can be to him, are to remain continually exposed to destruction, from an enterprising, cruel, now well-informed, and by success encouraged enemy. It seems as if heaven, justly displeased at our growing wickedness, and determined to punish this once favored land, had suffered our chiefs to engage in these foolish and mischievous contentions, for *little posts* and *paltry distinctions,* that our hands might be bound up, our understandings darkened and misled, and every means of our security neglected. It seems as if our greatest men, our *cives nobilissimi* of both parties, had *sworn the ruin of the country, and invited the French, our most inveterate enemy, to destroy it.* Where then shall we seek for succor and protection? The government we are immediately under denies it to us; and if the enemy comes, we are *far from* Zion, *and there is no deliverer near.* Our case indeed is dangerously bad; but perhaps there is yet a remedy, if we have but the prudence and the spirit to apply it . . .

If this now flourishing city, and greatly improving colony, is destroyed and ruined, it will not be for want of numbers of inhabitants able to bear arms in its defense. 'Tis computed that we have at least (exclusive of the Quakers) 60,000 fighting men, acquainted with firearms, many of them hunters and marksmen, hardy and bold. All we want is order, discipline, and a few cannon. At present we are like the separate filaments of flax before the thread is formed, without strength because without connection; but union would make us strong and even formidable: though the *great* should neither help nor join us; though they should even oppose our uniting from some mean views of their own, yet, if we resolve upon it, and it please God to inspire us with the necessary prudence and vigor, it *may* be effected . . .

The very fame of our strength and readiness would be a means of discouraging our enemies; for 'tis a wise and true saying, that *one sword often keeps another in the scabbard.*

The way to secure peace is to be prepared for war. They that are on their guard, and appear ready to receive their adversaries, are in much less danger of being attacked, than the supine, secure and negligent. We have yet a winter before us, which may afford a good and almost sufficient opportunity for this, if we seize and improve it with a becoming vigor. And if the hints contained in this paper are so happy as to meet with a suitable disposition of mind in his countrymen and fellow citizens, the writer of it will, in a few days, lay before them a form of an association for the purposes herein mentioned, together with a practicable scheme for raising the money necessary for the defense of our trade, city, and country, without laying a burthen on any man.

May the God *of* wisdom, strength *and* power, *the lord of the armies of Israel, inspire us with prudence in this time of* danger; *take away from us all the seeds of contention and division, and unite the hearts and counsels of all of us, of whatever* sect *or* nation, *in one bond of peace, brotherly love, and generous public spirit; may he give us strength and resolution to amend our lives, and remove from among us every thing that is displeasing to him; afford us his most gracious protection, confound the designs of our enemies, and give* peace *in all our borders, is the sincere prayer of*

A Tradesman of Philadelphia

THE UNIVERSITY OF PENNSYLVANIA

The ingenious lad who did not get to go to Harvard, who skewered that college's pretensions with ill-disguised envy as a teenaged essayist, and whose thirst for knowledge had made him the best self-taught writer and scientist of his times, had for years nurtured the dream of starting a college of his own. So in 1749 he published a pamphlet that described, with his usual indulgence in detail, why an academy was needed, what it should teach, and how the funds might be raised.

This was not to be a religiously affiliated elite bastion like the four colleges (Harvard, William and Mary, Yale and Princeton) that already existed in the colonies. The focus, as to be expected from Franklin, would be on practical instruction such as writing, arithmetic, accounting, oratory, history, and business skills, and earthly virtues should be instilled. Franklin's plan was that of an educational reformer taking on the rigid classicists. The new academy should not, he felt, train scholars merely to glorify God or to seek learning for its own sake. Instead, what should be cultivated was "an inclination joined with an ability to serve mankind, one's country, friends and family."

The pamphlet was crammed with footnotes citing ancient scholars and his own experience on everything from swimming to writing style. Franklin, like any good Enlightenment thinker, loved order and precise procedures. He had displayed this penchant by outlining, in the most incredibly minute detail imaginable, his rules for running the Junto, Masonic lodge, library, American Philosophical Society, fire corps, constable patrol and militia. His proposal for the academy was an extreme example, crammed with exhaustive procedures on the best ways to teach everything from pronunciation to military history.

Franklin quickly raised £2000 in donations (though not the £5000 he recalled in his autobiography), drew up a constitution that was as detailed as his original proposal, and was elected president of the board. The academy opened in January of 1751 as the first nonsectarian college in America (by 1791 it came to be known as the University of Pennsylvania).

OCTOBER, 1749

Proposals Relating to the Education of Youth in Pennsylvania

It has long been regretted as a misfortune to the youth of this province, that we have no academy, in which they might receive the accomplishments of a regular education.

The following paper of *hints* towards forming a plan for that purpose, is so far approved by some public-spirited gentlemen, to whom it has been privately communicated, that they have directed a number of copies to be made by the press, and properly distributed, in order to obtain the sentiments and advice of men of learning, understanding, and experience in these matters; and have determined to use their interest and best endeavors, to have the scheme, when completed, carried gradually into execution; in which they have reason to believe they shall have the hearty concurrence and assistance of many who are well-wishers to their country.

Those who incline to favor the design with their advice, either as to the parts of learning to be taught, the order of study, the method of teaching, the economy of the school, or any other matter of importance to the success of the undertaking, are desired to communicate their sentiments as soon as may be, by letter directed to B. Franklin, printer, in Philadelphia . . .

Proposals, &c.

The good education of youth has been esteemed by wise men in all ages, as the surest foundation of the happiness both of private families and of commonwealth, almost all governments have therefore made it a principal object of their attention, to establish and endow with proper revenues, such seminaries of learning, as might supply the succeeding age with men qualified to serve the public with honor to themselves, and to their country.

Many of the first settlers of these provinces, were men who had received a good education in Europe, and to their wisdom and good management we owe much of our present prosperity. But their hands were full, and they could not do all things. The present race are not thought to be generally of equal ability: for though the American youth are allowed not to want capacity; yet the best capacities require cultivation, it being truly with them, as with the best ground, which unless well tilled and sowed with profitable seed, produces only ranker weeds.

That we may obtain the advantages arising from an increase of knowledge, and prevent as much as may be the mischievous consequences that would attend general ignorance among us, the following *hints* are offered towards forming a plan for the education of the youth of Pennsylvania, viz.

It is proposed,

That some persons of leisure and public spirit, apply for a charter, by which they may be incorporated, with power to erect an academy for the education of youth, to govern the same, provide masters, make rules, receive donations, purchase lands, &c. and to add to their number, from time to time such other persons as they shall judge suitable.

That the members of the corporation make it their pleasure, and in some degree their business, to visit the academy often, encourage and countenance the youth, countenance and assist the masters, and by all means in their power advance the usefulness and reputation of the design; that they look on the students as in some sort their children, treat them with familiarity and affection, and when they have behaved well, and gone through their studies, and are to enter the world, zealously unite, and make all the interest that can be made to establish them, whether in business, offices, marriages, or any other thing for their advantage, preferably to all other persons whatsoever even of equal merit.

And if men may, and frequently do, catch such a taste for cultivating flowers, for planting, grafting, inoculating, and the like, as to despise all other amusements for their sake, why may not we expect they should acquire a relish for that *more useful* culture of young minds. Thompson says,

" 'Tis joy to see the human blossoms blow, when infant reason grows apace, and calls for the kind hand of an assiduous care; delightful task! To rear the tender thought, to teach the young idea how to shoot, to pour the fresh instruction over the mind, to breathe the enlivening spirit, and to fix the generous purpose in the glowing breast."

That a house be provided for the academy, if not in the town, not many miles from it; the situation high and dry, and if it may be, not far from a river, having a garden, orchard, meadow, and field or two.

That the house be furnished with a library (if in the country, if in the town, the town libraries may serve) with maps of all countries, globes, some mathematical instruments, an apparatus for experiments in natural philosophy, and for mechanics; prints, of all kinds, prospects, buildings, machines, &c.

That the rector be a man of good understanding; good morals, diligent and patient, learned in the languages and sciences, and a correct pure speaker and writer of the English tongue; to have such tutors under him as shall be necessary.

That the boarding scholars diet together, plainly, temperately, and frugally.

That to keep them in health, and to strengthen and render active their bodies, they be frequently, exercised in running, leaping, wrestling, and swimming, &c.

That they have peculiar habits to distinguish them from other youth, if the academy be in or near the town; for this, among other reasons, that their behavior may be the better observed.

As to their studies, it would be well if they could be taught *every thing* that is useful, and *everything* that is ornamental; but art is long, and their time is short. It is therefore proposed that they learn those things that are likely to be *most useful* and *most ornamental*, regard being had to the several professions for which they are intended.

All should be taught to write a *fair hand*, and swift, as that is useful to all. And with it may be learnt something of *drawing*, by imitation of prints, and some of the first principles of perspective.

Arithmetic, accounts, and some of the first principles of *geometry* and *astronomy.*

The English language might be taught by grammar; in which some of our best writers, as Tillotson, Addison, Pope, Algernon Sidney, Cato's letters, &c. should be classics: the *stiles* principally to be cultivated, being the *clear* and the *concise.* Reading should also be taught, and pronouncing, properly, distinctly, emphatically; not with an even tone, which *under-does,* nor a theatrical, which *over-does* nature.

To form their style, they should be put on writing letters to each other, making abstracts of what they read; or writing the same things in their own words; telling or writing stories lately read, in their own expressions. All to be revised and corrected by the tutor, who should give his reasons, explain the force and import of words, &c.

To form their pronunciation, they may be put on making declamations, repeating speeches, delivering orations, &c., the tutor assisting at the rehearsals, teaching, advising, correcting their accent, &c.

But if history be made a constant part of their reading, such as the translations of the Greek and roman historians, and the modern histories of ancient Greece and Rome, &c. may not almost all kinds of useful knowledge be that way introduced to advantage, and with pleasure to the student? As

Geography, by reading with maps, and being required to point out the places *where* the greatest actions were done, to give their old and new names, with the bounds, situation, extent of the countries concerned, &c.

Chronology, by the help of Helvicus or some other writer of the kind, who will enable them to tell *when* those events happened; what princes were cotemporaries, what states or famous men flourished about that time, &c. The several principal epochs to be first well fixed in their memories.

Ancient customs, religious and civil, being frequently mentioned in history, will give occasion for explaining them; in which the prints of medals, *basso relievos,* and ancient monuments will greatly assist.

Morality, by descanting and making continual observations on the causes of the rise or fall of any man's character, fortune, power, &c. mentioned in history; the advantages of temperance, order, frugality, industry, perseverance, &c. &c. Indeed the general natural tendency of reading good history must be to fix in the minds of youth deep impressions of the beauty and usefulness of virtue of all kinds, public spirit, fortitude, &c.

History will show the wonderful effects of oratory, in governing, turning and leading great bodies of mankind, armies, cities, nations. When the minds of youth are struck with admiration at this, then is the time to give them the principles of that art, which they will study with taste and application. Then they may be made acquainted with the best models among the ancients, their beauties being particularly pointed out to them. Modern political oratory being chiefly performed by the pen and press, its advantages over the ancient in some respects are to be shown; as that its effects are more extensive, more lasting, &c.

History will also afford frequent opportunities of showing the necessity of a *public religion,* from its usefulness to the public; the advantage of a religious character among private persons; the mischiefs of superstition, &c. and the excellency of the Christian religion above all others ancient or modern.

History will also give occasion to expatiate on the advantage of civil orders and constitutions, how men and their properties are protected by joining in societies and establishing government; their industry encouraged and rewarded, arts invented, and life made more comfortable: the advantages of *liberty,* mischiefs of *licentiousness,* benefits arising from good laws and a due execution of justice, &c. thus may the first principles of sound *politics* be fixed in the minds of youth.

On *historical* occasions, questions of right and wrong, justice and injustice, will naturally arise, and may be put to youth, which they may debate in conversation and in writing, when they ardently desire victory, for the sake of the praise attending it, they will begin to feel the want, and be sensible of the use of *logic,* or the art of reasoning to *discover* truth, and of arguing to *defend* it, and *convince* adversaries. This would be the time to acquaint them with the principles of that art. Grotius, Puffendorff, and some other writers of the same kind, may be used on these occasions to decide their disputes. Public disputes warm the imagination, whet the industry, and strengthen the natural abilities.

When youth are told, that the great men whose lives and actions they read in history, spoke two of the best languages that ever were, the most expressive, copious, beautiful; and that the finest writings, the most correct compositions, the most perfect productions of human wit and wisdom, are in those languages, which have endured ages, and will endure while there are men; that no translation can do them justice, or give the pleasure found in reading the originals; that those languages contain all science; that one of them is become almost universal, being the language of learned men in all countries; that to understand them is a distinguishing ornament, &c. They may be thereby made desirous of learning those languages, and their industry sharpened in the acquisition of them. All intended for divinity should be taught the Latin and Greek; for physic, the Latin, Greek and French; for law, the Latin and French; merchants, the French, German, and Spanish: and though all should not be compelled to learn Latin, Greek, or the modern foreign languages; yet none that have an ardent desire to learn them should be refused; their English, arithmetic, and other studies absolutely necessary, being at the same time not neglected.

If the new *universal history* were also read, it would give a *connected* idea of human affairs, so far as it goes, which should be followed by the best modern histories, particularly of our mother country; then of these colonies; which should be accompanied with observations on their rise, increase, use to Great Britain, encouragements, discouragements, &c. the means to make them flourish, secure their liberties, &c.

With the history of men, times and nations, should be read at proper hours or days, some of the best *histories of nature,* which would not only be delightful to youth, and furnish them with matter for their letters, &c. as well as other history; but afterwards of great use to them, whether they are merchants, handicrafts, or divines; enabling the first the better to understand many commodities, drugs, &c. The second to improve his trade or handicraft by new mixtures, material, &c. And the last to adorn his discourses by beautiful comparisons, and strengthen them by new proofs of divine providence. The conversation of all will be improved by it, as occasions frequently occur of making natural observations, which are instructive, agreeable, and entertaining in almost all companies. *Natural history* will also afford opportunities of introducing many observations, relating to the preservation of health, which may be afterwards of great use. Arbuthnot on air and aliment, Sanctorius on perspiration, Lemery on foods, and some others, may now be read, and a very little explanation will make them sufficiently intelligible to youth.

While they are reading natural history, might not a little *gardening, planting, grafting, inoculating,* &c. be taught and practiced; and now and then excursions made to the neighboring plantations of the best farmers, their methods observed and reasoned upon for the information of youth. The improvement of agriculture being useful to all, and skill in it no disparagement to any.

The history of *commerce,* of the invention of arts, rise of manufactures, progress of trade, change of its seats, with the reasons, causes, &c. may also be made entertaining to youth, and will be useful to all. And this, with the accounts in other history of the prodigious force and effect of engines and machines used in war, will naturally introduce a desire to be instructed in *mechanics,* and to be informed of the principles of that art by which weak men perform such wonders, labor is saved, manufactures expedited, &c. &c. This will be the time to show them prints of ancient and modern machines, to explain them, to let them be copied, and to give lectures in mechanical philosophy.

With the whole should be constantly inculcated and cultivated, that *benignity of mind,* which shows itself in *searching for* and *seizing* every opportunity *to serve* and *to oblige;* and is the foundation of what is called good breeding; highly useful to the possessor, and most agreeable to all.

The idea of what is *true merit,* should also be often presented to youth, explained and impressed on their minds, as consisting in an *inclination* joined with an *ability* to serve mankind, ones country, friends and family; which *ability* is (with the blessing of god) to be acquired or greatly increased by *true learning;* and should indeed be the great *aim* and *end* of all learning.

HOW TO BE A GOOD TRADESMAN

One of Franklin's goals in life was to provide useful advice for aspiring middle-class shopkeepers and tradesmen. He was America's godfather of self-help business books. By creating what he called a strong "middling class," he helped to lay the foundation for his vision of a stable civic society in America. Two pieces he wrote on this topic for his paper in 1750 show his different styles: the first is straightforward and earnest, the second a parody (along the lines of his fake list of talents for an almanac writer and the piece he wrote later on rules Britain could use for destroying its empire) listing the ways to make yourself disagreeable.

Rules Proper to be Observed in Trade

I. Endeavor to be perfect in the calling you are engaged in; and be assiduous in every part thereof; INDUSTRY being the natural means of acquiring *wealth, honor,* and *reputation;* as idleness is of *poverty, shame,* and *disgrace.*

II. Lay a good foundation in regard to principle: Be sure not willfully to overreach, or deceive your neighbor; but keep always in your eye the golden rule of *doing as you would be done unto.*

III. Be strict in discharging all legal debts: Do not evade your creditors by any shuffling arts, in giving notes under your hand, only to defer payment; but, if you have it in your power, discharge all debts when they become due. Above all, when you are straitened for want of money, be cautious of taking it up at an high interest. This has been the ruin of many, therefore endeavor to avoid it.

IV. Endeavor to be as much in your shop, or warehouse, or in whatever place your business properly lies, as possibly you can: Leave it not to servants to transact, for customers will not regard them as yourself; they generally think they shall not be so well served: Besides, mistakes may arise by the negligence, or inexperience, of servants; and therefore, your presence will prevent, probably, the loss of a good customer.

V. Be complaisant to the *meanest,* as well as greatest: You are as much obliged to use good manners for a farthing, as a pound; the one demands it from you, as well as the other.

VI. Be not too talkative, but speak as much as is necessary to recommend your goods, and always observe to keep within the rules of decency. If customers slight your goods, and undervalue them, endeavor to convince them of their mistake, if you can, but not affront them: Do not be pert in your answers, but with patience hear, and with meekness give an answer; for if you affront in a small matter, it may probably hinder you from a future good customer. They may think that you are dear in the articles they want; but, by going to another, may find it not so, and probably may return again; but if you behave rude and affronting, there is no hope either of returning, or their future custom.

VII. Take great care in keeping your accounts well: Enter every thing necessary in your books with neatness and exactness; often state your accounts, and examine whether you gain, or lose; and carefully survey your stock, and inspect into every particular of your affairs.

VIII. Take care, as much as you can, whom you trust: Neither take nor give long credit; but, at the farthest, annually settle your accounts. Deal at the fountain head for as many articles as you can; and, if it lies in your power, for ready money: This method you will find to be the most profitable in the end. Endeavor to keep a proper assortment in your way, but not over-stock yourself. Aim not at making a great figure in your shop, in unnecessary ornaments, but let it be neat and useful: Too great an appearance may rather prevent, than engage customers. Make your *business* your pleasure, and other entertainments will only appear necessary for relaxation therefrom.

IX. Strive to maintain a *fair character* in the world: That will be the best means for advancing your credit, gaining you the most flourishing trade, and enlarging your fortune. Condescend to no mean action, but add a luster to trade, by keeping up to the dignity of your nature.

THE PENNSYLVANIA GAZETTE, NOVEMBER 15, 1750

RULES, *by the Observation of which, a Man of Wit and Learning may nevertheless make himself a* disagreeable *Companion.*

Your business is to *shine;* therefore you must by all means prevent the shining of others, for their brightness may make yours the less distinguished. To this end,

1. If possible engross the whole discourse; and when other matter fails, talk much of yourself, your education, your knowledge, your circumstances, your successes in business, your victories in disputes, your own wise sayings and observations on particular occasions, &c. &c. &c.;

2. If when you are out of breath, one of the company should seize

the opportunity of saying something; watch his words, and, if possible, find somewhat either in his sentiment or expression, immediately to contradict and raise a dispute upon. Rather than fail, criticize even his grammar.

3. If another should be saying an indisputably good thing; either give no attention to it; or interrupt him; or draw away the attention of others; or, if you can guess what he would be at, be quick and say it before him; or, if he gets it said, and you perceive the company plea's with it, own it to be a good thing, and withal remark that it had been said by *Bacon, Locke, Bayle,* or some other eminent writer; thus you deprive him of the reputation he might have gained by it, and gain some yourself, as you hereby show your great reading and memory.

4. When modest men have been thus treated by you a few times, they will choose ever after to be silent in your company; then you may shine on without fear of a rival; rallying them at the same time for their dullness, which will be to you a new fund of wit.

Thus you will be sure to please *yourself.* The polite man aims at pleasing *others,* but you shall go beyond him even in that. A man can be present only in one company, but may at the same time be absent in twenty. He can please only where he *is,* you wherever you are *not.*

RATTLESNAKES FOR FELONS

Britain had been expelling convicts to America, which it justified as a way to help the colonies grow. Franklin sarcastically noted that "such a tender parental concern in our Mother Country for the welfare of her children calls aloud for the highest returns of gratitude." So he proposed that America ship a boatload of rattlesnakes back to England. Perhaps the change of climate might tame them, which is what the British had claimed would happen to the convicts.

THE PENNSYLVANIA GAZETTE, MAY 9, 1751

By a passage in one of your late papers, I understand that the government at home will not suffer our mistaken assemblies to make any law for preventing or discouraging the importation of convicts from great Britain, for this kind reason, *that such laws are against the public utility, as they tend to prevent the* improvement *and* well peopling of the colonies.

Such a tender *parental* concern in our *mother country* for the *welfare* of her children, calls aloud for the highest *returns* of gratitude and duty. This every one must be sensible of: but 'tis said, that in our present circumstances it is absolutely impossible for us to make *such* as are adequate to the favor. I own it; but nevertheless let us do our endeavor. 'Tis something to show a grateful disposition.

In some of the uninhabited parts of these provinces, there are numbers of these venomous reptiles we call rattle-snakes; felons-convict from the beginning of the world: these, whenever we meet with them, we put to death, by virtue of an old law, *thou shalt bruise his head.* But as this is a sanguinary law, and may seem too cruel; and as however mischievous those creatures are with us, they may possibly change their natures, if they were to change the climate; I would humbly propose, that this general sentence of *death* be changed for *transportation.*

In the spring of the year, when they first creep out of their holes, they are feeble, heavy, slow, and easily taken; and if a small bounty were allowed *per* head, some thousands might be collected annually, and *transported* to Britain. There I would propose to have them carefully distributed in St. James's Park, in the spring-gardens and other places of pleasure about London; in the gardens of all the nobility and gentry throughout the nation; but particularly in the gardens of the *Prime Ministers,* the *Lords of trade* and *Members of Parliament;* for to them we are *most particularly* obliged.

There is no human scheme so perfect, but some inconveniences may be objected to it: yet when the conveniences far exceed, the scheme is judged rational, and fit to be executed. Thus inconveniences have been objected to that *good* and *wise* act of Parliament, by virtue of which all the Newgates and dungeons in Britain are emptied into the colonies. It has been said, that these thieves and villains introduced among us, spoil the morals of youth in the neighborhoods that entertain them, and perpetrate many horrid crimes; but let not *private interests* obstruct *public utility.* Our *mother* knows what is best for us. What is a little *housebreaking, shoplifting,* or *highway robbing;* what is a *son* now and then *corrupted* and *hanged,* a daughter *debauched* and *poxed,* a wife *stabbed,* a husband's *throat cut,* or a child's *brains beat out* with an axe, compared with this improvement and well peopling of the colonies!

Thus it may perhaps be objected to my scheme, that the *rattle-snake* is a mischievous creature, and that his changing his nature with the clime is a mere supposition, not yet confirmed by sufficient facts. What then? Is not example more prevalent than precept? And may not the honest rough British gentry, by a familiarity with these reptiles, learn to *creep,* and to *insinuate,* and to *slaver,* and to *wriggle* into place (and perhaps to *poison* such as stand in their way) qualities of no small advantage to courtiers! In comparison of which *improvement* and *public utility,* what is a *child* now and then killed by their venomous bite, or even a favorite *lap-dog?*

I would only add, that this exporting of felons to the colonies, may be considered as a *trade,* as well as in the light of a *favor.* Now all commerce implies *returns:* justice requires them: there can be no trade without them. And *rattle-snakes* seem the most *suitable returns* for the *human serpents* sent us by our *mother* country. In this, however, as in every other branch of trade, she will have the advantage of us. She will reap *equal* benefits without equal risk of the inconveniencies and dangers. For the *rattle-snake* gives warning before he attempts his mischief; which the convict does not.

I am Yours, &c.
Americanus

MAGICAL SQUARES

As an Assembly clerk in Philadelphia, Franklin used to amuse himself with a mathematical curiosity: the creation of what he called magic squares. He sent a description of them to his friend in London, Peter Collinson.

To Peter Collinson, c. 1752

Sir,

According to your request, I now send you the Arithmetical Curiosity, of which this is the history.

Being one day in the country, at the house of our common friend, the late learned Mr. Logan, he showed me a folio French book, filled with magic squares, wrote, if I forget not, by one M. Frenicle, in which he said the author had discovered great ingenuity and dexterity in the management of numbers; and, though several other foreigners had distinguished themselves in the same way, he did not recollect that any one Englishman had done any thing of the kind remarkable.

I said, it was, perhaps, a mark of the good sense of our English mathematicians, that they would not spend their time in things that were merely *difficiles nugae,* incapable of any useful application. He answered, that many of the arithmetical or mathematical questions, publicly proposed and answered in England, were equally trifling and useless. Perhaps the considering and answering such questions, I replied, may not be altogether useless, if it produces by practice an habitual readiness and exactness in mathematical disquisitions, which readiness may, on many occasions, be of real use. In the same way, says he, may the making of these squares be of use. I then confessed to him, that in my younger days, having once some leisure, (which I still think I might have employed more usefully) I had amused myself in making these kind of magic squares, and, at length, had acquired such a knack at it, that I could fill the cells of any magic square, of reasonable size, with a series of numbers as fast as I could write them, disposed in such a manner, as that the sums of every row, horizontal, perpendicular, or diagonal, should be equal; but not being satisfied with these, which I looked on as common and easy things, I had imposed on myself more difficult tasks, and succeeded in making other magic squares, with a variety of properties, and much more curious. He then showed me several in the same book, of an uncommon and more curious kind; but as I thought none of them equal to some I remembered to have made, he desired me to let him see them; and accordingly, the next time I visited him, I carried him a square of 8, which I found among my old papers, and which I will now give you, with an account of its properties.

52	61	4	13	20	29	36	45
14	3	62	51	46	35	30	19
53	60	5	12	21	28	37	44
11	6	59	54	43	38	27	22
55	58	7	10	23	26	39	42
9	8	57	56	41	40	25	24
50	63	2	15	18	31	34	47
16	1	64	49	48	33	32	17

The properties are,

1. That every strait row (horizontal or vertical) of 8 numbers added together, makes 260, and half each row half 260.

2. That the bent row of 8 numbers, ascending and descending diagonally, viz, from 16 ascending to 10, and from 23 descending to 17; and every one of its parallel bent rows of 8 numbers, make 260. Also the bent row from 52, descending to 54, and from 43 ascending to 45; and every one of its parallel bent rows of 8 numbers, make 260. Also the bent row from 45 to 43 descending to the left, and from 23 to 17 descending to right, and every one of its parallel bent rows of 8 numbers make 260. Also the bent row from 52 to 54 descending to the right, and from 10 to 16 descending to the left, and every one of its parallel bent rows of 8 numbers make 260. Also the parallel bent rows next to the above-mentioned, which are shortened to 3 numbers ascending, and 3 descending, &c. as from 53 to 4 ascending, and from 29 to 44 descending, make, with the 2 corner numbers, 260. Also the 2 numbers 14, 61

ascending, and 36, 19 descending, with the lower 4 numbers situated like them, viz. 50, 1, descending, and 32, 47, ascending, make 260. And, lastly, the 4 corner numbers, with the 4 middle numbers, make 260.

So this magical square seems perfect in its kind. But these are not all its properties; there are 5 other curious ones, which, at some other time, I will explain to you.

Mr. Logan then showed me an old arithmetical book, in quarto, wrote, I think, by one Stifelius, which contained a square of 16, that he said he should imagine must have been a work of great labor; but if I forget not, it had only the common properties of making the same sum, viz. 2056, in every row, horizontal, vertical, and diagonal. Not willing to be out-done by Mr. Stifelius, even in the size of my square, I went home, and made, that evening, the following magical square of 16, which, be-sides having all the Properties of the foregoing square of 8, i.e. it would make the 2056 in all the same rows and diagonals, had this added, that a four square hole being cut in a piece of paper of such a size as to take in and show through it, just 16 of the little squares, when laid on the greater square, the sum of the 16 numbers so appearing through the hole, wherever it was placed on the greater square, should likewise make 2056. This I sent to our friend the next morning, who, after some days, sent it back in a letter, with these words: I return to thee thy astonishing or most stupendous piece of the magical square, in which but the com-pliment is too extravagant, and therefore, for his sake, as well as my own, I ought not to repeat it. Nor is it necessary; for I make no question but you will readily allow this square of 16 to be the most magically magical of any magic square ever made by any magician.

I did not, however, end with squares, but composed also a magic circle, consisting of 8 concentric circles, and 8 radial rows, filled with a series of numbers, from 12 to 75, inclusive, so disposed as that the numbers of each circle, or each radial row, being added to the central number 12, they made exactly 360, the number of degrees in a circle; and this circle had, moreover, all the properties of the square of 8. If you desire it, I will send it; but at present, I believe, you have enough on this subject. I am, &c.

B.F.

ON WELFARE DEPENDENCY

He also discoursed with Collinson on political philosophy. One such letter shows the emergence of Franklin's middle-class populist conservatism. Although he was a generous and charitable man, always concocting civic improvement schemes, he worried that welfare laws and government handouts might have an unintended effect of promoting laziness and dependency. He also praised the natural ways of the Indians and made fun of white colonists who tried to educate them to their own ways.

To Peter Collinson, May 9, 1753

Sir,

I received your favor of the 29th. August last and thank you for the kind and judicious remarks you have made on my little piece. Whatever further occurs to you on the same subject, you will much oblige me in communicating it.

I have often observed with wonder, that temper of the poor English Manufacturers and day laborers which you mention, and acknowledge it to be pretty general. When any of them happen to come here, where labor is much better paid than in England, their industry seems to diminish in equal proportion. But it is not so with the German laborers; They retain the habitual industry and frugality they bring with them, and now receiving higher wages an accumulation arises that makes them all rich.

When I consider, that the English are the offspring of Germans, that the climate they live in is much of the same temperature; when I can see nothing in nature that should create this Difference, I am apt to suspect it must arise from institution, and I have sometimes doubted, whether the laws peculiar to England which compel the rich to maintain the poor, have not given the latter a dependence that very much lessens the care of providing against the wants of old age.

I have heard it remarked that the poor in Protestant countries on the continent of Europe, are generally more industrious than those of

Popish countries, may not the more numerous foundations in the latter for the relief of the poor have some effect towards rendering them less provident. To relieve the misfortunes of our fellow creatures is concurring with the Deity, 'tis Godlike, but if we provide encouragements for laziness, and supports for folly, may it not be found fighting against the order of God and Nature, which perhaps has appointed want and misery as the proper punishments for, and cautions against as well as necessary consequences of idleness and extravagancy.

Whenever we attempt to mend the scheme of Providence and to interfere in the government of the world, we had need be very circumspect lest we do more harm than good. In New England they once thought Blackbirds useless and mischievous to their corn, they made laws to destroy them, the consequence was, the Blackbirds were diminished but a kind of worms which devoured their grass, and which the Blackbirds had been used to feed on increased prodigiously; then finding their loss in grass much greater than their saving in corn they wished again for their Blackbirds.

We had here some years since a Transylvanian Tartar, who had traveled much in the East, and came hither merely to see the West, intending to go home thro the Spanish West Indies, China &c. He asked me one day what I thought might be the reason that so many and such numerous nations, as the Tartars in Europe and Asia, the Indians in America, and the Negroes in Africa, continued a wandering careless life, and refused to live in cities, and to cultivate the arts they saw practiced by the civilized part of mankind. While I was considering what answer to make him; I'll tell you, says he in his broken English, God make man for Paradise, he make him for to live lazy; man make God angry, God turn him out of Paradise, and bid him work; man no love work; he want to go to Paradise again, he want to live lazy; so all mankind love lazy. However this may be it seems certain, that the hope of becoming at some time of life free from the necessity of care and labor, together with fear of penury, are the mainsprings of most people's industry.

To those indeed who have been educated in elegant plenty, even the provision made for the poor may appear misery, but to those who have scarce ever been better provided for, such provision may seem quite good and sufficient, these latter have then nothing to fear worse than their present conditions, and scarce hope for any thing better than a Parish maintenance; so that there is only the difficulty of getting that maintenance allowed while they are able to work, or a little shame they suppose attending it, that can induce them to work at all, and what they do will only be from hand to mouth.

The proneness of human nature to a life of ease, of freedom from care and labor appears strongly in the little success that has hitherto attended every attempt to civilize our American Indians, in their present way of living, almost all their wants are supplied by the spontaneous productions of Nature, with the addition of very little labor, if hunting and fishing may indeed be called labor when game is so plenty, they visit us frequently, and see the advantages that Arts, Sciences, and compact society procure us, they are not deficient in natural understanding and yet they have never shown any Inclination to change their manner of life for ours, or to learn any of our Arts; When an Indian Child has been brought up among us, taught our language and habituated to our Customs, yet if he goes to see his relations and make one Indian Ramble with them, there is no persuading him ever to return, and that this is not natural to them merely as Indians, but as men, is plain from this, that when white persons of either sex have been taken prisoners young by the Indians, and lived a while among them, though ransomed by their friends, and treated with all imaginable tenderness to prevail with them to stay among the English, yet in a short time they become disgusted with our manner of life, and the care and pains that are necessary to support it, and take the first good opportunity of escaping again into the woods, from whence there is no reclaiming them. One instance I remember to have heard, where the person was brought home to possess a good estate; but finding some care necessary to keep it together, he relinquished it to a younger brother, reserving to himself nothing but a gun and a match-coat, with which he took his way again to the wilderness.

Though they have few but natural wants and those easily supplied. But with us are infinite artificial wants, no less craving than those of Nature, and much more difficult to satisfy; so that I am apt to imagine that close societies subsisting by labor and arts, arose first not from choice, but from necessity: When numbers being driven by war from their hunting grounds and prevented by seas or by other nations were crowded together into some narrow territories, which without labor would not afford them food. However as matters stand with us, care and industry seem absolutely necessary to our well being; they should therefore have every encouragement we can invent, and not one motive to diligence be subtracted, and the support of the poor should not be by maintaining them in idleness, but by employing them in some kind of labor suited to their abilities of body &c. as I am informed of late begins to be the practice in many parts of England, where work houses are erected for that purpose. If these were general I should think the poor would be more careful and work voluntarily and lay up something for themselves against a rainy day, rather than run the risk of being obliged to work at the pleasure of others for a bare subsistence and that too under confinement.

The little value Indians set on what we prize so highly under the name of learning appears from a pleasant passage that happened some years since at a Treaty between one of our Colonies and the Six Nations; when every thing had been settled to the satisfaction of both sides, and nothing remained but a mutual exchange of civilities, the English Commissioners told the Indians, they had in their Country a College for the instruction of youth who were there taught various languages, Arts, and Sciences; that there was a particular foundation in favor of the Indians to defray the expense of the education of any of their sons who should desire to take the benefit of it. And now if the Indians would accept of the offer, the English would take half a dozen of their brightest lads and bring them up in the best manner; The Indians after consulting on the proposal replied that it was remembered some of their youths had formerly been educated in that College, but it had been observed that for a along time after they returned to their Friends, they were absolutely good for nothing being neither acquainted with the true methods of killing deer, catching beaver or surprising an enemy. The proposition however, they looked on as a mark of the kindness and good will of the English to the Indian Nations which merited a grateful return; and therefore if the English Gentlemen would send a dozen or two of their children to Onondago the great Council would take care of their education, bring them up in really what was the best manner and make men of them . . .

I pray God long to preserve to Great Britain the laws, manners, liberties and religion notwithstanding the complaints so frequent in your public papers, of the prevailing corruption and degeneracy of your people; I know you have a great deal of virtue still subsisting among you, and I hope the Constitution is not so near a dissolution, as some seem to apprehend; I do not think you are generally become such slaves to your vices, as to draw down that *Justice* Milton speaks of when he says that sometimes nations will descend so low from reason, which is virtue, that no wrong, but justice, and some fatal curse annexed deprives them of their *outward* liberty, Their *inward* lost.—Paradise Lost.

In history we find that piety, public spirit and military prowess have their flows, as well as their ebbs, in every nation, and that the tide is never so low but it may rise again; but should this dreaded fatal change happen in my time, how should I even in the midst of the affliction rejoice, if we have been able to preserve those invaluable treasures, and can invite the good among you to come and partake of them! O let not Britain seek to oppress us, but like an affectionate parent endeavor to secure freedom to her children; they may be able one day to assist her in defending her own whereas a mortification begun in the foot may spread upwards to the destruction of the nobler parts of the body. I fear I have extended this rambling letter beyond your patience, and therefore conclude with requesting your acceptance of the enclosed pamphlet from, Sir,

Your most humble servant,
B. Franklin

THE ALBANY PLAN FOR AN AMERICAN UNION

Pennsylvania and other colonies were plagued by recurring wars against the French and their Indian allies. In response, Britain's ministers asked each colony to send delegates to a conference in Albany, New York, in June of 1754. They would have two missions: meeting with the Iroquois Indian confederation to reaffirm their allegiance, and discussing among themselves ways to create a more unified colonial defense.

Cooperation among the colonies did not come naturally. Some of their assemblies declined the invitation, and most of the seven that accepted instructed their delegates to avoid any plan for colonial confederation. Franklin, on the other hand, was always eager to foster more unity. He wrote an editorial in the Gazette in which he blamed the French success "on the present disunited state of the British colonies." Next to the article he printed the first and most famous editorial cartoon in American history: a snake cut into pieces, labeled with names of the colonies, with the caption: "Join, or Die."

Franklin was appointed to be one of the commissioners at the Albany Conference. He carried with him a paper he had written proposing a union of the northern colonies. At its core was a somewhat new concept that became known as federalism. A "General Government" would handle matters such as national defense and westward expansion, but each colony would keep its own constitution and local governing power. Though he was sometimes dismissed as more of a practitioner than a visionary conceptualizer, Franklin in Albany had helped to devise a federal concept—orderly, balanced, and enlightened—that would eventually form the basis for a unified American nation.

The commissioners approved a plan along these lines and sent it to the colonial assemblies as well as to Parliament for approval. But it was rejected by all of the colonial assemblies for usurping too much of their power, and it was shelved in London for giving too much democratic power to voters in the colonies. "The assemblies did not adopt it as they all thought there was too much prerogative in it," Franklin recalled, "and in England it was judged to have too much of the democratic."

Looking back on it near the end of his life, Franklin was convinced that the acceptance of his Albany Plan could have prevented the Revolution and created a harmonious empire. "The colonies so united would have been sufficiently strong to have defended themselves," he reasoned. "There would then have been no need of troops from England; of course the subsequent pretence for taxing America, and the bloody contest it occasioned, would have been avoided."

On that score he was probably mistaken. Further conflicts over Britain's right to tax her colonies and keep them subservient were almost inevitable. But for the next two decades, Franklin would struggle to find a harmonious solution even as he became more convinced of the need for the colonies to unite.

THE ALBANY PLAN OF UNION, JULY 10, 1754

Plan of a Proposed Union of the Several Colonies of
Massachusetts-bay, New Hampshire, Connecticut,
Rhode Island, New York, New Jersey, Pennsylvania, Maryland,
Virginia, North Carolina, and South Carolina, For their
Mutual Defense and Security, and for Extending the
British Settlements in North America

That humble Application be made for an Act of the Parliament of Great Britain, by Virtue of which, one General Government may be formed in America, including all the said Colonies, within and under which Government, each Colony may retain its present Constitution, except in the Particulars wherein a Change may be directed by the said Act, as hereafter follows.

President General

Grand Council.

That the said General Government be administered by a President General, To be appointed and Supported by the Crown, and a Grand Council to be Chosen by the Representatives of the People of the Several Colonies, met in their respective Assemblies.

Election of Members.

That within Months after the passing of such Act, The House of Representatives in the Several Assemblies, that Happen to be Sitting within that time or that shall be Specially for that purpose Convened, may and Shall Choose Members for the Grand Council in the following Proportions, that is to say.

Massachusetts-Bay	7
New Hampshire	2
Connecticut	5
Rhode-Island	2
New-York	4
New-Jerseys	3
Pennsylvania	6
Maryland	4
Virginia	7
North-Carolina	4
South-Carolina	4
	48

Place of first meeting.

Who shall meet for the first time at the City of Philadelphia, in Pennsylvania, being called by the President General as soon as conveniently may be, after his Appointment.

New Election.

That there shall be a New Election of Members for the Grand Council every three years; And on the Death or Resignation of any Member his Place shall be Supplied by a New Choice at the next Sitting of the Assembly of the Colony he represented.

Proportion of Members after first 3 years.

That after the first three years, when the Proportion of Money arising out of each Colony to the General Treasury can be known, The Number of Members to be Chosen, for each Colony shall from time to time in all ensuing Elections be regulated by that proportion (yet so as that the Number to be Chosen by any one Province be not more than Seven nor less than Two).

Meetings of Grand Council.

Call.

That the Grand Council shall meet once in every Year, and oftener if Occasion require, at such Time and place as they shall adjourn to at the last preceding meeting, or as they shall be called to meet at by the President General, on any Emergency, he having first obtained in Writing the Consent of seven of the Members to such call, and sent due and timely Notice to the whole.

Speaker.

Continuance.

That the Grand Council have Power to Choose their Speaker, and shall neither be Dissolved, prorogued nor Continue Sitting longer than Six Weeks at one Time without their own Consent, or the Special Command of the Crown.

Member's Allowance.

That the Members of the Grand Council shall be Allowed for their Service ten shillings Sterling per Diem, during their Sessions or Journey to and from the Place of Meeting; Twenty miles to be reckoned a days Journey.

Assent of President General.

His Duty.

That the Assent of the President General be requisite, to all Acts of the Grand Council, and that it be His Office, and Duty to cause them to be carried into Execution.

Power of President and Grand Council.

Peace and War.

Indian Purchases.

New Settlements.

Laws to Govern them.

That the President General with the advice of the Grand Council, hold or direct all Indian Treaties in which the General Interest or Welfare of the Colony's may be Concerned; And make Peace or Declare War with the Indian Nations. That they make such Laws as they Judge Necessary for regulating all Indian Trade. That they make all Purchases from Indians for the Crown, of Lands not within the Bounds of Particular Colonies, or that shall not be within their Bounds when some of them are reduced to more Convenient Dimensions. That they make New Settlements on such Purchases, by Granting Lands in the King's Name, reserving a Quit Rent to the Crown, for the use of the General Treasury. That they make Laws for regulating and Governing such new Settlements, till the Crown shall think fit to form them into Particular Governments.

Raise Soldiers &c.

Lakes.

Not to Impress

Power to make Laws Duties &c.

That they raise and pay Soldiers, and build Forts for the Defense of any of the Colonies, and equip Vessels of Force to Guard the Coasts and Protect the Trade on the Ocean, Lakes, or Great Rivers; But they shall not Impress Men in any Colonies, without the Consent of its Legislature. That for these purposes they have Power to make Laws And lay and Levy such General Duties, Imposts, or Taxes, as to them shall appear most equal and Just, Considering the Ability and other Circumstances of the Inhabitants in the Several Colonies, and such as may be Collected with the least Inconvenience to the People, rather discouraging Luxury, than

Treasurer.

Money how to Issue.

Loading Industry with unnecessary Burdens.

That they may Appoint a General Treasurer and a Particular Treasurer in each Government, when Necessary, And from Time to Time may Order the Sums in the Treasuries of each Government, into the General Treasury, or draw on them for Special payments as they find most Convenient; Yet no money to Issue, but by joint Orders of the President General and Grand Council Except where Sums have been Appropriated to particular Purposes, And the President General is previously empowered By an Act to draw for such Sums.

Accounts.

That the General Accounts shall be yearly Settled and Reported to the

Several Assembly's.

Quorum.

Laws to be Transmitted.

That a Quorum of the Grand Council empowered to Act with the President General, do consist of Twenty-five Members, among whom there shall be one, or more from a Majority of the Colonies. That the Laws made by them for the Purposes aforesaid, shall not be repugnant but as near as may be agreeable to the Laws of England, and Shall be transmitted to the King in Council for Approbation, as Soon as may be after their Passing and if not disapproved within Three years after Presentation to remain in Force.

Death of President General.

That in case of the Death of the President General The Speaker of the Grand Council for the Time Being shall Succeed, and be Vested with the Same Powers, and Authority, to Continue until the King's Pleasure be known.

Officers how Appointed.

That all Military Commission Officers Whether for Land or Sea Service, to Act under this General Constitution, shall be Nominated by the President General But the Approbation of the Grand Council, is to be

Vacancies how Supplied.

Each Colony may defend itself on Emergency. Obtained before they receive their Commissions, And all Civil Officers are to be Nominated, by the Grand Council, and to receive the President General's Approbation, before they Officiate; But in Case of Vacancy by Death or removal of any Officer Civil or Military under this Constitution, The Governor of the Province, in which such Vacancy happens, may Appoint till the Pleasure of the President General and Grand Council can be known. That the Particular Military as well as Civil Establishments in each Colony remain in their present State, this General Constitution Notwithstanding. And that on Sudden Emergencies any Colony may Defend itself, and lay the Accounts of Expense thence Arisen, before the President General and Grand Council, who may allow and order payment of the same as far as they Judge such Accounts Just and reasonable.

CATHERINE RAY

After the Albany Conference, Franklin embarked on a tour of local post offices, in his capacity as postmaster that culminated in a visit to Boston. While staying with his brother John, he met an entrancing young woman who became the first intriguing example of his many amorous and romantic—but probably never consummated—flirtations.

Catherine Ray was a lively and fresh twenty-three-year-old woman from Block Island, whose sister was married to John Franklin's stepson. Franklin, then forty-eight, was both charmed and charming. She was a great talker; so too was Franklin, when he wanted to flatter, and he was also a great listener. They played a game where he tried to guess her thoughts; she called him a conjurer and relished his attention. She made sugarplums; he insisted they were the best he'd ever eaten.

When it came time, after a week, for her to leave Boston to visit another sister in Newport, he decided to accompany her. Along the way, their poorly-shod horses had trouble on the icy hills; they got caught in cold rains and on one occasion took a wrong turn. But they would recall, years later, the fun they had talking for hours, exploring ideas, gently flirting. After two days with her family in Newport, he saw her off on the boat to Block Island.

He left for Philadelphia slowly and with reluctance, loitering on the way for weeks. When he finally arrived home, there was a letter from her. Over the next few months he would write her six times, and through the course of their lives more than 40 letters would pass between them.

From reading their letters, and between the lines, one gets the impression that Franklin made a few playful advances that Caty (she signed herself Caty, though he addressed her as Katy) gently deflected, and he seemed to respect her all the more for it. There are no signs, at least in the letters that survive, of a sexual affair. "I write this during a Northeaster storm of snow," he said in the first one he sent after their meeting. "The snowy fleeces which are pure as your virgin innocence, white as your lovely bosom—and as cold." In a letter a few months later, he spoke of life, math and the role of "multiplication" in marriage, adding roguishly: "I would gladly have taught you that myself, but you thought it was time enough, and wouldn't learn."

How did his loyal and patient wife fit into this type of long-distance flirtation? Oddly enough, he seemed to use her as a shield, both with Caty and the other women he later toyed with, in order to keep his relationships just on the safe side of propriety. He invariably invoked Deborah's name, and praised her virtues, in almost every letter he wrote to Caty. It was as if he wanted her to keep her ardor in perspective and to realize that, though his affection was real, his flirtations were merely playful. Or, perhaps, once his sexual advances had been rebuffed, he wanted to show (or to pretend) that they had not been serious.

Instead of merely continuing their flirtation, Franklin also began to provide Caty with paternal exhortations about duty and virtue. "Be a good girl," he urged, "until you get a good husband; then stay at home, and nurse the children, and live like a Christian." He hoped that when he next visited her, he would find her surrounded by "plump, juicy, blushing pretty little rogues, like their mama." And so it happened. The next time they met, she was married to William Greene, a future governor of Rhode Island, with whom she would have six children.

So what are we to make of their relationship? Clearly there were sweet hints of romantic attractions. But unless Franklin was dissembling in his letters in order to protect her reputation (and his), the joy came from pleasant fancies rather than physical realities. It was probably typical of the many flirtations he would have with younger women over the years: slightly naughty in a playful way, flattering to both parties, filled with intimations of intimacy, engaging both the heart and the mind. Despite a reputation for lecherousness that he did little to dispel, there is no evidence of any serious sexual affair he had after his marriage to Deborah.

To Catharine Ray, March 4, 1755

Dear Katy,

Your kind letter of January 20 is but just come to hand, and I take this first opportunity of acknowledging the favor.

It gives me great pleasure to hear that you got home safe and well that day. I thought too much was hazarded, when I saw you put off to sea in that very little skiff, tossed by every wave. But the call was strong and just, a sick parent. I stood on the shore, and looked after you, till I could no longer distinguish you, even with my glass; then returned to your sister's, praying for your safe passage. Towards evening all agreed that you must certainly be arrived before that time, the weather having been so favorable; which made me more easy and cheerful, for I had been truly concerned for you.

I left New England slowly, and with great reluctance: short days journeys, and loitering visits on the road, for three or four weeks, manifested my unwillingness to quit a country in which I drew my first breath, spent my earliest and most pleasant days, and had now received so many fresh marks of the people's goodness and benevolence, in the kind and affectionate treatment I had every where met with. I almost forgot I had a home; till I was more than half-way towards it; till I had, one by one, parted with all my New England friends, and was got into the western borders of Connecticut, among mere strangers: then, like an old man, who, having buried all he loved in this world, begins to think of heaven, I begun to think of and wish for home; and as I drew nearer, I found the attraction stronger and stronger, my diligence and speed increased with my impatience, I drove on violently, and made such long stretches that a very few days brought me to my own house, and to the arms of my good old wife and children, where I remain, thanks to God, at present well and happy.

Persons subject to the hyp complain of the north east wind as increasing their malady. But since you promised to send me kisses in that wind, and I find you as good as your word, 'tis to me the gayest wind that blows, and gives me the best spirits. I write this during a n. East storm of snow, the greatest we have had this winter: your favors come mixed with the snowy fleeces which are pure as your virgin innocence, white as your lovely bosom,—and as cold:—but let it warm towards some worthy young man, and may heaven bless you both with every kind of happiness.

I desired Miss Anna Ward to send you over a little book I left with her; for your amusement in that lonely island. My respects to your good father and mother, and sister unknown. Let me often hear of your welfare, since it is not likely I shall ever again have the pleasure of seeing you. Accept mine, and my wife's sincere thanks for the many civilities I received from you and your relations; and do me the justice to believe me, dear girl, your affectionate faithful friend and humble servant.

My respectful compliments to your good brother Ward, and sister; and to the agreeable family of the Wards at Newport when you see them. Adieu.

To Catharine Ray, September 11, 1755

Begone, business, for an hour, at least, and let me chat a little with my Katy.

I have now before me, my dear girl, three of your favors, viz. of march the 3d. March the 30th. And May the 1st. The first I received just before I set out on a long journey and the others while I was on that journey, which held me near six weeks. Since my return, I have been in such a perpetual hurry of public affairs of various kinds, as rendered it impracticable for me to keep up my private correspondences, even those that afforded me the greatest pleasure.

You ask in your last, how I do, and what I am doing, and whether every body loves me yet, and why I make them do so? In the first place, I am so well. Thanks to God, that I do not remember I was ever better. I still relish all the pleasures of life that a temperate man can in reason desire, and thro favor I have them all in my power. This happy situation shall continue as long as God pleases, who knows what is best for his creatures, and I hope will enable me to bear with patience and dutiful submission any change he may think fit to make that is less agreeable. As to the second question, I must confess, (but don't you be jealous) that many more people love me now than ever did before: for since I saw you, I have been enabled to do some general services to the country, and to the army, for which both have thanked and praised me; and say they love me; they *say so,* as you used to do; and if I were to ask any favors of them, would, perhaps, as readily refuse me: so that I find little real advantage in being beloved, but it pleases my humor.

Now it is near four months since I have been favored with a single line from you; but I will not be angry with you, because 'tis my fault. I ran in debt to you three or four letters, and as I did not pay, you would not trust me any more, and you had some reason: but believe me, I am honest, and though I should never make equal returns, you shall see ill keep fair accounts. Equal returns I can never make, though I should write to you by every post: for the pleasure I receive from one of yours, is more than you can have from two of mine. The small news, the domestic occurrences among our friends, the natural pictures you draw of persons, the sensible observations and reflections you make, and the easy chatty manner in which you express every thing, all contribute to heighten the pleasure; and the more, as they remind me of those hours and miles that we talked away so agreeably, even in a winter journey, a wrong road, and a soaking shower.

I long to hear whether you have continued ever since in that monastery; or have broke into the world again, doing pretty mischief; how the lady Wards do, and how many of them are married, or about it; what is become of Mr. B. And Mr. L. And what the state of your heart is at this instant? But that, perhaps I ought not to know; and therefore I will not conjure, as you sometimes say I do. If I could conjure, it should be to know what was that *oddest question about me that ever was thought of,* which you tell me a lady had just sent to ask you.

I commend your prudent resolutions in the article of granting favors to lovers: but if I were courting you, I could not heartily approve such conduct. I should even be malicious enough to say you were too *knowing,* and tell you the old story of the girl and the miller.

I enclose you the songs you write for, and with them your Spanish letter with a translation. I honor that honest Spaniard for loving you: it showed the goodness of his taste and judgment. But you must forget him, and bless some worthy young Englishman.

You have spun a long thread, 5022 yards! It will reach almost from Block Island hither. I wish I had hold of one end of it, to pull you to me: but you would break it rather than come. The cords of love and friendship are longer and stronger, and in times past have drawn me farther; even back from England to Philadelphia. I guess that some of the same kind will one day draw you out of that island.

I was extremely pleased with the turff you sent me. The Irish people who have seen it, say, 'tis the right sort; but I cannot learn that we have anything like it here. The cheeses, particularly one of them, were excellent: all our friends have tasted it, and all agree that it exceeds any English cheese they ever tasted. Mrs. Franklin was very proud, that a young lady should have so much regard for her old husband, as to send him such a present. We talk of you every time it comes to table; she is sure you are a sensible girl, and a notable housewife; and talks of bequeathing me to you as a legacy; but I ought to wish you a better, and hope she will live these 100 years; for we are grown old together, and if she has any faults, I am so used to them that I don't perceive them, as the song says,

> *Some faults we have all, and so may my Joan,*
> *But then they're exceedingly small;*
> *And now I'm used to them they're just like my own,*
> *I scarcely can see them at all,*
> *My dear friends,*
> *I scarcely can see them at all.*

Indeed I begin to think she has none, as I think of you. And since she is willing I should love you as much as you are willing to be loved by me; let us join in wishing the old lady a long life and a happy.

With her respectful compliments to your good mother and sisters, present mine, though unknown, and believe me to be, dear girl, your affectionate friend and humble servant,

B. Franklin

To Catharine Ray, October 16, 1755

Dear Katy,

Your favor of the 28th of June came to hand but the 28th of September, just 3 months after it was written. I had, two weeks before, wrote you a long chat, and sent it to the care of your brother Ward. I hear you are now in Boston, gay and lovely as usual. Let me give you some fatherly advice. Kill no more pigeons than you can eat. Be a good girl, and don't forget your catechize. Go constantly to meeting—or church—till you get a good husband; then stay at home, and nurse the children, and live like a Christian. Spend your spare hours, in sober whisk, prayers, or learning to cipher. You must practice *addition* to your husband's estate, by industry and frugality; *subtraction* of all unnecessary expenses; multiplication (I would gladly have taught you that myself, but you thought it was time enough, and wouldn't learn) he will soon make you a mistress of it. As to *division*, I say with brother Paul, *let there be no divisions among ye.* But as your good sister Hubbard (my love to her) is well acquainted with *the rule of two*, I hope you will become as expert in the *rule of three;* that when I have again the pleasure of seeing you, I may find you like my grape vine, surrounded with clusters, plump, juicy, blushing, pretty little rogues, like their mama. Adieu. The bell rings, and I must go among the grave ones, and talk politics.

Your affectionate friend,
B. Franklin

P.S. The plums came safe, and were so sweet from the cause you mentioned, that I could scarce taste the sugar.

A PARABLE ON INTOLERANCE

As an apostle of tolerance, Franklin found many ways to express his disdain for religious persecution. Not surprisingly, he often used his favorite devices of the hoax or parody. One of these was a fabricated chapter of the Bible, which he wrote in 1755. Four years later, he was visiting Scotland where he stayed at the manor of Sir Alexander Dick, a renowned physician and scientist, and there he met the greats of the Scottish Enlightenment: the economist Adam Smith, the philosopher David Hume, and the jurist and historian Lord Kames. He read them his parable, which so amused his companions that he sent them all copies.

1755

CHAP. XXVII

1. And it came to pass after these Things, that Abraham sat in the Door of his Tent, about the going down of the Sun.

2. And behold a Man, bowed with Age, came from the Way of the Wilderness, leaning on a Staff.

3. And Abraham arose and met him, and said unto him, Turn in, I pray thee, and wash thy Feet, and tarry all Night, and thou shalt arise early on the Morrow, and go on thy Way.

4. And the Man said, Nay, for I will abide under this Tree.

5. But Abraham pressed him greatly; so he turned, and they went into the Tent; and Abraham baked unleavened Bread, and they did eat.

6. And when Abraham saw that the Man blessed not God, he said unto him, Wherefore dost thou not worship the most high God, Creator of Heaven and Earth?

7. And the Man answered and said, I do not worship the God thou speakest of; neither do I call upon his Name; for I have made to myself a God, which abideth always in mine House, and provideth me with all Things.

8. And Abraham's Zeal was kindled against the Man; and he arose, and fell upon him, and drove him forth with Blows into the Wilderness.

9. And at Midnight God called unto Abraham, saying, Abraham, where is the Stranger?

10. And Abraham answered and said, Lord, he would not worship thee, neither would he call upon thy Name; therefore have I driven him out from before my Face into the Wilderness.

11. And God said, Have I born with him these hundred ninety and eight Years, and nourished him, and clothed him, notwithstanding his Rebellion against me, and couldst not thou, that art thyself a Sinner, bear with him one Night?

12. And Abraham said, Let not the Anger of my Lord wax hot against his Servant. Lo, I have sinned; forgive me, I pray Thee:

13. And Abraham arose and went forth into the Wilderness, and sought diligently for the Man, and found him, and returned with him

to his Tent; and when he had entreated him kindly, he sent him away on the Morrow with Gifts.

14. And God spake again unto Abraham, saying, For this thy Sin shall thy Seed be afflicted four Hundred Years in a strange Land:

15. But for thy Repentance will I deliver them; and they shall come forth with Power, and with Gladness of Heart, and with much Substance.

THE WAY TO WEALTH

In the summer of 1757, Franklin was sent to London as an envoy for the Pennsylvania Assembly to lobby against the taxation policies of the Penn family, the proprietors who ran the colony, On his voyage over, he wrote the preface to what would be his final edition of Poor Richard's Almanac. In it he invented a character named Father Abraham who gives a speech that strings together all of the best and most famous maxims that Poor Richard had sprinkled in the margins of his almanacs over the years. Franklin's wry tone was, even then, still intact. Poor Richard, who is standing in the back of the crowd, reports at the end: "The people heard it, and approved the doctrine, and immediately practiced the contrary." Father Abraham's speech was soon published as *The Way to Wealth* and became, for a time, the most famous book to come out of colonial America. Within 40 years, it was reprinted in 145 editions and seven languages; the French one was entitled *La Science du Bonhomme Richard*.

JULY 7, 1757

Courteous Reader,

I have heard that nothing gives an author so great pleasure, as to find his works respectfully quoted by other learned authors. This pleasure I have seldom enjoyed; for though' I have been, if I may say it without vanity, an eminent author of almanacs annually now a full quarter of a century, my brother authors in the same way, for what reason I know not, have ever been very sparing in their applauses; and no other author has taken the least notice of me, so that did not my writings produce me some solid pudding, the great deficiency of praise would have quite discouraged me.

I concluded at length, that the people were the best judges of my merit; for they buy my works; and besides, in my rambles, where I am not personally known, I have frequently heard one or other of my adages repeated, with, as Poor Richard says, at the end of it; this gave me some satisfaction, as it showed not only that my instructions were regarded, but discovered likewise some respect for my authority; and I own, that to encourage the practice of remembering and repeating those wise sentences, I have sometimes quoted myself with great gravity.

Judge then how much I must have been gratified by an incident I am going to relate to you. I stopped my horse lately where a great number of people were collected at a vendue of merchant goods. The hour of sale not being come, they were conversing on the badness of the times, and one of the company called to a plain clean old man, with white locks, "Pray, Father Abraham, what think you of the times? Won't these heavy taxes quite ruin the country? How shall we be ever able to pay them? What would you advise us to do?" Father Abraham stood up, and replied, "If you'd have my advice, I'll give it you in short, for a *word to the wise is enough*, and *many words won't fill a bushel*, as *Poor Richard says*." They joined in desiring him to speak his mind, and gathering round him, he proceeded as follows:

"Friends, says he, and neighbors, the taxes are indeed very heavy, and if those laid on by the government were the only ones we had to pay, we might more easily discharge them; but we have many others, and much more grievous to some of us. We are taxed twice as much by our idleness, three times as much by our pride, and four times as much by our folly, and from these taxes the commissioners cannot ease or deliver us by allowing an abatement. However let us hearken to good advice, and something may be done for us; *God helps them that help themselves*, as Poor Richard says, in his almanac of 1733.

"It would be thought a hard government that should tax its people one tenth part of their time, to be employed in its service. But idleness taxes many of us much more, if we reckon all that is spent in absolute sloth, or doing of nothing, with that which is spent in idle employments or amusements, that amount to nothing. Sloth, by bringing on diseases, absolutely shortens life. *Sloth, like rust, consumes faster than labor wears, while the used key is always bright,* as Poor Richard says. But *dost thou love life, then do not squander time, for that's the stuff life is made of,* as Poor Richard says. How much more than is necessary do we spend in sleep! forgetting that *the sleeping fox catches no poultry,* and that *there will be sleeping enough in the grave,* as Poor Richard says. If time be of all things the most precious, *wasting time* must be, as Poor Richard says, *the greatest prodigality,* since, as he elsewhere tells us, *lost time is never found again,* and what we call *time-enough, always proves little enough:* let us then be up and be doing, and doing to the purpose; so by diligence shall we do more with less perplexity. *Sloth makes all things difficult, but industry all easy,* as Poor Richard says; and *he that riseth late, must trot all day, and shall scarce overtake his business at night.* While *laziness travels so slowly, that poverty soon overtakes him,* as we read in Poor Richard, who adds, *drive thy business, let not that drive thee;* and *early to bed, and early to rise, makes a man healthy, wealthy and wise.*

"So what signifies wishing and hoping for better times. We may make these times better if we bestir ourselves. *Industry need not wish,* as Poor Richard says, and *he that lives upon hope will die fasting. There are no gains, without pains,* then *help hands, for I have no lands,* or if I have, they are smartly taxed. And, as Poor Richard likewise observes, *he that hath a trade hath an estate,* and *he that hath a calling hath an office of profit and honor;* but then the trade must be worked at, and the calling well followed, or neither the estate, nor the office, will enable us to pay our taxes. If we are industrious we shall never starve; for, as Poor Richard says, *at the working man's house hunger looks in, but dares not enter.* Nor will the bailiff nor the constable enter, *for industry pays debts, while despair increaseth them,* says Poor Richard. What though you have found no treasure, nor has any rich relation left you a legacy, *diligence is the mother of good luck,* as Poor Richard says, and *God gives all things to industry.* Then *plough deep, while sluggards sleep, and you shall have corn to sell and to keep,* says Poor Dick. Work while it is called today, for you know not how much you may be hindered tomorrow, which makes Poor Richard say, *one today is worth two tomorrows;* and farther, *have you somewhat to do tomorrow, do it today.* If you were a servant, would you not be ashamed that a good master should catch you idle? Are you then your own master, *be ashamed to catch yourself idle,* as Poor Dick says. When there is so much to be done for yourself, your family, your country, and your gracious king, be up by peep of day; *let not the sun look down and say, inglorious here he lies.* Handle your tools without mittens; remember that *the cat in gloves catches no mice,* as Poor Richard says. 'Tis true there is much to be done, and perhaps you are weak handed, but stick to it steadily, and you will see great effects, for *constant dropping wears away stones,* and by *diligence and patience the mouse ate in two the cable;* and *little strokes fell great oaks,* as Poor Richard says in his almanac, the year I cannot just now remember.

"Methinks I hear some of you say, must a man afford himself no leisure? I will tell thee, my friend, what Poor Richard says, *employ thy time well if thou meanest to gain leisure;* and, *since thou art not sure of a minute, throw not away an hour.* Leisure is time for doing something useful; this leisure the diligent man will obtain, but the lazy man never; so that, as Poor Richard says, *a life of leisure and a life of laziness are two things.* Do you imagine that sloth will afford you more comfort than labor? No, for as Poor Richard says, *trouble springs from idleness, and grievous toil from needless ease. Many without labor would live by their wits only, but they break for want of stock.* Whereas industry gives comfort, and plenty, and respect: *fly pleasures, and they'll follow you. The diligent spinner has a large shift,* and *now I have a sheep and a cow, everybody bids me good morrow,* all which is well said by Poor Richard.

"But with our industry, we must likewise be steady, settled and careful, and oversee our own affairs with our own eyes, and not trust too much to others; for, as Poor Richard says,

> *I never saw an oft removed tree,*
> *Nor yet an oft removed family,*
> *That throve so well as those that settled be.*

"And again, *three removes is as bad as a fire,* and again, *keep the shop, and thy shop will keep thee;* and again, *if you would have your business done, go; if not, send.* And again,

> *He that by the plough would thrive,*
> *Himself must either hold or drive.*

"And again, *the eye of a master will do more work than both his hands;* and again, *want of care does us more damage than want of knowledge;* and again, *not to oversee workmen is to leave them your purse open.* Trusting too much to others' care is the ruin of many; for, as the almanac says, *in the affairs of this world men are saved not by faith, but by the want of it;* but a man's own care is profitable; for, saith Poor Dick, *learning is to the studious,* and *riches to the careful,* as well as *power to the bold,* and *Heaven to the virtuous.* And farther, *if you would have a faithful servant, and one that you like, serve yourself.* And again, he adviseth to circumspection and care, even in the smallest matters, because sometimes *a little neglect may breed great mischief;* adding, *for want of a nail the shoe was lost; for want of a shoe the horse was lost, and for want of a horse the rider was lost,* being overtaken and slain by the enemy, all for want of care about a horse-shoe nail.

"So much for industry, my friends, and attention to one's own business; but to these we must add frugality, if we would make our industry more certainly successful. A man may, if he knows not how to save as he gets, *keep his nose all his life to the grindstone,* and die not worth a *groat* at last. *A fat kitchen makes a lean will,* as Poor Richard says; and,

> *Many estates are spent in the getting,*
> *Since women for tea forsook spinning and knitting,*
> *And men for punch forsook hewing and splitting.*

"*If you would be wealthy,* says he, in another almanac, *think of saving as well as of getting: the Indies have not made Spain rich, because her outgoes are greater than her incomes.* Away then with your expensive follies, and you will not have so much cause to complain of hard times, heavy taxes, and chargeable families; for, as Poor Dick says,

Women and wine, game and deceit,
Make the wealth small, and the wants great.

"And farther, *what maintains one vice, would bring up two children.* You may think perhaps that a little tea, or a little punch now and then, diet a little more costly, clothes a little finer, and a little entertainment now and then, can be no great Matter; but remember what Poor Richard says, *many* a little *makes a mickle,* and farther, *beware of little expenses; a small leak will sink a great ship,* and again, *who dainties love, shall beggars prove,* and moreover, *fools make Feasts, and wise men eat them.*

"Here you are all got together at this vendue of fineries and knicknacks. You call them goods, but if you do not take care, they will prove evils to some of you. You expect they will be sold cheap, and perhaps they may for less than they cost; but if you have no occasion for them, they must be dear to you. Remember what Poor Richard says, *buy what thou hast no need of, and ere long thou shalt sell thy necessaries.* And again, *at a great pennyworth pause a while:* he means, that perhaps the cheapness is apparent only, and not real; or the bargain, by straitening thee in thy business, may do thee more harm than good. For in another place he says, *many have been ruined by buying good pennyworths.* Again, Poor Richard says, *'tis foolish to lay our money in a purchase of repentance;* and yet this folly is practiced every day at vendues, for want of minding the almanac. *Wise men,* as Poor Dick says, *learn by others' harms, fools scarcely by their own,* but, *felix quem faciunt aliena pericula cautum.* Many a one, for the sake of finery on the back, have gone with a hungry belly, and half starved their families; *silks and satins, scarlet and velvets,* as Poor Richard says, *put out the kitchen fire.* These are not the necessaries of life; they can scarcely be called the conveniencies, and yet only because they look pretty, how many want to have them. The artificial wants of mankind thus become more numerous than the natural; and, as Poor Dick says, *for one* poor *person, there are an hundred* indigent. By these, and other extravagancies, the genteel are reduced to poverty, and forced to borrow of those whom they formerly despised, but who through industry and frugality have maintained their standing; in which case it appears plainly, that a *ploughman on his legs is higher than a gentleman on his knees,* as Poor Richard says. Perhaps they have had a small estate left them, which they knew not the getting of; they think *'tis day, and will never be night;* that a little to be spent out of so much, is not worth minding; *(a child and a fool,* as Poor Richard says, *imagine twenty shillings and twenty years can never be spent)* but, *always taking out of the meal-tub, and never putting in, soon comes to the bottom;* then, as Poor Dick says, *when the well's dry, they know the worth of water.* But this they might have known before, if they had taken his advice; *if you would know the value of money, go and try to borrow some,* for, *he that goes a borrowing goes a sorrowing,* and indeed so does he that lends to such people, when he goes to get it in again. Poor Dick farther advises, and says,

> *Fond pride of dress, is sure a very curse;*
> *E'er fancy you consult, consult your purse.*

"And again, *pride is as loud a beggar as want, and a great deal more saucy.* When you have bought one fine thing you must buy ten more, that your appearance may be all of a piece; but Poor Dick says, *'tis easier to suppress the first desire than to satisfy all that follow it.* And 'tis as truly folly for the poor to ape the rich, as for the frog to swell, in order to equal the ox.

> *Great estates may venture more,*
> *But little boats should keep near shore.*

" 'Tis however a folly soon punished; for *pride that dines on vanity sups on contempt,* as Poor Richard says. And in another place, *pride breakfasted with plenty, dined with poverty, and supped with infamy.* And after all, of what use is this *pride of appearance,* for which so much is risked, so much is suffered? It cannot promote health; or ease pain; it makes no increase of merit in the person, it creates envy, it hastens misfortune.

> *What is a butterfly? At best*
> *He's but a caterpillar dressed.*
> *The gaudy fop's his picture just,*

as Poor Richard says.

"But what madness must it be to run in debt for these superfluities! We are offered, by the terms of this vendue, six months' credit; and that perhaps has induced some of us to attend it, because we cannot spare the ready money, and hope now to be fine without it. But, ah, think what you do when you run in debt; *you give to another power over your liberty.* If you cannot pay at the time, you will be ashamed to see your creditor; you will be in fear when you speak to him, you will make poor pitiful sneaking excuses, and by degrees come to lose you veracity, and sink into base downright lying; for, as Poor Richard says, *the second vice is lying, the first is running in debt.* And again to the same purpose, *lying rides upon debt's back.* Whereas a freeborn Englishman ought not to be ashamed or afraid to see or speak to any man living. But poverty often deprives a man of all spirit and virtue: *'tis hard for an empty bag to stand upright,* as Poor Richard truly says. What would you think of that Prince, or that government, who should issue an edict forbidding you to dress like a gentleman or a gentlewoman, on pain of imprisonment or servitude? Would you not say, that you are free, have a right to dress as you please, and that such an edict would be a breach of your privileges, and such a government tyrannical? And yet you are about to put yourself under that tyranny when you run in debt for such dress! Your creditor has authority at his pleasure to deprive you of your liberty, by confining you in jail for life, or to sell you for a servant, if you should not be able to pay him! When you have got your bargain, you may, perhaps, think little of payment; but *creditors,* Poor Richard tells us, *have better memories than debtors,* and in another place says, *creditors are a superstitious sect, great observers of set days and times.* The day comes round before you are aware, and the demand is made before you are prepared to satisfy it. Or if you bear your debt in mind, the term which at first seemed so long, will, as it lessens, appear extremely short. Time will seem to have added wings to his heels as well as shoulders. *Those have a short Lent,* saith Poor Richard, *who owe money to be paid at Easter.* Then since, as he says, *the borrower is a slave to the lender, and the debtor to the creditor,* disdain the chain, preserve your freedom; and maintain your independency: be industrious and free; be frugal and free. At present, perhaps, you may think yourself in thriving circumstances, and that you can bear a little extravagance without injury; but,

For age and want, save while you may;
No morning sun lasts a whole day,

as Poor Richard says. Gain may be temporary and uncertain, but ever while you live, expense is constant and certain; and *'tis easier to build two chimneys than to keep one in fuel,* as Poor Richard says. So *rather go to bed supperless than rise in debt.*

Get what you can, and what you get hold;
'Tis the stone that will turn all your lead into gold,

as Poor Richard says. And when you have got the philosopher's stone, sure you will no longer complain of bad times, or the difficulty of paying taxes.

"This doctrine, my friends, is reason and wisdom; but after all, do not depend too much upon your own industry, and frugality, and prudence, though excellent things, for they may all be blasted without the blessing of heaven; and therefore ask that blessing humbly, and be not uncharitable to those that at present seem to want it, but comfort and help them. Remember Job suffered, and was afterwards prosperous.

"And now to conclude, *experience keeps a dear school, but fools will learn in no other, and scarce in that,* for it is true, *we may give advice, but we cannot give conduct,* as Poor Richard says: however, remember this, *they that won't be counseled, can't be helped,* as Poor Richard says: and farther, that *if you will not hear reason, she'll surely rap your knuckles.*"

Thus the old gentleman ended his harangue. The people heard it, and approved the doctrine, and immediately practiced the contrary, just as if it had been a common sermon; for the vendue opened, and they began to buy extravagantly, notwithstanding all his cautions, and their own fear of taxes. I found the good man had thoroughly studied my almanacs, and digested all I had dropped on those topics during the course of five-and-twenty years. The frequent mention he made of me must have tired any one else, but my vanity was wonderfully delighted with it, though I was conscious that not a tenth part of the wisdom was my own which he ascribed to me, but rather the gleanings I had made of the sense of all ages and nations. However, I resolved to be the better for the echo of it; and though I had at first determined to buy stuff for a new coat, I went away resolved to wear my old one a little longer. Reader, if thou wilt do the same, thy profit will be as great as mine. I am, as ever, thine to serve thee,

Richard Saunders

PART 5

LOBBYIST IN LONDON

A Table of KINGS,

from the Time that *England* was first so called by King *Egbert*.

Kings Names.	Reigns began.	Reigned.	Kings Names.	Reigns began.	Reigned.
K. Egbert, *Sax.*	818	28	Henry 3.	1216	56
Ethelwolf,	836	21	Edward 1.	1272	35
Ethelbald,	857	1	Edward 2.	1307	19
Ethelbert,	858	5	Edward 3.	1326	51
Ethelfred,	863	10	Richard 2.	1377	22
Alfred,	873	27	*Lancaster Line.*		
Edward 1.	900	24	Henry 4.	1399	14
Athelston,	924	16	Henry 5.	1413	9
Edmund 1.	940	6	Henry 6.	1422	38
Eldred,	946	9	*York Line.*		
Edwin,	955	4	Edward 4.	1460	23
Edgar,	959	20	Edward 5.	1483	0
Edward 2.	979	3	Richard 3.	1483	2
Ethelred,	982	34	*Families united.*		
Edmund 2.	1016	1	Henry 7.	1485	24
Danish Line.			Henry 8.	1508	40
Canutus 1.	1017	20	Edward 6.	1547	6
Harold 1.	1037	3	Q. Mary 1.	1553	5
Canutus 2.	1040	2	Q. Elizabeth,	1558	44
Edward *Confessor.*	1042	23	*Kingdoms united.*		
Harold 2.	1065	1	James 1.	1602	22
Norman Line.			Charles 1.	1624	24
W. Conqueror,	1066	21	Charles 2.	1648	36
W. Rufus,	1087	13	James 2.	1684	4
Henry 1.	1100	35	Q. Mary 2.	1688	6
Stephen,	1135	19	William 3.	1688	13
Saxon Line vestor'd.			Q. Anne,	1702	12
Henry 2.	1154	35	George 1.	1714	13
Richard 1.	1189	10	GEORGE II.	1727	
John,	1199	17	*Whom God preserv.*		

"A Table of Kings," Poor Richard's Almanac, 1733

REASONS FOR RESTORING CANADA
TO FRANCE

Although Franklin's mission in England was to assert the rights of the colonists, he did so very much as a loyal supporter of the king and his empire. The French and Indian War had by then ended, with England and her colonies capturing control of Canada and many of the Caribbean sugar islands belonging to France and Spain. In Europe, however, the broader struggle between Britain and France, known as the Seven Years' War, would not be resolved until a Treaty of Paris was signed in 1763. Franklin's ardor for the expansion of the King's empire led him to wage a crusade to convince Britain to keep control of Canada, rather than cede it back to France in return for some Caribbean islands as part of a negotiated settlement. In an anonymous article in Strahan's London *Chronicle,* he used his old trick of parody and produced ten facetious reasons why Canada *should* be restored to France.

THE LONDON CHRONICLE, DECEMBER 27, 1759

Mr. *Chronicle,*

We Britons are a nation of statesmen and politicians; we are privy councilors by birthright; and therefore take it much amiss when we are told by some of your correspondents, 'that it is not proper to expose to public view the many good reasons there are for restoring Canada,' *(if we reduce it.)*

I have, with great industry, been able to procure a full account of those reasons, and shall make no secret of them among ourselves. Here they are.—Give them to all your readers; that is, to all that can read, in the King's dominions.

1. We should restore Canada; because an uninterrupted trade with the Indians throughout a vast country, where the communication by water is so easy, would increase our commerce, *already too great,* and occasion a large additional demand for our manufactures, *already too dear.*

2. We should restore it, lest, thro' a greater plenty of beaver, broad-brimmed hats become cheaper to that unmannerly sect, the Quakers.

3. We should restore Canada, that we may *soon* have a new war, and another opportunity of spending two or three millions a year in America; there being great danger of our growing too rich, our European expenses not being sufficient to drain our immense treasures.

4. We should restore it, that we may have occasion constantly to employ, in time of war, a fleet and army in those parts; for otherwise we might be too strong at home.

5. We should restore it, that the French may, by means of their Indians, carry on, (as they have done for these 100 years past even in times of peace between the two crowns) a constant scalping war against our colonies, and thereby stint their growth; for, otherwise, the children might in time be as tall as their mother.

7. Our colonies, 'tis true, have exerted themselves beyond their strength, on the expectations we gave them of driving the French from Canada; but though we ought to keep faith with our Allies, it is not necessary with our children. That might teach them (against Scripture) to *put their trust in Princes*: Let 'em learn to trust in God.

8. Should we not restore Canada, it would look as if our statesmen had *courage* as well as our soldiers; but what have statesmen to do with *courage*? Their proper character is *wisdom*.

9. What can be *braver*, than to show all Europe we can afford to lavish our best blood as well as our treasure, in conquests we do not intend to keep? Have we not plenty of *Howe's*, and *Wolfe's*, &c. &c. &c. in every regiment?

10. The French have long since openly declared, '*que les Anglois & les Fransois sont incompatible dans cette partie de l'Amerique;*' 'that our people and theirs were incompatible in that part of the continent of America:' '*que rien n'etoit plus important a l'etat, que de deliver leur colonie du facheux voisinage des Anglois;*' 'that nothing was of more importance to France, than delivering its colony from the troublesome neighborhood of the English,' to which end, there was an avowed project on foot '*pour chasser premierement les Anglois de la Nouvelle York;*' 'to drive the English in the first place out of the province of New York;' '*& apres la prise de la capitale, il falloit* (says the scheme) *la* BRULER & RUINER *le pays jusqu' a Orange;*' 'and after taking the capital, to *burn*

it, and *ruin* (that is, *make a desart* of) the whole country, quite up to Albany.' Now, if we do not fairly leave the French in Canada, till they have a favorable opportunity of putting their *burning* and *ruining* schemes in execution, will it not look as if we were afraid of them?

11. Their historian, Charlevoix, in his IVth book, also tells us, that when Canada was formerly taken by the English, it was a question at the court of France, whether they should endeavor to recover it; for, says he, *'bien de gens douterent si l'on avoit fait une veritable perte;'* 'many thought it was not really a loss.' But though various reasons were given why it was scarce worth recovering, *'le seul motive* (says he) *d'empecher les Anglois de se rendre trop puissans—atoit plus que suffissant pour nous engager a recouvrer Quebec, a quelque prix que ce fut;'* 'the single motive of preventing the increase of *English* power, was more than sufficient to engage us in recovering Quebec, *what price soever it might cost us.'* Here we see the high value they put on that country, and the reason of their valuing it so highly. Let us then, *oblige them* in this (to them) so important an article, and be assured they will *never prove ungrateful.*

I will not dissemble, Mr. *Chronicle;* that in answer to all these reasons and motives for restoring Canada, I have heard one that appears to have some weight on the other side of the question. It is said, that nations, as well as private persons, should, for their honor's sake, take care to preserve a *consistence of character:* that it has always been the character of the English to fight strongly, and negotiate weakly; generally agreeing to restore, at a peace, what they ought to have kept, and to keep what they had better have restored: then, if it would really, according to the preceding reasons, be prudent and right to restore Canada, we ought, say these objectors, to keep it; otherwise *we shall be inconsistent with ourselves.* I shall not take upon myself to weigh these different reasons, but offer the whole to the consideration of the public. Only permit me to suggest, that there is one method of avoiding fairly all future dispute about the propriety of *keeping* or *restoring* Canada; and that is, *let us never take it.* The French still hold out at Montreal and Trois Rivieres, in hopes of succor from France. Let us be but a *little too late* with our ships in the river St. Laurence, so that the enemy may get their supplies up next spring, as they did the last, with reinforcements sufficient to enable them to recover Quebec, and there is an end of the question. I am, Sir,

Yours, &c.

A. Z.

MARY STEVENSON

When Franklin arrived in London, he rented rooms on Craven Street, off the Strand, from a landlady named Margaret Stevenson, who also became his domestic (though probably not romantic) companion. More complex was his relation with her daughter Mary, known as Polly. She was a lively and endearing 18-year-old with the sort of inquisitive intellect that Franklin loved in women. In some respects, Polly served as the London counterpart to his daughter Sally. He treated her in an avuncular, and sometimes even paternal, manner, instructing her on life and morals as well as science and education. But she was also an English version of Caty Ray, a pretty young woman of playful demeanor and lively mind. His letters to her were flirtatious at times, and he flattered her with the focused attention that he lavished on women he liked.

Franklin spent hours talking to Polly and then, when she went to live with an aunt in the country, carried on an astonishing correspondence. During his years in London, he wrote to her far more often than he wrote to his real family. Some of the letters were flirtatious. "Not a day passes in which I do not think of you," he wrote less than a year after their first meeting. She sent him little gifts. "I have received the garters you have so kindly knit for me," he said in one letter. "Be assured that I shall think as often of you in the wearing as you did of me in the making."

As with Caty Ray, his relationship with Polly was an engagement of the mind as much as the heart. He wrote to her at great length and in sophisticated detail about how barometers work, colors absorb heat, electricity is conducted, waterspouts are formed, and the moon affects tidal flows. Eight of these letters were later included in a revised edition of his electricity papers. When he came up with the idea of a phonetic spelling system, he used it first in a letter to Polly.

His one concern was that Polly would take her studies *too* seriously. Even though he appreciated her mind, Franklin flinched when she hinted at her desire to devote herself to learning at the expense of getting married and raising a family. So he provided her with some paternal prodding. In response to her suggestion that she might "live single" the rest of her life, he lectured her about the "duty" of a woman to raise a family.

To Polly Stevenson, June 11, 1760

Dear Polly,

'Tis a very sensible question you ask, how the air can affect the barometer, when its opening appears covered with wood? If indeed it was so closely covered as to admit of no communication of the outward air to the surface of the mercury, the change of weight in the air could not possibly affect it. But the least crevice is sufficient for the purpose; a pinhole will do the business. And if you could look behind the frame to which your barometer is fixed, you would certainly find some small opening.

There are indeed some barometers in which the body of mercury at the lower end is contained in a close leather bag, and so the air cannot come into immediate contact with the mercury: yet the same effect is produced. For the leather being flexible, when the bag is pressed by any additional weight of air, it contracts, and the mercury is forced up into the tube; when the air becomes lighter, and its pressure less, the weight of the mercury prevails, and it descends again into the bag.

Your observation on what you have lately read concerning insects, is very just and solid. Superficial minds are apt to despise those who make that part of creation their study, as mere triflers; but certainly the world has been much obliged to them. Under the care and management of man, the labors of the little silkworm afford employment and subsistence to thousands of families, and become an immense article of commerce. The bee, too, yields us its delicious honey, and its wax useful to a multitude of purposes. Another insect, it is said, produces the cochineal, from whence we have our rich scarlet dye. The usefulness of the cantharides, or Spanish flies, in medicine, is known to all, and thousands owe their lives to that knowledge. By human industry and observation, other properties of other insects may possibly be hereafter discovered, and of equal utility. A thorough acquaintance with the nature of these little creatures, may also enable mankind to prevent the increase of such as are noxious or secure us against the mischiefs they occasion. These things doubtless your books make mention of: I can only add a particular late instance which I had from a Swedish gentleman of good credit. In the green timber intended for ship-building at the king's yards in that country, a kind of worms were found, which every year became more numerous and more pernicious, so that the ships were greatly damaged before they came into use. The king sent Linnaeus, the great naturalist, from Stockholm, to enquire into the affair, and see if the mischief was capable of any remedy. He found on examination, that the worm was produced from a small egg deposited in the little roughnesses on the surface of the wood, by a particular kind of fly or beetle; from whence the worm, as soon as it was hatched, began to eat into the substance of the wood, and after some time came out again a fly of the parent kind, and so the species increased. The season in which this fly laid its eggs, Linnaeus knew to be about a fortnight (I think) in the month of May, and at no other time of the year. He therefore advised, that some days before that season, all the green timber should be thrown into the water, and kept under water till the season was over. Which being done by the king's order, the flies missing their usual nests, could not increase; and the species was either destroyed or went elsewhere; and the wood was effectually preserved, for after the first year, it became too dry and hard for their purpose.

There is, however, a prudent moderation to be used in studies of this kind. The knowledge of nature may be ornamental, and it may be useful, but if to attain an eminence in that, we neglect the knowledge and practice of essential duties, we deserve reprehension. For there is no rank in natural knowledge of equal dignity and importance with that of being a good parent, a good child, a good husband, or wife, a good neighbor or friend, a good subject or citizen, that is, in short, a good Christian. Nicholas gimcrack, therefore, who neglected the care of his family, to pursue butterflies, was a just object of ridicule, and we must give him up as fair game to the satirist.

Adieu, my dear friend, and believe me ever, Yours affectionately,

B. Franklin

P.S. Your good Mother is well, and gives her Love and Blessing to you.

To Polly Stevenson, September 13, 1760

My dear Friend,

I have your agreeable letter from Bristol, which I take this first leisure hour to answer, having for some time been much engaged in business.

Your first question, *what is the reason the water at this place, though cold at the spring, becomes warm by pumping?* It will be most prudent in me to forbear attempting to answer, till, by a more circumstantial account, you assure me of the fact. I own I should expect that operation to warm, not so much the water pumped as the person pumping. The rubbing of dry solids together, has been long observed to produce heat; but the like effect has never yet, that I have heard, been produced by the mere agitation of fluids, or friction of fluids with solids. Water in a bottle shook for hours by a mill hopper, it is said, discovered no sensible addition of heat. The production of animal heat by exercise, is therefore to be accounted for in another manner, which I may hereafter endeavor to make you acquainted with.

This prudence of not attempting to give reasons before one is sure of facts, I learnt from one of your sex, who, as Selden tells us, being in company with some gentlemen that were viewing and considering something which they called a Chinese shoe, and disputing earnestly about the manner of wearing it, and how it could possibly be put on; put in her word, and said modestly, *Gentlemen, are you sure it is a shoe? Should not that be settled first?*

But I shall now endeavor to explain what I said to you about the tide in rivers, and to that end shall make a figure, which though not very like a river, may serve to convey my meaning . . .

[Editor's note: Here Franklin proceeds to describe in great detail the effects of tides on rivers.]

I have made this letter longer than I intended, and therefore reserve for another what I have farther to say on the subject of tides and rivers. I shall now only add, that I have not been exact in the numbers, because I would avoid perplexing you with minute calculations, my design at present being chiefly to give you distinct and clear ideas of the first principles.

After writing 6 folio pages of philosophy to a young girl, is it necessary to finish such a letter with a compliment? Is not such a letter of itself a compliment? Does it not say, she has a mind thirsty after knowledge, and capable of receiving it; and that the most agreeable things one can write to her are those that tend to the improvement of her understanding? It does indeed say all this, but then it is still no compliment; it is no more than plain honest truth, which is not the character of a compliment. So if I would finish my letter in the mode, I should yet add something that means nothing, and is *merely* civil and polite. But being naturally awkward at every circumstance of ceremony, I shall not attempt it. I had rather conclude abruptly with what pleases me more than any compliment can please you, that I am allowed to subscribe my self

Your affectionate Friend,
B. Franklin

DAVID HUME

David Hume was the greatest British philosopher of his era and one of the most important logical and analytic thinkers of all time. When Franklin met him in Scotland in 1759, Hume had already written the two seminal tracts, *A Treatise of Human Nature* and *Essays Concerning Human Understanding,* that are now considered among the most important works in the development of empirical thought, and he was completing the six-volume *History of England* that would make him rich and famous.

Franklin assiduously courted Hume to the colonial cause and

shared with him an interest in language. When Hume berated him for coining new words, Franklin agreed to quit using the terms "colonize" and "unshakeable." But he lamented that "I cannot but wish the usage of our tongue permitted making new words when we want them." He also included in one of his letters a delightful tale of a Puritan dispute over a maypole, another illustration of his deftness at poking fun at religious tolerance. Although they would later disagree, Hume was impressed by Franklin. "America has sent us many good things, gold, silver, sugar, tobacco, indigo," he wrote him. "But you are the first philosopher, and indeed the first great man of letters, for whom we are beholden to her."

To David Hume, September 27, 1760

Dear Sir,

I have too long postponed answering your obliging letter, a fault I will not attempt to excuse, but rather rely on your goodness to forgive it if I am more punctual for the future.

I am obliged to you for the favorable sentiments you express of the pieces sent you; though the volume relating to our Pennsylvania affairs was not written by me, nor any part of it, except the remarks on the proprietor's estimate of his estate, and some of the inserted messages and reports of the assembly which I wrote when at home, as a member of committees appointed by the house for that service; the rest was by another hand. But though I am satisfied by what you say, that the Duke of Bedford was hearty in the scheme of the expedition, I am not so clear that others in the administration were equally in earnest in that matter. It is certain that after the Duke of Newcastle's first orders to raise troops in the colonies, and promise to send over commissions to the officers, with arms, clothing, &c. for the men, we never had another syllable from him for 18 months; during all which time the army lay idle at Albany for want of orders and necessaries; and it began to be thought at least that if an expedition had ever been intended, the first design and the orders given, must, thro' the multiplicity of business here at home, have been quite forgotten.

I am not a little pleased to hear of your change of sentiments in some particulars relating to America; because I think it of importance to our general welfare that the people of this nation should have right notions of us, and I know no one that has it more in his power to rectify their notions, than Mr. Hume. I have lately read with great pleasure, as I do every thing of yours, the excellent essay on the *jealousy of commerce:* I think it cannot but have a good effect in promoting a certain interest too little thought of by selfish man, and scarce ever mentioned, so that we hardly have a name for it; I mean the *interest of humanity,* or common good of mankind: but I hope particularly from that essay, an abatement of the jealousy that reigns here of the commerce of the colonies, at least so far as such abatement may be reasonable.

I thank you for your friendly admonition relating to some unusual words in the pamphlet. It will be of service to me. The *pejorate,* and the *colonize,* since they are not in common use here, I give up as bad; for certainly in writings intended for persuasion and for general information, one cannot be too clear, and every expression in the least obscure is a fault. The *unshakeable* too, though clear, I give up as rather low. The introducing new words where we are already possessed of old ones sufficiently expressive, I confess must be generally wrong, as it tends to change the language; yet at the same time I cannot but wish the usage of our tongue permitted making new words when we want them, by composition of old ones whose meanings are already well understood. The German allows of it, and it is a common practice with their writers. Many of our present English words were originally so made; and many of the Latin words. In point of clearness such compound words would have the advantage of any we can borrow from the ancient or from foreign languages. For instance, the word *inaccessible,* though long in use among us, is not yet, I dare say, so universally understood by our people as the word *uncomeatable* would immediately be, which we are not allowed to write. But I hope with you, that we shall always in America make the best English of this island our standard, and I believe it will be so. I assure you, it often gives me pleasure to reflect how greatly the *audience* (if I may so term it) of a good English writer will in another century or two be increased, by the increase of English people in our colonies.

My son presents his respects with mine to you and Dr. Monro. We received your printed circular letter to the members of the society, and purpose some time next winter to send each of us a little philosophical essay. With the greatest esteem I am, dear sir, your most obedient and most humble servant,

B. Franklin

TO DAVID HUME, MAY 19, 1762

Dear sir,

It is no small pleasure to me to hear from you that my paper on the means of preserving buildings from damage by lightning, was acceptable to the philosophical society. Mr. Russel's proposals of improvement are very sensible and just. A leaden spout or pipe is undoubtedly a good conductor so far as it goes. If the conductor enters the ground just at the foundation, and from thence is carried horizontally to some well, or to a distant rod driven downright into the earth; I would then propose that the part under ground should be lead, as less liable to consume with rust than iron. Because if the conductor near the foot of the wall should be wasted, the lightning might act on the moisture of the earth, and by suddenly ratifying it occasion an explosion that may damage the foundation. In the experiment of discharging my large case of electrical bottles thro' a piece of small glass tube filled with water, the suddenly rarified water has exploded with a force equal, I think, to that of so much gunpowder; bursting the tube into many pieces, and driving them with violence in all directions and to all parts of the room. The shivering of trees into small splinters like a broom, is probably owing to this rarefaction of the sap in the longitudinal pores or capillary pipes in the substance of the wood. And the blowing-up of bricks or stones in a hearth, rending stones out of a foundation, and splitting of walls, is also probably an effect sometimes of rarified moisture in the earth, under the hearth, or in the walls. We should therefore have a durable conductor under ground, or convey the lightning to the earth at some distance.

It must afford Lord Mareschall a good deal of diversion to preside in a dispute so ridiculous as that you mention. Judges in their decisions often use precedents. I have somewhere met with one that is what the lawyers call *a case in point*. The church people and the Puritans in a country town, had once a bitter contention concerning the erecting of a maypole, which the former desired and the latter opposed. Each party endeavored to strengthen itself by obtaining the authority of the mayor, directing or forbidding a maypole. He heard their altercation with great patience, and then gravely determined thus; you that are for having no maypole shall have no maypole; and you that are for having a maypole shall have a maypole. Get about your business and let me hear no more of this quarrel. So methinks Lord Mareschal might say; you that are for no more damnation than is proportioned to your offences, have my consent that it may be so: and you that are for being damned eternally, God eternally damn you all, and let me hear no more of your disputes.

Your compliment of *gold* and *wisdom* is very obliging to me, but a little injurious to your country. The various value of every thing in every part of this world, arises you know from the various proportions of the quantity to the demand. We are told that gold and silver in Solomon's time were so plenty as to be of no more value in his country than the stones in the street. You have here at present just such a plenty of wisdom. Your people are therefore not to be censured for desiring no more among them than they have; and if I have *any*, I should certainly carry it where from its scarcity it may probably come to a better market.

I nevertheless regret extremely the leaving a country in which I have received so much friendship, and friends whose conversation has been so agreeable and so improving to me; and that I am henceforth to reside at so great a distance from them is no small mortification, to my dear friend, Yours most affectionately

B. Franklin

ON OBSERVING THE SABBATH

A trip to Flanders provided fodder for Franklin to continue his wry lampooning of Puritan dogma and rigid religious practices.

To Jared Ingersoll, Dec. 11, 1762

Dear Sir,

. . . I should be glad to know what it is that distinguishes Connecticut religion from common religion: Communicate, if you please, some of those particulars that you think will amuse me as a virtuoso. When I traveled in Flanders I thought of your excessively strict observation of Sunday; and that a man could hardly travel on that day among you upon his lawful occasions, without hazard of punishment; while where I was, everyone traveled, if he pleased, or diverted himself any other way; and in the afternoon both high and low went to the play or the opera, where there was plenty of singing, fiddling and dancing. I looked round for God's judgments but saw no signs of them. The cities were well built and full of inhabitants, the markets filled with plenty, the people well favored and well clothed; the fields well tilled; the cattle fat and strong; the fences, houses and windows all in repair; and *no old tenor* anywhere in the country; which would almost make one suspect, that the deity is not so angry at that offence as a New England justice.

WHEN OIL DOES NOT CALM TROUBLED WATERS

During his voyage back to Philadelphia for a brief home leave in 1762, Franklin resumed his longtime study of the calming effect of oil on water, which served as a metaphor for his attempts to still the political waves of the time. The lanterns aboard his ship had a thick layer of oil that floated atop a layer of water. The surface was always calm and flat, so viewed from above it would seem that the oil had stilled the roiling water. But when the lantern was viewed from the side, so that both layers could be seen, it became evident that "the water under the oil was in great commotion." This underlying turbulence, Franklin realized, was not something that could be easily calmed, even by the most judicious application of oil.

TO JOHN PRINGLE, DECEMBER 1, 1762

Sir,

During our passage of Madeira, the weather being warm, and the cabin windows constantly open for the benefit of the air, the candles at night flared and run very much, which was an inconvenience. At Madeira we got oil to burn, and with a common glass tumbler or beaker, slung in wire, and suspended to the ceiling of the cabin, and a little wire hoop for the wick, furnished with corks to float on the oil, I made an Italian lamp, that gave us very good light all over the table. The glass at bottom contained water to about one third of its height; another third was taken up with oil; the rest was left empty that the sides of the glass might protect the flame from the wind. There is nothing remarkable in all this; but what follows is particular. At supper, looking on the lamp, I remarked that though the surface of the oil was perfectly tranquil, and duly preserved its position and distance with regard to the brim of the glass, the water under the oil was in great commotion, rising and falling in irregular waves, which continued during the whole evening. The lamp was kept burning as a watch light all night, till the oil was spent, and the water only remained. In the morning I observed, that though the motion of the ship continued the same; the water was now quiet, and its surface as tranquil as that of the oil had been the evening before. At night again, when oil was put upon it, the water resumed its irregular motions, rising in high waves almost to the surface of the oil, but without disturbing the smooth level of that surface. And this was repeated every day during the voyage.

Since my arrival in America, I have repeated the experiment frequently thus. I have put a pack-thread round a tumbler, with strings of the same, from each side, meeting above it in a knot at about a foot distance from the top of the tumbler. Then putting in as much water as would fill about one third part of the tumbler, I lifted it up by the knot, and swung it to and fro in the air; when the water appeared to keep its place in the tumbler as steadily as if it had been ice. But pouring gently in upon the water about as much oil, and then again swinging it in the air as before, the tranquility before possessed by the water, was transferred to the surface of the oil, and the water under it was agitated with the same commotions as at sea.

I have shown this experiment to a number of ingenious persons. Those who are but slightly acquainted with the principles of hydrostatics, &c. are apt to fancy immediately that they understand it, and readily attempt to explain it; but their explanations have been different, and to me not very intelligible. Others more deeply skilled in those principles, seem to wonder at it, and promise to consider it. And I think it is worth considering: For a new appearance, if it cannot be explained by our old principles, may afford us new ones, of use perhaps in explaining some other obscure parts of natural knowledge.

I am, &c.

B.F.

RACE AND SLAVERY

One great moral issue historians must wrestle with when assessing America's Founders is slavery, and Franklin was wrestling with it as well. Slaves made up about 6 percent of Philadelphia's population at the time, and Franklin had facilitated the buying and selling of them through ads in his newspaper. "A likely Negro woman to be sold. Enquire at the Widow Read's," read one such ad on behalf of his mother-in-law. Another offered for sale "a likely young Negro fellow" and ended with the phrase "enquire of the printer hereof." He personally owned a slave couple, but in 1751 he decided to sell them because, as he told his mother, he did not like having "Negro servants" and he found them uneconomical. Yet later he would, at times, have a slave as a personal servant.

In "Observations on the Increase of Mankind," which he wrote in 1751, he had attacked slavery on economic grounds. But he had mainly focused on the ill effects to the owners rather than the immorality done to the slaves. The tract was, in fact, quite prejudiced in places. "Why increase the sons of Africa by planting them in America, where we have so fair an opportunity, by excluding all blacks and tawneys, of increasing the lovely white and red? But perhaps I am partial to the complexion of my country, for such kind of partiality is natural to mankind."

As the final sentence indicates, he was beginning to reexamine his "partiality" to his own race. In the first edition of "Observations," he remarked on "almost every slave being by nature a thief." When he reprinted it eighteen years later, he changed it to say that they became thieves "from the nature of slavery." He also omitted the entire section about the desirability of keeping America mainly white.

What helped shift his attitude was another of his philanthropic endeavors. He became, in the late 1750s, active in an organization that established schools for black children in Philadelphia and then elsewhere in America. After visiting the Philadelphia school in 1763, he wrote a reflective letter about his previous prejudices. In his later life, he became one of America's most active abolitionists. He denounced slavery on moral grounds and helped advance the rights of blacks.

TO JOHN WARING, DECEMBER 17, 1763

Reverend and dear Sir,

Being but just returned home from a tour through the northern colonies, that has employed the whole summer, my time at present is so taken up that I cannot now write fully in answer to the letters I have received from you, but purpose to do it shortly. This is chiefly to acquaint you, that I have visited the Negro school here in company with the Rev. Mr. Sturgeon and some others; and had the children thoroughly examined. They appeared all to have made considerable progress in reading for the time they had respectively been in the school, and most of them answered readily and well the questions of the catechism; they behaved very orderly, showed a proper respect and ready obedience to the mistress, and seemed very attentive to, and a good deal affected by, a serious exhortation with which Mr. Sturgeon concluded our visit. I was on the whole much pleased, and from what I then saw, have conceived a higher opinion of the natural capacities of the black race, than I had ever before entertained. Their apprehension seems as quick, their memory as strong, and their docility in every respect equal to that of white children. You will wonder perhaps that I should ever doubt it, and I will not undertake to justify all my prejudices, nor to account for them. I immediately advanced the two guineas you mentioned, for the mistress, and Mr. Sturgeon will therefore draw on you for 7 18s. only, which makes up the half year's salary of ten pounds. Be pleased to present my best respects to the associates, and believe me, with sincere esteem dear sir, Your most obedient servant,

B. Franklin

PROPAGANDA AGENT

Franklin left again for London in late 1764 to resume his lobbying on behalf of the colonial cause. But he found himself compromised when he appeared to accept the Stamp Act, a tax on colonial documents that caused an uproar in America. With his reputation as a defender of colonial rights in tatters because of his softness, Franklin faced one of the great challenges in the annals of political damage control.

So he unsheathed his great weapon, the pen. In a three month period in early 1766, he published in various papers 13 attacks, most of them anonymous, on the Stamp Act and Britain's repressive attitude toward her colonies. Franklin felt the best way to force repeal, one that appealed to his Poor Richard penchant for frugality and self-reliance, was for Americans to boycott British imports.

Writing as "Homespun," he ridiculed the notion that Americans could not get by without British imports of such things as tea. If need be, they would make tea from corn. Under the pseudonym Pacificus Secundus, he resorted to his old tactic of scathing satire by pretending to support the idea that military rule be imposed in the colonies. It would take only 50,000 British soldiers at a cost of merely £12 million a year. And he composed a satirical song comparing Britain to a peevish old mother.

Sir,

Pacificus in your paper of Friday last, tells us, that the inhabitants of New England are descended from the Stiff-Rumps in Oliver's time; and he accounts for their being so tenacious of what they call their rights and liberties; from the independent principles handed down to them by their forefathers, and that spirit of contradiction, which, he says, is the distinguishing characteristic of fanaticism. But it seems the inhabitants of Virginia and Maryland, who are descended from the royalists of the church of England, driven hence by those very Oliverian stiff-rumps, and never tinctured with fanaticism, are, in the present case, as stiff-rumped as the others, and even led the way in asserting what they call their rights. So that this hypothesis of fanaticism appears insufficient to account for the opposition universally given to the stamp-act in America; and I fancy the gentleman thought so himself, as he mends it a little after, by lumping all the Americans under the general character of house-breakers and felons.

Supposing them such, his proposal of vacating all their charters, taking away the power of their assemblies, and sending an armed force among them, to reduce them all to a military government, in which the order of the commanding officer is to be their law, will certainly be a very *justifiable* measure. I have only some doubts as to the expediency of it, and the facility of carrying it into execution. For I apprehend 'tis not unlikely they may set their rumps more stiffly against this method of government, than ever they did against that by act of parliament: but, on second thoughts, I conceive it may possibly do very well: for though there should be, as 'tis said there are, at least 250,000 fighting men among them, many of whom have lately seen service; yet, as one Englishman is to be sure as good as five Americans, I suppose it will not require armies of above 50,000 men in the whole, sent over to the different parts of that extensive continent, for reducing them; and that a three or four year's civil war, at perhaps a less expense than ten or twelve millions a year, transports and carriages included, will be sufficient to complete *Pacificus's pacification*, notwithstanding any disturbance our restless enemies in Europe might think fit to give us while engaged in this necessary work. I mention three or four years only; for I can never believe the Americans will be able to spin it out to seventy, as the Hollanders did the war for their liberties against Spain, how much soever it may be found the interest of our own numerous commissaries, contractors, and officers afraid of half pay, to continue and protract it.

It may be objected, that by ruining the colonies, killing one half the people, and driving the rest over the mountains, we may deprive ourselves of their custom for our manufactures: but a moment's consideration will satisfy us, that since we have lost so much of our European trade, it can only be the demand in America that keeps up, and has of late so greatly enhanced the price of those manufactures, and therefore a stop put to that demand will be an advantage to us all, as we may thereafter buy our own goods cheaper for our own use at home. I can think of but one objection more, which is, that multitudes of our poor may starve for want of employment. But our wise laws have provided a remedy for that. The rich are to maintain them. I am, Sir,

Your humble Servant,
Pacificus Secundus

THE GAZETTEER AND NEW DAILY ADVERTISER, JANUARY 2, 1766

Sir,

Vindex Patriae, a writer in your paper, comforts himself, and the India Company, with the fancy, that the Americans, should they resolve to drink no more tea, can by no means keep that resolution, their Indian corn not affording an agreeable, or easy digestible breakfast. Pray let me, an American, inform the gentleman, who seems quite ignorant of the matter, that Indian corn, take it for *all in all*, is one of the most agreeable and wholesome grains in the world; that its green ears roasted are a delicacy beyond expression; that *samp, hominy, succotash*, and *nokehock*, made of it, are so many pleasing varieties; and that a *johny* or *hoecake*, hot from the fire, is better than a Yorkshire muffin. But if Indian corn were as *disagreeable* and *indigestible* as the Stamp Act, does he imagine we can get nothing else for breakfast? Did he never hear that we have oatmeal in plenty, for water gruel or burgoo; as good wheat, rye, and barley as the world affords, to make frumenty; or toast and ale; that there is every where plenty of milk, butter, and cheese; that rice is one of our staple commodities; that for tea, we have sage and balm in our gardens, the young leaves of the sweet white hickory or walnut, and, above all, the buds of our pine, infinitely preferable to any tea from the Indies; while the islands yield us plenty of coffee and chocolate?

Let the gentleman do us the honor of a visit in America, and I will engage to breakfast him every day in the month with a fresh variety, without offering him either tea or Indian corn. As to the Americans using no more of the former, I am not sure they will take such a resolution; but if they do, I fancy they will not lightly break it. I question whether the army proposed to be sent among them, would oblige them to swallow a drop more of tea than they choose to swallow; for, as the proverb says, though one man may *lead* a horse to the water, one can't *make him drink.* Their resolutions have hitherto been pretty steadily kept. They resolved to wear no more mourning; and it is now totally out of fashion with near two millions of people; and yet nobody sighs for Norwich crapes, or any other of the expensive, flimsy, rotten, black stuffs and cloths you used to send us for that purpose, with the frippery gauzes, loves, ribbons, gloves, &c. thereunto belonging. They resolved last spring to eat no more lamb; and not a joint of lamb has since been seen on any of their tables, throughout a country of 1500 miles extent, but the sweet little creatures are all alive to this day, with the prettiest fleeces on their backs imaginable. Mr. Index's very civil letter will, I dare say, be printed in all our provincial news papers, from Nova Scotia to Georgia; and together with the other *kind, polite,* and *humane* epistles of your correspondents Pacific's, Tom Hint, &c. &c. contribute not a little to strengthen us in every resolution that may be of advantage, to *our* country at least, if not to *yours.*

Homespun

THE GAZETTEER AND NEW DAILY ADVERTISER, JANUARY 15, 1766

To the Printer.

John Bull shows in nothing more his great veneration for good eating, and how much he is always thinking of his belly, than in his making it the constant topic of his contempt for other nations, that *they do not eat so well as himself.* The *roast beef of Old England* he is always exulting in, as if no other country had beef to roast; reproaching, on every occasion, the Welsh with their leeks and toasted cheese, the Irish with their potatoes, and the Scotch with their oatmeal. And now that we are a little out of favor with him, he has begun, by his attorney Index Patria, to examine our eating and drinking, in order, I apprehend, to fix some horrible scandal of the same kind upon us poor Americans.

I did but say a word or two in favor of *Indian corn,* which he had treated as disagreeable and indigestible, and this vindictive gentleman grows angry. Let him tell the world, if he dares (says he) that the Americans prefer it to a place at their own tables. Ah, Sir, I see the dilemma you have prepared for me. If I should not *dare* to say, that we do prefer it to a place at our tables, then you demonstrate, that we must come to England for tea, or go without our breakfasts: and if I do *dare* to say it, you fix upon me and my countrymen for ever, the indelible disgrace of being *Indian corneaters.*

I am afraid, Mr. Printer, that you will think this too trifling a dispute to deserve a place in your paper: but pray, good Sir, consider, as you are yourself an Englishman, that we Americans, who are allowed even by Mr. Index to have some English blood in our veins, may think it a very serious thing to have the honor of our eating impeached in any particular whatsoever.

Why doth he not deny the fact (says Index) that it is assigned to the slaves for their food? To proclaim the *wholesomeness* of this corn, without assigning a reason why white men give it to their slaves, when they can get other food, is only satirizing the good sense of their brethren in America. In truth I cannot deny the fact, though it should reflect ever so much on the *good sense* of my countrymen. I own we do give food made of Indian corn to our slaves, as well as eat it ourselves; not, as you suppose, because it is *indigestible* and *unwholesome;* but because it keeps them healthy, strong and hearty, and fit to go through all the labor we require of them. Our slaves, Sir, cost us money, and we buy them to make money by their labor. If they are sick, they are not only unprofitable, but expensive. Where then was your *English good sense,* when you imagined we gave the slaves our Indian corn, because we knew it to be *unwholesome*?

In short, this is only another of Mr. Index's paradoxes, in which he is a great dealer. The first endeavored to persuade us, that we were represented in the British Parliament *virtually*, and by *fiction*: Then that we were *really* represented there, because the Manor of East Greenwich in Kent is represented there, and all the Americans live in East Greenwich. And now he undertakes to prove to us, that taxes are the most profitable things in the world to those that pay them; for that Scotland is grown rich since the Union, by paying English taxes. I wish he would accommodate himself a little better to our dull capacities. We Americans have a great many heavy taxes of our own, to support our several governments, and pay off the enormous debt contracted by the war; we never conceived ourselves the richer for paying taxes, and are willing to leave all new ones to those that like them. At least, if we must with Scotland, participate in your taxes, let us likewise, with Scotland, participate in the Union, and in all the privileges and advantages of commerce that accompanied it.

Index, however, will never consent to this. He has made us partakers in all the odium with which he thinks fit to load Scotland: They resemble the Scots in sentiments (says he) their religion is Scottish; their customs and *laws* are Scottish; like the Scotch they Judaically observe what *they call* the Sabbath, persecute old women for witches, are intolerant to other sects, &c. But we must not, like the Scots, be admitted into Parliament; for that, he thinks, would increase the Scotch interest in England, which is equally hostile to the cause of liberty, and the cause of our church.

Pray, Sir, who informed you that our *laws* are Scottish? The same, I suppose, that told you our Indian corn is unwholesome. Indeed, Sir, your information is very imperfect. The common law of England, is, I assure you, the common law of the colonies: and if the civil law is what you mean by the Scottish law, we have none of it but what is forced upon us by England, in its courts of Admiralty, depriving us of that inestimable part of the common law, trials by juries. And do you look upon keeping the *Sabbath,* as part of the Scottish law? The Americans, like the Scots, (you say,) observe what *they call* the Sabbath. Pray, Sir, you who are so zealous for your church (in abusing other Christians) what *do you call* it? and where the harm of their *observing* it? If you look into your prayer-book, or over your altars, you will find these words written, *Remember to keep holy the* Sabbath *Day.* This law, though it may be observed in Scotland, and has been *countenanced* by some of your statutes, is, Sir, originally one of *God's Commandments:* a body of laws still in force in America, though they may have become *obsolete* in *some other* countries.

Give me leave, Master John Bull, to remind you, that you are *related to all mankind;* and therefore it less become you than any body, to affront and abuse other nations. But you have mixed with your many virtues, a pride, a haughtiness, and an insolent contempt for all but yourself, that, I am afraid, will, if not abated, procure you one day or other a handsome drubbing. Besides your rudeness to foreigners, you are far from being civil even to your own family. The Welch you have always despised for submitting to your government: But why despise your own English, who conquered and settled Ireland for you; who conquered and settled America for you? Yet these you now think you may treat as you please, because, forsooth, they are a *conquered* people. Why despise the Scotch, who fight and die for you all over the world? Remember, you courted Scotland for one hundred years, and would fain have had your *wicked will* of her. She virtuously resisted all your importunities, but at length kindly consented to become your lawful wife. You then solemnly promised to *love, cherish,* and *honor* her, as long as you both should live; and yet you have ever since treated her with the utmost contumely, which you now begin to extend to your common children. But, pray, when your enemies are uniting in a *Family Compact* against you, can it be discreet in you to kick up in your own house a *Family Quarrel?* And at the very time you are inviting foreigners to settle on your lands, and when you have more to settle than ever you had before, it is [*sic*] prudent to suffer your lawyer, Vindex, to abuse those who have settled there already, because they cannot yet speak Plain English? It is my opinion, Master Bull, that the Scotch and Irish, as well as the colonists, are capable of speaking much *plainer English* than they have ever yet spoke, but which I hope they will never be provoked to speak.

To be brief, Mr. Vindex, I pass over your other accusations of the Americans, and of the Scotch, that we Persecute old women for witches, and are intolerant to other sects, observing only, that we were wise enough to leave off both those foolish tricks, long before Old England made the act of toleration, or repealed the statute against witchcraft; so that even *you yourself* may safely travel through all Scotland and the Colonies, without the least danger of being persecuted as a churchman, or taken (up) for a conjurer. And yet I own myself so far of an intolerant spirit, that though I thank you for the box-in-the-ear you have given Tom Hint, as being, what you justly call him, a futile calumniator, I cannot but wish he would give you another for the same reason.

One word more, however, about the *Indian corn*, which I began and must end with, even though I should hazard your remarking, that it is certainly indigestible, as it plainly appears to *stick in my stomach*. Let him tell the world, If he dares, (you say) that the Americans prefer it to a place at their tables. And, pray, if I should dare, what then? Why then You will enter upon a discussion of its salubrity and pleasant taste. Really? Would you venture to write on the salubrity and *pleasant taste* of Indian corn, when you never in your life have tasted a *single grain* of it? But why should that hinder you writing on it? Have you not written even on *politics?* Yours,

Homespun

c. 1765

The Mother Country. A Song
We have an old Mother that peevish is grown,
She snubs us like Children that scarce walk alone;
She forgets we're grown up and have Sense of our own;
Which nobody can deny, deny, Which no body can deny.
If we don't obey Orders, whatever the Case,
She frowns, and she chides, and she loses all Patience,
And sometimes she hits us a Slap in the Face,
Which nobody can deny, &c.
Her Orders so odd are, we often suspect,
That Age has impaired her sound Intellect:

But still an old Mother should have due Respect,
Which nobody can deny, &c.
Let's bear with her Humors as well as we can:
But why should we bear the Abuse of her Man?
When Servants make Mischief, they earn the Rattan,
Which nobody should deny, &c.
Know too, ye bad Neighbors, who aim to divide
The Sons from the Mother, that still she's our Prid;
And if ye attack her we're all of her side,
Which nobody can deny, &c.
Well join in her Lawsuits, to baffle all those,
Who, to get what she has, will be often her Foes:
For we know it must all be our own, when she goes,
Which nobody can deny, deny, Which nobody can deny.

A PAEAN TO DEBORAH

Largely due to Franklin's propaganda campaign and a stirring testimony he provided to Parliament, the Stamp Act was repealed. In celebration, he sent his wife a loving letter and a shipment of gifts. Deborah's frugality and self-reliance were symbols of America's ability to sacrifice rather than submit to an unfair tax.

To Deborah Franklin, April 6, 1766

My dear child,

As the Stamp Act is at length repealed, I am willing you should have a new gown, which you may suppose I did not send sooner, as I knew you would not like to be finer than your neighbors, unless in a gown of your own spinning. Had the trade between the two countries totally ceased, it was a comfort to me to recollect that I had once been clothed from head to foot in woolen and linen of my wife's manufacture, that I never was prouder of any dress in my life, and that she and her daughter might do it again if it was necessary. I told the Parliament that it was my opinion, before the old clothes of the Americans were worn out, they might have new ones of their own making. And indeed if they had all as many old clothes as your old man has, that would not be very unlikely; for I think you and George reckoned when I was last at home, at least 20 pair of old breeches.

Joking apart, I have sent you a fine piece of pompadour satin, 14 yards cost 11s. per yard. A silk negligee and petticoat of brocaded lutestring for my dear Sally, with 2 doz. gloves, 4 bottles of lavender water, and two little reels. The reels are to screw on the edge of a table, when she would wind silk or thread, the skein is to be put over them, and winds better than if held in two hands. There is also an ivory knob to each, to which she may with a bit of silk cord hang a pin hook to fasten her plain work to like the hooks on her weight. I send you also lace for two lappet caps, 3 ells of cambric (the cambric by Mr. Yates) 3 damask table cloths, a piece of crimson Morin for curtains, with tassels, line and binding. A large true turkey carpet cost 10 guineas, for the dining parlor. Some oiled silk; and a gimcrack corkscrew which you must get some brother gimcrack to show you the use of. In the chest is a parcel of books for my friend Mr. Coleman, and another for cousin Colbert. Pray did he receives those I sent him before? I send you also a box with three fine cheeses. Perhaps a bit of them may be left when I come home.

Mrs. Stevenson has been very diligent and serviceable in getting these things together for you, and presents her best respects, as does her daughter, to both you and Sally. There are two boxes included in your bill of lading for Billy.

I received your kind letter of Feb. 20. It gives me great pleasure to hear that our good old friend Mrs. Smith is on the recovery. I hope she has yet many happy years to live. My love to her.

I fear, from the account you give of brother Peter that he cannot hold it long. If it should please God that he leaves us before my return; I would have the post office remain under the management of their son, till Mr. Foxcroft and I agree how to settle it.

There are some droll prints in the box, which were given me by the painter; and being sent when I was not at home, were packed up without my knowledge. I think he was wrong to put in Lord Bute, who had nothing to do with the stamp act. But it is the fashion here to abuse that nobleman as the author of all mischief. I send you a few bush beans, a new sort for your garden. I shall write to my friends per packet, that goes next Saturday. I am very well, and hope this will find you and Sally so with all our relations and friends, to whom my love. I am, as ever, Your affectionate Husband,

B. Franklin

THE GRUMPY BOARDER

The good-humored domestic relationship that Franklin had with his landlady Margaret Stevenson was illustrated by the good-natured grumpiness he expressed when she left their home on Craven Street for a long weekend visit with relatives in the country.

To Margaret Stevenson, November 3, 1767

Dear Madam,

I breakfasted abroad this morning and nanny tells me that Mr. West called while I was out, and left word that you did not intend to come home till Sunday next, and that you expected me then to come and fetch you; that Mr. West also desired I would dine at his house that day: I know not whether nanny is right in all this, as she has but an indifferent memory. But it seems strange to me that you should think of staying so long.

People must have great confidence in their own agreeableness that can suppose themselves not to become tiresome guests at the end of three days at farthest. I did not imagine you had been so conceited. My advice to you is, to return with the stage tomorrow. And if it is proposed that we dine there on Sunday, I shall wait on Mr. and Mrs. West with pleasure on that day, taking you with me.

But, however, I pray you not to understand that I so want you at home as not to do very well without you. Everything goes on smoothly, and the house is very quiet; and very clean too, without my saying a word about it. I am willing to allow that the arrangements you made before you went may have contributed something towards the good order and comfort in which we go on; but yet you are really mistaken in your fancy that I should, by your absence, become more sensible of your usefulness to me, and the necessity of having you always near me; for in truth I find such a satisfaction in being a little more my own master, going any where and doing any thing just when and how I please without the advice or control of anybody's wisdom but my own small as it is, that I value my own liberty above all the advantage of other's services, and begin to think I should be still happier if nanny and the cat would follow their mistress, and leave me to the enjoyment of an empty house, in which I should never be disturbed by questions of whether I intend to dine at home, and what I would have for dinner; or by a mewing request to be let in or let out.

This happiness however is perhaps too great to be conferred on any but saints and holy hermits. Sinners like me, I might have said US, are condemned to live together and tease one another, so concluding you will be sentenced to come home tomorrow, I add no more but that I am as ever your affectionate friend and humble servant

B. Franklin

MORE ON WELFARE DEPENDENCY

Franklin's innate conservatism about government intervention and welfare was evident in the series of questions he had posed to Peter Collinson in 1753. Back then, he had asked whether laws "which com-

pel the rich to maintain the poor have not given the latter a dependence" and "provide encouragements for laziness"?

To Collinson these points were raised as questions. But in his essays in the late 1760s and early 1770s, Franklin asserted these ideas
more forcefully. Most notable was an anonymous piece in 1768 which
he signed as "Medius," from the Latin word for middle. He noted that in
England wealthy legislators had passed many laws to help support the
poor. These laws were compassionate, but he warned that they could
have unintended consequences and promote laziness.

Not only did he warn against welfare dependency, he offered his
own version of the trickle-down theory of economics. The more money
made by the rich and by all of society, the more money that would make
its way down to the poor. He also debunked the idea of imposing a
higher minimum wage.

ON THE LABORING POOR, *THE GENTLEMAN'S MAGAZINE*, APRIL, 1768

Sir,

I have met with much invective in the papers for these two years
past, against the hard-heartedness of the rich, and much complaint of
the great oppressions suffered in this country by the laboring poor.
Will you admit a word or two on the other side of the question? I do
not propose to be an advocate for oppression, or oppressors. But when
I see that the poor are by such writings exasperated against the rich,
and excited to insurrections, by which much mischief is done, and
some forfeit their lives, I could wish the true state of things were better
understood, the poor not made by these busy writers more uneasy and
unhappy than their situation subjects them to be, and the nation not
brought into disrepute among foreigners by public groundless accusations of ourselves, as if the rich in England had no compassion for the
poor, and Englishmen wanted common humanity.

In justice then to this country, give me leave to remark, that the
condition of the poor here is by far the best in Europe, for that, except
in England and her American colonies, there is not in any country of
the known world, not even in Scotland or Ireland, a provision by law to
enforce a support of the poor. Everywhere else necessity reduces to
beggary. This law was not made by the poor. The legislators were men

of fortune. By that act they voluntarily subjected their own estates, and the estates of all others, to the payment of a tax for the maintenance of the poor, encumbering those estates with a kind of rent charge for that purpose, whereby the poor are vested with an inheritance, as it were, in all the estates of the rich. I wish they were benefited by this generous provision in any degree equal to the good intention with which it was made, and is continued: But I fear the giving mankind a dependence on any thing for support in age or sickness, besides industry and frugality during youth and health, tends to flatter our natural indolence, to encourage idleness and prodigality, and thereby to promote and increase poverty, the very evil it was intended to cure; thus multiplying beggars, instead of diminishing them.

Besides this tax, which the rich in England have subjected themselves to in behalf of the poor, amounting in some places to five or six shillings in the pound of the annual income, they have, by donations and subscriptions, erected numerous schools in various parts of the kingdom, for educating gratis the children of the poor in reading and writing, and in many of those schools the children are also fed and clothed. They have erected hospitals, at an immense expense, for the reception and cure of the sick, the lame, the wounded, and the insane poor, for lying-in women, and deserted children. They are also continually contributing towards making up losses occasioned by fire, by storms, or by floods, and to relieve the poor in severe seasons of frost, in times of scarcity, &c. in which benevolent and charitable contributions no nation exceeds us. Surely there is some gratitude due for so many instances of goodness!

Add to this, all the laws made to discourage foreign manufactures, by laying heavy duties on them, or totally prohibiting them, whereby the rich are obliged to pay much higher prices for what they wear and consume, than if the trade was open: These are so many laws for the support of our laboring poor, made by the rich, and continued at their expense; all the difference of price between our own and foreign commodities, being so much given by our rich to our poor; who would indeed be enabled by it to get by degrees above poverty, if they did not, as too generally they do, consider every increase of wages, only as something that enables them to drink more and work less; so that their distress in sickness, age, or times of scarcity, continues to be the same as if such laws had never been made in their favor.

Much malignant censure have some writers bestowed upon the rich for their luxury and expensive living, while the poor are starving, &c. not considering that what the rich expend, the laboring poor receive in payment for their labor. It may seem a paradox if I should assert, that our laboring poor do in every year receive *the whole revenue of the nation;* I mean not only the public revenue, but also the revenue, or clear income, of all private estates, or a sum equivalent to the whole. In support of this position I reason thus. The rich do not work for one another. Their habitations, furniture, clothing, carriages, food, ornaments, and every thing in short that they, or their families use and consume, is the work or produce of the laboring poor, who are, and must be continually, paid for their labor in producing the same. In these payments the revenues of private estates are expended, for most people live up to their incomes. In clothing and provision for troops, in arms, ammunition, ships, tents, carriages, &c. &c. (every particular the produce of labor) much of the public revenue is expended. The pay of officers civil and military, and of the private soldiers and sailors, requires the rest; and they spend that also in paying for what is produced by the laboring poor. I allow that some estates may increase by the owners spending less than their income; but then I conceive that other estates do at the same time diminish, by the owners spending more than their income, so that when the enriched want to buy more land, they easily find lands in the hands of the impoverished, whose necessities oblige them to sell; and thus this difference is equaled. I allow also, that part of the expense of the rich is in foreign produce or manufactures, for producing which the laboring poor of other nations must be paid; but then I say, that we must first pay our own laboring poor for an equal quantity of our manufactures or produce, to exchange for those foreign productions, or we must pay for them in money, which money, not being the natural produce of our country, must first be purchased from abroad, by sending out its value in the produce or manufactures of this country, for which manufactures our laboring poor are to be paid. And indeed if we did not export more than we import, we could have no money at all. I allow farther, that there are middle men, who make a profit, and even get estates, by purchasing the labor of the poor and selling it at advanced prices to the rich; but then they cannot enjoy that profit or the incomes of estates, but by spending them and employing and paying our laboring poor, in some shape or other, for the products of industry. Even beggars, pensioners, hospitals, and all that are supported by charity, spend their incomes in the same manner. So that finally, as I said at first, *our laboring poor receive annually the whole of the clear revenues of the nation,* and from us they can have no more.

If it be said that their wages are too low, and that they ought to be better paid for their labor, I heartily wish any means could be fallen upon to do it, consistent with their interest and happiness; but as the cheapness of other things is owing to the plenty of those things, so the cheapness of labor is, in most cases, owing to the multitude of laborers, and to their underworking one another in order to obtain employment. How is this to be remedied? A law might be made to raise their wages; but if our manufactures are too dear, they will not vend abroad, and all that part of employment will fail, unless by fighting and conquering we compel other nations to buy our goods, whether they will or no, which some have been mad enough at times to propose. Among ourselves, unless we give our working people less employment, how can we, for what they do, pay them higher than we do? Out of what fund is the additional price of labor to be paid, when all our present incomes are, as it were, mortgaged to them? Should they get higher wages, would that make them less poor, if in consequence they worked fewer days of the week proportionally? I have said a law might be made to raise their wages; but I doubt much whether it could be executed to any purpose, unless another law, now indeed almost obsolete, could at the same time be revived and enforced; a law, I mean, that many have often heard and repeated, but few have ever duly considered. Six *days shalt thou labor.* This is as positive a part of the commandment as that which says, *the* Seventh *day thou shalt rest.* But we remember well to observe the indulgent part, and never think of the other. St. Monday is generally as duly kept by our working people as Sunday; the only difference is, that, instead of employing their time, cheaply, at church, they are wasting it expensively at the alehouse. I am, Sir, &c.

Medius

COLD AIR BATHS

Throughout his life, Franklin was a firm believer in good ventilation and that colds were caused not by chill but by breathing stale air that contained germs from other people. While living on Craven Street, he made a habit of sitting nude in front of an open window to help purify his body.

To Jacques Barbeu-Dubourg, July 28, 1768

I greatly approve the epithet, which you give in your letter of the 8th of June, to the new method of treating the small-pox, which you call the tonic or bracing method. I will take occasion from it, to mention a practice to which I have accustomed myself. You know the cold bath has long been in vogue here as a tonic; but the shock of the cold water has always appeared to me, generally speaking, as too violent: and I have found it much more agreeable to my constitution to bathe in another element, I mean cold air. With this view I rise early almost every morning, and sit in my chamber, without any clothes whatever, half an hour or an hour, according to the season, either reading or writing. This practice is not in the least painful, but on the contrary, agreeable; and if I return to bed afterwards, before I dress myself, as sometimes happens, I make a supplement to my night's rest, of one or two hours of the most pleasing sleep that can be imagined. I find no ill consequences whatever resulting from it, and that at least it does not injure my health, if it does not in fact contribute much to its preservation. I shall therefore call it for the future a bracing or tonic bath.

THE FABLE OF THE LION AND THE DOG

In his efforts to persuade the British that their tyrannical treatment of America would eventually backfire, Franklin continued to pour forth essays, letters, hoaxes and other pieces of propaganda. One of them, in January 1770, was a fable about a young lion cub and a large English dog traveling together on a ship. It was "humbly inscribed" to Lord Hillsborough, the colonial secretary who had become Franklin's most ardent opponent.

THE PUBLIC ADVERTISER, JANUARY 2, 1770

A lion's whelp was put on board a Guinea ship bound to America as a present to a friend in that country: it was tame and harmless as a kitten, and therefore not confined, but suffered to walk about the ship at pleasure. A stately, full-grown English mastiff, belonging to the captain, despising the weakness of the young lion, frequently took its *food* by force, and often turned it out of its lodging box, when he had a mind to repose therein himself. The young lion nevertheless grew daily in size and strength, and the voyage being long, he became at last a more equal match for the mastiff; who continuing his insults, received a stunning blow from the lion's paw that fetched his skin over his ears, and deterred him from any future contest with such growing strength; regretting that he had not rather secured its friendship than provoked its enmity.

POLLY GETS MARRIED

In late 1769, Polly Stevenson met a man that wanted to marry her. William Hewson was a good catch for Polly, who by then was 30. He was on the verge of what would be a prominent career as a medical researcher and lecturer. "He must be clever because he thinks as *we* do," Polly gushed in a letter from the country home where she was staying. But she played coy with Franklin by confessing (or feigning) her lack of enthusiasm for marrying Hewson. "He may be too young," she told her older admirer.

Franklin, who had just returned from a trip to Paris, replied the very

the next day with a letter that contained more flirtations than felicita-
tions. "If the truth were known, I have reason to be jealous of this in-
sinuating handsome young physician." He would flatter his vanity, he
said, by presuming "to suppose you were in spirits because of my safe
return."

For almost a year, Polly held off getting married because Franklin refused to advise her to accept Hewson's proposal. Finally, in May of
1770, Franklin wrote that he had no objections. It was hardly an over-
whelming endorsement. "I am sure you are a much better judge in this
affair of your own than I can possibly be," he said. As for her worry that
she would not bring much of a financial dowry, Franklin could not resist
noting that "I should think you a fortune sufficient for me without a
shilling."

Although he had missed the weddings of both of his real children,
this was one Franklin made sure not to miss. Even though it was held in
mid-summer when he usually traveled, he was there to walk Polly down
the aisle and play the role of her father. A few weeks later, he professed
to be pleased that she was happy, but he confessed that he was "now
and then in low spirits" at the prospect of having lost her friendship.
Fortunately for all, it was not to be. He became close to the new couple,
and he and Polly would exchange more than 130 more letters during
their lifelong friendship.

To Polly Stevenson, May 31, 1770

Dear Polly,

I received your letter early this morning, and as I am so engaged
that I cannot see you when you come today, I write this line just to say,
that I am sure you are a much better judge in this affair of your own
than I can possibly be; in that confidence it was that I forbore giving
my advice when you mentioned it to me, and not from any disapproba-
tion. My concern (equal to any father's) for your happiness, makes me
write this, lest having more regard for my opinion than you ought, and
imagining it against the proposal because I did not immediately advise
accepting it, you should let that weigh any thing in your deliberations.

I assure you that no objection has occurred to me; his person you
see, his temper and his understanding you can judge of, his character
for any thing I have ever heard is unblemished; his profession, with

that skill in it he is supposed to have, will be sufficient to support a family; and therefore considering the fortune you have in your hands, (though any future expectation from your aunt should be disappointed) I do not see but that the agreement may be a rational one on both sides. I see your delicacy; and your humility too; for you fancy that if you do not prove a great fortune you will not be beloved; but I am sure that were I in his situation in every respect, knowing you so well as I do, and esteeming you so highly, I should think you a fortune sufficient for me without a shilling.

Having thus more explicitly than before given my opinion, I leave the rest to your sound judgment, of which no one has a greater share; and shall not be too inquisitive after your particular reasons, your doubts, your fears, &c. for I shall be confident whether you accept or refuse, that you do right. I only wish you may do what will most contribute to your happiness, and of course to mine; being ever, my dear friend,

Yours most affectionately,
B.F.

P.S. Don't be angry with me for supposing your Determination not quite so fixed as you fancy it.

To Polly Stevenson Hewson, July 18, 1770

Dear Polly,

Yours of the 15th. informing me of your agreeable journey and safe arrival at Hexham gave me great pleasure, and would make your good mother happy if I knew how to convey it to her; but 'tis such an out-of-the-way place she is gone to, and the name so out of my head, that the good news must wait her return. Enclosed I send you a letter which came before she went, and, supposing it from my daughter Bache, she would have me open and read it to her, so you see if there had been any intrigue between the gentleman and you, how all would have been discovered. Your mother went away on Friday last, taking with her Sally and Temple, trusting me alone with nanny, who indeed has hitherto made no attempt upon my virtue. Neither Dolly nor Barwell, nor any other good female soul of your friends or mine have been nigh me, nor offered me the least consolation by letter in my present lonesome state. I hear the postman's bell, so can only add my affectionate respects to Mr. Hewson, and best wishes of perpetual happiness for you both. I am, as ever, my dear good girl, your affectionate friend,

B. Franklin

THE CRAVENSTREET GAZETTE

A few months after their wedding, Polly and William Hewson came to stay with Franklin while Mrs. Stevenson spent one of her long weekends visiting friends in the country. Together they published a fake newspaper to mark the occasion.

For four days, the newspaper poked fun at various Franklin foibles: how he violated his sermons about saving fuel by making a fire in his bedroom when everyone else was out, how he vowed to fix the front door but gave up because he was unable to decide whether it required buying a new lock or a new key, and how he pledged to go to church on Sunday. One particularly intriguing entry seems to refer to a woman named Lady Bardwell living nearby with whom Franklin had an unrequited flirtation.

The final edition contained one of Franklin's inimitable letters to the editor, signed with the pseudonym "Indignation," decrying the food and conditions. It was answered by "A Hater of Scandal," who wrote that the surly Franklin had been offered a wonderful dinner of beef ribs and had rejected it because it did not agree with his system.

THE CRAVENSTREET GAZETTE, SEPTEMBER 22–26, 1770

The Cravenstreet Gazette, No 113, Saturday, September 22, 1770

This Morning Queen Margaret, accompanied by her first Maid of Honor, Miss Franklin, set out for Rochester. Immediately on their departure, the whole Street was in Tears—from a heavy Shower of Rain.

It is whispered that the new Family Administration which took place on her Majesty's departure, promises, like all other new Administrations, to govern much better than the old one.

We hear that the *great* Person (so called from his enormous Size) of a certain Family in a certain Street, is grievously affected at the late changes, and could hardly be comforted this Morning, though the new Ministry promised him a roasted shoulder of mutton, and potatoes, for his dinner.

It is said, that the same *great* Person intended to pay his respects to another great personage this day, at St. James's, it being Coronation-Day; hoping thereby a little to amuse his Grief; but was prevented by an accident, Queen Margaret, or her Maid of Honor having carried off the key of the drawers, so that the Lady of the Bedchamber could not come at a laced shirt for his Highness. Great clamors were made on this occasion against her Majesty.

Other accounts say, that the shirts were afterwards found, though too late, in another Place. And some suspect, that the wanting a shirt from those drawers was only a ministerial Pretence to excuse Picking the Locks, that the new Administration might have every thing at command.

We hear that the Lady Chamberlain of the Household went to market this morning by her own self, gave the butcher whatever he asked for the mutton, and had no dispute with the potatoe woman—to their great amazement—at the change of times!

It is confidently asserted, that this Afternoon, the Weather being wet, the great *Person* a little chilly, and no body at home to find fault with the expense of fuel, he was indulged with a fire in his chamber, it seems the design is, to make him contented, by degrees, with the absence of the Queen.

A Project has been under consideration of Government, to take the opportunity of her Majesty's absence, for doing a Thing she was always averse to, viz. fixing a new lock on the street door, or getting a key made to the old one; it being found extremely inconvenient, that one or other of the Great Officers of State, should, whenever the Maid goes out for a hapworth of sand or a pint of porter, be obliged to attend the door to let her in again. But opinion, being divided, which of the two Expedients to adopt, the Project is for the present laid aside.

We have good Authority to assure our Readers, that a Cabinet Council was held this afternoon at tea; the subject of which was a Proposal for the Reformation of Manners, and a more strict Observation of the Lord's Day, the result was, an unanimous resolution that no meat should be dressed tomorrow; whereby the cook and the first minister will both be at liberty to go to church, the one having nothing to do, and the other no roast to rule. It seems the cold shoulder of mutton, and the apple pie, were thought sufficient for Sunday's dinner. All pious people applaud this measure, and 'tis thought the new Ministry will soon become popular.

We hear that Mr. Wilkes was at a certain House in Craven Street this day, and enquired after the absent Queen. His good Lady and the Children were well.

The Report that Mr. Wilkes the Patriot made the above Visit, is without Foundation, it being his Brother the Courtier.

Sunday, September 23

It is now found by sad Experience, that good Resolutions are easier made than executed. Notwithstanding yesterday's solemn Order of Council, no body went to Church to day. It seems the *great* Persons broad-built-bulk lay so long abed, that Breakfast was not over till it was too late to dress. At least this is the Excuse. In fine, it seems a vain thing to hope Reformation from the example of our great Folks. The cook and the minister, however, both took advantage of the order so far, as to save themselves all trouble, and the clause of *cold dinner* was enforced, though the *going to Church* was dispensed with; just as the common working People observe the Commandment; *the seventh Day thou shalt rest,* they think a sacred Injunction; but the other *Six Days shalt thou labor* is deemed a mere Piece of Advice which they may practice when they want Bread and are out of Credit at the Alehouse, and may neglect whenever they have Money in their Pockets. It must nevertheless be said in justice to our Court, that whatever Inclination they had to Gaming, no Cards were brought out to Day. Lord and Lady Hewson walked after Dinner to Kensington to pay their Duty to the Dowager, and Dr. Fatsides made 469 Turns in his Dining Room as the exact Distance of a Visit to the lovely Lady Barwell, whom he did not find at home, so there was no Struggle for and against a Kiss, and he sat down to dream in the Easy Chair that he had it without any trouble.

Monday, September 24

We are credibly informed, that the *great* Person dined this Day with the Club at the Cat-and-Bagpipes in the City, on cold round of boiled beef. This, it seems, he was under some necessity of doing (though he rather dislikes beef) because truly the Ministers were to be all abroad somewhere to dine on hot roast Venison. It is thought that if the Queen had been at home, he would not have been so slighted. And though he shows outwardly no Marks of Dissatisfaction, it is suspected that he begins to wish for her Majesty's Return.

It is currently reported, that poor Nanny had nothing for Dinner in the Kitchen, for herself and Puss, but the Scrapings of the Bones of Saturday's Mutton.

This Evening there was high Play at the Groom Porters in Cravenstreet House. The Great Person lost Money. It is supposed the Ministers, as is usually supposed of all Ministers, shared the Emoluments among them.

Tuesday, September 25

This Morning the good Lord Hutton called at Cravenstreet House, and enquired very respectfully and affectionately concerning the Welfare of the absent Queen. He then imparted to the big Man a piece of intelligence important to them both, which he had just received from Lady Hawkesworth, viz. That amiable and excellent Companion Miss Dorothea Blount had made a vow to marry absolutely him of the two, whose wife should first depart this life. It is impossible to express with Words the various Agitations of Mind appearing in both their Faces on this Occasion. *Vanity* at the Preference given them to the rest of Mankind; *Affection* to their present Wives; *Fear* of losing them; *Hope,* (if they must lose them) to obtain the proposed Comfort; *Jealousy* of each other, in case both Wives should die together; &c. &c. &c. all working at the same time, jumbled their features into inexplicable confusion. They parted at length with

Professions and outward Appearances indeed of ever-during Friendship; but it was shrewdly suspected that each of them sincerely wished Health and long Life to the other's Wife; and that however long either of those Friends might like to live himself, the other would be very well pleased to survive him.

It is remarked that the skies have wept every day in Cravenstreet the Absence of the Queen.

The Public may be assured, that this Morning a certain *great Person* was asked very complaisantly by the Mistress of the Household, if he would choose to have the blade bone of Saturday's Mutton that had been kept for his dinner today, *broiled* or *cold?* He answered gravely, *If there is any flesh on it, it may be broiled; if not, it may as well be cold.* Orders were accordingly given for broiling it. But when it came to table, there was indeed so very little flesh, or rather none at all (Puss having dined on it yesterday after Nanny) that if our new Administration had been as good Economists as they would be thought, the Expense of Broiling might well have been saved to the Public, and carried to the Sinking Fund. It is assured the great Person bears all with infinite Patience. But the Nation is astonished at the insolent presumption that dares treat so much mildness in so cruel a manner.

A terrible accident had *like to have happened* this Afternoon at Tea. The boiler was set too near the end of the little square table. The first Ministress was sitting at one end of the table to administer the Tea; the great Person was about to sit down at the other End where the Boiler stood. By a sudden motion, the Lady gave the table a tilt. Had it gone over, the great *Person* must have been scalded; perhaps to Death. Various are the Surmises and Observations on this Occasion. The Godly say, it would have been a just Judgment on him, for preventing by his Laziness, the Family's going to Church last Sunday. The Opposition do not stick to insinuate that there was a design to scald him, prevented only by his quick catching the table. The Friends of the Ministry give out, that he carelessly jogged the Table himself, and would have been inevitably scalded had not the Ministress saved him. It is hard for the Public to come at the Truth in these Cases. At six o'clock this Afternoon News came by the Post, that her Majesty arrived safely at Rochester on Saturday Night. The Bells immediately rang for Candles, to illuminate the Parlor; the Court went into Cribbage, and the Evening concluded with every other Demonstration of Joy.

It is reported that all the principal Officers of the State, have received an Invitation from the Duchess Dowager of Rochester to go down thither on Saturday next. But it is not yet known whether the great Affairs they have on their hands will permit them to make this excursion.

We hear that from the Time of her Majesty's leaving Craven Street House to this Day, no care is taken to file the Newspapers; but they lie about in every room, in every window, and on every chair, just where the Doctor lays them when he has read them. It is impossible Government can long go on in such Hands.

To the Publisher of the Craven Street Gazette

Sir,

I make no doubt of the truth of what the papers tell us, that a certain great *person* has been half-starved on the bare blade-bone, *of a sheep* (I cannot call it *of Mutton* because none was on it) by a Set of the most careless, thoughtless, inconsiderate, corrupt, ignorant, blundering, foolish, crafty, and Knavish Ministers, that ever got into a House and pretended to govern a Family and provide a Dinner. Alas, for the poor Old England of Craven Street! If these nefarious Wretches continue in power another week, the nation will be ruined! Undone!— totally undone, if the Queen does not return; or (which is better) turn them all out and appoint me and my Friends to succeed them. I am a great Admirer of your useful and impartial Paper; and therefore request you will insert this without fail; from Your humble Servant,

Indignation

To the Publisher of the Craven Street Gazette

Sir,

Your Correspondent *Indignation* has made a fine Story in your Paper against our excellent Cravenstreet Ministry, as if they meant to starve his Highness, giving him only a bare Blade Bone for his Dinner, while they riot upon roast Venison, &c. The Wickedness of Writers in this Age is truly amazing! I believe we never had since the Foundation of our State, a more faithful, upright, worthy, careful, considerate, incorrupt, discreet, wise, prudent and beneficent Ministry than the present. But if even the Angel Gabriel would condescend to be our Minister and provide our Dinners, he could scarcely escape Newspaper Defamation from a Gang of hungry ever-restless, discontented and malicious Scribblers. It is, Sir, a piece of Justice you owe our righteous Administration to undeceive the Public on this Occasion, by assuring them of the Fact, which is, that there was provided; and actually smoking on the Table under his Royal Nose at the same Instant, as fine a Piece of Ribs of Beef, roasted, as ever Knife was put into; with Potatoes, Horse radish, pickled Walnuts, &c. which Beef his Highness might have eaten of, if so he had pleased to do; and which he forbore to do, merely from a whimsical Opinion (with Respect be it spoken) that Beef doth not with him perspire well, but makes his Back itch, to his no small Vexation, now that he hath lost the little Chinese Ivory Hand at the End of a Stick, commonly called a *Scratchback,* presented to him by her Majesty. This is the Truth; and if your boasted Impartiality is real, you will not hesitate a Moment to insert this Letter in your very next Paper. I am, though a little angry with you at present. Yours as you behave,

A Hater of Scandal

Junius and Cinna *came to Hand too late for this Day's Paper, but shall have Place in our next.*

Marriages. None since our last; but Puss begins to go a Courting.

Deaths. In the back Closet, and elsewhere, many poor Mice.

Stocks. Biscuit very low. Buckwheat and Indian meal, both sour. Tea, lowering daily in the Canister.

A SHOWDOWN WITH LORD HILLSBOROUGH

Franklin's battles with the colonial secretary, Lord Hillsborough, became more heated after Britain imposed new duties, especially on tea imports. Franklin, who was the agent for Pennsylvania and other colonies, was appointed by the Massachusetts House of Representatives to represent them as well. In January 1771 he obtained an audience with Hillsborough to present his new credentials. The meeting was so acrimonious that Franklin immediately went back to Craven Street to write a transcript of it. Hillsborough "took great offense at some of my last words, which he calls extremely rude and abusive," Franklin reported to a friend in Boston. "I find that he did not mistake me."

JANUARY 16, 1771

I went this morning to wait on Lord Hillsborough. The porter at first denied his lordship, on which I left my name, and drove off. But before the coach got out of the square, the coachman heard a call, turned, and went back to the door, when the porter came and said, his lordship will see you, sir. I was shown into the levee room, where I found Governor Barnard, who I understand attends there constantly. Several other gentlemen were there attending, with whom I sat down a few minutes. When Secretary Pownall came out to us, and said his lordship desired I would come in.

I was pleased with this ready admission, and preference, (having sometimes waited 3 or 4 hours for my turn) and being pleased, I could more easily put on the open cheerful countenance that my friends advised me to wear. His lordship came towards me, and said I was dressing in order to go to court; but hearing that you were at the door, who are a man of business, I determined to see you immediately. I thanked his lordship and said that my business at present was not much, it was only to pay my respects to his lordship and to acquaint him with my appointment by the House of Representatives of the province of Massachusetts Bay, to be their agent here, in which station if I could be of any service I was going on to say, to the public I should be very happy; but his lordship whose countenance changed at my naming that province cut me short, by saying, with something between a smile and a sneer,

Lord H.: I must set you right there, Mr. Franklin, you are not Agent.

Franklin: Why; my Lord?

Lord H.: You are not appointed.

Franklin: I do not understand your Lordship. I have the Appointment in my Pocket.

Lord H.: You are mistaken. I have later and better advices. I have a letter from Governor Hutchinson. He would not give his Assent to the Bill.

Franklin: There was no Bill, my Lord; it is a vote of the House.

Lord H.: There was a Bill presented to the Governor, for the purpose of appointing you, and another, one Dr. Lee, I think he is called, to which the Governor refused his Assent.

Franklin: I cannot understand this, my Lord. I think There must be some mistake in it. Is your Lordship quite sure that you have such a Letter?

Lord H.: I will convince you of it directly. *Rings the Bell.* Mr. Pownall will come in and satisfy you.

Franklin: You are going to Court. I will wait on your Lordship another time.

Lord H.: No, stay, He will come in immediately. *To the Servant.* Tell Mr. Pownall I want him. *Mr. Pownall comes in.*

Lord H.: Have not you at hand Governor Hutchinson's letter mentioning his refusing his Assent to the Bill for appointing Dr. Franklin Agent?

Secretary Pownall: My Lord?

Lord H.: Is there not such a Letter?

Secretary Pownall: No, my Lord. There is a Letter relating to some Bill for payment of Salary to Mr. DeBerdt and I think to some other Agent, to which the Governor had refused his Assent.

Lord H.: And is there nothing in that Letter to the purpose I mention?

Secretary Pownall: No, my Lord.

Franklin: I thought it could not well be, my Lord, as my Letters are by the last Ships and mention no such Thing. Here is an authentic Copy of the Vote of the House appointing me, in which there is no Mention of any Act intended. Will your Lordship please to look at it? (*With some seeming Unwillingness he takes it, but does not look into it*).

Lord H.: An Information of this kind is not properly brought to me as Secretary of State. The Board of Trade is the proper Place.

Franklin: I will leave the Paper then with Mr. Pownall, to be

Lord H.: (*Hastily*) To what End would you leave it with him?

Franklin: To be entered on the Minutes of that Board, as usual.

Lord H.: (*Angrily*) It shall not be entered there. No such Paper shall be entered there while I have any thing to do with the Business of that Board. The House of Representatives has no Right to appoint an Agent. We shall take no Notice of any Agents but such as are appointed by Acts of Assembly to which the Governor gives his Assent. We have had Confusion enough already. Here is one Agent appointed by the Council, another by the House of Representatives; Which of these is Agent for the Province? Who are we to hear on Provincial Affairs? An Agent appointed by Act of Assembly we can understand. No other will be attended to for the future, I can assure you.

Franklin: I cannot conceive, my Lord, why the Consent of the *Governor* should be thought necessary to the Appointment of an Agent for the *People*. It seems to me, that

Lord H.: (*With a mixed Look of Anger and Contempt*) I shall not enter into a Dispute with you, Sir, upon this Subject.

Franklin: I beg your Lordships Pardon. I do not presume to dispute with your

Lordship: I would only say, that it seems to me, that every Body of Men, who cannot appear in Person where Business relating to them may be transacted, should have a Right to appear by an Agent; The Concurrence of the Governor does not seem to me necessary. It is the Business of the People that is to be done, he is not one of them, he is himself an Agent.

Lord H.: Whose Agent is he? (*Hastily*).

Franklin: The King's, my Lord.

Lord H.: No such Matter. He is one of the Corporation, by the Province Charter. No Agent can be appointed but by an Act, nor any

Act pass without his Assent. Besides, This Proceeding is directly contrary to express Instructions.

Franklin: I did not know there had been such Instructions, I am not concerned in any Offence against them, and

Lord H.: Yes, your Offering such a Paper to be entered is an Offence against them. (*Folding it up again, without having read a Word of it.*) No such Appointment shall be entered. When I came into the Administration of American Affairs, I found them in great Disorder; By *my Firmness* they are now something mended; and while I have the Honor to hold the Seals, I shall continue the same Conduct, the same *Firmness.* I think My Duty to the Master I serve and to the Government of this Nation require it of me. If that Conduct is not approved, They may take my Office from me when they please. I shall make em a Bow, and thank em. I shall resign with Pleasure. That Gentleman knows it. (*Pointing to Mr. Pownall.*) But while I continue in it, I shall resolutely persevere in the same firmness. (*Spoken with great Warmth, and turning pale in his Discourse, as if he was angry at something or somebody besides the Agent; and of more Importance*) Consequence to himself.

Franklin: (*Reaching out his Hand for the Paper, which his Lordship returned to him*) I beg your Lordship's Pardon for taking up so much of your time. It is I believe of no great Importance whether the Appointment is acknowledged or not, for I have not the least Conception that an Agent can *at present* be of any Use, to any of the Colonies. I shall therefore give your Lordship no farther Trouble. *Withdrew.*

THE SEEDS OF A TOTAL DISUNION

The showdown with Hillsborough caused Franklin to contemplate the worst: that the dispute between Britain and America might lead to revolution and total separation. He did, however, hold out hope that prudent conduct could thwart those in Britain who favored even more repressive measures.

To the Massachusetts House of Representatives, May 15, 1771

Gentlemen,

. . . I think one may clearly see, in the system of customs to be exacted in America by act of Parliament, the seeds sown of a total disunion of the two countries, though, as yet, that event may be at a
considerable distance. The course and natural progress seems to be,
first, the appointment of needy men as officers, for others do not care
to leave England; then, their necessities make them rapacious, their office makes them proud and insolent, their insolence and rapacity make
them odious, and, being conscious that they are hated, they become
malicious; their malice urges them to a continual abuse of the inhabitants in their letters to administration, representing them as disaffected
and rebellious, and (to encourage the use of severity) as weak, divided,
timid, and cowardly. Government believes all; thinks it necessary to
support and countenance its officers; their quarrelling with the people
is deemed a mark and consequence of their fidelity; they are therefore
more highly rewarded, and this makes their conduct still more insolent
and provoking.

The resentment of the people will, at times and on particular incidents, burst into outrages and violence upon such officers, and this naturally draws down severity and acts of further oppression from hence.
The more the people are dissatisfied, the more rigor will be thought
necessary; severe punishments will be inflicted to terrify; rights and
privileges will be abolished; greater force will then be required to secure
execution and submission; the expense will become enormous; it will
then be thought proper, by fresh exactions, to make the people defray
it; thence, the British nation and government will become odious, the
subjection to it will be deemed no longer tolerable; war ensues, and the
bloody struggle will end in absolute slavery to America, or ruin to
Britain by the loss of her colonies; the latter most probable, from
America's growing strength and magnitude.

But, as the whole empire must, in either case, be greatly weakened,
I cannot but wish to see much patience and the utmost discretion in
our general conduct, that the fatal period may be postponed, and that,
whenever this catastrophe shall happen, it may appear to all mankind,

that the fault has not been ours. And, since the collection of these duties has already cost Britain infinitely more, in the loss of commerce, than they amount to, and that loss is likely to continue and increase by the encouragement given to our manufactures through resentment; and since the best pretence for establishing and enforcing the duties is the regulation of trade for the general advantage, it seems to me, that it would be much better for Britain to give them up, on condition of the colonies undertaking to enforce and collect such, as are thought fit to be continued, by laws of their own, and officers of their own appointment, for the public uses of their respective governments. This would alone destroy those seeds of disunion, and both countries might thence much longer continue to grow great together, more secure by their united strength, and more formidable to their common enemies. But the power of appointing friends and dependents to profitable offices is too pleasing to most administrations, to be easily parted with or lessened; and therefore such a proposition, if it were made, is not very likely to meet with attention.

I do not pretend to the gift of prophecy. History shows, that, by these steps, great empires have crumbled heretofore; and the late transactions we have so much cause to complain of show, that we are in the same train, and that, without a greater share of prudence and wisdom, than we have seen both sides to be possessed of, we shall probably come to the same conclusion.

The Parliament, however, is prorogued, without having taken any of the steps we had been threatened with, relating to our charter. Their attention has been engrossed by other affairs, and we have therefore longer time to operate in making such impressions, as may prevent a renewal of this particular attempt by our adversaries. With great esteem and respect, I have the honor to be, &c.

B. Franklin

HOW TO WEIGH A DECISION

Franklin was a very orderly man, and around the time he had been considering getting married he came up with a method for making complex decisions. He described it in a letter he wrote to one of his closest London friends, the scientist Joseph Priestley, who wrote a history of electricity that featured Franklin's kite experiment and who isolated the element oxygen.

JOSEPH PRIESTLEY, SEPTEMBER 19, 1772

Dear Sir,

In the affair of so much importance to you, wherein you ask my advice, I cannot for want of sufficient premises, advise you *what* to determine, but if you please I will tell you *how*. When these difficult cases occur, they are difficult chiefly because while we have them under consideration all the reasons *pro* and *con* are not present to the mind at the same time; but sometimes one set present themselves, and at other times another, the first being out of sight. Hence the various purposes or inclinations that alternately prevail, and the uncertainty that perplexes us. To get over this, my way is, to divide half a sheet of paper by a line into two columns, writing over the one *pro*, and over the other *con*. Then during three or four day's consideration I put down under the different heads short hints of the different motives that at different times occur to me for or against the measure. When I have thus got them all together in one view, I endeavor to estimate their respective weights; and where I find two, one on each side, that seem equal, I strike them both out: if I find a reason *pro* equal to some two reasons *con*, I strike out the three. If I judge some two reasons *con* equal to some three reasons *pro*, I strike out the five; and thus proceeding I find at length where the balance lies; and if after a day or two of farther consideration nothing new that is of importance occurs on either side, I come to a determination accordingly. And though the weight of reasons cannot be taken with the precision of algebraic quantities, yet when each is thus considered separately and comparatively, and the whole lies before me, I think I can judge better, and am less likely to make a rash step; and in fact I have found great advantage from this kind of equation, in what may be called *moral* or *prudential algebra*. Wishing sincerely that you may determine for the best, I am ever, my dear friend, yours most affectionately,

B. Franklin

ODE TO A SQUIRREL

In the summer of 1771, Franklin had begun writing his autobiography at the home of Jonathan Shipley, an Anglican bishop who had five spirited daughters. Franklin delighted in the company of young women, and he had his wife send over a pet squirrel from America as a gift to the girls. When it met an untimely end the following year in the jaws of a dog, Franklin composed a flowery eulogy, that reflected on the perils of liberty, and then added a little epitaph that would become famous.

To Georgiana Shipley, September 26, 1772

Dear Miss,

I lament with you most sincerely the unfortunate end of poor *Mungo*: few squirrels were better accomplished; for he had had a good education, had traveled far, and seen much of the world. As he had the honor of being for his virtues your favorite, he should not go like common Skuggs without an elegy or an epitaph. Let us give him one in the monumental stile and measure, which being neither prose nor verse, is perhaps the properest for grief; since to use common language would look as if we were not affected, and to make rhymes would seem trifling in sorrow.

Alas! poor Mungo!
Happy wert thou, hadst thou known

Thy own Felicity!
Remote from the fierce Bald-Eagle,
Tyrant of thy native Woods,
Thou hadst nought to fear from his piercing Talons;
Nor from the murdering Gun Of the thoughtless Sportsman.
Safe in thy wired Castle,
Grimalkin never could annoy thee.
Daily wert thou fed with the choicest Viands
By the fair Hand Of an indulgent Mistress.
But, discontented, thou wouldst have more Freedom.
Too soon, alas! didst thou obtain it,
And, wandering, Fell by the merciless Fangs,
Of wanton, cruel Ranger.
Learn hence, ye who blindly wish more Liberty,
Whether Subjects, Sons, Squirrels or Daughters,
That apparent Restraint *may be real* protection
Yielding Peace, Plenty, and Security.

You see how much more decent and proper this broken style, interrupted as it were with sighs, is for the occasion, than if one were to say, by way of epitaph,

Here Skugg Lies
Snug As a Bug In a Rug.

And yet perhaps there are people in the world of so little feeling as to think, *that* would be a good-enough Epitaph for our poor Mungo!

If you wish it, I shall procure another to succeed him. But perhaps you will now choose some other Amusement. Remember me respectfully to all the good Family; and believe me ever, Your affectionate Friend,

B. Franklin

THE CAUSE OF COLDS

Franklin's penchant for air baths were part of his theory about the cause of the common cold. Although germs and viruses had yet to be discovered, Franklin was one of the first to argue that colds and flu "may possibly be spread by contagion" rather than cold air. The best defense was good ventilation. Throughout his life, Franklin liked open windows, even in the midst of winter.

To Benjamin Rush, July 14, 1773

Dear Sir,

. . . I shall communicate your judicious remark relating to air transpired by patients in putrid diseases to my friend Dr. Priestley. I hope that after having discovered the benefit of fresh and cool air applied to the *sick,* people will begin to suspect that possibly it may do no harm to the *well.* I have not seen Dr. Cullen's book, but am glad to hear that he speaks of catarrhs or colds *by contagion.* I have long been satisfied from observation, that besides the general colds now termed *influenzas,* which may possibly spread by contagion as well as by a particular quality of the air, people often catch cold from one another when shut up together in small close rooms, coaches, &c. and when sitting near and conversing so as to breathe in each other's transpiration, the disorder being in a certain state. I think too that it is the frowzy corrupt air from animal substances, and the perspired matter from our bodies, which, being long confined in beds not lately used, and clothes not lately worn, and books long shut up in close rooms, obtains that kind of putridity which infects us, and occasions the colds observed upon sleeping in, wearing, or turning over, such beds, clothes or books, and not their coldness or dampness. From these causes, but more from *too full living* with too *little exercise,* proceed in my opinion most of the disorders which for 100 years past the English have called *colds.* As to Dr. Cullen's cold or catarrh *frigore,* I question whether such an one ever existed.

Traveling in our severe winters, I have suffered cold sometimes to an extremity only short of freezing, but this did not make me *catch cold*. And for moisture, I have been in the river every evening two or three hours for a fortnight together, when one would suppose I might imbibe enough of it to *take cold* if humidity could give it; but no such effect followed: boys never get cold by swimming. Nor are people at sea, or who live at Bermudas, or St. Helena, where the air must be ever moist, from the dashing and breaking of waves against their rocks on all sides, more subject to colds than those who inhabit parts of a continent where the air is driest. Dampness may indeed assist in producing putridity, and those miasmas which infect us with the disorder we call a cold, but of itself can never by a little addition of moisture hurt a body filled with watery fluids from head to foot . . .

With great esteem and sincere wishes for your welfare, I am, sir, your most obedient humble servant,

B. Franklin

PARODY RULES AND AN EDICT DIRECTED AT BRITAIN

In the fall of 1773, Franklin anonymously published in the London papers two of his most famous parodies designed to make the British come to their senses about their treatment of the American colonies. They reflected his youthful love of satire. The first referred to "an ancient sage" (it was Themistocles) who had described how to turn a little city into a great one, and Franklin turned it around to produce the rules by which an empire could do the reverse. The second purported to be a declaration issued by Prussia's King Frederick II.

THE PUBLIC ADVERTISER, SEPTEMBER 11, 1773

Rules by which a Great Empire may be reduced to a Small One.
An ancient Sage valued himself upon this, that though he could not

fiddle, he knew how to make a *great City* of a *little one*. The Science that I, a modern Simpleton, am about to communicate is the very reverse.

I address myself to all Ministers who have the management of extensive dominions, which from their very greatness are become troublesome to govern, because the multiplicity of their affairs leaves no time for *fiddling.*

I. In the first Place, Gentlemen, you are to consider, that a great Empire, like a great Cake, is most easily diminished at the Edges. Turn your Attention therefore first to your remotest Provinces; that as you get rid of them, the next may follow in Order.

II. That the Possibility of this Separation may always exist, take special Care the Provinces are never incorporated with the Mother Country, that they do not enjoy the same common Rights, the same Privileges in Commerce, and that they are governed by *severer* Laws, all of *your enacting,* without allowing them any Share in the Choice of the Legislators. By carefully making and preserving such Distinctions, you will (to keep to my Simile of the Cake) act like a wise Gingerbread Baker, who, to facilitate a Division, cuts his Dough half through in those Places, where, when baked, he would have it *broken to Pieces.*

III. These remote Provinces have perhaps been acquired, purchased, or conquered, at the *sole Expense* of the Settlers or their Ancestors, without the Aid of the Mother Country. If this should happen to increase her *Strength* by their growing Numbers ready to join in her Wars, her *Commerce* by their growing Demand for her Manufactures, or her *Naval Power* by greater Employment for her Ships and Seamen, they may probably suppose some Merit in this, and that it entitles them to some Favor; you are therefore to *forget it all,* or resent it as if they had done you Injury. If they happen to be zealous Whigs, Friends of Liberty, nurtured in Revolution Principles, *remember all that* to their Prejudice, and contrive to punish it: For such Principles, after a Revolution is thoroughly established, are of *no more Use,* they are even *odious* and *abominable.*

IV. However peaceably your Colonies have submitted to your Government, shown their Affection to your Interest, and patiently borne their Grievances, you are to *suppose* them always inclined to revolt, and treat them accordingly. Quarter Troops among them, who by their Insolence may *provoke* the rising of Mobs, and by their Bullets and Bayonets *suppress* them. By this Means, like the Husband who uses his Wife ill *from Suspicion,* you may in Time convert your *Suspicions* into *Realities.*

V. Remote Provinces must have *Governors,* and *Judges,* to represent the Royal Person, and execute every where the delegated Parts of his Office and Authority. You Ministers know, that much of the Strength of Government depends on the *Opinion* of the People; and much of that Opinion on the Choice of Rulers placed immediately over them. If you send them wise and good Men for Governors, who study the Interest of the Colonists, and advance their Prosperity, they will think their King wise and good, and that he wishes the Welfare of his Subjects. If you send them learned and upright Men for judges, they will think him a Lover of Justice. This may attach your Provinces more to his Government. You are therefore to be careful who you recommend for those Offices. If you can find Prodigals who have ruined their Fortunes, broken Gamesters or Stock-Jobbers, these may do well as *Governors;* for they will probably be rapacious, and provoke the People by their Extortions. Wrangling Proctors and pettyfogging Lawyers too are not amiss, for they will be for ever disputing and quarrelling with their little Parliaments, if withal they should be ignorant, wrong-headed and insolent, so much the better. Attorneys Clerks and New-gate Solicitors will do for *Chief-Justices,* especially if they hold their Places *during your Pleasure:* And all will contribute to impress those ideas of your Government that are proper for a People *you would wish to renounce it.*

VI. To confirm these Impressions, and strike them deeper, whenever the Injured come to the Capital with Complaints of Mal-administration, Oppression, or Injustice, punish such Suitors with long Delay, enormous Expense, and a final Judgment in Favor of the Oppressor. This will have an admirable Effect every Way. The Trouble of future Complaints will be prevented, and Governors and Judges will be encouraged to farther Acts of Oppression and Injustice; and thence the People may become more disaffected, *and at length desperate.*

VII. When such Governors have crammed their Coffers, and made themselves so odious to the People that they can no longer remain among them with Safety to their Persons, recall and *reward* them with Pensions. You may make them *Baronets* too, if that respectable Order should not think fit to resent it. All will contribute to encourage new Governors in the same Practices, and make the supreme Government *detestable.*

VIII. If when you are engaged in War, your Colonies should vie in liberal Aids of Men and Money against the common Enemy, upon your simple Requisition, and give far beyond their Abilities, reflect, that a Penny taken from them by your Power is more honorable to you than a Pound presented by their Benevolence. Despise therefore their voluntary Grants, and resolve to harass them with novel Taxes. They will probably complain to your Parliaments that they are taxed by a Body in which they have no Representative, and that this is contrary to common Right. They will petition for Redress. Let the Parliaments flout their Claims, reject their Petitions, refuse even to suffer the reading of them, and treat the Petitioners with the utmost Contempt. Nothing can have a better Effect, in producing the Alienation proposed; for though many can forgive Injuries, *none ever forgave Contempt.*

IX. In laying these Taxes, never regard the heavy burdens those remote People already undergo, in defending their own Frontiers, supporting their own provincial Governments, making new Roads, building Bridges, Churches and other public Edifices, which in old Countries have been done to your Hands by your Ancestors, but which occasion constant Calls and Demands on the Purses of a new People. Forget the *Restraints* you lay on their Trade for *your own* Benefit, and the Advantage a *Monopoly* of this Trade gives your exacting Merchants. Think nothing of the Wealth those Merchants and your Manufacturers acquire by the Colony Commerce; their increased Ability thereby to pay Taxes at home; their accumulating, in the Price of their Commodities, most of those Taxes, and so levying them from their consuming Customers: All this, and the Employment and Support of thousands of your Poor by the Colonists, you are *entirely to forget.* But remember to make your arbitrary Tax more grievous to your Provinces, by public Declarations importing that your Power of taxing them has *no limits,* so that when you take from them without their Consent a Shilling in the Pound, you have a clear Right to the other nineteen. This will probably weaken every Idea of *Security in their Property,* and convince them that under such a Government *they have nothing they can call their own;* which can scarce fail of producing *the happiest Consequences!*

X. Possibly indeed some of them might still comfort themselves, and say, Though we have no Property, we have yet *something* left that is valuable; we have constitutional *Liberty* both of Person and of Conscience. This King, these Lords, and these Commons, who it seems are too remote from us to know us and feel for us, cannot take from us our *Habeas Corpus* Right, or our Right of Trial *by a Jury of our Neighbors:* They cannot deprive us of the Exercise of our Religion, alter our ecclesiastical Constitutions, and compel us to be Papists if they please, or Mahometans. To annihilate this Comfort, begin by Laws to perplex their Commerce with infinite Regulations impossible to be remembered and observed; ordain Seizures of their Property for every Failure; take away the Trial of such Property by Jury, and give it to arbitrary Judges of your own appointing, and of the lowest Characters in the Country, whose Salaries and Emoluments are to arise out of the Duties or Condemnations, and whose Appointments are *during Pleasure.* Then let there be a formal Declaration of both Houses, that Opposition to your Edicts is *Treason,* and that Persons suspected of Treason in the Provinces may, according to some obsolete Law, be seized and sent to the Metropolis of the Empire for Trial; and pass an Act that those there charged with certain other Offences shall be sent away in Chains from their Friends and Country to be tried in the same Manner for Felony. Then erect a new Court of Inquisition among them, accompanied by an armed Force, with Instructions to transport all such suspected Persons, to be ruined by the Expense if they bring over Evidences to prove their Innocence, or be found guilty and hanged if they can't afford it. And lest the People should think you cannot possibly go any farther, pass another solemn declaratory Act, that King, Lords, and Commons had, hath, and of Right ought to have, full Power and Authority to make Statutes of sufficient Force and Validity to bind the unrepresented Provinces in all cases whatsoever. This will include *Spiritual* with temporal; and taken together, must operate wonderfully to your Purpose, by convincing them, that they are at present under a Power something like that spoken of in the Scriptures, which can not only *kill their Bodies,* but *damn their Souls* to all Eternity, by compelling them, if it pleases, *to worship the Devil.*

XI. To make your Taxes more odious, and more likely to procure Resistance, send from the Capital a Board of Officers to superintend the Collection, composed of the most *indiscreet, illbred* and *insolent* you can find. Let these have large salaries out of the extorted revenue, and live in open grating Luxury upon the Sweat and Blood of the Industrious, whom they are to worry continually with groundless and expensive Prosecutions before the above-mentioned arbitrary Revenue-Judges, all *at the Cost of the Party prosecuted* though acquitted, because *the King is to pay no Costs.* Let these Men *by your Order* be exempted from all the common Taxes and Burdens of the Province, though they and their Property are protected by its Laws. If any Revenue Officers are *suspected* of the least Tenderness for the People, discard them. If others are justly complained of, protect and reward them. If any of the Under-officers behave so as to provoke the People to drub them, promote those to better Offices: This will encourage others to procure for themselves such profitable Drubbings, by multiplying and enlarging such Provocations, and *all with work towards the End you aim at.*

XII. Another Way to make your Tax odious, is to misapply the Produce of it. If it was originally appropriated for the *Defense* of the Provinces and the better Support of Government, and the Administration of Justice where it may be *necessary,* then apply none of it to that *Defense,* but bestow it where it is *not necessary,* in augmented Salaries or Pensions to every Governor who has distinguished himself by his Enmity to the People, and by calumniating them to their Sovereign. This will make them pay it more unwillingly, and be more apt to quarrel with those that collect it, and those that imposed it, who will quarrel again with them, and all shall contribute to your *main Purpose* of making them *weary of your Government.*

XIII. If the People of any Province have been accustomed to support their own Governors and Judges to Satisfaction, you are to apprehend that such Governors and Judges may be thereby influenced to treat the People kindly, and to do them Justice. This is another Reason for applying Part of that Revenue in larger Salaries to such Governors and Judges, given, as their Commissions are, *during your Pleasure* only, forbidding them to take any Salaries from their Provinces; that thus the People may no longer hope any Kindness from their Governors, or (in Crown Cases) any Justice from their Judges. And as the Money thus misapplied in one Province is extorted from all, probably *all will resent the Misapplication.*

XIV. If the Parliaments of your Provinces should dare to claim Rights or complain of your Administration, order them to be harassed with repeated *Dissolutions.* If the same Men are continually returned by new Elections, adjourn their Meetings to some Country Village where they cannot be accommodated, and there keep them *during Pleasure;* for this, you know, is your Prerogative; and an excellent one it is, as you may manage it, to promote Discontents among the People, diminish their Respect, and *increase their Disaffection.*

XV. Convert the brave honest Officers of your Navy into pimping Tide-waiters and Colony Officers of the Customs. Let those who in Time of War fought gallantly in Defense of the Commerce of their Countrymen, in Peace be taught to prey upon it. Let them learn to be corrupted by great and real Smugglers; but (to show their Diligence) scour with armed Boats every Bay, Harbor, River, Creek, Cove or Nook throughout the Coast of your Colonies, stop and detain every Coaster, every Wood-boat, every Fisherman, tumble their Cargoes, and even their Ballast, inside out and upside down; and if a Pennorth of Pins is found un-entered, let the Whole be seized and confiscated. Thus shall the Trade of your Colonists suffer more from their Friends in Time of Peace, than it did from their Enemies in War. Then let these Boats Crews land upon every Farm in their Way, rob the Orchards, steal the Pigs and Poultry, and insult the Inhabitants. If the injured and exasperated Farmers, unable to procure other Justice, should attack the Aggressors, drub them and burn their Boats, you are to call this *High Treason* and *Rebellion,* order Fleets and Armies into their Country, and threaten to carry all the Offenders three thousand Miles to be hanged, drawn and quartered. *O! this will work admirably!*

XVI. If you are told of Discontents in your Colonies, never believe that they are general, or that you have given Occasion for them; therefore do not think of applying any Remedy, or of changing any offensive Measure. Redress no Grievance, lest they should be encouraged to demand the Redress of some other Grievance. Grant no Request that is just and reasonable, lest they should make another that is unreasonable. Take all your Informations of the State of the Colonies from your Governors and Officers in Enmity with them. Encourage and reward these *Leasingmakers;* secrete their lying Accusations lest they should be confuted; but act upon them as the clearest Evidence, and believe nothing you hear from the Friends of the People. Suppose all *their* Complaints to be invented and promoted by a few factious Demagogues, whom if you could catch and hang, all would be quiet. Catch and hang a few of them accordingly; and the *Blood of the Martyrs* shall *work Miracles* in favor of your Purpose.

XVII. If you see *rival Nations* rejoicing at the Prospect of your Disunion with your Provinces, and endeavoring to promote it: If they translate, publish and applaud all the Complaints of your discontented Colonists, at the same Time privately stimulating you to severer Measures; let not that *alarm* or offend you. Why should it? since you all mean *the same Thing*.

XVIII. If any Colony should at their own charge erect a Fortress to secure their Port against the Fleets of a foreign Enemy, get your Governor to betray that Fortress into your Hands. Never think of paying what it cost the Country, for that would *look*, at least, like some Regard for Justice; but turn it into a Citadel to awe the Inhabitants and curb their Commerce. If they should have lodged in such Fortress the very Arms they bought and used to aid you in your Conquests, seize them all, twill provoke like *Ingratitude* added to *Robbery*. One admirable effect of these operations will be, to discourage every other Colony from erecting such Defenses, and so their and your Enemies may more easily invade them, to the great Disgrace of your Government, and of course *the Furtherance of your Project*.

XIX. Send Armies into their Country under Pretence of protecting the Inhabitants; but instead of garrisoning the Forts on their Frontiers with those Troops, to prevent Incursions, demolish those Forts, and order the Troops into the Heart of the Country, that the Savages may be encouraged to attack the Frontiers, and that the Troops may be protected by the Inhabitants: This will seem to proceed from your Ill will or your Ignorance, and contribute farther to produce and strengthen an Opinion among them, *that you are no longer fit to govern them.*

XX. Lastly, Invest the General of your Army in the Provinces with great and unconstitutional Powers, and free him from the Control of even your own Civil Governors. Let him have Troops enough under his Command, with all the Fortresses in his Possession; and who knows but (like some provincial Generals in the Roman Empire, and encouraged by the universal Discontent you have produced) he may take it into his Head to set up for himself. If he should, and you have carefully practiced these few *excellent Rules* of mine, take my Word for it, all the Provinces will immediately join him, and you will that Day (if you have not done it sooner) get rid of the Trouble of governing them, and all the *Plagues* attending their *Commerce* and Connection from thenceforth and for ever.

Q.E.D.

AN EDICT BY THE KING OF PRUSSIA, *THE PUBLIC ADVERTISER,* SEPTEMBER 22, 1773

The Subject of the following Article of Foreign Intelligence being exceeding extraordinary, is the Reason of its being separated from the usual Articles of *Foreign News.*

Dantzick, September 5.

We have long wondered here at the Supineness of the English Nation, under the Prussian impositions upon its trade entering our Port. We did not till lately know the *Claims,* ancient and modern, that hang over that Nation, and therefore could not suspect that it might submit to those impositions from a Sense of *Duty,* or from Principles of *Equity.* The following *Edict,* just made public, may, if serious, throw some Light upon this Matter.

Frederick, by the Grace of God, King of Prussia, &c. &c. &c. to all present and to come, Health. The Peace now enjoyed throughout our Dominions, having afforded us Leisure to apply ourselves to the Regulation of Commerce, the Improvement of our Finances, and at the same time the easing our *Domestic Subjects* in their Taxes: For these Causes, and other good Considerations us thereunto moving, We hereby make known, that after having deliberated these Affairs in our Council, present our dear Brothers, and other great Officers of the State, members of the same, We, of our certain Knowledge, full Power and Authority Royal, have made and issued this present Edict, viz.

Whereas it is well known to all the World, that the first German Settlements made in the Island of Britain, were by Colonies of People, Subjects to our renowned Ducal Ancestors, and drawn from *their* Dominions, under the Conduct of Hengist, Horsa, Hella, Uffa, Cerdicus, Ida, and others; and that the said Colonies have flourished under the Protection of our august House, for Ages past, have never been *emancipated* therefrom, and yet have hitherto yielded little Profit to the same. And whereas We ourself have in the last War fought for and defended the said Colonies against the Power of France, and thereby enabled them to make conquests from the said Power in America, for which we have not yet received adequate compensation. And whereas it is just and expedient that a Revenue should be raised from the said Colonies in Britain towards our Indemnification; and that those who are Descendants of our ancient Subjects, and thence still owe us due Obedience, should contribute to the replenishing of our Royal Coffers, as they must have done had their Ancestors remained in the Territories now to us appertaining: We do therefore hereby ordain and command, That from and after the Date of these Presents, there shall be levied and paid to our Officers of the Customs, on all goods, wares and merchandises, and on all grain and other produce of the earth exported from the said Island of Britain, and on all Goods of whatever Kind imported into the same, a *Duty* of *Four and an Half* per Cent. *ad Valorem*, for the Use of us and our Successors. And that the said Duty may more effectually be collected, We do hereby ordain, that all Ships or Vessels bound from Great Britain to any other Part of the World, or from any other Part of the World to Great Britain, shall in their respective Voyages touch at our Port of Koningsberg, there to be unladen, searched, and charged with the said Duties.

And whereas there have been from time to time discovered in the said Island of Great Britain by our Colonists there, many mines or beds of iron stone; and sundry subjects of our ancient dominion, skilful in converting the said stone into metal, have in times past transported themselves thither, carrying with them and communicating that art; and the inhabitants of the said island, *presuming* that they had a natural right to make the best use they could of the natural productions of their country for their own benefit, have not only built furnaces for smelting the said stone into iron, but have erected plating forges, slitting mills, and steel furnaces, for the more convenient manufacturing of the same, thereby endangering a diminution of the said manufacture in our ancient dominion. We *do therefore* hereby farther ordain, that from and after the date hereof, no mill or other engine for slitting or rolling of iron, or any plating forge to work with a tilt-hammer, or any furnace for making steel, shall be erected or continued in the said Island of Great Britain: And the Lord Lieutenant of every County in the said Island is hereby commanded, on Information of any such Erection within his County, to order and by Force to cause the same to be abated and destroyed, as he shall answer the neglect thereof to us at his peril. But We are nevertheless graciously pleased to permit the inhabitants of the said island to transport their iron into Prussia, there to be manufactured, and to them returned, they paying our Prussian subjects for the workmanship, with all the costs of commission, freight and risk coming and returning, any thing herein contained to the contrary notwithstanding.

We do not however think fit to extend this our indulgence to the article of *wool,* but meaning to encourage not only the manufacturing of woolen cloth, but also the raising of wool in our ancient dominions, and to prevent *both,* as much as may be, in our said island, We do hereby absolutely forbid the Transportation of Wool from thence even to the Mother Country Prussia; and that those Islanders may be farther and more effectually restrained in making any Advantage of their own Wool in the Way of Manufacture, We command that none shall be carried *out of one County into another,* nor shall any Worsted-Bay, or Yam-Yam, Cloth, Says, Bays, Kerseys, Surges, Frizzes, Druggist, Cloth Surges, Saloons, or any other Drapery Stuffs, or Woolen Manufactures whatsoever, made up or mixed with Wool in any of the said Counties, be carried into any other County, or be Waterborne even across the smallest River or Creek, on Penalty of Forfeiture of the same, together with the Boats, Carriages, Horses, &c. that shall be employed in removing them. *Nevertheless* Our loving Subjects there are hereby permitted, (if they think proper) to use all their Wool as *Manure for the Improvement of their Lands.*

And whereas the Art and Mystery of making *Hats* hath arrived at great Perfection in Prussia, and the making of Hats by our remote Subjects ought to be as much as possible restrained. And forasmuch as the Islanders before-mentioned, being in possession of wool, beaver, and other furs, have *presumptuously* conceived they had a right to make some advantage thereof, by manufacturing the same into hats, to the prejudice of our domestic manufacture, We do therefore hereby strictly command and ordain, that no hats or felts whatsoever, dyed or undyed, finished or unfinished, shall be laden or put into or upon any vessel, cart, carriage or horse, to be transported or conveyed *out of one County* in the said Island *into another County,* or to *any other Place whatsoever,* by any Person or Persons whatsoever, on Pain of forfeiting the same, with a Penalty of *Five Hundred Pounds* Sterling for every Offence. Nor shall any Hat-maker in any of the said Counties employ more than two Apprentices, on Penalty of *Five Pounds* Sterling per Month: We intending hereby that such Hat-makers, being so restrained both in the Production and Sale of their Commodity, may find no Advantage in continuing their Business. But lest the said Islanders should suffer Inconveniency by the Want of Hats, We are farther graciously pleased to permit them to send their Beaver Furs to Prussia; and We also permit Hats made thereof to be exported from Prussia to Britain, the People thus favored to pay all costs and charges of manufacturing, interest, commission to our merchants, insurance and freight going and returning, as in the case of iron.

And lastly, Being willing farther to favor Our said Colonies in Britain, We do hereby also ordain and command, that all the Thieves, Highway and Street-Robbers, House-breakers, Forgerers, Murderers, Sodomites, and Villains of every Denomination, who have forfeited their Lives to the Law in Prussia, but whom We, in Our great Clemency, do not think fit here to hang, shall be emptied out of our jails into the said Island of Great Britain *for the* better peopling *of that Country.*

We flatter Ourselves that these Our Royal Regulations and Commands will be thought *just* and *reasonable* by Our much-favored Colonists in England, the said Regulations being copied from their own Statutes of 10 and 11 Will. iii. C. 10, 5 Geo. ii. C. 22, 23 Geo. ii. C. 29, 4 Geo. I. C. 11, and from other equitable Laws made by their Parliaments, or from Instructions given by their Princes, or from Resolutions of both Houses entered into for the good *Government* of their own Colonies in Ireland and America.

And all Persons in the said Island are hereby cautioned not to oppose in any wise the Execution of this Our Edict, or any Part thereof, such Opposition being High Treason, of which all who are *suspected* shall be transported in Fetters from Britain to Prussia, there to be tried and executed according to the *Prussian Law.*

Such is our Pleasure.

Given at Potsdam this twenty-fifth Day of the Month of August, One Thousand Seven Hundred and Seventy-three, and in the Thirty-third Year of our Reign.

By the King in his Council

RECHTMAESSIG, *Secretary.*

Some take this Edict to be merely one of the King's *Jeux d'Esprit:* Others suppose it serious, and that he means a quarrel with England: But all here think the assertion it concludes with, that these Regulations are copied from Acts of the English Parliament respecting their Colonies, a very *injurious* one: it being impossible to believe, that a People distinguished for their *Love of Liberty*, a Nation so *wise*, so *liberal in its sentiments*, so *just and equitable* towards its *neighbors*, should, from mean and *injudicious* Views of *petty immediate Profit*, treat *its own Children* in a Manner so *arbitrary* and tyrannical!

In a letter the following month to his son William, who was the royal governor of New Jersey and showing dangerous signs of being too loyal to the British, Franklin described how the pieces were received and the pleasure he got watching an English house party believe the Prussian hoax.

TO WILLIAM FRANKLIN, OCTOBER 6, 1773

Dear Son,

. . . From a long and thorough consideration of the subject, I am indeed of the opinion that the Parliament has no right to make any law whatever binding on the colonies. That the king, and not the king, lords, and commons collectively, is their sovereign; and that the king with their respective parliaments, is their only legislator. I know your sentiments differ from mine on these subjects. You are a thorough government man, which I do not wonder at, nor do I aim at converting you. I only wish you to act uprightly and steadily, avoiding that duplicity, which in [the case of Governor] Hutchinson, adds contempt to indignation. If you can promote the prosperity of your people, and leave them happier than you found them, whatever your political principles are, your memory will be honored.

I have written two pieces here lately for the *Public Advertiser,* on American affairs, designed to expose the conduct of this country towards the colonies, in a short, comprehensive, and striking view, and stated therefore in out-of-the-way forms, as most likely to take the general attention. The first was called, *Rules by which a great empire may be reduced to a small one*; the second, *An Edict of the king of Prussia.* I sent you one of the first, but could not get enough of the second to spare you one, though my clerk went the next morning to the printers, and wherever they were sold. They were all gone but two.

In my own mind I preferred the first, as a composition for the quantity and variety of the matter contained, and a kind of spirited ending of each paragraph. But I find that others here generally prefer the second. I am not suspected as the author, except by one or two friends; and have heard the latter spoken of in the highest terms as the keenest and severest piece that has appeared here a long time. Lord Mansfield I hear said of it, that it *was very* able *and very* artful indeed; and would do mischief by giving here a bad impression of the measures of government; and in the colonies, by encouraging them in their contumacy. It is reprinted in the *Chronicle,* where you will see it, but stripped of all the capitalling and italicking, that intimate the allusions and mark the emphasis of written discourses, to bring them as near as possible to those spoken: printing such a piece all in one even small character seems to me like repeating one of Whitfield's Sermons in the monotony of a school-boy.

What made it the more noticed here was that people in reading it were, as the phrase is, *taken in,* till they had got half through it, and imagined it a real edict, to which mistake I suppose the King of Prussia's *character* must have contributed. I was down at Lord Le Despencer's when the post brought that day's papers. Mr. Whitehead was there too (Paul Whitehead, the author of Manners) who runs early through all the papers, and tells the company what he finds remarkable. He had them in another room, and we were chatting in the breakfast parlor, when he came running in to us, out of breath, with the paper in his hand. Here! says he, here's news for ye! *Here's the King of Prussia, claiming a right to this kingdom!* All stared, and I as much as any body; and he went on to read it. When he had read two or three paragraphs, a gentleman present said, *Damn his impudence, I dare say, we shall hear by next post that he is upon his march with one hundred thousand men to back this.* Whitehead, who is very shrewd, soon after began to smoke it, and looking in my face said, *I'll be hanged if this is not some of your American jokes upon us.* The reading went on, and ended with abundance of laughing, and a general verdict that it was a fair hit: and the piece was cut out of the paper and preserved in my lord's collection.

I don't wonder that Hutchinson should be dejected. It must be an uncomfortable thing to live among people who he is conscious universally detest him. Yet I fancy he will not have leave to come home, both because they know not well what to do with him, and because they do not very well like his conduct. I am ever your affectionate father,

B. Franklin

Franklin continued his satirical attacks a few months later with a piece that gave advice about what General Gage, the British commander in America, should do if he truly wanted to prevail. In it Franklin suggests that potential rebels such as John Hancock and Samuel Adams might be castrated, though he uses dashes to avoid spelling out the offensive word.

Sir,

Permit me, through the channel of your paper, to convey to the premier, by him to be laid before his mercenaries, our constituents, my own opinion, and that of many of my brethren, freeholders of this imperial kingdom of the most feasible method of humbling our rebellious vassals of North America. As we have declared by our representatives that we are the supreme lords of their persons and property, and their occupying our territory at such a remote distance without a proper control from us, except at a very great expense, encourages a mutinous disposition, and may, if not timely prevented, dispose them in perhaps less than a century to deny our authority, slip their necks out of the collar, and from being slaves set up for masters, more especially when it is considered that they are a robust, hardy people, encourage early marriages, and their women being amazingly prolific, they must of consequence in 100 years be very numerous, and of course be able to set us at defiance. Effectually to prevent which, as we have an undoubted right to do, it is humbly proposed, and we do hereby give it as part of our instructions to our representatives, that a bill be brought in and passed, and orders immediately transmitted to General Gage, our commander in chief in north America, in consequence of it, that all the males there be c-st—ed.

He may make a progress through the several towns of North America at the head of five battalions, which we hear our experienced generals, who have been consulted, think sufficient to subdue America if they were in open rebellion; for who can resist the intrepid sons of Britain, the terror of France and Spain, and the conquerors of America in Germany. Let a company of sow-gelders, consisting of 100 men, accompany the army. On their arrival at any town or village, let orders be given that on the blowing of the horn all the males be assembled in the market place. If the corps are men of skill and ability in their profession, they will make great dispatch, and retard but very little the progress of the army. There may be a clause in the bill to be left at the discretion of the general, whose powers ought to be very extensive, that the most notorious offenders, such as Hancock, Adams, &c. who have been the ringleaders in the rebellion of our servants, should be shaved quite close. But that none of the offenders may escape in the town of Boston, let all the males there suffer the latter operation, as it will be conformable to the modern maxim that is now generally adopted by our worthy constituents, that it is better that ten innocent persons should suffer than that one guilty should escape.

It is true, blood will be shed, but probably not many lives lost. Bleeding to a certain degree is salutary. The English, whose humanity is celebrated by all the world, but particularly by themselves, do not desire the death of the delinquent, but his reformation. The advantages arising from this scheme being carried into execution are obvious. In the course of fifty years it is probable we shall not have one rebellious subject in north America. This will be laying the axe to the root of the tree. In the mean time a considerable expense may be saved to the managers of the opera, and our nobility and gentry be entertained at a cheaper rate by the fine voices of our own c-st——-i, and the specie remain in the kingdom, which now, to an enormous amount, is carried every year to Italy. It might likewise be of service to our Levant trade, as we could supply the grand signors seraglio, and the harems of the grandees of the Turkish dominions with cargos of eunuchs, as also with handsome women, for which America is as famous as Circassia. I could enumerate many other advantages. I shall mention but one: it would effectually put a stop to the emigrations from this country now grown so very fashionable.

No doubt you will esteem it expedient that this useful project shall have an early insertion, that no time may be lost in carrying it into execution. I am, Mr. Printer, (for myself, and in behalf of a number of independent freeholders of great Britain) your humble servant,

A Freeholder of Old Sarum

PART 6

AMERICAN REBEL

America's first political cartoon, by Franklin, 1754

YOU ARE MY ENEMY

Defeated in his efforts to prevent a split, Franklin returned to America in 1775. That July, even after hostilities had erupted in Lexington and Concord, most Americans were not yet in favor of independence. The Continental Congress sent an "Olive Branch Petition" to the king seeking reconciliation. But Franklin proclaimed his own sentiments in favor of outright rebellion in a short and sharp letter he sent to his closest friend in London, the printer William Strahan. Franklin allowed the letter to be published to show his ardent views. But interestingly, he never actually mailed it to Strahan, with whom he in fact remained friends.

To WILLIAM STRAHAN, JULY 5, 1775

Mr. Strahan,

You are a Member of Parliament, and one of that majority which has doomed my country to destruction. You have begun to burn our towns, and murder our people. Look upon your hands! They are stained with the blood of your relations! You and I were long friends: you are now my Enemy, and I am, Yours,

B. Franklin

PROPOSED ARTICLES OF CONFEDERATION

In order for the colonies to become independent of Britain, they had to become less independent of each other. As one of the most traveled and least parochial of colonial leaders, Franklin had long espoused some form of confederation, beginning with his Albany Plan of 1754.

In July 1775, Franklin put forth the idea again in a proposed draft for Articles of Confederation that contained the seeds of the conceptual breakthrough that would eventually define America's federal system: a division of powers between a central government and those of the states. Franklin was, however, ahead of his time. His proposed central government was far more powerful than other Americans yet envisioned, indeed more powerful than the one eventually created by the actual Articles of Confederation that Congress began to draft the following year.

Much of the wording in Franklin's proposal was drawn from New England confederation plans that stretched back to one forged by settlements in Massachusetts and Connecticut in 1643. But the scope and powers went far beyond anything previously proposed. Congress would have only a single chamber, in which there would be proportional representation from each state based on population. It would have the power to levy taxes, make war, manage the military, enter into foreign alliances, settle disputes between colonies, form new colonies, issue a unified currency, establish a postal system, regulate commerce, and enact laws "necessary to the general welfare." Franklin also proposed that, instead of a single president, Congress appoint a twelve-person "executive council" whose members would serve for staggered three-year terms.

As Franklin fully realized, this pretty much amounted to a declaration of independence from Britain and a declaration of dependence by the colonies on each other, neither of which had widespread support yet. So he read his proposal into the record but did not force a vote on it. He was content to wait for history, and the rest of the Continental Congress, to catch up with him.

PROPOSED ARTICLES OF CONFEDERATION, JULY 21, 1775

Art. I. The Name of the Confederacy shall henceforth be *The United Colonies of North America.*

Art. II. The said United Colonies hereby severally enter into a firm League of Friendship with each other, binding on themselves and their Posterity, for their common Defense against their Enemies, for the Security of their Liberties and Properties, the Safety of their Persons and Families, and their mutual and general welfare.

Art. III. That each Colony shall enjoy and retain as much as it may think fit of its own present Laws, Customs, Rights, Privileges, and peculiar Jurisdictions within its own Limits; and may amend its own Constitution as shall seem best to its own Assembly or Convention.

Art. IV. That for the more convenient Management of general Interests, Delegates shall be annually elected in each Colony to meet in General Congress at such Time and Place as shall be agreed on in the next preceding Congress. Only where particular Circumstances do not make a Deviation necessary, it is understood to be a Rule, that each succeeding Congress be held in a different Colony till the whole Number be gone through, and so in perpetual Rotation; and that accordingly the next Congress after the present shall be held at Annapolis in Maryland.

Art. V. That the Power and Duty of the Congress shall extend to the Determining on War and Peace, to sending and receiving Ambassadors, and entering into Alliances, the Reconciliation with Great Britain; the Settling all Disputes and Differences between Colony and Colony about Limits or any other cause if such should arise; and the Planting of new Colonies when proper. The Congress shall also make such general Ordinances as thought necessary to the General Welfare, particular Assemblies cannot be competent to; viz. those that may relate to our general Commerce or general Currency; to the Establishment of Posts; and the Regulation of our common Forces. The Congress shall also have the Appointment of all Officers civil and military, appertaining to the general Confederacy, such as General Treasurer Secretary, &c.

Art. VI. All Charges of Wars, and all other general Expenses to be incurred for the common Welfare, shall be defrayed out of a common Treasury, which is to be supplied by each Colony in proportion to its Number of Male Polls between 16 and 60 Years of Age; the Taxes for paying that proportion are to be laid and levied by the Laws of each Colony.

Art. VII. The Number of Delegates to be elected and sent to the Congress by each Colony, shall be regulated from time to time by the Number of such Polls returned, so as that one Delegate be allowed for every [5000] Polls. And the Delegates are to bring with them to every Congress an authenticated Return of the number of Polls in their respective Provinces, which is to be annually taken, for the Purposes above-mentioned.

Art. VIII. Each Delegate at the Congress, shall have a Vote in all Cases; and if necessarily absent, shall be allowed to appoint any other Delegate from the same Colony to be his Proxy, who may vote for him.

Art. IX. An executive Council shall be appointed by the Congress out of their own Body, consisting of 12 persons; of whom in the first appointment four shall be for one Year, four for two Years, and four for three Years; and as the said Terms expire, the vacancies shall be filled by Appointments for three Years, whereby One Third of the Members will be changed annually. This Council in the Recess of the Congress is to execute what shall have been enjoined thereby; to manage the general Business and Interests to receive Applications from foreign Countries; to prepare Matters for the Consideration of the Congress; to fill up (*pro tempore*) continental Offices that fall vacant; and to draw on the General Treasurer for such Monies as may be necessary for general Services, and appropriated by the Congress to such Services.

Art. X. No Colony shall engage in an offensive War with any Nation of Indians without the Consent of the Congress, or great Council above-mentioned, who are first to consider the Justice and Necessity of such War.

Art. XI. A perpetual Alliance offensive and defensive, is to be entered into as soon as may be with the Six Nations; their Limits to be secured to them; their Land not to be encroached on, nor any private Purchases made of them hereafter to be held good; nor any Contract for Lands to be made but between the Great Council of the Indians at Onondaga and the General Congress. The Boundaries and Lands of all the other Indians shall also be ascertained and secured to them in the same manner; and Persons appointed to reside among them in proper Districts, who shall take care to prevent Injustice in the Trade with them. And all Purchases from them shall be by the Congress for the General Advantage and Benefit of the United Colonies.

Art. XII. As all new Institutions may have Imperfections which only Time and Experience can discover, it is agreed, that the General Congress from time to time shall propose such Amendment of this Constitution as may be found necessary; which being approved by a Majority of the Colony Assemblies, shall be equally binding with the rest of the Articles of this Confederation.

Art. XIII. Any and every Colony from Great Britain upon the Continent of North America not at present engaged in our Association, may upon be received into this Confederation, viz. the West India Islands, Quebec, St. Johns, Nova Scotia, Bermudas, and the East and West Floridas: and shall thereupon be entitled to all the Advantages of our Union, mutual Assistance and Commerce.

These Articles shall be proposed to the Several Provincial Conventions or Assemblies, to be by them considered, and if approved they are advised to empower their Delegates to agree to and ratify the same in the ensuing Congress. After which the *Union* thereby established is to continue firm till the Terms of Reconciliation proposed in the Petition of the last Congress to the King are agreed to; till the Acts since made restraining the American Commerce and Fisheries are repealed; till Reparation is made for the Injury done to Boston by shutting up its Port; for the Burning of Charlestown; and for the Expense of this unjust War; and till all the British Troops are withdrawn from America. On the Arrival of these Events the Colonies are to return to their former Connection and Friendship with Britain: But on Failure thereof this Confederation is to be perpetual.

THE RATTLESNAKE AS AMERICA'S SYMBOL

In Philadelphia, a group of Marine units were being organized to try to capture British arms shipments. Franklin noticed that one of their drummers had painted a rattlesnake on his drum emblazoned with the words "Don't tread on me." In an anonymous article, filled with bold humor and a touch of venom, Franklin suggested that this should be the symbol and motto of America's fight. Christopher Gadsen, a delegate to Congress from South Carolina, picked up the suggestion in Franklin's article and subsequently designed a yellow flag with a rattlesnake emblazoned "Don't Tread on Me." It was flown in early 1776 by America's first Marine units and later many other militias.

THE PENNSYLVANIA JOURNAL, DECEMBER 27, 1775

Messrs. Printers,

I observed on one of the drums belonging to the marines now rais-ing, there was painted a Rattle-Snake, with this modest motto under it, "Don't tread on me." As I know it is the custom to have some device on the arms of every country, I supposed this may have been intended for the arms of America; and as I have nothing to do with public affairs, and as my time is perfectly my own, in order to divert an idle hour, I sat down to guess what could have been intended by this uncommon de-vice—I took care, however, to consult on this occasion a person who is acquainted with heraldry, from whom I learned, that it is a rule among the learned in that science "That the worthy properties of the animal, in the crest-born, shall be considered," and, "That the base ones cannot have been intended;" he likewise informed me that the ancients con-sidered the serpent as an emblem of wisdom, and in a certain attitude of endless duration—both which circumstances I suppose may have been had in view.

Having gained this intelligence, and recollecting that countries are sometimes represented by animals peculiar to them, it occurred to me that the Rattle-Snake is found in no other quarter of the world besides America, and may therefore have been chosen, on that account, to rep-resent her.

But then "the worthy properties" of a Snake I judged would be hard to point out—This rather raised than suppressed my curiosity, and having frequently seen the Rattle-Snake, I ran over in my mind every property by which she was distinguished, not only from other animals, but from those of the same genus or class of animals, endeavoring to fix some meaning to each, not wholly inconsistent with common sense.

I recollected that her eye excelled in brightness, that of any other animal, and that she has no eye-lids—She may therefore be esteemed an emblem of vigilance.—She never begins an attack, nor, when once engaged, ever surrenders: She is therefore an emblem of magnanimity and true courage.—As if anxious to prevent all pretensions of quar-relling with her, the weapons with which nature has furnished her, she conceals in the roof of her mouth, so that, to those who are unacquainted with her, she appears to be a most defenseless animal; and even when those weapons are shown and extended for her defense, they appear weak and contemptible; but their wounds however small, are decisive and fatal: Conscious of this, she never wounds till she has generously given notice, even to her enemy, and cautioned him against the danger of treading on her.

Was I wrong, Sir, in thinking this a strong picture of the temper and conduct of America? The poison of her teeth is the necessary means of digesting her food, and at the same time is certain destruction to her enemies. This may be understood to intimate that those things which are destructive to our enemies, may be to us not only harmless, but absolutely necessary to our existence.

I confess I was wholly at a loss what to make of the rattles, till I went back and counted them and found them just thirteen, exactly the number of the Colonies united in America; and I recollected too that this was the only part of the Snake which increased in numbers— Perhaps it might be only fancy, but, I conceited the painter had shown a half formed additional rattle, which, I suppose, may have been intended to represent the province of Canada.—'Tis curious and amazing to observe how distinct and independent of each other the rattles of this animal are, and yet how firmly they are united together, so as never to be separated but by breaking them to pieces.—One of those rattles singly, is incapable of producing sound, but the ringing of thirteen together, is sufficient to alarm the boldest man living. The Rattle-Snake is solitary, and associates with her kind only when it is necessary for their preservation. In winter, the warmth of a number together will preserve their lives, while singly, they would probably perish. The power of fascination attributed to her, by a generous construction, may be understood to mean, that those who consider the liberty and blessings which America affords, and once come over to her, never afterwards leave her, but spend their lives with her. She strongly resembles America in this, that she is beautiful in youth and her beauty increaseth with her age, "her tongue also is blue and forked as the lightning, and her abode is among impenetrable rocks."

Having pleased myself with reflections of this kind, I communicated my sentiments to a neighbor of mine, who has a surprising readiness at guessing at every thing which relates to public affairs, and indeed I should be jealous of his reputation, in that way, was it not that the event constantly shows that he has guessed wrong. He instantly declared it as his sentiments, that the Congress meant to allude to Lord North's declaration in the House of Commons, that he never would relax his measures until he had brought America to his feet, and to intimate to his Lordship, that were she brought to his feet, it would be dangerous treading on her. But, I am positive he has guessed wrong, for I am sure the Congress would not condescend, at this time of day, to take the least notice of his Lordship in that or any other way. In which opinion, I am determined to remain your humble servant,

An American Guesser

PART 7

AMBASSADOR IN PARIS

Sir, Passy, Feb. 22. 1781

I received the Letter your Excellency did me the honour of writing to me the 15th Instant, respecting Bills presented to you for Acceptance; drawn by Congress in favour of N. Tracey for 10,000 £ Sterling, payable at 90 Days sight; and desiring to know if I can furnish Funds for the Payment.

I have lately made a fresh & strong Application for more Money. I have not yet received a positive Answer. I have, however, two of the Christian Graces, Faith and Hope: But my Faith is only that of which the Apostle speaks, the Evidence of Things not seen. For in Truth I do not see at present how so many Bills drawn at random on our Ministers in France, Spain and Holland, are to be paid; nor that any thing but omnipotent Necessity can excuse the Imprudence of it. — Yet I think the Bills drawn upon us by the Congress ought at all Risques to be accepted. I shall accordingly use my best Endeavours to procure Money for their honourable Discharge against they become due; if you should not in the mean time be provided: And if those Endeavours fail, I shall be ready to break, run away, or go to Prison with you, as it shall please God.

Sir George Grand has return'd to me the Remainder of the Book of Promesses, sign'd by us, which his House had not an Opportunity of issuing. Perhaps the late Change of Affairs in that Country may

open

His Excellt. John Adams, Esqr.

Letter to John Adams, February 22, 1781

AN APPEAL TO FRANCE'S INTERESTS

Franklin arrived in Paris at the end of 1776 as America's envoy attempting to enlist the support of the French in the revolution. His diplomacy was an adroit mix of realism and idealism. After meeting with the French foreign minister, the Comte de Vergennes, Franklin wrote a memo on behalf of the three American commissioners explaining why it was in France's national interest to side with the Americans and reap the balance of power benefits (including islands in the West Indies) that would come from such a successful alliance.

To THE COMTE DE VERGENNES, JANUARY 5, 1777

To his Excellency the Comte de Vergennes, one of his most Christian Majesty's principal Secretaries of State, and Minister for Foreign Affairs.

The Congress, the better to defend their coasts, protect the trade, and drive off the enemy, have instructed us to apply to France for 8 ships of the line, completely manned, the expense of which they will undertake to pay. As other princes of Europe are lending or hiring their troops to Britain against America, it is apprehended that France may, if she thinks fit, afford our independent states the same kind of aid, without giving England just cause of complaint: but if England should on that account declare war we conceive that by the united force of France, Spain and America, she will lose all her possessions in the West Indies, much the greatest part of that commerce that has rendered her so opulent, and be reduced to that state of weakness and humiliation, she has by her perfidy, her insolence, and her cruelty both in the east and west, so justly merited.

We are also instructed to solicit the court of France for an immediate supply of twenty or thirty thousand muskets and bayonets, and a large quantity of ammunition and brass field pieces, to be sent under convoy. The united states engage for the payment of the arms, artillery and ammunition, and to defray the expense of the convoy. This application is now become the more necessary, as the private purchase made by Mr. Deane of those articles, is rendered ineffectual by an order forbidding their exportation.

We also beg it may be particularly considered, while the English are masters of the American seas and can, without fear of interruption, transport with such ease their army from one part of our extensive coast to another, and we can only meet them by land-marches, we may possibly, unless some powerful aid is given us, or some strong diversion made in our favor be so harassed, and put to such immense expense, as that finally our people will find themselves reduced to the necessity of ending the war by an accommodation.

The courts of France and Spain may rely with the fullest confidence, that whatever stipulations are made by us in case of granting such aid, will be ratified and punctually fulfilled by the Congress, who are determined to found their future character, with regard to justice and fidelity, on a full and perfect performance of all their present engagements.

North America now offers to France and Spain her amity and commerce. She is also ready to guarantee in the firmest manner to those nations all their present possessions in the West Indies, as well as those they shall acquire from the enemy in a war that may be consequential of such assistance as she requests. The interest of the three nations is the same. The opportunity of cementing them, and of securing all the advantages of that commerce, which in time will be immense, now presents itself. If neglected, it may never again return. We cannot help suggesting that a considerable delay may be attended with fatal consequences.

> B. Franklin, Silas Deane, Arthur Lee
> Plenipotentiaries from the Congress of the
> United States of North America

THE SALE OF THE HESSIANS

Franklin also waged a propaganda campaign, and the device he often used, once again, was that of satire. Along the lines of his Edict from the King of Prussia, Franklin published anonymously what purported to be a letter to the commander of the Hessian troops in America from a German count who got paid a bounty for the death of each of the soldiers he sent over. Because Britain had decided not to pay for any wounded soldiers, only for those who died, the count encouraged his commander to make sure that as many died as possible.

THE SALE OF THE HESSIANS, FEBRUARY 18, 1777

The Sale of the Hessians
FROM THE COUNT DE SCHAUMBERGH
TO THE BARON HOHENDORF,
COMMANDING THE HESSIAN TROOPS IN AMERICA
Rome, February 18, 1777

Monsieur Le Baron: On my return from Naples, I received at Rome your letter of the 27th December of last year. I have learned with unspeakable pleasure the courage our troops exhibited at Trenton, and you cannot imagine my joy on being told that of the 1,950 Hessians engaged in the fight, but 345 escaped. There were just 1,605 men killed, and I cannot sufficiently commend your prudence in sending an exact list of the dead to my minister in London. This precaution was the more necessary, as the report sent to the English ministry does not give but 1,455 dead. This would make 483,450 florins instead of 643,500 which I am entitled to demand under our convention. You will comprehend the prejudice which such an error would work in my finances, and I do not doubt you will take the necessary pains to prove that Lord North's list is false and yours correct.

The court of London objects that there were a hundred wounded who ought not to be included in the list, nor paid for as dead; but I trust you will not overlook my instructions to you on quitting Cassel, and that you will not have tried by human succor to recall the life of the unfortunates whose days could not be lengthened but by the loss of a leg or an arm. That would be making them a pernicious present, and I am sure they would rather die than live in a condition no longer fit for my service. I do not mean by this that you should assassinate them; we should be humane, my dear Baron, but you may insinuate to the surgeons with entire propriety that a crippled man is a reproach to their profession, and that there is no wiser course than to let every one of them die when he ceases to be fit to fight.

I am about to send to you some new recruits. Don't economize them. Remember glory before all things. Glory is true wealth. There is nothing degrades the soldier like the love of money. He must care only for honor and reputation, but this reputation must be acquired in the midst of dangers. A battle gained without costing the conqueror any blood is an inglorious success, while the conquered cover themselves with glory by perishing with their arms in their hands. Do you remember that of the 300 Lacedaemonians who defended the defile of Thermopylae, not one returned? How happy should I be could I say the same of my brave Hessians!

It is true that their king, Leonidas, perished with them: but things have changed, and it is no longer the custom for princes of the empire to go and fight in America for a cause with which they have no concern. And besides, to whom should they pay the thirty guineas per man if I did not stay in Europe to receive them? Then, it is necessary also that I be ready to send recruits to replace the men you lose. For this purpose I must return to Hesse. It is true, grown men are becoming scarce there, but I will send you boys. Besides, the scarcer the commodity the higher the price. I am assured that the women and little girls have begun to till our lands, and they get on not badly. You did right to send back to Europe that Dr. Crumerus who was so successful in curing dysentery. Don't bother with a man who is subject to looseness of the bowels. That disease makes bad soldiers. One coward will do more mischief in an engagement than ten brave men will do good. Better that they burst in their barracks than fly in a battle, and tarnish the glory of our arms. Besides, you know that they pay me as killed for all who die from disease, and I don't get a farthing for runaways. My trip to Italy, which has cost me enormously, makes it desirable that there should be a great mortality among them. You will therefore promise promotion to all who expose themselves; you will exhort them to seek glory in the midst of dangers; you will say to Major Maundorff that I am not at all content with his saving the 345 men who escaped the massacre of Trenton. Through the whole campaign he has not had ten men killed in consequence of his orders. Finally, let it be your principal object to prolong the war and avoid a decisive engagement on either side, for I have made arrangements for a grand Italian opera, and I do not wish to be obliged to give it up. Meantime I pray God, my dear Baron de Hohendorf, to have you in his holy and gracious keeping.

A FORM LETTER OF RECOMMENDATION

Franklin spent much of his first years in France coping with European supplicants who sought commissions to serve as officers in the American army. His collected letters are clogged with requests, more than 400 in all, some valiant and others vain. There was the mother who offered up three of her flock of sons, the Dutch surgeon who wanted to study bodies that had been blown apart, and the Benedictine monk who promised to pray for America if it would pay off his gambling debts. Franklin's favorite was a less than effusive recommendation he received from a mother which began: "Sir, If in your America one knows the secret of how to reform a detestable subject who has been the cross of his family . . ."

Not all the supplicants were vagabonds. Franklin was able to find, among those seeking commissions, a few great officers to recommend: the Marquis de Lafayette, Baron von Steuben (whose rank in the Prussian army Franklin inflated in his eagerness to get General Washington to take him), and Count Pulaski, a famed Polish fighter who became a heroic brigadier general for America. Nevertheless, Washington quickly grew testy about the number of aspiring officers Franklin was sending his way. "Our corps being already formed and fully officered," he wrote, "every new arrival is only a source of embarrassment to Congress and myself and of disappointment and chagrin to the gentlemen who come over."

So Franklin tried as best he could to reject most of the commission-seekers. To cope with the constant flood of requests—or perhaps merely to make fun of them—he even composed a form letter which he had printed up.

APRIL 2, 1777

Sir,

The Bearer of this who is going to America, presses me to give him a Letter of Recommendation, though I know nothing of him, not even his Name. This may seem extraordinary, but I assure you it is not un-common here. Sometimes indeed one unknown Person brings me an-other equally unknown, to recommend him; and sometimes they recommend one another! As to this Gentleman, I must refer you to himself for his Character and Merits, with which he is certainly better acquainted than I can possibly be; I recommend him however to those Civilities which every Stranger, of whom one knows no Harm, has a Right to, and I request you will do him all the good Offices and show him all the Favor that on further Acquaintance you shall find him to deserve. I have the honor to be, &c.

THE TWELVE COMMANDMENTS, TO MADAME BRILLON

Among Franklin's many reputations was that of a legendary and lecherous old lover who had many mistresses among the ladies of Paris. The reality was, truth be told, somewhat less titillating. His famed female friends were mistresses only of his mind and soul. Yet that hardly made their relationships less intriguing.

The first of these was with a talented and high-strung neighbor in Passy, Madame Brillon de Jouy, an accomplished musician who was noted for her performances on the harpsichord and the new pianos that were becoming fashionable in France. Madame Brillon, who was 33 when she met Franklin, was buffeted by conflicting passions and variable moods. Her husband, 24 years her senior (but 14 years younger than Franklin), was wealthy, doting and unfaithful. She had two daughters with beautiful singing voices and one of the most elegant estates in Passy, yet she was prone to fits of depression and self-pity. Although she spoke no English, she and Franklin exchanged more than 130 letters in French during their eight-year relationship, and she was able not only to enchant him but also to manipulate him.

Madame Brillon's letters were suggestive. "I know my penitent's weak spot, I shall tolerate it! As long as he loves God, America, and me above all things, I absolve him of all of his sins, present, past and *future*." She went on to describe the seven cardinal sins, merrily noting that he had conquered well the first six, ranging from pride to sloth. When she got to the seventh, the sin of lust, she became a bit coy: "The seventh—I shall not name it. All great men are tainted with it . . . You have loved, my dear brother; you have been kind and lovable; you have been loved in return! What is so damnable about that?"

Franklin responded with his own revision of the Ten Commandments.

To Madame Brillon, March 10, 1778

I am charmed with the goodness of my spiritual guide, and resign myself implicitly to her conduct, as she promises to lead me to heaven in a road so delicious, when I could be content to travel thither even in the roughest of all the ways with the pleasure of her company.

How kindly partial to her penitent, in finding him, on examining his conscience, guilty of only one capital sin, and to call that by the gentle name of a *foible!*

I lay fast hold of your promise to absolve me of all sins past, present, and *future*, on the easy and pleasing condition of loving God, America, and my Guide above all things. I am in raptures when I think of being absolved of the future.

People commonly speak of *Ten* Commandments. I have been taught that there are *twelve*. The *first* was, *Increase and multiply* and replenish the Earth. The *twelfth* is a new Commandment I give unto you, *that ye love one another.* It seems to me that they are a little misplaced, and that the last should have been the first. However, I never made any difficulty about that, but was always willing to obey them both whenever I had an opportunity. Pray tell me, my dear Casuist, whether my keeping religiously these two commandments, though not in the Decalogue, may not be accepted in compensation for my breaking so often one of the ten, I mean that which forbids coveting my neighbor's wife, and which *I confess* I break constantly, God forgive me, as often as I see or think of my lovely Confessor: And I am afraid I should never be able to repent of the Sin, even if I had the full possession of her.

And now I am consulting you upon a case of conscience, I will mention the opinion of a certain father of the church, which I find myself willing to adopt, though I am not sure it is orthodox. It is this, that the most effectual way to get rid of a certain temptation, is, as often as it returns, to comply with and satisfy it. Pray instruct me how far, I may venture to practice upon this principle?

But why should I be so scrupulous, when you have promised to absolve me of the *future!* Adieu, my charming Conductress, and believe me ever, with the sincerest Esteem and Affection,

Your most obedient humble Servant

A PROPOSED TREATY WITH MADAME BRILLON

Franklin was not successful in turning their relationship into a sexual one. Madame Brillon retreated by insisting that she be more like a flirtatious child to him than a lover. Yet despite being unwilling to satisfy his ardor, she remained jealous whenever he flirted or spent evenings with other ladies. "When you scatter your friendship, as you have done, my friendship does not diminish, but from now on I shall try to be somewhat sterner to your faults," she threatened. Franklin replied with a letter complaining that he got from her only small kisses and that he was able to share his affections without depriving her of any. He also used a salacious metaphor to describe how she had starved his "poor little boy" instead of making it "fat and jolly."

To Madame Brillon, July 27, 1778

What a difference, my dear friend, between you and me! You find my faults so many as to be innumerable, while I can see but one in you; and perhaps that is the fault of my spectacles. The fault I mean is that kind of covetousness, by which you would engross all my affection, and permit me none for the other amiable ladies of your country. You seem to imagine that it cannot be divided without being diminished: in which you mistake the nature of the thing and forget the situation in which you have placed and hold me.

You renounce and exclude arbitrarily everything corporal from our amour, except such a merely civil embrace now and then as you would permit to a country cousin; what is there then remaining that I may not afford to others without a diminution of what belongs to you? The operations of the mind, esteem, admiration, respect, and even affection for one object, may be multiplied as more objects that merit them present themselves, and yet remain the same to the first, which therefore has no room to complain of injury. They are in their nature as divisible as the sweet sounds of the forte piano produced by your exquisite skill: twenty people may receive the same pleasure from them, without lessening that which you kindly intend for me; and I might as reasonably require of your friendship, that they should reach and delight no ears but mine.

You see by this time how unjust you are in your demands, and in the open war you declare against me if I do not comply with them. Indeed it is I that have the most reason to complain. My poor little boy, whom you ought methinks to have cherished, instead of being fat and jolly like those in your elegant drawings, is meager and starved almost to death for want of the substantial nourishment which you his mother inhumanly deny him, and yet would now clip his little wings to prevent his seeking it elsewhere!

I fancy we shall neither of us get any thing by this war, and therefore as feeling my self the weakest, I will do what indeed ought always to be done by the wisest, be first in making the propositions for peace. That a peace may be lasting, the articles of the treaty should be regulated upon the principles of the most perfect equity and reciprocity. In this view I have drawn up and offer the following, viz.

ARTICLE 1.

There shall be eternal peace, friendship and love, between Madame B. and Mr. F.

ARTICLE 2.

In order to maintain the same inviolably, Madame B. on her part stipulates and agrees, that Mr. F. shall come to her whenever she sends for him.

ART. 3.

That he shall stay with her as long as she pleases.

ART. 4.

That when he is with her, he shall be obliged to drink tea, play chess, hear music; or do any other thing that she requires of him.

ART. 5.

And that he shall love no other woman but herself.

ART. 6.

And the said Mr. F. in his part stipulates and agrees, that he will go away from Madame B's whenever he pleases.

ART. 7.

That he will stay away as long as he please.

ART. 8.

That when he is with her he will do what he pleases.

ART. 9.

And that he will love any other woman as far as he finds her amiable.

Let me know what you think of these preliminaries. To me they seem to express the true meaning and intention of each party more plainly than most treaties. I shall insist pretty strongly on the eighth article, though without much hope of your consent to it; and on the ninth also, though I despair of ever finding any other woman that I could love with equal tenderness: being ever, my dear dear friend,

Yours most sincerely, B.F.

BAGATELLE OF THE EPHEMERA

The frustration of their relationship evoked from Franklin one of his most wistful and self-revealing little tales, *The Ephemera,* written to her after a stroll in the garden. (The theme came from an article he had printed in the *Pennsylvania Gazette* fifty years earlier.) He called these stories bagatelles, the French term for a sprightly musical piece. He had happened to overhear, he wrote, a lament by one of the tiny short-lived flies who realized that his seven hours on this planet were nearing an end. He ends with a pun on her name.

To Madame Brillon, September 20, 1778

You may remember, my dear friend, that when we lately spent that happy day in the delightful garden and sweet society of the *Moulin-Joli,* I stopped a little in one of our walks, and staid some time behind the company. We had been shown numberless skeletons of a kind of little fly, called an ephemere, all whose successive generations we were told were bred and expired within the day. I happened to see a living company of them on a leaf, who appeared to be engaged in conversation. You know I understand all the inferior animal tongues: my too great application to the study of them is the best excuse I can give for the little progress I have made in your charming language. I listened thro curiosity to the discourse of these little creatures, but as they in their national vivacity spoke three or four together, I could make but little of their discourse. I found however, by some broken expressions that I caught now and then, they were disputing warmly the merit of two foreign musicians, one a *cousin,* the other a *mosquito;* in which dispute they spent their time seemingly as regardless of the shortness of life, as if they had been sure of living a month. Happy people! Thought I, you live certainly under a wise, just and mild government, since you have no public grievances to complain of, nor any subject of contention but the perfections or imperfections of foreign music. I turned from them to an old greyheaded one, who was single on another leaf, and talking to himself. Being amused with his soliloquy, I have put it down in writing, in hopes it will likewise amuse her to whom I am so much indebted for the most pleasing of all amusements, her delicious company, and her heavenly harmony.

It was, says he, the opinion of learned philosophers of our race, who lived and flourished long before my time, that this vast world, the *Moulin-Joli,* could not itself subsist more than 18 hours; and I think there was some foundation for that opinion, since by the apparent motion of the great luminary that gives life to all nature, and which in my time has evidently declined considerably towards the ocean at the end of our earth, it must then finish its course, be extinguished in the waters that surround us, and leave the world in cold and darkness, necessarily producing universal death and destruction. I have lived seven of those hours; a great age, being no less than 420 minutes of time. How very few of us continue so long! I have seen generations born, flourish, and expire. My present friends are the children and grandchildren of the friends of my youth, who are now, alas, no more! And I must soon follow them; for by the course of nature, though still in health, I cannot expect to live above 7 or 8 minutes longer. What now avails all my toil and labor in amassing honey-dew on this leaf, which I cannot live to enjoy! What the political struggles I have been engaged in for the good of my *compatriots,* inhabitants of this bush; or my philosophical studies for the benefit of our race in general! For in politics, *what can laws do without morals!* Our present race of ephemeres will in a course of minutes, become corrupt like those of other and older bushes, and consequently as wretched. And in philosophy how small our progress! Alas, *art is long, and life short!* My friends would comfort me with the idea of a name they say I shall leave behind me; and they tell me I have *lived long enough, to nature and to glory:* but what will fame be to an *ephemere* who no longer exists? And what will become of all history, in the 18th hour, when the world itself, even the whole *Moulin-Joli,* shall come to its end, and be buried in universal ruin? To me, after all my eager pursuits, no solid pleasures now remain, but the reflection of a long life spent in meaning well, the sensible conversation of a few good lady-ephemeres, and now and then a kind smile, and a tune from the ever-amiable *Brillante.*

MADAME HELVÉTIUS AND ELYSIAN FIELDS

Franklin's other great female friend in Paris was Madame Helvétius, the widow of a noted French philosophe. She was a lively, outgoing and free-spirited bohemian who enjoyed projecting an earthy aura even at age 60. Franklin did more than flirt with her; by September of 1779, he was ardently proposing marriage in a way that was more than half-serious but retained enough ironic detachment to preserve their dignities. She led him on lightly. "I hoped that after putting such pretty things on paper," she scrawled, "you would come and tell me some." But she declined his marriage proposal, citing her loyalty to her late husband. That prompted Franklin to write her one of his most amusing bagatelles, Elysian Fields, in which he recounted a dream about going to heaven and discussing the matter with her late husband and his late wife, who had themselves married. Praising Madame Helvétius's looks over those of his departed wife, he suggested they take revenge.

TO MADAME HELVÉTIUS, DECEMBER 7, 1778

The Elysian Fields

Vexed by your barbarous resolution, announced so positively last evening, to remain single all your life in respect to your dear husband, I went home, fell on my bed, and, believing myself dead, found myself in the Elysian Fields.

I was asked if I desired to see anybody in particular. "Lead me to the home of the philosophers."

"There are two who live nearby in the garden: they are very good neighbors, and close friends of each other."

"Who are they?"

"Socrates and H———."

"I esteem them both prodigiously; but let me see first H———, because I understand a little French, but not one word of Greek."

He received me with great courtesy, having known me for some time, he said, by the reputation I had there. He asked me a thousand things about the war, and about the present state of religion, liberty, and the government in France.

"You ask nothing then of your dear friend Madame H———; nevertheless she still loves you excessively and I was at her place but an hour ago."

"Ah!" said he, "you make me remember my former felicity. But it is necessary to forget it in order to be happy here. During several of the early years, I thought only of her. Finally I am consoled. I have taken another wife. The most like her that I could find. She is not, it is true, so completely beautiful, but she has as much good sense, a little more of Spirit, and she loves me infinitely. Her continual study is to please me; and she has actually gone to hunt the best Nectar and the best Ambrosia in order to regale me this evening; remain with me and you will see her."

"I perceive," I said, "that your old friend is more faithful than you: for several good offers have been made her, all of which she has refused. I confess to you that I myself have loved her to the point of distraction; but she was hard-hearted to my regard, and has absolutely rejected me for love of you."

"I pity you," he said, "for your bad fortune; for truly she is a good and beautiful woman and very loveable. But the Abbé de la R———, and the Abbé M———, are they not still sometimes at her home?"

"Yes, assuredly, for she has not lost a single one of your friends."

"If you had won over the Abbé M——— (with coffee and cream)

to speak for you, perhaps you would have succeeded; for he is a subtle logician like Duns Scotus or St. Thomas; he places his arguments in such good order that they become nearly irresistible. Also, if the Abbé de la R——— had been bribed (by some beautiful edition of an old classic) to speak against you, that would have been better: for I have always observed, that when he advises something, she has a very strong penchant to do the reverse."

At these words the new Madame H———entered with the Nectar: at which instant I recognized her to be Madame F———, my old American friend. I reclaimed to her. But she told me coldly, "I have been your good wife forty-nine years and four months, nearly a half century; be content with that. Here I have formed a new connection, which will endure to eternity."

Offended by this refusal of my Eurydice, I suddenly decided to leave these ungrateful spirits, to return to the good earth, to see again the sunshine and you. Here I am! Let us revenge ourselves.

JOHN PAUL JONES

One of Franklin's duties in Paris was overseeing John Paul Jones, the brave and erratic sea commander who was conducting naval raids against Britain from a base in France. On one of these raids, Jones decided to kidnap a Scottish earl named Lord Selkirk, but the man was away, so the crew instead forced his wife to hand over the family silver. In a fit of noble guilt, Jones decided to buy the booty from his crew so that he could return it to the family. Franklin tried to help Jones resolve the problem, but it led to such a convoluted exchange of letters with the outraged earl that the silver was not returned until after the end of the war.

Franklin was able to help secure for Jones, in February of 1779, an old 40-gun man-of-war named the *Duras,* which Jones rechristened the *Bonhomme Richard* in his patron's honor. Jones was so thrilled that he paid a visit to Franklin's home in the Paris suburb of Passy to thank Franklin and his landlord Chaumont, who had helped supply Jones with uniforms and funds. There was perhaps another reason for the visit: Jones may have been having an illicit affair with Madame de Chaumont.

During this stay, an incident occurred that resembled a French farce. A wizened old woman, who was the wife of the Chaumonts' gardener, alleged that Jones tried to rape her. Franklin made a passing allusion to the alleged incident in a postscript to a letter, and Jones mistakenly assumed that "the mystery you so delicately mention" referred to the controversy that surrounded his killing of a rebellious crewmember years earlier. So he provided a long and anguished account of that old travail.

Franklin, bemused by Jones's detailed explanation about impaling the mutineer, replied that he had never heard that story and informed Jones that the "mystery" he alluded to referred, instead, to an allegation made by the gardener's wife that Jones had "attempted to ravish her" in the bushes of the estate. But Jones should not worry, Franklin said, because everyone at Passy found the tale to be the subject of great merriment. Madame Chaumont, whose own familiarity with Jones's sexual appetites did not prevent her from a great display of French insouciance, declared that "it gave a high idea of the strength of appetite and courage of the Americans."

They all ended up concluding, Franklin assured Jones, that it must have been a case of mistaken identity. As part of the Mardi Gras festivities, a chamber girl had apparently dressed up in one of his uniforms and, so they surmised, attacked the gardener's wife as a prank. It seems quite implausible that the gardener's wife, even in the dimness of early evening, could have been so easily fooled, but the explanation was satisfactory enough that the event was not mentioned in subsequent letters.

TO JOHN PAUL JONES, MARCH 14, 1779

Dear Sir,

I yesterday received your favor of the 6th. I did not understand from M. Alexander that Lord Selkirk had any particular objection to receiving the plate from you. It was general, that though he might not refuse it if offered him by a public body, as the Congress, he could not accept it from any private person whatever. I know nothing of m. Alexander's having any enmity to you, nor can I imagine any reason for it. But on the whole it seems to me not worth your while to give yourself any farther trouble about Lord Selkirk. You have now the disposal of what belongs to the Congress; and may give it with your own share if you think fit, in little encouragements to your men on particular occasions . . .

I have looked over the copy of my letter to you of February 24, not being able to imagine what part of it could give you the idea that I hinted at an affair I never knew. Not finding any thing in the letter, I suppose it must have been the postscript of which I have no copy; and which I know now that you could not understand, though I did not when I wrote it. The story I alluded to is this: l'abbé Rochon had just been telling me & Madame Chaumont that the old gardener & his wife had complained to the curate, of your having attacked her in the garden about 7 o'clock the evening before your departure; and attempted to ravish her, relating all the circumstances, some of which are not fit for me to write. The serious part of it was that three of her sons were determined to kill you, if you had not gone off; the rest occasioned some laughing: for the old woman being one of the grossest, coarsest, dirtiest & ugliest that one may find in a thousand, Madame Chaumont said it gave a high idea of the strength of appetite & courage of the Americans. A day or two after, I learnt that it was the femme de chambre of Mademoiselle Chaumont who had disguised herself in a suit I think of your clothes, to divert herself under that masquerade, as is customary the last evening of carnival: and that meeting the old woman in the garden, she took it into her head to try her chastity, which it seems was found proof.

As to the unhappy affair of which you give me an acct., there is no doubt but the facts being as you state them, the person must have been acquitted if he had been tried, it being merely *se defendendo.*

I wish you all the imaginable success in your present undertaking; being ever with sincere esteem &c.

B. Franklin

TO HIS DAUGHTER ON FAME, FRUGALITY, AND GRANDCHILDREN

Among Franklin's cards was his fame, and he was among a long line of statesmen, from Richelieu to Mettemich to Kissinger, to realize that with celebrity came cachet, and with that came influence. His lightning theories had been proved in France in 1752, his collected works published there in 1773, and a new edition of Poor Richard's *The Way to Wealth,* entitled *La Science du Bonhomme Richard,* was published soon after his arrival.

His fame was so great that, all of fashionable Paris seemed to desire some display of his benign countenance. Medallions were struck in various sizes, engravings and portraits were hung in homes, and his likeness graced snuff boxes and signet rings. "The numbers sold are incredible," he wrote his daughter Sarah "Sally" Franklin Bache. The fad went so far as to mildly annoy, though still amuse, the King himself. He gave a female friend, who had bored him with her praise of Franklin, a Sevres porcelain chamber pot with his cameo embossed inside.

In his letter to Sally, Franklin praises her industriousness, but he lapses into stern outrage at her request that she send him some fashionable French finery and instead offers an amusing solution to creating feathers and lace on her own. He also talks of his grandchildren. Temple, the illegitimate son of his own illegitimate son William, was serving as his secretary in Paris. But his enemies in Congress were trying to have Temple recalled, partly because his father had remained a loyalist. Sally's son Benjamin Bache was also in Paris, and Franklin was overseeing his education. Her other son, Will, was a toddler back in Philadelphia, and she had written an account of how he was offering his evening prayers to Hercules.

TO SARAH "SALLY" FRANKLIN BACHE, PASSY, JUNE 3, 1779

Dear Sally,

I have before me your letters of Oct. 22, and Jan. 17th: they are the only ones I received from you in the course of eighteen months. If you knew how happy your letters make me, and considered how many miscarry, I think you would write oftener . . .

The clay medallion of me you say you gave to Mr. Hopkinson was the first of the kind made in France. A variety of others have been made since of different sizes; some to be set in lids of snuff boxes, and some so small as to be worn in rings; and the numbers sold are incredible. These, with the pictures, busts, and prints, (of which copies upon copies are spread every where) have made your father's face as well known as that of the moon, so that he durst not do any thing that would oblige him to run away, as his phiz would discover him wherever he should venture to show it. It is said by learned etymologists that the name *Doll*, for the images children play with, is derived from the word IDOL; from the number of *dolls* now made of him, he may be truly said, *in that sense*, to be *i-dollized* in this country.

I think you did right to stay out of town till the summer was over for the sake of your child's health. I hope you will get out again this summer during the hot months; for I begin to love the dear little creature from your description of her.

I was charmed with the account you give me of your industry, the tablecloths of your own spinning, &c. but the latter part of the paragraph, that you had sent for linen from France because weaving and flax were grown dear; alas, that dissolved the charm; and your sending for long black pins, and lace, and *feathers!* disgusted me as much as if you had put salt into my strawberries. The spinning, I see, is laid aside, and you are to be dressed for the ball! you seem not to know, my dear daughter, that of all the dear things in this world, idleness is the dearest, except mischief.

The project you mention of removing *Temple* from me was an unkind one; to deprive an old man sent to serve his country in a foreign one, of the comfort of a child to attend him, to assist him in health and take care of him in sickness, would be cruel, if it was practicable. In this case it could not be done; for as the pretended suspicions of him are groundless, and his behavior in every respect unexceptionable; I should not part with the child, but with the employment. But I am confident that whatever may be proposed by weak or malicious people, the Congress is too wise and too good to think of treating me in that manner.

Ben, if I should live long enough to want it, is like to be another comfort to me: as I intend him for a Presbyterian as well as a Republican, I have sent him to finish his education at Geneva. He is much grown, in very good health, draws a little, as you will see by the enclosed, learns Latin, writing, arithmetic and dancing, and speaks French better than English. He made a translation of your last letter to him, so that some of your works may now appear in a foreign language. He has not been long from me. I send the accounts I have of him, and I shall put him in mind of writing to you. I cannot propose to you to part with your own dear *Will:* I must one of these days go back to see him; happy to be once more all together! But futurities are uncertain. Teach him however in the mean time to direct his worship more properly, for the deity of *Hercules* is now quite out of fashion.

The present you mention as sent by me, was rather that of a merchant at Bourdeaux, for he would never give me any account of it, and neither Temple nor I know any thing of the particulars.

When I began to read your account of the high prices of goods, *a pair of gloves seven dollars, a yard of common gause twenty-four dollars, and that it now required a fortune to maintain a family in a very plain way,* I expected you would conclude with telling me, that every body as well as yourself was grown frugal and industrious; and I could scarce believe my eyes in reading forward, that *there never was so much dressing and pleasure going on;* and that you yourself wanted *black pins and feathers from France,* to appear, I suppose, in the mode! This leads me to imagine that perhaps, it is not so much that the goods are grown dear, as that the money is grown cheap, as every thing else will do when excessively plenty; and that people are still as easy nearly in their circumstances as when a pair of gloves might be had for half a crown. The war indeed may in some degree raise the prices of goods, and the high taxes which are necessary to support the war may make our frugality necessary; and as I am always preaching that doctrine, I cannot in conscience or in decency encourage the contrary, by my example, in furnishing my children with foolish modes and luxuries. I therefore send all the articles you desire that are useful and necessary, and omit the rest; for as you say you should *have great pride in wearing any thing I send, and showing it as your father's taste;* I must avoid giving you an opportunity of doing that with either lace or feathers. If you wear your cambric ruffles as I do, and take care not to mend the holes, they will come in time to be lace; and feathers, my dear girl, may be had in America from every cocks tail.

If you happen again to see General Washington, assure him of my very great and sincere respect, and tell him that all the old Generals here amuse themselves in studying the accounts of his operations, and approve highly of his conduct.

Present my affectionate regards to all friends that enquire after me, particularly Mr. Duffield and family, and write oftener, my dear child, to Your loving father,

B. Franklin

THE MORALS OF CHESS

One of Franklin's famous passions was chess, a game he even played late at night as Madame Brillon was soaking in her tub. During one of his late-night matches in Passy, a messenger arrived with an important set of dispatches from America. Franklin waved him off until the game was finished. Another time, he was playing with his equal, the Duchess of Bourbon, who made a move that inadvertently exposed her king. Ignoring the rules of the game, he promptly captured it. "Ah," said the duchess, "we do not take Kings so." Replied Franklin in a famous quip: "We do in America."

He saw the game as a metaphor for both diplomacy and life, a point that he made explicit in a bagatelle he wrote in 1779, which was based on an essay he had drafted in 1732 for his Philadelphia Junto. Chess, he said, taught foresight, circumspection, caution and the importance of not being discouraged.

THE MORALS OF CHESS, JUNE, 1779

Sir,

Playing at Chess, is the most ancient and the most universal game known among men; for its original is beyond the memory of history, and it has, for numberless ages, been the amusement of all the civilized nations of Asia, the Persians, the Indians, and the Chinese. Europe has had it above 1,000 years; the Spaniards have spread it over their part of America, and it begins lately to make its appearance in these northern states. It is so interesting in itself, as not to need the view of gain to induce engaging in it; and thence it is never played for money. Those, therefore, who have leisure for such diversions, cannot find one that is more *innocent;* and the following piece, written with a view to correct (among a few young friends) some little improprieties in the practice of it, shows at the same time, that it may, in its effects on the mind, be not merely *innocent,* but *advantageous,* to the vanquished as well as to the victor.

The MORALS of CHESS

The game of Chess is not merely an idle amusement. Several very valuable qualities of the mind, useful in the course of human life, are to be acquired or strengthened by it, so as to become habits, ready on all occasions. For life is a kind of chess, in which we have often points to gain, and competitors or adversaries to contend with, and in which there is a vast variety of good and ill events, that are, in some degree, the effects of prudence or the want of it. By playing at chess, then, we may learn:

1. *Foresight,* which looks a little into futurity, and considers the consequences that may attend an action: for it is continually occurring to the player, If I move this piece, what will be the advantages of my new situation? What use can my adversary make of it to annoy me? What other moves can I make to support it, and to defend myself from his attacks?

2. *Circumspection,* which surveys the whole chess-board, or scene of action, the relations of the several pieces and situations, the dangers they are respectively exposed to, the several possibilities of their aiding each other; the probabilities that the adversary may make this or that move, and attack this or the other piece; and what different means can be used to avoid his stroke, or turn its consequences against him.

3. *Caution,* not to make our moves too hastily. This habit is best ac-

quired by observing strictly the laws of the game, such as, *if you touch a piece, you must move it somewhere; if you set it down, you must let it stand.* And it is therefore best that these rules should be observed, as the game thereby becomes more the image of human life, and particularly of war; in which, if you have incautiously put yourself into a bad and dangerous position, you cannot obtain your enemy's leave to withdraw your troops, and place them more securely; but you must abide all the consequences of your rashness.

And, *lastly,* we learn by chess the habit of *not being discouraged* by *present* bad appearances in the state of our affairs, the habit of *hoping for a favorable change,* and that of *persevering in the search of resources.* The game is so full of events, there is such a variety of turns in it, the fortune of it is so subject to sudden vicissitudes, and one so frequently, after long contemplation, discovers the means of extricating ones self from a supposed insurmountable difficulty, that one is encouraged to continue the contest to the last, in hopes of victory by our own skill, or, at least, of giving a *stale mate,* by the negligence of our adversary. And whoever considers, what in chess he often sees instances of, that particular pieces of success are apt to produce *presumption,* and its consequent, inattention, by which more is afterwards lost than was gained by the preceding advantage; while misfortunes produce more care and attention, by which the loss may be recovered, will learn not to be too much discouraged by the present success of his adversary, nor to despair of final good fortune, upon every little check he receives in the pursuit of it.

That we may, therefore, be induced more frequently to choose this beneficial amusement, in preference to others which are not attended with the same advantages, every circumstance, that may increase the pleasure of it, should be regarded; and every action or word that is unfair, disrespectful, or that in any way may give uneasiness, should be avoided, as contrary to the immediate intention of both the players, which is to pass the time agreeably.

Therefore, 1*st.* If it is agreed to play according to the strict rules, then those rules are to be exactly observed by both parties; and should not be insisted on for one side, while deviated from by the other: for this is not equitable.

2. If it is agreed not to observe the rules exactly, but one party demands indulgencies, he should then be as willing to allow them to the other.

3. No false move should ever be made to extricate yourself out of a difficulty, or to gain an advantage. There can be no pleasure in playing with a person once detected in such unfair practice.

4. If your adversary is long in playing, you ought not to hurry him, or express any uneasiness at his delay. You should not sing, nor whistle, nor look at your watch, nor take up a book to read, nor make a tapping with your feet on the floor, or with your fingers on the table, nor do anything that may disturb his attention. For all these things displease. And they do not show your skill in playing, but your craftiness or your rudeness.

5. You ought not to endeavor to amuse and deceive your adversary, by pretending to have made bad moves, and saying you have now lost the game, in order to make him secure and careless, and inattentive to your schemes; for this is fraud, and deceit, not skill in the game.

6. You must not, when you have gained a victory, use any triumphing or insulting expression, nor show too much pleasure; but endeavor to console your adversary, and make him less dissatisfied with himself by every kind and civil expression, that may be used with truth, such as, You understand the game better than I, but you are a little inattentive; or, You play too fast; or, You had the best of the game but something happened to divert your thoughts, and that turned it in my favor.

7. If you are a spectator, while others play, observe the most perfect silence. For if you give advice, you offend both parties; him, against whom you give it, because it may cause the loss of his game; him, in whose favor you give it, because, though it be good, and he follows it, he loses the pleasure he might have had, if you had permitted him to think till it occurred to himself. Even after a move or moves, you must not, by replacing the pieces, show how it might have been played better: for that displeases, and may occasion disputes or doubts about their true situation. All talking to the players, lessens or diverts their attention, and is therefore unpleasing; nor should you give the least hint to

either party, by any kind of noise or motion. If you do, you are unworthy to be a spectator. If you have a mind to exercise or show your judgments, do it in playing your own game when you have an opportunity, not in criticizing or meddling with, or counseling, the play of others.

Lastly. If the game is not to be played rigorously, according to the rules above-mentioned, then moderate your desire of victory over your adversary, and be pleased with one over yourself. Snatch not eagerly at every advantage offered by his unskilfulness or inattention; but point out to him kindly that by such a move he places or leaves a piece in danger and unsupported; that by another he will put his king in a dangerous situation. &c. By this generous civility (so opposite to the unfairness above forbidden) you may indeed happen to lose the game to your opponent, but you will win what is better, his esteem, his respect, and his affection; together with the silent approbation and good will of impartial spectators.

BAGATELLE ON ST. PETER'S TOLERANCE

The bagatelle that most enchanted his French friends, entitled "Conte" [story], was a parable about religious tolerance. A French officer who is about to die recounts a dream in which he arrives at the gates of heaven and watches St. Peter ask people about their religion.

"CONTE," C. DECEMBER, 1778

There was once an officer, a worthy man, named Montresor, who was very ill. His parish priest, thinking he would die, advised him to make his peace with God, so that he would be received into Paradise. "I don't feel much uneasiness on that score," said Montresor; "for last night I had a vision which set me entirely at rest." "What vision did you have?" asked the good Priest. "I was," he said, "at the Gate of Paradise with a crowd of people who wanted to enter. And St. Peter asked each of them what Religion he belonged to. One answered, 'I am a Roman Catholic.' 'Very well,' said St. Peter; 'come in, & take your place over there among the Catholics.' Another said he belonged to the Anglican Church. 'Very well,' said St. Peter; 'come in, & take your place over there among the Anglicans.' Another said he was a Quaker. 'Very well,' said St. Peter; 'come in, & take a place among the Quakers.' Finally he asked me what my religion was. 'Alas!' I replied, 'unfortunately, poor Jacques Montresor belongs to none at all.' 'That's a pity,' said the Saint. 'But enter anyway and take any place you wish.' "

ON WINE AND THE ELBOW

Although he was a temperate man, Franklin built a wine collection in Paris that soon included more than 1,200 bottles of Bordeaux, champagne and sherry. In a letter and illustration to Madame Helvétius's friend the Abbé Morellet, he has fun with some mock science to praise both wine and the human elbow.

c. JULY, 1779

From the Abbé Franklin to the Abbé Morellet.

You have often entertained me, my very dear friend, by your excellent drinking-songs; in return, I beg to edify you by some Christian, moral, and philosophical reflections upon the same subject.

In vino veritas, says the sage, *Truth is in wine.*

Before the days of Noah, men, having nothing but water to drink, could not discover the truth. Thus they went astray, became abominably wicked, and were justly exterminated by water, which they loved to drink.

The good man Noah, seeing that through this pernicious beverage all his contemporaries had perished, took it in aversion; and to quench his thirst God created the vine, and revealed to him the means of converting its fruit into wine. By means of this liquor he discovered numberless important truths; so that ever since his time the word to *divine* has been in common use, signifying originally, to discover by means of WINE. (VIN) Thus the patriarch Joseph took upon himself to *divine* by means of a cup or glass of wine, a liquor which obtained this name to show that it was not of human but *divine* invention (another proof of the antiquity of the French language, in opposition to M. Geebelin); nay, since that time, all things of peculiar excellence, even the Deities themselves, have been called *Divine* or Divinities.

We hear of the conversion of water into wine at the marriage in Cana as of a miracle. But this conversion is, through the goodness of God, made every day before our eyes. Behold the rain which descends from heaven upon our vineyards; there it enters the roots of the vines, to be changed into wine; a constant proof that God loves us, and loves to see us happy. The miracle in question was only performed to hasten the operation, under circumstances of present necessity, which required it.

It is true that God has also instructed man to reduce wine into water. But into what sort of water?—Water of Life. (*Eau de Vie.*) And this, that man may be able upon occasion to perform the miracle of Cana, and convert common water into that excellent species of wine which we call punch. My Christian brother, be kind and benevolent like God, and do not spoil his good drink.

He made wine to gladden the heart of man; do not, therefore when at table you see your neighbor pour wine into his glass, be eager to mingle water with it. Why would you drown truth? It is probable that your neighbor knows better than you what suits him. Perhaps he does not like water; perhaps he would only put in a few drops for fashion's sake; perhaps he does not wish any one to observe how little he puts in his glass. Do not, then, offer water, except to children; 't is a mistaken piece of politeness, and often very inconvenient. I give you this hint as a man of the world; and I will finish as I began, like a good Christian, in making a religious observation of high importance, taken from the Holy Scriptures. I mean that the apostle Paul counseled Timothy very seriously to put wine into his water for the sake of his health; but that not one of the apostles or holy fathers ever recommended putting water to wine.

P.S. To confirm still more your piety and gratitude to Divine Providence, reflect upon the situation which it has given to the *elbow*. You see in animals, who are intended to drink the waters that flow upon the earth, that if they have long legs, they have also a long neck, so that they can get at their drink without kneeling down. But man, who was destined to drink wine, must be able to raise the glass to his mouth. If the elbow had been placed nearer the hand (as in Figure 3), the part in advance would have been too short to bring the glass up to the mouth; and if it had been placed nearer the shoulder, (as in Figure 4) that part would have been so long that it would have carried the wine far beyond the mouth. But by the actual situation, (represented in Figure 5), we are enabled to drink at our ease, the glass going exactly to the mouth. Let us, then, with glass in hand, adore this benevolent wisdom;—let us adore and drink!

TO GEORGE WASHINGTON
ON REPUTATION

At times, Franklin worried that his enemies back home were hurting his reputation. In a ruminative mood, he wrote George Washington in 1780 a letter that ostensibly offered reassurance about the general's reputation but clearly reflected his worries about his own. "I must soon quit the scene," Franklin wrote, in an unusually introspective way, referring not to his post in France but his life in this world. Washington's own great reputation in France, he said, was "free from those little shades that the jealousy and envy of a man's countrymen and contemporaries are ever endeavoring to cast over living merit." It was clear that he was trying to reassure not only Washington but also himself that history would treat them more kindly.

Sir,

I received but lately the letter your excellency did me the honor of writing to me in recommendation of the Marquis de Lafayette. His modesty detained it long in his own hands. We became acquainted however, from the time of his arrival at Paris, and his zeal for the honor of our country, his activity in our affairs here, and his firm attachment to our cause, and to you, impressed me with the same regard & esteem for him that your excellency's letter would have done, had it been immediately delivered to me.

Should peace arrive after another campaign or two, and afford us a little leisure, I should be happy to see your excellency in Europe, and to accompany you, if my age & strength would permit, in visiting some of its ancient and most famous kingdoms. You would on this side of the sea, enjoy the great reputation you have acquired, pure and free from those little shades that the jealousy and envy of a man's countrymen & contemporaries are ever endeavoring to cast over living merit. Here you would know, and enjoy, what posterity will say of Washington. For a 1000 leagues have nearly the same effect with 1000 years. The feeble voice of those groveling passions cannot extend so far either in time or distance. At present I enjoy that pleasure for you: as I frequently hear the old generals of this martial country, (who study the maps of America, and mark upon them all your operations) speak with sincere approbation & great applause of your conduct, and join in giving you the character of one of the greatest captains of the age.

I must soon quit the scene, but you may live to see our country flourish, as it will amazingly and rapidly after the war is over. Like a field of young Indian corn, which long fair weather & sunshine had enfeebled and discolored, and which in that weak state, by a thunder gust of violent wind, hail & rain seemed to be threatened with absolute destruction; yet the storm being past, it recovers fresh verdure, shoots up with double vigor, and delights the eye not of its owner only, but of every observing traveler.

The best wishes that can be formed for your health honor and happiness, ever attend you, from your excellency's most obedient and most humble servant,

B. Franklin

JOHN ADAMS

During his tenure in Paris, Franklin was joined by John Adams as a co-commissioner. When they had served together in Congress, Adams had initially distrusted Franklin, then gone through a blender of· emotions: bemusement, resentment, admiration, and jealousy. So when he arrived in Paris, it was rather inevitable that he and Franklin would, as they did, enjoy and suffer a complex mix of disdain and grudging admiration for one another.

Some have found the relationship baffling: Did Adams resent or respect Franklin? Did Franklin find Adams maddening or solid? Did they like or dislike each other? The answer, which is not all that baffling because it is often true of the relationship between two great and strong people, is that they felt all of these conflicting emotions about each other, and more.

Adams, who was 42 when he arrived, was thirty years younger than Franklin. They were both very smart, but they had quite different personalities. Adams was unbending and outspoken and argumentative, Franklin charming and taciturn and flirtatious. Adams was rigid in his personal morality and lifestyle, Franklin famously playful. Adams learned French by pouring over grammar books and memorizing a collection of funeral orations, Franklin (who cared little about the grammar) learned the language by lounging on the pillows of his female friends and writing them amusing little tales. Adams felt comfortable confronting people, while Franklin preferred to seduce them, and the same was true of the way they dealt with nations.

Their most significant rift occurred in 1780. Previously the tension had been based more on their differences in personality and style, but this one was caused by a fundamental disagreement over policy:

whether or not America should show gratitude, allegiance and fealty to France. Franklin felt it should; Adams disagreed.

Foreign Minister Vergennes, not surprisingly, was eager to deal only with Franklin, and by the end of July 1780 he had exchanged enough strained correspondence with Adams that he felt justified in sending him a stinging letter that managed to be both formally diplomatic and undiplomatic at the same time. On behalf of the court of Louis XVI, he declared: "The King did not stand in need of your solicitations to direct his attentions to the interests of the United States." In other words, France would not deal with Adams any more.

Vergennes informed Franklin of this decision and sent him copies of all his testy correspondence with Adams, with the request that Franklin "lay the whole before Congress." Although Franklin could have, and perhaps should have, dispatched the letters without comment, he took the opportunity to write ("with reluctance") a letter of his own to Congress that detailed his disagreement with Adams.

TO SAMUEL HUNTINGTON, AUGUST 9, 1780

Sir,

. . . Mr. Adams has given offence to the court here by some sentiments and expressions contained in several of his letters written to the Comte de Vergennes. I mention this with reluctance, though perhaps it would have been my duty to acquaint you with such a circumstance, even were it not required of me by the minister himself. He has sent me copies of the correspondence, desiring I would communicate them to Congress; and I send them herewith. Mr. Adams did not show me his letters before he sent them.

I have in a former letter to Mr. Lovell, mentioned some of the inconveniences that attend the having more than one minister at the same court, one of which inconveniencies is, that they do not always hold the same language, and that the impressions made by one and intended for the service of his constituents, may be effaced by the discourse of the other. It is true that Mr. Adams's proper business is elsewhere, but the time not being come for that business, and having nothing else here wherewith to employ himself, he seems to have endeavored supplying what he may suppose my negotiations defective in.

He thinks, as he tells me himself, that America has been too free in expressions of gratitude to France; for that she is more obliged to us than we to her, and that we should show spirit in our applications. I apprehend that he mistakes his ground, and that this court is to be treated with decency and delicacy. The king, a young and virtuous prince, has, I am persuaded, a pleasure in reflecting on the generous benevolence of the action, in assisting an oppressed people, and proposes it as a part of the glory of his reign: I think it right to increase this pleasure by our thankful acknowledgements; and that such an expression of gratitude is not only our duty but our interest. A different conduct seems to me what is not only improper and unbecoming, but what may be hurtful to us.

Mr. Adams, on the other hand, who at the same time means our welfare and interest as much as I, or any man can do, seems to think a little apparent stoutness and greater air of independence and boldness in our demands, will procure us more ample assistance. It is for the Congress to judge and regulate their affairs accordingly.

M. De Vergennes, who appears much offended, told me yesterday, that he would enter into no further discussions with Mr. Adams, nor answer any more of his letters. He is gone to Holland to try, as he told me, whether something might not be done to render us a little less dependent on France. He says the ideas of this court and those of the people in America are so totally different, as that it is impossible for any minister to please both.

He ought to know America better than I do, having been there lately; and he may choose to do what he thinks will best please the people of America: but when I consider the expressions of Congress in many of their public acts, and particularly in their letter to the Chevalier de la Luzerne of the 24th of May last, I cannot but imagine that he mistakes the sentiments of a few for a general opinion. It is my intention while I stay here, to procure what advantages I can for our country, by endeavoring to please this court; and I wish I could prevent anything being said by any of our countrymen here that may have a contrary effect, and increase an opinion lately showing itself in Paris that we seek a difference, and with a view of reconciling ourselves to England: some of them have of late been very indiscreet in their conversations . . .

Despite their dispute, Franklin remained cordial, or retained the pretense of cordiality, in letters he wrote to Adams, who had gone to Holland to try to elicit a loan for America.

To John Adams, February 22, 1781

Sir,

I have lately made a fresh and strong application for more money. I have not yet received a positive answer. I have, however, two of the Christian Graces, Faith and Hope: But my Faith is only that of which the Apostle speaks, the Evidence of Things not seen. For in truth I do not see at present how so many bills drawn at random on our ministers in France, Spain and Holland, are to be paid; nor that any thing but omnipotent necessity can excuse the imprudence of it. Yet I think the bills drawn upon us by the Congress ought at all risks to be accepted. I shall accordingly use my best endeavors to procure money for their honorable discharge against they become due, if you should nor in the mean time be provided. And if those endeavors fail, I shall be ready to break, run away, or go to prison with you, as it shall please God . . .

With great Respect, I have the honor to be, Sir, Your most obedient and most humble Servant,

B. Franklin

DIALOGUE BETWEEN THE GOUT AND MR. FRANKLIN

One product of Franklin's flirtations at Passy and Auteuil was the collection of fables and bagatelles—such as "The Ephemera" and "The Elysian Fields" mentioned above—that he wrote to amuse his friends. He published many of the bagatelles on the private press he installed at Passy. They were similar to little stories he had written in the past, such as "The Trial of Polly Baker," but the dozen or so written in Passy have a slight French accent to them.

They have been the subject of much critical fawning. "Franklin's bagatelles combine delight with moral truth," declares Alfred Owen Aldridge. "They are among the world's masterpieces of light literature." Not exactly. Their value lies more in the glimpse they give into Franklin's personality than in their literary merit, which is somewhat slight. They are *jeux d'esprit,* lively little five-finger exercises. Most display Franklin's typical wry self-awareness, though some are a bit heavy-handed in their attempt to teach a moral lesson.

One of the most amusing is a dialogue he pretended to have with the gout. When he was bedridden by the malady in October 1780, Madame Brillon wrote him a poem, "Le Sage et la Goutte," that implied that his malady was caused by his love for "one pretty mistress, sometimes two three, four." Among the lines:

"Moderation, dear Doctor," said the Gout,/ "Is no virtue for which you stand out./ You like food, you like ladies' sweet talk,/ You play chess when you should walk . . ."

Franklin replied one midnight with a long and rollicking dialogue in which the gout chided him for his indulgences and also, since Franklin liked to be instructive, prescribed a course of exercise and fresh air. He sent it to Madame Brillon along with a letter that, in a cheeky way, rebutted her poem's contention "that mistresses have had a share in producing this painful malady." As he pointed out: "When I was a young man and enjoyed more of the favors of the fair sex than I do at present, I had no gout. Hence, if the ladies of Passy had shown more of that Christian charity that I have so often recommended to you in vain, I should not be suffering from the gout right now." Sex had become, by then, a topic of banter rather than of tension for them. "I will do my best for you, in a spirit of Christian charity," she wrote back, "but to the exclusion of *your* brand of Christian charity."

Dialogue Between the Gout and Mr. Franklin, October 22, 1780

MIDNIGHT, OCTOBER 22, 1780

Mr. F.: Eh! oh! eh! What have I done to merit these cruel sufferings?

The Gout: Many things; you have ate and drank too freely, and too much indulged those legs of yours in their indolence.

Mr. F.: Who is it that accuses me?

The Gout: It is I, even I, The Gout.

Mr. F.: What! my enemy in person?

The Gout: No, not your enemy.

Mr. F.: I repeat it, my enemy; for you would not only torment my body to death, but ruin my good name; you reproach me as a glutton and a tippler; now all the world, that knows me, will allow that I am neither the one nor the other.

The Gout: The world may think as it pleases; it is always very complaisant to itself, and sometimes to its friends; but I very well know that the quantity of meat and drink proper for a man who takes a reasonable degree of exercise, would be too much for another who never takes any.

Mr. F.: I take—eh! oh!—as much exercise—eh!—as I can, Madam Gout. You know my sedentary state, and on that account, it would seem, Madam Gout, as if you might spare me a little, seeing it is not altogether my own fault.

The Gout: Not a jot; your rhetoric and your politeness are thrown away; your apology avails nothing. If your situation in life is a sedentary one, your amusements, your recreation, at least, should be active. You ought to walk or ride; or, if the weather prevents that, play at billiards. But let us examine your course of life. While the mornings are long, and you have leisure to go abroad, what do you do? Why, instead of gaining an appetite for breakfast by salutary exercise, you amuse yourself with books, pamphlets, or newspapers, which commonly are not worth the reading. Yet you eat an inordinate breakfast, four dishes of tea with cream, and one or two buttered toasts, with slices of hung beef, which I fancy are not things the most easily digested. Immediately afterwards you sit down to write at your desk, or converse with persons who apply to you on business. Thus the time passes till one, without any kind of bodily exercise. But all this I could pardon, in regard, as you say, to your sedentary condition. But what is your practice after dinner? Walking in the beautiful gardens of those friends with whom you have dined would be the choice of men of sense; yours is to be fixed down to chess, where you are found engaged for two or three hours! This is your perpetual recreation, which is the least eligible of any for a sedentary man, because, instead of accelerating the motion of the fluids, the rigid attention it requires helps to retard the circulation and obstruct internal secretions. Wrapt in the speculations of this wretched game, you destroy your constitution. What can be expected from such a course of living but a body replete with stagnant humors, ready to fall a prey to all kinds of dangerous maladies, if I, The Gout, did not occasionally bring you relief by agitating those humors, and so purifying or dissipating them? If it was in some nook or alley in Paris, deprived of walks, that you played a while at chess after dinner, this might be excusable; but the same taste prevails with you in Passy, Auteuil, Montmartre, or Sanoy, places where there are the finest gardens and walks, a pure air, beautiful women, and most agreeable and instructive conversation: all which you might enjoy by frequenting the walks. But these are rejected for this abominable game of chess. Fie, then, Mr. Franklin! But amidst my instructions, I had almost forgot to administer my wholesome corrections; so take that twinge—and that.

Mr. F.: Oh! eh! oh! ohhh! As much instruction as you please, Madam Gout, and as many reproaches; but pray, Madam, a truce with your corrections!

The Gout: No, Sir, no, I will not abate a particle of what is so much for your good.

Mr. F.: Oh! ehhh!—It is not fair to say I take no exercise, when I do very often, going out to dine and returning in my carriage.

The Gout: That, of all imaginable exercises, is the most slight and insignificant, if you allude to the motion of a carriage suspended on springs. By observing the degree of heat obtained by different kinds of motion, we may form an estimate of the quantity of exercise given by each. Thus, for example, if you turn out to walk in winter with cold feet, in an hour's time you will be in a glow all over; ride on horseback, the same effect will scarcely be perceived by four hours' round trotting; but if you loll in a carriage, such as you have mentioned, you may travel all day and gladly enter the last inn to warm your feet by a fire. Flatter yourself then no longer that half an hour's airing in your carriage deserves the name of exercise. Providence has appointed few to roll in carriages, while he has given to all a pair of legs, which are machines infinitely more commodious and serviceable. Be grateful, then, and make a proper use of yours. Would you know how they forward the circulation of your fluids in the very action of transporting you from place to place, observe when you walk that all your weight is alternately thrown from one leg to the other; this occasions a great pressure on the vessels of the foot, and repels their contents; when relieved, by the weight being thrown on the other foot, the vessels of the first are allowed to replenish, and by a return of this weight, this repulsion again succeeds; thus accelerating the circulation of the blood. The heat produced in any given time depends on the degree of this acceleration; the fluids are shaken, the humors attenuated, the secretions facilitated, and all goes well; the cheeks are ruddy, and health is established. Behold your fair friend at Auteuil; a lady who received from bounteous nature more really useful science than half a dozen such pretenders to philosophy as you have been able to extract from all your books. When she honors you with a visit, it is on foot. She walks all hours of the day, and leaves indolence, and its concomitant maladies, to be endured by her horses. In this, see at once the preservative of her health and personal charms. But when you go to Auteuil, you must have your carriage, though it is no farther from Passy to Auteuil than from Auteuil to Passy.

Mr. F.: Your reasonings grow very tiresome.

The Gout: I stand corrected. I will be silent and continue my office; take that, and that.

Mr. F.: Oh! Ohh! Talk on, I pray you.

The Gout: No, no; I have a good number of twinges for you tonight, and you may be sure of some more tomorrow.

Mr. F.: What, with such a fever! I shall go distracted. Oh! eh! Can no one bear it for me?

The Gout: Ask that of your horses; they have served you faithfully.

Mr. F.: How can you so cruelly sport with my torments?

The Gout: Sport! I am very serious. I have here a list of offences against your own health distinctly written, and can justify every stroke inflicted on you.

Mr. F.: Read it then.

The Gout: It is too long a detail; but I will briefly mention some particulars.

Mr. F.: Proceed. I am all attention.

The Gout: Do you remember how often you have promised yourself, the following morning, a walk in the grove of Boulogne, in the garden de La Muette, or in your own garden, and have violated your promise, alleging, at one time, it was too cold, at another too warm, too windy, too moist, or what else you pleased; when in truth it was too nothing but your insuperable love of ease?

Mr. F.: That I confess may have happened occasionally, probably ten times in a year.

The Gout: Your confession is very far short of the truth; the gross amount is one hundred and ninety-nine times.

Mr. F.: Is it possible?

The Gout: So possible that it is fact; you may rely on the accuracy of my statement. You know M. Brillon's gardens, and what fine walks they contain; you know the handsome flight of an hundred steps which lead from the terrace above to the lawn below. You have been in the practice of visiting this amiable family twice a week, after dinner, and it is a maxim of your own, that "a man may take as much exercise in walking a mile up and down stairs, as in ten on level ground." What an opportunity was here for you to have had exercise in both these ways! Did you embrace it, and how often?

Mr. F.: I cannot immediately answer that question.

The Gout: I will do it for you; not once.

Mr. F.: Not once?

The Gout: Even so. During the summer you went there at six o'clock. You found the charming lady, with her lovely children and friends, eager to walk with you, and entertain you with their agreeable conversation; and what has been your choice? Why, to sit on the terrace, satisfying yourself with the fine prospect, and passing your eye over the beauties of the garden below, without taking one step to descend and walk about in them. On the contrary, you call for tea and the chessboard; and lo! you are occupied in your seat till nine o'clock, and that besides two hours' play after dinner; and then, instead of walking home, which would have bestirred you a little, you step into your carriage. How absurd to suppose that all this carelessness can be reconcilable with health, without my interposition!

Mr. F.: I am convinced now of the justness of Poor Richard's remark, that "Our debts and our sins are always greater than we think for."

The Gout: So it is. You philosophers are sages in your maxims, and fools in your conduct.

Mr. F.: But do you charge among my crimes that I return in a carriage from M. Brillon's?

The Gout: Certainly; for having been seated all the while, you cannot object the fatigue of the day, and cannot want therefore the relief of a carriage.

Mr. F.: What then would you have me do with my carriage?

The Gout: Burn it if you choose; you would at least get heat out of it once in this way; or if you dislike that proposal, here's another for you; observe the poor peasants who work in the vineyards and grounds about the villages of Passy, Auteuil, Chaillot, etc.; you may find every day among these deserving creatures four or five old men and women, bent and perhaps crippled by weight of years, and too long and too great labor. After a most fatiguing day these people have to trudge a mile or two to their smoky huts. Order your coachman to set them down. This is an act that will be good for your soul; and, at the same time, after your visit to the Brillons, if you return on foot, that will be good for your body.

Mr. F.: Ah! how tiresome you are!

The Gout: Well, then, to my office; it should not be forgotten that I am your physician. There.

Mr. F.: Ohhh! what a devil of a physician!

The Gout: How ungrateful you are to say so! Is it not I who, in the character of your physician, have saved you from the palsy, dropsy, and apoplexy? One or other of which would have done for you long ago but for me.

Mr. F.: I submit, and thank you for the past, but entreat the discontinuance of your visits for the future; for in my mind, one had better die than be cured so dolefully. Permit me just to hint that I have also not been unfriendly to you. I never feed physician or quack of any kind, to enter the list against you; if then you do not leave me to my repose, it may be said you are ungrateful too.

The Gout: I can scarcely acknowledge that as any objection. As to quacks, I despise them; they may kill you indeed, but cannot injure me. And as to regular physicians, they are at last convinced that The Gout, in such a subject as you are, is no disease, but a remedy; and wherefore cure a remedy?—but to our business—there.

Mr. F.: Oh! oh! For Heaven's sake leave me! and I promise faithfully never more to play at chess, but to take exercise daily, and live temperately.

The Gout: I know you too well. You promise fair; but, after a few months of good health, you will return to your old habits; your fine promises will be forgotten like the forms of the last year's clouds. Let us then finish the account, and I will go. But I leave you with an assurance of visiting you again at a proper time and place; for my object is your good, and you are sensible now that I am your *real friend.*

THE SCIENCE OF FARTS

A similar spoof, even wittier and more famous (or perhaps notorious), was the mock proposal he made to the Royal Academy of Brussels that they study the causes and cures of farting. Noting that the academy's leaders, in soliciting questions to study, claimed to "esteem utility," he suggested an enquiry that would be worthy of "this enlightened age."

Although he printed this farce privately at his press in Passy, Franklin apparently had qualms and never published it publicly. He did, however, send it to friends, and he noted in particular that it might be of interest to one of them, the famous chemist and gas specialist Joseph Priestley, "who is apt to give himself airs."

To the Royal Academy of Brussels, c. 1780

*To the Royal Academy of * * * * * **

Gentlemen,

I have perused your late mathematical Prize Question, proposed in lieu of one in Natural Philosophy, for the ensuing year, viz. *Une figure quelconque donne, on demande dy inscrire le plus grand nombre de fois possible une autre figure plus petite quelconque, qui est aussi donne.* I was glad to find by these following Words, *l'Académie a jug que cette découverte, en tendant les bornes de nos connoissances, ne seroit pas sans UTILITÉ,* that you esteem *Utility* an essential Point in your Enquiries, which has not always been the case with all Academies; and I conclude therefore that you have given this Question instead of a philosophical, or as the learned express it, a physical one, because you could not at the time think of a physical one that promised greater *Utility*.

Permit me then humbly to propose one of that sort for your consideration, and through you, if you approve it, for the serious enquiry of learned physicians, chemists, &c. of this enlightened age.

It is universally well known, that in digesting our common food, there is created or produced in the bowels of human creatures, a great quantity of wind.

That the permitting this air to escape and mix with the atmosphere, is usually offensive to the company, from the fetid smell that accompanies it.

That all well-bred people therefore, to avoid giving such offence, forcibly restrain the efforts of nature to discharge that wind.

That so retained contrary to Nature, it not only gives frequently great present pain, but occasions future diseases, such as habitual colics, ruptures, tympanis, &c. often destructive of the constitution, & sometimes of life itself.

Were it not for the odiously offensive smell accompanying such escapes, polite people would probably be under no more restraint in discharging such wind in company, than they are in spitting, or in blowing their noses.

My Prize Question therefore should be, *To discover some drug wholesome & not disagreeable, to be mixed with our common food, or sauces, that shall render the natural discharges of wind from our bodies, not only inoffensive, but agreeable as perfumes.*

That this is not a chimerical project, and altogether impossible, may appear from these considerations. That we already have some knowledge of means capable of *varying* that smell. He that dines on stale flesh, especially with much addition of onions, shall be able to afford a stink that no company can tolerate; while he that has lived for some time on vegetables only, shall have that breath so pure as to be insensible to the most delicate noses; and if he can manage so as to avoid the report, he may any where give vent to his griefs, unnoticed. But as there are many to whom an entire vegetable diet would be inconvenient, and as a little quick-lime thrown into a jakes will correct the amazing quantity of fetid air arising from the vast mass of putrid matter contained in such places, and render it rather pleasing to the smell, who knows but that a little powder of lime (or some other thing equivalent) taken in our food, or perhaps a glass of limewater drank at dinner, may have the same effect on the air produced in and issuing from our bowels? This is worth the experiment.

Certain it is also that we have the power of changing by slight means the smell of another discharge, that of our water. A few stems of asparagus eaten, shall give our urine a disagreeable odor; and a pill of turpentine no bigger than a pea, shall bestow on it the pleasing smell of violets. And why should it be thought more impossible in nature, to find means of making a perfume of our *wind* than of our *water?*

For the encouragement of this enquiry, (from the immortal honor to be reasonably expected by the inventor) let it be considered of how small importance to mankind, or to how small a part of mankind have been useful those discoveries in science that have heretofore made philosophers famous. Are there twenty men in Europe at this day, the happier, or even the easier, for any knowledge they have picked out of Aristotle? What comfort can the vortices of Descartes give to a man who has whirlwinds in his bowels! The knowledge of Newton's mutual *attraction* of the particles of matter, can it afford ease to him who is racked by their mutual *repulsion,* and the cruel distensions it occasions? The pleasure arising to a few philosophers, from seeing, a few times in their life, the threads of light untwisted, and separated by the Newtonian prism into seven colors, can it be compared with the ease and comfort every man living might feel seven times a day, by discharging freely the wind from his bowels? Especially if it be converted into a perfume: for the pleasures of one sense being little inferior to those of another, instead of pleasing the *sight* he might delight the *smell* of those about him, & make numbers happy, which to a benevolent mind must afford infinite satisfaction.

The generous soul, who now endeavors to find out whether the friends he entertains like best Claret or Burgundy, Champagne or Madeira, would then enquire also whether they chose musk or lily, rose or bergamot, and provide accordingly. And surely such a liberty of *expressing* ones *scent-iments,* and *pleasing one another,* is of infinitely more importance to human happiness than that liberty of the *press,* or *abusing one another,* which the English are so ready to fight & die for. In short, this invention, if completed, would be, as *Bacon* expresses it, *bringing philosophy home to men's business and bosoms.* And I cannot but conclude, that in Comparison therewith, for *universal* and *continual UTILITY,* the Science of the Philosophers above-mentioned, even with the addition, Gentlemen, of your *figure quelconque* and the figures inscribed in it, are, all together, scarcely worth a

FART-HING.

A FABLE ABOUT MISGUIDED LOYALISTS

The most contentious issue when Franklin was negotiating a peace treaty with Britain in 1782 was the treatment of those in America who had remained loyal to the king during the revolution. It was a particularly sore subject for Franklin, who had split bitterly with his son William, a noted loyalist. Should restitution be made by America for the property it confiscated from such loyalists? Franklin ardently (and successfully) insisted not, and he wrote a fable about the noble lion who stood up against such mongrel dogs.

c. NOVEMBER, 1782

Apologue

Lion, king of a certain forest, had among his subjects a body of faithful dogs, in principle and affection strongly attached to his person and government, but through whose assistance he had extended his dominions, and had become the terror of his enemies.

Lion, however, influenced by evil counselors, took an aversion to the dogs, condemned them unheard, and ordered his tigers, leopards, and panthers to attack and destroy them.

The dogs petitioned humbly, but their petitions were rejected haughtily; and they were forced to defend themselves, which they did with bravery.

A few among them, of a mongrel race, derived from a mixture with wolves and foxes, corrupted by royal promises of great rewards, deserted the honest dogs and joined their enemies.

The dogs were finally victorious: a treaty of peace was made, in which Lion acknowledged them to be free, and disclaimed all future authority over them.

The mongrels not being permitted to return among them, claimed of the royalists the reward that had been promised.

A council of the beasts was held to consider their demand.

The wolves and the foxes agreed unanimously that the demand was just, that royal promises ought to be kept, and that every loyal subject should contribute freely to enable his majesty to fulfill them.

The horse alone, with a boldness and freedom that became the nobleness of his nature, delivered a contrary opinion.

"The King," said he, "has been misled, by bad ministers, to war unjustly upon his faithful subjects. Royal promises, when made to encourage us to act for the public good, should indeed be honorably acquitted; but if to encourage us to betray and destroy each other, they are wicked and void from the beginning. The advisers of such promises, and those who murdered in consequence of them, instead of being recompensed, should be severely punished. Consider how greatly our common strength is already diminished by our loss of the dogs. If you enable the King to reward those fratricides, you will establish a precedent that may justify a future tyrant to make like promises; and every example of such an unnatural brute rewarded will give them additional weight. Horses and bulls, as well as dogs, may thus be divided against their own kind, and civil wars produced at pleasure, till we are so weakened that neither liberty nor safety is any longer to be found in the forest, and nothing remains but abject submission to the will of a despot, who may devour us as he pleases."

The council had sense enough to resolve: *that the demand be rejected.*

SEDUCING THE FRENCH

After he had concluded a peace agreement with Britain in November 1782, Franklin had the difficult duty of explaining to foreign minister Vergennes why the Americans had breached their obligations to France, which was still at war with Britain, by negotiating a treaty without consulting him. After sending Vergennes a copy of the signed accord, which he stressed was provisional, Franklin called upon him at Versailles the following week. The French minister remarked, coolly but politely, that "proceeding in this abrupt signature of the articles" was not "agreeable to the [French] King."

When Franklin followed up with a brash request for yet another French loan, along with the information that he was transmitting the peace accord to Congress, Vergennes took the opportunity to protest officially. It was lacking in propriety, he wrote Franklin, for him "to hold out a certain hope of peace to America without even informing yourself on the state of negotiation on our part." America was under an obligation not to consider ratifying any peace until France had also come to terms with Britain.

Franklin's response, which has been called "a diplomatic masterpiece" and "one of the most famous of all diplomatic letters," combined a few dignified expressions of contrition with appeals to France's national interest. Using the French word *bienséance,* which roughly translates to "propriety," Franklin sought to minimize the American transgression.

There was little Vergennes could do. Forcing a showdown, as Franklin had warned, would drive the Americans into an even faster and closer alliance with Britain. So, reluctantly, he let the matter drop, and he even agreed to supply yet another French loan.

"Two great diplomatic duelists had formally crossed swords," the Franklin scholar Carl Van Doren noted, "and the philosopher had exquisitely disarmed the minister." Yes, but perhaps a better analogy would be to Franklin's own favorite game of chess. From his opening gambit that led to America's treaty of alliance with France to the endgame that produced a peace with England while preserving French friendship, Franklin mastered a three-dimensional game against two aggressive players by exhibiting great patience when the pieces were not properly aligned and carefully exploiting strategic advantages when they were.

To Vergennes, December 17, 1782

Sir,

. . . Nothing has been agreed in the preliminaries contrary to the interests of France; and no peace is to take place between us and England till you have concluded yours. Your observation is however apparently just, that in not consulting you before they were signed, we have been guilty of neglecting a point of *bienséance*. But as this was not from want of respect for the king whom we all love and honor, we hope it may be excused; and that the great work which has hitherto been so happily conducted, is so nearly brought to perfection, and is so glorious to his reign, will not be ruined by a single indiscretion of ours. And certainly the whole edifice falls to the ground immediately, if you refuse on this account to give us any farther assistance. I have not yet dispatched the ship, and shall wait upon you on Friday for your answer.

It is not possible for any one to be more sensible than I am, of what I and every American owe to the king, for the many and great benefits and favors he has bestowed upon us. All my letters to America are proofs of this; all tending to make the same impressions on the minds of my countrymen, that I felt in my own. And I believe that no prince was ever more beloved and respected by his own subjects, than the king is by the people of the United States. The English, I just now learn, flatter themselves they have already divided us. I hope this little misunderstanding will therefore be kept a perfect secret, and that they will find themselves totally mistaken.

With great and sincere respect, I am, sir, your excellency's most obedient and most humble Servant,

B. Franklin

TO POLLY ON HER MOTHER AND THE FUTILITY OF WAR

During his final year in France, Franklin learned that his dear land-lady and companion from London, Margaret Stevenson, had died. To her daughter Polly, who had remained his affectionate friend, Franklin expressed his grief and also the hope that she would join him in Paris before he returned to America. Polly did so, and she also would later join him in America where she would be with him until he died.

TO POLLY STEVENSON HEWSON, JANUARY 27, 1783

The departure of my dearest friend, which I learn from your last let-ter, greatly affects me. To meet with her once more in this life, was one of the principal motives of my proposing to visit England again before my return to America. The last year carried off my friends Dr. Pringle and Dr. Fothergill, and Lord Kames, and Lord le Despencer; this has begun to take away the rest, and strikes the hardest. Thus the ties I had to that country, and indeed to the world in general, are loosened one by one, and I shall soon have no attachment left to make me unwilling to follow.

I intended writing when I sent the 11 books, but I lost the time in looking for the 12th. I wrote with that; and I hope it came to hand. I therein asked your counsel about my coming to England. On reflec-tion, I think I can from my knowledge of your prudence foresee what it will be; viz. Not to come too soon, lest it should seem braving and in-sulting some who ought to be respected. I shall therefore omit that journey till I am near going to America; and then just step over to take leave of my friends, and spend a few days with you. I purpose bringing Ben with me, and perhaps may leave him under your care.

At length we are in peace, God be praised; and long, very long may it continue. All wars are follies, very expensive and very mischievous ones. When will mankind be convinced of this, and agree to settle their differences by arbitration? Were they to do it even by the cast of a dye, it would be better than by fighting and destroying each other.

Spring is coming on, when traveling will be delightful. Can you not, when your children are all at school, make a little party, and take a trip hither? I have now a large house, delightfully situated, in which I could accommodate you and two or three friends; and I am but half an hours drive from Paris.

In looking forward twenty five years seems a long period; but in looking back, how short! Could you imagine that 'tis now full a quarter of a century since we were first acquainted! It was in 1757. During the greatest part of the time I lived in the same house with my dear deceased friend your mother; of course you and I saw and conversed with each other much and often. It is to all our honors, that in all that time we never had among us the smallest misunderstanding. Our friendship has been all clear sunshine, without any the least cloud in its hemisphere. Let me conclude by saying to you what I have had too frequent occasions to say to my other remaining old friends, *the fewer we become, the more let us love one another.* Adieu, and believe me ever, Yours most affectionately,

B. Franklin

A CRITIQUE OF EXCESS WEALTH

Franklin's affection for the middle class, and its virtues of hard work and frugality, meant that his social theories tended to be a blend of conservatism (as we have seen, he was dubious of generous welfare laws that led to dependency among the poor) and populism (he was opposed to the privileges of inheritance and to wealth idly gained through ownership of large estates). From Paris he expanded on these ideas by questioning the morality of excess personal wealth, most notably in letters to his friends Robert Morris in America and Benjamin Vaughan in London. Franklin's antipathy to excess wealth also led him to defend high taxes, especially on luxuries.

To some of his contemporaries, both rich and poor, Franklin's social philosophy seemed an odd mix. In fact, however, it formed a very coherent leather-apron outlook. Franklin's blend of beliefs would become part of the outlook of much of America's middle class: its faith in the virtues of hard work and frugality, its benevolent belief in voluntary associations to help others, its conservative opposition to handouts that led to laziness and dependency, and its slightly ambivalent resentment of unnecessary luxury, hereditary privileges, and an idle landowning leisure class.

TO ROBERT MORRIS, DECEMBER 25, 1783

Sir,

. . . The remissness of our people in paying taxes is highly blamable, the unwillingness to pay them is still more so. I see in some resolutions of town meetings, a remonstrance against giving Congress a power to take as they call it, *the people's money* out of their pockets though only to pay the interest and principal of debts duly contracted. They seem to mistake the point. Money justly due from the people is their creditor's money, and no longer the money of the people, who, if they withhold it, should be compelled to pay by some law.

All property indeed, except the savage's temporary cabin, his bow, his matchcoat, and other little acquisitions absolutely necessary for his subsistence, seems to me to be the creature of public convention. Hence the public has the right of regulating descents & all other conveyances of property, and even of limiting the quantity & the uses of it. All the property that is necessary to a man for the conservation of the individual & the propagation of the species, is his natural right which none can justly deprive him of: but all property of the public, who by their laws have created it, and who may therefore by other laws dispose of it, whenever the welfare of the public shall demand such disposition. He that does not like civil society on these terms, let him retire & live among savages. He can have no right to the benefits of society who will not pay his club towards the support of it . . .

With sincere regard & attachment, I am ever, dear sir, your most &c

TO BENJAMIN VAUGHAN, JULY 26, 1784

Dear friend,

. . . You ask what remedy I have for the growing luxury of my country, which gives so much *offence* to all *English travelers* without exception. I answer that I think it exaggerated, and that travelers are no good judges whether our luxury is growing or diminishing. Our people are hospitable, and have indeed too much pride in displaying upon their tables before strangers the plenty and variety that our country affords. They have the vanity too of sometimes borrowing one another's plate to entertain more splendidly strangers being invited from house to house, and meeting every day with a feast, imagine what they see is the ordinary way of living of all the families where they dine; when perhaps each family lives a week after upon the remains of the dinner given. It is, I own, a folly in our people to give *such offence* to *English* travelers. The first part of the proverb is thereby verified, that *fools make feasts*. I wish in this case the other were as true, *and wise men eat them.* These travelers might one would think find some fault they could more decently reproach us with, than that of our excessive civility to them as strangers.

I have not indeed yet thought of a remedy for luxury. I am not sure that in a great state it is capable of a remedy. Nor that the evil is in itself always so great as it is represented. Suppose we include in the definition of luxury all unnecessary expense, and then let us consider whether laws to prevent such expense are possible to be executed in a great country; and whether if they could be executed, our people generally would be happier or even richer. Is not the hope of one day being able to purchase and enjoy luxuries a great spur to labor and industry? May not luxury therefore produce more than it consumes, if without such a spur people would be as they are naturally enough inclined to be, lazy and indolent?

To this purpose I remember a circumstance. The skipper of a shallop employed between Cape May and Philadelphia, had done us some small service for which he refused pay. My wife understanding that he had a daughter, sent her as a present a new-fashioned cap. Three years after, this skipper being at my house with an old farmer of Cape May his passenger, he mentioned the cap and how much his daughter had been pleased with it; but says he it proved a dear cap to our congregation. How so? When my daughter appeared in it at meeting, it was so much admired, that all the girls resolved to get such caps from Philadelphia; and my wife and I computed that the whole could not have cost less than a hundred pound. True says the farmer, but you do not tell all the story; I think the cap was nevertheless an advantage to us; for it was the first thing that put our girls upon knitting worsted mittens for sale at Philadelphia, that they might have wherewithal to buy caps and ribbons there; and you know that that industry has continued and is likely to continue and increase to a much greater value, and answers better purposes. Upon the whole I was more reconciled to this little piece of luxury; since not only the girls were made happier by having fine caps, but the Philadelphians by the supply of warm mittens.

In our commercial towns upon the seacoast, fortunes will occasionally be made. Some of those who grow rich, will be prudent, live within bounds, and preserve what they have gained for their posterity. Others fond of showing their wealth, will be extravagant and ruin themselves. Laws cannot prevent this, and perhaps it is not always an evil to the public. A shilling spent idly by a fool, may be picked up by a wiser person who knows better what to do with it. It is therefore not lost. A vain silly fellow builds a fine house, furnishes it richly, lives in it expensively, and in a few years ruins himself, but the masons, carpenters, smiths and other honest tradesmen have been by his employ assisted in maintaining and raising their families, the farmer has been paid for his labor and encouraged, and the estate is now in better hands.

In some cases indeed certain modes of luxury may be a public evil in the same manner as it is a private one. If there be a nation for instance, that exports its beef and linen to pay for its importations of claret and porter, while a great part of its people live upon potatoes and wear no shirts, wherein does it differ from the sot who lets his family starve and sells his clothes to buy drink? Our American commerce is I confess a little in this way. We sell our victuals to your islands for rum and sugar; the substantial necessaries of life for superfluities. But we have plenty and live well nevertheless; though by being soberer we might be richer. By the by, here is just issued an arret of council, taking off all the duties upon the exportation of brandies, which it is said will render them cheaper in America than your rum, in which case there is no doubt but they will be preferred, and we shall be better able to bear your restrictions on our commerce. There are views here by augmenting their settlements of being able to supply the growing people of North America with the sugar that may be wanted there. On the whole I guess England will get as little by the commercial war she has begun with us as she did by the military. But to return to *luxury.*

The vast quantity of forest lands we yet have to clear and put in order for cultivation, will for a long time keep the body of our nation laborious and frugal. Forming an opinion of our people and their manners by what is seen among the inhabitants of the seaports, is judging from an improper sample. The people of the trading towns may be rich and luxurious, while the country possesses all the virtues that tend to private happiness and public prosperity. Those towns are not much regarded by the country. They are hardly considered as an essential part of the states. And the experience of the last war has shown, that their being in possession of the enemy, did not necessarily draw on the subjection of the country, which bravely continued to maintain its freedom and independence not withstanding.

It has been computed by some political arithmetician, that if every man and woman would work four hours each day on something useful, that labor would produce sufficient to procure all the necessaries and comforts of life, want and misery would be banished out of the world, and the rest of the 24 hours might be leisure and pleasure.

What occasions then so much want and misery? It is the employment of men and women in works that produce neither the necessaries nor conveniences of life, who, with those who do nothing, consume the necessaries raised by the laborious.

To explain this: the first elements of wealth are obtained by labor from the earth and waters. I have land and raise corn. With this if I feed a family that does nothing, my corn will be consumed and at the end of the year I shall be no richer than I was at the beginning. But if while I feed them I employ them, some in spinning others in hewing timber and sawing boards, others in making bricks &c for building; the value of my corn will be arrested, and remain with me, and at the end of the year we may all be better clothed and better lodged. And if instead of employing a man I feed, in making bricks, I employ him in fiddling for me, the corn he eats is gone, and no part of his manufacture remains to augment the wealth and the conveniences of the family. I shall therefore be the poorer for this fiddling man, unless the rest of my family work more or eat less to make up for the deficiency he occasions.

Look round the world and see the millions employed in doing nothing, or in something that amounts to nothing when the necessaries and conveniences of life are in question. What is the bulk of commerce, for which we fight and destroy each other but the toil of millions for superfluities to the great hazard and loss of many lives by the constant dangers of the sea. How much labor spent in building and fitting great ships to go to China and Arabia for tea and for coffee, to the West Indies for sugar, to America for tobacco! These things cannot be called the necessaries of life, for our ancestors lived very comfortably without them.

A question may be asked, could all these people now employed in raising, making or carrying superfluities, be subsisted by raising necessaries? I think they might. The world is large, and a great part of it still uncultivated. Many hundred millions of acres in Asia, Africa and America, are still forest, and a great deal even in Europe. On 100 acres of this forest a man might become a substantial farmer; and 100,000 men employed in clearing each his 100 acres, (instead of being as they are French hairdressers) would hardly brighten a spot big enough to be visible from the moon, unless with Herschel's telescope, so vast are the regions still in [the] world unimproved.

'Tis however some comfort to reflect that upon the whole the quantity of industry and prudence among mankind exceeds the quantity of idleness and folly. Hence the increase of good buildings, farms cultivated, and populous cities filled with wealth all over Europe, which a few ages since were only to be found on the coasts of the Mediterranean. And this notwithstanding the mad wars continually raging, by which are often destroyed in one year the works of many years' peace. So that we may hope the luxury of a few merchants on the sea coast, will not be the ruin of America.

One reflection more, and I will end this long rambling letter. Almost all the parts of our bodies require some expense. The feet demand shoes, the legs stockings, the rest of the body clothing, and the belly a good deal of victuals. *Our* eyes, though exceedingly useful, ask when reasonable, only the cheap assistance of *spectacles,* which could not much impair our finances. But *the eyes of other people* are the eyes that ruin us. If all but myself were blind, I should want neither fine clothes, fine houses nor fine furniture. Adieu, my Dear Friend. I am Yours ever,

B. Franklin

ON HEREDITARY HONORS
AND THE TURKEY

Franklin focused much of his writing on his egalitarian, anti-elitist ideas for building a new American society based on middle-class virtues. His daughter Sally sent him newspaper clippings about the formation of a hereditary order of merit called the Society of the Cincinnati, which was headed by General Washington and open to distinguished officers of the American army who would pass the title down to their eldest sons. Franklin ridiculed the concept. The Chinese were right, he said, to honor the parents of people who earned distinction, for they had some role in it. But honoring a worthy person's descendants, who had nothing to do with achieving the merit, "is not only groundless and absurd but often hurtful to that posterity." Any form of hereditary aristocracy or nobility was, he declared, "in direct opposition to the solemnly declared sense of their country."

He also, in the letter, made fun of the symbol of the new Cincinnati order, a bald eagle, which had also been selected as a national symbol. That provoked one of Franklin's most famous riffs about America's values and the question of a national bird.

To Sarah Bache, January 26, 1784

My dear Child,

Your care in sending me the news papers is very agreeable to me. I received by Capt. Barney those relating to the Cincinnati. My opinion of the institution cannot be of much importance. I only wonder that

when the united wisdom of our nation had, in the articles of confederation, manifested their dislike of establishing ranks of nobility, by authority either of the Congress or of any particular state, a number of
private persons should think proper to distinguish themselves and
their posterity from their fellow citizens, and form an order of hereditary knights, in direct opposition to the solemnly declared sense of
their country. I imagine it must be likewise contrary to the good sense
of most of those drawn into it, by the persuasion of its projectors, who
have been too much struck with the ribbons and crosses they have seen
among them, hanging to the button-holes of foreign officers. And I
suppose those who disapprove of it have not hitherto given it much opposition, from a principle a little like that of your mother, relating to
punctilious persons, who are always exacting little observances of respect, that *if people can be pleased with small matters, it is pity but they
should have them.*

In this view, perhaps I should not myself, if my advice had been
asked, have objected to their wearing their ribbon and badge according
to their fancy, though I certainly should to the entailing it as an honor
on their posterity. For honor worthily obtained, as that for example of
our officers, is in its nature a personal thing, and incommunicable to
any but those who had some share in obtaining it. Thus among the
Chinese, the most ancient, and, from long experience, the wisest of nations, honor does not *descend* but *ascends.* If a man from his learning, his
wisdom or his valor, is promoted by the emperor to the rank of mandarin, his parents are immediately entitled to all the same ceremonies
of respect from the people, that are established as due to the mandarin
himself; on this supposition, that it must have been owing to the education, instruction, and good example afforded him by his parents
that he was rendered capable of serving the public. This *ascending honor*
is therefore useful to the state as it encourages parents to give their
children a good and virtuous education. But the *descending honor,* to
posterity who could have had no share in obtaining it, is not only
groundless and absurd, but often hurtful to that posterity, since it is
apt to make them proud, disdaining to be employed in useful arts,
and thence falling into poverty and all the meannesses, servility and
wretchedness attending it; which is the present case with much of what

is called the *noblesse* in Europe. Or if, to keep up the dignity of the family, estates are entailed entire on the eldest male heir, another pest to industry and improvement of the country is introduced, which will be followed by all the odious mixture of pride and beggary, and idleness that have half depopulated Spain, occasioning continual extinction of families by the discouragements of marriage and improvement of estates.

I wish therefore that the Cincinnati, if they must go on with their project, would direct the badges of their order to be worn by their parents instead of handing them down to their children. It would be a good precedent, and might have good effects. It would also be a kind of obedience to the fourth commandment, in which God enjoins us to *honor* our father and mother, but has no where directed us to *honor* our children. And certainly no mode of honoring those immediate authors of our being can be more effectual, than that of doing praiseworthy actions, which reflect honor on those who gave us our education; or more becoming than that of manifesting by some public expression or token that it is to their instruction and example we ascribe the merit of those actions.

But the absurdity of *descending* honors is not a mere matter of philosophical opinion, it is capable of mathematical demonstration. A man's son, for instance, is but half of his family, the other half belonging to the family of his wife. His son too, marrying into another family, his share in the grandson is but a fourth; in the great grandson, by the same process, it is but an eighth. In the next generation a sixteenth: the next a thirty-second. The next a sixty-fourth. The next an hundred and twenty-eighth. The next a two hundred and fifty-sixth: and the next a five hundred and twelfth. Thus in nine generations, which will not require more than 300 years, (no very great antiquity for a family) our present chevalier of the order of Cincinnatus share in the then existing knight will be but a 512th part; which, allowing the present certain fidelity of American wives to be insured down thro' all those nine generations, is so small a consideration, that methinks no reasonable man would hazard for the sake of it the disagreeable consequences of the jealousy, envy and ill-will of his countrymen.

Let us go back with our calculation from this young noble, the

512th. part of the present knight, thro' his nine generations till we return to the year of the institution. He must have had a father and mother, they are two. Each of them had a father and mother, they are four. Those of the next preceding generation will be eight; the next sixteen; the next thirty-two; the next sixty-four; the next one hundred and twenty-eight; the next two hundred and fifty-six; and the ninth in this retrocession five hundred and twelve, who must be now existing, and all contribute their proportion of this future Chevalier de Cincinnatus. These with the rest make together as follows: 2 4 8 16 32 64 128 256 512 total 1022.

One thousand and twenty-two men and women contributors to the formation of one knight. And if we are to have a thousand of these future knights there must be now and hereafter existing one million and twenty two thousand fathers and mothers who are to contribute to their production, unless a part of the number are employed in making more knights than one. Let us strike off then the 22,000 on the supposition of this double employ, and then consider whether after a reasonable estimation of the number of rogues, and fools, and royalists and scoundrels and prostitutes that are mixed with and help to make up necessarily their million of predecessors, posterity will have much reason to boast of the noble blood of the then existing set of Chevaliers de Cincinnatus. I hope therefore that the order will drop this part of their project, and content themselves as the knights of the garter, bath, thistle, St. Louis and other orders of Europe do, with a life enjoyment of their little badge and ribbon, and let the distinction die with those who have merited it. This I imagine will give no offence. For my own part, I shall think it a convenience when I go into a company where there may be faces unknown to me, if I discover by this badge the persons who merit some particular expression of my respect; and it will save modest virtue the trouble of calling for our regard, by awkward round-about intimations of having been heretofore employed in the continental service.

The gentleman who made the voyage to France to provide the ribbons and medals has executed his commission. To me they seem tolerably done, but all such things are criticized. Some find fault with the Latin, as wanting classic elegance and correctness; and since our nine universities were not able to furnish better Latin, it was pity, they say, that the mottos had not been in English. Others object to the title, as not properly assumable by any but General Washington, who served without pay. Others object to the bald eagle, as looking too much like a *dindon,* or turkey.

For my own part I wish the bald eagle had not been chosen as the representative of our country. He is a bird of bad moral character. He does not get his living honestly. You may have seen him perched on some dead tree near the river, where, too lazy to fish for himself, he watches the labor of the fishing hawk; and when that diligent bird has at length taken a fish, and is bearing it to his nest for the support of his mate and young ones, the bald eagle pursues him and takes it from him. With all this injustice, he is never in good case but like those among men who live by sharping and robbing he is generally poor and often very lousy. Besides he is a rank coward: the little *king bird* not bigger than a sparrow attacks him boldly and drives him out of the district. He is therefore by no means a proper emblem for the brave and honest Cincinnati of America who have driven all the *king birds* from our country, though exactly fit for that order of knights which the French call *chevaliers d'industrie.* I am on this account not displeased that the figure is not known as a bald eagle, but looks more like a turkey. For in truth the turkey is in comparison a much more respectable bird, and withal a true original native of America. Eagles have been found in all countries, but the turkey was peculiar to ours, the first of the species seen in Europe being brought to France by the Jesuits from Canada, and served up at the wedding table of Charles the Ninth. He is besides, though a little vain and silly, a bird of courage, and would not hesitate to attack a grenadier of the British guards who should presume to invade his farm yard with a red coat on.

I shall not enter into the criticisms made upon their Latin. The gallant officers of America may not have the merit of being great scholars, but they undoubtedly merit much as brave soldiers from their country, which should therefore not leave them merely *fame* for their *virtutis premium;* which is one of their Latin mottos. Their *esto perpetua* another is an excellent wish, if they mean it for their country, bad, if intended for their order. The states should not only restore to them the *omnia* of their first motto which many of them have left and lost, but pay them justly, and reward them generously. They should not be suffered to remain with their new created chivalry *entirely* in the situation of the gentleman in the story, which their *omnia reliquit* reminds me of. You know every thing makes me recollect some story. He had built a very fine house, and thereby much impaired his fortune. He had a pride however in showing it to his acquaintance. One of them after viewing it all, remarked a motto over the door, *o-ia vanitas*. What, says he, is the meaning of this *o-ia?* 'Tis a word I don't understand. I will tell you says the gentleman; I had a mind to have the motto cut on a piece of smooth marble, but there was not room for it between the ornaments to be put in characters large enough to be read. I therefore made use of a contraction anciently very common in Latin manuscripts, by which the *ms* and *ns* in words are omitted, and the omission noted by a little dash above, which you may see there, so that the word is *omnia, omnia vanitas*. O, says his friend, I now comprehend the meaning of your motto, it relates to your edifice; and signifies, that if you have abridged your *omnia,* you have nevertheless left your vanitas legible at full length. I am ever,

Your affectionate Father,
B. Franklin

A VISION OF AMERICA

Franklin heard so frequently from people who wanted to emigrate to America that in early 1784 he printed a pamphlet, in French and in English, designed to encourage the more industrious of them while discouraging those who sought a life of upper-class leisure. His essay, "Information to Those Who Would Remove to America," is one of the clearest expressions of his belief that American society was based on the virtues of the middle (or "mediocre," as he sometimes called them, meaning it as a word of praise) classes of which he still considered himself a part. He purported to be describing the way America was, but he was also subtly prescribing what he wanted it to become. All in all, it was his best paean to the middle-class values he represented and helped to make integral to the new nation's character.

FEBRUARY, 1784

Information to Those Who Would Remove to America

Many persons in Europe having directly or by letters, expressed to the writer of this, who is well acquainted with North America, their desire of transporting and establishing themselves in that country; but who appear to him to have formed thro' ignorance, mistaken ideas & expectations of what is to be obtained there; he thinks it may be useful, and prevent inconvenient, expensive & fruitless removals and voyages of improper persons, if he gives some clearer & truer notions of that part of the world than appear to have hitherto prevailed.

He finds it is imagined by numbers that the inhabitants of North America are rich, capable of rewarding, and disposed to reward all sorts of ingenuity; that they are at the same time ignorant of all the sciences; & consequently that strangers possessing talents in the belles-lettres, fine arts, &c. must be highly esteemed, and so well paid as to become easily rich themselves; that there are also abundance of profitable offices to be disposed of, which the natives are not qualified to fill; and that having few persons of family among them, strangers of birth must be greatly respected, and of course easily obtain the best of those offices, which will make all their fortunes: that the governments too, to encourage emigrations from Europe, not only pay the expense of personal transportation, but give lands gratis to strangers, with Negroes to work for them, utensils of husbandry, & stocks of cattle. These are all wild imaginations; and those who go to America with expectations founded upon them, will surely find themselves disappointed.

The truth is, that though there are in that country few people so miserable as the poor of Europe, there are also very few that in Europe would be called rich: it is rather a general happy mediocrity that prevails. There are few great proprietors of the soil, and few tenants; most people cultivate their own lands, or follow some handicraft or merchandise; very few rich enough to live idly upon their rents or incomes;

or to pay the high prices given in Europe, for paintings, statues, architecture and the other works of art that are more curious than useful. Hence the natural geniuses that have arisen in America, with such talents, have uniformly quitted that country for Europe, where they can be more suitably rewarded. It is true that letters and mathematical knowledge are in esteem there, but they are at the same time more common than is apprehended; there being already existing nine colleges or universities, viz. Four in New England, and one in each of the provinces of New York, New Jersey, Pennsylvania, Maryland and Virginia, all furnished with learned professors; besides a number of smaller academies: these educate many of their youth in the languages and those sciences that qualify men for the professions of divinity, law or physic. Strangers indeed are by no means excluded from exercising those professions, and the quick increase of inhabitants every where gives them a chance of employ, which they have in common with the natives. Of civil offices or employments there are few; no superfluous ones as in Europe; and it is a rule established in some of the states, that no office should be so profitable as to make it desirable . . .

Much less is it advisable for a person to go thither who has no other quality to recommend him but his birth. In Europe it has indeed its value, but it is a commodity that cannot be carried to a worse market than to that of America, where people do not enquire concerning a stranger, *what is he?* but *what can he do?* If he has any useful art, he is welcome; and if he exercises it and behaves well, he will be respected by all that know him; but a mere man of quality, who on that account wants to live upon the public, by some office or salary, will be despised and disregarded. The husbandman is in honor there, & even the mechanic, because their employments are useful. The people have a saying, that God almighty is himself a mechanic, the greatest in the universe; and he is respected and admired more for the variety, ingenuity and utility of his handiworks, than for the antiquity of his family. They are pleased with the observation of a Negro, and frequently mention it, that *boccarorra* (meaning the whiteman) make de blackman workee, make de horse workee, make de ox workee, make ebery ting workee; only de hog. He de hog, no workee; he eat, he drink, he walk about, he go to sleep when he please, *he libb like a gentleman.*

According to these opinions of the Americans, one of them would think himself more obliged to a genealogist, who could prove for him that his ancestors & relations for ten generations had been ploughmen, smiths, carpenters, turners, weavers, tanners, or even shoemakers, & consequently that they were useful members of society; than if he could only prove that they were gentlemen, doing nothing of value, but living idly on the labor of others, mere *fruges consumere nati*, and otherwise *good* for *nothing*, till by their death, their estates like the carcass of the Negro's gentleman-hog, come to be *cut up*.

There are a number of us born merely to eat up the corn. —Watts

With regard to encouragements for strangers from government, they are really only what are derived from good laws & liberty. Strangers are welcome because there is room enough for them all, and therefore the old inhabitants are not jealous of them; the laws protect them sufficiently, so that they have no need of the patronage of great men; and every one will enjoy securely the profits of his industry. But if he does not bring a fortune with him, he must work and be industrious to live. One or two years' residence give him all the rights of a citizen; but the government does not at present, whatever it may have done in former times, hire people to become settlers, by paying their passages, giving land, Negroes, utensils, stock, or any other kind of emolument whatsoever. In short America is the land of labor, and by no means what the English call *lubberland,* and the French *pays de cocagne,* where the streets are said to be paved with half-peck loaves, the houses tiled with pancakes, and where the fowls fly about ready roasted, crying, *come eat me!*

Who then are the kind of persons to whom an emigration to America may be advantageous? And what are the advantages they may reasonably expect?

Land being cheap in that country, from the vast forests still void of inhabitants, and not likely to be occupied in an age to come, insomuch that the propriety of an hundred acres of fertile soil full of wood may be obtained near the frontiers in many places for eight or ten guineas, hearty young laboring men, who understand the husbandry of corn and cattle, which is nearly the same in that country as in Europe, may easily establish themselves there. A little money saved of the good wages they receive there while they work for others, enables them to buy the land and begin their plantation, in which they are assisted by the good will of their neighbors and some credit. Multitudes of poor people from England, Ireland, Scotland and Germany, have by this means in a few years become wealthy farmers, who in their own countries, where all the lands are fully occupied, and the wages of labor low, could never have emerged from the mean condition wherein they were born.

From the salubrity of the air, the healthiness of the climate, the plenty of good provisions, and the encouragement to early marriages, by the certainty of subsistence in cultivating the earth, the increase of inhabitants by natural generation is very rapid in America, and becomes still more so by the accession of strangers; hence there is a continual demand for more artisans of all the necessary and useful kinds, to supply those cultivators of the earth with houses, and with furniture & utensils of the grosser sorts which cannot so well be brought from Europe. Tolerably good workmen in any of those mechanic arts, are sure to find employ, and to be well paid for their work, there being no restraints preventing strangers from exercising any art they understand, nor any permission necessary. If they are poor, they begin first as servants or journeymen; and if they are sober, industrious & frugal, they soon become masters, establish themselves in business, marry, raise families, and become respectable citizens.

Also, persons of moderate fortunes and capitals, who having a number of children to provide for, are desirous of bringing them up to industry, and to secure estates for their posterity, have opportunities of doing it in America, which Europe does not afford. There they may be taught & practice profitable mechanic arts, without incurring disgrace on that account; but on the contrary acquiring respect by such abilities. There small capitals laid out in lands, which daily become more valuable by the increase of people, afford a solid prospect of ample fortunes thereafter for those children. The writer of this has known several instances of large tracts of land, bought on what was then the frontier of Pennsylvania, for ten pounds per hundred acres, which, after twenty years, when the settlements had been extended far beyond them, sold readily, without any improvement made upon them, for three pounds per acre. The acre in America is the same with the English acre or the acre of Normandy.

Those who desire to understand the state of government in America, would do well to read the Constitutions of the several states, and the Articles of Confederation that bind the whole together for general purposes under the direction of one assembly called the Congress. These Constitutions have been printed by order of Congress in America; two editions of them have also been printed in London, and a good translation of them into French has lately been published at Paris.

Several of the princes of Europe having of late years, from an opinion of advantage to arise by producing all commodities & manufactures within their own dominions, so as to diminish or render useless their importations, have endeavored to entice workmen from other countries, by high salaries, privileges, &c. Many persons pretending to be skilled in various great manufactures, imagining that America must be in want of them, and that the Congress would probably be disposed to imitate the princes above-mentioned, have proposed to go over, on condition of having their passages paid, lands given, salaries appointed, exclusive privileges for terms of years, &c. Such persons on reading the Articles of Confederation will find that the Congress have no power committed to them, or money put into their hands, for such purposes; and that if any such encouragement is given, it must be by the government of some separate state. This however has rarely been done in America; and when it has been done it has rarely succeeded, so as to establish a manufacture which the country was not yet so ripe for as to encourage private persons to set it up; labor being generally too dear there, & hands difficult to be kept together, every one desiring to be a master, and the cheapness of land inclining many to leave trades for agriculture.

Some indeed have met with success, and are carried on to advantage; but they are generally such as require only a few hands, or wherein great part of the work is performed by machines. Goods that are bulky, & of so small value as not well to bear the expense of freight, may often be made cheaper in the country than they can be imported; and the manufacture of such goods will be profitable wherever there is a sufficient demand. The farmers in America produce indeed a good deal of wool & flax; and none is exported, it is all worked up; but it is in the way of domestic manufacture for the use of the family. The buying up quantities of wool & flax with the design to employ spinners, weavers, &c and form great establishments, producing quantities of linen and woolen goods for sale, has been several times attempted in different provinces; but those projects have generally failed, goods of equal value being imported cheaper. And when the governments have been solicited to support such schemes by encouragements, in money, or by imposing duties on importation of such goods, it has been generally refused, on this principle, that if the country is ripe for the manufacture, it may be carried on by private persons to advantage; and if not, it is a folly to think of forcing nature.

Great establishments of manufacture, require great numbers of poor to do the work for small wages; these poor are to be found in Europe, but will not be found in America, till the lands are all taken up and cultivated, and the excess of people who cannot get land, want employment. The manufacture of silk, they say, is natural in France, as that of cloth in England, because each country produces in plenty the first material: but if England will have a manufacture of silk as well as that of cloth, and France one of cloth as well as that of silk, these unnatural operations must be supported by mutual prohibitions or high duties on the importation of each other's goods, by which means the workmen are enabled to tax the home-consumer by greater prices, while the higher wages they receive makes them neither happier nor richer, since they only drink more and work less. Therefore the governments in America do nothing to encourage such projects. The people by this means are not imposed on, either by the merchant or mechanic; if the merchant demands too much profit on imported shoes, they buy of the shoemaker: and if he asks too high a price, they take them of the merchant: thus the two professions are checks on each other. The shoemaker however has on the whole a considerable profit upon his labor in America, beyond what he had in Europe, as he can add to his price a sum nearly equal to all the expenses of freight & commission, risk or insurance, &c. necessarily charged by the merchant. And the case is the same with the workmen in every other mechanic art. Hence it is that artisans generally live better and more easily in America than in Europe, and such as are good; economists make a comfortable provision for age, & for their children. Such may therefore remove with advantage to America.

In the old long settled countries of Europe, all arts, trades, professions, farms, &c. are so full that it is difficult for a poor man who has children, to place them where they may gain, or learn to gain a decent livelihood. The artisans, who fear creating future rivals in business, refuse to take apprentices, but upon conditions of money, maintenance or the like, which the parents are unable to comply with. Hence the youth are dragged up in ignorance of every gainful art, and obliged to become soldiers or servants or thieves, for a subsistence. In America the rapid increase of inhabitants takes away that fear of rivalship, & artisans willingly receive apprentices from the hope of profit by their labor during the remainder of the time stipulated after they shall be instructed. Hence it is easy for poor families to get their children instructed; for the artisans are so desirous of apprentices, that many of them will even give money to the parents to have boys from ten to fifteen years of age bound apprentices to them till the age of twenty one; and many poor parents have by that means, on their arrival in the country, raised money enough to buy land sufficient to establish themselves, and to subsist the rest of their family by agriculture. These contracts for apprentices are made before a magistrate, who regulates the agreement according to reason and justice; and having in view the formation of a future useful citizen, obliges the master to engage by a written indenture, not only that during the time of service stipulated, the apprentice shall be duly provided with meat, drink, apparel, washing & lodging, and at its expiration with a complete new suit of clothes, but also that he shall be taught to read, write & cast accounts, & that he shall be well instructed in the art or profession of his master, or some other, by which he may afterwards gain a livelihood, and be able in his turn to raise a family. A copy of this indenture is given to the apprentice or his friends, & the magistrate keeps a record of it, to which recourse may be had, in case of failure by the master in any point of performance. This desire among the masters to have more hands employed in working for them, induces them to pay the passages of young persons, of both sexes, who on their arrival agree to serve them one, two, three or four years; those who have already learnt a trade agreeing for a shorter term in proportion to their skill and the consequent immediate value of their service; and those who have none, agreeing for a longer term, in consideration of being taught an art their poverty would not permit them to acquire in their own country.

The almost general mediocrity of fortune that prevails in America, obliging its people to follow some business for subsistence, those vices that arise usually from idleness are in a great measure prevented. Industry and constant employment are great preservatives of the morals and virtue of a nation. Hence bad examples to youth are more rare in America, which must be a comfortable consideration to parents. To this may be truly added, that serious religion under its various denominations, is not only tolerated but respected and practiced. Atheism is unknown there, infidelity rare & secret, so that persons may live to a great age in that country without having their piety shocked by meeting with either an atheist or an infidel. And the divine being seems to have manifested his approbation of the mutual forbearance and kindness with which the different sects treat each other, by the remarkable prosperity with which he has been pleased to favor the whole country.

NO LONGER HIS ENEMY

The end of the war permitted the resumption of amiable correspondence with old friends in England, most notably his fellow printer William Strahan, to whom he had written the famous but unsent letter nine years earlier declaring "you are now my enemy." By 1780, he had mellowed enough to draft a letter signed "your formerly affectionate friend," which he then changed to "your long affectionate humble servant." By 1784, he was signing himself "most affectionately."

Once again they debated Franklin's theories that top government officials should serve without pay and that England's society and government were inherently corrupt. Now, however, the tone was bantering as

Franklin suggested that the Americans, who "have some remains of affection" for the British, perhaps should help govern them. "If you have not sense and virtue enough left to govern yourselves," he wrote, "dissolve your present old crazy constitution and send members to Congress." Lest Strahan not realize he was joking, Franklin confessed: "You will say my advice smells of Madeira. You are right. This foolish letter is mere chitchat between ourselves over the second bottle."

To William Strahan, February 16, 1784

Dear Sir,

I received and read with pleasure your kind letter of the first as it informed me of the welfare of you and yours. I am glad the accounts you have from your kinswomen at Philadelphia are agreeable, and I shall be happy if any recommendations from me can be serviceable to Dr. Ross or any other friend of yours going to America.

Your arguments persuading me to come once more to England, are very powerful. To be sure I long to see again my friends there, whom I love abundantly: but there are difficulties and objections of several kinds which at present I do not see how to get over.

I lament with you the political disorders England at present labors under. Your papers are full of strange accounts of anarchy and confusion in America, of which we know nothing; while your own affairs are really in a situation deplorable. In my humble opinion the root of the evil lies, not so much in too long or too unequally chosen parliaments, as in the enormous salaries, emoluments, and patronage of your great offices; and that you will never be at rest till they are all abolished, and every place of *honor* made, at the same time, in stead of a place of *profit*, a place of *expense* and *burthen*. *Ambition* and *avarice* are each of them strong passions, and when they are united in the same persons, and have the same objects in view for their gratification, they are too strong for public spirit and love of country, and are apt to produce the most violent factions and contentions. They should therefore be separated, and made to act one against the other. Those places, to speak in our own old style, (*brother type*) may be *for the good of the chapel*, but they are bad for the *master*, as they create constant quarrels that hinder the business.

For example, here are near two months that your government has been employed in *getting its form to press*; which is not yet fit to *work on*, every page of it being *squabbled*, and the whole ready to *fall into pie*. The founts too must be very scanty, or strangely *out of sorts*, since your *compositors* cannot find either *upper-* or *lower-case* letters sufficient to set the word *administration*, but are forced to be continually *turning for them*. However, to return to common (though perhaps too saucy) language, don't despair; you have still one resource left, and that not a bad one since it may reunite the empire. We have some remains of affection for you, and shall always be ready to receive and take care of you in case of distress. So, if you have not sense and virtue enough left to govern yourselves, even dissolve your present old crazy constitution, *and send members to Congress.*

You will say my *advice* smells of *Madeira*. You are right. This foolish letter is mere chit-chat *between ourselves,* over the *second* bottle: if therefore you show it to any body (except our indulgent friends Dagge and Lady Strahan) I will positively *solless* you.

Yours ever most affectionately,
B.F.

To William Strahan, August 19, 1784

Dear friend,

. . . You press me much to come to England; I am not without strong inducements to do so; the fund of knowledge you promise to communicate to me is an addition to them, and no small one. At present it is impracticable. But when my grandson returns, come with him. We will then talk the matter over, and perhaps you may take me back with you. I have a bed at your service, and will try to make your residence, while you can stay with us, as agreeable to you if possible, as I am sure it will be to me.

You do not approve the annihilation of profitable places, for you do not see why a statesman who does his business well, should not be paid for his labor as well as any other workman. Agreed. But why more than any other workman? The less the salary the greater the honor. In so great a nation there are many rich enough to afford giving their time to the public, and there are, I make no doubt many wise and able men who would take as much pleasure in governing for nothing as they do in playing chess for nothing. It would be one of the noblest of amusements. That this opinion is not chimerical the country I now live in affords a proof, its whole civil and criminal law administration being done for nothing, or in some sense for less than nothing, since the members of its judiciary parliaments buy their places, and do not make more than three per cent, for their money, by their fees and emoluments, while the legal interest is five: so that in fact they give two per cent, to be allowed to govern, and all their time and trouble into the bargain. Thus *profit*, one motive for desiring place, being abolished, there remains only ambition; and that being in some degree balanced by *loss*, you may easily conceive that there will not be very violent factions and contentions for such places; nor much of the mischief to the country that attends your factions, which have often occasioned wars, and overloaded you with debts impayable.

I allow all the force of your joke upon the vagrancy of our Congress. They have a right to sit *where* they please, of which perhaps they have made too much use by shifting too often but they have two other rights; those of sitting *when* they please, and as *long* as they please, in which methinks they have the advantage of your Parliament; for they cannot be dissolved by the breath of a minister, and sent packing as you were the other day, when it was your earnest desire to have remained longer together.

You fairly acknowledge that the late war terminated quite contrary to your expectation. Your expectation was ill founded; for you would not believe your old friend, who told you repeatedly that by those measures England would lose her colonies, as Epictetus warned in vain his master that he would break his leg. You believed rather the tales you heard of our poltroonery and impotence of body and mind. Do you not remember the story you told me of the Scotch sergeant, who met with a party of forty American soldiers, and though alone disarmed them all and brought them in prisoners; a story almost as improbable as that of the Irishman, who pretended to have alone taken and brought in five of the enemy, by *surrounding* them. And yet, my friend, sensible and judicious as you are, but partaking of the general infatuation, you seemed to believe it. The word general puts me in mind of a general, your general Clarke, who had the folly to say in my hearing at Sir John Pringle's, that with a thousand British grenadiers he would undertake to go from one end of America to the other and geld all the males partly by force and partly by a little coaxing. It is plain he took us for a species of animals very little superior to brutes. The Parliament too believed the stories of another foolish general, I forget his name, that the Yankees never *felt bold.* Yankee was understood to be a sort of yahoo, and the Parliament did not think the petitions of such creatures were fit to be received and read in so wise an assembly.

What was the consequence of this monstrous pride and insolence? You first send small armies to subdue us, believing them more than sufficient, but soon found yourselves obliged to send greater; these whenever they ventured to penetrate our country beyond the protection of their ships, were either repulsed and obliged to scamper out, or were surrounded, beaten, and taken prisoners.

An American planter who had never seen Europe, was chosen by us to command our troops and continued during the whole war. This man sent home to you, one after another, five of your best generals, baffled, their heads bare of laurels, disgraced even in the opinion of their employers. Your contempt of our understandings in comparison with your own appeared to be not much better founded than that of our courage, if we may judge by this circumstance, that in whatever court of Europe a Yankee negotiator appeared, the wise British minister was put in a passion, picked a quarrel with your friends, and was sent home with a flea in his ear.

But after all my dear friend, do not imagine that I am vain enough to ascribe our success to any superiority in any of those points. I am too well acquainted with all the springs and levers of our machine, not to see that our human means were unequal to our undertaking, and that if it had not been for the justice of our cause, and the consequent interposition of providence in which we had faith we must have been ruined. If I had ever before been an atheist I should now have been convinced of the being and government of a deity. It is he who abases the proud and favors the humble! May we never forget his goodness to us, and may our future conduct manifest our gratitude.

But let us leave these serious reflections and converse with our usual pleasantry. I remember your observing once to me, as we sat together in the House of Commons, that no two journeymen printers within your knowledge had met with such success in the world as ourselves. You were then at the head of your profession, and soon afterward became a member of that Parliament. I was an agent for a few provinces and now act for them all. But we have risen by different modes. I as a republican printer, always liked a form well *planed down;* being averse to those *overbearing* letters that hold their heads so *high* as to hinder their neighbors from *appearing.* You as a monarchist chose to work upon *crown* paper, and found it profitable; while I worked upon *pro-patria* (often indeed called fools-cap) with no less advantage. Both our *heaps hold out* very well, and we seem likely to make a pretty good day's work of it. With regard to public affairs, (to continue in the same stile) it seems to me that the compositors in your chapel do not *cast off their copy* well, nor perfectly understand *imposing,* their *forms* too are continually pestered by the *outs,* and *doubles,* that are not easy to be corrected. And I think they were wrong in laying aside some *faces,* and particularly certain *head-pieces,* that would have been both useful and ornamental. But, courage! The business may still flourish with good management; and the master become as rich as any of the company.

By the way, the rapid growth and extension of the English language in America, must become greatly advantageous to the booksellers, and holders of copy rights in England. A vast audience is assembling there for English authors, ancient, present and future, our people doubling every twenty years; and this will demand large, and of course profitable, impressions of your most valuable books. I would therefore if I possessed such rights, entail them, if such a thing be practicable, upon my posterity; for their worth will be continually augmenting. This may look a little like advice, and yet I have drank no Madeira these ten months. The subject however leads me to another thought, which is, that you do wrong to discourage the emigration of Englishmen to America. In my piece on population, I have proved, I think, that emigration does not diminish but multiplies a nation. You will not have fewer at home for those that go abroad, and as every man who comes among us, and takes up a piece of land, becomes a citizen, and by our constitution has a voice in elections and a share in the government of the country, why should you be against acquiring by this fair means a repossession of it, and leave it to be taken by foreigners of all nations and languages who by their numbers may drown and stifle the English, which otherwise would probably become in the course of two centuries the most extensive language in the world, the Spanish only excepted. It is a fact that the Irish emigrants and their children are now in possession of the government of Pennsylvania, by their majority in the assembly, as well as of a great part of the territory; and I remember well the first ship that brought any of them over. I am ever, my dear friend,

> Yours most Affectionately,
> B. Franklin

DAYLIGHT SAVINGS TIME

One night in Passy, Franklin was absorbed in a game when the candles flickered out. Refusing to quit, he sent his opponent to find more. The man quickly returned with a surprised look and the news that it was already light outside. Franklin threw open the shutters. "You are right, it is daytime," he said. "Let's go to bed."

The incident was the inspiration for a bagatelle he wrote about his surprise at discovering that the sun rose and poured forth light at six in the morning. By this stage in his life, it should be noted, he no longer shared Poor Richard's belief in being early to bed and early to rise. This incident led him to conclude that if people would simply get up much earlier, they could save a lot of money on candles. He even included some pseudo-scientific calculations of what could be saved by this "Economical Project" if Parisians during the summer months would shift their sleeping time seven hours earlier.

The essay, which parodied both human habits and scientific treatises, reflected (as did his writings as a youth) the influence of Jonathan Swift. Franklin concluded by bestowing the idea to the public without any request for royalty or reward. "I expect only to have the honor of it," he declared. He ended up with far more honor than he could have imagined: most histories of the invention of Daylight Savings Time credit the idea to this essay by Franklin, even though he wrote it mockingly and did not come up with the idea of actually shifting clocks by an hour during the summer.

JOURNAL OF PARIS, APRIL 26, 1784

An Economical Project

Messieurs,

You often entertain us with accounts of new discoveries. Permit me to communicate to the public through your paper, one that has been late made by myself, and which I conceive may be of great utility.

I was the other evening in a grand company, where the new lamp of Messrs. Quinquet and Lange was introduced, and much admired for its splendor; but a general enquiry was made, whether the oil it consumed was not in proportion to the light it afforded, in which case there would be no saving in the use of it. No one present could satisfy us in this point, which all agreed ought to be known, it being a very desirable thing to lessen, if possible, the expense of lighting our apartments, when every other article of family expense was so much augmented.

I was much pleased to see this general concern for economy; for I love economy exceedingly.

I went home, and to bed, three or four hours after midnight, with my head full of the subject. An accidental sudden noise waked me about six in the morning, when I was surprised to find my room filled with light; and I imagined at first that a number of those lamps had been brought into it; but rubbing my eyes I perceived the light came in at the windows. I got up and looked out to see what might be the occasion of it, when I saw the sun just rising above the horizon, from whence he poured his rays plentifully into my chamber, my domestic having negligently omitted the preceding night to close the shutters.

I looked at my watch, which goes very well, and found that it was but six o'clock; and still thinking it something extraordinary that the sun should rise so early, I looked into the almanac, where I found it to be the hour given for his rising on that day. I looked forward too, and found he was to rise still earlier every day till towards the end of June, and that at no time in the year he retarded his rising so long as till eight o'clock. Your readers, who with me have never seen any signs of sunshine before noon, and seldom regard the astronomical part of the almanac, will be as much astonished as I was, when they hear of his rising so early; and especially when I assure them *that he gives light as soon as he rises;* I am convinced of this. I am certain of my fact. One cannot be more certain of any fact. I saw it with my own eyes. And having repeated this observation the three following mornings, I found always precisely the same result.

Yet so it happens, that when I speak of this discovery to others, I can easily perceive by their countenances, though they forbear expressing it in words, that they do not quite believe me. One indeed, who is a learned natural philosopher, has assured me that I must certainly be mistaken as to the circumstance of the light *coming* into my room; for it being well known, as he says, that there could be no light *abroad* at that hour, it follows that none could enter from *without;* and that of consequence my windows being accidentally left open, instead of *letting in the light,* had only served *to let out the darkness;* and he used many ingenious arguments to show me how I might by that means have been deceived. I own that he puzzled me a little, but he did not satisfy me; and the subsequent observations I made, as above-mentioned, confirmed me in my first opinion.

This event has given rise in my mind to several serious and important reflections. I considered that if I had not been awakened so early that morning, I should have slept six hours longer by the light of the sun, and in exchange have lived six hours the following night by candle light; and the latter being a much more expensive light than the former, my love of economy induced me to muster up what little arithmetic I was master of, and to make some calculations, which I shall give you, after observing that utility is, in my opinion, the test of value in matters of invention, and that a discovery which can be applied to no use, or is not good for something, is good for nothing.

I took for the basis of my calculation the supposition that there are 100,000 families in Paris, and that these families consume in the night half a pound of bougies, or candles, per hour. I think this a moderate allowance, taking one family with another, for though I believe some consume less, I know that many consume a great deal more. Then estimating seven hours per day, as the medium quantity between the time of the sun's rising and ours, he rising during the six following months from six to eight hours before noon; and there being seven hours of course per night in which we burn candles, the account will stand thus:

In the six months between the 20th of March and the 20th of September, there are:

Nights, 183

Hours of each night in which we burn candles, 7

Multiplication gives us for the total number of hours, 1,281

These 1,281 hours, multiplied by 1,000,000, the number of families, give, 128,000,000

One hundred twenty-eight millions and one hundred thousand hours, spent at Paris by candle-light, which at half a pound of wax and tallow per hour, gives the weight of: 64,050,000

Sixty-four millions and fifty thousand of pounds, which, estimating the whole at the medium price of thirty sols the pound, makes the sum of ninety-six millions and seventy-five thousand livres tournois, 96,075,000.

An immense sum! that the city of Paris might save every year, only by the economy of using sun-shine instead of candles.

If it should be said that people are apt to be obstinately attached to old customs, and that it will be difficult to induce them to rise before noon, consequently my discovery can be of but little use; I answer, *nil desperandum*, I believe all who have common sense, as soon as they have learnt from this paper that it is day-light when the sun rises, will contrive to rise with him; and to compel the rest, I would propose the following regulations:

First. Let a tax be laid of a Louis per window, on every window that is provided with shutters to keep out the light of the sun.

Second. Let the same salutary operation of police be made use of to prevent our burning candles that inclined us last winter to be more economical in burning wood; that is, let guards be placed in the shops of all the wax and tallow chandlers, and no family permitted to be supplied with more than one pound of candles per week.

Third. Let guards also be posted to stop all the coaches, &c. that would pass the streets after sun-set, except those of physicians, surgeons, and midwives.

Fourth. Every morning, as soon as the sun rises, let all the bells in every church be set ringing; and if that is not sufficient, let cannon be fired in every street, to wake the sluggards effectually, and make them open their eyes to see their true interest.

All the difficulty will be in the first two or three days; after which the reformation will be as natural and easy, as the present irregularity: for *ce n'est que le premier pas qui coute.* Oblige a man to rise at four in the morning, and it is more than probably he shall go willingly to bed at eight in the evening; and having had eight hours sleep, he will rise more willingly at four the morning following.

But this sum of ninety-six millions and seventy-five thousand livres, is not the whole of what may be saved by my economical project. You may observe, that I have calculated upon only one-half of the year, and much may be saved in the other, though the days are shorter. Besides the immense flock of wax and tallow left unconsumed during the summer, will probably make candles much cheaper for the ensuing winter, and continue cheaper as long as the proposed reformation shall be supported.

For the great benefit of this discovery, thus freely communicated and bestowed by me on the public, I demand neither place, pension, exclusive privilege, or any other reward whatever. I expect only to have the honor of it. And yet I know there are little envious minds who will, as usual, deny me this, and say that my invention was known to the ancients, and perhaps they may bring passages out of old books in proof if it. I will not dispute with these people that the ancients might know the sun would rise at certain hours; they possibly had, as we have, almanacs that predicted it; but it does not follow from thence that they knew *he gave light as soon as he rose.* This is what I claim as my discovery.

If the ancients knew it, it must have been long since forgotten, for it certainly was unknown to the moderns, at least to the Parisians, which to prove, I need use but one plain simple argument. They are as well-instructed, judicious, and prudent a people as exist any where in the world, all professing like myself to be lovers of economy; and from the many heavy taxes required from them by the necessities of the state, have surely an abundant reason to be economical. I say it is impossible that so sensible a people, under such circumstances, should have lived so long by the smoky unwholesome and enormously-expensive light of candles, if they had really known that they might have had as much as pure light of the sun for nothing. I am, &c.

An Abonne

THE PRODIGAL WILLIAM

The end of the Revolution was, for both men and nations, a season or reconciliation. If America could repair its relationship with Britain, there was hope that Franklin could do so with his son. "Dear and honored father," William wrote from England that summer. "Ever since the termination of the unhappy contest between Great Britain and America, I have been anxious to write to you, and to endeavor to revive that affectionate intercourse and connection which, until the commencement of the late troubles, had been the pride and happiness of my life."

It was a noble and plaintive gesture from a son who had, through it all, never said anything bad about his estranged father nor stopped loving him. But William was still a Franklin, and he could not bring himself to admit that he had been in the wrong, nor to apologize. "If I have been mistaken, I cannot help it. It is an error of judgment that the maturest reflection I am capable of cannot rectify; and I verily believe were the same circumstances to occur again tomorrow, my conduct would be exactly similar to what it was." He offered to come to Paris, if his father did not want to come to England, so they could settle their issues with "a personal interview."

Franklin's response revealed his pain, but it also offered some hints of hope. He began by saying he was "glad to find that you desire to revive the affectionate intercourse," and he even brought himself to add, "it will be agreeable to me." Yet he immediately segued from love to anger.

TO WILLIAM FRANKLIN, AUGUST 16, 1784

Dear Son,

I received your letter of the 22d past, and am glad to find that you desire to revive the affectionate intercourse that formerly existed between us. It will be very agreeable to me. Indeed nothing has ever hurt me so much and affected me with such keen sensations, as to find myself deserted in my old age by my only son; and not only deserted, but to find him taking up arms against me, in a cause wherein my good fame, fortune and life were all at stake.

You conceived, you say, that your duty to your king and regard for your country required this. I ought not to blame you for differing in sentiment with me in public affairs. We are men, all subject to errors. Our opinions are not in our power; they are formed and governed much by circumstances that are often as inexplicable as they are irresistible. Your situation was such that few would have censured your remaining neuter, though *there are natural duties which precede political ones, and cannot be extinguished by them.* This is a disagreeable subject. I drop it. And we will endeavor as you propose mutually to forget what has happened relating to it, as well as we can.

I send your son over to pay his duty to you. You will find him much improved. He is greatly esteemed and beloved in this country, and will make his way anywhere. It is my desire that he should study the law, as a necessary part of knowledge for a public man, and profitable if he should have occasion to practice it. I would have you therefore put into his hands those law-books you have viz. Blackstone, Coke, Bacon, Viner, etc. He will inform you, that he received the letter sent him by Mr. Galloway, and the *paper* it enclosed, safe. On my leaving America I deposited with that friend for you a chest of papers, among which was a manuscript of 9 or 10 volumes relating to manufactures, agriculture, commerce, finance, etc. Which cost me in England about 70 guineas; and eight quire books containing the rough drafts of all my letters while I lived in London. These are missing. I hope you have got them. If not, they are lost. Mr. Vaughan has published in London a volume of what he calls my political works. He proposes a second edition. But as the first was very incomplete, and you had many things that are omitted, for I used to send you sometimes the rough drafts, and sometimes the printed pieces I wrote in London, I have directed him to apply to you for what may be in your power to furnish him with, or to delay his publication till I can be at home again if that may ever happen. I did intend returning this year, but the Congress, instead of giving me leave to do so, have sent me another commission, which will keep me here at least a year longer, and perhaps I may then be too old and feeble to bear the voyage. I am here among a people that love and respect me, a most amiable nation to live with, and perhaps I may conclude to die among them; for my friends in America are dying off one after another, and I have been so long abroad that I should now be almost a stranger in my own country. I shall be glad to see you when convenient, but would not have you come here at present. You may confide to your son the family affairs you wished to confer upon with me, for he is discreet. And I trust that you will prudently avoid introducing him to company that it may be improper for him to be seen with. I shall hear from you by him, and any letters to me afterwards, will come safe, under cover directed to Mr. Ferdinand Grand, Banker at Paris.

Wishing you Health, and more Happiness than it seems you have lately experienced, I remain,

Your affectionate Father,
B. Franklin

ON WISHES, AGE, AND BIFOCALS

In his spare time, Franklin perfected one of his most famous and useful inventions, bifocal glasses. Writing to a friend in August of 1784, he announced himself "happy in the invention of Double Spectacles, which, serving for distant objects as well as near ones, make my eyes as useful to me as ever they were." A few months later, in response to a request for more information about "your invention," Franklin provided details. A portrait by Charles Willson Peale, done in 1785, shows him wearing his new spectacles.

TO GEORGE WHATLEY, MAY 23, 1785

Dear old Friend,

I sent you a few Lines the other Day, with the Medallion, when I should have written more but was prevented by the coming in of a Bavard, who worried me till Evening. I bore with him, and now you are to bear with me: For I shall probably *bavarder* in answering your Letter.

I am not acquainted with the saying of Alphonsus which you allude to, as a Sanctification of your Rigidity in refusing to allow me the Plea of Old Age as an Excuse for my want of exactitude in correspondence. What was that Saying? You do not it seems, feel any occasion for such an excuse, though you are, as you say, rising 75. But I am rising (perhaps more properly falling) 80, and I leave the excuse with you till you arrive at that Age; perhaps you may then be more sensible of its validity, and see fit to use it for your self.

I must agree with you that the Gout is bad, and that the Stone is worse. I am happy in not having them both together: and I join in your Prayer that you may live till you die without either. But I doubt the Author of the Epitaph you send me was a little mistaken, when he speaking of the world, he says that

> *He never cared a pin, What they said or may say*
> *of the Mortal within,*

It is so natural to wish to be well spoken of, whether alive or dead, that I imagine he could not be quite exempt from that desire, and that at least he wished to be thought a wit, or he would not have given himself the trouble of writing so good an epitaph to leave behind him. Was it not as worthy of his care that the world should say he was an honest and a good man? I like better the concluding sentiment in the old song called the *Old Man's Wish,* wherein after wishing for a warm house in a country town, an easy horse, some good old authors, ingenious and cheerful companions, a pudding on Sundays with stout ale and a bottle of burgundy, &c. &c. in separate stanzas, each ending with this burden

> *May I govern my Passions with an absolute sway*
> *Grow wise and better as my Strength wears away*
> *Without Gout, or Stone, by a gentle Decay,*

he adds,

> *With a Courage undaunted may I face my last day;*
> *And when I am gone, may the better Sort say,*
> *In the Morning when sober, in the Evening when mellow,*
> *He's gone, and has not left behind him his Fellow;*
> *For he governed his Passions, &c*

But what signifies our wishing? Things happen after all as they will happen. I have sung that *Wishing Song* a thousand times when I was young, and now find at Fourscore that the three Contraries have befallen me; being subject to the Gout, and the Stone, and not being yet Master of all my Passions. Like the proud girl in my country, who wished and resolved not to marry a Parson, nor a Presbyterian, nor an Irishman, and at length found herself married to an Irish Presbyterian Parson. You see I have some reason to wish that in a future State I may not only be *as well as I was,* but a little better. And I hope it: For I too, with your Poet, *trust in God.* And when I observe that there is great frugality as well as wisdom in his works, since he has been evidently sparing both of labor and materials; for by the various wonderful inventions of propagation he has provided for the continual peopling his world with plants and animals without being at the trouble of repeated new creations; and by the natural reduction of compound substances to their original elements, capable of being employed in new compositions, he has presented the necessity of creating new matter; for that the earth, water, air and perhaps fire which, being compounded, from wood, do when the wood is dissolved return and again become air, earth, fire and water: I say that when I see nothing annihilated, and not even a drop of water wasted, I cannot suspect the annihilation of souls, or believe that he will suffer the daily waste of millions of minds ready made that now exist, and put himself to the continual trouble of making new ones, thus finding myself in the world, I believe I shall in some shape or other always exist: and with all the inconveniences human life is liable to, I shall not object to a new edition of mine; hoping however that the Errata of the last may be corrected . . .

What you call the Cincinnati Institution is no Institution of our Government, but a private Convention among the Officers of our late Army, and so universally disliked by the people that it is supposed it will be dropt. It was considered as an attempt to establish something like an hereditary Rank or Nobility. I hold with you that it was wrong; may I add that all descending honors are wrong and absurd; that the honor of virtuous actions appertains only to him that performs them, and is in its nature incommunicable. If it were communicable by descent, it must also be divisible among the descendants, and the more ancient the family, the less would be found existing in any one branch of it; to say nothing of the greater chance of unlucky interruptions.

Our Constitution seems not to be well understood with you. If the Congress were a permanent body, there would be more reason in being jealous of giving it powers. But its members are chosen annually, cannot be chosen more than three years successively, nor more than three years in seven, and any of them may be recalled at any time, whence their constituents shall be dissatisfied with their conduct. They are of the people and return again to mix with the people, having no more durable pre-eminence than the different grains of sand in an hourglass. Such an assembly cannot easily become dangerous to liberty. They are the servants of the people, sent together to do the people's business and promote the public welfare; their powers must be sufficient, or their duties cannot be performed. They have no profitable appointments, but a mere payment of daily wages, such as are scarcely equivalent to their expenses, so that having no chance for great places and enormous salaries or pensions as in some countries, there is no *bruiging* or bribing for elections. I wish old England were as happy in its government, but I do not see it. Your people however think their constitution the best in the world, and affect to despise ours. It is comfortable to have a good opinion of one's self and of every thing that belongs to us, to think one's own religion, king and wife the best of all possible wives, kings and religions. I remember three Greenlanders, who had traveled two years in Europe, under the care of some Moravian missionaries, and had visited Germany, Denmark, Holland and England, when I asked them at Philadelphia, (where they were in their way home) whether now they had seen how much more commodiously the white people lived by the help of the arts, they would not choose to remain among us, their answer was that they were pleased with having had an opportunity of seeing so many fine things, *but they chose to live in their own country,* which country by the way consisted of rock only; for the Moravians were obliged to carry earth in their ship from New York for the purpose of making there a cabbage garden.

By Mr. Dolland's saying that my double spectacles can only serve particular eyes, I doubt he has not been rightly informed of their construction. I imagine it will be found pretty generally true, that the same convexity of glass through which a man sees clearest and best at the distance proper for reading, is not the best for greater distances. I therefore had formerly two pair of spectacles, which I shifted occasionally, as in traveling I sometimes read and often wanted to regard the prospects. Finding this change troublesome and not always sufficiently ready, I had the glasses cut, and half of each kind associated in the same circle, thus by this means, as I wear my spectacles constantly, I have only to move my eyes up or down as I want to see distinctly far or near, the proper glasses being always ready. This I find more particularly convenient since my being in France, the glasses that serve me best at table to see what I eat, not being the best to see the faces of those on the other side of the table who speak to me; and when one's ears are not well accustomed to the sounds of a language, a sight of the movements in the features of him that speaks helps to explain, so that I understand French better by the help of my spectacles . . .

We shall always be ready to take your children if you send them to us. I only wonder that since London draws to itself and consumes such numbers of your country-people, your country should not to supply their places, want and willingly receive the children you have to dispose of. That circumstance, together with the multitude who voluntarily part with their freedom as men, to serve for a time as lackeys, or for life as soldiers in consideration of small wages, seems to me a proof that your island is over-peopled. And yet it is afraid of emigrations!

> Adieu, my dear Friend, and believe me ever,
> Yours very affectionately,
> B. Franklin

PART 8

CONSTITUTIONAL SAGE

I Benjamin Franklin of

Philadelphia, Printer, late Minister Plenipotentiary from the United States of
America to the Court of France, now President of the State of Pennsylvania, do
make and declare my last Will and Testament as follows.—

To my Son William Franklin late Governor of the Jerseys, I give and
devise all the Lands I hold or have a Right to in the Province of Nova —
Scotia, to hold to him his Heirs and Assigns forever. I also give to him
all my Books and Papers which he has in his Possession, and all Debts
standing against him on my Account Books, willing that no Payment for,
nor Restitution of the same be required of him by my Executors: The part
he acted against me in the late War, which is of public Notoriety, will
account for my leaving him no more of an Estate he endeavoured to deprive
me of.—

Having since my return from France demolished the three Houses in
Market Street, between third and fourth Streets, fronting my dwelling House,
and erected two new and larger Houses on the Ground, and having also
erected another House on the Lot which formerly was the Passage to my
Dwelling; and also a Printing Office between my Dwelling and the Front
Houses; Now I do give and devise my said Dwelling House wherein I now
live, & the three new Houses, my Printing Office & the Lots of Ground
thereto respectively belonging; also my small House and Lot in Sixth Street,
which I bought of the Widow Henmarsh; also my Pasture Ground which
I have in Hickory Lane with the Buildings thereon: also my House —
and Lot on the North side of Market Street now occupied by Mary Jacobs,
together with two Houses and Lots behind the same and fronting on Sixth or
Hatter Alley; also my Lot of Ground in Arch Street opposite the Church
Burying Ground, with the Buildings thereon erected; also all my Silver
Plate, Pictures, and Household Goods of every kind, now in my said Dwelling
House, to my Daughter Sarah Bache and to her Husband Richard Bache,
to hold to them for and during their natural Lives and the Life of the longest
liver of them; and from and after the decease of the Survivor of them I do
give devise and bequeath the same, to all Children already born, or to be born,
of my said Daughter, and to their Heirs and Assigns for ever, as Tenants
in Common and not as joint Tenants. And if any or either of them shall
happen to die under Age and without Issue, the Part and Share of him
her or them so dying, shall go to, and be equally divided among the —
Survivors, or Survivor of them. But my intention is that if any or either —
of them should happen to die under Age and [without] Issue, such Issue shall

First page of Franklin's last will and testament

THE CONSTITUTIONAL CONVENTION

Franklin arrived back in Philadelphia in 1785, and two years later he was elected to the convention meeting there to write a new Constitution to replace the weak Articles of Confederation. At 81, Franklin was the oldest member by 15 years and was exactly twice the average age of the rest of the members. His benign countenance and venerable grace as he took his seat every morning, and his preference for wry storytelling over argumentative oratory, added a calming presence.

The greatest issue facing the convention was whether America would remain 13 separate states, or become one nation, or some magical combination of both, as Franklin had first suggested in his Albany Plan of Union back in 1754. This issue was manifest in various specific ways: Would Congress be directly elected by the people or chosen by the state legislatures? Would representation be based on population or be equal for each state? Would the national government or the state governments be sovereign?

America was deeply split on this set of issues. Some people, Franklin initially among them, were in favor of creating a supreme national government and reducing the states to a subordinate role. On the other side were those fervently opposed to any surrender of state sovereignty, which had been enshrined in the Articles of Confederation.

The debate grew heated, threatening to break up the convention, and on June 11 Franklin decided it was time to try to restore a spirit of compromise. He had written his speech in advance, and because of his health he asked another delegate to read it aloud. Some of the suggestions that Franklin proposed seemed sensible, others rather odd. With his love of detail, he provided a lengthy set of calculations showing how smaller states could garner enough votes to match the power of larger ones. There were other remedies to be considered. Perhaps the larger states could give up some of their land to the smaller ones. If that was not feasible, he suggested an even more complex option: There could be equal tax contributions requisitioned from each state, and equal votes in Congress from each state on how to spend this money, then a supplemental requisition from larger states, with proportional votes in Congress on how to spend that fund.

Franklin's speech was long, complex and at times baffling. Were these all serious suggestions or were some of them merely theoretical discourses? Members seemed not to know. He made no motion to vote on his suggestion for adjusting borders or creating separate treasury funds. More important than his specific ideas was his tone of moderation and conciliation. His speech, with its openness to new ideas and absence of one-sided advocacy, provided time for tempers to cool, and his call for creative compromises had an effect.

In the Convention, June 11, 1787

Mr. Chairman,

It has given me great pleasure to observe that till this point, *the proportion of representation,* came before us, our debates were carried on with great coolness and temper. If any thing of a contrary kind has on this occasion appeared, I hope it will not be repeated; for we are sent hither to *consult,* not to *contend,* with each other; and declaration of a fixed opinion and of determined resolutions never to change it; neither enlighten nor convince us. Positiveness and warmth on one side naturally beget their like on the other; and tend to create and augment discord, and division, in a great concern, wherein harmony and union are extremely necessary, to give weight to our counsels, and render them effectual in promoting and securing the common good.

I must own that I was originally of opinion it would be better if every member of Congress, or our national council, were to consider himself rather as a representative of the whole, than as an agent for the interests of a particular state, in which case the proportion of members for each state would be of less consequence, and it would not be very material whether they voted by states or individually. But I find as this is not to be expected, I now think the number of representatives should bear some proportion to the number of the represented, and that the decisions should be by the majority of members, not by the majority of states. This is objected to, from an apprehension that the greater states would then swallow up the smaller. I do not at present clearly see what advantage the greater states could propose to themselves by swallowing the smaller and therefore do not apprehend they would attempt it. I recollect that in the beginning of this century, when the union was proposed of the two kingdoms, England and Scotland, the Scotch patriots were full of fears, that unless they had an equal number of representatives in Parliament they should be ruined by the superiority of the English. They finally agreed however that the different proportions of importance in the union, of the two nations should be attended to, whereby they were to have only forty members in the house of commons, and only sixteen of their peers were to sit in the house of lords, a very great inferiority of numbers! And yet to this day I do not recollect that any thing has been done in the Parliament of great Britain to the prejudice of Scotland; and whoever looks over the lists of public officers civil and military of that nation will find, I believe, that the north Britons enjoy at least their full proportion of emolument.

But, sir, in the present mode of voting by states, it is equally in the power of the lesser states to swallow up the greater; and this is mathematically demonstrable. Suppose, for example, that 7 smaller states had each 3 members in the house, and the six larger to have one with another 6 members. And that upon a question, two members of each smaller state should be in the affirmative, and one in the negative, they will make:

Affirmatives 14—Negatives 7

and that all the larger states should be unanimously in the negative, they would make:

Negatives 36—In all, 43

It is then apparent that the 14 carry the question against the 41, and the minority overpowers the majority, contrary to the common practice of assemblies in all countries and ages.

The greater states, sir, are naturally as unwilling to have their property left in the disposition of the smaller, as the smaller are to leave theirs in the disposition of the greater. An honorable gentleman has to avoid this difficulty, hinted a proposition of equalizing the states. It appears to me an equitable one, and I should for my own part, not be against such a measure, if it might be found practicable. Formerly, indeed, when almost every province had a different constitution some with greater others with fewer privileges, it was of importance to the borderers when their boundaries were contested, whether, by running the division lines they were placed on one side or the other. At present when such differences are done away, it is less material. The interest of a state is made up of the interests of its individual members. If they are not injured, the state is not injured. Small states are more easily well and happily governed than large ones. If therefore in such an equal division, it should be found necessary to diminish Pennsylvania, I should not be averse to the giving a part of it to n. Jersey, and another to Delaware; but as there would probably be considerable difficulties in adjusting such a division; and however equally made at first, it would be continually varying by the augmentation of inhabitants in some states and their more fixed proportion in others; and thence frequent occasion for new divisions; I beg leave to propose for the consideration of the committee another mode, which appears to me, to be as equitable, more easily carried into practice, and more permanent in its nature.

Let the weakest state say what proportion of money or force it is able and willing to furnish for the general purposes of the union.

Let all the others oblige themselves to furnish, even an equal proportion.

The whole of these joins supplies to be absolutely in the disposition of Congress.

The Congress in this case to be composed of an equal number of delegates from each state:

And their decisions to be by the majority of individual members voting.

If these joint and equal supplies should on particular occasions not be sufficient, let Congress make requisitions on the richer and more powerful states for farther aids, to be voluntarily afforded; leaving to each state the right of considering the necessity and utility of the aid desired, and of giving more or less as it should be found proper.

This mode is not new; it formerly was practiced with success by the British government, with respect to Ireland and the colonies. We sometimes gave even more than they expected or thought just to accept; and in the last war, carried on while we were united, they gave us back in 5 years a million sterling. We should probably have continued such voluntary contributions, whenever the occasions appeared to require them for the common good of the empire: it was not till they chose to force us, and to deprive us of the merit and pleasure of voluntary contributions, that we refused and resisted. Those contributions however were to be disposed of at the pleasure of a government in which we had no representative. I am therefore persuaded that they will not be refused to one in which the representation shall be equal.

MOTION FOR PRAYERS

As the days grew even hotter, so again did the dispute over representation.

Once again it was time for Franklin to try to restore equanimity, and this time he did so in an unexpected way. In a speech on June 28, he suggested that they open each session with a prayer.

Franklin was a believer, even more so as he grew older, in a rather general and at times nebulous divine providence, the principle that God had a benevolent interest in the affairs of men. But he never showed much faith in the more specific notion of providence which held that God would intervene directly based on personal prayer. So the question arises: Did he make his proposal for prayer out of a deep religious faith or out of a pragmatic political belief that it would encourage calm in the deliberations?

There was, as usual, probably an element of both, but perhaps a bit more of the latter. Franklin was never known to pray publicly himself, and he rarely attended church. Yet he thought it useful to remind this assembly of demi-gods that they were in the presence of a God far greater, and that history was watching as well. In order to succeed they had to be awed by the magnitude of their task and be humbled, not assertive.

Alexander Hamilton warned that the sudden hiring of a chaplain might frighten the public into thinking that "embarrassments and dissensions within the convention had suggested this measure." Franklin replied that a sense of alarm outside the hall might help rather than hurt the deliberations within. Another objection was raised, that there was no money to pay a chaplain. The idea was quietly shelved.

THE CONSTITUTIONAL CONVENTION, JUNE 28, 1787

Mr. President,

The small progress we have made after 4 or 5 weeks close attendance and continual reasonings with each other, our different sentiments on almost every question, several of the last producing as many *noes* as *ayes*, is methinks a melancholy proof of the imperfection of the human understanding. We indeed seem to feel our own want of political wisdom, since we have been running all about in search of it. We have gone back to ancient history for models of government, and examined the different forms of those republics, which, having been originally formed with the seeds of their own dissolution, now no longer exist. And we have viewed modern states all round Europe, but find none of their constitutions suitable to our circumstances.

In this situation of this assembly, groping, as it were, in the dark, to find political truth, and scarce able to distinguish it when presented to us, how has it happened, sir, that we have not, hitherto once thought of humbly applying to the father of lights to illuminate our understandings? In the beginning of the contest with Britain, when we were sensible of danger, we had daily prayers in this room for the divine protection! Our prayers, sir, were heard; and they were graciously answered. All of us, who were engaged in the struggle, must have observed frequent instances of a superintending providence in our favor. To that kind providence we owe this happy opportunity of consulting in peace on the means of establishing our future national felicity. And have we now forgotten that powerful friend? Or do we imagine we no longer need its assistance?

I have lived, sir, a long time; and the longer I live, the more convincing proofs I see of this truth, *that God governs in the affairs of men!* And if a sparrow cannot fall to the ground without his notice, is it probable that an empire can rise without his aid? We have been assured, sir, in the sacred writings, that except the lord build the house, they labor in vain that build it. I firmly believe this; and I also believe that without his concurring aid, we shall succeed in this political building no better than the builders of Babel: we shall be divided by our little partial local interests, our projects will be confounded and we ourselves shall become a reproach and a byword down to future ages. And what is worse, mankind may hereafter, from this unfortunate instance, despair of establishing government by human wisdom, and leave it to chance, war and conquest. I therefore beg leave to move,

That henceforth prayers, imploring the assistance of heaven, and its blessing on our deliberations, be held in this assembly every morning before we proceed to business; and that one or more of the clergy of this city be requested to officiate in that service.

Note by Franklin: The Convention except three or four Persons, thought Prayers unnecessary!!

FRANKLIN'S CLOSING SPEECH

The convention did finally compromise on a proportional House and a Senate with equal votes per state, a motion that was formally made by Franklin. It was a triumph of conciliation and humility and the respect for other opinions that undergirds a democracy.

Franklin's final triumph was to express these sentiments, with a wry but powerful charm, in a remarkable closing address to the convention. The speech was a testament to the virtue of intellectual tolerance and to the evil of presumed infallibility, and it proclaimed for the ages the enlightened creed that became central to America's freedom. With his deft and self-deprecating use of double negatives—"I am not sure I shall never approve it," "I am not sure that it is not the best"—he emphasized the humility and appreciation for human fallibility that was necessary to form a nation. They were the most eloquent words Franklin ever wrote—and perhaps the best ever written by anyone about the magic of the American system and the spirit that created it. Compromisers may not make great heroes, but they do make great democracies.

Mr. President,

I confess that I do not entirely approve this Constitution at present, but sir, I am not sure I shall never approve it: for having lived long, I have experienced many instances of being obliged, by better information or fuller consideration, to change opinions even on important subjects, which I once thought right, but found to be otherwise. It is therefore that the older I grow the more apt I am to doubt my own judgment, and to pay more respect to the judgment of others. Most men indeed as well as most sects in religion, think themselves in possession of all truth, and that wherever others differ from them it is so far error. Steele, a Protestant, in a dedication tells the pope, that the only difference between our two churches in their opinions of the certainty of their doctrine, is, the Romish church is infallible, and the Church of England is never in the wrong. But though many private persons think almost as highly of their own infallibility, as of that of their sect, few express it so naturally as a certain French lady, who in a little dispute with her sister, said, I don't know how it happens, sister, but I meet with no body but myself that's *always* in the right. *Il n'y a que moi a toujours raison.*

In these sentiments, sir, I agree to this Constitution, with all its faults, if they are such; because I think a general government necessary for us, there is no *form* of government but what may be a blessing to the people if well administered; and I believe farther that this is likely to be well administered for a course of years, and can only end in despotism as other forms have done before it, when the people shall become so corrupted as to need despotic government, being incapable of any other. I doubt too whether any other convention we can obtain, may be able to make a better Constitution: for when you assemble a number of men to have the advantage of their joint wisdom, you inevitably assemble with those men all their prejudices, their passions, their errors of opinion, their local interests, and their selfish views. From such an assembly can a perfect production be expected? It therefore astonishes me, sir, to find this system approaching so near to perfection as it does;

and I think it will astonish our enemies, who are waiting with confidence to hear that our councils are confounded, like those of the builders of Babel, and that our states are on the point of separation, only to meet hereafter for the purpose of cutting one another's throats.

Thus I consent, sir, to this Constitution because I expect no better, and because I am not sure that it is not the best. The opinions I have had of its errors, I sacrifice to the public good. I have never whispered a syllable of them abroad. Within these walls they were born, and here they shall die. If every one of us in returning to our constituents were to report the objections he has had to it, and endeavor to gain partisans in support of them, we might prevent its being generally received, and thereby lose all the salutary effects and great advantages resulting naturally in our favor among foreign nations, as well as among ourselves, from our real or apparent unanimity.

Much of the strength and efficiency of any government in procuring and securing happiness to the people depends on opinion, on the general opinion of the goodness of that government as well as of the wisdom and integrity of its governors. I hope therefore that for our own sakes, as a part of the people, and for the sake of our posterity we shall act heartily and unanimously in recommending this Constitution, wherever our influence may extend, and turn our future thoughts and endeavors to the means of having it well administered.

On the whole, sir, I cannot help expressing a wish, that every member of the convention, who may still have objections to it, would with me on this occasion doubt a little of his own infallibility, and to make *manifest* our *unanimity* put his name to this instrument.

A MIFFY FAMILY

Franklin's closest sibling was his sister Jane Franklin Mecom. His letters to her were always informative and affectionate, and he lamented that he was unlikely ever to see her again. He could, however, still chide her for her sloppiness in keeping post office accounts and make fun of the edgy qualities of their relatives.

TO JANE MECOM, AUGUST 3, 1789

Dear Sister,

I have received your kind letter of the 23rd past, and am glad to learn that you have at length got some of those I so long since wrote to you. I think your post office is very badly managed. I expect your bill, and shall pay it when it appears. I would have you put the books into cousin Jonathan's hands who will dispose of them for you if he can, or return them hither. I am very much pleased to hear that you have had no misunderstanding with his good father. Indeed if there had been any such, I should have concluded that it was your fault for I think our family were always subject to being a little miffy. By the way, is our relationship in Nantucket quite worn out? I have met with none from thence of late years who were disposed to be acquainted with me, except Capt. Timothy Foulger. They are wonderfully shy. But I admire their honest plainness of speech. About a year ago I invited two of them to dine with me. Their answer was that they would if they could not do better. I suppose they did better, for I never saw them afterwards; and so had no opportunity of showing my miff, if I had one. Give my love to cousin Williams's, and thank them from me for all their kindess to you, which I have always been acquainted with by you, and take as if done to myself. I am sorry to learn from his son, that his health is not so firm as formerly. A journey hither by land might do him good, and I should be happy to see him. I shall make the addition you desire to my superscriptions, desiring in return that you would make a subtraction from yours. The word excellency does not belong to me, and dr. Will be sufficient to distinguish me from my grandson. This family joins in love to you and yours, with

Your affectionate Brother,
B. Franklin

WEBSTER'S DICTIONARY

To Noah Webster, the famous lexicographer who had dedicated his *Dissertations on the English Language* to him, Franklin lamented the loose new word usages infecting the language, a common complaint of curmudgeonly writers but a bit atypical of the jovial Franklin, who had once taken pleasure in inventing new English words and, with even more pleasure, amusing the ladies of Paris with new French ones.

To Noah Webster, December 26, 1789

Dear Sir,

I received some time since your *Dissertations on the English Language*. (The book was not accompanied by any letter or message, informing me to whom I am obliged for it; but I suppose it is to yourself.) It is an excellent work, and will be greatly useful in turning the thoughts of our countrymen to correct writing. Please to accept my thanks for it, as well as for the great honor you have done me, in its dedication. I ought to have made this acknowledgment sooner, but much indisposition prevented me.

I cannot but applaud your zeal for preserving the purity of our language, both in its expressions and pronunciation, and in correcting the popular errors, several of our states are continually falling into with respect to both. Give me leave to mention some of them, though possibly they may already have occurred to you. I wish however that in some future publication of yours, you would set a discountenancing mark upon them. The first I remember is the word *improved*. When I left New England in the year 23, this word had never been used among us, as far as I know, but in the sense of *ameliorated* or *made better*, except once in a very old book of Dr. Mather's entitled *remarkable providences*. As that eminent man wrote a very obscure hand, I remember that when I read that word in his book, used instead of the word *employed*, I conjectured that it was an error of the printer, who had mistaken a too short *l* in the writing for an *r*, and a *y* with too short a tail for a *v*, whereby *employed* was converted into *improved*; but when I returned to Boston in 1733, I found this change had obtained favor, and was then become common; for I met with it often in perusing the newspapers, where it frequently made an appearance rather ridiculous: such, for instance, as the advertisement of a country-house to be sold, which had been many years *improved* as a tavern; and in the character of a deceased country-gentleman, that he had been, for more than 30 years, *improved* as a justice-of-peace. This use of the word *improve* is peculiar to New England, and not to be met with among any other speakers of English, either on this or the other side of the water.

During my late absence in France I find that several other new words have been introduced into our parliamentary language; for example, I find a verb formed from the substantive *notice, I should not have* noticed this, were it not that the gentleman &c. Also another verb, from the substantive, *advocate, the gentleman who* advocates, or *who has* advocated that motion, &c. Another from the substantive *progress,* the most awkward and abominable of the three, *the committee having* progressed resolved to adjourn. The word *opposed,* though not a new word, I find used in a new manner, as, *the gentlemen who are* opposed to this measure, to which I have *also myself always been* opposed. If you should happen to be of my opinion with respect to these innovations you will use your authority in reprobating them . . .

I congratulate you on your marriage of which the newspapers inform me. My best wishes attend you, being, with sincere esteem sir,

> Your most obedient and most humble Servant,
> B. Franklin

ON THE ABOLITION OF SLAVERY

In the very last year of his life, Franklin embarked on one final public mission, a moral crusade that would help ameliorate one of the few blemishes on a life spent fighting for freedom. Throughout much of the 18th century, slavery had been an institution that few White Americans questioned. Even in brotherly Philadelphia, ownership continued to climb until about 1760, when almost 10% of the city's population were slaves. But views had begun to evolve, especially after the ringing words of the Declaration and the awkward compromises of the Constitution. Franklin's views had evolved as well. His conversion culminated in 1787 when he accepted the presidency of the Pennsylvania Society for Promoting the Abolition of Slavery. In that capacity, he wrote a stirring address that called for both abolition and a system to help bring free blacks into the economic and social mainstream of society.

BENJAMIN FRANKLIN'S ADDRESS TO THE PUBLIC, NOVEMBER 9, 1789

It is with peculiar satisfaction we assure the friends of humanity that, in prosecuting the design of our association, our endeavors have proved successful, far beyond our most sanguine expectations.

Encouraged by this success, and by the daily progress of that luminous and benign spirit of liberty which is diffusing itself throughout the world, and humbly hoping for the continuance of the divine blessing on our labors, we have ventured to make an important addition to our original plan; and do therefore earnestly solicit the support and assistance of all who can feel the tender emotions of sympathy and compassion, or relish the exalted pleasure of beneficence.

Slavery is such an atrocious debasement of human nature, that its very extirpation, if not performed with solicitous care, may sometimes open a source of serious evils.

The unhappy man, who has long been treated as a brute animal, too frequently sinks beneath the common standard of the human species. The galling chains that bind his body do also fetter his intellectual faculties, and impair the social affections of his heart. Accustomed to move like a mere machine, by the will of a master, reflection is suspended; he has not the power of choice; and reason and conscience have but little influence over his conduct, because he is chiefly governed by the passion of fear. He is poor and friendless; perhaps worn out by extreme labor, age, and disease.

Under such circumstances, freedom may often prove a misfortune to himself, and prejudicial to society.

Attention to emancipated black people, it is therefore to be hoped, will become a branch of our national police; but, as far as we contribute to promote this emancipation, so far that attention is evidently a serious duty incumbent on us, and which we mean to discharge to the best of our judgment and abilities.

To instruct, to advise, to qualify those who have been restored to freedom, for the exercised and enjoyment of civil liberty; to promote in them habits of industry; to furnish them with employments suited to their age, sex, talents, and other circumstances; and to procure their children an education calculated for their future situation in life, these are the great outlines of the annexed plan, which we have adopted, and which we conceive will essentially promote the public good, and the happiness of these our hitherto too much neglected fellow-creatures.

A plan so extensive cannot be carried into execution without considerable pecuniary resources, beyond the present ordinary funds of the Society. We hope much from the generosity of enlightened and benevolent freemen, and will gratefully receive any donations of subscriptions for this purpose which may be made to our Treasurer, James Starr, or to James Pemberton, Chairman of our Committee of Correspondence.

Signed, by order of the society, B. Franklin, President

One of the arguments against immediate abolition, which Franklin had heretofore accepted, was that it was not practical or safe to free hundreds of thousands of adult slaves into a society for which they were not prepared. (There were about 700,000 slaves in the U.S. out of a total population of 4 million in 1790.) So his abolition society dedicated itself not only to freeing slaves but also to helping them become good citizens. As was typical of Franklin, he drew up for the society a meticulously detailed charter and procedures.

Plan for Improving the Condition of the Free Blacks, 1789

The business relative to free blacks shall be transacted by a committee of twenty-four persons, annually elected by ballot, at the meeting of this Society, in the month called April; and, in order to perform the different services with expedition, regularity, and energy, this committee shall resolve itself into the following sub-committees, viz.

I. A Committee of Inspection, who shall superintend the morals, general conduct, and ordinary situation of the free Negroes, and afford them advice and instruction, protection from wrongs, and other friendly offices.

II. A Committee of Guardians, who shall place out children and young people with suitable persons, that they may (during a moderate time of apprenticeship or servitude) learn some trade or other business of subsistence. The committee may effect this partly by a persuasive influence on parents and the persons concerned, and partly by cooperating with the laws, which are, or may be, enacted for this and similar purposes. In forming contracts on these occasions, the committee shall secure to the Society, as far as may be practicable, the right of guardianship over the persons so bound.

III. A Committee of Education, who shall superintend the school instruction of the children and youth of the free blacks. They may either influence them to attend regularly the schools already established in this city, or form others with this view; they shall, in either case, provide, that the pupils may receive such learning as is necessary for their future situation in life, and especially a deep impression of the most important and generally acknowledged moral and religious principles. They shall also procure and preserve a regular record of the marriages, births, and manumissions of all free blacks.

IV. A Committee of Employ, who shall endeavor to procure constant employment for those free Negroes who are able to work; as the want of this would occasion poverty, idleness, and many vicious habits. This committee will, by sedulous inquiry, be enabled to find common labor for a great number; they will also provide, that such as indicate proper talents may learn various trades, which may be done by prevailing upon them to bind themselves for such a term of years as shall compensate their masters for the expense and trouble of instruction and maintenance. The committee may attempt the institution of some useful and simple manufactures, which require but little skill, and also may assist, in commencing business, such as appear to be qualified for it.

Whenever the committee of inspection shall find persons of any particular description requiring attention, they shall immediately direct them to the committee of whose care they are the proper objects.

In matters of a mixed nature, the committees shall confer, and, if necessary, act in concert. Affairs of great importance shall be referred to the whole committee. The expense, incurred by the prosecution of this plan, shall be defrayed by a fund, to be formed by donations or subscriptions for these particular purposes, and to be kept separate from the other funds of this Society.

The committee shall make a report of their proceedings, and of the state of their stock, to the Society, at their quarterly meetings, in the months called April and October.

THE FINAL PARODY, ON SLAVERY

On behalf of the society, Franklin presented a formal abolition petition to Congress in February 1790. "Mankind are all formed by the same Almighty Being, alike objects of his care, and equally designed for the enjoyment of happiness," it declared. The duty of Congress was to secure "the blessings of liberty to the People of the United States," and this should be done "without distinction of color." Therefore Congress should grant "liberty to those unhappy men who alone in this land of freedom are degraded into perpetual bondage."

Franklin and his petition were roundly denounced by the defenders of slavery, most notably Congressman James Jackson of Georgia, who declared on the House floor that the Bible had sanctioned slavery and, without it, there would be no one to do the hard and hot work on plantations. It was the perfect setup for Franklin's last great parody, written less than a month before he died.

He had begun his literary career 68 years earlier when, as a 16-year-old apprentice, he pretended to be a prudish widow named Silence Dogood, and he made a subsequent career of enlightening readers with similar hoaxes such as "The Trial of Polly Baker" and "An

Edict from the King of Prussia." In the spirit of the second of these essays, he anonymously published in a local newspaper, with appropriate scholarly source citations, a purported speech given by a member of the divan of Algiers 100 years earlier.

It bore a scathing mirror resemblance to Congressman Jackson's speech. "God is great, and Mahomet is his prophet," it began realistically. Then it went on to attack a petition by a purist sect asking for an end to the practice of capturing and enslaving European Christians to work in Algeria.

THE FEDERAL GAZETTE, MARCH 23, 1790

Sir,

Reading last night in your excellent paper the speech of Mr. Jackson in Congress, against meddling with the affair of slavery, or attempting to mend the condition of slaves, it put me in mind of a similar one made about one hundred years since, by Sidi Mehemet Ibrahim, a member of the Divan of Algiers, which may be seen in Martin's account of his consulship, anno 1687. It was against granting the petition of the Sect called Erika or Purists, who prayed for the abolition of piracy and slavery, as being unjust. Mr. Jackson does not quote it; perhaps he has not seen it. If therefore some of its reasonings are to be found in his eloquent speech, it may only show that men's interests and intellects operate and are operated on with surprising similarity in all countries and climates, whenever they are under similar circumstances. The African's speech, as translated, is as follows:

"Allah Bismillah, &c. God is great, and Mahomet is his Prophet.

"Have these Erika considered the consequences of granting their petition? If we cease our cruises against the Christians, how shall we be furnished with the commodities their countries produce, and which are so necessary for us? If we forbear to make slaves of their people, who, in this hot climate, are to cultivate our lands? Who are to perform the common labors of our city, and in our families? Must we not then be our own slaves? And is there not more compassion and more favor due to us Mussulmen, than to these Christian dogs? We have now above 50,000 slaves in and near Algiers. This number, if not kept up by fresh supplies, will soon diminish, and be gradually annihilated. If then we cease taking and plundering the Infidel ships, and making slaves of the seamen and passengers, our lands will become of no value for want of cultivation; the rents of houses in the city will sink one half, and the revenues of government arising from its share of prizes must be totally destroyed.

"And for what? To gratify the whim of a whimsical sect! who would have us not only forbear making more slaves, but even to manumit those we have. But who is to indemnify their masters for the loss? Will the state do it? Is our treasury sufficient? Will the Erika do it? Can they do it? Or would they, to do what they think justice to the slaves, do a greater injustice to the owners? And if we set our slaves free, what is to be done with them? Few of them will return to their countries, they know too well the greater hardships they must there be subject to: they will not embrace our holy religion: they will not adopt our manners: our people will not pollute themselves by intermarrying with them: must we maintain them as beggars in our streets; or suffer our properties to be the prey of their pillage; for men accustomed to slavery, will not work for a livelihood when not compelled. And what is there so pitiable in their present condition? Were they not slaves in their own countries? Are not Spain, Portugal, France and the Italian states, governed by despots, who hold all their subjects in slavery, without exception?

"Even England treats its sailors as slaves, for they are, whenever the government pleases, seized and confined in ships of war, condemned not only to work but to fight for small wages or a mere subsistence, not better than our slaves are allowed by us. Is their condition then made worse by their falling into our hands? No, they have only exchanged one slavery for another: and I may say a better: for here they are brought into a land where the sun of Islamism gives forth its light, and shines in full splendor, and they have an opportunity of making themselves ac-quainted with the true doctrine, and thereby saving their immortal souls. Those who remain at home have not that happiness. Sending the slaves home then, would be sending them out of light into darkness.

"I repeat the question, what is to be done with them? I have heard it suggested, that they may be planted in the wilderness, where there is plenty of land for them to subsist on, and where they may flourish as a free state; but they are, I doubt, too little disposed to labor without compulsion, as well as too ignorant to establish a good government, and the wild Arabs would soon molest and destroy or again enslave them. While serving us, we take care to provide them with every thing; and they are treated with humanity. The laborers in their own countries, are, as I am well informed, worse fed, lodged and clothed. The condition of most of them is therefore already mended, and requires no farther improvement. Here their lives are in safety. They are not liable to be impressed for soldiers, and forced to cut one another's Christian throats, as in the wars of their own countries.

"If some of the religious mad bigots who now tease us with their silly petitions, have in a fit of blind zeal freed their slaves, it was not generosity, it was not humanity that moved them to the action; it was from the conscious burthen of a load of sins, and hope from the supposed merits of so good a work to be excused from damnation. How grossly are they mistaken in imagining slavery to be disallowed by the Al Koran! Are not the two precepts, to quote no more, Masters treat your slaves with kindness: Slaves serve your masters with cheerfulness and fidelity, clear proofs to the contrary? Nor can the plundering of infidels be in that sacred book forbidden, since it is well known from it, that God has given the world and all that it contains to his faithful Mussulmen, who are to enjoy it of right as fast as they can conquer it.

"Let us then hear no more of this detestable proposition, the manumission of Christian slaves, the adoption of which would, by depreciating our lands and houses, and thereby depriving so many good citizens of their properties, create universal discontent, and provoke insurrections, to the endangering of government, and producing general confusion. I have therefore no doubt, but this wise Council will prefer the comfort and happiness of a whole nation of true believers, to the whim of a few Erika, and dismiss their petition."

The result was, as Martin tells us, that the Divan came to this resolution, The doctrine that plundering and enslaving the Christians is unjust, is at best *problematical;* but that it is the interest of this state to continue the practice, is clear; therefore let the petition be rejected.

And it was rejected accordingly.

And since like motives are apt to produce in the minds of men like opinions and resolutions, may we not, Mr. Brown, venture to predict, from this account, that the petitions to the Parliament of England for abolishing the slave trade, to say nothing of other legislatures, and the debates upon them, will have a similar conclusion. I am, Sir,

Your constant reader and humble servant,

Historicus

ON JESUS CHRIST

It is not surprising that, at the end of their lives, many people take stock of their religious beliefs. Franklin had never fully joined a church nor subscribed to a sectarian dogma, and he found it more useful to focus on earthly issues rather than spiritual ones. When he narrowly escaped a shipwreck as he neared the English coast in 1757, he had joked to Debbie that "were I a Roman Catholic, perhaps I should on this occasion vow to build a chapel to some saint; but as I am not, if I were to vow at all, it should be to build a *lighthouse*." Likewise, when a town in Massachusetts named itself Franklin in 1785 and asked him to donate a church bell, he told them to forsake the steeple and build a library, for which he sent "books instead of a bell, sense being preferable to sound."

As he grew older, Franklin's amorphous faith in a benevolent God seemed to become more firm. "If it had not been for the justice of our cause and the consequent interposition of Providence, in which we had faith, we must have been ruined," he wrote Strahan after the war. "If I had ever before been an atheist, I should now have been convinced of the Being and government of a Deity!"

The most important religious role Franklin played—and it was an exceedingly important one in shaping his enlightened new republic—was as an apostle of tolerance. He had contributed to the building funds of each and every sect in Philadelphia, including £5 for the Congregation Mikveh Israel for its new synagogue in April 1788, and he had opposed

religious oaths and tests in both the Pennsylvania and federal constitutions. During the July 4 celebrations in 1788, Franklin was too sick to
leave his bed, but the parade marched under his window. For the first
time, as per arrangements that Franklin had overseen, "the clergy of
different Christian denominations, with the rabbi of the Jews, walked
arm in arm."

His final summation of his religious thinking came the month before
he died, in response to questions from the Rev. Ezra Stiles, president
of Yale. Franklin began by restating his basic belief in God and of the
deist creed that he felt was fundamental to all religions; anything else
was mere embellishment.

Then he addressed Stiles's question about whether he believed in
Jesus, which was, he said, the first time he had ever been asked directly.

To Ezra Stiles, March 9, 1790

Reverend and Dear Sir,

I received your kind Letter of January 28, and am glad you have at
length received the portraits of Governor Yale from his family, and deposited it in the College Library. He was a great and good man, and has
the merit of doing infinite service to your country by his munificence to
that institution. The honor you propose doing me by placing in the
same room with his, is much too great for my deserts; but you always
had a partiality for me, and to that it must be ascribed. I am however
too much obliged to Yale College, the first learned society that took
notice of me, and adorned me with its honors, to refuse a request that
comes from it thro' so esteemed a friend. But I do not think any one of
the portraits you mention as in my possession worthy of the place and
company you propose to place it in. You have an excellent artist lately
arrived. If he will undertake to make one for you, I shall cheerfully pay
the expense: but he must not long delay setting about it, or I may slip
thro' his fingers, for I am now in my 85th year and very infirm.

I send with this a very learned work, (as it seems to me) on the ancient Samaritan coins, lately printed in Spain, and at least curious for
the beauty of the impression. Please to accept it for your college library.
I have subscribed for the encyclopedia now printing here, with the in-

tention of presenting it to the college; I shall probably depart before the work is finished, but shall leave directions for its continuance to the end. With this you will receive some of the first numbers.

You desire to know something of my religion. *It is the first time I have been questioned upon it*: but I do not take your curiosity amiss, and shall endeavor in a few words to gratify it. Here is my creed: I believe in one God, creator of the universe. That he governs it by his providence. That he ought to be worshipped. That the most acceptable service we can render to him, is doing good to his other children. That the soul of man is immortal, and will be treated with justice in another life respecting its conduct in this. These I take to be the fundamental principles of all sound religion, and I regard them as you do, in whatever sect I meet with them.

As to Jesus of Nazareth, my opinion of whom you particularly desire, I think the system of morals and his religion as he left them to us, the best the world ever saw, or is likely to see; but I apprehend it has received various corrupting changes, and I have with most of the present dissenters in England, some doubts as to his divinity: though it is a question I do not dogmatise upon, having never studied it, and think it needless to busy myself with it now, when I expect soon an opportunity of knowing the truth with less trouble. I see no harm however in its being believed, if that belief has the good consequence as probably it has, of making his doctrines more respected and better observed, especially as I do not perceive that the Supreme takes it amiss, by distinguishing the believers, in his government of the world, with any particular marks of his displeasure.

I shall only add respecting myself, that having experienced the goodness of that Being, in conducting me prosperously thro' a long life, I have no doubt of its continuance in the next, though without the smallest conceit of meriting such goodness . . .

With great and sincere esteem and affection, I am, dear sir, your obliged old friend and most obedient humble servant,

B. Franklin

TO THOMAS JEFFERSON

The last letter Franklin wrote was, fittingly, to Thomas Jefferson, his spiritual heir as the nation's foremost apostle of the Enlightenment's faith in reason, experiment and tolerance. Jefferson had come to call at Franklin's bedside and provide news of their beleaguered friends in France. "He went over all in succession," Jefferson noted, "with a rapidity and animation almost too much for his strength." Jefferson praised him for getting so far in his memoirs, which he predicted would be very instructive. "I cannot say much of that," replied Franklin, "but I will give you a sample." Then he pulled out a page that described the last weeks of his negotiations in London to avert the war, which he insisted that Jefferson keep as a memento.

Jefferson followed up by asking about an arcane issue that needed resolving: Which maps had been used to draw America's western boundaries in the Paris peace talks? After Jefferson left, Franklin studied the matter and then wrote his final letter. His mind was clear enough to describe, with precision, the decisions they had made and the maps they had used regarding various rivers running into the Bay of Passamaquoddy.

To Thomas Jefferson, April 8, 1790

Sir,

I received your letter of the 31st past, relating to encroachments made on the eastern limits of the United States, by settlers under the British government, pretending that it is the western and not the eastern river of the bay of Passamaquoddy, which was designated by the name of St. Croix in the treaty of peace with that nation; and requesting of me to communicate any facts, which my memory or papers may enable me to recollect, and which may indicate the true river the commissioners on both sides had in their view to establish as the boundary between the two nations. Your letter found me under a severe fit of my malady, which prevented my answering it sooner, or attending indeed to any kind of business. I now can assure you that I am perfectly clear in the remembrance that the map we used in tracing the boundary was brought to the treaty by the commissioners from England, and that it was the same that was published by Mitchell above 20 years before. Having a copy of that map by me in loose sheets I send you that sheet which contains the bay of Passamaquoddy, where you will see that part of the boundary traced. I remember too that in that part of the boundary, we relied much on the opinion of Mr. Adams, who had been concerned in some former disputes concerning those territories. I think therefore that you may obtain still far their lights from him. That the map we used was Mitchell's map, Congress were acquainted, at the time, by a letter to their secretary for foreign affairs, which I suppose may be found upon their files. I have the honor to be with the greatest esteem and respect, Sir,

Your most obedient and most humble servant,
B. Franklin

LAST WILL AND CODICIL

In his will, which begins with his identifying himself by the occupation that he loved most, Franklin bequeathed his loyalist son William nothing more than some worthless land claims in Canada and the forgiveness of any debts that he still owed him. "The part he acted against me in the late war, which is of public notoriety, will account for my leaving him no more of an estate he endeavored to deprive me of." William complained about the "shameful injustice" of the will, but he still revered his father's memory, and he did not permit himself another harsh public word about him.

Franklin's loyal daughter Sally and her husband Richard Bache got most of his property, including the Market Street houses, on the condition that Richard "set free his Negro man Bob." He did, but Bob took to drink, couldn't support himself and asked to be restored to slavery; the Baches did not do that, but they let him live in their home the rest of his life. Sally was also given a miniature encircled with diamonds given to

Franklin by King Louis XVI. She sold the diamonds to fulfill her lifelong desire to see England. With her husband, she went to stay with William, with whom she had always remained close.

The most unusual provision was a trust he established in his codicil to his will. He noted that, unlike the other founders of the country, he was born poor and had been helped in his rise by those who supported him as a struggling artisan. So he designated £2,000 he had earned as President of Pennsylvania to be split between the towns of Boston and Philadelphia and provided as loans, "at 5% per annum, to such young married artificers" who had served apprenticeships and were now seeking to establish their own businesses. With his usual obsession with detail, he described precisely how the loans and repayments would work, and he calculated that after 100 years the annuities would each be worth £131,000. At that time, the cities could spend £100,000 of it on public projects, while keeping the remainder in the trust, which after another hundred years of loans and compounded interest would, he calculated, be worth £4,061,000. At that point the money would go into the public treasury.

Did it work as he envisioned? In Boston, after 100 years, the fund was worth about $400,000, a little bit less than he had calculated. At that point a trade school, Franklin Union (now the Benjamin Franklin Institute of Technology), was founded with three-fourths of the money plus a matching bequest from Andrew Carnegie, who considered Franklin a hero; the rest remained in the trust. A century later, that amount had grown to nearly $5 million, not quite the equivalent of £4 million but still a sizeable sum. After a legal struggle that was settled by an act of the legislature, the funds went to the Benjamin Franklin Institute of Technology.

In Philadelphia, the bequest did not accumulate quite as well. A century after his death, it totaled $172,000, about one-quarter of what he had projected. Of that sum, three-fourths went to establish Philadelphia's Franklin Institute, still a thriving science museum, with the remainder continued as a loan fund for young tradesmen. A century later, in 1990, this fund had reached $2.3 million.

At that point, Philadelphia Mayor Wilson Goode suggested, one assumes jokingly, that the Ben Franklin money be used to pay for a party featuring BEN Vereen and Aretha FRANKLIN. Others, more serious, proposed it be used to promote tourism, which caused a popular uproar.

The mayor finally appointed a panel of historians, and the state divvied up the money in accordance with their general recommendations. Among the recipients were The Franklin Institute, a variety of community libraries and fire companies, and a group called the Philadelphia Academies that funds scholarships at vocational training programs in the city schools. One of the small but appropriate examples of his legacy occurred at the 2001 Tour de Sol, a race of experimental cars. Some scholarship recipients from a poor high school in West Philadelphia used a $4,300 grant from the father of electricity to build a battery-powered car that won the race's Power of Dreams award.

LAST WILL AND TESTAMENT, JULY 17, 1788

I, Benjamin Franklin of Philadelphia, printer, late Minister Plenipotentiary from the United States of America to the Court of France, now President of the State of Pennsylvania, do make and declare my last will and testament as follows:

To my Son William Franklin late Governor of the Jerseys, I give and devise all the lands I hold or have a right to, in the province of Nova Scotia, to hold to him, his heirs, and assigns forever. I also give to him all my books and papers, which he has in his possession, and all debts standing against him on my account books, willing that no payment for, nor restitution of, the same be required of him, by my executors. The part he acted against me in the late war, which is of public notoriety, will account for my leaving him no more of an estate he endeavored to deprive me of.

Having since my return from France demolished the three houses in Market Street, between Third and Fourth Streets, fronting my dwelling-house, and erected two new and larger ones on the ground, and having also erected another house on the lot which formerly was the passage to my dwelling, and also a printing-office between my dwelling and the front houses; now I do give and devise my said dwelling-house, wherein I now live, my said three new houses, my printing-office and the lots of ground thereto belonging; also my small lot and house in Sixth Street, which I bought of the widow Henmarsh; also my pasture-ground which I have in Hickory Lane, with the buildings thereon; also my house and lot on the north side of Market Street, now occupied by Mary Jacobs, together with two houses and lots behind the same, and fronting on Pewter-Platter Alley; also my lot of ground in Arch Street, opposite the church burying-ground, with the buildings thereon erected; also all my silver plate, pictures, and household goods, of every kind, now in my said dwelling-house, to my daughter Sarah Bache and to her husband Richard Bache to hold to them for and during their natural lives, and the life of the longest liver of them, and from and after the decease of the survivor of them, I do give, devise, and bequeath to all children already born, or to be born of my said daughter, and to their heirs and assigns forever, as tenants in common, and not as joint tenants. And if any or either of them shall happen to die under age, and without issue, the part and share of him, her, or them, so dying, shall go to and be equally divided among the survivors or survivor of them. But my intention is, that, if any or either of them should happen to die under age, leaving issue, such issue shall inherit the part and share that would have passed to his, her, or their parent, had he, she, or they been living . . .

All the Lands near the Ohio, and the lots near the Center of Philadelphia, which I lately purchased of the State, I give to my son-in-law, Richard Bache, his heirs and assigns forever; I also give him the bond I have against him, of two thousand and one hundred and seventy-two pounds, five shillings, together with the interest that shall or may accrue thereon, and direct the same to be delivered up to him by my executors, cancelled, requesting that, in consideration thereof, he would immediately after my decease manumit and set free his Negro man Bob. I leave to him, also, the money due to me from the State of Virginia for types. I also give to him the bond of William Goddard and his sister, and the counter bond of the late Robert Grace, and the bond and judgment of Francis Childs, if not recovered before my decease, or any other bonds, except the bond due from Killan, of Delaware State, which I give to my grandson, Benjamin Franklin Bache. I also discharge him, my said son-in-law, from all claim and rent of moneys due to me, on book account or otherwise. I also give him all my musical instruments.

The King of France's picture set with four hundred and eight diamonds, I give to my daughter Sarah Bache, requesting however that she would not form any of those diamonds into ornaments either for herself or daughters, and thereby introduce or countenance the expensive, vain, and useless fashion of wearing jewels in this country; and those immediately connected with the picture may be preserved with the same.

I give and devise to my dear sister Jane Mecom a house and lot I have in Unity Street, Boston, now or late under the care of Mr. Jonathan Williams, to her and to her heirs and assigns for ever. I also give her the yearly sum of fifty pounds sterling, during life, to commence at my death, and to be paid to her annually out of the interests of dividends arising on twelve shares which I have since my arrival at Philadelphia purchased in the Bank of North America, and, at her decease, I give the said twelve shares in the bank to my daughter Sarah Bache and her husband Richard Bache. But it is my express will and desire that, after Payment of the above fifty pounds sterling annually to my said sister, my said daughter be allowed to apply the residue of the interest or dividends on those shares to her sole and separate use, during the life of my said sister, and afterwards the whole of the interest or dividends thereof as her private pocket money.

I give the right I have to take up three thousand acres of land in the State of Georgia, granted to me by the government of that State, to my grandson William Temple Franklin, his heirs and assigns for ever. I also give to my grandson William Temple Franklin the bond and judgment I have against him of four thousand pounds sterling, my right to the same to cease upon the day of his marriage; and if he dies unmarried, my will is, that the same be recovered and divided among my other grandchildren, the children of my daughter Sarah Bache, in such manner and form as I have herein before given to them the other parts of my estate.

The Philosophical Instruments I have in Philadelphia I give to my ingenious Friend Francis Hopkinson.

To the Children, Grand Children, and Great Grand Children of my brother Samuel Franklin that may be living at the time of my decease, I give fifty pounds sterling, to be equally divided among them. To the children, grandchildren, and great-grandchildren of my sister Anne Harris that may be living at the time of my decease, I give fifty pounds sterling, to be equally divided among them. To the children, grandchildren, and great-grandchildren of my brother James Franklin, that may be living at the time of my decease, I give fifty pounds sterling, to be equally divided among them. To the children, grandchildren, and great-grandchildren of my sister Sarah Davenport, that may be living at the time of my decease, I give fifty pounds sterling to be equally divided among them. To the children, grandchildren, and great-grandchildren of my sister Lydia Scott that may be living at the time of my decease, I give fifty pounds sterling, to be equally divided among them. To the children, grandchildren, and great-grandchildren of my sister Jane Mecom that may be living at the time of my decease, I give fifty pounds sterling, to be equally divided among them.

I give to my grandson Benjamin Franklin Bache all the types and printing materials, which I now have in Philadelphia, with the complete letter foundry, which, in the whole, I suppose to be worth near one thousand pounds; but if he should die under age, then I do order the same to be sold by my executors, the survivors or survivor of them, and the moneys thence arising to be equally divided among all the rest of my said daughter's children, or their representatives, each one on coming of age to take his or her share, and the children of such of them as may die under age to represent, and to take the share and proportion of, the parent so dying, each one to receive his or her part of such share as they come of age.

With regard to my books, those I had in France and those I left in Philadelphia, being now assembled together here, and a catalogue made of them, it is my intention to dispose of the same as follows: My History of the Academy of Sciences in sixty or seventy volumes quarto, I give to the Philosophical Society of Philadelphia, of which I have the honor to be President. My collection in folio of Les Arts et les Métiers I give to the American Philosophical Society, established in New England, of which I am a member. My quarto edition of the same, Arts et Métiers, I give to the Library Company of Philadelphia. Such and so many of my books as I shall mark on the said catalogue with the name of my grandson, Benjamin Franklin Bache, I do hereby give to him; and such and so many of my books as I shall mark on the said catalogue with the name of my grandson, William Bache, I do hereby give to him; and such as shall be marked with the name of Jonathan Williams, I hereby give to my cousin of that name. The residue and remainder of all my books, manuscripts, and papers, I do give to my grandson, William Temple Franklin. My share in the Library Company of Philadelphia, I give to my grandson, Benjamin Franklin Bache, confiding that he will permit his brothers and sisters to share in the use of it.

I was born in Boston, New England, and owe my first instructions in literature to the free grammar-schools established there. I therefore give one hundred pounds sterling to my executors, to be by them, the survivors or survivor of them, paid over to the managers or directors of the free schools in my native town of Boston, to be by them, or by those person or persons, who shall have the superintendence and management of the said schools, put out to interest, and so continued at interest for ever, which interest annually shall be laid out in silver medals, and given as honorary rewards annually by the directors of the said free schools belonging to the said town, in such manner as to the discretion of the selectmen of the said town shall seem meet.

Out of the salary that may remain due to me as President of the State, I do give the sum of two thousand pounds to my executors, to be by them, the survivors or survivor of them, paid over to such person or persons as the legislature of this state by an act of Assembly shall appoint to receive the same in trust, to be employed for making the river Schuylkill navigable.

And what money of mine shall, at the time of my decease, remain in the hands of my bankers, Messrs. Ferdinand Grand and Son, at Paris, or Messrs. Smith, Wright, and Gray, of London, I will that, after my debts are paid and deducted, with the money legacies of this my will, the same be divided into four equal parts, two of which I give to my dear daughter, Sarah Bache, one to her son Benjamin, and one to my grandson, William Temple Franklin.

During the number of years I was in business as a stationer, printer, and postmaster, a great many small sums became due for books, advertisements, postage of letters, and other matters, which were not collected when, in 1757, I was sent by the Assembly to England as their agent, and by subsequent appointments continued there till 1775, when on my return, I was immediately engaged in the affairs of Congress, and sent to France in 1776, where I remained nine years, not returning till 1785: and the said debts, not being demanded in such a length of time, are become in a manner obsolete, yet are nevertheless justly due. These, as they are stated in my great folio ledger E, I bequeath to the contributors to the Pennsylvania Hospital, hoping that those debtors, and the descendants of such as are deceased, who now, as I find, make some difficulty of satisfying such antiquated demands as just debts, may, however, be induced to pay or give them as charity to that excellent institution. I am sensible that much must inevitably be lost, but I hope something considerable may be recovered. It is possible, too, that some of the parties charged may have existing old, unsettled accounts against me; in which case the managers of the said hospital will allow and deduct the amount, or pay the balance if they find it against me.

My debts and legacies being all satisfied and paid, the rest and residue of all my estate, real and personal, not herein expressly disposed of, I do give and bequeath to my son and daughter, Richard and Sarah Bache.

I request my friends, Henry Hill, Esquire, John Jay, Esquire, Francis Hopkinson, Esquire, and Mr. Edward Duffield, of Benfield, in Philadelphia County, to be the executors of this my last will and testament; and I hereby nominate and appoint them for that purpose.

I would have my body buried with as little expense or ceremony as may be. I revoke all former wills by me made, declaring this only to be my last.

In witness thereof, I have hereunto set my hand and seal, this seventeenth day of July, in the year of our Lord one thousand seven hundred and eighty-eight.

B. Franklin

Codicil to the Will, June 23, 1789

I Benjamin Franklin in the foregoing or annexed last will and testament named, having further considered the same, do think proper to make and publish the following codicil or addition thereto.

It having long been a fixed political opinion of mine, that in a democratical state there ought to be no offices of profit, for the reasons I had given in an article of my drawing in our constitution, it was my intention when I accepted the office of President, to devote the appointed salary to some public uses. Accordingly, I had already, before I made my will in July last, given large sums of it to colleges, schools, building of churches, etc.; and in that will I bequeathed two thousand pounds more to the State for the purpose of making the Schuylkill navigable. But understanding since that such a sum will do but little towards accomplishing such a work, and that the project is not likely to be undertaken for many years to come, and having entertained another idea, that I hope may be more extensively useful, I do hereby revoke and annul that bequest, and direct that the certificates I have for what remains due to me of that salary be sold, towards raising the sum of two thousand pounds sterling, to be disposed of as I am now about to order.

It has been an opinion, that he who receives an estate from his ancestors is under some kind of obligation to transmit the same to their posterity. This obligation does not lie on me, who never inherited a shilling from any ancestor or relation. I shall, however, if it is not diminished by some accident before my death, leave a considerable estate among my descendants and relations. The above observation is made merely as some apology to my family for making bequests that do not appear to have any immediate relation to their advantage.

I was born in Boston, New England, and owe my first instructions in literature to the free grammar-schools established there. I have, therefore, already considered these schools in my will. But I am also under obligations to the State of Massachusetts for having, unasked, appointed me formerly their agent in England, with a handsome salary, which continued some years; and although I accidentally lost in their service, by transmitting Governor Hutchinson's letters, much more than the amount of what they gave me, I do not think that ought in the least to diminish my gratitude.

I have considered that, among artisans, good apprentices are most likely to make good citizens, and, having myself been bred to a manual art, printing, in my native town, and afterwards assisted to set up my business in Philadelphia by kind loans of money from two friends there, which was the foundation of my fortune, and of all the utility in life that may be ascribed to me, I wish to be useful even after my death, if possible, in forming and advancing other young men, that may be serviceable to their country in both these towns. To this end, I devote two thousand pounds sterling, of which I give one thousand thereof to the inhabitants of the town of Boston, in Massachusetts, and the other thousand to the inhabitants of the city of Philadelphia, in trust, to and for the uses, intents, and purposes hereinafter mentioned and declared.

The said sum of one thousand pounds sterling, if accepted by the inhabitants of the town of Boston, shall be managed under the direction of the selectmen, united with the ministers of the oldest Episcopalian, Congregational, and Presbyterian churches in that town, who are to let out the sum upon interest, at five per cent. per annum, to such young married artificers, under the age of twenty-five years, as have served an apprenticeship in the said town, and faithfully fulfilled the duties required in their indentures, so as to obtain a good moral character from at least two respectable citizens, who are willing to become their sureties, in a bond with the applicants, for the repayment of the moneys so lent, with interest, according to the terms hereinafter prescribed; all which bonds are to be taken for Spanish milled dollars, or the value thereof in current gold coin; and the managers shall keep a bound book or books, wherein shall be entered the names of those who shall apply for and receive the benefits of this institution, and of their sureties, together with the sums lent, the dates, and other necessary and proper records respecting the business and concerns of this institution. And as these loans are intended to assist young married artificers in setting up their business, they are to be proportioned by the discretion of the managers, so as not to exceed sixty pounds sterling to one person, nor to be less than fifteen pounds; and if the number of appliers so entitled should be so large as that the sum will not suffice to afford to each as much as might otherwise not be improper, the proportion to each shall be diminished so as to afford to every one some assistance. These aids may, therefore, be small at first, but, as the capital increases by the accumulated interest, they will be more ample. And in order to serve as many as possible in their turn, as well as to make the repayment of the principal borrowed more easy, each borrower shall be obliged to pay, with the yearly interest, one tenth part of the principal, which sums of principal and interest, so paid in, shall be again let out to fresh borrowers.

And, as it is presumed that there will always be found in Boston virtuous and benevolent citizens, willing to bestow a part of their time in doing good to the rising generation, by superintending and managing this institution gratis, it is hoped that no part of the money will at any time be dead, or be diverted to other purposes, but be continually augmenting by the interest; in which case there may, in time, be more than the occasions in Boston shall require, and then some may be spared to the neighboring or other towns in the said State of Massachusetts, who may desire to have it; such towns engaging to pay punctually the interest and the portions of the principal, annually, to the inhabitants of the town of Boston.

If this plan is executed, and succeeds as projected without interruption for one hundred years, the sum will then be one hundred and thirty-one thousand pounds; of which I would have the managers of the donation to the town of Boston then lay out, at their discretion, one hundred thousand pounds in public works, which may be judged of most general utility to the inhabitants, such as fortifications, bridges, aqueducts, public buildings, baths, pavements, or whatever may make living in the town more convenient to its people, and render it more agreeable to strangers resorting thither for health or a temporary residence. The remaining thirty-one thousand pounds I would have continued to be let out on interest, in the manner above directed, for another hundred years, as I hope it will have been found that the institution has had a good effect on the conduct of youth, and been of service to many worthy characters and useful citizens. At the end of this second term, if no unfortunate accident has prevented the operation, the sum will be four millions and sixty one thousand pounds sterling, of which I leave one million sixty one thousand pounds to the disposition of the inhabitants of the town of Boston, and three millions to the disposition of the government of the state, not presuming to carry my views farther.

All the directions herein given, respecting the disposition and management of the donation to the inhabitants of Philadelphia, only, as Philadelphia is incorporated, I request the corporation of that city to undertake the management agreeably to the said directions; and I do hereby vest them with full and ample powers for that purpose. And, having considered that the covering a ground plot with buildings and pavements, which carry off most of the rain and prevent its soaking into the Earth and renewing and purifying the Springs, whence the water of wells must gradually grow worse, and in time be unfit for use, as I find has happened in all old cities, I recommend that at the end of the first hundred years, if not done before, the corporation of the city Employ a part of the hundred thousand pounds in bringing, by pipes, the water of Wissahickon Creek into the town, so as to supply the inhabitants, which I apprehend may be done without great difficulty, the level of the creek being much above that of the city, and may be made higher by a dam. I also recommend making the Schuylkill completely navigable. At the end of the second hundred years, I would have the disposition of the four million and sixty one thousand pounds divided between the inhabitants of the city of Philadelphia and the government of Pennsylvania, in the same manner as herein directed with respect to that of the inhabitants of Boston and the government of Massachusetts.

It is my desire that this institution should take place and begin to operate within one year after my decease, for which purpose due notice should be publicly given previous to the expiration of that year, that those for whose benefit this establishment is intended may make their respective applications. And I hereby direct my executors, the survivors or survivor of them, within six months after my decease, to pay over the said sum of two thousand pounds sterling to such persons as shall be duly appointed by the Selectmen of Boston and the corporation of Philadelphia, to receive and take charge of their respective sums, of one thousand pounds each, for the purpose aforesaid. Considering the accidents to which all human affairs and projects are subject in such a length of time, I have, perhaps, too much flattered myself with a vain fancy that these dispositions, if carried into execution, will be continued without interruption and have the effects proposed. I hope, however, that if the inhabitants of the two cities should not think fit to undertake the execution, they will, at least, accept the offer of these donations as a mark of my good will, a token of my gratitude, and a testimony of my earnest desire to be useful to them after my departure.

I wish, indeed, that they may both undertake to endeavor the execution of the project, because I think that, though unforeseen difficulties may arise, expedients will be found to remove them, and the scheme be found practicable. If one of them accepts the money, with the conditions, and the other refuses, my will then is, that both Sums be given to the inhabitants of the city accepting the whole, to be applied to the same purposes, and under the same regulations directed for the separate parts; and if both refuse, the money of course remains in the mass of my Estate, and is to be disposed of therewith according to my will made the Seventeenth day of July, 1788.

I wish to be buried by the side of my wife, if it may be, and that a marble stone, to be made by Chambers, six feet long, four feet wide, plain, with only a small molding round the upper edge, and this inscription:

Benjamin and Deborah
Franklin

to be placed over us both. My fine crab-tree walking-stick, with a gold head curiously wrought in the form of the cap of liberty, I give to my friend, and the friend of mankind, General Washington. If it were a Scepter, he has merited it, and would become it. It was a present to me from that excellent woman, Madame de Forbach, the dowager Duchess of Deux-Ponts, connected with some verses which should go with it. I give my gold watch to my son-in-law, Richard Bache, and also the gold watch chain of the Thirteen United States, which I have not yet worn. My timepiece, that stands in my library, I give to my grandson William Temple Franklin. I give him also my Chinese gong. To my dear old friend, Mrs. Mary Hewson, I give one of my silver tankards marked for her use during her life, and after her decease I give it to her daughter Eliza. I give to her son, William Hewson, who is my godson, my new quarto Bible, Oxford edition, to be for his family Bible, and also the botanic description of the plants in the Emperor's garden at Vienna, in folio, with colored cuts.

And to her son, Thomas Hewson, I give a set of Spectators, Tatlers, and Guardians handsomely bound.

There is an error in my will, where the Bond of William Temple Franklin is mentioned as being four thousand pounds sterling, whereas it is but for three thousand five hundred pounds.

I give to my executors, to be divided equally among those that act, the sum of sixty pounds sterling, as some compensation for their trouble in the execution of my will; and I request my friend, Mr. Duffield, to accept moreover my French wayweiser, a piece of clockwork in Brass, to be fixed to the wheel of any carriage; and that my friend, Mr. Hill, may also accept my silver cream pot, formerly given to me by the good Doctor Fothergill, with the motto, Keep bright the Chain. My reflecting telescope, made by Short, which was formerly Mr. Canton's, I give to my friend, Mr. David Rittenhouse, for the use of his observatory.

My picture, drawn by Martin, in 1767, I give to the Supreme Executive Council of Pennsylvania, if they shall be pleased to do me the honor of accepting it and placing it in their chamber. Since my will was made I have bought some more city lots, near the center part of the estate of Joseph Dean. I would have them go with the other lots, disposed of in my will, and I do give the same to my Son-in-law, Richard Bache, to his heirs and assigns forever.

In addition to the annuity left to my sister in my will, of fifty pounds sterling during her life, I now add thereto ten pounds sterling more, in order to make the Sum sixty pounds. I give twenty guineas to my good friend and physician, Dr. John Jones.

With regard to the separate bequests made to my daughter Sarah in my will, my intention is, that the same shall be for her sole and separate use, notwithstanding her coverture, or whether she be covert or sole; and I do give my executors so much right and power therein as may be necessary to render my intention effectual in that respect only. This provision for my daughter is not made out of any disrespect I have for her husband. And lastly, it is my desire that this, my present codicil, be annexed to, and considered as part of, my last will and testament to all intents and purposes.

In witness whereof, I have hereunto set my hand and Seal this twenty-third day of June, Anno Domini one thousand Seven hundred and eighty nine.

B. Franklin

THE AUTOBIOGRAPHY

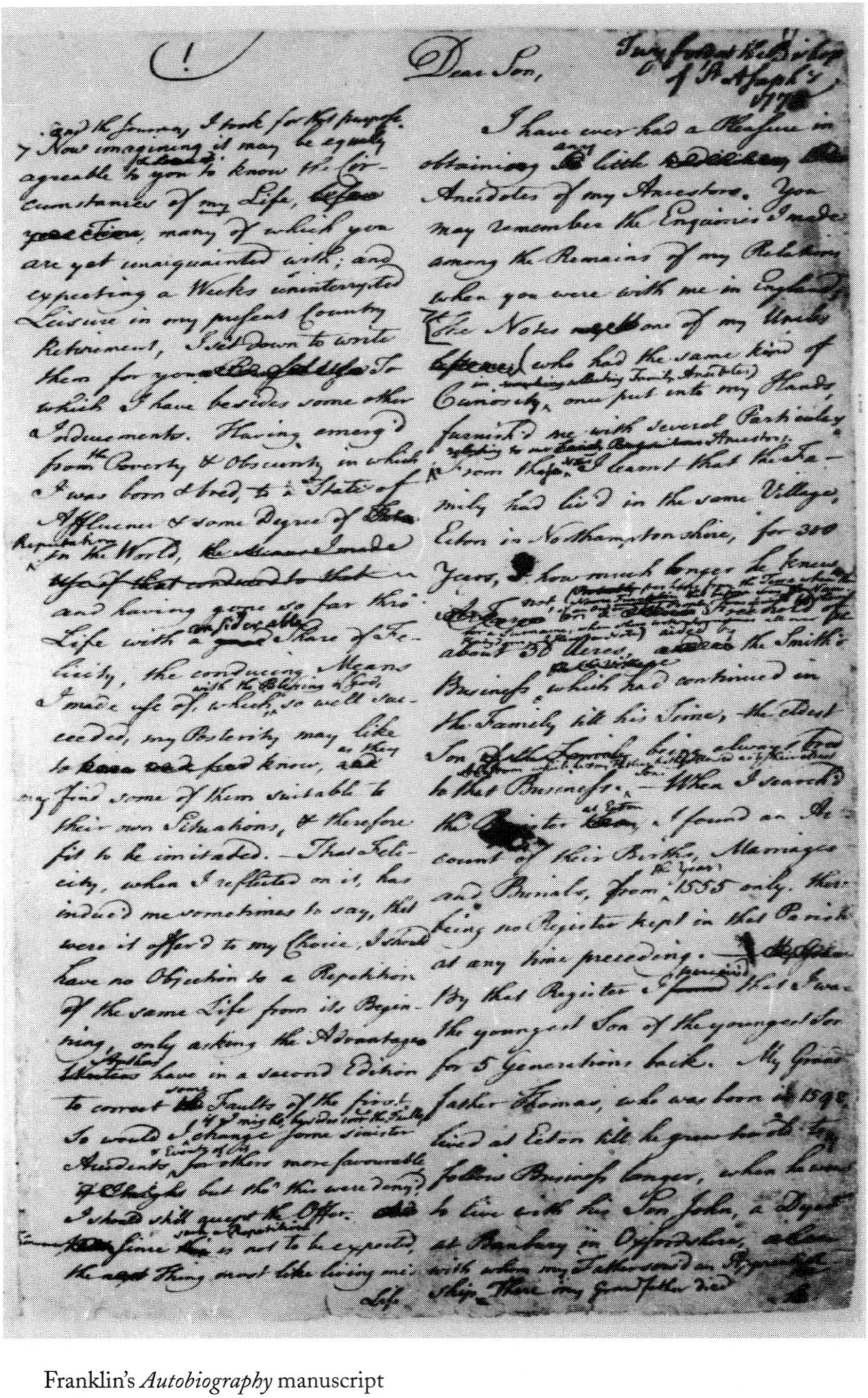
Twyford, at the Bishop of St Asaph's 1771.

Dear Son,

I have ever had a Pleasure in obtaining any little Anecdotes of my Ancestors. You may remember the Enquiries I made among the Remains of my Relations when you were with me in England; and the Journey I took for that purpose. The Notes one of my Uncles (who had the same kind of Curiosity in collecting Family Anecdotes) once put into my Hands, furnish'd me with several Particulars relating to our Ancestors. From these Notes I learnt that the Family had liv'd in the same Village, Ecton in Northamptonshire, for 300 Years, and how much longer he knew not, on a Freehold of about 30 Acres, aided by the Smith's Business which had continued in the Family till his Time, the eldest Son being always bred to that Business. When I search'd the Register at Ecton, I found an Account of their Births, Marriages and Burials, from the Year 1555 only, there being no Register kept in that Parish at any time preceding. By that Register I perceiv'd that I was the youngest Son of the youngest Son for 5 Generations back. My Grandfather Thomas, who was born in 1598, lived at Ecton till he grew too old to follow Business longer, when he went to live with his Son John, a Dyer at Banbury in Oxfordshire, with whom my Father serv'd an Apprenticeship. There my Grandfather died

Now imagining it may be equally agreable to you to know the Circumstances of my Life, many of which you are yet unacquainted with; and expecting a Weeks uninterrupted Leisure in my present Country Retirement, I sit down to write them for you. To which I have besides some other Inducements. Having emerg'd from the Poverty & Obscurity in which I was born & bred, to a State of Affluence & some Degree of Reputation in the World, and having gone so far thro' Life with a considerable Share of Felicity, the conducing Means I made use of, which, with the Blessing of God, so well succeeded, my Posterity may like to know, as they may find some of them suitable to their own Situations, & therefore fit to be imitated. That Felicity, when I reflected on it, has induc'd me sometimes to say, that were it offer'd to my Choice, I should have no Objection to a Repetition of the same Life from its Beginning, only asking the Advantage Authors have in a second Edition to correct some Faults of the first. So would I if I might, besides correcting the Faults, change some sinister Accidents & Events of it for others more favourable. But tho' this were deny'd, I should still accept the Offer. Since such a Repetition is not to be expected, the Thing most like living one's Life

Franklin's *Autobiography* manuscript

buried and there buried. We saw
his Gravestone in 1758. The
eldest Son Thomas liv'd in the House
at Eton, and left it with the Land
to his only Child, a Daughter, who
with her Husband, one Fisher of
Wellingborough sold it to Mr Isted
now Lord of the Manor there. My
Grandfather had 4 Sons that grew
up, viz. Thomas, John, Benjamin
and Josiah. I will give you what
Account I can of them at this
distance from my Papers, and if
these are not lost in
my Absence, you will among
them find many more Particulars.

Thomas was bred a Smith under
his Father, but being ingenious,
and encourag'd in Learning, by an
Esquire Palmer then the principal Gentleman
in that Parish, he qualify'd himself for the Business of Scrivener;
became a considerable Man in the
County Affairs, was a chief
Mover of all publick Spirited Undertakings
much taken Notice of
by the then Lord Halifax. He died
in 1702 just 4 years to a Day before I was born. The Account we
receiv'd of from some old People at Eton, I remember struck
you as something extraordinary from its
Similarity to what you knew
of mine. John was bred a Dyer,
I believe of Woollens. Benjamin, was bred a Silk Dyer, serving an Apprenticeship at London.

Life over again, seems to be a Recollection
of that Life; and to make that Recollection as
durable as possible, the putting it down
in Writing. Hereby, too, I shall indulge the Inclination so natural in
old Men, to be talking of themselves
and their own past Actions, and I shall
indulge it, without being troublesome
to others who thro' respect to Age
might think themselves oblig'd to give me a
Hearing, since this may be read or not
as any one pleases. And lastly,
(I may as well confess it,
since my Denial of it will be believ'd by
no body) I shall a good deal gratify
my own Vanity. Indeed I scarce
ever heard or saw the introductory
Words, Without Vanity I may say, &c. but
some vain thing immediately follow'd.
Most People dislike Vanity in others
whatever Share they have of it themselves, but I give it fair Quarter
wherever I meet with it, being
persuaded that it is often productive
of Good to the Possessor & to others that
are within his Sphere of Action: And
therefore in many Cases it would not be
quite absurd if a Man were to thank
God for his Vanity among the other
Comforts of Life.

And now I speak of thanking
God, I desire with all Humility to
acknowledge, that I owe the mention'd Happiness of my past Life
to his kind Providence, which led me to the Means I
us'd & gave them Success. My Belief of This,
induces me to hope, tho'
I must not presume, that the same
Goodness will still be exercis'd towards me in continuing that Happiness, or in enabling me to bear a fatal
Reverse, which I may experience as
others have done; the Complexion of
my future Fortune being known to
him only: and in whose Power is it
that to bless to us even our Afflictions

THE AUTOBIOGRAPHY

In the summer of 1771, Franklin was in a reflective mood. His mission as Pennsylvania's lobbyist in London was not going well, and he was drifting away from his son, who was a royalist with social aspirations. On a visit to the Tudor country home of his friend Jonathan Shipley, an Anglican bishop, Franklin began the first installment of the most enduring of his literary efforts, *The Autobiography of Benjamin Franklin.*

"Dear son," he began, casting his account as a letter to William, whom he had not seen for seven years. The epistolary guise gave him the opportunity to be chatty and casual in his prose. He pretended, at least initially, that this was merely a personal communication rather than a work of literature. "I used to write more methodically," he said in a paragraph he inserted into the text after rereading some of the rambling genealogical digressions he had composed on the first day. "But one does not dress for private company as for a public ball."

So was the autobiography really just for the private company of his son? No. It was clear from the outset that Franklin was writing for public consumption as well. The family information that would most interest his son was omitted completely: the identity and description of William's own mother. Nor did Franklin write the letter on regular stationery; instead, he used the left half of large folio sheets, leaving the right half blank for revisions and additions.

At the beginning of his second day of writing, he stopped to make an outline of his entire career, showing his intention to construct a full memoir. He also, that second morning, used the blank right-hand columns of his first pages to insert a long section justifying the "vanity" of his decision to "indulge the inclination so natural in old men to be talking of themselves." His goal, he declared, was to describe how he rose from obscurity to prominence and to provide some useful hints about how he succeeded, expressing hope that others might find them suitable to be imitated.

This was obviously directed at an audience beyond that of his son, who was already forty and the governor of New Jersey. There was, however, a subtext that was directed at him: William had taken on airs since becoming a governor, and he was far more enamored of the aristocracy and establishment than his father. The autobiography would be a reminder of their humble origins and a paean to hard work, thrift, shopkeeping values, and the role of a proud middle class that resisted rather than emulated the pretensions of the well-born elite.

For almost three weeks, Franklin wrote by day and then read aloud portions to the Shipleys in the evening. Because the work was cast as a letter, and because it was read aloud, Franklin's prose took on the voice of a lovable old raconteur. Lacking in literary flair, with nary a metaphor nor poetic flourish, the narrative flowed as a string of wry anecdotes and instructive lessons. Occasionally, when he found himself writing with too much pride about an event, he would revise it by adding a self-deprecating comment or ironic aside, just as would a good after-dinner storyteller.

By the time he left for London, Franklin had finished about 40 percent of what would later be called *The Autobiography.* In Paris thirteen years later, just after the end of the American Revolution, he added another 10 percent of the work. His focus by then was on the need to build a new American character, and most of the section he wrote in 1784 was devoted to an explanation of the famous self-improvement project in which he sought to train himself in the thirteen virtues ranging from frugality and industry to temperance and humility. He began what would be the final installment in 1788, after he had returned to Philadelphia, and continued writing through May 1789, a year before his death.

The Autobiography features Franklin's most delightful literary creation: the portrait he painted of his younger self. With a mix of wry detachment and amused self-awareness, Franklin was able to keep his creation at a bit of a distance, to be modestly revealing but never deeply so. He included, amid all the enlightening anecdotes, few intimations of inner torment, no struggles of the soul nor reflections of the deeper spirit. More pregnant than profound, his recollections provide a cheerful look at a simple approach to life that only hints at the deeper meanings he found in serving his fellow man and thus his God. What he wrote had little pretension other than pretending to poke fun at all pretensions. It was the work of a gregarious man who loved to recount stories, turn them into down-home parables that could lead to a better life, and delve into the shallows of simple lessons.

To some, this simplicity is its failing. The great literary critic Charles

Angoff declares that "it is lacking in almost everything necessary to a really great work of *belles lettres:* grace of expression, charm of personality, and intellectual flight." But surely it is unfair to say that it lacks charm of personality, and as the historian Henry Steele Commager points out, its "artless simplicity, lucidity, homely idiom, freshness and humor have commended it anew to each generation of readers." Indeed, read with an unjaundiced eye, it is a pure delight as well as an archetype of homespun American literature. And it was destined to become, through hundreds of editions published in almost every language, the world's most popular autobiography.

In this age of instant memoirs, it is important to note that Franklin was producing something relatively new for his time. St. Augustine's *Confessions* had mainly been about his religious conversion, and Rousseau's *Confessions* had not yet been published. As Carl Van Doren points out, "his book was the first masterpiece of autobiography by a self-made man." The closest model that he had, in terms of narrative style, was one of his favorite books, John Bunyan's allegorical dream, *A Pilgrim's Progress* that he had read at 14. But Franklin's was the story of a very real pilgrim, albeit a lapsed one, in a very real world.

The Autobiography
Twyford, at the Bishop of St. Asaph's, 1771

Dear Son,

I have ever had pleasure in obtaining any little anecdotes of my ancestors. You may remember the inquiries I made among the remains of my relations when you were with me in England, and the journey I undertook for that purpose. Now imagining it may be equally agreeable to some of you to know the circumstances of *my* life, many of which you are yet unacquainted with, and expecting a week's uninterrupted leisure in my present country retirement, I sit down to write them for you. To which I have besides some other inducements. Having emerged from the poverty and obscurity in which I was born and bred, to a state of affluence and some degree of reputation in the world, and having gone so far through life with a considerable share of felicity, the conducing means I made use of, which with the blessing of God, so well succeeded, my posterity may like to know, as they may find some of them suitable to their own situations, and therefore fit to be imitated.

That felicity, when I reflected on it, has induced me sometimes to say, that were it offered to my choice, I should have no objection to a repetition of the same life from its beginning, only asking the advantages authors have in a second edition to correct some faults of the first. So would I if I might, besides correcting the faults, change some sinister accidents and events of it for others more favorable. But though this were denied, I should still accept the offer. However, since such a repetition is not to be expected, the next thing most like living one's life over again seems to be a *recollection* of that life, and to make that recollection as durable as possible by the putting it down in writing.

Hereby, too, I shall indulge the inclination so natural in old men, to be talking of themselves and their own past actions; and I shall indulge it, without being tiresome to others, who, through respect to age, might conceive themselves obliged to give me a hearing, since this may be read or not as any one pleases. And, lastly (I may as well confess it, since my denial of it will be believed by nobody), perhaps I shall a good deal gratify my own vanity. Indeed, I scarce ever heard or saw the introductory words, "Without vanity I may say," &c., but some vain thing immediately followed. Most people dislike vanity in others, whatever share they have of it themselves; but I give it fair quarter wherever I meet with it, being persuaded that it is often productive of good to the possessor, and to others that are within his sphere of action; and therefore, in many cases, it would not be altogether absurd if a man were to thank God for his vanity among the other comforts of life.

And now I speak of thanking God, I desire with all humility to acknowledge that I owe the mentioned happiness of my past life to his kind providence, which lead me to the means I used and gave them success. My belief of this induces me to hope, though I must not presume, that the same goodness will still be exercised toward me, in continuing that happiness, or enabling me to bear a fatal reverse, which I may experience as others have done: the complexion of my future fortune being known to Him only in whose power it is to bless to us even our afflictions.

The notes one of my uncles (who had the same kind of curiosity in collecting family anecdotes) once put into my hands, furnished me with several particulars relating to our ancestors. From these notes I learned that the family had lived in the same village, Ecton in Northamptonshire, for three hundred years, and how much longer he knew not (perhaps from the time when the name of Franklin, that before was the name of an order of people, was assumed by them as a surname when others took surnames all over the kingdom), on a freehold of about thirty acres, aided by the smith's business, which had continued in the family till his time, the eldest son being always bred to that business; a custom which he and my father followed as to their eldest sons. When I searched the registers at Ecton, I found an account of their births, marriages and burials from the year 1555 only, there being no registers kept in that parish at any time preceding. By that register I perceived that I was the youngest son of the youngest son for five generations back. My grandfather Thomas, who was born in 1598, lived at Ecton till he grew too old to follow business longer, when he went to live with his son John, a dyer at Banbury, in Oxfordshire, with whom my father served an apprenticeship. There my grandfather died and lies buried. We saw his gravestone in 1758. His eldest son Thomas lived in the house at Ecton, and left it with the land to his only child, a daughter, who, with her husband, one Fisher, of Wellingborough, sold it to Mr. Isted, now lord of the manor there. My grandfather had four sons that grew up, viz.: Thomas, John, Benjamin and Josiah. I will give you what account I can of them, at this distance from my papers, and if these are not lost in my absence, you will among them find many more particulars.

Thomas was bred a smith under his father; but, being ingenious, and encouraged in learning (as all my brothers were) by an Esquire Palmer, then the principal gentleman in that parish, he qualified himself for the business of scrivener; became a considerable man in the county; was a chief mover of all public-spirited undertakings for the county or town of Northampton, and his own village, of which many instances were related of him; and much taken notice of and patronized by the then Lord Halifax. He died in 1702, January 6, old style, just four years to a day before I was born. The account we received of his life and character from some old people at Ecton, I remember, struck you as something extraordinary, from its similarity to what you knew of mine.

"Had he died on the same day," you said, "one might have supposed a transmigration."

John was bred a dyer, I believe of woolens. Benjamin was bred a silk dyer, serving an apprenticeship at London. He was an ingenious man. I remember him well, for when I was a boy he came over to my father in Boston, and lived in the house with us some years. He lived to a great age. His grandson, Samuel Franklin, now lives in Boston. He left behind him two quarto volumes, MS., of his own poetry, consisting of little occasional pieces addressed to his friends and relations, of which the following, sent to me, is a specimen.

To my Namesake upon a Report of his Inclination to
Martial Affairs, July 7th, 1710
Believe me, Ben, war is a dangerous trade.
The sword has marred as well as made;
By it do many fall, not many rise—
Makes many poor, few rich, and fewer wise;
Fills towns with ruin, fields with blood, beside
'Tis sloth's maintainer and the shield of Pride.
Fair cities, rich today in plenty flow,
War fills with want tomorrow, and with woe.
Ruined states, vice, broken limbs, and scars
Are the effects of desolating wars.

He had formed a shorthand of his own, which he taught me, but never practicing it I have now forgot it. I was named after this uncle, there being a particular affection between him and my father. He was very pious, a great attender of sermons of the best preachers, which he took down in his shorthand and had with him many volumes of them. He was also much of a politician, too much, perhaps, for his station. There fell lately into my hands, in London, a collection he had made of all the principal pamphlets, relating to public affairs, from 1641 to 1717. Many of the volumes are wanting as appears by the numbering, but there still remain eight volumes in folio, and twenty-four in quarto and octavo. A dealer in old books met with them, and knowing me by my sometimes buying of him, he brought them to me. It seems my uncle must have left them here, when he went to America, which was about 50 years since. There are many of his notes in the margins.

This obscure family of ours was early in the Reformation, and continued Protestants through the reign of Queen Mary, when they were sometimes in danger of trouble on account of their zeal against popery. They had got an English Bible, and to conceal and secure it, it was fastened open with tapes under and within the cover of a joint-stool. When my great great grandfather read it to his family, he turned up the joint-stool upon his knees, turning over the leaves then under the tapes. One of the children stood at the door to give notice if he saw the apparitor coming, who was an officer of the spiritual court. In that case the stool was turned down again upon its feet, when the Bible remained concealed under it as before. This anecdote I had from my uncle Benjamin. The family continued all of the Church of England till about the end of Charles the 2d's reign, when some of the ministers that had been outed for nonconformity, holding conventicles in Northamptonshire, Benjamin and Josiah adhered to them, and so continued all their lives. The rest of the family remained with the Episcopal Church.

Josiah, my father, married young, and carried his wife with three children into New England, about 1682. The conventicles having been forbidden by law, and frequently disturbed, induced some considerable men of his acquaintance to remove to that country, and he was prevailed with to accompany them thither, where they expected to enjoy their mode of religion with freedom. By the same wife he had four children more born there, and by a second wife ten more, in all seventeen; of which I remember thirteen sitting at one time at his table, who all grew up to be men and women, and married; I was the youngest son, and the youngest child but two, and was born in Boston, New England.

My mother, the second wife, was Abiah Folger, daughter of Peter Folger, one of the first settlers of New England, of whom honorable mention is made by Cotton Mather in his church history of that country, entitled Magnalia Christi Americana, as "a godly, learned Englishman," if I remember the words rightly. I have heard that he wrote sundry small occasional pieces, but only one of them was printed, which I saw now many years since. It was written in 1675, in the homespun verse of that time and people, and addressed to those then concerned in the government there. It was in favor of liberty of conscience, and in behalf of the Baptists, Quakers, and other sectaries that had been under persecution, ascribing the Indian wars, and other distresses that had befallen the country, to that persecution, as so many judgments of God to punish so heinous an offense, and exhorting a repeal of those uncharitable laws. The whole appeared to me as written with a good deal of decent plainness and manly freedom. The six concluding lines I remember, though I have forgotten the two first of the stanza; but the purport of them was that his censures proceeded from *good-will,* and therefore he would be known to be the author,

> *Because to be a libeler (says he)*
> *I hate it with my heart;*
> *From Sherburne town, where now I dwell*
> *My name I do put here;*
> *Without offense your real friend,*
> *It is Peter Folger.*

My elder brothers were all put apprentices to different trades. I was put to the grammar school at eight years of age, my father intending to devote me, as the tithe of his sons, to the service of the Church. My early readiness in learning to read (which must have been very early, as I do not remember when I could not read), and the opinion of all his friends, that I should certainly make a good scholar, encouraged him in this purpose of his. My uncle Benjamin, too, approved of it, and proposed to give me all his shorthand volumes of sermons, I suppose as a stock to set up with, if I would learn his character. I continued, however, at the grammar-school not quite one year, though in that time I had risen gradually from the middle of the class of that year to be the head of it, and farther was removed into the next class above it, in order to go with that into the third at the end of the year. But my father, in the meantime, from a view of the expense of a college education, which having so large a family he could not well afford, and the mean living many so educated were afterwards able to obtain—reasons that he gave to his friends in my hearing—altered his first intention, took me from the grammar-school, and sent me to a school for writing and arithmetic, kept by a then famous man, Mr. George Brownell, very successful in his profession generally, and that by mild, encouraging methods. Under him I acquired fair writing pretty soon, but I failed in the arithmetic, and made no progress in it. At ten years old I was taken home to assist my father in his business, which was that of a tallow-chandler and soap-boiler; a business he was not bred to, but had assumed on his arrival in New England, and on finding his dying trade would not maintain his family, being in little request. Accordingly, I was employed in cutting wick for the candles, filling the dipping mold and the molds for cast candles, attending the shop, going of errands, etc.

I disliked the trade, and had a strong inclination for the sea, but my father declared against it; however, living near the water, I was much in and about it, learned early to swim well, and to manage boats; and when in a boat or canoe with other boys, I was commonly allowed to govern, especially in any case of difficulty; and upon other occasions I was generally a leader among the boys, and sometimes led them into scrapes, of which I will mention one instance, as it shows an early projecting public spirit, though not then justly conducted.

There was a salt-marsh that bounded part of the mill-pond, on the edge of which, at high water, we used to stand to fish for minnows. By much trampling, we had made it a mere quagmire. My proposal was to build a wharf there fit for us to stand upon, and I showed my comrades a large heap of stones, which were intended for a new house near the marsh, and which would very well suit our purpose. Accordingly, in the evening, when the workmen were gone, I assembled a number of my play-fellows, and working with them diligently like so many emmets, sometimes two or three to a stone, we brought them all away and built our little wharf. The next morning the workmen were surprised at missing the stones, which were found in our wharf. Inquiry was made after the removers; we were discovered and complained of; several of us were corrected by our fathers; and though I pleaded the usefulness of the work, mine convinced me that nothing was useful which was not honest.

I think you may like to know something of his person and character. He had an excellent constitution of body, was of middle stature, but well set, and very strong. He was ingenious, could draw prettily, was skilled a little in music, and had a clear pleasing voice, so that when he played psalm tunes on his violin and sung withal, as he sometimes did in an evening after the business of the day was over, it was extremely agreeable to hear. He had a mechanical genius too, and, on occasion, was very handy in the use of other tradesmen's tools; but his great excellence lay in a sound understanding and solid judgment in prudential matters, both in private and public affairs. In the latter, indeed, he was never employed, the numerous family he had to educate and the straitness of his circumstances keeping him close to his trade; but I remember well his being frequently visited by leading people, who consulted him for his opinion in affairs of the town or of the church he belonged to, and showed a good deal of respect for his judgment and advice: he was also much consulted by private persons about their affairs when any difficulty occurred, and frequently chosen an arbitrator between contending parties.

At his table he liked to have, as often as he could, some sensible friend or neighbor to converse with, and always took care to start some ingenious or useful topic for discourse, which might tend to improve the minds of his children. By this means he turned our attention to what was good, just, and prudent in the conduct of life; and little or no notice was ever taken of what related to the victuals on the table, whether it was well or ill dressed, in or out of season, of good or bad flavor, preferable or inferior to this or that other thing of the kind, so that I was brought up in such a perfect inattention to those matters as to be quite indifferent what kind of food was set before me, and so unobservant of it, that to this day if I am asked I can scarce tell a few hours after dinner what I dined upon. This has been a convenience to me in traveling, where my companions have been sometimes very unhappy for want of a suitable gratification of their more delicate, because better instructed, tastes and appetites.

My mother had likewise an excellent constitution: she suckled all her ten children. I never knew either my father or mother to have any sickness but that of which they died, he at 89, and she at 85 years of age. They lie buried together at Boston, where I some years since placed a marble over their grave, with this inscription:

> *Josiah Franklin,*
> *And Abiah his Wife,*
> *Lie here interred.*
> *They lived lovingly together in wedlock*
> *Fifty-five years.*
> *Without an estate, or any gainful employment,*
> *By constant labor and industry,*
> *With God's blessing,*
> *They maintained a large family*
> *Comfortably;*
> *And brought up thirteen children*
> *And seven grandchildren*
> *Reputably.*
> *From this instance, Reader,*
> *Be encouraged to diligence in thy calling,*
> *And distrust not Providence.*
> *He was a pious and prudent man,*
> *She, a discreet and virtuous woman.*
> *Their youngest son,*
> *In filial regard to their memory,*
> *Place this stone.*
> *J.F. born 1655—Died 1744—Ætat. 89.*
> *A.F. born 1667—Died 1752,——85.*

By my rambling digressions I perceive myself to be grown old. I used to write more methodically. But one does not dress for private company as for a public ball. 'Tis perhaps only negligence.

To return: I continued thus employed in my father's business for two years, that is, till I was twelve years old; and my brother John, who was bred to that business, having left my father, married, and set up for himself at Rhode Island, there was all appearance that I was destined to supply his place, and become a tallow chandler. But my dislike to the trade continuing, my father was under apprehensions that if he did not find one for me more agreeable, I should break away and get to sea, as his son Josiah had done, to his great vexation. He therefore sometimes took me to walk with him, and see joiners, bricklayers, turners, braziers, etc., at their work, that he might observe my inclination, and endeavor to fix it on some trade or other on land. It has ever since been a pleasure to me to see good workmen handle their tools; and it has been useful to me, having learnt so much by it as to be able to do little jobs myself in my house when a workman could not readily be got, and to construct little machines for my experiments, while the intention of making the experiment was fresh and warm in my mind. My father at last fixed upon the cutler's trade, and my uncle Benjamin's son Samuel, who was bred to that business in London, being about that time established in Boston, I was sent to be with him some time on liking. But his expectations of a fee with me displeasing my father, I was taken home again.

From a child I was fond of reading, and all the little money that came into my hands was ever laid out in books. Pleased with the Pilgrim's Progress, my first collection was of John Bunyan's works in separate little volumes. I afterward sold them to enable me to buy R. Burton's Historical Collections; they were small chapmen's books, and cheap, 40 or 50 in all. My father's little library consisted chiefly of books in polemic divinity, most of which I read, and have since often regretted that, at a time when I had such a thirst for knowledge, more proper books had not fallen in my way since it was now resolved I should not be a clergyman. Plutarch's Lives there was in which I read abundantly, and I still think that time spent to great advantage. There was also a book of De Foe's, called an Essay on Projects, and another of Dr. Mather's, called Essays to do Good, which perhaps gave me a turn of thinking that had an influence on some of the principal future events of my life.

This bookish inclination at length determined my father to make me a printer, though he had already one son (James) of that profession. In 1717 my brother James returned from England with a press and letters to set up his business in Boston. I liked it much better than that of my father, but still had a hankering for the sea. To prevent the apprehended effect of such an inclination, my father was impatient to have me bound to my brother. I stood out some time, but at last was persuaded, and signed the indentures when I was yet but twelve years old. I was to serve as an apprentice till I was twenty-one years of age, only I was to be allowed journeyman's wages during the last year. In a little time I made great proficiency in the business, and became a useful hand to my brother. I now had access to better books. An acquaintance with the apprentices of booksellers enabled me sometimes to borrow a small one, which I was careful to return soon and clean. Often I sat up in my room reading the greatest part of the night, when the book was borrowed in the evening and to be returned early in the morning, lest it should be missed or wanted.

And after some time an ingenious tradesman, Mr. Matthew Adams, who had a pretty collection of books, and who frequented our printing-house, took notice of me, invited me to his library, and very kindly lent me such books as I chose to read. I now took a fancy to poetry, and made some little pieces; my brother, thinking it might turn to account, encouraged me, and put me on composing occasional ballads. One was called The Lighthouse Tragedy, and contained an account of the drowning of Captain Worthilake, with his two daughters: the other was a sailor's song, on the taking of Teach (or Blackbeard) the pirate. They were wretched stuff, in the rub-street-ballad style; and when they were printed he sent me about the town to sell them. The first sold wonderfully, the event being recent, having made a great noise. This flattered my vanity; but my father discouraged me by ridiculing my performances, and telling me verse-makers were generally beggars. So I escaped being a poet, most probably a very bad one; but as prose writing has been of great use to me in the course of my life, and was a principal means of my advancement, I shall tell you how, in such a situation, I acquired what little ability I have in that way.

There was another bookish lad in the town, John Collins by name, with whom I was intimately acquainted. We sometimes disputed, and very fond we were of argument, and very desirous of confuting one another, which disputatious turn, by the way, is apt to become a very bad habit, making people often extremely disagreeable in company by the contradiction that is necessary to bring it into practice; and thence, besides souring and spoiling the conversation, is productive of disgusts and, perhaps enmities where you may have occasion for friendship. I had caught it by reading my father's books of dispute about religion. Persons of good sense, I have since observed, seldom fall into it, except lawyers, university men, and men of all sorts that have been bred at Edinborough.

A question was once, somehow or other, started between Collins and me, of the propriety of educating the female sex in learning, and their abilities for study. He was of opinion that it was improper, and that they were naturally unequal to it. I took the contrary side, perhaps a little for dispute's sake. He was naturally more eloquent, had a ready plenty of words; and sometimes, as I thought, bore me down more by his fluency than by the strength of his reasons. As we parted without settling the point, and were not to see one another again for some time, I sat down to put my arguments in writing, which I copied fair and sent to him. He answered, and I replied. Three or four letters of a side had passed, when my father happened to find my papers and read them. Without entering into the discussion, he took occasion to talk to me about the manner of my writing; observed that, though I had the advantage of my antagonist in correct spelling and pointing (which I owed to the printing-house), I fell far short in elegance of expression, in method and in perspicuity, of which he convinced me by several instances. I saw the justice of his remark, and thence grew more attentive to the manner in writing, and determined to endeavor at improvement.

About this time I met with an odd volume of the Spectator. It was the third. I had never before seen any of them. I bought it, read it over and over, and was much delighted with it. I thought the writing excellent, and wished, if possible, to imitate it. With this view I took some of the papers, and, making short hints of the sentiment in each sentence, laid them by a few days, and then, without looking at the book, tried to complete the papers again, by expressing each hinted sentiment at length, and as fully as it had been expressed before, in any suitable words that should come to hand. Then I compared my Spectator with the original, discovered some of my faults, and corrected them. But I found I wanted a stock of words, or a readiness in recollecting and using them, which I thought I should have acquired before that time if I had gone on making verses; since the continual occasion for words of the same import, but of different length, to suit the measure, or of different sound for the rhyme, would have laid me under a constant necessity of searching for variety, and also have tended to fix that variety in my mind, and make me master of it. Therefore I took some of the tales and turned them into verse; and, after a time, when I had pretty well forgotten the prose, turned them back again. I also sometimes jumbled my collections of hints into confusion, and after some weeks endeavored to reduce them into the best order, before I began to form the full sentences and complete the paper. This was to teach me method in the arrangement of thoughts. By comparing my work afterwards with the original, I discovered many faults and amended them; but I sometimes had the pleasure of fancying that, in certain particulars of small import, I had been lucky enough to improve the method or the language, and this encouraged me to think I might possibly in time come to be a tolerable English writer, of which I was extremely ambitious. My time for these exercises and for reading was at night, after work or before it began in the morning, or on Sundays, when I contrived to be in the printing-house alone, evading as much as I could the common attendance on public worship which my father used to exact on me when I was under his care, and which indeed I still thought a duty, though I could not, as it seemed to me, afford time to practice it.

When about 16 years of age I happened to meet with a book, written by one Tryon, recommending a vegetable diet. I determined to go into it. My brother, being yet unmarried, did not keep house, but boarded himself and his apprentices in another family. My refusing to eat flesh occasioned an inconveniency, and I was frequently chid for my singularity. I made myself acquainted with Tryon's manner of preparing some of his dishes, such as boiling potatoes or rice, making hasty pudding, and a few others, and then proposed to my brother, that if he would give me, weekly, half the money he paid for my board, I would board myself. He instantly agreed to it, and I presently found that I could save half what he paid me. This was an additional fund for buying books. But I had another advantage in it. My brother and the rest going from the printing-house to their meals, I remained there alone, and, dispatching presently my light repast, which often was no more than a biscuit or a slice of bread, a handful of raisins or a tart from the pastry-cook's, and a glass of water, had the rest of the time till their return for study, in which I made the greater progress, from that greater clearness of head and quicker apprehension which usually attend temperance in eating and drinking.

And now it was that, being on some occasion made ashamed of my ignorance in figures, which I had twice failed in learning when at school, I took Cocker's book of Arithmetic, and went through the whole by myself with great ease. I also read Seller's and Shermy's books of Navigation, and became acquainted with the little geometry they contain; but never proceeded far in that science. And I read about this time Locke, On Human Understanding, and the Art of Thinking, by Messrs. du Port Royal.

While I was intent on improving my language, I met with an English grammar (I think it was Greenwood's), at the end of which there were two little sketches of the arts of rhetoric and logic, the latter finishing with a specimen of a dispute in the Socratic method; and soon after I procured Xenophon's Memorable Things of Socrates, wherein there are many instances of the same method. I was charmed with it, adopted it, dropt my abrupt contradiction and positive argumentation, and put on the humble inquirer and doubter. And being then, from reading Shaftesbury and Collins, become a real doubter in many points of our religious doctrine, I found this method safest for myself and very embarrassing to those against whom I used it; therefore I took a delight in it, practiced it continually, and grew very artful and expert in drawing people, even of superior knowledge, into concessions, the consequences of which they did not foresee, entangling them in difficulties out of which they could not extricate themselves, and so obtaining victories that neither myself nor my cause always deserved. I continued this method some few years, but gradually left it, retaining only the habit of expressing myself in terms of modest diffidence; never using, when I advanced any thing that may possibly be disputed, the words certainly, undoubtedly, or any others that give the air of positiveness to an opinion; but rather say, I conceive or apprehend a thing to be so and

so; it appears to me, or I should think it so or so, for such and such reasons; or I imagine it to be so; or it is so, if I am not mistaken. This habit,
I believe, has been of great advantage to me when I have had occasion
to inculcate my opinions, and persuade men into measures that I have
been from time to time engaged in promoting; and, as the chief ends of
conversation are to inform or to be informed, to please or to persuade,
I wish well-meaning, sensible men would not lessen their power of
doing good by a positive, assuming manner, that seldom fails to disgust, tends to create opposition, and to defeat every one of those purposes for which speech was given to us, to wit, giving or receiving
information or pleasure. For, if you would inform, a positive and dogmatical manner in advancing your sentiments may provoke contradiction and prevent a candid attention. If you wish information and
improvement from the knowledge of others, and yet at the same time
express yourself as firmly fixed in your present opinions, modest, sensible men, who do not love disputation, will probably leave you undisturbed in the possession of your error. And by such a manner, you can
seldom hope to recommend yourself in pleasing your hearers, or to persuade those whose concurrence you desire. Pope says, judiciously:

> *Men should be taught as if you taught them not,*
> *And things unknown proposed as things forgot;*

farther recommending to us,

> *To speak, though' sure, with seeming diffidence.*

And he might have coupled with this line that which he has coupled with another, I think less properly,

> *For want of modesty is want of sense.*

If you ask, *Why less properly?* I must repeat the lines,

> *Immodest words admit of no defense,*
> *For want of modesty is want of sense.*

Now, is not *Want of sense* (where a man is so unfortunate as to want it) some apology for his *Want of modesty*? and would not the lines stand more justly thus?

> *Immodest works admit* but this *defense,*
> *That want of modesty is want of sense.*

This, however, I should submit to better judgments.

My brother had, in 1720 or 1721, begun to print a newspaper. It was the second that appeared in America, and was called the New-England Courant. The only one before it was the Boston News-Letter. I remember his being dissuaded by some of his friends from the undertaking, as not likely to succeed, one newspaper being, in their judgment, enough for America. At this time (1771) there are not less than five-and-twenty. He went on, however, with the undertaking, and after having worked in composing the types and printing off the sheets, I was employed to carry the papers thro' the streets to the customers.

He had some ingenious men among his friends, who amused themselves by writing little pieces for this paper, which gained it credit and made it more in demand, and these gentlemen often visited us. Hearing their conversations, and their accounts of the approbation their papers were received with, I was excited to try my hand among them; but, being still a boy, and suspecting that my brother would object to printing anything of mine in his paper if he knew it to be mine, I contrived to disguise my hand, and, writing an anonymous paper, I put it in at night under the door of the printing-house. It was found in the morning, and communicated to his writing friends when they called in as usual. They read it, commented on it in my hearing, and I had the exquisite pleasure of finding it met with their approbation, and that, in their different guesses at the author, none were named but men of some character among us for learning and ingenuity. I suppose now that I was rather lucky in my judges, and that perhaps they were not really so very good ones as I then esteemed them.

Encouraged, however, by this, I wrote and conveyed in the same way to the press several more papers which were equally approved; and I kept my secret till my small fund of sense for such performances was pretty well exhausted and then I discovered it, when I began to be considered a little more by my brother's acquaintance, and in a manner that did not quite please him, as he thought, probably with reason, that it tended to make me too vain. And, perhaps, this might be one occasion of the differences that we began to have about this time. Though a brother, he considered himself as my master, and me as his apprentice, and accordingly, expected the same services from me as he would from another, while I thought he demeaned me too much in some he required of me, who from a brother expected more indulgence. Our disputes were often brought before our father, and I fancy I was either generally in the right, or else a better pleader, because the judgment was generally in my favor. But my brother was passionate, and had often beaten me, which I took extremely amiss;* and, thinking my apprenticeship very tedious, I was continually wishing for some opportunity of shortening it, which at length offered in a manner unexpected.

One of the pieces in our newspaper on some political point, which I have now forgotten, gave offense to the Assembly. He was taken up, censured, and imprisoned for a month by the speaker's warrant, I suppose, because he would not discover his author. I too was taken up and examined before the council; but, though I did not give them any satisfaction, they contented themselves with admonishing me, and dismissed me, considering me, perhaps, as an apprentice, who was bound to keep his master's secrets.

During my brother's confinement, which I resented a good deal, notwithstanding our private differences, I had the management of the paper; and I made bold to give our rulers some rubs in it, which my brother took very kindly, while others began to consider me in an unfavorable light, as a young genius that had a turn for libeling and satyr. My brother's discharge was accompanied with an order of the House (a very odd one), that "James Franklin should no longer print the paper called the *New-England Courant.*"

There was a consultation held in our printing-house among his friends, what he should do in this case. Some proposed to evade the

---

* I fancy his harsh & tyrannical treatment of me, might be a means of impressing me with that aversion to arbitrary power that has stuck to me through my entire life.

order by changing the name of the paper, but my brother, seeing inconveniences in that, it was finally concluded on as a better way, to let it be printed for the future under the name of Benjamin Franklin; and to avoid the censure of the Assembly, that might fall on him as still printing it by his apprentice, the contrivance was that my old indenture should be returned to me, with a full discharge on the back of it, to be shown on occasion, but to secure to him the benefit of my service, I was to sign new indentures for the remainder of the term, which were to be kept private. A very flimsy scheme it was; however, it was immediately executed, and the paper went on accordingly, under my name for several months.

At length, a fresh difference arising between my brother and me, I took upon me to assert my freedom, presuming that he would not venture to produce the new indentures. It was not fair in me to take this advantage, and this I therefore reckon one of the first errata of my life; but the unfairness of it weighed little with me, when under the impressions of resentment for the blows his passion too often urged him to bestow upon me, though he was otherwise not an ill-natured man: perhaps I was too saucy and provoking.

When he found I would leave him, he took care to prevent my getting employment in any other printing-house of the town, by going round and speaking to every master, who accordingly refused to give me work. I then thought of going to New York, as the nearest place where there was a printer; and I was rather inclined to leave Boston when I reflected that I had already made myself a little obnoxious to the governing party, and, from the arbitrary proceedings of the Assembly in my brother's case, it was likely I might, if I stayed, soon bring myself into scrapes; and farther, that my indiscrete disputations about religion began to make me pointed at with horror by good people as an infidel or atheist. I determined on the point, but my father now siding with my brother, I was sensible that, if I attempted to go openly, means would be used to prevent me. My friend Collins, therefore, undertook to manage a little for me. He agreed with the captain of a New York sloop for my passage, under the notion of my being a young acquaintance of his, that had got a naughty girl with child, whose friends would compel me to marry her, and therefore I could not appear or come away publicly. So I sold some of my books to raise a little money, was taken on board privately, and as we had a fair wind, in three days I found myself in New York, near 300 miles from home, a boy of but 17, without the least recommendation to, or knowledge of any person in the place, and with very little money in my pocket.

My inclinations for the sea were by this time worn out, or I might now have gratified them. But, having a trade, and supposing myself a pretty good workman, I offered my service to the printer in the place, old Mr. William Bradford, who had been the first printer in Pennsylvania, but removed from thence upon the quarrel of George Keith. He could give me no employment, having little to do, and help enough already; but says he, "My son at Philadelphia has lately lost his principal hand, Aquila Rose, by death; if you go thither, I believe he may employ you." Philadelphia was a hundred miles further; I set out, however, in a boat for Amboy, leaving my chest and things to follow me round by sea.

In crossing the bay, we met with a squall that tore our rotten sails to pieces, prevented our getting into the Kill and drove us upon Long Island. In our way, a drunken Dutchman, who was a passenger too, fell overboard; when he was sinking, I reached through the water to his shock pate, and drew him up, so that we got him in again. His ducking sobered him a little, and he went to sleep, taking first out of his pocket a book, which he desired I would dry for him. It proved to be my old favorite author, Bunyan's Pilgrim's Progress, in Dutch, finely printed on good paper, with copper cuts, a dress better than I had ever seen it wear in its own language. I have since found that it has been translated into most of the languages of Europe, and suppose it has been more generally read than any other book, except perhaps the Bible. Honest John was the first that I know of who mixed narration and dialogue; a method of writing very engaging to the reader, who in the most interesting parts finds himself, as it were, brought into the company and present at the discourse. De Foe in his Cruso, his Moll Flanders, Religious Courtship, Family Instructor, and other pieces, has imitated it with success; and Richardson has done the same, in his Pamela, etc.

When we drew near the island, we found it was at a place where there could be no landing, there being a great surf on the stony beach. So we dropt anchor, and swung round towards the shore. Some people came down to the water edge and hallowed to us, as we did to them; but the wind was so high, and the surf so loud, that we could not hear so as to understand each other. There were canoes on the shore, and we made signs, and hallowed that they should fetch us; but they either did not understand us, or thought it impracticable, so they went away, and night coming on, we had no remedy but to wait till the wind should abate; and, in the meantime, the boatman and I concluded to sleep, if we could; and so crowded into the scuttle, with the Dutchman, who was still wet, and the spray beating over the head of our boat, leaked thro' to us, so that we were soon almost as wet as he. In this manner we lay all night, with very little rest; but, the wind abating the next day, we made a shift to reach Amboy before night, having been thirty hours on the water, without victuals, or any drink but a bottle of filthy rum, and the water we sailed on being salt.

In the evening I found myself very feverish, and went in to bed; but, having read somewhere that cold water drank plentifully was good for a fever, I followed the prescription, sweat plentiful most of the night, my fever left me, and in the morning, crossing the ferry, I proceeded on my journey on foot, having fifty miles to Burlington, where I was told I should find boats that would carry me the rest of the way to Philadelphia.

It rained very hard all the day; I was thoroughly soaked, and by noon a good deal tired; so I stopped at a poor inn, where I staid all night, beginning now to wish that I had never left home. I cut so miserable a figure, too, that I found, by the questions asked me, I was suspected to be some runaway servant, and in danger of being taken up on that suspicion. However, I proceeded the next day, and got in the evening to an inn, within eight or ten miles of Burlington, kept by one Dr. Brown. He entered into conversation with me while I took some refreshment, and, finding I had read a little, became very sociable and friendly. Our acquaintance continued as long as he lived. He had been, I imagine, an itinerant doctor, for there was no town in England, or country in Europe, of which he could not give a very particular account. He had some letters, and was ingenious, but much of an unbeliever, and wickedly undertook, some years after, to travesty the Bible in doggerel verse, as Cotton had done Virgil. By this means he set many of the facts in a very ridiculous light, and might have hurt weak minds if his work had been published; but it never was.

At his house I lay that night, and the next morning reached Burlington, but had the mortification to find that the regular boats were gone a little before my coming, and no other expected to go before Tuesday, this being Saturday; wherefore I returned to an old woman in the town, of whom I had bought gingerbread to eat on the water, and asked her advice. She invited me to lodge at her house till a passage by water should offer; and being tired with my foot traveling, I accepted the invitation. She understanding I was a printer, would have had me stay at that town and follow my business, being ignorant of the stock necessary to begin with. She was very hospitable, gave me a dinner of ox-cheek with great good will, accepting only a pot of ale in return; and I thought myself fixed till Tuesday should come. However, walking in the evening by the side of the river, a boat came by, which I found was going towards Philadelphia, with several people in her. They took me in, and, as there was no wind, we rowed all the way; and about midnight, not having yet seen the city, some of the company were confident we must have passed it, and would row no farther; the others knew not where we were; so we put toward the shore, got into a creek, landed near an old fence, with the rails of which we made a fire, the night being cold, in October, and there we remained till daylight. Then one of the company knew the place to be Cooper's Creek, a little above Philadelphia, which we saw as soon as we got out of the creek, and arrived there about eight or nine o'clock on the Sunday morning, and landed at the Market Street wharf.

I have been the more particular in this description of my journey, and shall be so of my first entry into that city, that you may in your mind compare such unlikely beginnings with the figure I have since made there. I was in my working dress, my best clothes being to come round by sea. I was dirty from my journey; my pockets were stuffed out with shirts and stockings, and I knew no soul nor where to look for lodging. I was fatigued with traveling, rowing, and want of rest, I was very hungry; and my whole stock of cash consisted of a Dutch dollar, and about a shilling in copper. The latter I gave the people of the boat for my passage, who at first refused it, on account of my rowing; but I insisted on their taking it. A man being sometimes more generous when he has but a little money than when he has plenty, perhaps thro' fear of being thought to have but little.

Then I walked up the street, gazing about till near the market-house I met a boy with bread. I had made many a meal on bread, and, inquiring where he got it, I went immediately to the baker's he directed me to, in Second Street, and asked for biscuit, intending such as we had in Boston; but they, it seems, were not made in Philadelphia. Then I asked for a three-penny loaf, and was told they had none such. So not considering or knowing the difference of money, and the greater cheapness nor the names of his bread, I made him give me three-penny worth of any sort. He gave me, accordingly, three great puffy rolls. I was surprised at the quantity, but took it, and, having no room in my pockets, walked off with a roll under each arm, and eating the other. Thus I went up Market Street as far as Fourth-street, passing by the door of Mr. Read, my future wife's father; when she, standing at the door, saw me, and thought I made, as I certainly did, a most awkward, ridiculous appearance. Then I turned and went down Chestnut-street and part of Walnut-street, eating my roll all the way, and, corning round, found myself again at Market Street wharf, near the boat I came in, to which I went for a draught of the river water; and, being filled with one of my rolls, gave the other two to a woman and her child that came down the river in the boat with us, and were waiting to go farther.

Thus refreshed, I walked again up the street, which by this time had many clean-dressed people in it, who were all walking the same way. I joined them, and thereby was led into the great meeting-house of the Quakers near the market. I sat down among them, and, after looking round awhile and hearing nothing said, being very drowsy through labor and want of rest the preceding night, I fell fast asleep, and continued so till the meeting broke up, when one was kind enough to rouse me. This was, therefore, the first house I was in, or slept in, in Philadelphia.

Walking down again toward the river, and, looking in the faces of people, I met a young Quaker man, whose countenance I liked, and, accosting him, requested he would tell me where a stranger could get lodging. We were then near the sign of the Three Mariners. "Here," says he, "is one place that entertains strangers, but it is not a reputable house; if thee wilt walk with me, I'll show thee a better." He brought me to the Crooked Billet in Water Street. Here I got a dinner; and, while I was eating it, several sly questions were asked me, as it seemed to be suspected from my youth and appearance, that I might be some runaway.

After dinner, my sleepiness returned, and being shown to a bed, I lay down without undressing, and slept till six in the evening, was called to supper, went to bed again very early, and slept soundly till next morning. Then I made myself as tidy as I could, and went to Andrew Bradford the printer's. I found in the shop the old man his father, whom I had seen at New York, and who, traveling on horseback, had got to Philadelphia before me. He introduced me to his son, who received me civilly, gave me a breakfast, but told me he did not at present want a hand, being lately supplied with one; but there was another printer in town, lately set up, one Keimer, who, perhaps, might employ me; if not, I should be welcome to lodge at his house, and he would give me a little work to do now and then till fuller business should offer.

The old gentleman said he would go with me to the new printer; and when we found him, "Neighbor," says Bradford, "I have brought to see you a young man of your business; perhaps you may want such a one." He asked me a few questions, put a composing stick in my hand to see how I worked, and then said he would employ me soon, though he had just then nothing for me to do; and, taking old Bradford, whom he had never seen before, to be one of the town's people that had a good will for him, entered into a conversation on his present undertaking and projects; while Bradford, not discovering that he was the other printer's father, on Keimer's saying he expected soon to get the greatest part of the business into his own hands, drew him on by artful questions, and starting little doubts, to explain all his views, what interests he relied on, and in what manner he intended to proceed. I, who stood by and heard all, saw immediately that one of them was a crafty old sophister, and the other a mere novice. Bradford left me with Keimer, who was greatly surprised when I told him who the old man was.

Keimer's printing-house, I found, consisted of an old shattered press, and one small, worn-out font of English which he was then using himself, composing an Elegy on Aquila Rose, before mentioned, an ingenious young man, of excellent character, much respected in the town, clerk of the Assembly, and a pretty poet. Keimer made verses too, but very indifferently. He could not be said to write them, for his manner was to compose them in the types directly out of his head. So there being no copy, but one pair of cases, and the Elegy likely to require all the letter, no one could help him. I endeavored to put his press (which he had not yet used, and of which he understood nothing) into order fit to be worked with; and, promising to come and print off his Elegy as soon as he should have got it ready, I returned to Bradford's, who gave me a little job to do for the present, and there I lodged and dieted. A few days after, Keimer sent for me to print off the Elegy. And now he had got another pair of cases, and a pamphlet to reprint, on which he set me to work.

These two printers I found poorly qualified for their business. Bradford had not been bred to it, and was very illiterate; and Keimer, though something of a scholar, was a mere compositor, knowing nothing of presswork. He had been one of the French prophets, and could act their enthusiastic agitations. At this time he did not profess any particular religion, but something of all on occasion; was very ignorant of the world, and had, as I afterward found, a good deal of the knave in his composition. He did not like my lodging at Bradford's while I worked with him. He had a house, indeed, but without furniture, so he could not lodge me; but he got me a lodging at Mr. Read's, before mentioned, who was the owner of his house; and, my chest and clothes being come by this time, I made rather a more respectable appearance in the eyes of Miss Read than I had done when she first happened to see me eating my roll in the street.

I began now to have some acquaintance among the young people of the town, that were lovers of reading, with whom I spent my evenings very pleasantly; and gaining money by my industry and frugality, I lived very agreeably, forgetting Boston as much as I could, and not desiring that any there should know where I resided, except my friend Collins, who was in my secret, and kept it when I wrote to him. At length, an incident happened that sent me back again much sooner than I had intended. I had a brother-in-law, Robert Holmes, master of a sloop that traded between Boston and Delaware. He being at Newcastle, forty miles below Philadelphia, heard there of me, and wrote me a letter mentioning the concern of my friends in Boston at my abrupt departure, assuring me of their good will to me, and that every thing would be accommodated to my mind if I would return, to which he exhorted me very earnestly. I wrote an answer to his letter, thanked him for his advice, but stated my reasons for quitting Boston fully and in such a light as to convince him I was not so wrong as he had apprehended.

Sir William Keith, governor of the province, was then at Newcastle, and Captain Holmes, happening to be in company with him when my letter came to hand, spoke to him of me, and showed him the letter. The governor read it, and seemed surprised when he was told my age. He said I appeared a young man of promising parts, and therefore should be encouraged; the printers at Philadelphia were wretched ones; and, if I would set up there, he made no doubt I should succeed; for his part, he would procure me the public business, and do me every other service in his power. This my brother-in-law afterwards told me in Boston, but I knew as yet nothing of it; when, one day, Keimer and I being at work together near the window, we saw the governor and another gentleman (which proved to be Colonel French, of Newcastle), finely dressed, come directly across the street to our house, and heard them at the door.

Keimer ran down immediately, thinking it a visit to him; but the governor inquired for me, came up, and with a condescension of politeness I had been quite unused to, made me many compliments, desired to be acquainted with me, blamed me kindly for not having made myself known to him when I first came to the place, and would have me away with him to the tavern, where he was going with Colonel French to taste, as he said, some excellent Madeira. I was not a little surprised, and Keimer stared like a pig poisoned. I went, however, with the governor and Colonel French to a tavern, at the corner of Third-street, and over the Madeira he proposed my setting up my business, laid before me the probabilities of success, and both he and Colonel French assured me I should have their interest and influence in procuring the public business of both governments. On my doubting whether my father would assist me in it, Sir William said he would give me a letter to him, in which he would state the advantages, and he did not doubt of prevailing with him. So it was concluded I should return to Boston in the first vessel, with the governor's letter recommending me to my father. In the mean time the intention was to be kept a secret, and I went on working with Keimer as usual, the governor sending for me now and then to dine with him, a very great honor I thought it, and conversing with me in the most affable, familiar, and friendly manner imaginable.

About the end of April, 1724, a little vessel offered for Boston. I took leave of Keimer as going to see my friends. The governor gave me an ample letter, saying many flattering things of me to my father, and strongly recommending the project of my setting up at Philadelphia as a thing that must make my fortune. We struck on a shoal in going down the bay, and sprung a leak; we had a blustering time at sea, and were obliged to pump almost continually, at which I took my turn. We arrived safe, however, at Boston in about a fortnight. I had been absent seven months, and my friends had heard nothing of me; for my brother Holmes was not yet returned, and had not written about me. My unexpected appearance surprised the family; all were, however, very glad to see me, and made me welcome, except my brother. I went to see him at his printing-house. I was better dressed than ever while in his service, having a genteel new suit from head to foot, a watch, and my pockets lined with near five pounds sterling in silver. He received me not very frankly, looked me all over, and turned to his work again.

The journeymen were inquisitive where I had been, what sort of a country it was, and how I liked it. I praised it much, the happy life I led in it, expressing strongly my intention of returning to it; and, one of them asking what kind of money we had there, I produced a handful of silver, and spread it before them, which was a kind of raree-show they had not been used to, paper being the money of Boston. Then I took an opportunity of letting them see my watch; and, lastly (my brother still glum and sullen), I gave them a piece of eight to drink, and took my leave. This visit of mine offended him extremely; for, when my mother some time after spoke to him of a reconciliation, and of her wishes to see us on good terms together, and that we might live for the future as brothers, he said I had insulted him in such a manner before his people that he could never forget or forgive it. In this, however, he was mistaken.

My father received the governor's letter with some apparent surprise, but said little of it to me for some days, when Capt. Holmes returning he showed it to him, asked him if he knew Keith, and what kind of man he was; adding his opinion that he must be of small discretion to think of setting a boy up in business who wanted yet three years of being at man's estate. Holmes said what he could in favor of the project, but my father was clear in the impropriety of it, and at last gave a flat denial to it. Then he wrote a civil letter to Sir William, thanking him for the patronage he had so kindly offered me, but declining to assist me as yet in setting up, I being, in his opinion, too young to be trusted with the management of a business so important, and for which the preparation must be so expensive.

My friend and companion Collins, who was a clerk in the post-office, pleased with the account I gave him of my new country, determined to go thither also; and, while I waited for my father's determination, he set out before me by land to Rhode Island, leaving his books, which were a pretty collection of mathematics and natural philosophy, to come with mine and me to New York, where he proposed to wait for me.

My father, though he did not approve Sir William's proposition, was yet pleased that I had been able to obtain so advantageous a character from a person of such note where I had resided, and that I had been so industrious and careful as to equip myself so handsomely in so short a time; therefore, seeing no prospect of an accommodation between my brother and me, he gave his consent to my returning again to Philadelphia, advised me to behave respectfully to the people there, endeavor to obtain the general esteem, and avoid lampooning and libeling, to which he thought I had too much inclination; telling me, that by steady industry and a prudent parsimony I might save enough by the time I was one-and-twenty to set me up; and that, if I came near the matter, he would help me out with the rest. This was all I could obtain, except some small gifts as tokens of his and my mother's love, when I embarked again for New York, now with their approbation and their blessing.

The sloop putting in at Newport, Rhode Island, I visited my brother John, who had been married and settled there some years. He received me very affectionately, for he always loved me. A friend of his, one Vernon, having some money due to him in Pennsylvania, about thirty-five pounds currency, desired I would receive it for him, and keep it till I had his directions what to remit it in. Accordingly, he gave me an order. This afterwards occasioned me a good deal of uneasiness.

At Newport we took in a number of passengers for New York, among which were two young women, companions, and a grave, sensible, matron-like Quaker woman, with her attendants. I had shown an obliging readiness to do her some little services, which impressed her I suppose with a degree of good will toward me; therefore, when she saw a daily growing familiarity between me and the two young women, which they appeared to encourage, she took me aside, and said: "Young man, I am concerned for thee, as thou has no friend with thee, an seems not to know much of the world, or of the snares youth is exposed to; depend upon it, those are very bad women; I can see it in all their actions; and if thee art not upon thy guard, they will draw thee into some danger; they are strangers to thee, and I advise thee, in a friendly concern for thy welfare, to have no acquaintance with them." As I seemed at first not to think so ill of them as she did, she mentioned some things she had observed and heard that had escaped my notice, but now convinced me she was right. I thanked her for her kind advice, and promised to follow it. When we arrived at New York, they told me where they lived, and invited me to come and see them; but I avoided it, and it was well I did; for the next day the captain missed a silver spoon and some other things, that had been taken out of his cabin, and, knowing that these were a couple of strumpets, he got a warrant to search their lodgings, found the stolen goods, and had the thieves punished. So, though we had escaped a sunken rock, which we scraped upon in the passage, I thought this escape of rather more importance to me.

At New York I found my friend Collins, who had arrived there some time before me. We had been intimate from children, and had read the same books together; but he had the advantage of more time for reading and studying, and a wonderful genius for mathematical learning, in which he far outstript me. While I lived in Boston most of my hours of leisure for conversation were spent with him, and he continued a sober as well as an industrious lad; was much respected for his learning by several of the clergy and other gentlemen, and seemed to promise making a good figure in life. But, during my absence, he had acquired a habit of sotting with brandy; and I found by his own account, and what I heard from others, that he had been drunk every day since his arrival at New York, and behaved very oddly. He had gamed, too, and lost his money, so that I was obliged to discharge his lodgings, and defray his expenses to and at Philadelphia, which proved extremely inconvenient to me.

The then governor of New York, Burnet (son of Bishop Burnet), hearing from the captain that a young man, one of his passengers, had a great many books, desired he would bring me to see him. I waited upon him accordingly, and should have taken Collins with me but that he was not sober. The governor treated me with great civility, showed me his library, which was a very large one, and we had a good deal of conversation about books and authors. This was the second governor who had done me the honor to take notice of me; which, to a poor boy like me, was very pleasing.

We proceeded to Philadelphia. I received on the way Vernon's money, without which we could hardly have finished our journey. Collins wished to be employed in some counting-house, but, whether they discovered his dramming by his breath, or by his behavior, though' he had some recommendations, he met with no success in any application, and continued lodging and boarding at the same house with me, and at my expense. Knowing I had that money of Vernon's, he was continually borrowing of me, still promising repayment as soon as he should be in business. At length he had got so much of it that I was distressed to think what I should do in case of being called on to remit it.

His drinking continued, about which we sometimes quarreled, for, when a little intoxicated, he was very fractious. Once, in a boat on the Delaware with some other young men, he refused to row in his turn. "I will be rowed home," says he. "We will not row you," says I. "You must, or stay all night on the water," says he, "just as you please." The others said, "Let us row; what signifies it?"

But, my mind being soured with his other conduct, I continued to refuse. So he swore he would make me row, or throw me overboard; and coming along, stepping on the thwarts, toward me, when he came up and struck at me, I clapped my hand under his crutch, and, rising, pitched him head-foremost into the river. I knew he was a good swimmer, and so was under little concern about him; but before he could get round to lay hold of the boat, we had with a few strokes pulled her out of his reach; and ever when he drew near the boat, we asked if he would row, striking a few strokes to slide her away from him. He was ready to die with vexation, and obstinately would not promise to row. However, seeing him at last beginning to tire, we lifted him in and brought him home dripping wet in the evening. We hardly exchanged a civil word afterwards, and a West India captain, who had a commission to procure a tutor for the sons of a gentleman at Barbados, happening to meet with him, agreed to carry him thither. He left me then, promising to remit me the first money he should receive in order to discharge the debt; but I never heard of him after.

The breaking into this money of Vernon's was one of the first great errata of my life; and this affair showed that my father was not much out in his judgment when he supposed me too young to manage business of importance. But Sir William, on reading his letter, said he was too prudent. There was great difference in persons; and discretion did not always accompany years, nor was youth always without it. "And since he will not set you up," says he, "I will do it myself. Give me an inventory of the things necessary to be had from England, and I will send for them. You shall repay me when you are able; I am resolved to have a good printer here, and I am sure you must succeed." This was spoken with such an appearance of cordiality, that I had not the least doubt of his meaning what he said. I had hitherto kept the proposition of my setting up, a secret in Philadelphia, and I still kept it. Had let been known that I depended on the governor, probably some friend, that knew him better, would have advised me not to rely on him, as I afterwards heard it as his known character to be liberal of promises which he never meant to keep. Yet, unsolicited as he was by me, how could I think his generous offers insincere? I believed him one of the best men in the world.

I presented him an inventory of a little printing-house, amounting by my computation to about one hundred pounds sterling. He liked it, but asked me if my being on the spot in England to choose the types, and see that every thing was good of the kind, might not be of some advantage. "Then," says he, "when there, you may make acquaintances, and establish correspondences in the bookselling and stationery way." I agreed that this might be advantageous. "Then," says he, "get yourself ready to go with Annis;" which was the annual ship, and the only one at that time usually passing between London and Philadelphia. But it would be some months before Annis sailed, so I continued working with Keimer, fretting about the money Collins had got from me, and in daily apprehensions of being called upon by Vernon, which, however, did not happen for some years after.

I believe I have omitted mentioning that, in my first voyage from Boston, being becalmed off Block Island, our people set about catching cod, and hauled up a great many. Hitherto I had stuck to my resolution of not eating animal food, and on this occasion considered, with my master Tryon, the taking every fish as a kind of unprovoked murder, since none of them had, or ever could do us any injury that might justify the slaughter. All this seemed very reasonable. But I had formerly been a great lover of fish, and, when this came hot out of the frying-pan, it smelt admirably well. I balanced some time between principle and inclination, till I recollected that, when the fish were opened, I saw smaller fish taken out of their stomachs; then thought I, "If you eat one another, I don't see why we mayn't eat you." So I dined upon cod very heartily, and continued to eat with other people, returning only now and then occasionally to a vegetable diet. So convenient a thing it is to be a reasonable creature, since it enables one to find or make a reason for everything one has a mind to do.

Keimer and I lived on a pretty good familiar footing, and agreed tolerably well, for he suspected nothing of my setting up. He retained a great deal of his old enthusiasms and loved argumentation. We therefore had many disputations. I used to work him so with my Socratic method, and had trepanned him so often by questions apparently so distant from any point we had in hand, and yet by degrees lead to the point, and brought him into difficulties and contradictions, that at last he grew ridiculously cautious, and would hardly answer me the most common question, without asking first, "What do you intend to infer from that?" However, it gave him so high an opinion of my abilities in the confuting way, that he seriously proposed my being his colleague in a project he had of setting up a new sect. He was to preach the doctrines, and I was to confound all opponents. When he came to explain with me upon the doctrines, I found several conundrums which I objected to, unless I might have my way a little too, and introduce some of mine.

Keimer wore his beard at full length, because somewhere in the Mosaic law it is said, "Thou shalt not mar the corners of thy beard." He likewise kept the Seventh day, Sabbath; and these two points were essentials with him. I disliked both; but agreed to admit them upon condition of his adopting the doctrine of using no animal food. "I doubt," said he, "my constitution will not bear that." I assured him it would, and that he would be the better for it. He was usually a great glutton, and I promised myself some diversion in half starving him. He agreed to try the practice, if I would keep him company. I did so, and we held it for three months. We had our victuals dressed, and brought to us regularly by a woman in the neighborhood, who had from me a list of forty dishes to be prepared for us at different times, in all which there was neither fish, flesh, nor fowl, and the whim suited me the better at this time from the cheapness of it, not costing us above eighteen pence sterling each per week. I have since kept several Lents most strictly, leaving the common diet for that, and that for the common, abruptly, without the least inconvenience, so that I think there is little in the advice of making those changes by easy gradations. I went on pleasantly, but poor Keimer suffered grievously, tired of the project, longed for the flesh-pots of Egypt, and ordered a roast pig. He invited me and two women friends to dine with him; but, it being brought too soon upon table, he could not resist the temptation, and ate the whole before we came.

I had made some courtship during this time to Miss Read. I had a great respect and affection for her, and had some reason to believe she had the same for me; but, as I was about to take a long voyage, and we were both very young, only a little above eighteen, it was thought most prudent by her mother to prevent our going too far at present, as a marriage, if it was to take place, would be more convenient after my return, when I should be, as I expected, set up in my business. Perhaps, too, she thought my expectations not so well founded as I imagined them to be.

My chief acquaintances at this time were Charles Osborne, Joseph Watson, and James Ralph, all lovers of reading. The two first were clerks to an eminent scrivener or conveyancer in the town, Charles Brogden; the other was clerk to a merchant. Watson was a pious, sensible young man, of great integrity; the others rather more lax in their principles of religion, particularly Ralph, who, as well as Collins, had been unsettled by me, for which they both made me suffer. Osborne was sensible, candid, frank; sincere and affectionate to his friends; but, in literary matters, too fond of criticizing. Ralph was ingenious, genteel in his manners, and extremely eloquent; I think I never knew a prettier talker. Both of them great admirers of poetry, and began to try their hands in little pieces. Many pleasant walks we four had together on Sundays into the woods, near Schuylkill, where we read to one another, and conferred on what we read.

Ralph was inclined to pursue the study of poetry, not doubting but he might become eminent in it, and make his fortune by it, alleging that the best poets must, when they first began to write, make as many faults as he did. Osborne dissuaded him, assured him he had no genius for poetry, and advised him to think of nothing beyond the business he was bred to; that, in the mercantile way, though he had no stock, he might, by his diligence and punctuality, recommend himself to employment as a factor, and in time acquire wherewith to trade on his own account. I approved the amusing one's self with poetry now and then, so far as to improve one's language, but no farther.

On this it was proposed that we should each of us, at our next meeting, produce a piece of our own composing, in order to improve by our mutual observations, criticisms, and corrections. As language and expression were what we had in view, we excluded all considerations of invention by agreeing that the task should be a version of the eighteenth Psalm, which describes the descent of a Deity. When the time of our meeting drew nigh, Ralph called on me first, and let me know his piece was ready. I told him I had been busy, and, having little inclination, had done nothing. He then showed me his piece for my opinion, and I much approved it, as it appeared to me to have great merit. "Now," says he, "Osborne never will allow the least merit in any thing of mine, but makes 1000 criticisms out of mere envy. He is not so jealous of you; I wish, therefore, you would take this piece, and produce it as yours; I will pretend not to have had time, and so produce nothing. We shall then see what he will say to it." It was agreed, and I immediately transcribed it, that it might appear in my own hand.

We met; Watson's performance was read; there were some beauties in it, but many defects. Osborne's was read; it was much better; Ralph did it justice; remarked some faults, but applauded the beauties. He himself had nothing to produce. I was backward; seemed desirous of being excused; had not had sufficient time to correct, etc.; but no excuse could be admitted; produce I must. It was read and repeated; Watson and Osborne gave up the contest, and joined in applauding it. Ralph only made some criticisms, and proposed some amendments; but I defended my text. Osborne was against Ralph, and told him he was no better a critic than poet, so he dropt the argument. As they two went home together, Osborne expressed himself still more strongly in favor of what he thought my production; having restrained himself before, as he said, lest I should think it flattery. "But who would have imagined," said he, "that Franklin had been capable of such a performance; such painting, such force, such fire! He has even improved the original. In his common conversation he seems to have no choice of words; he hesitates and blunders; and yet, good God! how he writes!" When we next met, Ralph discovered the trick we had plaid him, and Osborne was a little laughed at.

This transaction fixed Ralph in his resolution of becoming a poet. I did all I could to dissuade him from it, but he continued scribbling verses till Pope cured him. He became, however, a pretty good prose writer. More of him hereafter. But, as I may not have occasion again to mention the other two, I shall just remark here, that Watson died in my arms a few years after, much lamented, being the best of our set. Osborne went to the West Indies, where he became an eminent lawyer and made money, but died young. He and I had made a serious agreement, that the one who happened first to die should, if possible, make a friendly visit to the other, and acquaint him how he found things in that separate state. But he never fulfilled his promise.

The governor, seeming to like my company, had me frequently to his house, and his setting me up was always mentioned as a fixed thing. I was to take with me letters recommendatory to a number of his friends, besides the letter of credit to furnish me with the necessary money for purchasing the press and types, paper, etc. For these letters I was appointed to call at different times, when they were to be ready, but a future time was still named. Thus he went on till the ship, whose departure too had been several times postponed, was on the point of sailing. Then, when I called to take my leave and receive the letters, his secretary, Dr. Bard, came out to me and said the governor was extremely busy in writing, but would be down at Newcastle before the ship, and there the letters would be delivered to me.

Ralph, though married, and having one child, had determined to accompany me in this voyage. It was thought he intended to establish a correspondence, and obtain goods to sell on commission; but I found afterwards, that, thro' some discontent with his wife's relations, he purposed to leave her on their hands, and never return again. Having taken leave of my friends, and interchanged some promises with Miss Read, I left Philadelphia in the ship, which anchored at Newcastle. The governor was there; but when I went to his lodging, the secretary came to me from him with the civilest message in the world, that he could not then see me, being engaged in business of the utmost importance, but should send the letters to me on board, wished me heartily a good voyage and a speedy return, etc. I returned on board a little puzzled, but still not doubting.

Mr. Andrew Hamilton, a famous lawyer of Philadelphia, had taken passage in the same ship for himself and son, and with Mr. Denham, a Quaker merchant, and Messrs. Onion and Russel, masters of an iron work in Maryland, had engaged the great cabin; so that Ralph and I were forced to take up with a berth in the steerage, and none on board knowing us, were considered as ordinary persons. But Mr. Hamilton and his son (it was James, since governor) returned from Newcastle to Philadelphia, the father being recalled by a great fee to plead for a seized ship; and, just before we sailed, Colonel French coming on board, and showing me great respect, I was more taken notice of, and, with my friend Ralph, invited by the other gentlemen to come into the cabin, there being now room. Accordingly, we removed thither.

Understanding that Colonel French had brought on board the governor's dispatches, I asked the captain for those letters that were to be under my care. He said all were put into the bag together and he could not then come at them; but, before we landed in England, I should have an opportunity of picking them out; so I was satisfied for the present, and we proceeded on our voyage. We had a sociable company in the cabin, and lived uncommonly well, having the addition of all Mr. Hamilton's stores, who had laid in plentifully. In this passage Mr. Denham contracted a friendship for me that continued during his life. The voyage was otherwise not a pleasant one, as we had a great deal of bad weather.

When we came into the Channel, the captain kept his word with me, and gave me an opportunity of examining the bag for the governor's letters. I found none upon which my name was put as under my care. I picked out six or seven, that, by the handwriting, I thought might be the promised letters, especially as one of them was directed to Basket, the king's printer, and another to some stationer. We arrived in London the 24th of December, 1724. I waited upon the stationer, who came first in my way, delivering the letter as from Governor Keith. "I don't know such a person," says he; but, opening the letter, "O! this is from Riddlesden. I have lately found him to be a complete rascal, and I will have nothing to do with him, nor receive any letters from him." So, putting the letter into my hand, he turned on his heel and left me to serve some customer. I was surprised to find these were not the governor's letters; and, after recollecting and comparing circumstances, I began to doubt his sincerity. I found my friend Denham, and opened the whole affair to him. He let me into Keith's character; told me there was not the least probability that he had written any letters for me; that no one, who knew him, had the smallest dependence on him; and he laughed at the notion of the governor's giving me a letter of credit, having, as he said, no credit to give. On my expressing some concern about what I should do, he advised me to endeavor getting some employment in the way of my business. "Among the printers here," said he, "you will improve yourself, and when you return to America, you will set up to greater advantage."

We both of us happened to know, as well as the stationer, that Riddlesden, the attorney, was a very knave. He had half ruined Miss Read's father by persuading him to be bound for him. By this letter it appeared there was a secret scheme on foot to the prejudice of Hamilton (supposed to be then coming over with us); and that Keith was concerned in it with Riddlesden. Denham, who was a friend of Hamilton's thought he ought to be acquainted with it; so, when he arrived in England, which was soon after, partly from resentment and ill-will to Keith and Riddlesden, and partly from good-will to him, I waited on him, and gave him the letter. He thanked me cordially, the information being of importance to him; and from that time he became my friend, greatly to my advantage afterwards on many occasions.

But what shall we think of a governor's playing such pitiful tricks, and imposing so grossly on a poor ignorant boy! It was a habit he had acquired. He wished to please everybody; and, having little to give, he gave expectations. He was otherwise an ingenious, sensible man, a pretty good writer, and a good governor for the people, though not for his constituents, the proprietaries, whose instructions he sometimes disregarded. Several of our best laws were of his planning and passed during his administration.

Ralph and I were inseparable companions. We took lodgings together in Little Britain at three shillings and sixpence per week, as much as we could then afford. He found some relations, but they were poor, and unable to assist him. He now let me know his intentions of remaining in London, and that he never meant to return to Philadelphia. He had brought no money with him, the whole he could muster having been expended in paying his passage. I had fifteen pistoles; so he borrowed occasionally of me to subsist, while he was looking out for business. He first endeavored to get into the playhouse, believing himself qualified for an actor; but Wilkes, to whom he applied, advised him candidly not to think of that employment, as it was impossible he should succeed in it. Then he proposed to Roberts, a publisher in Paternoster Row, to write for him a weekly paper like the Spectator, on certain conditions, which Roberts did not approve. Then he endeavored to get employment as a hackney writer, to copy for the stationers and lawyers about the Temple, but could find no vacancy.

I immediately got into work at Palmer's, then a famous printing-house in Bartholomew Close, and here I continued near a year. I was pretty diligent, but spent with Ralph a good deal of my earnings in going to plays and other places of amusement. We had together consumed all my pistoles, and now just rubbed on from hand to mouth. He seemed quite to forget his wife and child, and I, by degrees, my engagements with Miss Read, to whom I never wrote more than one letter, and that was to let her know I was not likely soon to return. This was another of the great errata of my life, which I should wish to correct if I were to live it over again. In fact, by our expenses, I was constantly kept unable to pay my passage.

At Palmer's I was employed in composing for the second edition of Wollaston's Religion of Nature. Some of his reasonings not appearing to me well founded, I wrote a little metaphysical piece in which I made remarks on them. It was entitled "A Dissertation on Liberty and Necessity, Pleasure and Pain." I inscribed it to my friend Ralph; I printed a small number. It occasioned my being more considered by Mr. Palmer as a young man of some ingenuity, though he seriously expostulated with me upon the principles of my pamphlet, which to him appeared abominable. My printing this pamphlet was another erratum. While I lodged in Little Britain, I made an acquaintance with one Wilcox, a bookseller, whose shop was at the next door. He had an immense collection of second-hand books. Circulating libraries were not then in use; but we agreed that, on certain reasonable terms, which I have now forgotten, I might take, read, and return any of his books. This I esteemed a great advantage, and I made as much use of it as I could.

My pamphlet by some means falling into the hands of one Lyons, a surgeon, author of a book entitled The Infallibility of Human Judgment, it occasioned an acquaintance between us. He took great notice of me, called on me often to converse on those subjects, carried me to the Horns, a pale alehouse in—Lane, Cheapside, and introduced me to Mr. Mandeville, author of the Fable of the Bees, who had a club there, of which he was the soul, being a most facetious, entertaining companion. Lyons, too, introduced me to Dr. Pemberton, at Batson's Coffeehouse, who promised to give me an opportunity, some time or other, of seeing Sir Isaac Newton, of which I was extremely desirous; but this never happened.

I had brought over a few curiosities, among which the principal was a purse made of the asbestos, which purifies by fire. Sir Hans Sloane heard of it, came to see me, and invited me to his house in Bloomsbury Square, where he showed me all his curiosities, and persuaded me to let him add that to the number, for which he paid me handsomely.

In our house there lodged a young woman, a milliner, who, I think, had a shop in the Cloisters. She had been genteelly bred, was sensible and lively, and of most pleasing conversation. Ralph read plays to her in the evenings, they grew intimate, she took another lodging, and he followed her. They lived together some time; but, he being still out of business, and her income not sufficient to maintain them with her child, he took a resolution of going from London, to try for a country school, which he thought himself well qualified to undertake, as he wrote an excellent hand, and was a master of arithmetic and accounts. This, however, he deemed a business below him, and confident of future better fortune, when he should be unwilling to have it known that he once was so meanly employed, he changed his name, and did me the honor to assume mine; for I soon after had a letter from him, acquainting me that he was settled in a small village (in Berkshire, I think it was, where he taught reading and writing to ten or a dozen boys, at sixpence each per week), recommending Mrs. T——to my care, and desiring me to write to him, directing for Mr. Franklin, schoolmaster, at such a place.

He continued to write frequently, sending me large specimens of an epic poem which he was then composing, and desiring my remarks and corrections. These I gave him from time to time, but endeavored rather to discourage his proceeding. One of Young's Satires was then just published. I copied and sent him a great part of it, which set in a strong light the folly of pursuing the Muses with any hope of advancement by them. All was in vain; sheets of the poem continued to come by every post. In the mean time, Mrs. T——, having on his account lost her friends and business, was often in distresses, and used to send for me, and borrow what I could spare to help her out of them. I grew fond of her company, and, being at that time under no religious restraint, and presuming upon my importance to her, I attempted familiarities (another erratum) which she repulsed with a proper resentment, and acquainted him with my behavior. This made a breach between us; and, when he returned again to London, he let me know he thought I had cancelled all the obligations he had been under to me. So I found I was never to expect his repaying me what I lent to him, or advanced for him. This, however, was not then of much consequence, as he was totally unable; and in the loss of his friendship I found myself relieved from a burthen. I now began to think of getting a little money beforehand, and, expecting better work, I left Palmer's to work at Watts's, near Lincoln's Inn Fields, a still greater printing-house. Here I continued all the rest of my stay in London.

At my first admission into this printing-house I took to working at press, imagining I felt a want of the bodily exercise I had been used to in America, where presswork is mixed with composing. I drank only water; the other workmen, near fifty in number, were great guzzlers of beer. On occasion, I carried up and down stairs a large form of types in each hand, when others carried but one in both hands. They wondered to see, from this and several instances, that the Water-American, as they called me, was stronger than themselves, who drank strong beer! We had an alehouse boy who attended always in the house to supply the workmen. My companion at the press drank every day a pint before breakfast, a pint at breakfast with his bread and cheese, a pint between breakfast and dinner, a pint at dinner, a pint in the afternoon about six o'clock, and another when he had done his day's work. I thought it a detestable custom; but it was necessary, he supposed, to drink strong beer, that he might be strong to labor. I endeavored to convince him that the bodily strength afforded by beer could only be in proportion to the grain or flour of the barley dissolved in the water of which it was made; that there was more flour in a pennyworth of bread; and therefore, if he would eat that with a pint of water, it would give him more strength than a quart of beer. He drank on, however, and had four or five shillings to pay out of his wages every Saturday night for that muddling liquor; an expense I was free from. And thus these poor devils keep themselves always under.

Watts, after some weeks, desiring to have me in the composing-room, I left the pressmen; a new bien venu or sum for drink, being five shillings, was demanded of me by the compositors. I thought it an imposition, as I had paid below; the master thought so too, and forbad my paying it. I stood out two or three weeks, was accordingly considered as an excommunicate, and had so many little pieces of private mischief done me, by mixing my sorts, transposing my pages, breaking my matter, etc., etc., if I were ever so little out of the room, and all ascribed to the chapel ghost, which they said ever haunted those not regularly admitted, that, notwithstanding the master's protection, I found myself obliged to comply and pay the money, convinced of the folly of being on ill terms with those one is to live with continually.

I was now on a fair footing with them, and soon acquired considerable influence. I proposed some reasonable alterations in their chapel laws, and carried them against all opposition. From my example, a great part of them left their muddling breakfast of beer, and bread, and cheese, finding they could with me be supplied from a neighboring house with a large porringer of hot water-gruel, sprinkled with pepper, crumbled with bread, and a bit of butter in it, for the price of a pint of beer, viz., three half-pence. This was a more comfortable as well as cheaper breakfast, and kept their heads clearer. Those who continued sotting with beer all day, were often, by not paying, out of credit at the alehouse, and used to make interest with me to get beer; their light, as they phrased it, being out. I watched the pay-table on Saturday night, and collected what I stood engaged for them, having to pay sometimes near thirty shillings a week on their account. This, and my being esteemed a pretty good riggite, that is, a jocular verbal satirist, supported my consequence in the society. My constant attendance (I never making a St. Monday) recommended me to the master; and my uncommon quickness at composing occasioned my being put upon all work of dispatch, which was generally better paid. So I went on now very agreeably.

My lodging in Little Britain being too remote, I found another in Dukestreet, opposite to the Romish Chapel. It was two pair of stairs backwards, at an Italian warehouse. A widow lady kept the house; she had a daughter, and a maid servant, and a journeyman who attended the warehouse, but lodged abroad. After sending to inquire my character at the house where I last lodged she agreed to take me in at the same rate, 3s. 6d. per week; cheaper, as she said, from the protection she expected in having a man lodge in the house. She was a widow, an elderly woman; had been bred a Protestant, being a clergyman's daughter, but was converted to the Catholic religion by her husband, whose memory she much revered; had lived much among people of distinction, and knew a thousand anecdotes of them as far back as the times of Charles the Second. She was lame in her knees with the gout, and, therefore, seldom stirred out of her room, so sometimes wanted company; and hers was so highly amusing to me, that I was sure to spend an evening with her whenever she desired it. Our supper was only half an anchovy each, on a very little strip of bread and butter, and half a pint of ale between us; but the entertainment was in her conversation. My always keeping good hours, and giving little trouble in the family, made her unwilling to part with me; so that, when I talked of a lodging I had heard of, nearer my business, for two shillings a week, which, intent as I now was on saving money, made some difference, she bid me not think of it, for she would abate me two shillings a week for the future; so I remained with her at one shilling and sixpence as long as I staid in London.

In a garret of her house there lived a maiden lady of seventy, in the most retired manner, of whom my landlady gave me this account: that she was a Roman Catholic, had been sent abroad when young, and lodged in a nunnery with an intent of becoming a nun; but, the country not agreeing with her, she returned to England, where, there being no nunnery, she had vowed to lead the life of a nun, as near as might be done in those circumstances. Accordingly, she had given all her estate to charitable uses, reserving only twelve pounds a year to live on, and out of this sum she still gave a great deal in charity, living herself on water-gruel only, and using no fire but to boil it. She had lived many years in that garret, being permitted to remain there gratis by successive Catholic tenants of the house below, as they deemed it a blessing to have her there. A priest visited her to confess her every day. "I have asked her," says my landlady, "how she, as she lived, could possibly find so much employment for a confessor?" "Oh," said she, "it is impossible to avoid vain thoughts." I was permitted once to visit her. She was cheerful and polite, and conversed pleasantly. The room was clean, but had no other furniture than a mattress, a table with a crucifix and book, a stool which she gave me to sit on, and a picture over the chimney of Saint Veronica displaying her handkerchief, with the miraculous figure of Christ's bleeding face on it, which she explained to me with great seriousness. She looked pale, but was never sick; and I give it as another instance on how small an income life and health may be supported.

At Watts's printing-house I contracted an acquaintance with an ingenious young man, one Wygate, who, having wealthy relations, had been better educated than most printers; was a tolerable Latinist, spoke French, and loved reading. I taught him and a friend of his to swim at twice going into the river, and they soon became good swimmers. They introduced me to some gentlemen from the country, who went to Chelsea by water to see the College and Don Saltero's curiosities. In our return, at the request of the company, whose curiosity Wygate had excited, I stripped and leaped into the river, and swam from near Chelsea to Blackfryar's, performing on the way many feats of activity, both upon and under water, that surprised and pleased those to whom they were novelties.

I had from a child been ever delighted with this exercise, had studied and practiced all Thevenot's motions and positions, added some of my own, aiming at the graceful and easy as well as the useful. All these I took this occasion of exhibiting to the company, and was much flattered by their admiration; and Wygate, who was desirous of becoming a master, grew more and more attached to me on that account, as well as from the similarity of our studies. He at length proposed to me traveling all over Europe together, supporting ourselves everywhere by working at our business. I was once inclined to it; but, mentioning it to my good friend Mr. Denham, with whom I often spent an hour when I had leisure, he dissuaded me from it, advising me to think only of returning to Pennsylvania, which he was now about to do.

I must record one trait of this good man's character. He had formerly been in business at Bristol, but failed in debt to a number of people, compounded and went to America. There, by a close application to business as a merchant, he acquired a plentiful fortune in a few years. Returning to England in the ship with me, he invited his old creditors to an entertainment, at which he thanked them for the easy composition they had favored him with, and, when they expected nothing but the treat, every man at the first remove found under his plate an order on a banker for the full amount of the unpaid remainder with interest.

He now told me he was about to return to Philadelphia, and should carry over a great quantity of goods in order to open a store there. He proposed to take me over as his clerk, to keep his books, in which he would instruct me, copy his letters, and attend the store. He added that, as soon as I should be acquainted with mercantile business, he would promote me by sending me with a cargo of flour and bread, etc., to the West Indies, and procure me commissions from others which would be profitable; and, if I managed well, would establish me handsomely. The thing pleased me; for I was grown tired of London, remembered with pleasure the happy months I had spent in Pennsylvania, and wished again to see it; therefore I immediately agreed on the terms of fifty pounds a year, Pennsylvania money; less, indeed, than my present gettings as a compositor, but affording a better prospect.

I now took leave of printing, as I thought, for ever, and was daily employed in my new business, going about with Mr. Denham among the tradesmen to purchase various articles, and seeing them packed up, doing errands, calling upon workmen to dispatch, etc.; and, when all was on board, I had a few days' leisure. On one of these days, I was, to my surprise, sent for by a great man I knew only by name, a Sir William Wyndham, and I waited upon him. He had heard by some means or other of my swimming from Chelsea to Blackfriar's, and of my teaching Wygate and another young man to swim in a few hours. He had two sons, about to set out on their travels; he wished to have them first taught swimming, and proposed to gratify me handsomely if I would teach them. They were not yet come to town, and my stay was uncertain, so I could not undertake it; but, from this incident, I thought it likely that, if I were to remain in England and open a swimming-school, I might get a good deal of money; and it struck me so strongly, that, had the overture been sooner made me, probably I should not so soon have returned to America. After many years, you and I had something of more importance to do with one of these sons of Sir William Wyndham, become Earl of Egremont, which I shall mention in its place.

Thus I spent about eighteen months in London; most part of the time I worked hard at my business, and spent but little upon myself except in seeing plays and in books. My friend Ralph had kept me poor; he owed me about twenty-seven pounds, which I was now never likely to receive; a great sum out of my small earnings! I loved him, notwithstanding, for he had many amiable qualities. I had by no means improved my fortune; but I had picked up some very ingenious acquaintance, whose conversation was of great advantage to me; and I had read considerably.

We sailed from Gravesend on the 23d of July, 1726. For the incidents of the voyage, I refer you to my journal, where you will find them all minutely related. Perhaps the most important part of that journal is the plan to be found in it, which I formed at sea, for regulating my future conduct in life. It is the more remarkable, as being formed when I was so young, and yet being pretty faithfully adhered to quite thro' to old age.

We landed in Philadelphia on the 11th of October, where I found sundry alterations. Keith was no longer governor, being superseded by Major Gordon. I met him walking the streets as a common citizen. He seemed a little ashamed at seeing me, but passed without saying anything. I should have been as much ashamed at seeing Miss Read, had not her friends, despairing with reason of my return after the receipt of my letter, persuaded her to marry another, one Rogers, a potter, which was done in my absence. With him, however, she was never happy, and soon parted from him, refusing to cohabit with him or bear his name, it being now said that he had another wife. He was a worthless fellow, though an excellent workman, which was the temptation to her friends. He got into debt, ran away in 1727 or 1728, went to the West Indies, and died there. Keimer had got a better house, a shop well supplied with stationery, plenty of new types, a number of hands, though none good, and seemed to have a great deal of business.

Mr. Denham took a store in Water-street, where we opened our goods; I attended the business diligently, studied accounts, and grew, in a little time, expert at selling. We lodged and boarded together; he counseled me as a father, having a sincere regard for me. I respected and loved him, and we might have gone on together very happy; but, in the beginning of February, 1726–7, when I had just passed my twenty-first year, we both were taken ill. My distemper was a pleurisy, which very nearly carried me off. I suffered a good deal, gave up the point in my own mind, and was rather disappointed when I found myself recovering, regretting, in some degree, that I must now, some time or other, have all that disagreeable work to do over again. I forget what his distemper was; it held him a long time, and at length carried him off. He left me a small legacy in a nuncupative will, as a token of his kindness for me, and he left me once more to the wide world; for the store was taken into the care of his executors, and my employment under him ended.

My brother-in-law, Holmes, being now at Philadelphia, advised my return to my business; and Keimer tempted me, with an offer of large wages by the year, to come and take the management of his printing-house, that he might better attend his stationer's shop. I had heard a bad character of him in London from his wife and her friends, and was not fond of having any more to do with him. I tried for farther employment as a merchant's clerk; but, not readily meeting with any, I closed again with Keimer. I found in his house these hands: Hugh Meredith, a Welsh Pennsylvanian, thirty years of age, bred to country work; honest, sensible, had a great deal of solid observation, was something of a reader, but given to drink. Stephen Potts, a young countryman of full age, bred to the same, of uncommon natural parts, and great wit and humor, but a little idle. These he had agreed with at extreme low wages per week, to be raised a shilling every three months, as they would deserve by improving in their business; and the expectation of these high wages, to come on hereafter, was what he had drawn them in with. Meredith was to work at press, Potts at book-binding, which he, by agreement, was to teach them, though he knew neither one nor t'other. John—, a wild Irishman, brought up to no business, whose service, for four years, Keimer had purchased from the captain of a ship; he, too, was to be made a pressman. George Webb, an Oxford scholar, whose time for four years he had likewise bought, intending him for a compositor, of whom more presently; and David Harry, a country boy, whom he had taken apprentice.

I soon perceived that the intention of engaging me at wages so much higher than he had been used to give, was, to have these raw, cheap hands formed thro' me; and, as soon as I had instructed them, then they being all articled to him, he should be able to do without me. I went on, however, very cheerfully, put his printing-house in order, which had been in great confusion, and brought his hands by degrees to mind their business and to do it better.

It was an odd thing to find an Oxford scholar in the situation of a bought servant. He was not more than eighteen years of age, and gave me this account of himself; that he was born in Gloucester, educated at a grammar-school there, had been distinguished among the scholars for some apparent superiority in performing his part, when they exhibited plays; belonged to the Witty Club there, and had written some pieces in prose and verse, which were printed in the Gloucester newspapers; thence he was sent to Oxford; where he continued about a year, but not well satisfied, wishing of all things to see London, and become a player. At length, receiving his quarterly allowance of fifteen guineas, instead of discharging his debts he walked out of town, hid his gown in a furze bush, and footed it to London, where, having no friend to advise him, he fell into bad company, soon spent his guineas, found no means of being introduced among the players, grew necessitous, pawned his clothes, and wanted bread. Walking the street very hungry, and not knowing what to do with himself, a crimp's bill was put into his hand, offering immediate entertainment and encouragement to such as would bind themselves to serve in America.

He went directly, signed the indentures, was put into the ship, and came over, never writing a line to acquaint his friends what was become of him. He was lively, witty, good-natured, and a pleasant companion, but idle, thoughtless, and imprudent to the last degree.

John, the Irishman, soon ran away; with the rest I began to live very agreeably, for they all respected me the more, as they found Keimer incapable of instructing them, and that from me they learned something daily. We never worked on Saturday, that being Keimer's Sabbath, so I

had two days for reading. My acquaintance with ingenious people in
the town increased. Keimer himself treated me with great civility and
apparent regard, and nothing now made me uneasy but my debt to
Vernon, which I was yet unable to pay, being hitherto but a poor economist. He, however, kindly made no demand of it.

Our printing-house often wanted sorts, and there was no letter-
founder in America; I had seen types cast at James's in London, but
without much attention to the manner; however, I now contrived a
mould, made use of the letters we had as puncheons, struck the matri-
ces in lead, and thus supplied in a pretty tolerable way all deficiencies.
I also engraved several things on occasion; I made the ink; I was ware-
houseman, and everything, and, in short, quite a factotum.

But, however serviceable I might be, I found that my services became every day of less importance, as the other hands improved in the
business; and, when Keimer paid my second quarter's wages, he let
me know that he felt them too heavy, and thought I should make an
abatement. He grew by degrees less civil, put on more of the master,
frequently found fault, was captious, and seemed ready for an out-
breaking. I went on, nevertheless, with a good deal of patience, thinking that his encumbered circumstances were partly the cause. At
length a trifle snapped our connections; for, a great noise happening
near the court-house, I put my head out of the window to see what
was the matter. Keimer, being in the street, looked up and saw me,
called out to me in a loud voice and angry tone to mind my business,
adding some reproachful words, that nettled me the more for their
publicity, all the neighbors who were looking out on the same occasion being witnesses how I was treated. He came up immediately into
the printing-house, continued the quarrel, high words passed on both
sides, he gave me the quarter's warning we had stipulated, expressing
a wish that he had not been obliged to so long a warning. I told him
his wish was unnecessary, for I would leave him that instant; and
so, taking my hat, walked out of doors, desiring Meredith, whom I
saw below, to take care of some things I left, and bring them to my
lodgings.

Meredith came accordingly in the evening, when we talked my affair over. He had conceived a great regard for me, and was very unwill-

ing that I should leave the house while he remained in it. He dissuaded me from returning to my native country, which I began to think of; he reminded me that Keimer was in debt for all he possessed; that his creditors began to be uneasy; that he kept his shop miserably, sold often without profit for ready money, and often trusted without keeping accounts; that he must therefore fall, which would make a vacancy I might profit of. I objected my want of money. He then let me know that his father had a high opinion of me, and, from some discourse that had passed between them, he was sure would advance money to set us up, if I would enter into partnership with him. "My time," says he, "will be out with Keimer in the spring; by that time we may have our press and types in from London. I am sensible I am no workman. If you like it, your skill in the business shall be set against the stock I furnish, and we will share the profits equally."

The proposal was agreeable, and I consented; his father was in town and approved of it; the more as he saw I had great influence with his son, had prevailed on him to abstain long from dram-drinking, and he hoped might break him off that wretched habit entirely, when we came to be so closely connected. I gave an inventory to the father, who carried it to a merchant; the things were sent for, the secret was to be kept till they should arrive, and in the mean time I was to get work, if I could, at the other printing-house. But I found no vacancy there, and so remained idle a few days, when Keimer, on a prospect of being employed to print some paper money in New Jersey, which would require cuts and various types that I only could supply, and apprehending Bradford might engage me and get the job from him, sent me a very civil message, that old friends should not part for a few words, the effect of sudden passion, and wishing me to return. Meredith persuaded me to comply, as it would give more opportunity for his improvement under my daily instructions; so I returned, and we went on more smoothly than for some time before. The New Jersey job was obtained, I contrived a copperplate press for it, the first that had been seen in the country; I cut several ornaments and checks for the bills. We went together to Burlington, where I executed the whole to satisfaction; and he received so large a sum for the work as to be enabled thereby to keep his head much longer above water.

At Burlington I made an acquaintance with many principal people of the province. Several of them had been appointed by the Assembly a committee to attend the press, and take care that no more bills were printed than the law directed. They were therefore, by turns, constantly with us, and generally he who attended, brought with him a friend or two for company. My mind having been much more improved by reading than Keimer's, I suppose it was for that reason my conversation seemed to he more valued. They had me to their houses, introduced me to their friends, and showed me much civility; while he, though the master, was a little neglected. In truth, he was an odd fish; ignorant of common life, fond of rudely opposing received opinions, slovenly to extreme dirtiness, enthusiastic in some points of religion, and a little knavish withal.

We continued there near three months; and by that time I could reckon among my acquired friends, Judge Allen, Samuel Bustill, the secretary of the Province, Isaac Pearson, Joseph Cooper, and several of the Smiths, members of Assembly, and Isaac Decow, the surveyor-general. The latter was a shrewd, sagacious old man, who told me that he began for himself, when young, by wheeling clay for the brick-makers, learned to write after he was of age, carried the chain for surveyors, who taught him surveying, and he had now by his industry, acquired a good estate; and says he, "I foresee that you will soon work this man out of business, and make a fortune in it at Philadelphia." He had not then the least intimation of my intention to set up there or anywhere. These friends were afterwards of great use to me, as I occasionally was to some of them. They all continued their regard for me as long as they lived.

Before I enter upon my public appearance in business, it may be well to let you know the then state of my mind with regard to my principles and morals, that you may see how far those influenced the future events of my life. My parents had early given me religious impressions, and brought me through my childhood piously in the Dissenting way. But I was scarce fifteen, when, after doubting by turns of several points, as I found them disputed in the different books I read, I began to doubt of Revelation itself. Some books against Deism fell into my hands; they were said to be the substance of sermons preached at Boyle's Lectures.

It happened that they wrought an effect on me quite contrary to what was intended by them; for the arguments of the Deists, which were quoted to be refuted, appeared to me much stronger than the refutations; in short, I soon became a thorough Deist. My arguments perverted some others, particularly Collins and Ralph; but, each of them having afterwards wronged me greatly without the least compunction, and recollecting Keith's conduct towards me (who was another freethinker), and my own towards Vernon and Miss Read, which at times gave me great trouble, I began to suspect that this doctrine, though it might be true, was not very useful. My London pamphlet, which had for its motto these lines of Dryden:

> *Whatever is, is right.*
> *Though purblind man*
> *Sees but a part o' the chain, the nearest link,*
> *His eyes not carrying to the equal beam, m*
> *That poises all above.*

And from the attributes of God, his infinite wisdom, goodness and power, concluded that nothing could possibly be wrong in the world, and that vice and virtue were empty distinctions, no such things existing, appeared now not so clever a performance as I once thought it; and I doubted whether some error had not insinuated itself unperceived into my argument, so as to infect all that followed, as is common in metaphysical reasonings.

I grew convinced that truth, sincerity and integrity in dealings between man and man were of the utmost importance to the felicity of life; and I formed written resolutions, which still remain in my journal book, to practice them ever while I lived. Revelation had indeed no weight with me, as such; but I entertained an opinion that, though certain actions might not be bad because they were forbidden by it, or good because it commanded them, yet probably these actions might be forbidden because they were bad for us, or commanded because they were beneficial to us, in their own natures, all the circumstances of things considered. And this persuasion, with the kind hand of Providence, or some guardian angel, or accidental favorable circumstances and situations, or all together, preserved me, through this dangerous time of youth, and the hazardous situations I was sometimes in among strangers, remote from the eye and advice of my father, without any willful gross immorality or injustice, that might have been expected from my want of religion. I say willful, because the instances I have mentioned had something of necessity in them, from my youth, inexperience, and the knavery of others. I had therefore a tolerable character to begin the world with; I valued it properly, and determined to preserve it.

We had not been long returned to Philadelphia before the new types arrived from London. We settled with Keimer, and left him by his consent before he heard of it. We found a house to hire near the market, and took it. To lessen the rent, which was then but twenty-four pounds a year, though I have since known it to let for seventy, we took in Thomas Godfrey, a glazier, and his family, who were to pay a considerable part of it to us, and we to board with them. We had scarce opened our letters and put our press in order, before George House, an acquaintance of mine, brought a countryman to us, whom he had met in the street inquiring for a printer. All our cash was now expended in the variety of particulars we had been obliged to procure, and this countryman's five shillings, being our first-fruits, and coming so seasonably, gave me more pleasure than any crown I have since earned; and the gratitude I felt toward House has made me often more ready than perhaps I should otherwise have been to assist young beginners.

There are croakers in every country, always boding its ruin. Such a one then lived in Philadelphia; a person of note, an elderly man, with a wise look and a very grave manner of speaking; his name was Samuel Mickle. This gentleman, a stranger to me, stopped one day at my door, and asked me if I was the young man who had lately opened a new printing-house. Being answered in the affirmative, he said he was sorry for me, because it was an expensive undertaking, and the expense would be lost; for Philadelphia was a sinking place, the people already half-bankrupts, or near being so; all appearances to the contrary, such as new buildings and the rise of rents, being to his certain knowledge fallacious; for they were, in fact, among the things that would soon ruin us. And he gave me such a detail of misfortunes now existing, or that were soon to exist, that he left me half melancholy. Had I known him before I engaged in this business, probably I never should have done it. This man continued to live in this decaying place, and to declaim in the same strain, refusing for many years to buy a house there, because all was going to destruction; and at last I had the pleasure of seeing him give five times as much for one as he might have bought it for when he first began his croaking.

I should have mentioned before, that, in the autumn of the preceding year, I had formed most of my ingenious acquaintance into a club of mutual improvement, which we called the JUNTO; we met on Friday evenings. The rules that I drew up required that every member, in his turn, should produce one or more queries on any point of Morals, Politics, or Natural Philosophy, to be discussed by the company; and once in three months produce and read an essay of his own writing, on any subject he pleased. Our debates were to be under the direction of a president, and to be conducted in the sincere spirit of inquiry after truth, without fondness for dispute, or desire of victory; and, to prevent warmth, all expressions of positiveness in opinions, or direct contradiction, were after some time made contraband, and prohibited under small pecuniary penalties.

The first members were Joseph Breintnal, a copier of deeds for the scriveners, a good-natured, friendly, middle-aged man, a great lover of poetry, reading all he could meet with, and writing some that was tolerable; very ingenious in many little Nicknackeries, and of sensible conversation.

Thomas Godfrey, a self-taught mathematician, great in his way, and afterward inventor of what is now called Hadley's Quadrant. But he knew little out of his way, and was not a pleasing companion; as, like most great mathematicians I have met with, he expected universal precision in everything said, or was for ever denying or distinguishing upon trifles, to the disturbance of all conversation. He soon left us.

Nicholas Scull, a surveyor, afterwards surveyor-general, who loved books, and sometimes made a few verses.

William Parsons, bred a shoemaker, but loving reading, had acquired a considerable share of mathematics, which he first studied with a view to astrology, that he afterwards laughed at it. He also became surveyor-general.

William Maugridge, a joiner, a most exquisite mechanic, and a solid, sensible man.

Hugh Meredith, Stephen Potts, and George Webb I have characterized before.

Robert Grace, a young gentleman of some fortune, generous, lively, and witty; a lover of punning and of his friends.

And William Coleman, then a merchant's clerk, about my age, who had the coolest, dearest head, the best heart, and the exactest morals of almost any man I ever met with. He became afterwards a merchant of great note, and one of our provincial judges. Our friendship continued without interruption to his death, upward of forty years; and the club continued almost as long, and was the best school of philosophy, morality, and politics that then existed in the province; for our queries, which were read the week preceding their discussion, put us upon reading with attention upon the several subjects, that we might speak more to the purpose; and here, too, we acquired better habits of conversation, every thing being studied in our rules which might prevent our disgusting each other. From hence the long continuance of the club, which I shall have frequent occasion to speak further of hereafter.

But my giving this account of it here is to show something of the interest I had, every one of these exerting themselves in recommending business to us. Breintnal particularly procured us from the Quakers the printing forty sheets of their history, the rest being to be done by Keimer; and upon this we worked exceedingly hard, for the price was low. It was a folio, pro patria size, in pica, with long primer notes. I composed of it a sheet a day, and Meredith worked it off at press; it was often eleven at night, and sometimes later, before I had finished my distribution for the next day's work, for the little jobs sent in by our other friends now and then put us back. But so determined I was to continue doing a sheet a day of the folio, that one night, when, having imposed my forms, I thought my day's work over, one of them by accident was broken, and two pages reduced to pi, I immediately distributed and composed it over again before I went to bed; and this industry, visible to our neighbors, began to give us character and credit; particularly, I was told, that mention being made of the new printing-office at the merchants' Every-night club, the general opinion was that it must fail, there being already two printers in the place, Keimer and Bradford; but Dr. Baird (whom you and I saw many years after at his native place, St. Andrew's in Scotland) gave a contrary opinion: "For the industry of that Franklin," says he, "is superior to any thing I ever saw of the kind; I see him still at work when I go home from club, and he is at work again before his neighbors are out of bed." This struck the rest, and we soon after had offers from one of them to supply us with stationery; but as yet we did not choose to engage in shop business.

I mention this industry the more particularly and the more freely, though it seems to be talking in my own praise, that those of my posterity, who shall read it, may know the use of that virtue, when they see its effects in my favor throughout this relation.

George Webb, who had found a female friend that lent him wherewith to purchase his time of Keimer, now came to offer himself as a journeyman to us. We could not then employ him; but I foolishly let him know as a secret that I soon intended to begin a newspaper, and might then have work for him. My hopes of success, as I told him, were founded on this, that the then only newspaper, printed by Bradford, was a paltry thing, wretchedly managed, no way entertaining, and yet was profitable to him; I therefore thought a good paper would scarcely fail of good encouragement. I requested Webb not to mention it; but he told it to Keimer, who immediately, to be beforehand with me, published proposals for printing one himself, on which Webb was to be employed. I resented this; and, to counteract them, as I could not yet begin our paper, I wrote several pieces of entertainment for Bradford's paper, under the title of the BUSY-BODY, which Breintnal continued some months. By this means the attention of the public was fixed on that paper, and Keimer's proposals, which we burlesqued and ridiculed, were disregarded. He began his paper, however, and, after carrying it on three quarters of a year, with at most only ninety subscribers, he offered it to me for a trifle; and I, having been ready some time to go on with it, took it in hand directly; and it proved in a few years extremely profitable to me.

I perceive that I am apt to speak in the singular number, though our partnership still continued; the reason may be that, in fact, the whole management of the business lay upon me. Meredith was no compositor, a poor pressman, and seldom sober. My friends lamented my connection with him, but I was to make the best of it.

Our first papers made a quite different appearance from any before in the province; a better type, and better printed; but some spirited remarks of my writing, on the dispute then going on between Governor Burnet and the Massachusetts Assembly, struck the principal people, occasioned the paper and the manager of it to be much talked of, and in a few weeks brought them all to be our subscribers.

Their example was followed by many, and our number went on growing continually. This was one of the first good effects of my having learnt a little to scribble; another was, that the leading men, seeing a newspaper now in the hands of one who could also handle a pen, thought it convenient to oblige and encourage me. Bradford still printed the votes, and laws, and other public business. He had printed an address of the House to the governor, in a coarse, blundering manner, we reprinted it elegantly and correctly, and sent one to every member. They were sensible of the difference: it strengthened the hands of our friends in the House, and they voted us their printers for the year ensuing.

Among my friends in the House I must not forget Mr. Hamilton, before mentioned, who was then returned from England, and had a seat in it. He interested himself for me strongly in that instance, as he did in many others afterward, continuing his patronage till his death.

Mr. Vernon, about this time, put me in mind of the debt I owed him, but did not press me. I wrote him an ingenuous letter of acknowledgment, craved his forbearance a little longer, which he allowed me, and as soon as I was able, I paid the principal with interest, and many thanks; so that erratum was in some degree corrected.

But now another difficulty came upon me which I had never the least reason to expect. Mr. Meredith's father, who was to have paid for our printing-house, according to the expectations given me, was able to advance only one hundred pounds currency, which had been paid; and a hundred more was due to the merchant, who grew impatient, and sued us all. We gave bail, but saw that, if the money could not be raised in time, the suit must soon come to a judgment and execution, and our hopeful prospects must, with us, be ruined, as the press and letters must be sold for payment, perhaps at half price.

In this distress two true friends, whose kindness I have never forgotten, nor ever shall forget while I can remember any thing, came to me separately, unknown to each other, and, without any application from me, offering each of them to advance me all the money that should be necessary to enable me to take the whole business upon myself, if that should be practicable; but they did not like my continuing the partnership with Meredith, who, as they said, was often seen drunk in the streets, and playing at low games in alehouses, much to our discredit. These two friends were William Coleman and Robert Grace. I told them I could not propose a separation while any prospect remained of the Merediths' fulfilling their part of our agreement, because I thought myself under great obligations to them for what they had done, and would do if they could; but, if they finally failed in their performance, and our partnership must be dissolved, I should then think myself at liberty to accept the assistance of my friends.

Thus the matter rested for some time, when I said to my partner, "Perhaps your father is dissatisfied at the part you have undertaken in this affair of ours, and is unwilling to advance for you and me what he would for you alone. If that is the case, tell me, and I will resign the whole to you, and go about my business." "No," said he, "my father has really been disappointed, and is really unable; and I am unwilling to distress him farther. I see this is a business I am not fit for. I was bred a farmer, and it was a folly in me to come to town, and put myself, at thirty years of age, an apprentice to learn a new trade. Many of our Welsh people are going to settle in North Carolina, where land is cheap. I am inclined to go with them, and follow my old employment. You may find friends to assist you. If you will take the debts of the company upon you; return to my father the hundred pound he has advanced; pay my little personal debts, and give me thirty pounds and a new saddle, I will relinquish the partnership, and leave the whole in your hands." I agreed to this proposal: it was drawn up in writing, signed, and sealed immediately. I gave him what he demanded, and he went soon after to Carolina, from whence he sent me next year two long letters, containing the best account that had been given of that country, the climate, the soil, husbandry, etc., for in those matters he was very judicious. I printed them in the papers, and they gave great satisfaction to the public.

As soon as he was gone, I recurred to my two friends; and because I would not give an unkind preference to either, I took half of what each had offered and I wanted of one, and half of the other; paid off the company's debts, and went on with the business in my own name, advertising that the partnership was dissolved. I think this was in or about the year 1729.

About this time there was a cry among the people for more paper money, only fifteen thousand pounds being extant in the province, and that soon to be sunk. The wealthy inhabitants opposed any addition, being against all paper currency, from an apprehension that it would depreciate, as it had done in New England, to the prejudice of all creditors. We had discussed this point in our Junto, where I was on the side of an addition, being persuaded that the first small sum struck in 1723 had done much good by increasing the trade, employment, and number of inhabitants in the province, since I now saw all the old houses inhabited, and many new ones building; whereas I remembered well, that when I first walked about the streets of Philadelphia, eating my roll, I saw most of the houses in Walnut-street, between Second and Front streets, with bills on their doors, "To be let"; and many likewise in Chestnut-street and other streets, which made me then think the inhabitants of the city were deserting it one after another.

Our debates possessed me so fully of the subject, that I wrote and printed an anonymous pamphlet on it, entitled The Nature and Necessity of a Paper Currency. It was well received by the common people in general; but the rich men disliked it, for it increased and strengthened the clamor for more money, and they happening to have no writers among them that were able to answer it, their opposition slackened, and the point was carried by a majority in the House. My friends there, who conceived I had been of some service, thought fit to reward me by employing me in printing the money; a very profitable job and a great help to me. This was another advantage gained by my being able to write.

The utility of this currency became by time and experience so evident as never afterwards to be much disputed; so that it grew soon to fifty-five thousand pounds, and in 1739 to eighty thousand pounds, since which it arose during war to upwards of three hundred and fifty thousand pounds, trade, building, and inhabitants all the while increasing, till I now think there are limits beyond which the quantity may be hurtful.

I soon after obtained, thro' my friend Hamilton, the printing of the Newcastle paper money, another profitable job as I then thought it; small things appearing great to those in small circumstances; and these, to me, were really great advantages, as they were great encouragements. He procured for me, also, the printing of the laws and votes of that government, which continued in my hands as long as I followed the business.

I now opened a little stationer's shop. I had in it blanks of all sorts, the correctest that ever appeared among us, being assisted in that by my friend Breintnal. I had also paper, parchment, chapmen's books, etc. One Whitemash, a compositor I had known in London, an excellent workman, now came to me, and worked with me constantly and diligently; and I took an apprentice, the son of Aquila Rose.

I began now gradually to pay off the debt I was under for the printing-house. In order to secure my credit and character as a tradesman, I took care not only to be in reality industrious and frugal, but to avoid all appearances to the contrary. I dressed plainly; I was seen at no places of idle diversion. I never went out a fishing or shooting; a book, indeed, sometimes debauched me from my work, but that was seldom, snug, and gave no scandal; and, to show that I was not above my business, I sometimes brought home the paper I purchased at the stores thro' the streets on a wheelbarrow. Thus being esteemed an industrious, thriving young man, and paying duly for what I bought, the merchants who imported stationery solicited my custom; others proposed supplying me with books, and I went on swimmingly. In the mean time, Keimer's credit and business declining daily, he was at last forced to sell his printing-house to satisfy his creditors. He went to Barbados, and there lived some years in very poor circumstances.

His apprentice, David Harry, whom I had instructed while I worked with him, set up in his place at Philadelphia, having bought his materials. I was at first apprehensive of a powerful rival in Harry, as his friends were very able, and had a good deal of interest. I therefore proposed a partnership to him which he, fortunately for me, rejected with scorn. He was very proud, dressed like a gentleman, lived expensively, took much diversion and pleasure abroad, ran in debt, and neglected his business; upon which, all business left him; and, finding nothing to do, he followed Keimer to Barbados, taking the printing-house with him. There this apprentice employed his former master as a journeyman; they quarreled often; Harry went continually behindhand, and at length was forced to sell his types and return to his country work in Pennsylvania. The person that bought them employed Keimer to use them, but in a few years he died.

There remained now no competitor with me at Philadelphia but the old one, Bradford; who was rich and easy, did a little printing now and then by straggling hands, but was not very anxious about the business. However, as he kept the post-office, it was imagined he had better opportunities of obtaining news; his paper was thought a better distributor of advertisements than mine, and therefore had many, more, which was a profitable thing to him, and a disadvantage to me; for, though I did indeed receive and send papers by the post, yet the public opinion was otherwise, for what I did send was by bribing the riders, who took them privately, Bradford being unkind enough to forbid it, which occasioned some resentment on my part; and I thought so meanly of him for it, that, when I afterward came into his situation, I took care never to imitate it.

I had hitherto continued to board with Godfrey, who lived in part of my house with his wife and children, and had one side of the shop for his glazier's business, though he worked little, being always absorbed in his mathematics. Mrs. Godfrey projected a match for me with a relation's daughter, took opportunities of bringing us often together, till a serious courtship on my part ensued, the girl being in herself very deserving. The old folks encouraged me by continual invitations to supper, and by leaving us together, till at length it was time to explain. Mrs. Godfrey managed our little treaty. I let her know that I expected as much money with their daughter as would pay off my remaining debt for the printing-house, which I believe was not then above a hundred pounds. She brought me word they had no such sum to spare; I said they might mortgage their house in the loan-office. The answer to this, after some days, was, that they did not approve the match; that, on inquiry of Bradford, they had been informed the printing business was not a profitable one; the types would soon be worn out, and more wanted; that S. Keimer and D. Harry had failed one after the other, and I should probably soon follow them; and, therefore, I was forbidden the house, and the daughter shut up.

Whether this was a real change of sentiment or only artifice, on a supposition of our being too far engaged in affection to retract, and therefore that we should steal a marriage, which would leave them at liberty to give or withhold what they pleased, I know not; but I suspected the latter, resented it, and went no more. Mrs. Godfrey brought me afterward some more favorable accounts of their disposition, and would have drawn me on again; but I declared absolutely my resolution to have nothing more to do with that family. This was resented by the Godfreys; we differed, and they removed, leaving me the whole house, and I resolved to take no more inmates.

But this affair having turned my thoughts to marriage, I looked round me and made overtures of acquaintance in other places; but soon found that, the business of a printer being generally thought a poor one, I was not to expect money with a wife, unless with such a one as I should not otherwise think agreeable. In the mean time, that hard-to-be-governed passion of youth hurried me frequently into intrigues with low women that fell in my way, which were attended with some expense and great inconvenience, besides a continual risk to my health by a distemper which of all things I dreaded, though by great good luck I escaped it. A friendly correspondence as neighbors and old acquaintances had continued between me and Mrs. Read's family, who all had a regard for me from the time of my first lodging in their house. I was often invited there and consulted in their affairs, wherein I sometimes was of service. I pitied poor Miss Read's unfortunate situation, who was generally dejected, seldom cheerful, and avoided company. I considered my giddiness and inconstancy when in London as in a great degree the cause of her unhappiness, though the mother was good

enough to think the fault more her own than mine, as she had prevented our marrying before I went thither, and persuaded the other
match in my absence. Our mutual affection was revived, but there were
now great objections to our union. The match was indeed looked upon
as invalid, a preceding wife being said to be living in England; but this
could not easily be proved, because of the distance; and, though there
was a report of his death, it was not certain. Then, though it should be
true, he had left many debts, which his successor might be called upon
to pay. We ventured, however, over all these difficulties, and I took her
to wife, September 1st, 1730. None of the inconveniences happened
that we had apprehended, she proved a good and faithful helpmate, assisted me much by attending the shop; we throve together, and have
ever mutually endeavored to make each other happy. Thus I corrected
that great erratum as well as I could.

About this time, our club meeting, not at a tavern, but in a little
room of Mr. Grace's, set apart for that purpose, a proposition was made
by me, that, since our books were often referred to in our disquisitions
upon the queries, it might be convenient to us to have them altogether
where we met, that upon occasion they might be consulted; and by thus
clubbing our books to a common library, we should, while we liked to
keep them together, have each of us the advantage of using the books
of all the other members, which would be nearly as beneficial as if each
owned the whole. It was liked and agreed to, and we filled one end of
the room with such books as we could best spare. The number was not
so great as we expected; and though they had been of great use, yet
some inconveniences occurring for want of due care of them, the collection, after about a year, was separated, and each took his books home
again.

And now I set on foot my first project of a public nature, that for a
subscription library. I drew up the proposals, got them put into form by
our great scrivener, Brockden, and, by the help of my friends in the
Junto, procured fifty subscribers of forty shillings each to begin with,
and ten shillings a year for fifty years, the term our company was to
continue. We afterwards obtained a charter, the company being increased to one hundred: this was the mother of all the North American
subscription libraries, now so numerous. It is become a great thing it-

self, and continually increasing. These libraries have improved the general conversation of the Americans, made the common tradesmen and farmers as intelligent as most gentlemen from other countries, and perhaps have contributed in some degree to the stand so generally made throughout the colonies in defense of their privileges.

Memo: Thus far was written with the intention expressed in the beginning and therefore contains several little family anecdotes of no importance to others. What follows was written many years after in compliance with the advice contained in these letters, and accordingly intended for the public. The affairs of the Revolution occasioned the interruption.

PART TWO

Continuation of the Account of my Life, begun at Passy, near Paris, 1784

It is some time since I received the above letters [Editor's note: from friends urging him to continue writing his autobiography], but I have been too busy till now to think of complying with the request they contain. It might, too, be much better done if I were at home among my papers, which would aid my memory, and help to ascertain dates; but my return being uncertain and having just now a little leisure, I will endeavor to recollect and write what I can; if I live to get home, it may there be corrected and improved.

Not having any copy here of what is already written, I know not whether an account is given of the means I used to establish the Philadelphia public library, which, from a small beginning, is now become so considerable, though I remember to have come down to near the time of that transaction (1730). I will therefore begin here with an account of it, which may be struck out if found to have been already given.

At the time I established myself in Pennsylvania, there was not a good bookseller's shop in any of the colonies to the southward of Boston. In New York and Philadelphia the printers were indeed stationers; they sold only paper, etc., almanacs, ballads, and a few common school-books. Those who loved reading were obliged to send for their books from England; the members of the Junto had each a few. We had left the alehouse, where we first met, and hired a room to hold our club in. I proposed that we should all of us bring our books to that room, where they would not only be ready to consult in our conferences, but become a common benefit, each of us being at liberty to borrow such as he wished to read at home. This was accordingly done, and for some time contented us.

Finding the advantage of this little collection, I proposed to render the benefit from books more common, by commencing a public subscription library. I drew a sketch of the plan and rules that would be necessary, and got a skilful conveyancer, Mr. Charles Brockden, to put the whole in form of articles of agreement to be subscribed, by which each subscriber engaged to pay a certain sum down for the first purchase of books, and an annual contribution for increasing them. So few were the readers at that time in Philadelphia, and the majority of us so poor, that I was not able, with great industry, to find more than fifty persons, mostly young tradesmen, willing to pay down for this purpose forty shillings each, and ten shillings per annum. On this little fund we began. The books were imported; the library wag opened one day in the week for lending to the subscribers, on their promissory notes to pay double the value if not duly returned. The institution soon manifested its utility, was imitated by other towns, and in other provinces. The libraries were augmented by donations; reading became fashionable; and our people, having no public amusements to divert their attention from study, became better acquainted with books, and in a few years were observed by strangers to be better instructed and more intelligent than people of the same rank generally are in other countries.

When we were about to sign the above-mentioned articles, which were to be binding upon us, our heirs, etc., for fifty years, Mr. Brockden, the scrivener, said to us, "You are young men, but it is scarcely probable that any of you will live to see the expiration of the term fixed in the instrument." A number of us, however, are yet living; but the instrument was after a few years rendered null by a charter that incorporated and gave perpetuity to the company.

The objections and reluctances I met with in soliciting the subscriptions, made me soon feel the impropriety of presenting one's self as the proposer of any useful project, that might be supposed to raise one's reputation in the smallest degree above that of one's neighbors, when one has need of their assistance to accomplish that project. I therefore put myself as much as I could out of sight, and stated it as a scheme of a number of friends, who had requested me to go about and propose it to such as they thought lovers of reading. In this way my affair went on more smoothly, and I ever after practiced it on such occasions; and, from my frequent successes, can heartily recommend it. The present little sacrifice of your vanity will afterwards be amply repaid. If it remains a while uncertain to whom the merit belongs, some one more vain than yourself will be encouraged to claim it, and then even envy will be disposed to do you justice by plucking those assumed feathers, and restoring them to their right owner.

This library afforded me the means of improvement by constant study, for which I set apart an hour or two each day, and thus repaired in some degree the loss of the learned education my father once intended for me. Reading was the only amusement I allowed myself. I spent no time in taverns, games, or frolics of any kind; and my industry in my business continued as indefatigable as it was necessary. I was indebted for my printing-house; I had a young family coming on to be educated, and I had to contend with for business two printers, who were established in the place before me. My circumstances, however, grew daily easier. My original habits of frugality continuing, and my father having, among his instructions to me when a boy, frequently repeated a proverb of Solomon, "Seest thou a man diligent in his calling, he shall stand before kings, he shall not stand before mean men," I from thence considered industry as a means of obtaining wealth and distinction, which encouraged me, though I did not think that I should ever literally stand before kings, which, however, has since happened; for I have stood before five, and even had the honor of sitting down with one, the King of Denmark, to dinner.

We have an English proverb that says, "He that would thrive, must ask his wife." It was lucky for me that I had one as much disposed to industry and frugality as myself. She assisted me cheerfully in my business, folding and stitching pamphlets, tending shop, purchasing old linen rags for the papermakers, etc., etc. We kept no idle servants, our table was plain and simple, our furniture of the cheapest. For instance, my breakfast was a long time bread and milk (no tea), and I ate it out of a twopenny earthen porringer, with a pewter spoon. But mark how luxury will enter families, and make a progress, in spite of principle: being called one morning to breakfast, I found it in a China bowl, with a spoon of silver! They had been bought for me without my knowledge by my wife, and had cost her the enormous sum of three-and-twenty shillings, for which she had no other excuse or apology to make, but that she thought her husband deserved a silver spoon and China bowl as well as any of his neighbors. This was the first appearance of plate and China in our house, which afterward, in a course of years, as our wealth increased, augmented gradually to several hundred pounds in value.

I had been religiously educated as a Presbyterian; and though some of the dogmas of that persuasion, such as the eternal decrees of God, election, reprobation, etc., appeared to me unintelligible, others doubtful, and I early absented myself from the public assemblies of the sect, Sunday being my studying day, I never was without some religious principles. I never doubted, for instance, the existence of the Deity; that he made the world, and governed it by his Providence; that the most acceptable service of God was the doing good to man; that our souls are immortal; and that all crime will be punished, and virtue rewarded, either here or hereafter. These I esteemed the essentials of every religion; and, being to be found in all the religions we had in our country, I respected them all, though with different degrees of respect, as I found them more or less mixed with other articles, which, without any tendency to inspire, promote, or confirm morality, served principally to divide us, and make us unfriendly to one another. This respect to all, with an opinion that the worst had some good effects, induced me to avoid all discourse that might tend to lessen the good opinion another might have of his own religion; and as our province increased in people, and new places of worship were continually wanted, and generally erected by voluntary contributions, my mite for such purpose, whatever might be the sect, was never refused.

Though I seldom attended any public worship, I had still an opinion of its propriety, and of its utility when rightly conducted, and I regularly paid my annual subscription for the support of the only Presbyterian minister or meeting we had in Philadelphia. He used to visit me sometimes as a friend, and admonish me to attend his administrations, and I was now and then prevailed on to do so, once for five Sundays successively. Had he been in my opinion a good preacher, perhaps I might have continued, notwithstanding the occasion I had for the Sunday's leisure in my course of study; but his discourses were chiefly either polemic arguments, or explications of the peculiar doctrines of our sect, and were all to me very dry, uninteresting, and unedifying, since not a single moral principle was inculcated or enforced, their aim seeming to be rather to make us Presbyterians than good citizens.

At length he took for his text that verse of the fourth chapter of Philippians, "Finally, brethren, whatsoever things are true, honest, just, pure, lovely, or of good report, if there be any virtue, or any praise, think on these things." And I imagined, in a sermon on such a text, we could not miss of having some morality. But he confined himself to five points only, as meant by the apostle, viz.: 1. Keeping holy the Sabbath day. 2. Being diligent in reading the holy Scriptures. 3. Attending duly the public worship. 4. Partaking of the Sacrament. 5. Paying a due respect to God's ministers. These might be all good things; but, as they were not the kind of good things that I expected from that text, I despaired of ever meeting with them from any other, was disgusted, and attended his preaching no more. I had some years before composed a little Liturgy, or form of prayer, for my own private use (viz., in 1728), entitled, Articles of Belief and Acts of Religion. I returned to the use of this, and went no more to the public assemblies. My conduct might be blamable, but I leave it, without attempting further to excuse it; my present purpose being to relate facts, and not to make apologies for them.

It was about this time I conceived the bold and arduous project of arriving at moral perfection. I wished to live without committing any fault at any time; I would conquer all that either natural inclination, custom, or company might lead me into. As I knew, or thought I knew, what was right and wrong, I did not see why I might not always do the one and avoid the other. But I soon found I had undertaken a task of more difficulty than I had imagined. While my care was employed in guarding against one fault, I was often surprised by another; habit took the advantage of inattention; inclination was sometimes too strong for reason. I concluded, at length, that the mere speculative conviction that it was our interest to be completely virtuous, was not sufficient to prevent our slipping; and that the contrary habits must be broken, and good ones acquired and established, before we can have any dependence on a steady, uniform rectitude of conduct. For this purpose I therefore contrived the following method.

In the various enumerations of the moral virtues I had met with in my reading, I found the catalogue more or less numerous, as different writers included more or fewer ideas under the same name. Temperance, for example, was by some confined to eating and drinking, while by others it was extended to mean the moderating every other pleasure, appetite, inclination, or passion, bodily or mental, even to our avarice and ambition. I proposed to myself, for the sake of clearness, to use rather more names, with fewer ideas annexed to each, than a few names with more ideas; and I included under thirteen names of virtues all that at that time occurred to me as necessary or desirable, and annexed to each a short precept, which fully expressed the extent I gave to its meaning.

These names of virtues, with their precepts, were:

Temperance:	Eat not to dullness; drink not to elevation.
Silence:	Speak not but what may benefit others or yourself; avoid trifling conversation.
Order:	Let all your things have their places; let each part of your business have its time.
Resolution:	Resolve to perform what you ought; perform without fail what you resolve.
Frugality:	Make no expense but to do good to others or yourself; i.e., waste nothing.
Industry:	Lose no time; be always employed in something useful; cut off all unnecessary actions.
Sincerity:	Use no hurtful deceit; think innocently and justly, and, if you speak, speak accordingly.
Justice:	Wrong none by doing injuries, or omitting the benefits that are your duty.

Moderation:	Avoid extremes; forbear resenting injuries so much as you think they deserve.
Cleanliness:	Tolerate no uncleanliness in body, clothes, or habitation.
Tranquility:	Be not disturbed at trifles, or at accidents common or unavoidable.
Chastity:	Rarely use venery but for health or offspring, never to dullness, weakness, or the injury of your own or another's peace or reputation.
Humility:	Imitate Jesus and Socrates.

My intention being to acquire the habitude of all these virtues, I judged it would be well not to distract my attention by attempting the whole at once, but to fix it on one of them at a time; and, when I should be master of that, then to proceed to another, and so on, till I should have gone thro' the thirteen; and, as the previous acquisition of some might facilitate the acquisition of certain others, I arranged them with that view, as they stand above. Temperance first, as it tends to procure that coolness and clearness of head, which is so necessary where constant vigilance was to be kept up, and guard maintained against the unremitting attraction of ancient habits, and the force of perpetual temptations. This being acquired and established, Silence would be more easy; and my desire being to gain knowledge at the same time that I improved in virtue, and considering that in conversation it was obtained rather by the use of the ears than of the tongue, and therefore wishing to break a habit I was getting into of prattling, punning, and joking, which only made me acceptable to trifling company, I gave Silence the second place. This and the next, Order, I expected would allow me more time for attending to my project and my studies. Resolution, once become habitual, would keep me firm in my endeavors to obtain all the subsequent virtues; Frugality and Industry freeing me from my remaining debt, and producing affluence and independence, would make more easy the practice of Sincerity and Justice, etc., etc. Conceiving then, that, agreeably to the advice of Pythagoras in his

Golden Verses, daily examination would be necessary, I contrived the following method for conducting that examination.

I made a little book, in which I allotted a page for each of the virtues. I ruled each page with red ink, so as to have seven columns, one for each day of the week, marking each column with a letter for the day. I crossed these columns with thirteen red lines, marking the beginning of each line with the first letter of one of the virtues, on which line, and in its proper column, I might mark, by a little black spot, every fault I found upon examination to have been committed respecting that virtue upon that day.

Form of the pages:

TEMPERANCE

Eat not to dullness;
Drink not to elevation.

	S	M	T	W	T	F	S
T							
S	x x	x		x		x	
O	x	x	x		x	x	x
R			x			x	
F		x			x		
I			x				
S							
J							
M							
Cl							
T							
Ch							
H							

I determined to give a week's strict attention to each of the virtues successively. Thus, in the first week, my great guard was to avoid every the least offence against Temperance, leaving the other virtues to their ordinary chance, only marking every evening the faults of the day. Thus, if in the first week I could keep my first line, marked T, clear of spots, I supposed the habit of that virtue so much strengthened and its opposite weakened, that I might venture extending my attention to include the next, and for the following week keep both lines clear of spots. Proceeding thus to the last, I could go thro' a course complete in thirteen weeks, and four courses in a year. And like him who, having a garden to weed, does not attempt to eradicate all the bad herbs at once, which would exceed his reach and his strength, but works on one of the beds at a time, and, having accomplished the first, proceeds to a second, so I should have, I hoped, the encouraging pleasure of seeing on my pages the progress I made in virtue, by clearing successively my lines of their spots, till in the end, by a number of courses, I should be happy in viewing a clean book, after a thirteen weeks' daily examination.

This my little book had for its motto these lines from Addison's Cato:

> *Here will I hold. If there's a power above us*
> *(And that there is all nature cries aloud*
> *Thro' all her works), He must delight in virtue;*
> *And that which he delights in must be happy.*

Another from Cicero,

O vitae Philosophia dux! O virtutum indagatrix expultrixque vitiorum! Unus dies, bene et ex praeceptis tuis actus, peccanti immortalitati est anteponendus.

Another from the Proverbs of Solomon, speaking of wisdom or virtue:

Length of days is in her right hand, and in her left hand riches and honors. Her ways are ways of pleasantness, and all her paths are peace. (III,. 16, 17).

And conceiving God to be the fountain of wisdom, I thought it right and necessary to solicit his assistance for obtaining it; to this end I formed the following little prayer, which was prefixed to my tables of examination, for daily use.

O powerful Goodness! bountiful Father! merciful Guide!
increase in me that wisdom which discovers my truest interest.
strengthen my resolutions to perform what that wisdom dictates.
Accept my kind offices to thy other children as the only return
in my power for thy continual favors to me.

I used also sometimes a little prayer which I took from Thomson's Poems, viz.:

Father of light and life, thou Good Supreme!
O teach me what is good; teach me Thyself!
Save me from folly, vanity, and vice,
From every low pursuit; and fill my soul
With knowledge, conscious peace, and virtue pure;
Sacred, substantial, never-fading bliss!

The precept of Order requiring that every part of my business should have its allotted time, one page in my little book contained the following scheme of employment for the twenty-four hours of a natural day:

The morning question, What good shall I do this day?	5 6 7	Rise, wash, and address Powerful Goodness; Contrive day's business, and take the resolution of the day; prosecute the present study, and breakfast.
	8 9 10 11	Work

	12 1	Read or overlook my accounts and dine
	2 3 4 5	Work
The evening question, What good have I done to– day?	6 7 8 9	Put things in their places. Supper. Music or diversion, or conversation. Examination of the day.
	10 11 12 1 2 3 4	Sleep

I entered upon the execution of this plan for self-examination, and continued it with occasional intermissions for some time. I was surprised to find myself so much fuller of faults than I had imagined; but I had the satisfaction of seeing them diminish. To avoid the trouble of renewing now and then my little book, which, by scraping out the marks on the paper of old faults to make room for new ones in a new course, became full of holes, I transferred my tables and precepts to the ivory leaves of a memorandum book, on which the lines were drawn with red ink, that made a durable stain, and on those lines I marked my faults with a black-lead pencil, which marks I could easily wipe out with a wet sponge. After a while I went thro' one course only in a year, and afterward only one in several years, till at length I omitted them entirely, being employed in voyages and business abroad, with a multiplicity of affairs that interfered; but I always carried my little book with me.

My scheme of Order gave me the most trouble; and I found that, though it might be practicable where a man's business was such as to leave him the disposition of his time, that of a journeyman printer, for instance, it was not possible to be exactly observed by a master, who must mix with the world, and often receive people of business at their own hours. Order, too, with regard to places for things, papers, etc., I found extremely difficult to acquire. I had not been early accustomed to it, and, having an exceeding good memory, I was not so sensible of the inconvenience attending want of method. This article, therefore, cost me so much painful attention, and my faults in it vexed me so much, and I made so little progress in amendment, and had such frequent relapses, that I was almost ready to give up the attempt, and content myself with a faulty character in that respect, like the man who, in buying an ax of a smith, my neighbor, desired to have the whole of its surface as bright as the edge. The smith consented to grind it bright for him if he would turn the wheel; he turned, while the smith pressed the broad face of the ax hard and heavily on the stone, which made the turning of it very fatiguing. The man came every now and then from the wheel to see how the work went on, and at length would take his ax as it was, without farther grinding. "No," said the smith, "turn on, turn on; we shall have it bright by-and-by; as yet, it is only speckled." "Yes," said the man, "but I think I like a speckled ax best." And I believe this may have been the case with many, who, having, for want of some such means as I employed, found the difficulty of obtaining good and breaking bad habits in other points of vice and virtue, have given up the struggle, and concluded that "a speckled ax was best"; for something, that pretended to be reason, was every now and then suggesting to me that such extreme nicety as I exacted of myself might be a kind of foppery in morals, which, if it were known, would make me ridiculous; that a perfect character might be attended with the inconvenience of being envied and hated; and that a benevolent man should allow a few faults in himself, to keep his friends in countenance.

In truth, I found myself incorrigible with respect to Order; and now I am grown old, and my memory bad, I feel very sensibly the want of it. But, on the whole, though I never arrived at the perfection I had been so ambitious of obtaining, but fell far short of it, yet I was, by the endeavor, a better and a happier man than I otherwise should have been if I had not attempted it; as those who aim at perfect writing by imitating the engraved copies, though they never reach the excellence of those copies, their hand is mended by the endeavor, and is tolerable while it continues fair and legible.

It may be well my posterity should be informed that to this little artifice, with the blessing of God, their ancestor owed the constant felicity of his life, down to his 79th year, in which this is written. What reverses may attend the remainder is in the hand of Providence; but, if they arrive, the reflection on past happiness enjoyed ought to help his bearing them with more resignation. To Temperance he ascribes his long-continued health, and what is still left to him of a good constitution; to Industry and Frugality, the early easiness of his circumstances and acquisition of his fortune, with all that knowledge that enabled him to be a useful citizen, and obtained for him some degree of reputation among the learned; to Sincerity and Justice, the confidence of his country, and the honorable employs it conferred upon him; and to the joint influence of the whole mass of the virtues, even in the imperfect state he was able to acquire them, all that evenness of temper, and that cheerfulness in conversation, which makes his company still sought for, and agreeable even to his younger acquaintance. I hope, therefore, that some of my descendants may follow the example and reap the benefit.

It will be remarked that, though my scheme was not wholly without religion, there was in it no mark of any of the distinguishing tenets of any particular sect. I had purposely avoided them; for, being fully persuaded of the utility and excellency of my method, and that it might be serviceable to people in all religions, and intending some time or

other to publish it, I would not have any thing in it that should prejudice any one, of any sect, against it. I purposed writing a little comment
on each virtue, in which I would have shown the advantages of possessing it, and the mischiefs attending its opposite vice; and I should
have called my book The Art of Virtue, because it would have shown
the means and manner of obtaining virtue, which would have distinguished it from the mere exhortation to be good, that does not instruct
and indicate the means, but is like the apostle's man of verbal charity,
who only without showing to the naked and hungry how or where they
might get clothes or victuals, exhorted them to be fed and clothed.—
James II: 15, 16.

But it so happened that my intention of writing and publishing this
comment was never fulfilled. I did, indeed, from time to time, put
down short hints of the sentiments, reasonings, etc., to be made use of
in it, some of which I have still by me; but the necessary close attention
to private business in the earlier part of thy life, and public business
since, have occasioned my postponing it; for, it being connected in my
mind with a great and extensive project, that required the whole man
to execute, and which an unforeseen succession of employs prevented
my attending to, it has hitherto remained unfinished.

In this piece it was my design to explain and enforce this doctrine,
that vicious actions are not hurtful because they are forbidden, but forbidden because they are hurtful, the nature of man alone considered;
that it was, therefore, every one's interest to be virtuous who wished to
be happy even in this world; and I should, from this circumstance
(there being always in the world a number of rich merchants, nobility,
states, and princes, who have need of honest instruments for the management of their affairs, and such being so rare), have endeavored to
convince young persons that no qualities were so likely to make a poor
man's fortune as those of probity and integrity.

My list of virtues contained at first but twelve; but a Quaker friend
having kindly informed me that I was generally thought proud; that
my pride showed itself frequently in conversation; that I was not content with being in the right when discussing any point, but was overbearing, and rather insolent, of which he convinced me by mentioning

several instances; I determined endeavoring to cure myself, if I could, of this vice or folly among the rest, and I added Humility to my list giving an extensive meaning to the word.

I cannot boast of much success in acquiring the reality of this virtue, but I had a good deal with regard to the appearance of it. I made it a rule to forbear all direct contradiction to the sentiments of others, and all positive assertion of my own. I even forbid myself, agreeably to the old laws of our Junto, the use of every word or expression in the language that imported a fixed opinion, such as certainly, undoubtedly, etc., and I adopted, instead of them, I conceive, I apprehend, or I imagine a thing to be so or so; or it so appears to me at present. When another asserted something that I thought an error, I denied myself the pleasure of contradicting him abruptly, and of showing immediately some absurdity in his proposition; and in answering I began by observing that in certain cases or circumstances his opinion would be right, but in the present case there appeared or seemed to me some difference, etc. I soon found the advantage of this change in my manner; the conversations I engaged in went on more pleasantly. The modest way in which I proposed my opinions procured them a readier reception and less contradiction; I had less mortification when I was found to be in the wrong, and I more easily prevailed with others to give up their mistakes and join with me when I happened to be in the right.

And this mode, which I at first put on with some violence to natural inclination, became at length so easy, and so habitual to me, that perhaps for these fifty years past no one has ever heard a dogmatical expression escape me. And to this habit (after my character of integrity) I think it principally owing that I had early so much weight with my fellow-citizens when I proposed new institutions, or alterations in the old, and so much influence in public councils when I became a member; for I was but a bad speaker, never eloquent, subject to much hesitation in my choice of words, hardly correct in language, and yet I generally carried my points.

In reality, there is, perhaps, no one of our natural passions so hard to subdue as pride. Disguise it, struggle with it, beat it down, stifle it, mortify it as much as one pleases, it is still alive, and will every now and then peep out and show itself; you will see it, perhaps, often in this history; for, even if I could conceive that I had completely overcome it, I should probably be proud of my humility.

[Thus far written at Passy, 1784.]

PART THREE

I am now about to write at home, August, 1788, but can not have the help expected from my papers, many of them being lost in the war. I have, however, found the following.

Having mentioned a great and extensive project which I had conceived, it seems proper that some account should be here given of that project and its object. Its first rise in my mind appears in the following little paper, accidentally preserved, viz.:

Observations on my reading history, in Library, May 19th, 1731.
That the great affairs of the world, the wars, revolutions, etc., are carried on and affected by parties.
That the view of these parties is their present general interest, or what they take to be such.
That the different views of these different parties occasion all confusion.
That while a party is carrying on a general design, each man has his particular private interest in view.
That as soon as a party has gained its general point, each member becomes intent upon his particular interest; which, thwarting others, breaks that party into divisions, and occasions more confusion.
That few in public affairs act from a mere view of the good of their country, whatever they may pretend; and, though their actings bring real good to their country, yet men primarily considered that their own and their country's interest was united, and did not act from a principle of benevolence.
That fewer still, in public affairs, act with a view to the good of mankind. There seems to me at present to be great occasion for raising a United Party for Virtue, by forming the virtuous and

good men of all nations into a regular body, to be governed by suitable good and wise rules, which good and wise men may probably be more unanimous in their obedience to, than common people are to common laws. I at present think that whoever attempts this aright, and is well qualified, can not fail of pleasing God, and of meeting with success. B. F.

Revolving this project in my mind, as to be undertaken hereafter, when my circumstances should afford me the necessary leisure, I put down from time to time, on pieces of paper, such thoughts as occurred to me respecting it. Most of these are lost; but I find one purporting to be the substance of an intended creed) containing, as I thought, the essentials of every known religion, and being free of every thing that might shock the professors of any religion. It is expressed in these words, viz.:

That there is one God, who made all things.
That he governs the world by his providence.
That he ought to be worshipped by adoration, prayer,
and thanksgiving.
But that the most acceptable service of God is doing good to man.
That the soul is immortal.

And that God will certainly reward virtue and punish vice either here or hereafter.

My ideas at that time were, that the sect should be begun and spread at first among young and single men only; that each person to be initiated should not only declare his assent to such creed, but should have exercised himself with the thirteen weeks' examination and practice of the virtues) as in the before-mentioned model; that the existence of such a society should he kept a secret, till it was become considerable, to prevent solicitations for the admission of improper persons, but that the members should each of them search among his acquaintance for ingenuous, well-disposed youths, to whom, with prudent caution, the scheme should be gradually communicated; that the members should engage to afford their advice, assistance, and support to each other in promoting one another's interests, business, and advancement in life; that, for distinction, we should be called The Society of the Free and Easy: free, as being, by the general practice and habit of the virtues, free from the dominion of vice; and particularly by the practice of industry and frugality, free from debt, which exposes a man to confinement, and a species of slavery to his creditors.

This is as much as I can now recollect of the project, except that I communicated it in part to two young men, who adopted it with some enthusiasm; but my then narrow circumstances, and the necessity I was under of sticking close to my business, occasioned my postponing the further prosecution of it at that time; and my multifarious occupations, public and private, induced me to continue postponing, so that it has been omitted till I have no longer strength or activity left sufficient for such an enterprise; though I am still of opinion that it was a practicable scheme, and might have been very useful, by forming a great number of good citizens; and I was not discouraged by the seeming magnitude of the undertaking, as I have always thought that one man of tolerable abilities may work great changes, and accomplish great affairs among mankind, if he first forms a good plan, and, cutting off all amusements or other employments that would divert his attention, makes the execution of that same plan his sole study and business.

In 1732 I first published my Almanac, under the name of Richard Saunders; it was continued by me about twenty-five years, commonly called Poor Richard's Almanac. I endeavored to make it both entertaining and useful, and it accordingly came to be in such demand, that I reaped considerable profit from it, vending annually near ten thousand. And observing that it was generally read, scarce any neighborhood in the province being without it, I considered it as a proper vehicle for conveying instruction among the common people, who bought scarcely any other books; I therefore filled all the little spaces that occurred between the remarkable days in the calendar with proverbial sentences, chiefly such as inculcated industry and frugality, as the means of procuring wealth, and thereby securing virtue; it being more difficult for a man in want, to act always honestly, as, to use here one of those proverbs, it is hard for an empty sack to stand up-right.

These proverbs, which contained the wisdom of many ages and nations, I assembled and formed into a connected discourse prefixed to the Almanac of 1757, as the harangue of a wise old man to the people attending an auction. The bringing all these scattered counsels thus into a focus enabled them to make greater impression. The piece, being universally approved, was copied in all the newspapers of the Continent; reprinted in Britain on a broad side, to be stuck up in houses; two translations were made of it in French, and great numbers bought by the clergy and gentry, to distribute gratis among their poor parishioners and tenants. In Pennsylvania, as it discouraged useless expense in foreign superfluities, some thought it had its share of influence in producing that growing plenty of money which was observable for several years after its publication.

I considered my newspaper, also, as another means of communicating instruction, and in that view frequently reprinted in it extracts from the Spectator, and other moral writers; and sometimes published little pieces of my own, which had been first composed for reading in our Junto. Of these are a Socratic dialogue, tending to prove that, whatever might be his parts and abilities, a vicious man could not properly be called a man of sense; and a discourse on self-denial, showing that virtue was not secure till its practice became a habitude, and was free from the opposition of contrary inclinations. These may be found in the papers about the beginning of 1735.

In the conduct of my newspaper, I carefully excluded all libeling and personal abuse, which is of late years become so disgraceful to our country. Whenever I was solicited to insert anything of that kind, and the writers pleaded, as they generally did, the liberty of the press, and that a newspaper was like a stagecoach, in which any one who would pay had a right to a place, my answer was, that I would print the piece separately if desired, and the author might have as many copies as he pleased to distribute himself, but that I would not take upon me to spread his detraction; and that, having contracted with my subscribers to furnish them with what might be either useful or entertaining, I could not fill their papers with private altercation, in which they had no concern, without doing them manifest injustice. Now, many of our printers make no scruple of gratifying the malice of individuals by false accusations of the fairest characters among ourselves, augmenting animosity even to the producing of duels; and are, moreover, so indiscreet as to print scurrilous reflections on the government of neighboring states, and even on the conduct of our best national allies, which may be attended with the most pernicious consequences. These things I mention as a caution to young printers, and that they may be encouraged not to pollute their presses and disgrace their profession by such infamous practices, but refuse steadily, as they may see by my example that such a course of conduct will not, on the whole, be injurious to their interests.

In 1733 I sent one of my journeymen to Charleston, South Carolina, where a printer was wanting. I furnished him with a press and letters, on an agreement of partnership, by which I was to receive one-third of the profits of the business, paying one-third of the expense. He was a man of learning, and honest but ignorant in matters of account; and, though he sometimes made me remittances, I could get no account from him, nor any satisfactory state of our partnership while he lived. On his decease, the business was continued by his widow, who, being born and bred in Holland, where, as I have been informed, the knowledge of accounts makes a part of female education, she not only sent me as clear a state as she could find of the transactions past, but continued to account with the greatest regularity and exactness every quarter afterwards, and managed the business with such success, that she not only brought up reputably a family of children, but, at the expiration of the term, was able to purchase of me the printing-house, and establish her son in it.

I mention this affair chiefly for the sake of recommending that branch of education for our young females, as likely to be of more use to them and their children, in case of widowhood, than either music or dancing, by preserving them from losses by imposition of crafty men, and enabling them to continue, perhaps, a profitable mercantile house, with established correspondence, till a son is grown up fit to undertake and go on with it, to the lasting advantage and enriching of the family.

About the year 1734 there arrived among us from Ireland a young Presbyterian preacher, named Hemphill, who delivered with a good voice, and apparently extempore, most excellent discourses, which drew together considerable numbers of different persuasion, who joined in admiring them. Among the rest, I became one of his constant hearers, his sermons pleasing me, as they had little of the dogmatical kind, but inculcated strongly the practice of virtue, or what in the religious stile are called good works. Those, however, of our congregation, who considered themselves as orthodox Presbyterians, disapproved his doctrine, and were joined by most of the old clergy, who arraigned him of heterodoxy before the synod, in order to have him silenced. I became his zealous partisan, and contributed all I could to raise a party in his favor, and we combated for him a while with some hopes of success. There was much scribbling pro and con upon the occasion; and finding that, though an elegant preacher, he was but a poor writer, I lent him my pen and wrote for him two or three pamphlets, and one piece in the Gazette of April, 1735. Those pamphlets, as is generally the case with controversial writings, though eagerly read at the time, were soon out of vogue, and I question whether a single copy of them now exists.

During the contest an unlucky occurrence hurt his cause exceedingly. One of our adversaries having heard him preach a sermon that was much admired, thought he had somewhere read the sermon before, or at least a part of it. On search he found that part quoted at length, in one of the British Reviews, from a discourse of Dr. Foster's. This detection gave many of our party disgust, who accordingly abandoned his cause, and occasioned our more speedy discomfiture in the synod. I stuck by him, however, as I rather approved his giving us good sermons composed by others, than bad ones of his own manufacture, though the latter was the practice of our common teachers. He afterward acknowledged to me that none of those he preached were his own; adding, that his memory was such as enabled him to retain and repeat any sermon after one reading only. On our defeat, he left us in search elsewhere of better fortune, and I quitted the congregation, never joining it after, though I continued many years my subscription for the support of its ministers.

I had begun in 1733 to study languages; I soon made myself so much a master of the French as to be able to read the books with ease. I then undertook the Italian. An acquaintance, who was also learning it, used often to tempt me to play chess with him. Finding this took up too much of the time I had to spare for study, I at length refused to play any more, unless on this condition, that the victor in every game should have a right to impose a task, either in parts of the grammar to be got by heart, or in translations, etc., which tasks the vanquished was to perform upon honor, before our next meeting. As we played pretty equally, we thus beat one another into that language. I afterwards with a little painstaking, acquired as much of the Spanish as to read their books also.

I have already mentioned that I had only one year's instruction in a Latin school, and that when very young, after which I neglected that language entirely. But, when I had attained an acquaintance with the French, Italian, and Spanish, I was surprised to find, on looking over a Latin Testament, that I understood so much more of that language than I had imagined, which encouraged me to apply myself again to the study of it, and I met with more success, as those preceding languages had greatly smoothed my way.

From these circumstances, I have thought that there is some inconsistency in our common mode of teaching languages. We are told that it is proper to begin first with the Latin, and, having acquired that, it will be more easy to attain those modern languages which are derived from it; and yet we do not begin with the Greek, in order more easily to acquire the Latin. It is true that, if you can clamber and get to the top of a staircase without using the steps, you will more easily gain them in descending; but certainly, if you begin with the lowest you will with more ease ascend to the top; and I would therefore offer it to the consideration of those who superintend the education of our youth, whether, since many of those who begin with the Latin quit the same after spending some years without having made any great proficiency, and what they have learnt becomes almost useless, so that their time has been lost, it would not have been better to have begun with the French, proceeding to the Italian, etc.; for, though, after spending the same time, they should quit the study of languages and never arrive at the Latin, they would, however, have acquired another tongue or two, that, being in modern use, might be serviceable to them in common life.

After ten years' absence from Boston, and having become easy in my circumstances, I made a journey thither to visit my relations, which

I could not sooner well afford. In returning, I called at Newport to see my brother, then settled there with his printing-house. Our former differences were forgotten, and our meeting was very cordial and affectionate. He was fast declining in his health, and requested of me that, in case of his death, which he apprehended not far distant, I would take home his son, then but ten years of age, and bring him up to the printing business. This I accordingly performed, sending him a few years to school before I took him into the office. His mother carried on the business till he was grown up, when I assisted him with an assortment of new types, those of his father being in a manner worn out. Thus it was that I made my brother ample amends for the service I had deprived him of by leaving him so early.

In 1736 I lost one of my sons, a fine boy of four years old, by the small-pox, taken in the common way. I long regretted bitterly, and still regret that I had not given it to him by inoculation. This I mention for the sake of parents who omit that operation, on the supposition that they should never forgive themselves if a child died under it; my example showing that the regret may be the same either way, and that, therefore, the safer should be chosen.

Our club, the Junto, was found so useful, and afforded such satisfaction to the members, that several were desirous of introducing their friends, which could not well be done without exceeding what we had settled as a convenient number, viz., twelve. We had from the beginning made it a rule to keep our institution a secret, which was pretty well observed; the intention was to avoid applications of improper persons for admittance, some of whom, perhaps, we might find it difficult to refuse. I was one of those who were against any addition to our number, but, instead of it, made in writing a proposal, that every member separately should endeavor to form a subordinate club, with the same rules respecting queries, etc., and without informing them of the connection with the Junto. The advantages proposed were, the improvement of so many more young citizens by the use of our institutions; our better acquaintance with the general sentiments of the inhabitants on any occasion, as the Junto member might propose what queries we should desire, and was to report to the Junto what passed in his separate club; the promotion of our particular interest in business by more extensive recommendation, and the increase of our influence in public affairs, and our power of doing good by spreading thro' the several clubs the sentiments of the Junto.

The project was approved, and every member undertook to form his club, but they did not all succeed. Five or six only were completed, which were called by different names, as the Vine, the Union, the Band, etc. They were useful to themselves, and afforded us a good deal of amusement, information, and instruction, besides answering, in some considerable degree, our views of influencing the public opinion on particular occasions, of which I shall give some instances in course of time as they happened.

My first promotion was my being chosen, in 1736, clerk of the General Assembly. The choice was made that year without opposition; but the year following, when I was again proposed (the choice, like that of the members, being annual), a new member made a long speech against me, in order to favor some other candidate. I was, however, chosen, which was the more agreeable to me, as, besides the pay for the immediate service as clerk, the place gave me a better opportunity of keeping up an interest among the members, which secured to me the business of printing the votes, laws, paper money, and other occasional jobs for the public, that, on the whole, were very profitable.

I therefore did not like the opposition of this new member, who was a gentleman of fortune and education, with talents that were likely to give him, in time, great influence in the House, which, indeed, afterwards happened. I did not, however, aim at gaining his favor by paying any servile respect to him, but, after some time, took this other method. Having heard that he had in his library a certain very scarce and curious book, I wrote a note to him, expressing my desire of perusing that book, and requesting he would do me the favor of lending it to me for a few days. He sent it immediately, and I returned it in about a week with another note, expressing strongly my sense of the favor. When we next met in the House, he spoke to me (which he had never done before), and with great civility; and he ever after manifested a readiness to serve me on all occasions, so that we became great friends, and our friendship continued to his death. This is another instance of the truth of an old maxim I had learned, which says, "He that has once done you a kindness will be more ready to do you another, than he whom you yourself have obliged." And it shows how much more profitable it is prudently to remove, than to resent, return, and continue inimical proceedings.

In 1737, Colonel Spotswood, late governor of Virginia, and then postmaster-general, being dissatisfied with the conduct of his deputy at Philadelphia, respecting some negligence in rendering, and inexactitude of his accounts, took from him the commission and offered it to me. I accepted it readily, and found it of great advantage; for, though the salary was small, it facilitated the correspondence that improved my newspaper, increased the number demanded, as well as the advertisements to be inserted, so that it came to afford me a considerable income. My old competitor's newspaper declined proportionally, and I was satisfied without retaliating his refusal, while postmaster, to permit my papers being carried by the riders. Thus he suffered greatly from his neglect in due accounting; and I mention it as a lesson to those young men who may be employed in managing affairs for others, that they should always render accounts, and make remittances, with great clearness and punctuality. The character of observing such a conduct is the most powerful of all recommendations to new employments and increase of business.

I began now to turn my thoughts a little to public affairs, beginning, however, with small matters. The city watch was one of the first things that I conceived to want regulation. It was managed by the constables of the respective wards in turn; the constable warned a number of housekeepers to attend him for the night. Those who chose never to attend paid him six shillings a year to be excused, which was supposed to be for hiring substitutes, but was, in reality, much more than was necessary for that purpose, and made the constableship a place of profit; and the constable, for a little drink, often got such ragamuffins about him as a watch, that respectable housekeepers did not choose to mix with. Walking the rounds, too, was often neglected, and most of the nights spent in tippling. I thereupon wrote a paper, to be read in Junto, representing these irregularities, but insisting more particularly on the inequality of this six-shilling tax of the constables, respecting the circumstances of those who paid it, since a poor widow housekeeper, all whose property to be guarded by the watch did not perhaps exceed the value of fifty pounds, paid as much as the wealthiest merchant, who had thousands of pounds worth of goods in his stores.

On the whole, I proposed as a more effectual watch, the hiring of proper men to serve constantly in that business; and as a more equitable way of supporting the charge the levying a tax that should be proportioned to the property. This idea, being approved by the Junto, was communicated to the other clubs, but as arising in each of them; and though the plan was not immediately carried into execution, yet, by preparing the minds of people for the change, it paved the way for the law obtained a few years after, when the members of our clubs were grown into more influence.

About this time I wrote a paper (first to be read in Junto, but it was afterward published) on the different accidents and carelessnesses by which houses were set on fire, with cautions against them, and means proposed of avoiding them. This was much spoken of as a useful piece, and gave rise to a project, which soon followed it, of forming a company for the more ready extinguishing of fires, and mutual assistance in removing and securing the goods when in danger. Associates in this scheme were presently found, amounting to thirty. Our articles of agreement obliged every member to keep always in good order, and fit for use, a certain number of leather buckets, with strong bags and baskets (for packing and transporting of goods), which were to be brought to every fire; and we agreed to meet once a month and spend a social evening together, in discoursing and communicating such ideas as occurred to us upon the subject of fires, as might be useful in our conduct on such occasions.

The utility of this institution soon appeared, and many more desiring to be admitted than we thought convenient for one company, they were advised to form another, which was accordingly done; and this went on, one new company being formed after another, till they became so numerous as to include most of the inhabitants who were men of property; and now, at the time of my writing this, though upward of fifty years since its establishment, that which I first formed, called the Union Fire Company, still subsists and flourishes, though the first members are all deceased but myself and one, who is older by a year than I am. The small fines that have been paid by members for absence at the monthly meetings have been applied to the purchase of fire-engines, ladders, fire-hooks, and other useful implements for each company, so that I question whether there is a city in the world better provided with the means of putting a stop to beginning conflagrations; and, in fact, since these institutions, the city has never lost by fire more than one or two houses at a time, and the flames have often been extinguished before the house in which they began has been half consumed.

In 1739 arrived among us from Ireland the Reverend Mr. Whitefield, who had made himself remarkable there as an itinerant preacher. He was at first permitted to preach in some of our churches; but the clergy, taking a dislike to him, soon refused him their pulpits, and he was obliged to preach in the fields. The multitudes of all sects and denominations that attended his sermons were enormous, and it was a matter of speculation to me, who was one of the number, to observe the extraordinary influence of his oratory on his hearers, and how much they admired and respected him, notwithstanding his common abuse of them, by assuring them that they were naturally half beasts and half devils. It was wonderful to see the change soon made in the manners of our inhabitants. From being thoughtless or indifferent about religion, it seemed as if all the world were growing religious, so that one could not walk thro' the town in an evening without hearing psalms sung in different families of every street.

And it being found inconvenient to assemble in the open air, subject to its inclemencies, the building of a house to meet in was no sooner proposed, and persons appointed to receive contributions, but sufficient sums were soon received to procure the ground and erect the building, which was one hundred feet long and seventy broad, about the size of Westminster Hall; and the work was carried on with such spirit as to be finished in a much shorter time than could have been expected. Both house and ground were vested in trustees, expressly for the use of any preacher of any religious persuasion who might desire to say something to the people at Philadelphia; the design in building not being to accommodate any particular sect, but the inhabitants in general; so that even if the Mufti of Constantinople were to send a missionary to preach Mohammedanism to us, he would find a pulpit at his service.

Mr. Whitefield, in leaving us, went preaching all the way thro' the colonies to Georgia. The settlement of that province had lately been begun, but, instead of being made with hardy, industrious husband-men, accustomed to labor, the only people fit for such an enterprise, it was with families of broken shop-keepers and other insolvent debtors, many of indolent and idle habits, taken out of the jails, who, being set down in the woods, unqualified for clearing land, and unable to endure the hardships of a new settlement, perished in numbers, leaving many helpless children unprovided for. The sight of their miserable situation inspired the benevolent heart of Mr. Whitefield with the idea of building an Orphan House there, in which they might be supported and educated. Returning northward, he preached up this charity, and made large collections, for his eloquence had a wonderful power over the hearts and purses of his hearers, of which I myself was an instance.

I did not disapprove of the design, but, as Georgia was then destitute of materials and workmen, and it was proposed to send them from Philadelphia at a great expense, I thought it would have been better to have built the house here, and brought the children to it. This I advised; but he was resolute in his first project, rejected my counsel, and I therefore refused to contribute. I happened soon after to attend one of his sermons, in the course of which I perceived he intended to finish with a collection, and I silently resolved he should get nothing from me, I had in my pocket a handful of copper money, three or four silver dollars, and five pistoles in gold. As he proceeded I began to soften, and concluded to give the coppers. Another stroke of his oratory made me ashamed of that, and determined me to give the silver; and he finished so admirably, that I emptied my pocket wholly into the collector's dish, gold and all. At this sermon there was also one of our club, who, being of my sentiments respecting the building in Georgia, and suspecting a collection might be intended, had, by precaution, emptied his pockets before he came from home. Towards the conclusion of the discourse, however, he felt a strong desire to give, and applied to a neighbor, who stood near him, to borrow some money for the purpose. The application was unfortunately [made] to perhaps the only man in the company who had the firmness not to be affected by the preacher. His answer was, "At any other time, Friend Hopkinson, I would lend to thee freely; but not now, for thee seems to be out of thy right senses."

Some of Mr. Whitefield's enemies affected to suppose that he would apply these collections to his own private emolument; but I who was intimately acquainted with him (being employed in printing his Sermons and Journals, etc.), never had the least suspicion of his integrity, but am to this day decidedly of opinion that he was in all his conduct a perfectly honest man, and methinks my testimony in his favor ought to have the more weight, as we had no religious connection. He used, indeed, sometimes to pray for my conversion, but never had the satisfaction of believing that his prayers were heard. Ours was a mere civil friendship, sincere on both sides, and lasted to his death.

The following instance will show something of the terms on which we stood. Upon one of his arrivals from England at Boston, he wrote to me that he should come soon to Philadelphia, but knew not where he could lodge when there, as he understood his old friend and host, Mr. Benezet, was removed to Germantown. My answer was, "You know my house; if you can make shift with its scanty accommodations, you will be most heartily welcome." He replied, that if I made that kind offer for Christ's sake, I should not miss of a reward. And I returned, "Don't let me be mistaken; it was not for Christ's sake, but for your sake." One of our common acquaintance jocosely remarked, that, knowing it to be the custom of the saints, when they received any favor, to shift the burden of the obligation from off their own shoulders, and place it in heaven, I had contrived to fix it on earth.

The last time I saw Mr. Whitefield was in London, when he consulted me about his Orphan House concern, and his purpose of appropriating it to the establishment of a college.

He had a loud and clear voice, and articulated his words and sentences so perfectly, that he might be heard and understood at a great distance, especially as his auditories, however numerous, observed the most exact silence. He preached one evening from the top of the Court-house steps, which are in the middle of Market-street, and on the west side of Second-street, which crosses it at right angles. Both streets were filled with his hearers to a considerable distance. Being among the hindmost in Market-street, I had the curiosity to learn how far he could be heard, by retiring backwards down the street towards the river; and I found his voice distinct till I came near Front-street, when some noise in that street obscured it. Imagining then a semi-circle, of which my distance should be the radius, and that it were filled with auditors, to each of whom I allowed two square feet, I computed that he might well be heard by more than thirty thousand. This reconciled me to the newspaper accounts of his having preached to twenty-five thousand people in the fields, and to the ancient histories of generals haranguing whole armies, of which I had sometimes doubted.

By hearing him often, I came to distinguish easily between sermons newly composed, and those which he had often preached in the course of his travels. His delivery of the latter was so improved by frequent repetitions that every accent, every emphasis, every modulation of voice, was so perfectly well turned and well placed, that, without being interested in the subject, one could not help being pleased with the discourse; a pleasure of much the same kind with that received from an excellent piece of music. This is an advantage itinerant preachers have over those who are stationary, as the latter can not well improve their delivery of a sermon by so many rehearsals.

His writing and printing from time to time gave great advantage to his enemies; unguarded expressions, and even erroneous opinions, delivered in preaching, might have been afterwards explained or qualified by supposing others that might have accompanied them, or they might have been denied; but litera scripta monet. Critics attacked his writings violently, and with so much appearance of reason as to diminish the number of his votaries and prevent their increase; so that I am of opinion if he had never written any thing, he would have left behind him a much more numerous and important sect, and his reputation might in that case have been still growing, even after his death, as there being nothing of his writing on which to found a censure and give him a lower character, his proselytes would be left at liberty to feign for him as great a variety of excellence as their enthusiastic admiration might wish him to have possessed.

My business was now continually augmenting, and my circumstances growing daily easier, my newspaper having become very profitable, as being for a time almost the only one in this and the neighboring provinces. I experienced, too, the truth of the observation, "that after getting the first hundred pound, it is more easy to get the second," money itself being of a prolific nature.

The partnership at Carolina having succeeded, I was encouraged to engage in others, and to promote several of my workmen, who had behaved well, by establishing them with printing-houses in different colonies, on the same terms with that in Carolina. Most of them did well, being enabled at the end of our term, six years, to purchase the types of me and go on working for themselves, by which means several families were raised. Partnerships often finish in quarrels; but I was happy in this, that mine were all carried on and ended amicably, owing, I think, a good deal to the precaution of having very explicitly settled, in our articles, every thing to be done by or expected from each partner, so that there was nothing to dispute, which precaution I would therefore recommend to all who enter into partnerships; for, whatever esteem partners may have for, and confidence in each other at the time of the contract, little jealousies and disgusts may arise, with ideas of inequality in the care and burden of the business, etc., which are attended often with breach of friendship and of the connection, perhaps with lawsuits and other disagreeable consequences.

I had, on the whole, abundant reason to be satisfied with my being established in Pennsylvania. There were, however, two things that I regretted, there being no provision for defense, nor for a complete education of youth; no militia, nor any college. I therefore, in 1743, drew up a proposal for establishing an academy; and at that time, thinking the Reverend Mr. Peters, who was out of employ, a fit person to superintend such an institution, I communicated the project to him; but he, having more profitable views in the service of the proprietaries, which succeeded, declined the undertaking; and, not knowing another at that time suitable for such a trust, I let the scheme lie a while dormant. I succeeded better the next year, 1744, in proposing and establishing a Philosophical Society. The paper I wrote for that purpose will be found among my writings, when collected.

With respect to defense, Spain having been several years at war against Great Britain, and being at length joined by France, which brought us into great danger; and the labored and long-continued endeavor of our governor, Thomas, to prevail with our Quaker Assembly to pass a militia law, and make other provisions for the security of the province, having proved abortive, I determined to try what might be done by a voluntary association of the people. To promote this, I first wrote and published a pamphlet, entitled Plain Truth, in which I stated our defenseless situation in strong lights, with the necessity of union and discipline for our defense, and promised to propose in a few days an association, to be generally signed for that purpose. The pamphlet had a sudden and surprising effect. I was called upon for the instrument of association, and having settled the draft of it with a few friends, I appointed a meeting of the citizens in the large building before mentioned. The house was pretty full; I had prepared a number of printed copies, and provided pens and ink dispersed all over the room. I harangued them a little on the subject, read the paper, and explained it, and then distributed the copies, which were eagerly signed, not the least objection being made.

When the company separated, and the papers were collected, we found above twelve hundred hands; and, other copies being dispersed in the country, the subscribers amounted at length to upward of ten thousand. These all furnished themselves as soon as they could with arms, formed themselves into companies and regiments, chose their own officers, and met every week to be instructed in the manual exercise, and other parts of military discipline. The women, by subscriptions among themselves, provided silk colors, which they presented to the companies, painted with different devices and mottos, which I supplied.

The officers of the companies composing the Philadelphia regiment, being met, chose me for their colonel; but, conceiving myself unfit, I declined that station, and recommended Mr. Lawrence, a fine person, and man of influence, who was accordingly appointed. I then proposed a lottery to defray the expense of building a battery below the town, and furnishing it with cannon. It filled expeditiously, and the battery was soon erected, the merlons being framed of logs and filled with earth. We bought some old cannon from Boston, but, these not being sufficient, we wrote to England for more, soliciting, at the same time, our proprietaries for some assistance, though without much expectation of obtaining it.

Meanwhile, Colonel Lawrence, William Allen, Abram Taylor, Esq., and myself were sent to New York by the associators, commissioned to borrow some cannon of Governor Clinton. He at first refused us peremptorily; but at dinner with his council, where there was great drinking of Madeira wine, as the custom of that place then was, he softened by degrees, and said he would lend us six. After a few more bumpers he advanced to ten; and at length he very good-naturedly conceded eighteen. They were fine cannon, eighteen-pounders, with their carriages, which we soon transported and mounted on our battery, where the associators kept a nightly guard while the war lasted, and among the rest I regularly took my turn of duty there as a common soldier.

My activity in these operations was agreeable to the governor and council; they took me into confidence, and I was consulted by them in every measure wherein their concurrence was thought useful to the association. Calling in the aid of religion, I proposed to them the proclaiming a fast, to promote reformation, and implore the blessing of Heaven on our undertaking. They embraced the motion; but, as it was the first fast ever thought of in the province, the secretary had no precedent from which to draw the proclamation. My education in New England, where a fast is proclaimed every year, was here of some advantage: I drew it in the accustomed stile, it was translated into German, printed in both languages, and divulged thro' the province. This gave the clergy of the different sects an opportunity of influencing their congregations to join in the association, and it would probably have been general among all but Quakers if the peace had not soon intervened.

It was thought by some of my friends that, by my activity in these affairs, I should offend that sect, and thereby lose my interest in the Assembly of the province, where they formed a great majority. A young gentleman who had likewise some friends in the House, and wished to succeed me as their clerk, acquainted me that it was decided to displace me at the next election; and he, therefore, in good will, advised me to resign, as more consistent with my honor than being turned out. My answer to him was, that I had read or heard of some public man who made it a rule never to ask for an office, and never to refuse one when offered to him. "I approve," says I, "of his rule, and will practice it with a small addition; I shall never ask, never refuse, nor ever resign an office. If they will have my office of clerk to dispose of to another, they shall take it from me. I will not, by giving it up, lose my right of some time or other making reprisals on my adversaries." I heard, however, no more of this; I was chosen again unanimously as usual at the next election. Possibly, as they disliked my late intimacy with the members of council, who had joined the governors in all the disputes about military preparations, with which the House had long been harassed, they might have been pleased if I would voluntarily have left them; but they did not care to displace me on account merely of my zeal for the association, and they could not well give another reason.

Indeed I had some cause to believe that the defense of the country was not disagreeable to any of them, provided they were not required to assist in it. And I found that a much greater number of them than I could have imagined, though against offensive war, were clearly for the defensive. Many pamphlets pro and con were published on the subject, and some by good Quakers, in favor of defense, which I believe convinced most of their younger people.

A transaction in our fire company gave me some insight into their prevailing sentiments. It had been proposed that we should encourage the scheme for building a battery by laying out the present stock, then about sixty pounds, in tickets of the lottery. By our rules, no money could be disposed of till the next meeting after the proposal. The company consisted of thirty members, of which twenty-two were Quakers, and eight only of other persuasions. We eight punctually attended the meeting; but, though we thought that some of the Quakers would join us, we were by no means sure of a majority. Only one Quaker, Mr. James Morris, appeared to oppose the measure. He expressed much sorrow that it had ever been proposed, as he said Friends were all against it, and it would create such discord as might break up the company. We told him that we saw no reason for that; we were the minority, and if Friends were against the measure, and outvoted us, we must and should, agreeably to the usage of all societies, submit. When the hour for business arrived it was moved to put the vote; he allowed we might then do it by the rules, but, as he could assure us that a number of members intended to be present for the purpose of opposing it, it would be but candid to allow a little time for their appearing.

While we were disputing this, a waiter came to tell me two gentlemen below desired to speak with me. I went down, and found they were two of our Quaker members. They told me there were eight of them assembled at a tavern just by; that they were determined to come and vote with us if there should be occasion, which they hoped would not be the case, and desired we would not call for their assistance if we could do without it, as their voting for such a measure might embroil them with their elders and friends. Being thus secure of a majority, I went up, and after a little seeming hesitation, agreed to a delay of another hour. This Mr. Morris allowed to be extremely fair. Not one of his opposing friends appeared, at which he expressed great surprise; and, at the expiration of the hour, we carried the resolution eight to one; and as, of the twenty-two Quakers, eight were ready to vote with us, and thirteen, by their absence, manifested that they were not inclined to oppose the measure, I afterward estimated the proportion of Quakers sincerely against defense as one to twenty-one only; for these were all regular members of that society, and in good reputation among them, and had due notice of what was proposed at that meeting.

The honorable and learned Mr. Logan, who had always been of that sect, was one who wrote an address to them, declaring his approbation of defensive war, and supporting his opinion by many strong arguments. He put into my hands sixty pounds to be laid out in lottery tickets for the battery, with directions to apply what prizes might be drawn wholly to that service. He told me the following anecdote of his old master, William Penn, respecting defense. He came over from England, when a young man, with that proprietary, and as his secretary. It was war-time, and their ship was chased by an armed vessel, supposed to be an enemy. Their captain prepared for defense; but told William Penn and his company of Quakers, that he did not expect their assistance, and they might retire into the cabin, which they did, except James Logan, who chose to stay upon deck, and was quartered to a gun. The supposed enemy proved a friend, so there was no fighting; but when the secretary went down to communicate the intelligence, William Penn rebuked him severely for staying upon deck, and undertaking to assist in defending the vessel, contrary to the principles of Friends, especially as it had not been required by the captain. This reproof, being before all the company, piqued the secretary, who answered, "I being thy servant, why did thee not order me to come down? But thee was willing enough that I should stay and help to fight the ship when thee thought there was danger."

My being many years in the Assembly, the majority of which were constantly Quakers, gave me frequent opportunities of seeing the embarrassment given them by their principle against war, whenever application was made to them, by order of the crown, to grant aids for military purposes. They were unwilling to offend government, on the one hand, by a direct refusal; and their friends, the body of the Quakers, on the other, by a compliance contrary to their principles; hence a variety of evasions to avoid complying, and modes of disguising the compliance when it became unavoidable. The common mode at last was, to grant money under the phrase of its being "for the king's use," and never to inquire how it was applied.

But, if the demand was not directly from the crown, that phrase was found not so proper, and some other was to be invented. As, when powder was wanting (I think it was for the garrison at Louisburg), and the government of New England solicited a grant of some from Pennsylvania, which was much urged on the House by Governor Thomas, they could not grant money to buy powder, because that was an ingredient of war; but they voted an aid to New England of £3,000, to be put into the hands of the governor, and appropriated it for the purchasing of bread, flour, wheat, or other grain. Some of the council, desirous of giving the House still further embarrassment, advised the governor not to accept provision, as not being the thing he had demanded; but he replied, "I shall take the money, for I understand very well their meaning; other grain is gunpowder," which he accordingly bought, and they never objected to it.

It was in allusion to this fact that, when in our fire company we feared the success of our proposal in favor of the lottery, and I had said to my friend Mr. Syng, one of our members, "If we fail, let us move the purchase of a fire-engine with the money; the Quakers can have no objection to that; and then, if you nominate me and I you as a committee for that purpose, we will buy a great gun, which is certainly a fire-engine." "I see," says he, "you have improved by being so long in the Assembly; your equivocal project would be just a match for their wheat or other grain."

These embarrassments that the Quakers suffered from having established and published it as one of their principles that no kind of war was lawful, and which, being once published, they could not afterwards, however they might change their minds, easily get rid of, reminds me of what I think a more prudent conduct in another sect among us, that of the Dunkers. I was acquainted with one of its founders, Michael Welfare, soon after it appeared. He complained to me that they were grievously calumniated by the zealots of other persuasions, and charged with abominable principles and practices, to which they were utter strangers. I told him this had always been the case with new sects, and that, to put a stop to such abuse, I imagined it might be well to publish the articles of their belief, and the rules of their discipline. He said that it had been proposed among them, but not agreed to, for this reason: "When we were first drawn together as a society," says he, "it had pleased God to enlighten our minds so far as to see that some doctrines, which we once esteemed truths, were errors; and that others, which we had esteemed errors, were real truths. From time to time He has been pleased to afford us farther light, and our principles have been improving, and our errors diminishing. Now we are not sure that we are arrived at the end of this progression, and at the perfection of spiritual or theological knowledge; and we fear that, if we should once print our confession of faith, we should feel ourselves as if bound and confined by it, and perhaps be unwilling to receive farther improvement, and our successors still more so, as conceiving what we their elders and founders had done, to be something sacred, never to be departed from."

This modesty in a sect is perhaps a singular instance in the history of mankind, every other sect supposing itself in possession of all truth, and that those who differ are so far in the wrong; like a man traveling in foggy weather, those at some distance before him on the road he sees wrapped up in the fog, as well as those behind him, and also the people in the fields on each side, but near him all appears clear, though in truth he is as much in the fog as any of them. To avoid this kind of embarrassment, the Quakers have of late years been gradually declining the public service in the Assembly and in the magistracy, choosing rather to quit their power than their principle.

In order of time, I should have mentioned before, that having, in 1742, invented an open stove for the better warming of rooms, and at the same time saving fuel, as the fresh air admitted was warmed in entering, I made a present of the model to Mr. Robert Grace, one of my early friends, who, having an iron-furnace, found the casting of the plates for these stoves a profitable thing, as they were growing in demand. To promote that demand, I wrote and published a pamphlet, entitled An Account of the new-invented Pennsylvania Fireplaces; Wherein their Construction and Manner of Operation is Particularly Explained; their Advantages Above Every Other Method of Warming Rooms Demonstrated; and all Objections That Have Been Raised against the Use of Them Answered and Obviated, etc. This pamphlet had a good effect. Governor Thomas was so pleased with the construction of this stove, as described in it, that he offered to give me a patent for the sole vending of them for a term of years; but I declined it from a principle which has ever weighed with me on such occasions, viz., that, as we enjoy great advantages from the inventions of others, we should be glad of an opportunity to serve others by any invention of ours; and this we should do freely and generously.

An ironmonger in London however, assuming a good deal of my pamphlet, and working it up into his own, and making some small changes in the machine, which rather hurt its operation, got a patent for it there, and made, as I was told, a little fortune by it. And this is not the only instance of patents taken out for my inventions by others, though not always with the same success, which I never contested, as having no desire of profiting by patents myself, and hating disputes. The use of these fireplaces in very many houses, both of this and the neighboring colonies, has been, and is, a great saving of wood to the inhabitants.

Peace being concluded, and the association business therefore at an end, I turned my thoughts again to the affair of establishing an academy. The first step I took was to associate in the design a number of active friends, of whom the Junto furnished a good part; the next was to write and publish a pamphlet, entitled Proposals Relating to the Education of Youth in Pennsylvania. This I distributed among the principal inhabitants gratis; and as soon as I could suppose their minds a little prepared by the perusal of it, I set on foot a subscription for opening and supporting an academy; it was to be paid in quotas yearly for five years; by so dividing it, I judged the subscription might be larger, and I believe it was so, amounting to no less, if I remember right, than £5,000.

In the introduction to these proposals, I stated their publication, not as an act of mine, but of some spirited-spirited gentlemen, avoiding as much as I could, according to my usual rule, the presenting myself to the public as the author of any scheme for their benefit.

The subscribers, to carry the project into immediate execution, chose out of their number twenty-four trustees, and appointed Mr. Francis, then attorney-general, and myself to draw up constitutions for the government of the academy; which being done and signed, a house was hired, masters engaged, and the schools opened, I think, in the same year, 1749.

The scholars increasing fast, the house was soon found too small, and we were looking out for a piece of ground, properly situated, with intention to build, when Providence threw into our way a large house ready built, which, with a few alterations, might well serve our purpose. This was the building before mentioned, erected by the hearers of Mr. Whitefield, and was obtained for us in the following manner.

It is to be noted that the contributions to this building being made by people of different sects, care was taken in the nomination of trustees, in whom the building and ground was to be vested, that a predominancy should not be given to any sect, lest in time that predominancy might be a means of appropriating the whole to the use of such sect, contrary to the original intention. It was therefore that one of each sect was appointed, viz., one Church-of-England man, one Presbyterian, one Baptist, one Moravian, etc., those, in case of vacancy by death, were to fill it by election from among the contributors. The Moravian happened not to please his colleagues, and on his death they resolved to have no other of that sect. The difficulty then was, how to avoid having two of some other sect, by means of the new choice.

Several persons were named, and for that reason not agreed to. At length one mentioned me, with the observation that I was merely an honest man, and of no sect at all, which prevailed with them to choose me. The enthusiasm which existed when the house was built had long since abated, and its trustees had not been able to procure fresh contributions for paying the ground-rent, and discharging some other debts the building had occasioned, which embarrassed them greatly. Being now a member of both sets of trustees, that for the building and that for the Academy, I had a good opportunity of negotiating with both, and brought them finally to an agreement, by which the trustees for the building were to cede it to those of the academy, the latter undertaking to discharge the debt, to keep for ever open in the building a large hall for occasional preachers, according to the original intention, and maintain a free school for the instruction of poor children. Writings were accordingly drawn, and on paying the debts the trustees of the academy were put in possession of the premises; and by dividing the great and lofty hall into stories, and different rooms above and below for the several schools, and purchasing some additional ground, the whole was soon made fit for our purpose, and the scholars removed into the building. The care and trouble of agreeing with the workmen, purchasing materials, and superintending the work, fell upon me; and I went thro' it the more cheerfully, as it did not then interfere with my private business, having the year before taken a very able, industrious, and honest partner, Mr. David Hall, with whose character I was well acquainted, as he had worked for me four years. He took off my hands all care of the printing-office, paying me punctually my share of the profits. This partnership continued eighteen years, successfully for us both.

The trustees of the academy, after a while, were incorporated by a charter from the governor; their funds were increased by contributions in Britain and grants of land from the proprietaries, to which the Assembly has since made considerable addition; and thus was established the present University of Philadelphia. I have been continued one of its trustees from the beginning, now near forty years, and have had the very great pleasure of seeing a number of the youth who have received their education in it, distinguished by their improved abilities, serviceable in public stations and ornaments to their country.

When I disengaged myself, as above-mentioned, from private business, I flattered myself that, by the sufficient though moderate fortune I had acquired, I had secured leisure during the rest of my life for philosophical studies and amusements. I purchased all Dr. Spence's apparatus, who had come from England to lecture here, and I proceeded in my electrical experiments with great alacrity; but the public, now considering me as a man of leisure, laid hold of me for their purposes, every part of our civil government, and almost at the same time, imposing some duty upon me. The governor put me into the commission of the peace; the corporation of the city chose me of the common council, and soon after an alderman; and the citizens at large chose me a burgess to represent them in Assembly. This latter station was the more agreeable to me, as I was at length tired with sitting there to hear debates, in which, as clerk, I could take no part, and which were often so unentertaining that I was induced to amuse myself with making magic squares or circles, or any thing to avoid weariness; and I conceived my becoming a member would enlarge my power of doing good. I would not, however, insinuate that my ambition was not flattered by all these promotions; it certainly was; for, considering my low beginning, they were great things to me; and they were still more pleasing, as being so many spontaneous testimonies of the public good opinion, and by me entirely unsolicited.

The office of justice of the peace I tried a little, by attending a few courts, and sitting on the bench to hear causes; but finding that more knowledge of the common law than I possessed was necessary to act in that station with credit, I gradually withdrew from it, excusing myself by my being obliged to attend the higher duties of a legislator in the Assembly. My election to this trust was repeated every year for ten years, without my ever asking any elector for his vote, or signifying, either directly or indirectly, any desire of being chosen. On taking my seat in the House, my son was appointed their clerk.

The year following, a treaty being to be held with the Indians at Carlisle, the governor sent a message to the House, proposing that they should nominate some of their members, to be joined with some members of council, as commissioners for that purpose. The House named the speaker (Mr. Norris) and myself; and, being commissioned, we went to Carlisle, and met the Indians accordingly.

As those people are extremely apt to get drunk, and, when so, are very quarrelsome and disorderly, we strictly forbad the selling any liquor to them; and when they complained of this restriction, we told them that if they would continue sober during the treaty, we would give them plenty of rum when business was over. They promised this, and they kept their promise, because they could get no liquor, and the treaty was conducted very orderly, and concluded to mutual satisfaction. They then claimed and received the rum; this was in the afternoon; they were near one hundred men, women, and children, and were lodged in temporary cabins, built in the form of a square, just without the town. In the evening, hearing a great noise among them, the commissioners walked out to see what was the matter. We found they had made a great bonfire in the middle of the square; they were all drunk, men and women, quarreling and fighting. Their dark-colored bodies, half naked, seen only by the gloomy light of the bonfire, running after and beating one another with firebrands, accompanied by their horrid yellings, formed a scene the most resembling our ideas of hell that could well be imagined; there was no appeasing the tumult, and we retired to our lodging. At midnight a number of them came thundering at our door, demanding more rum, of which we took no notice.

The next day, sensible they had misbehaved in giving us that disturbance, they sent three of their old counselors to make their apology. The orator acknowledged the fault, but laid it upon the rum; and then endeavored to excuse the rum by saying, "The Great Spirit, who made all things, made every thing for some use, and whatever use he designed any thing for, that use it should always be put to. Now, when he made rum, he said 'Let this be for the Indians to get drunk with,' and it must be so." And, indeed, if it be the design of Providence to extirpate these savages in order to make room for cultivators of the earth, it seems not improbable that rum may be the appointed means. It has already annihilated all the tribes who formerly inhabited the sea-coast.

In 1751, Dr. Thomas Bond, a particular friend of mine, conceived the idea of establishing a hospital in Philadelphia (a very beneficent design, which has been ascribed to me, but was originally his), for the reception and cure of poor sick persons, whether inhabitants of the province or strangers. He was zealous and active in endeavoring to procure subscriptions for it, but the proposal being a novelty in America, and at first not well understood, he met with but small success.

At length he came to me with the compliment that he found there was no such thing as carrying a public-spirited project through without my being concerned in it. "For," says he, "I am often asked by those to whom I propose subscribing, Have you consulted Franklin upon this business? And what does he think of it? And when I tell them that I have not (supposing it rather out of your line), they do not subscribe, but say they will consider of it." I enquired into the nature and probable utility of his scheme, and receiving from him a very satisfactory explanation, I not only subscribed to it myself, but engaged heartily in the design of procuring subscriptions from others. Previously, however, to the solicitation, I endeavored to prepare the minds of the people by writing on the subject in the newspapers, which was my usual custom in such cases, but which he had omitted.

The subscriptions afterwards were more free and generous; but, beginning to flag, I saw they would be insufficient without some assistance from the Assembly, and therefore proposed to petition for it, which was done. The country members did not at first relish the project; they objected that it could only be serviceable to the city, and therefore the citizens alone should be at the expense of it; and they doubted whether the citizens themselves generally approved of it. My allegation on the contrary, that it met with such approbation as to leave no doubt of our being able to raise £2,000 by voluntary donations, they considered as a most extravagant supposition, and utterly impossible.

On this I formed my plan; and asking leave to bring in a bill for incorporating the contributors according to the prayer of their petition, and granting them a blank sum of money, which leave was obtained chiefly on the consideration that the House could throw the bill out if they did not like it, I drew it so as to make the important clause a conditional one, viz., "And be it enacted, by the authority aforesaid, that when the said contributors shall have met and chosen their managers and treasurer, and shall have raised by their contributions a capital stock of £2,000 value (the yearly interest of which is to be applied to the accommodating of the sick poor in the said hospital, free of charge for diet, attendance, advice, and medicines), and shall make the same appear to the satisfaction of the Speaker of the Assembly for the time being, that then it shall and may be lawful for the said speaker, and he is hereby required, to sign an order on the provincial treasurer for the payment of £2,000, in two yearly payments, to the treasurer of the said hospital, to be applied to the founding, building, and finishing of the same."

This condition carried the bill through; for the members, who had opposed the grant, and now conceived they might have the credit of being charitable without the expense, agreed to its passage; and then, in soliciting subscriptions among the people, we urged the conditional promise of the law as an additional motive to give, since every man's donation would be doubled; thus the clause worked both ways. The subscriptions accordingly soon exceeded the requisite sum, and we claimed and received the public gift, which enabled us to carry the design into execution. A convenient and handsome building was soon erected; the institution has by constant experience been found useful, and flourishes to this day; and I do not remember any of my political maneuvers, the success of which gave me at the time more pleasure, or wherein, after thinking of it, I more easily excused myself for having made some use of cunning.

It was about this time that another projector, the Rev. Gilbert Tennent, came to me with a request that I would assist him in procuring a subscription for erecting a new meeting-house. It was to be for the use of a congregation he had gathered among the Presbyterians, who were originally disciples of Mr. Whitefield. Unwilling to make myself disagreeable to my fellow-citizens by too frequently soliciting their contributions, I absolutely refused. He then desired I would furnish him with a list of the names of persons I knew by experience to be generous and public-spirited. I thought it would be unbecoming in me, after their kind compliance with my solicitations, to mark them out to be worried by other beggars, and therefore refused also to give such a list.

He then desired I would at least give him my advice. "That I will readily do," said I; "and, in the first place, I advise you to apply to all those whom you know will give something; next, to those whom you are uncertain whether they will give any thing or not, and show them the list of those who have given; and, lastly, do not neglect those who you are sure will give nothing, for in some of them you may be mistaken." He laughed and thanked me, and said he would take my advice. He did so, for he asked of everybody, and he obtained a much larger sum than he expected, with which he erected the capacious and very elegant meeting-house that stands in Arch-street.

Our city, though laid out with a beautiful regularity, the streets large, strait, and crossing each other at right angles, had the disgrace of suffering those streets to remain long unpaved, and in wet weather the wheels of heavy carriages ploughed them into a quagmire, so that it was difficult to cross them; and in dry weather the dust was offensive. I had lived near what was called the Jersey Market, and saw with pain the inhabitants wading in mud while purchasing their provisions. A strip of ground down the middle of that market was at length paved with brick, so that, being once in the market, they had firm footing, but were often over shoes in dirt to get there. By talking and writing on the subject, I was at length instrumental in getting the street paved with stone between the market and the bricked foot-pavement, that was on each side next to the houses. This, for some time, gave an easy access to the market dry-shod; but, the rest of the street not being paved, whenever a carriage came out of the mud upon this pavement, it shook off and left its dirt upon it, and it was soon covered with mire, which was not removed, the city as yet having no scavengers.

After some inquiry I found a poor industrious man, who was willing to undertake keeping the pavement clean, by sweeping it twice a week, carrying off the dirt from before all the neighbors' doors, for the sum of sixpence per month, to be paid by each house. I then wrote and printed a paper setting forth the advantages to the neighborhood that might be obtained by this small expense; the greater ease in keeping our houses clean, so much dirt not being brought in by people's feet; the benefit to the shops by more custom, etc., etc., as buyers could more easily get at them; and by not having, in windy weather, the dust blown in upon their goods, etc., etc. I sent one of these papers to each house, and in a day or two went round to see who would subscribe an agreement to pay these sixpences; it was unanimously signed, and for a time well executed. All the inhabitants of the city were delighted with the cleanliness of the pavement that surrounded the market, it being a convenience to all, and this raised a general desire to have all the streets paved, and made the people more willing to submit to a tax for that purpose.

After some time I drew a bill for paving the city, and brought it into the Assembly. It was just before I went to England, in 1757, and did not pass till I was gone, and then with an alteration in the mode of assessment, which I thought not for the better, but with an additional provision for lighting as well as paving the streets, which was a great improvement. It was by a private person, the late Mr. John Clifton, his giving a sample of the utility of lamps, by placing one at his door, that the people were first impressed with the idea of enlighting all the city. The honor of this public benefit has also been ascribed to me but it belongs truly to that gentleman. I did but follow his example, and have only some merit to claim respecting the form of our lamps, as differing from the globe lamps we were at first supplied with from London. Those we found inconvenient in these respects: they admitted no air below; the smoke, therefore, did not readily go out above, but circulated in the globe, lodged on its inside, and soon obstructed the light they were intended to afford; giving, besides, the daily trouble of wiping them clean; and an accidental stroke on one of them would demolish it, and render it totally useless. I therefore suggested the composing them of four flat panes, with a long funnel above to draw up the smoke, and crevices admitting air below, to facilitate the ascent of the smoke; by this means they were kept clean, and did not grow dark in a few hours, as the London lamps do, but continued bright till morning, and an accidental stroke would generally break but a single pane, easily repaired.

I have sometimes wondered that the Londoners did not, from the effect holes in the bottom of the globe lamps used at Vauxhall have in keeping them clean, learn to have such holes in their street lamps. But, these holes being made for another purpose, viz., to communicate flame more suddenly to the wick by a little flax hanging down thro' them, the other use, of letting in air, seems not to have been thought of; and therefore, after the lamps have been lit a few hours, the streets of London are very poorly illuminated.

The mention of these improvements puts me in mind of one I proposed, when in London, to Dr. Fothergill, who was among the best men I have known, and a great promoter of useful projects. I had observed that the streets, when dry, were never swept, and the light dust carried away; but it was suffered to accumulate till wet weather reduced it to mud, and then, after lying some days so deep on the pavement that there was no crossing but in paths kept clean by poor people with brooms, it was with great labor raked together and thrown up into carts open above, the sides of which suffered some of the slush at every jolt on the pavement to shake out and fall, sometimes to the annoyance of foot-passengers. The reason given for not sweeping the dusty streets was, that the dust would fly into the windows of shops and houses.

An accidental occurrence had instructed me how much sweeping might be done in a little time. I found at my door in Craven-street, one morning, a poor woman sweeping my pavement with a birch broom; she appeared very pale and feeble, as just come out of a fit of sickness. I asked who employed her to sweep there; she said, "Nobody, but I am very poor and in distress, and I sweeps before gentlefolks's doors, and hopes they will give me something." I bid her sweep the whole street clean, and I would give her a shilling; this was at nine o'clock; at 12 she came for the shilling. From the slowness I saw at first in her working, I could scarce believe that the work was done so soon, and sent my servant to examine it, who reported that the whole street was swept perfectly clean, and all the dust placed in the gutter, which was in the middle; and the next rain washed it quite away, so that the pavement and even the kennel were perfectly clean.

I then judged that, if that feeble woman could sweep such a street in three hours, a strong, active man might have done it in half the time. And here let me remark the convenience of having but one gutter in such a narrow street, running down its middle, instead of two, one on each side, near the footway; for where all the rain that falls on a street runs from the sides and meets in the middle, it forms there a current strong enough to wash away all the mud it meets with; but when divided into two channels, it is often too weak to cleanse either, and only makes the mud it finds more fluid, so that the wheels of carriages and feet of horses throw and dash it upon the foot-pavement, which is thereby rendered foul and slippery, and sometimes splash it upon those who are walking. My proposal, communicated to the good doctor, was as follows:

For the more effectual cleaning and keeping clean the streets of London and Westminster, it is proposed that the several watchmen be contracted with to have the dust swept up in dry seasons, and the mud raked up at other times, each in the several streets and lanes of his round; that they be furnished with brooms and other proper instruments for these purposes, to be kept at their respective stands, ready to furnish the poor people they may employ in the service.

That in the dry summer months the dust be all swept up into heaps at proper distances, before the shops and windows of houses are usually opened, when the scavengers, with close-covered carts, shall also carry it all away.

That the mud, when raked up, be not left in heaps to be spread abroad again by the wheels of carriages and trampling of horses, but that the scavengers be provided with bodies of carts, not placed high upon wheels, but low upon sliders, with lattice bottoms, which, being covered with straw, will retain the mud thrown into them, and permit the water to drain from it, whereby it will become much lighter, water making the greatest part of its weight; these bodies of carts to be placed at convenient distances, and the mud brought to them in wheelbarrows; they remaining where placed till the mud is drained, and then horses brought to draw them away.

I have since had doubts of the practicability of the latter part of this proposal, on account of the narrowness of some streets, and the difficulty of placing the draining-sleds so as not to encumber too much the passage; but I am still of opinion that the former, requiring the dust to be swept up and carried away before the shops are open, is very practicable in the summer, when the days are long; for, in walking thro' the Strand and Fleet-street one morning at seven o'clock, I observed there was not one shop open, though it had been daylight and the sun up above three hours; the inhabitants of London choosing voluntarily to live much by candle-light, and sleep by sunshine, and yet often complain, a little absurdly, of the duty on candles and the high price of tallow.

Some may think these trifling matters not worth minding or relating; but when they consider that though dust blown into the eyes of a single person, or into a single shop on a windy day, is but of small importance, yet the great number of the instances in a populous city, and its frequent repetitions give it weight and consequence, perhaps they will not censure very severely those who bestow some attention to affairs of this seemingly low nature. Human felicity is produced not so much by great pieces of good fortune that seldom happen, as by little advantages that occur every day. Thus, if you teach a poor young man to shave himself, and keep his razor in order, you may contribute more to the happiness of his life than in giving him a thousand guineas. The money may be soon spent, the regret only remaining of having foolishly consumed it; but in the other case, he escapes the frequent vexation of waiting for barbers, and of their sometimes dirty fingers, offensive breaths, and dull razors; he shaves when most convenient to him, and enjoys daily the pleasure of its being done with a good instrument. With these sentiments I have hazarded the few preceding pages, hoping they may afford hints which some time or other may be useful to a city I love, having lived many years in it very happily—and perhaps to some of our towns in America.

Having been for some time employed by the postmaster-general of America as his comptroller in regulating several offices, and bringing the officers to account, I was, upon his death in 1753, appointed, jointly with Mr. William Hunter, to succeed him, by a commission from the postmaster-general in England. The American office never had hitherto paid any thing to that of Britain. We were to have £600 a year between us, if we could make that sum out of the profits of the office. To do this, a variety of improvements were necessary; some of these were inevitably at first expensive, so that in the first four years the office became above £900 in debt to us. But it soon after began to repay us; and before I was displaced by a freak of the ministers, of which I shall speak hereafter, we had brought it to yield three times as much clear revenue to the crown as the post office of Ireland. Since that imprudent transaction, they have received from it—not one farthing!

The business of the post office occasioned my taking a journey this year to New England, where the College of Cambridge, of their own motion, presented me with the degree of Master of Arts. Yale College, in Connecticut, had before made me a similar compliment. Thus, without studying in any college, I came to partake of their honors. They were conferred in consideration of my improvements and discoveries in the electric branch of natural philosophy.

In 1754, war with France being again apprehended, a congress of commissioners from the different colonies was, by an order of the Lords of Trade, to be assembled at Albany, there to confer with the chiefs of the Six Nations concerning the means of defending both their country and ours. Governor Hamilton, having received this order, acquainted the House with it, requesting they would furnish proper presents for the Indians, to be given on this occasion; and naming the speaker (Mr. Norris) and myself to join Mr. Thomas Penn and Mr. Secretary Peters as commissioners to act for Pennsylvania. The House approved the nomination, and provided the goods for the present, though they did not much like treating out of the province, and we met the other commissioners at Albany about the middle of June.

In our way thither, I projected and drew a plan for the union of all the colonies under one government, so far as might be necessary for defense, and other important general purposes. As we passed thro' New York, I had there shown my project to Mr. James Alexander and Mr. Kennedy, two gentlemen of great knowledge in public affairs, and, being fortified by their approbation, I ventured to lay it before the Congress. It then appeared that several of the commissioners had formed plans of the same kind. A previous question was first taken, whether a union should be established, which passed in the affirmative unanimously. A committee was then appointed, one member from each colony, to consider the several plans and report. Mine happened to be preferred, and, with a few amendments, was accordingly reported.

By this plan the general government was to be administered by a president-general, appointed and supported by the crown, and a grand council was to be chosen by the representatives of the people of the several colonies, met in their respective assemblies. The debates upon it in Congress went on daily, hand in hand with the Indian business. Many objections and difficulties were started, but at length they were all overcome, and the plan was unanimously agreed to, and copies ordered to be transmitted to the Board of Trade and to the assemblies of the several provinces. Its fate was singular: the assemblies did not adopt it, as they all thought there was too much prerogative in it, and in England it was judged to have too much of the democratic.

The Board of Trade therefore did not approve of it, nor recommend it for the approbation of his majesty; but another scheme was formed, supposed to answer the same purpose better, whereby the governors of the provinces, with some members of their respective councils, were to meet and order the raising of troops, building of forts, etc., and to draw on the treasury of Great Britain for the expense, which was afterwards to be refunded by an act of Parliament laying a tax on America. My plan, with my reasons in support of it, is to be found among my political papers that are printed.

Being the winter following in Boston, I had much conversation with Governor Shirley upon both the plans. Part of what passed between us on the occasion may also be seen among those papers. The different and contrary reasons of dislike to my plan makes me suspect that it was really the true medium; and I am still of opinion it would have been happy for both sides of the water if it had been adopted. The colonies, so united, would have been sufficiently strong to have defended themselves; there would then have been no need of troops from England; of course, the subsequent pretence for taxing America, and the bloody contest it occasioned, would have been avoided. But such mistakes are not new; history is full of the errors of states and princes.

> *Look round the habitable world, how few*
> *Know their own good, or, knowing it, pursue!*

Those who govern, having much business on their hands, do not generally like to take the trouble of considering and carrying into execution new projects. The best public measures are therefore seldom adopted from previous wisdom, but forced by the occasion.

The Governor of Pennsylvania, in sending it down to the Assembly, expressed his approbation of the plan, "as appearing to him to be drawn up with great clearness and strength of judgment, and therefore recommended it as well worthy of their closest and most serious attention." The House, however, by the management of a certain member, took it up when I happened to be absent, which I thought not very fair, and reprobated it without paying any attention to it at all, to my no small mortification.

In my journey to Boston this year, I met at New York with our new governor, Mr. Morris, just arrived there from England, with whom I had been before intimately acquainted. He brought a commission to supersede Mr. Hamilton, who, tired with the disputes his proprietary instructions subjected him to, had resigned. Mr. Morris asked me if I thought he must expect as uncomfortable an administration. I said, "No; you may, on the contrary, have a very comfortable one, if you will only take care not to enter into any dispute with the Assembly." "My dear friend," says he, pleasantly, "how can you advise my avoiding disputes? You know I love disputing; it is one of my greatest pleasures; however, to show the regard I have for your counsel, I promise you I will, if possible, avoid them." He had some reason for loving to dispute, being eloquent, an acute sophister, and, therefore, generally successful in argumentative conversation. He had been brought up to it from a boy, his father, as I have heard, accustoming his children to dispute with one another for his diversion, while sitting at table after dinner; but I think the practice was not wise; for, in the course of my observation, these disputing, contradicting, and confuting people are generally unfortunate in their affairs. They get victory sometimes, but they never get good will, which would be of more use to them. We parted, he going to Philadelphia, and I to Boston.

In returning, I met at New York with the votes of the Assembly, by which it appeared that, notwithstanding his promise to me, he and the House were already in high contention; and it was a continual battle between them as long as he retained the government. I had my share of it; for, as soon as I got back to my seat in the Assembly, I was put on every committee for answering his speeches and messages, and by the committees always desired to make the drafts. Our answers, as well as his messages, were often tart, and sometimes indecently abusive; and, as he knew I wrote for the Assembly, one might have imagined that, when we met, we could hardly avoid cutting throats; but he was so good-natured a man that no personal difference between him and me was occasioned by the contest, and we often dined together.

One afternoon, in the height of this public quarrel, we met in the street. "Franklin," says he, "you must go home with me and spend the evening; I am to have some company that you will like;" and, taking me by the arm, he led me to his house. In gay conversation over our wine, after supper, he told us, jokingly, that he much admired the idea of Sancho Panza, who, when it was proposed to give him a government, requested it might be a government of blacks, as then, if he could not agree with his people, he might sell them. One of his friends, who sat next to me, says, "Franklin, why do you continue to side with these damned Quakers? Had not you better sell them? The proprietor would give you a good price." "The governor," says I, "has not yet blacked them enough." He, indeed, had labored hard to blacken the Assembly in all his messages, but they wiped off his coloring as fast as he laid it on, and placed it, in return, thick upon his own face; so that, finding he was likely to be Negrofied himself, he, as well as Mr. Hamilton, grew tired of the contest, and quitted the government.

These public quarrels were all at bottom owing to the proprietaries, our hereditary governors, who, when any expense was to be incurred for the defense of their province, with incredible meanness instructed their deputies to pass no act for levying the necessary taxes, unless their vast estates were in the same act expressly excused; and they had even taken bonds of these deputies to observe such instructions. The Assemblies for three years held out against this injustice, though constrained to bend at last. At length Captain Denny, who was Governor Morris's successor, ventured to disobey those instructions; how that was brought about I shall show hereafter.

But I am got forward too fast with my story: there are still some transactions to be mentioned that happened during the administration of Governor Morris.

War being in a manner commenced with France, the government of Massachusetts Bay projected an attack upon Crown Point, and sent

Mr. Quincy to Pennsylvania, and Mr. Pownall, afterward Governor Pownall, to New York, to solicit assistance. As I was in the Assembly, knew its temper, and was Mr. Quincy's countryman, he applied to me for my influence and assistance. I dictated his address to them, which was well received. They voted an aid of £10,000, to be laid out in provisions. But the governor refusing his assent to their bill (which included this with other sums granted for the use of the crown), unless a clause were inserted exempting the proprietary estate from bearing any part of the tax that would be necessary, the Assembly, though very desirous of making their grant to New England effectual, were at a loss how to accomplish it. Mr. Quincy labored hard with the governor to obtain his assent, but he was obstinate.

I then suggested a method of doing the business without the governor, by orders on the trustees of the Loan Office, which, by law, the Assembly had the right of drawing. There was, indeed, little or no money at that time in the office, and therefore I proposed that the orders should be payable in a year, and to bear an interest of five per cent. With these orders I supposed the provisions might easily be purchased. The Assembly, with very little hesitation, adopted the proposal. The orders were immediately printed, and I was one of the committee directed to sign and dispose of them. The fund for paying them was the interest of all the paper currency then extant in the province upon loan, together with the revenue arising from the excise, which being known to be more than sufficient, they obtained instant credit, and were not only received in payment for the provisions, but many moneyed people, who had cash lying by them, vested it in those orders, which they found advantageous, as they bore interest while upon hand, and might on any occasion be used as money; so that they were eagerly all bought up, and in a few weeks none of them were to be seen. Thus this important affair was by my means completed. Mr. Quincy returned thanks to the Assembly in a handsome memorial, went home highly pleased with the success of his embassy, and ever after bore for me the most cordial and affectionate friendship.

The British government, not choosing to permit the union of the colonies as proposed at Albany, and to trust that union with their defense, lest they should thereby grow too military, and feel their own strength, suspicions and jealousies at this time being entertained of them, sent over General Braddock with two regiments of regular English troops for that purpose. He landed at Alexandria, in Virginia, and thence marched to Frederictown, in Maryland, where he halted for carriages. Our Assembly apprehending, from some information, that he had conceived violent prejudices against them, as averse to the service, wished me to wait upon him, not as from them, but as postmaster-general, under the guise of proposing to settle with him the mode of conducting with most celerity and certainty the dispatches between him and the governors of the several provinces, with whom he must necessarily have continual correspondence, and of which they proposed to pay the expense. My son accompanied me on this journey.

We found the general at Frederictown, waiting impatiently for the return of those he had sent thro' the back parts of Maryland and Virginia to collect wagons. I stayed with him several days, dined with him daily, and had full opportunity of removing all his prejudices, by the information of what the Assembly had before his arrival actually done, and were still willing to do, to facilitate his operations. When I was about to depart, the returns of wagons to be obtained were brought in, by which it appeared that they amounted only to twenty-five, and not all of those were in serviceable condition. The general and all the officers were surprised, declared the expedition was then at an end, being impossible, and exclaimed against the ministers for ignorantly landing them in a country destitute of the means of conveying their stores, baggage, etc., not less than one hundred and fifty wagons being necessary.

I happened to say I thought it was a pity they had not been landed rather in Pennsylvania, as in that country almost every farmer had his wagon. The general eagerly laid hold of my words, and said, "Then you, sir, who are a man of interest there, can probably procure them for us; and I beg you will undertake it." I asked what terms were to be offered the owners of the wagons; and I was desired to put on paper the terms that appeared to me necessary. This I did, and they were agreed to, and a commission and instructions accordingly prepared immediately. What those terms were will appear in the advertisement I published as soon as I arrived at Lancaster, which being, from the great and sudden effect it produced, a piece of some curiosity, I shall insert it at length, as follows:

ADVERTISEMENT

LANCASTER, APRIL 26, 1753

Whereas, one hundred and fifty wagons, with four horses to each wagon, and fifteen hundred saddle or pack horses, are wanted for the service of his majesty's forces now about to rendezvous at Will's Creek, and his excellency General Braddock having been pleased to empower me to contract for the hire of the same, I hereby give notice that I shall attend for that purpose at Lancaster from this day to next Wednesday evening, and at York from next Thursday morning till Friday evening, where I shall be ready to agree for wagons and teams, or single horses, on the following terms, viz.:

1. That there shall be paid for each wagon, with four good horses and a driver, fifteen shillings per diem; and for each able horse with a pack-saddle, or other saddle and furniture, two shillings per diem; and for each able horse without a saddle, eighteen pence per diem.

2. That the pay commence from the time of their joining the forces at Will's Creek, which must be on or before the 20th of May ensuing, and that a reasonable allowance be paid over and above for the time necessary for their traveling to Will's Creek and home again after their discharge.

3. Each wagon and team, and every saddle or pack horse, is to be valued by indifferent persons chosen between me and the owner; and in case of the loss of any wagon, team, or other horse in the service, the price according to such valuation is to be allowed and paid.

4. Seven days' pay is to be advanced and paid in hand by me to the owner of each wagon and team, or horse, at the time of contracting, if required, and the remainder to be paid by General Braddock, or by the paymaster of the army, at the time of their discharge, or from time to time, as it shall be demanded.

5. No drivers of wagons, or persons taking care of the hired horses, are on any account to be called upon to do the duty of soldiers, or be otherwise employed than in conducting or taking care of their carriages or horses. 6. All oats, Indian corn, or other forage that wagons or horses bring to the camp, more than is necessary for the subsistence of the horses, is to be taken for the use of the army, and a reasonable price paid for the same.

Note.—My son, William Franklin, is empowered to enter into like contracts with any person in Cumberland county.

B. Franklin

To the inhabitants of the Counties of Lancaster, York and Cumberland.
Friends and Countrymen,

Being occasionally at the camp at Frederic a few days since, I found the general and officers extremely exasperated on account of their not being supplied with horses and carriages, which had been expected from this province, as most able to furnish them; but, through the dissensions between our governor and Assembly, money had not been provided, nor any steps taken for that purpose.

It was proposed to send an armed force immediately into these counties, to seize as many of the best carriages and horses as should be wanted, and compel as many persons into the service as would be necessary to drive and take care of them.

I apprehended that the progress of British soldiers through these counties on such an occasion, especially considering the temper they are in, and their resentment against us, would be attended with many and great inconveniences to the inhabitants, and therefore more willingly took the trouble of trying first what might be done by fair and equitable means. The people of these back counties have lately complained to the Assembly that a sufficient currency was wanting; you have an opportunity of receiving and dividing among you a very considerable sum; for, if the service of this expedition should continue, as it is more than probable it will, for one hundred and twenty days, the hire of these wagons and horses will amount to upward of £30,000, which will be paid you in silver and gold of the king's money.

The service will be light and easy, for the army will scarce march above twelve miles per day, and the wagons and baggage-horses, as they carry those things that are absolutely necessary to the welfare of the army, must march with the army, and no faster; and are, for the army's sake, always placed where they can be most secure, whether in a march or in a camp.

If you are really, as I believe you are, good and loyal subjects to his majesty, you may now do a most acceptable service, and make it easy to yourselves; for three or four of such as can not separately spare from the business of their plantations a wagon and four horses and a driver, may do it together, one furnishing the wagon, another one or two horses, and another the driver, and divide the pay proportionately between you; but if you do not this service to your king and country voluntarily, when such good pay and reasonable terms are offered to you, your loyalty will be strongly suspected. The king's business must be done; so many brave troops, come so far for your defense, must not stand idle through your backwardness to do what may be reasonably expected from you; wagons and horses must be had; violent measures will probably be used, and you will be left to seek for a recompense where you can find it, and your case, perhaps, be little pitied or regarded.

I have no particular interest in this affair, as, except the satisfaction of endeavoring to do good, I shall have only my labor for my pains. If this method of obtaining the wagons and horses is not likely to succeed, I am obliged to send word to the general in fourteen days; and I suppose Sir John St. Clair, the hussar, with a body of soldiers, will immediately enter the province for the purpose, which I shall be sorry to hear, because I am very sincerely and truly

Your friend and well-wisher,
B. Franklin

I received of the general about £800, to be disbursed in advance-money to the wagon owners, etc.; but, that sum being insufficient, I advanced upward of £200 more, and in two weeks the one hundred and fifty wagons, with two hundred and fifty-nine carrying horses, were on their march for the camp. The advertisement promised payment according to the valuation, in case any wagon or horse should be lost. The owners, however, alleging they did not know General Braddock, or what dependence might be had on his promise, insisted on my bond for the performance, which I accordingly gave them.

While I was at the camp, supping one evening with the officers of Colonel Dunbar's regiment, he represented to me his concern for the subalterns, who, he said, were generally not in affluence, and could ill afford, in this dear country, to lay in the stores that might be necessary in so long a march, thro' a wilderness, where nothing was to be purchased. I commiserated their case, and resolved to endeavor procuring them some relief. I said nothing, however, to him of my intention, but wrote the next morning to the committee of the Assembly, who had the disposition of some public money, warmly recommending the case of these officers to their consideration, and proposing that a present should be sent them of necessaries and refreshments. My son, who had some experience of a camp life, and of its wants, drew up a list for me, which I enclosed in my letter. The committee approved, and used such diligence that, conducted by my son, the stores arrived at the camp as soon as the wagons. They consisted of twenty parcels, each containing:

6 lbs. loaf sugar.	*1 Gloucester cheese.*
6 lbs. good Muscovado do.	*1 keg containing 20 lbs. good butter.*
1 lb. good green tea.	*2 doz. old Madeira wine.*
1 lb. good bohea do.	*2 gallons Jamaica spirits.*
6 lbs. good ground coffee.	*1 bottle flour of mustard.*
6 lbs. chocolate.	*2 well-cured hams.*
1–2 cwt. best white biscuit.	*1–2 dozen dried tongues.*
1–2 lb. pepper.	*6 lbs. rice.*
1 quart best white wine vinegar.	*6 lbs. raisins.*

These twenty parcels, well packed, were placed on as many horses, each parcel, with the horse, being intended as a present for one officer. They were very thankfully received, and the kindness acknowledged by letters to me from the colonels of both regiments, in the most grateful terms. The general, too, was highly satisfied with my conduct in procuring him the wagons, etc., and readily paid my account of disbursements, thanking me repeatedly, and requesting my farther assistance in sending provisions after him. I undertook this also, and was busily employed in it till we heard of his defeat, advancing for the service of my own money, upwards of £1000 sterling, of which I sent him an account. It came to his hands, luckily for me, a few days before the battle, and he returned me immediately an order on the paymaster for the round sum of £1,000, leaving the remainder to the next account. I consider this payment as good luck, having never been able to obtain that remainder, of which more hereafter.

This general was, I think, a brave man, and might probably have made a figure as a good officer in some European war. But he had too much self-confidence, too high an opinion of the validity of regular troops, and too mean a one of both Americans and Indians. George Croghan, our Indian interpreter, joined him on his march with one hundred of those people, who might have been of great use to his army as guides, scouts, etc., if he had treated them kindly; but he slighted and neglected them, and they gradually left him.

In conversation with him one day, he was giving me some account of his intended progress. "After taking Fort Duquesne," says he, "I am to proceed to Niagara; and, having taken that, to Frontenac, if the season will allow time; and I suppose it will, for Duquesne can hardly detain me above three or four days; and then I see nothing that can obstruct my march to Niagara." Having before revolved in my mind the long line his army must make in their march by a very narrow road, to be cut for them thro' the woods and bushes, and also what I had read of a former defeat of fifteen hundred French, who invaded the Iroquois country, I had conceived some doubts and some fears for the event of the campaign. But I ventured only to say, "To be sure, sir, if you arrive well before Duquesne, with these fine troops, so well provided with artillery, that place not yet completely fortified, and as we hear with no very strong garrison, can probably make but a short resistance. The only danger I apprehend of obstruction to your march is from ambuscades of Indians, who, by constant practice, are dexterous in laying and executing them; and the slender line, near four miles long, which your army must make, may expose it to be attacked by surprise in its flanks, and to be cut like a thread into several pieces, which, from their distance, can not come up in time to support each other."

He smiled at my ignorance, and replied, "These savages may, indeed, be a formidable enemy to your raw American militia, but upon the king's regular and disciplined troops, sir, it is impossible they should make any impression." I was conscious of an impropriety in my disputing with a military man in matters of his profession, and said no more. The enemy, however, did not take the advantage of his army which I apprehended its long line of march exposed it to, but let it advance without interruption till within nine miles of the place; and then, when more in a body (for it had just passed a river, where the front had halted till all were come over), and in a more open part of the woods than any it had passed, attacked its advanced guard by a heavy fire from behind trees and bushes, which was the first intelligence the general had of an enemy's being near him. This guard being disordered, the general hurried the troops up to their assistance, which was done in great confusion, thro' wagons, baggage, and cattle; and presently the fire came upon their flank: the officers, being on horseback, were more easily distinguished, picked out as marks, and fell very fast; and the soldiers were crowded together in a huddle, having or hearing no orders, and standing to be shot at till two-thirds of them were killed; and then, being seized with a panic, the whole fled with precipitation.

The wagoners took each a horse out of his team and scampered; their example was immediately followed by others; so that all the wagons, provisions, artillery, and stores were left to the enemy. The general, being wounded, was brought off with difficulty; his secretary, Mr. Shirley, was killed by his side; and out of eighty-six officers, sixty-three were killed or wounded, and seven hundred and fourteen men killed out of eleven hundred. These eleven hundred had been picked men from the whole army; the rest had been left behind with Colonel Dunbar, who was to follow with the heavier part of the stores, provisions, and baggage. The flyers, not being pursued, arrived at Dunbar's camp, and the panic they brought with them instantly seized him and all his people; and, though he had now above one thousand men, and the enemy who had beaten Braddock did not at most exceed four hundred Indians and French together, instead of proceeding, and endeavoring to recover some of the lost honor, he ordered all the stores, ammunition, etc., to be destroyed, that he might have more horses to assist his flight towards the settlements, and less lumber to remove. He was there met with requests from the governors of Virginia, Maryland, and Pennsylvania, that he would post his troops on the frontiers, so as to afford some protection to the inhabitants; but he continued his hasty march thro' all the country, not thinking himself safe till he arrived at Philadelphia, where the inhabitants could protect him. This whole transaction gave us Americans the first suspicion that our exalted ideas of the prowess of British regulars had not been well founded.

In their first march, too, from their landing till they got beyond the settlements, they had plundered and stripped the inhabitants, totally ruining some poor families, besides insulting, abusing, and confining the people if they remonstrated. This was enough to put us out of conceit of such defenders, if we had really wanted any. How different was the conduct of our French friends in 1781, who, during a march thro' the most inhabited part of our country from Rhode Island to Virginia, near seven hundred miles, occasioned not the smallest complaint for the loss of a pig, a chicken, or even an apple.

Captain Orme, who was one of the general's aids-de-camp, and, being grievously wounded, was brought off with him, and continued with him to his death, which happened in a few days, told me that he was totally silent all the first day, and at night only said, "Who would have thought it?" That he was silent again the following day, saying only at last, "We shall better know how to deal with them another time;" and died in a few minutes after.

The secretary's papers, with all the general's orders, instructions, and correspondence, falling into the enemy's hands, they selected and translated into French a number of the articles, which they printed, to prove the hostile intentions of the British court before the declaration of war. Among these I saw some letters of the general to the ministry, speaking highly of the great service I had rendered the army, and recommending me to their notice. David Hume, too, who was some years after secretary to Lord Hertford, when minister in France, and afterward to General Conway, when secretary of state, told me he had seen among the papers in that office, letters from Braddock highly recommending me. But, the expedition having been unfortunate, my service, it seems, was not thought of much value, for those recommendations were never of any use to me.

As to rewards from himself, I asked only one, which was, that he would give orders to his officers not to enlist any more of our bought servants, and that he would discharge such as had been already enlisted. This he readily granted, and several were accordingly returned to their masters, on my application. Dunbar, when the command devolved on him, was not so generous. He being at Philadelphia, on his retreat, or rather flight, I applied to him for the discharge of the servants of three poor farmers of Lancaster county that he had enlisted, reminding him of the late general's orders on that bead. He promised me that, if the masters would come to him at Trenton, where he should be in a few days on his march to New York, he would there deliver their men to them. They accordingly were at the expense and trouble of going to Trenton, and there he refused to perform his promise, to their great loss and disappointment.

As soon as the loss of the wagons and horses was generally known, all the owners came upon me for the valuation which I had given bond to pay. Their demands gave me a great deal of trouble, my acquainting them that the money was ready in the paymaster's hands, but that orders for paying it must first be obtained from General Shirley, and my assuring them that I had applied to that general by letter; but, he being at a distance, an answer could not soon be received, and they must have patience, all this was not sufficient to satisfy, and some began to sue me. General Shirley at length relieved me from this terrible situation by appointing commissioners to examine the claims, and ordering payment. They amounted to near £20,000, which to pay would have ruined me.

Before we had the news of this defeat, the two Doctors Bond came to me with a subscription paper for raising money to defray the expense of a grand firework, which it was intended to exhibit at a rejoicing on receipt of the news of our taking Fort Duquesne. I looked grave, and said it would, I thought, be time enough to prepare for the rejoicing when we knew we should have occasion to rejoice. They seemed surprised that I did not immediately comply with their proposal. "Why the d—l!" says one of them, "you surely don't suppose that the fort will not be taken?" "I don't know that it will not be taken, but I know that the events of war are subject to great uncertainty." I gave them the reasons of my doubting; the subscription was dropt, and the projectors thereby missed the mortification they would have undergone if the firework had been prepared. Dr. Bond, on some other occasion afterward, said that he did not like Franklin's forebodings.

Governor Morris, who had continually worried the Assembly with message after message before the defeat of Braddock, to beat them into the making of acts to raise money for the defense of the province, without taxing, among others, the proprietary estates, and had rejected all their bills for not having such an exempting clause, now redoubled his attacks with more hope of success, the danger and necessity being greater. The Assembly, however, continued firm, believing they had justice on their side, and that it would be giving up an essential right if they suffered the governor to amend their money-bills. In one of the last, indeed, which was for granting £50,000, his proposed amendment was only of a single word. The bill expressed "that all estates, real and personal, were to be taxed, those of the proprietaries not excepted." His amendment was, for "not" read "only"—a small, but very material alteration. However, when the news of this disaster reached England, our friends there, whom we had taken care to furnish with all the Assembly's answers to the governor's messages, raised a clamor against the proprietaries for their meanness and injustice in giving their governor such instructions; some going so far as to say that, by obstructing the defense of their province, they forfeited their right to it. They were intimidated by this, and sent orders to their receiver-general to add £5,000 of their money to whatever sum might be given by the Assembly for such purpose.

This, being notified to the House, was accepted in lieu of their share of a general tax, and a new bill was formed, with an exempting clause, which passed accordingly. By this act I was appointed one of the commissioners for disposing of the money, £60,000. I had been active in modeling the bill and procuring its passage, and had, at the same time, drawn a bill for establishing and disciplining of a voluntary militia, which I carried thro' the House without much difficulty, as care was taken in it to leave the Quakers at their liberty. To promote the association necessary to form the militia, I wrote a dialogue, stating and answering all the objections I could think of to such a militia, which was printed, and had, as I thought, great effect.

While the several companies in the city and country were forming and learning their exercise, the governor prevailed with me to take charge of our North-western frontier, which was infested by the enemy, and provide for the defense of the inhabitants by raising troops and building a line of forts. I undertook this military business, though I did not conceive myself well qualified for it. He gave me a commission with full powers, and a parcel of blank commissions for officers, to be given to whom I thought fit. I had but little difficulty in raising men, having soon five hundred and sixty under my command. My son, who had in the preceding war been an officer in the army raised against Canada, was my aide-de-camp, and of great use to me. The Indians had burned Gnadenhut, a village settled by the Moravians, and massacred the inhabitants; but the place was thought a good situation for one of the forts.

In order to march thither, I assembled the companies at Bethlehem, the chief establishment of those people. I was surprised to find it in so good a posture of defense; the destruction of Gnadenhut had made them apprehend danger. The principal buildings were defended by a stockade; they had purchased a quantity of arms and ammunition from New York, and had even placed quantities of small paving stones between the windows of their high stone houses, for their women to throw down upon the heads of any Indians that should attempt to force into them. The armed brethren, too, kept watch, and relieved as methodically as in any garrison town. In conversation with the bishop, Spangenberg, I mentioned my surprise; for, knowing they had obtained an act of Parliament exempting them from military duties in the colonies, I had supposed they were conscientiously scrupulous of bearing arms. He answered me that it was not one of their established principles, but that, at the time of their obtaining that act, it was thought to be a principle with many of their people. On this occasion, however, they, to their surprise, found it adopted by but a few. It seems they were either deceived in themselves, or deceived the Parliament; but common sense, aided by present danger, will sometimes be too strong for whimsical opinions.

It was the beginning of January when we set out upon this business of building forts. I sent one detachment toward the Minisink, with instructions to erect one for the security of that upper part of the country, and another to the lower part, with similar instructions; and I concluded to go myself with the rest of my force to Gnadenhut, where a fort was thought more immediately necessary. The Moravians procured me five wagons for our tools, stores, baggage, etc.

Just before we left Bethlehem, eleven farmers, who had been driven from their plantations by the Indians, came to me requesting a supply of firearms, that they might go back and fetch off their cattle. I gave them each a gun with suitable ammunition. We had not marched many miles before it began to rain, and it continued raining all day; there were no habitations on the road to shelter us, till we arrived near night at the house of a German, where, and in his barn, we were all huddled together, as wet as water could make us. It was well we were not attacked in our march, for our arms were of the most ordinary sort, and our men could not keep their gun locks dry. The Indians are dexterous in contrivances for that purpose, which we had not. They met that day the eleven poor farmers above-mentioned, and killed ten of them. The one who escaped informed that his and his companions' guns would not go off, the priming being wet with the rain.

The next day being fair, we continued our march, and arrived at the desolated Gnadenhut. There was a saw-mill near, round which were left several piles of boards, with which we soon hutted ourselves; an operation the more necessary at that inclement season, as we had no tents. Our first work was to bury more effectually the dead we found there, who had been half interred by the country people.

The next morning our fort was planned and marked out, the circumference measuring four hundred and fifty-five feet, which would require as many palisades to be made of trees, one with another, of a foot diameter each. Our axes, of which we had seventy, were immediately set to work to cut down trees, and, our men being dexterous in the use of them, great dispatch was made. Seeing the trees fall so fast, I had the curiosity to look at my watch when two men began to cut at a pine;

in six minutes they had it upon the ground, and I found it of fourteen inches diameter. Each pine made three palisades of eighteen feet long, pointed at one end. While these were preparing, our other men dug a trench all round, of three feet deep, in which the palisades were to be planted; and, our wagons, the bodies being taken off, and the fore and hind wheels separated by taking out the pin which united the two parts of the perch, we had ten carriages, with two horses each, to bring the palisades from the woods to the spot. When they were set up, our carpenters built a stage of boards all round within, about six feet high, for the men to stand on when to fire thro' the loopholes. We had one swivel gun, which we mounted on one of the angles, and fired it as soon as fixed, to let the Indians know, if any were within hearing, that we had such pieces; and thus our fort, if such a magnificent name may be given to so miserable a stockade, was finished in a week, though it rained so hard every other day that the men could not work.

This gave me occasion to observe, that, when men are employed, they are best contented; for on the days they worked they were good-natured and cheerful, and, with the consciousness of having done a good day's work, they spent the evening jollily; but on our idle days they were mutinous and quarrelsome, finding fault with their pork, the bread, etc., and in continual ill-humor, which put me in mind of a sea-captain, whose rule it was to keep his men constantly at work; and, when his mate once told him that they had done every thing, and there was nothing further to employ them about, "Oh," says he, "Make them scour the anchor."

This kind of fort, however contemptible, is a sufficient defense against Indians, who have no cannon. Finding ourselves now posted securely, and having a place to retreat to on occasion, we ventured out in parties to scour the adjacent country. We met with no Indians, but we found the places on the neighboring hills where they had lain to watch our proceedings. There was an art in their contrivance of those places, that seems worth mention. It being winter, a fire was necessary for them; but a common fire on the surface of the ground would by its light have discovered their position at a distance. They had therefore dug holes in the ground about three feet diameter, and somewhat deeper; we saw where they had with their hatchets cut off the charcoal from the sides of burnt logs lying in the woods. With these coals they had made small fires in the bottom of the holes, and we observed among the weeds and grass the prints of their bodies, made by their laying all round, with their legs hanging down in the holes to keep their feet warm, which, with them, is an essential point. This kind of fire, so managed, could not discover them, either by its light, flame, sparks, or even smoke: it appeared that their number was not great, and it seems they saw we were too many to be attacked by them with prospect of advantage.

We had for our chaplain a zealous Presbyterian minister, Mr. Beatty, who complained to me that the men did not generally attend his prayers and exhortations. When they enlisted, they were promised, besides pay and provisions, a gill of rum a day, which was punctually served out to them, half in the morning, and the other half in the evening; and I observed they were as punctual in attending to receive it; upon which I said to Mr. Beatty, "It is, perhaps, below the dignity of your profession to act as steward of the rum, but if you were to deal it out and only just after prayers, you would have them all about you." He liked the thought, undertook the office, and, with the help of a few hands to measure out the liquor, executed it to satisfaction, and never were prayers more generally and more punctually attended; so that I thought this method preferable to the punishment inflicted by some military laws for non-attendance on divine service.

I had hardly finished this business, and got my fort well stored with provisions, when I received a letter from the governor, acquainting me that he had called the Assembly, and wished my attendance there, if the posture of affairs on the frontiers was such that my remaining there was no longer necessary. My friends, too, of the Assembly, pressing me by their letters to be, if possible, at the meeting, and my three intended forts being now completed, and the inhabitants contented to remain on their farms under that protection, I resolved to return; the more willingly, as a New England officer, Colonel Clapham, experienced in Indian war, being on a visit to our establishment, consented to accept the command. I gave him a commission, and, parading the garrison, had it read before them, and introduced him to them as an officer who, from his skill in military affairs, was much more fit to command them than myself; and, giving them a little exhortation, took my leave. I was escorted as far as Bethlehem, where I rested a few days to recover from the fatigue I had undergone. The first night, being in a good bed, I could hardly sleep, it was so different from my hard lodging on the floor of our hut at Gnaden wrapped only in a blanket or two.

While at Bethlehem, I inquired a little into the practice of the Moravians: some of them had accompanied me, and all were very kind to me. I found they worked for a common stock, eat at common tables, and slept in common dormitories, great numbers together. In the dormitories I observed loopholes, at certain distances all along just under the ceiling, which I thought judiciously placed for change of air. I was at their church, where I was entertained with good music, the organ being accompanied with violins, hautboys, flutes, clarinets, etc. I understood that their sermons were not usually preached to mixed congregations of men, women, and children, as is our common practice, but that they assembled sometimes the married men, at other times their wives, then the young men, the young women, and the little children, each division by itself. The sermon I heard was to the latter, who came in and were placed in rows on benches; the boys under the conduct of a young man, their tutor, and the girls conducted by a young woman. The discourse seemed well adapted to their capacities, and was delivered in a pleasing, familiar manner, coaxing them, as it were, to be good. They behaved very orderly, but looked pale and unhealthy, which made me suspect they were kept too much within doors, or not allowed sufficient exercise.

I inquired concerning the Moravian marriages, whether the report was true that they were by lot. I was told that lots were used only in particular cases; that generally, when a young man found himself disposed to marry, he informed the elders of his class, who consulted the elder ladies that governed the young women. As these elders of the different sexes were well acquainted with the tempers and dispositions of their respective pupils, they could best judge what matches were suitable, and their judgments were generally acquiesced in; but if, for example, it should happen that two or three young women were found to be equally proper for the young man, the lot was then recurred to. I objected, if the matches are not made by the mutual choice of the parties,

some of them may chance to be very unhappy. "And so they may," answered my informer, "if you let the parties choose for themselves;"—
which, indeed, I could not deny.

Being returned to Philadelphia, I found the association went on
swimmingly, the inhabitants that were not Quakers having pretty generally come into it, formed themselves into companies, and chose their
captains, lieutenants, and ensigns, according to the new law. Dr. B. visited me, and gave me an account of the pains he had taken to spread a
general good liking to the law, and ascribed much to those endeavors. I
had had the vanity to ascribe all to my Dialogue; however, not knowing
but that he might be in the right, I let him enjoy his opinion, which I
take to be generally the best way in such cases. The officers, meeting,
chose me to be colonel of the regiment, which I this time accepted. I
forget how many companies we had, but we paraded about twelve hundred well-looking men, with a company of artillery, who had been furnished with six brass field-pieces, which they had become so expert in
the use of as to fire twelve times in a minute. The first time I reviewed
my regiment they accompanied me to my house, and would salute me
with some rounds fired before my door, which shook down and broke
several glasses of my electrical apparatus. And my new honor proved
not much less brittle; for all our commissions were soon after broken by
a repeal of the law in England.

During this short time of my colonelship, being about to set out on
a journey to Virginia, the officers of my regiment took it into their
heads that it would be proper for them to escort me out of town, as far
as the Lower Ferry. Just as I was getting on horseback they came to my
door, between thirty and forty, mounted, and all in their uniforms. I
had not been previously acquainted with the project, or I should have
prevented it, being naturally averse to the assuming of state on any occasion; and I was a good deal chagrined at their appearance, as I could
not avoid their accompanying me. What made it worse was, that, as
soon as we began to move, they drew their swords and rode with them
naked all the way. Somebody wrote an account of this to the proprietor,
and it gave him great offense. No such honor had been paid him when
in the province, nor to any of his governors; and he said it was only

proper to princes of the blood royal, which may be true for aught I know, who was, and still am, ignorant of the etiquette in such cases.

This silly affair, however, greatly increased his rancor against me, which was before not a little, on account of my conduct in the Assembly respecting the exemption of his estate from taxation, which I had always opposed very warmly, and not without severe reflections on his meanness and injustice of contending for it. He accused me to the ministry as being the great obstacle to the king's service, preventing, by my influence in the House, the proper form of the bills for raising money, and he instanced this parade with my officers as a proof of my having an intention to take the government of the province out of his hands by force. He also applied to Sir Everard Fawkener, the postmaster-general, to deprive me of my office; but it had no other effect than to procure from Sir Everard a gentle admonition.

Notwithstanding the continual wrangle between the governor and the House, in which I, as a member, had so large a share, there still subsisted a civil intercourse between that gentleman and myself, and we never had any personal difference. I have sometimes since thought that his little or no resentment against me, for the answers it was known I drew up to his messages, might be the effect of professional habit, and that, being bred a lawyer, he might consider us both as merely advocates for contending clients in a suit, he for the proprietaries and I for the Assembly. He would, therefore, sometimes call in a friendly way to advise with me on difficult points, and sometimes, though not often, take my advice.

We acted in concert to supply Braddock's army with provisions; and, when the shocking news arrived of his defeat, the governor sent in haste for me, to consult with him on measures for preventing the desertion of the back counties. I forget now the advice I gave; but I think it was, that Dunbar should be written to, and prevailed with, if possible, to post his troops on the frontiers for their protection, till, by re-enforcements from the colonies, he might be able to proceed on the expedition. And, after my return from the frontier, he would have had me undertake the conduct of such an expedition with provincial troops, for the reduction of Fort Duquesne, Dunbar and his men being otherwise employed; and he proposed to commission me as general. I had not so good an opinion of my military abilities as he professed to have, and I believe his professions must have exceeded his real sentiments; but probably he might think that my popularity would facilitate the raising of the men, and my influence in Assembly, the grant of money to pay them, and that, perhaps, without taxing the proprietary estate. Finding me not so forward to engage as he expected, the project was dropt, and he soon after left the government, being superseded by Captain Denny.

Before I proceed in relating the part I had in public affairs under this new governor's administration, it may not be amiss here to give some account of the rise and progress of my philosophical reputation.

In 1746, being at Boston, I met there with a Dr. Spence, who was lately arrived from Scotland, and showed me some electric experiments. They were imperfectly performed, as he was not very expert; but, being on a subject quite new to me, they equally surprised and pleased me. Soon after my return to Philadelphia, our library company received from Mr. P. Collinson, Fellow of the Royal Society of London, a present of a glass tube, with some account of the use of it in making such experiments. I eagerly seized the opportunity of repeating what I had seen at Boston; and, by much practice, acquired great readiness in performing those, also, which we had an account of from England, adding a number of new ones. I say much practice, for my house was continually full, for some time, with people who came to see these new wonders.

To divide a little this encumbrance among my friends, I caused a number of similar tubes to be blown at our glass-house, with which they furnished themselves, so that we had at length several performers. Among these, the principal was Mr. Kinnersley, an ingenious neighbor, who, being out of business, I encouraged to undertake showing the experiments for money, and drew up for him two lectures, in which the experiments were ranged in such order, and accompanied with such explanations in such method, as that the foregoing should assist in comprehending the following. He procured an elegant apparatus for the purpose, in which all the little machines that I had roughly made for myself were nicely formed by instrument-makers. His lectures were well attended, and gave great satisfaction; and after some time he went thro' the colonies, exhibiting them in every capital town, and picked up some money. In the West India islands, indeed, it was with difficulty the experiments could be made, from the general moisture of the air.

Obliged as we were to Mr. Collinson for his present of the tube, etc., I thought it right he should be informed of our success in using it, and wrote him several letters containing accounts of our experiments. He got them read in the Royal Society, where they were not at first thought worth so much notice as to be printed in their Transactions. One paper, which I wrote for Mr. Kinnersley, on the sameness of lightning with electricity, I sent to Dr. Mitchel, an acquaintance of mine, and one of the members also of that society, who wrote me word that it had been read, but was laughed at by the connoisseurs. The papers, however, being shown to Dr. Fothergill, he thought them of too much value to be stifled, and advised the printing of them. Mr. Collinson then gave them to Cave for publication in his Gentleman's Magazine; but he chose to print them separately in a pamphlet, and Dr. Fothergill wrote the preface. Cave, it seems, judged rightly for his profit, for by the additions that arrived afterward they swelled to a quarto volume, which has had five editions, and cost him nothing for copy-money.

It was, however, some time before those papers were much taken notice of in England. A copy of them happening to fall into the hands of the Count de Buffon, a philosopher deservedly of great reputation in France, and, indeed, all over Europe, he prevailed with M. Dalibard to translate them into French, and they were printed at Paris. The publication offended the Abbé Nollet, preceptor in Natural Philosophy to the royal family, and an able experimenter, who had formed and published a theory of electricity, which then had the general vogue. He could not at first believe that such a work came from America, and said it must have been fabricated by his enemies at Paris, to decry his system. Afterwards, having been assured that there really existed such a person as Franklin at Philadelphia, which he had doubted, he wrote and published a volume of Letters, chiefly addressed to me, defending his theory, and denying the verity of my experiments, and of the positions deduced from them.

I once purposed answering the Abbé, and actually began the answer; but, on consideration that my writings contained a description of experiments which any one might repeat and verify, and if not to be verified, could not be defended; or of observations offered as conjectures, and not delivered dogmatically, therefore not laying me under any obligation to defend them; and reflecting that a dispute between two persons, writing in different languages, might be lengthened greatly by mistranslations, and thence misconceptions of one another's meaning, much of one of the Abbé's letters being founded on an error in the translation, I concluded to let my papers shift for themselves, believing it was better to spend what time I could spare from public business in making new experiments, than in disputing about those already made. I therefore never answered M. Nollet, and the event gave me no cause to repent my silence; for my friend M. le Roy, of the Royal Academy of Sciences, took up my cause and refuted him; my book was translated into the Italian, German, and Latin languages; and the doctrine it contained was by degrees universally adopted by the philosophers of Europe, in preference to that of the Abbé; so that he lived to see himself the last of his sect, except Monsieur B—, of Paris, his élève and immediate disciple.

What gave my book the more sudden and general celebrity, was the success of one of its proposed experiments, made by Messrs. Dalibard and De Lor at Marly, for drawing lightning from the clouds. This engaged the public attention every where. M. de Lor, who had an apparatus for experimental philosophy, and lectured in that branch of science, undertook to repeat what he called the Philadelphia Experiments; and, after they were performed before the king and court, all the curious of Paris flocked to see them. I will not swell this narrative with an account of that capital experiment, nor of the infinite pleasure I received in the success of a similar one I made soon after with a kite at Philadelphia, as both are to be found in the histories of electricity.

Dr. Wright, an English physician, when at Paris, wrote to a friend, who was of the Royal Society, an account of the high esteem my experiments were in among the learned abroad, and of their wonder that my writings had been so little noticed in England. The society, on this, resumed the consideration of the letters that had been read to them; and the celebrated Dr. Watson drew up a summary account of them, and of all I had afterwards sent to England on the subject, which he accompanied with some praise of the writer. This summary was then printed in their Transactions; and some members of the society in London, particularly the very ingenious Mr. Canton, having verified the experiment of procuring lightning from the clouds by a pointed rod, and acquainting them with the success, they soon made me more than amends for the slight with which they had before treated me. Without my having made any application for that honor, they chose me a member, and voted that I should be excused the customary payments, which would have amounted to twenty-five guineas; and ever since have given me their Transactions gratis. They also presented me with the gold medal of Sir Godfrey Copley for the year 1753, the delivery of which was accompanied by a very handsome speech of the president, Lord Macclesfield, wherein I was highly honored.

Our new governor, Captain Denny, brought over for me the before-mentioned medal from the Royal Society, which he presented to me at an entertainment given him by the city. He accompanied it with very polite expressions of his esteem for me, having, as he said, been long acquainted with my character. After dinner, when the company, as was customary at that time, were engaged in drinking, he took me aside into another room, and acquainted me that he had been advised by his friends in England to cultivate a friendship with me, as one who was capable of giving him the best advice, and of contributing most effectually to the making his administration easy; that he therefore desired of all things to have a good understanding with me, and he begged me to be assured of his readiness on all occasions to render me every service that might be in his power. He said much to me, also, of the proprietor's good disposition towards the province, and of the advantage it might be to us all, and to me in particular, if the opposition that had been so long continued to his measures was dropt, and harmony restored between him and the people; in effecting which, it was thought no one could be more serviceable than myself; and I might depend on adequate acknowledgments and recompenses, etc., etc. The drinkers, finding we did not return immediately to the table, sent us a decanter of Madeira, which the governor made liberal use of, and in proportion became more profuse of his solicitations and promises.

My answers were to this purpose: that my circumstances, thanks to God, were such as to make proprietary favors unnecessary to me; and that, being a member of the Assembly, I could not possibly accept of any; that, however, I had no personal enmity to the proprietary, and that, whenever the public measures he proposed should appear to be for the good of the people, no one should espouse and forward them more zealously than myself; my past opposition having been founded on this, that the measures which had been urged were evidently intended to serve the proprietary interest, with great prejudice to that of the people; that I was much obliged to him (the governor) for his professions of regard to me, and that he might rely on every thing in my power to make his administration as easy as possible, hoping at the same time that he had not brought with him the same unfortunate instruction his predecessor had been hampered with.

On this he did not then explain himself; but when he afterwards came to do business with the Assembly, they appeared again, the disputes were renewed, and I was as active as ever in the opposition, being the penman, first, of the request to have a communication of the instructions, and then of the remarks upon them, which may be found in the votes of the time, and in the Historical Review I afterward published. But between us personally no enmity arose; we were often together; he was a man of letters, had seen much of the world, and was very entertaining and pleasing in conversation. He gave me the first information that my old friend Jas. Ralph was still alive; that he was esteemed one of the best political writers in England; had been employed in the dispute between Prince Frederic and the king, and had obtained a pension of three hundred a year; that his reputation was indeed small as a poet, Pope having damned his poetry in the Dunciad; but his prose was thought as good as any man's.

The Assembly finally finding the proprietary obstinately persisted in manacling their deputies with instructions inconsistent not only with the privileges of the people, but with the service of the crown, resolved to petition the king against them, and appointed me their agent to go over to England, to present and support the petition. The House had sent up a bill to the governor, granting a sum of £60,000 for the king's use (£10,000 of which was subjected to the orders of the then general, Lord Loudoun), which the governor absolutely refused to pass, in compliance with his instructions.

I had agreed with Captain Morris, of the packet at New York, for my passage, and my stores were put on board, when Lord Loudoun arrived at Philadelphia, expressly, as he told me, to endeavor an accommodation between the governor and Assembly, that his majesty's service might not be obstructed by their dissensions. Accordingly, he desired the governor and myself to meet him, that he might hear what was to be said on both sides. We met and discussed the business. In behalf of the Assembly, I urged all the various arguments that may be found in the public papers of that time, which were of my writing, and are printed with the minutes of the Assembly; and the governor pleaded his instructions; the bond he had given to observe them, and his ruin if he disobeyed, yet seemed not unwilling to hazard himself if Lord Loudoun would advise it. This his lordship did not choose to do, though I once thought I had nearly prevailed with him to do it; but finally he rather chose to urge the compliance of the Assembly; and he entreated me to use my endeavors with them for that purpose, declaring that he would spare none of the king's troops for the defense of our frontiers, and that, if we did not continue to provide for that defense ourselves, they must remain exposed to the enemy.

I acquainted the House with what had passed, and, presenting them with a set of resolutions I had drawn up, declaring our rights, and that we did not relinquish our claim to those rights, but only suspended the exercise of them on this occasion thro' force, against which we protested, they at length agreed to drop that bill, and frame another conformable to the proprietary instructions. This of course the governor passed, and I was then at liberty to proceed on my voyage. But, in the meantime, the packet had sailed with my sea-stores, which was some loss to me, and my only recompense was his lordship's thanks for my service, all the credit of obtaining the accommodation falling to his share.

He set out for New York before me; and, as the time for dispatching the packet-boats was at his disposition, and there were two then remaining there, one of which, he said, was to sail very soon, I requested to know the precise time, that I might not miss her by any delay of mine. His answer was, "I have given out that she is to sail on Saturday next; but I may let you know, entre nous, that if you are there by Monday morning, you will be in time, but do not delay longer." By some accidental hindrance at a ferry, it was Monday noon before I arrived, and I was much afraid she might have sailed, as the wind was fair; but I was soon made easy by the information that she was still in the harbor, and would not move till the next day. One would imagine that I was now on the very point of departing for Europe. I thought so; but I was not then so well acquainted with his lordship's character, of which indecision was one of the strongest features. I shall give some instances. It was about the beginning of April that I came to New York, and I think it was near the end of June before we sailed. There were then two of the packet-boats, which had been long in port, but were detained for the general's letters, which were always to be ready to-morrow. Another packet arrived; she too was detained; and, before we sailed, a fourth was expected. Ours was the first to be dispatched, as having been there longest. Passengers were engaged in all, and some extremely impatient to be gone, and the merchants uneasy about their letters, and the orders they had given for insurance (it being war time) for fall goods! but their anxiety availed nothing; his lordship's letters were not ready; and yet whoever waited on him found him always at his desk, pen in hand, and concluded he must needs write abundantly.

Going myself one morning to pay my respects, I found in his antechamber one Innis, a messenger of Philadelphia, who had come from thence express with a packet from Governor Denny for the General. He delivered to me some letters from my friends there, which occasioned my inquiring when he was to return, and where be lodged, that I might send some letters by him. He told me he was ordered to call to-morrow at nine for the general's answer to the governor, and should set off immediately. I put my letters into his hands the same day. A fortnight after I met him again in the same place. "So, you are soon returned, Innis?" "Returned! no, I am not gone yet." "How so?" "I have called here by order every morning these two weeks past for his lordship's letter, and it is not yet ready." "Is it possible, when he is so great a writer? for I see him constantly at his escritoire." "Yes," says Innis, "but he is like St. George on the signs, always on horseback, and never rides on." This observation of the messenger was, it seems, well founded; for, when in England, I understood that Mr. Pitt gave it as one reason for removing this general, and sending Generals Amherst and Wolfe, that the minister never heard from him, and could not know what he was doing.

This daily expectation of sailing, and all the three packets going down to Sandy Hook, to join the fleet there, the passengers thought it best to be on board, lest by a sudden order the ships should sail, and they be left behind. There, if I remember right, we were about six weeks, consuming our sea-stores, and obliged to procure more. At length the fleet sailed, the General and all his army on board, bound to Louisburg, with intent to besiege and take that fortress; all the packet-boats in company ordered to attend the General's ship, ready to receive his dispatches when they should be ready. We were out five days before we got a letter with leave to part, and then our ship quitted the fleet and steered for England. The other two packets he still detained, carried them with him to Halifax, where he stayed some time to exercise the men in sham attacks upon sham forts, then altered his mind as to besieging Louisburg, and returned to New York, with all his troops, together with the two packets above-mentioned, and all their passengers! During his absence the French and savages had taken Fort George, on the frontier of that province, and the savages had massacred many of the garrison after capitulation.

I saw afterwards in London Captain Bonnell, who commanded one of those packets. He told me that, when he had been detained a month, he acquainted his lordship that his ship was grown foul, to a degree that must necessarily hinder her fast sailing, a point of consequence for a packet-boat, and requested an allowance of time to leave her down and clean her bottom. He was asked how long time that would require. He answered, three days. The general replied, "If you can do it in one day, I give leave; otherwise not; for you must certainly sail the day after to-morrow." So he never obtained leave, though detained afterwards from day to day during full three months.

I saw also in London one of Bonnell's passengers, who was so enraged against his lordship for deceiving and detaining him so long at New York, and then carrying him to Halifax and back again, that he swore he would sue for damages. Whether he did or not, I never heard; but, as he represented the injury to his affairs, it was very considerable.

On the whole, I wondered much how such a man came to be entrusted with so important a business as the conduct of a great army; but, having since seen more of the great world, and the means of obtaining, and motives for giving places, my wonder is diminished. General Shirley, on whom the command of the army devolved upon the death of Braddock, would, in my opinion, if continued in place, have made a much better campaign than that of Loudoun in 1757, which was frivolous, expensive, and disgraceful to our nation beyond conception; for, though Shirley was not a bred soldier, he was sensible and sagacious in himself, and attentive to good advice from others, capable of forming judicious plans, and quick and active in carrying them into execution. Loudoun, instead of defending the colonies with his great army, left them totally exposed while he paraded idly at Halifax, by which means Fort George was lost, besides, he deranged all our mercantile operations, and distressed our trade, by a long embargo on the exportation of provisions, on pretence of keeping supplies from being obtained by the enemy, but in reality for beating down their price in favor of the contractors, in whose profits, it was said, perhaps from suspicion only, he had a share. And, when at length the embargo was taken off, by neglecting to send notice of it to Charlestown, the Carolina fleet was detained near three months longer, whereby their bottoms were so much damaged by the worm that a great part of them foundered in their passage home.

Shirley was, I believe, sincerely glad of being relieved from so burdensome a charge as the conduct of an army must be to a man unacquainted with military business. I was at the entertainment given by the city of New York to Lord Loudoun, on his taking upon him the command. Shirley, though thereby superseded, was present also. There was a great company of officers, citizens, and strangers, and, some chairs having been borrowed in the neighborhood, there was one among them very low, which fell to the lot of Mr. Shirley. Perceiving it as I sat by him, I said, "They have given you, sir, too low a seat." "No matter," says he, "Mr. Franklin, I find a low seat the easiest."

While I was, as afore mentioned, detained at New York, I received all the accounts of the provisions, etc., that I had furnished to Braddock, some of which accounts could not sooner be obtained from the different persons I had employed to assist in the business. I presented them to Lord Loudoun, desiring to be paid the balance. He caused them to be regularly examined by the proper officer, who, after comparing every article with its voucher, certified them to be right; and the balance due for which his lordship promised to give me an order on the paymaster. This was, however, put off from time to time; and, though I called often for it by appointment, I did not get it. At length, just before my departure, he told me he had, on better consideration, concluded not to mix his accounts with those of his predecessors. "And you," says he, "when in England, have only to exhibit your accounts at the treasury, and you will be paid immediately."

I mentioned, but without effect, the great and unexpected expense I had been put to by being detained so long at New York, as a reason for my desiring to be presently paid; and on my observing that it was not right I should be put to any further trouble or delay in obtaining the money I had advanced, as I charged no commission for my service, "O, sir," says he, "you must not think of persuading us that you are no gainer; we understand better those affairs, and know that every one concerned in supplying the army finds means, in the doing it, to fill his own pockets." I assured him that was not my case, and that I had not pocketed a farthing; but he appeared clearly not to believe me; and, indeed, I have since learnt that immense fortunes are often made in such employments. As to my balance, I am not paid it to this day, of which more hereafter.

Our captain of the packet had boasted much, before we sailed, of the swiftness of his ship; unfortunately, when we came to sea, she proved the dullest of ninety-six sail, to his no small mortification. After many conjectures respecting the cause, when we were near another ship almost as dull as ours, which, however, gained upon us, the captain ordered all hands to come aft, and stand as near the ensign staff as possible. We were, passengers included, about forty persons. While we stood there, the ship mended her pace, and soon left her neighbor far behind, which proved clearly what our captain suspected, that she was loaded too much by the head. The casks of water, it seems, had been all placed forward; these he therefore ordered to be moved further aft, on which the ship recovered her character, and proved the sailor in the fleet.

The captain said she had once gone at the rate of thirteen knots, which is accounted thirteen miles per hour. We had on board, as a passenger, Captain Kennedy, of the Navy, who contended that it was impossible, and that no ship ever sailed so fast, and that there must have been some error in the division of the log-line, or some mistake in heaving the log. A wager ensued between the two captains, to be decided when there should be sufficient wind. Kennedy thereupon examined rigorously the log-line, and, being satisfied with that, he determined to throw the log himself. Accordingly some days after, when the wind blew very fair and fresh, and the captain of the packet, Lutwidge, said he believed she then went at the rate of thirteen knots, Kennedy made the experiment, and owned his wager lost.

The above fact I give for the sake of the following observation. It has been remarked, as an imperfection in the art of ship-building, that it can never be known, till she is tried, whether a new ship will or will not be a good sailor; for that the model of a good-sailing ship has been exactly followed in a new one, which has proved, on the contrary, remarkably dull. I apprehend that this may partly be occasioned by the different opinions of seamen respecting the modes of lading, rigging, and sailing of a ship; each has his system; and the same vessel, laden by the judgment and orders of one captain, shall sail better or worse than when by the orders of another. Besides, it scarce ever happens that a ship is formed, fitted for the sea, and sailed by the same person. One man builds the hull, another rigs her, a third lades and sails her. No one of these has the advantage of knowing all the ideas and experience of the others, and, therefore, can not draw just conclusions from a combination of the whole.

Even in the simple operation of sailing when at sea, I have often observed different judgments in the officers who commanded the successive watches, the wind being the same. One would have the sails trimmed sharper or flatter than another, so that they seemed to have no certain rule to govern by. Yet I think a set of experiments might be instituted, first, to determine the most proper form of the hull for swift sailing; next, the best dimensions and properest place for the masts: then the form and quantity of sails, and their position, as the wind may be; and, lastly, the disposition of the lading. This is an age of experiments, and I think a set accurately made and combined would be of great use. I am persuaded, therefore, that ere long some ingenious philosopher will undertake it, to whom I wish success.

We were several times chased in our passage, but outsailed every thing, and in thirty days had soundings. We had a good observation, and the captain judged himself so near our port, Falmouth, that, if we made a good run in the night, we might be off the mouth of that harbor in the morning, and by running in the night might escape the notice of the enemy's privateers, who often cruised near the entrance of the channel. Accordingly, all the sail was set that we could possibly make, and the wind being very fresh and fair, we went right before it, and made great way. The captain, after his observation, shaped his course, as he thought, so as to pass wide of the Scilly Isles; but it seems there is sometimes a strong indraught setting up St. George's Channel, which deceives seamen and caused the loss of Sir Cloudesley Shovel's squadron. This indraught was probably the cause of what happened to us.

We had a watchman placed in the bow, to whom they often called, "Look well out before there," and he as often answered, "Ay ay;" but perhaps had his eyes shut, and was half asleep at the time, they sometimes answering, as is said, mechanically; for he did not see a light just before us, which had been hid by the studdingsails from the man at the helm, and from the rest of the watch, but by an accidental yaw of the ship was discovered, and occasioned a great alarm, we being very near it, the light appearing to me as big as a cart-wheel. It was midnight, and our captain fast asleep; but Captain Kennedy, jumping upon deck, and seeing the danger, ordered the ship to wear round, all sails standing; an operation dangerous to the masts, but it carried us clear, and we escaped shipwreck, for we were running right upon the rocks on which the light-house was erected. This deliverance impressed me strongly with the utility of light-houses, and made me resolve to encourage the building more of them in America, if I should live to return there.

In the morning it was found by the soundings, etc., that we were near our port, but a thick fog hid the land from our sight. About nine o'clock the fog began to rise, and seemed to be lifted up from the water like the curtain at a play-house, discovering underneath, the town of Falmouth, the vessels in its harbor, and the fields that surrounded it. This was a most pleasing spectacle to those who had been so long without any other prospects than the uniform view of a vacant ocean, and it gave us the more pleasure as we were now free from the anxieties which the state of war occasioned.

I set out immediately, with my son, for London, and we only stopped a little by the way to view Stonehenge on Salisbury Plain, and Lord Pembroke's house and gardens, with his very curious antiquities at Wilton. We arrived in London the 27th of July, 1757.

PART FOUR

As soon as I was settled in a lodging Mr. Charles had provided for me, I went to visit Dr. Fothergill, to whom I was strongly recommended, and whose counsel respecting my proceedings I was advised to obtain. He was against an immediate complaint to government, and thought the proprietaries should first be personally applied to, who might possibly be induced by the interposition and persuasion of some private friends, to accommodate matters amicably. I then waited on my old friend and correspondent, Mr. Peter Collinson, who told me that John Hanbury, the great Virginia merchant, had requested to be informed when I should arrive, that he might carry me to Lord Granville's, who was then President of the Council and wished to see me as soon as possible. I agreed to go with him the next morning. Accordingly Mr. Hanbury called for me and took me in his carriage to that nobleman's, who received me with great civility; and after some questions respecting the present state of affairs in America and discourse thereupon, he said to me: "You Americans have wrong ideas of the nature of your constitution; you contend that the king's instructions to his governors are not laws, and think yourselves at liberty to regard or disregard them at your own discretion. But those instructions are not like the pocket instructions given to a minister going abroad, for regulating his conduct in some trifling point of ceremony. They are first drawn up by judges learned in the laws; they are then considered, debated, and perhaps amended in Council, after which they are signed by the king. They are then, so far as they relate to you, the law of the land, for the king is the LEGISLATOR OF THE COLONIES." I told his lordship this was new doctrine to me. I had always understood from our charters that our laws were to be made by our Assemblies, to be presented indeed to the king for his royal assent, but that being once given the king could not repeal or alter them. And as the Assemblies could not make permanent laws without his assent, so neither could he make a law for them without theirs. He assured me I was totally mistaken. I did not think so, however, and his lordship's conversation having a little alarmed me as to what might be the sentiments of the court concerning us, I wrote it down as soon as I returned to my lodgings. I recollected that about 20 years before, a clause in a bill brought into Parliament by the ministry had proposed to make the king's instructions laws in the colonies, but the clause was thrown out by the Commons, for which we adored them as our friends and friends of liberty, till by their conduct towards us in 1765 it seemed that they had refused that point of sovereignty to the king only that they might reserve it for themselves.

After some days, Dr. Fothergill having spoken to the proprietaries, they agreed to a meeting with me at Mr. T. Penn's house in Spring Garden. The conversation at first consisted of mutual declarations of disposition to reasonable accommodations, but I suppose each party had its own ideas of what should be meant by reasonable. We then went into consideration of our several points of complaint, which I enumerated. The proprietaries justified their conduct as well as they could, and I the Assembly's. We now appeared very wide, and so far from each other in our opinions as to discourage all hope of agreement. However, it was concluded that I should give them the heads of our complaints in writing, and they promised then to consider them. I did so soon after, but they put the paper into the hands of their solicitor, Ferdinand John Paris, who managed for them all their law business in their great suit with the neighboring proprietary of Maryland, Lord Baltimore, which had subsisted 70 years, and wrote for them all their papers and messages in their dispute with the Assembly. He was a proud, angry man, and as I had occasionally in the answers of the Assembly treated his papers with some severity, they being really weak in point of argument and haughty in expression, he had conceived a mortal enmity to me, which discovering itself whenever we met, I declined the proprietary's proposal that he and I should discuss the heads of complaint between our two selves, and refused treating with any one but them. They then by his advice put the paper into the hands of the Attorney and Solicitor-General for their opinion and counsel upon it, where it lay unanswered a year wanting eight days, during which time I made frequent demands of an answer from the proprietaries, but without obtaining any other than that they had not yet received the opinion of the Attorney and Solicitor-General. What it was when they did receive it I never learnt, for they did not communicate it to me, but sent a long message to the Assembly drawn and signed by Paris, reciting my paper, complaining of its want of formality, as a rudeness on my part, and giving a flimsy justification of their conduct, adding that they should be willing to accommodate matters if the Assembly would send out "some person of candor" to treat with them for that purpose, intimating thereby that I was not such.

The want of formality or rudeness was, probably, my not having addressed the paper to them with their assumed titles of True and Absolute Proprietaries of the Province of Pennsylvania, which I omitted as not thinking it necessary in a paper, the intention of which was only to reduce to a certainty by writing, what in conversation I had delivered viva voce.

But during this delay, the Assembly having prevailed with Governor Denny to pass an act taxing the proprietary estate in common with the estates of the people, which was the grand point in dispute, they omitted answering the message.

When this act however came over, the proprietaries, counseled by Paris, determined to oppose its receiving the royal assent. Accordingly they petitioned the king in Council, and a hearing was appointed in which two lawyers were employed by them against the act, and two by me in support of it. They alleged that the act was intended to load the proprietary estate in order to spare those of the people, and that if it were suffered to continue in force, and the proprietaries who were in odium with the people, left to their mercy in proportioning the taxes, they would inevitably be ruined. We replied that the act had no such intention, and would have no such effect. That the assessors were honest and discreet men under an oath to assess fairly and equitably, and that any advantage each of them might expect in lessening his own tax by augmenting that of the proprietaries was too trifling to induce them to perjure themselves. This is the purport of what I remember as urged by both sides, except that we insisted strongly on the mischievous consequences that must attend a repeal, for that the money, £100,000, being printed and given to the king's use, expended in his service, and now spread among the people, the repeal would strike it dead in their hands to the ruin of many, and the total discouragement of future grants, and the selfishness of the proprietors in soliciting such a general catastrophe, merely from a groundless fear of their estate being taxed too highly, was insisted on in the strongest terms. On this, Lord Mansfield, one of the counsel rose, and beckoning me took me into the clerk's chamber, while the lawyers were pleading, and asked me if I was really of opinion that no injury would be done the proprietary estate in the execution of the act. I said certainly. "Then," says he, "you can have little objection to enter into an engagement to assure that point." I answered, "None at all." He then called in Paris, and after some discourse, his lordship's proposition was accepted on both sides; a paper to the purpose was drawn up by the Clerk of the Council, which I signed with Mr. Charles, who was also an Agent of the Province for their ordinary affairs, when Lord Mansfield returned to the Council Chamber, where finally the law was allowed to pass. Some changes were however recommended and we also engaged they should be made by a subsequent law, but the Assembly did not think them necessary; for one year's tax having been levied by the act before the order of Council arrived, they appointed a committee to examine the proceedings of the assessors, and on this committee they put several particular friends of the proprietaries. After a full enquiry, they unanimously signed a report that they found the tax had been assessed with perfect equity.

The Assembly looked into my entering into the first part of the engagement, as an essential service to the Province, since it secured the credit of the paper money then spread over all the country. They gave me their thanks in form when I returned. But the proprietaries were enraged at Governor Denny for having passed the act, and turned him out with threats of suing him for breach of instructions which he had given bond to observe. He, however, having done it at the insistence of the General, and for His Majesty's service, and having some powerful interest at court, despised the threats and they were never put in execution.

Here ends Franklin's text. By May 1789, a year before his death, he was facing ever greater pain from his kidney stones, and he had resorted to using Laudanium, a tincture of opium and alcohol. "I am so interrupted by extreme pain, which obliges me to have recourse to opium, that between the effects of both, I have but little time in which I can write anything," he complained to his friend Benjamin Vaughan, who had urged him to complete his narrative. He also worried that what he had written was not worth publishing. "Give me your candid opinion whether I had best publish it or suppress it," he asked, "for I am grown so old and feeble in mind, as well as body, that I cannot place any confidence in my own judgment."

Back in 1728, when he was a fledgling printer imbued with the pride that he believed an honest man should have in his trade, Franklin had composed for himself, or at least for his amusement, a cheeky epitaph that reflected his wry perspective on his pilgrim's progress through this world:

> *The body of*
> *B. Franklin, Printer;*
> *(Like the cover of an old book,*
> *Its contents worn out,*
> *and stripped of its lettering and gilding)*
> *Lies here, food for worms.*
> *But the work shall not be lost:*
> *For it will, (as he believed) appear once more,*
> *In a new and more elegant edition,*
> *Revised and corrected*
> *By the Author.*

Shortly before he died, however, he prescribed something simpler to be placed over the gravesite that he would share with his wife. His tombstone should be, he wrote, a marble stone "six feet long, four feet wide, plain, with only a small molding round the upper edge, and this inscription: Benjamin and Deborah Franklin."

Close to 20,000 mourners, more than had ever before gathered in Philadelphia, watched as his funeral procession made its way to the Christ Church burying ground, a few blocks from his home. In front marched the clergymen of the city, all of them, of every faith.

ABOUT THE AUTHOR

Walter Isaacson is the author of *Benjamin Franklin: An American Life* and the president and CEO of the Aspen Institute. He has been the chairman and CEO of CNN and the managing editor of *Time* magazine. He is the author of *Kissinger: A Biography* and coauthor of *The Wise Men: Six Friends and the World They Made.* He lives with his wife and daughter in Washington, D.C., and Aspen, Colorado.